THE CHANGING HIGH SCHOOL CURRICULUM: READINGS
Second Edition

WILLIAM M. ALEXANDER
University of Florida

HOLT, RINEHART AND WINSTON, INC.
New York Chicago San Francisco Atlanta
Dallas Montreal Toronto London Sydney

THE CHANGING SECONDARY SCHOOL CURRICULUM: READINGS,
by William M. Alexander
Copyright © 1967 by Holt, Rinehart and Winston, Inc.

THE CHANGING HIGH SCHOOL CURRICULUM: READINGS,
by William M. Alexander
Copyright © 1972 by Holt, Rinehart and Winston, Inc.
Library of Congress Catalog Card Number: 71–184307
ISBN: 0–03–084243–3
Printed in the United States of America
2 3 4 5   090   9 8 7 6 5 4 3 2 1

PREFACE

This book is intended to serve as a basic guide and resource for all students of the American high school curriculum. Planned as a comprehensive text on the high school curriculum, it is much more than the traditional textbook based upon the author's point of view alone; this book is a collection of research, theory, and practice deliberately selected to reflect various positions on complex and controversial educational issues.

Students, practitioners, researchers, and theorists, including both widely published authorities and popular journalists, are included among the contributors. The reader is encouraged to formulate his own conclusions using the various selections as a resource guide.

The high school curriculum has been ferociously attacked, drastically modified in many situations, and, in general, has been in an upheaval since publication of my earlier text, *The Changing Secondary School Curriculum: Readings,* in 1967. During the ensuing five years, students have become more actively involved in curriculum development by their own efforts, such as protests and demonstrations, as well as their participation in activities arranged by the schools. Considerable disenchantment has spread regarding the academic college preparatory emphasis of the high school. The burgeoning movement to replace the grade 7–9 junior high school with the grade 5–8 or 6–8 middle school has tended to reestablish the four-year high school. Significant research about high school students, their school, and its curriculum has become available. In addition, a host of innovations in curriculum, instruction, and organization and a mass of publications about the high school have been introduced.

Hence this book is as completely new and current as its author–editor and publisher can make it to reflect all these developments. Only three of the sixty-nine articles herein were included in the 1967 edition. Twelve of the articles are reports of research relevant to the high school curriculum.

Despite the present divergence in high school education, I believe there is a basic structure for its study and have organized the selections according to the structure developed in my own teaching. Part I relates to the bases of high school curriculum improvement; Part II describes curriculum changes in process; Part III reports and analyzes trends and issues; and Part IV presents various proposals for the high school curriculum of the future. Selections on student alienation and disruption are reviewed in Chapters 3 and 4; emergent curriculum areas are described in Chapter 6, including career education, interdisciplinary humanities, Black Studies, sex education, drug education, and others; articles in Chapters 8 and 9, respectively, focus on making the curriculum more relevant and individually oriented; and Chapters 11 and 12 illustrate the movement toward alternative schools and programs and the role of teachers and technology. The selections are tied together and briefly interpreted by my own introductory sections for each part and chapter.

To aid students and instructors, the original bibliography that accompanied each selection is retained. The introductory sections include other references and questions for investigation and discussion. A detailed table of contents and comprehensive index are also provided.

Appreciation is expressed to the organizations, publishers, and authors who have permitted me to use their selections in this book. It is hoped that my mesh and interpretation of these materials will help to bring about some resolution of the issues confronting high school education and its continuing improvement.

WILLIAM M. ALEXANDER
Gainesville, Florida
December 1971

CONTRIBUTORS*

ALEXANDER, WILLIAM M., Professor of Education, University of Florida, Gainesville

ALLEN, DWIGHT W., Dean, School of Education, University of Massachusetts, Amherst

BAILEY, STEPHEN K., Chairman, Policy Institute, Syracuse University Research Corporation, Syracuse, New York

BARNES, DONALD E., Vice President, Institute for Educational Development, New York

BERG, DAVID W., Teacher of English, University School, Northern Illinois University, DeKalb, Illinois

BLACK, JONATHAN, Staffwriter, *Village Voice*, New York

CATALINA, JOHN, Student, Tucson, Arizona

CONANT, JAMES B., Former President, Harvard University, and Director, Study of The American High School, and other educational studies

COOPER, GEORGIA, Director, Publications and Publicity, Dade County Classroom Teachers Association, Miami, Florida

DANIEL, WALTER G., Editor-in-Chief, *The Journal of Negro Education*, Howard University, Washington, D.C.

DARBY, CHARLES A., JR., American Institutes for Research, Washington Office, Silver Spring, Maryland

DEBOER, JOHN, Professor of Secondary Education, University of Illinois, Urbana

DIVOKY, DIANE, Free-lance writer, Colrain, Massachusetts

ELLIOTT, ROBERT, Administrative Assistant, Oak Park-River Forest School District, Oak Park, Illinois

ENGLISH, FENWICK, Professor of Secondary Education, Arizona State University, Tempe

ESTES, NOLAN, General Superintendent of Schools, Dallas Independent School District, Texas

FALTERMAYER, EDMUND K., Member, Board of Editors, *Fortune*

* The position listed for each contributor is as it appeared in the original publication or as otherwise known to the author as this book goes to press.

FENNER, JAMES L.,   Chairman, Department of English, Lafayette High School, Brooklyn, New York

FORD, ROBERT R.,   Principal, West High School, Torrance, California

FRASER, DOROTHY,   Coordinator of Social Studies, Hunter College, New York

GARDNER, JOHN W.,   Chairman, Common Cause, Washington, D.C.

GEORGIADES, WILLIAM,   Professor of Education, University of Southern California, Los Angeles

GLATTHORN, ALLAN A.,   Principal, Abington High School, Abington, Pennsylvania

GLINES, DON E.,   Director, Wilson Campus School, Mankato State College, Mankato, Minnesota

GUTHRIE, JAMES W.,   Assistant Professor of Education, University of California, Berkeley

HARNACK, ROBERT S.,   Professor of Education and Director, Center for Curriculum Planning, State University of New York at Buffalo

HAVIGHURST, ROBERT J.,   Professor of Education and Human Development, University of Chicago

HILL, CHARLES H.

HIPPLE, THEODORE W.,   Associate Professor of Education, University of Florida, Gainesville

HOLT, JOHN,   Consultant, Fayerweather Street School, Cambridge, Massachusetts

HOUSE, JAMES E.,   Secondary Education Consultant, Wayne County Intermediate School District, Detroit, Michigan

JEWETT, ANN E.,   Professor of Physical Education, University of Wisconsin, Madison

JONES, RICHARD V., JR.,   Assistant Professor of Education, Stanislaus State College, Turlock, California

KAULFERS, WALTER V.,   Professor of Education, University of Illinois, Urbana

KELLER, CHARLES R.,   Friend-in-residence, Greenwich, Connecticut Public Schools, and educational consultant

KING, ARTHUR R., JR.,   Researcher, Educational Research and Development Center, and Professor of Education, University of Hawaii, Honolulu

KLEINDORFER, GEORGE B.,   Lecturer in Education, University of California, Berkeley

KLEINERT, E. JOHN,   Professor of Education, University of Miami, Coral Gables, Florida

KOOB, C. ALBERT,   President, National Catholic Educational Association, Washington, D.C.

KOROTKIN, ARTHUR L.,   American Institutes for Research, Washington Office, Silver Spring, Maryland

KRUGER, W. STANLEY, Area Chief, Demonstration Projects Branch, Bureau of Elementary and Secondary Education, United States Office of Education

LEONDAR, BARBARA, Assistant Professor, Graduate School of Education, Harvard University, Cambridge, Massachusetts

LESSINGER, LEON, Callaway Professor of Education and Urban Life, Georgia State University, Atlanta

LEVIN, HENRY M., Associate Professor of Education, Stanford University, Stanford, California

MARLAND, SIDNEY P., JR., U.S. Commissioner of Education, Department of Health, Education, and Welfare, Washington, D.C.

MIEL, ALICE, Professor of Education, Teachers College, Columbia University, New York City

NOVAK, JOSEPH D., Professor and Chairman, Division of Science and Environmental Education, Cornell University, Ithaca, New York

OFIESH, GABRIEL D., Professor of Education and Director, Center for Educational Technology, Catholic University of America, Washington, D.C.

OGLE, JOHN W., Mathematics Consultant, North Carolina State Department of Public Instruction, Raleigh

REUBEN, GABRIEL, Former Superintendent, University City Schools, University City, Missouri

ROBINSON, DONALD W., Associate Professor of Secondary Education, Indiana University, Bloomington

ROMASHKO, TANIA, American Institutes for Research, Washington Office, Silver Spring, Maryland

SAYLOR, GALEN, Professor of Secondary Education, University of Nebraska, Lincoln

SHANE, HAROLD, University Professor of Education, Indiana University, Bloomington

SILBERMAN, CHARLES E., Member, Board of Editors, *Fortune*

SMITH, WILLIAM L., Director, Division of School Programs, Bureau of Educational Personnel Development, U.S. Office of Education, Washington, D.C.

SOLBERG, JAMES R., Principal, Seaside High School, Monterey Peninsula Unified School District, Monterey, California

STOUT, ROBERT T., Associate Professor, Claremont Graduate School, Claremont, California

THOMSON, SCOTT D., Superintendent, Evanston Township High School, Evanston, Illinois

TRUMP, J. LLOYD, Associate Secretary, National Association of Secondary School Principals, Washington, D.C.

TYLER, RALPH W.,   former Director, Center for Advanced Study in the Behavioral Sciences, Stanford, California

WILHELMS, FRED,   Senior Associate, Association for Supervision and Curriculum Development, NEA, Washington, D.C.

WILLIAMS, EMMETT L.,   Associate Dean, College of Education, University of Florida, Gainesville

WRIGHT, GRACE S.,   Specialist in Secondary Education, U.S. Office of Education, Washington, D.C.

CONTENTS

PART I

THE BASES OF HIGH SCHOOL CURRICULUM DEVELOPMENT

The pattern of the American high school curriculum established in
the late nineteenth century has persisted with little fundamental change
in its subject-centered design, but with many additions of subjects,
activities, and services. As the United States placed ever greater emphasis
on education and still encountered bewildering problems in the third
quarter of the twentieth century, education came under closer scrutiny
and many demands for greater change in the high school curriculum
emerged. Students themselves became increasingly vocal critics of the
high school. Major changes in the content of the subject curriculum
introduced in the 1960s were proving too few, perhaps almost too late, as
the turn of the decade witnessed a mounting crescendo of arguments
and proposals for social and educational improvement.

The readings in Part I have been selected to define and illustrate the
forces, problems, and demands underlying the changing high school
curriculum. Chapter 1 deals with goals of the high school and their
achievement, including the problems of relating goals and outcomes.
Chapter 2 focuses on the status of the traditional, and still common,
high school program of studies, but attention is also given to the
problems of the comprehensive high school, which is generally considered
the most desirable one in the United States. Chapter 3 is concerned
with the high school student—particularly with students' concerns,
protests, and problems in the early 1970s, which seem likely to persist until
more substantial changes are made in the high school curriculum. Chapter
4 presents several statements that actually, or in effect, demand change
in the high school curriculum. Thus Part I is intended to present a
context in which the curriculum changes described, proposed, and
argued about in later sections can be related and evaluated.

Chapter 1

GOALS AND OUTCOMES OF HIGH SCHOOL EDUCATION IN THE UNITED STATES

In its more than 300 years of evolution from Latin grammar school to comprehensive high school, the American school for adolescents has reflected many goals of our people. Various historic statements of the goals and purposes of the high school (early colonial acts pertaining to the Latin grammar schools; Benjamin Franklin's tract on the academy he instituted in Philadelphia; the 1893 report of the Committee of Ten; the Cardinal Principles of Secondary Education of 1918; the Educational Policies Commission's "imperative educational needs of youth" of 1944; and many influential Congressional acts and professional organization reports of the past two decades) may be read in many sources and therefore are not included in this collection. Study of these sources suggests that the historical trend of the American high school has been for it to become an institution in which each and every American can optimally advance his own self-fulfillment and thereby his participation in an ever-improving society. Some statements have emphasized preparation for further study, for citizenship, or for work; some have given more importance to the individual than to the social purposes, and vice-versa; but the two almost inextricably related notions of self-fulfillment and social improvement have been and still remain persistent. Nowhere, in this writer's judgment, have these aims been stated more eloquently than in John W. Gardner's chapter on "National Goals in Education" in *Goals for Americans*, the 1960 report of the President's Commission on National Goals. This was also the opening selection in the first edition of this anthology and is retained in this second edition as a clearcut definition of the goals to which high school curriculum change should continue to be directed.

Many problems in American society during past decades were, by the 1970s, causing citizens, legislatures, and educators to turn their attention from statements of goals to reports of outcomes of schooling. Student unrest in high schools and colleges, sparked by heightened awareness of grave racial and ideological conflicts, the burdens of the Vietnam War, and economic difficulties such as increasing taxes, inflation, and unemployment, brought pressure on the schools to account for their expenditures by showing some results of schooling. Educators can derive some reassurance, but little ground for complacency, from research on the relationship between schooling and postschool success: Schooling does make a difference in some measures of success, but the challenge to make it count more in solving the human problems which confound us also exists. A comprehensive review of research on school achievement and postschool success is included in this chapter to help students identify the positive outcomes of schooling as well as questions needing further study.

The researches reviewed by Levin, Guthrie, Kleindorfer, and Stout were considered by them as conclusive regarding the positive effect of schooling on earnings; they stated that "there are few social science hypotheses that have been tested so intensively with such consistent results." Furthermore, the individual's choice of occupations is significantly affected by the quality and quantity of his schooling, and upward mobility over generations is enhanced by schooling: "Higher educational attainment not only increases the opportunity of the individual receiving the schooling, but also enhances the prospects of his children." As to the social improvement goal, they noted from the research that "persons with higher educational attainment are more able and more likely to become involved in political processes and to influence the outcomes of the issues that affect them." Research that relates educational attainment to juvenile delinquency, crime, mental health, military training choices, and geographic mobility is also reviewed, the indication being that the poorly educated individual is more likely to be charged with delinquency or crime, to suffer mental illness, to have poor choices in the military, and to have less mobility. Although these researches tend to confirm long-time popular arguments for schooling, it is timely to have their confirmation. It is also timely to review related issues: Are earnings, occupational choices, and job mobility significant criteria of individual self-fulfillment? Are there other criteria as well that should be the subject of research? And if the quantity and quality of schooling are significantly related to individual success, how can the United States more rapidly equalize educational opportunities for all? And if more education increases civic participation, how can it more rapidly widen and improve citizenship education—for example, how can the high school help the new 18-year-old voters to make effective use of their franchise?

The movement toward educational accountability encompasses the National Assessment project, which has been hotly debated by educators beginning in the mid-1960s. To help the student using this book evaluate National Assessment, a selection from the project is included: a partial report in 1971 of the assessment in writing and citizenship. What inferences, if any, can you draw from this report as to the status of writing and citizenship instruction in the schools? What implications, if any, do you see as to the need for curriculum improvement in the high school? To deal with these questions students may wish to examine complete reports of the project to be published as they become available by the National Assessment of Educational Progress, A Project of the Education Commission of the States.

As National Assessment was getting under way, another project, also initially supported by the Carnegie Corporation, was finding much evidence of a lack of concern for individual self-fulfillment in American schools. This study by Charles E. Silberman was originally termed the Carnegie Study of the Education of Educators, and is reported in the best-seller *Crisis in the Classroom: The Remaking of American Education* (Random House, 1970). A portion of that report dealing with the high school, as originally published in an article entitled "High Schools That Work," is reproduced here to indicate Silberman's principal conclusions about the major goal of the high school and its past outcomes. He sees the goal as "helping students develop the knowledge and skills they need to make sense out of their experience—their experience with themselves, with others, with the world—not just during adolescence, but for the rest of their lives," and he thinks the schools are falling far short of meeting it. He did find signs of change, and his full report included descriptions of what he considered promising approaches to reform.

The final selection of this chapter reflects the concern of the early 1970s for increasing "humaneness in education" and also the long-time goals cited earlier in this introduction to Chapter 1. This report from the National Education Association's Center for the Study of Instruction on *Schools for the 70s and Beyond* calls for the schools to prepare their students "to become totally realized *individuals*—humane, self-renewing, self-directing individuals—who will not only survive in society, but will take a conscious role in *shaping* it for the better, as George Counts asked us to do years ago in *Dare the School Build a New Social Order?*" To this writer, the NEA volume is emphasizing the same two goals that have been persistent in high school education—indeed in public education in general—and stated by Gardner as "to foster individual fulfillment and to nurture the free, rational, and responsible men and women without whom our society cannot endure." The perhaps more direct charge of *Schools for the 70s and Beyond* to prepare youth to "shape" society for the better reflects the unhappy realizations of Americans during the decade between the publication of the Gardner and NEA reports (and also between the latter published one and its NEA predecessor, *Schools for the 60s*) that we are confronted with awesome and onerous problems no longer to be neglected in school and society.

NATIONAL GOALS IN EDUCATION*

John W. Gardner

Education is important in any modern society, whatever its political or economic forms. But a society such as ours, dedicated to the worth of the individual, committed to the nurture of free, rational and responsible men and women, has special reasons for valuing education. Our deepest convictions impel us to foster individual fulfillment. We wish each one to achieve the promise that is in him. We wish each one to be worthy of a free society, and capable of strengthening a free society.

Education is essential not only to individual fulfillment but to the vitality of our national life. The vigor of our free institutions depends upon educated men and women at every level of the society. And at this moment in history, free institutions are on trial.

Ultimately, education serves all of our purposes—liberty, justice and all our other aims—but the one it serves most directly is equality of opportunity. We promise such equality, and education is the instrument by which we hope to make good the promises. It is the high road of individual opportunity, the great avenue that all may travel. That is why we must renew our efforts to remove the barriers to education that still exist for disadvantaged individuals—barriers of poverty, of prejudice and of ignorance. The fulfillment of the individual must not be dependent on his color, religion, economic status or place of residence.

Our devotion to equality does not ignore the fact that individuals differ greatly in their talents and motivations. It simply asserts that each should be enabled to develop to the full, in his own style and to his own limit. Each is worthy of respect as a human being. This means that there must be diverse programs within the educational system to take care of the diversity of individuals; and that each of these programs should be accorded respect and stature. . . .

* Reprinted from The Report of the President's Commission on National Goals, *Goals for Americans*, pp. 81, 100, © 1960, by the American Assembly, Columbia University, New York, N.Y. Reprinted by permission of Prentice-Hall, Inc., Englewood Cliffs, N.J.

And in striving for excellence, we must never forget that American education has a clear mission to accomplish with every single child who walks into the school. Modern life has pressed some urgent and sharply defined tasks on education, tasks of producing certain specially needed kinds of educated talent. For the sake of our future we had better succeed in these tasks—but they cannot and should not crowd out the great basic goals of our educational system: to foster individual fulfillment and to nurture the free, rational and responsible men and women without whom our kind of society cannot endure. Our schools must prepare *all* young people, whatever their talents, for the serious business of being free men and women.

SCHOOL ACHIEVEMENT AND POST-SCHOOL SUCCESS: A REVIEW*

HENRY M. LEVIN
    Stanford University

JAMES W. GUTHRIE
    University of California—Berkeley

GEORGE B. KLEINDORFER
    University of California—Berkeley

ROBERT T. STOUT
    Claremont Graduate School

Education . . . prevents being poor.
Horace Mann

For centuries education has been viewed as a general remedy for improving one's lot in life. As early as the 17th century, the English political economist, Sir William Petty, noted the link between education and in-

* Reprinted from *Review of Educational Research* (February 1971), 41:1–16, by permission. Copyright by American Educational Research Association, Washington, D.C.

come. Indeed, the assumption that education would raise the economic status of the poor was an important factor in the United States in stimulating the universal free-schooling movement of the late 19th century. This same assumption contributed to the enactment of compulsory education laws in the early 20th century. Education came to be looked on as a primary means for keeping American society open and for enabling men to break the social, economic, and political bonds of poverty. The famous American educator, Horace Mann, reflected this tenet when, with uncommon insight for that time, he issued the statement at the head of this page (Mann, 1968).

Our purpose in this paper is to explore the link between education, individual opportunity, and individual success. Specifically, we wish to examine the proposition that: the post-school opportunity and performance of a pupil is related to his achievement in school, and the relationship is such that higher achievement is associated with "success" and lower achievement is associated with lack of "success."

At first glance, this appears to be little more than a statement of the obvious. Unfortunately, the step from what seems so obvious to empirical verification of the phenomenon is not an easy one. While it may be true that schooling improves the social and economic situations of an individual, it is difficult to demonstrate this relationship. The prime obstacle to systematic verification is the impossibility of conducting a controlled experiment in which the different lifetime possibilities of one set of persons can be observed in different sets of lifetime situations which vary *only* in the amount and quality of formal education.

The everyday connections frequently made between educational attainment and life success are based on observations of different individuals at each level of educational attainment. Consequently, it is not known, in any controlled or scientific way, what would have happened to a particular individual had he obtained more schooling or had he not gone to school at all. Our knowledge is limited even further by the tendency of highly educated individuals to have other attributes which might explain their greater success. The quantity and quality of one's schooling may be directly related to an individual's ability, his family's location and wealth, his motivation, his cultural milieu, his race, etc. Thus, the ostensible connection between schooling and success may merely reflect the greater possibilities open to persons with a number of other helpful attributes rather than being an effect of education per se. In all likelihood, attributing the gross improvement in an individual's potential lifetime opportunity to higher educational attainment probably understates the effects of the other traits of persons who receive more schooling. Accordingly, in reviewing evidence that links schooling to an individual's post-school opportunity, we attempt to take into account other factors which frequently occur in close association with various degrees of educational attainment.

DEFINING "EDUCATION" AND "OPPORTUNITY"

By "education" we refer specifically to the quality and quantity of an individual's schooling. Usually, educational *quality* is measured by student performance on standardized achievement tests, and *quantity* is denoted by the years of schooling completed. Other studies have demonstrated that both of these measures often seem to be related directly to the quality and availability of school resources (Guthrie, Kleindorfer, Levin, & Stout, in press).

In this review we are concerned with the following question: If improvement in school services can increase student achievement and expand the number of years of schooling for a representative individual student, will such increases in educational performance improve that same individual's lifetime opportunity?

By "opportunity" we mean the quality and quantity of alternatives available to an individual for improving his and his family's overall economic, social, and political well being. Thus, if educational attainment is to be judged to produce increased opportunity, it must provide an individual with a larger number of higher quality alternatives from which to choose in determining his destiny and the destiny of those in his household.

It should be noted that many of the measures used in the studies we review reflect post-school *success* rather than *opportunity per se*. The concept of "opportunity" reflects the existence of an option whereas attainment refers also to having taken advantage of that option. In many studies only an outcome or "attainment" is examined. In such cases, optional opportunities do not appear in the data. For example, assume that more education can lead to an opportunity for better occupations, but the recipients of such added education choose to ignore this option. In this instance, the "opportunity" would exist, but it would not be reflected in our data on attainment or "success." Where such a situation is obvious, however, we take it into account in reviewing the evidence.

In estimating whether education produces higher opportunity, we have chosen what we believe to be several critical dimensions of opportunity: lifetime earnings, occupational attainment, political participation, social, economic, and geographic mobility for the individual and his children, school choice, military service options, and social deviance. Available studies on each of these dimensions are reviewed separately with attention given to the conceptual linkages between educational attainment as well as the particular dimension of opportunity and to specific research findings.

EDUCATION AND EARNINGS

The opportunity dimension which has received the most attention from social scientists is the relationship between educational attainment and monetary earnings. The explanation for this intensive examination is threefold. First, education has been viewed traditionally as one of the most important means by which poverty can be eliminated. The federal anti-poverty efforts of the "New Frontier" and the "Great Society" were aimed largely at increasing the quality and quantity of schooling available to the poor. Project Head Start and Title I of the Elementary and Secondary Education Act of 1965 are two notable examples of such programs. Second, earnings can be readily measured. And third, there are easily available sources of data on both education and earnings.

There is a sound theoretical reason for expecting education to improve an individual's earning capacity. This logic asserts that schooling is an investment in "human capital" capable of raising the productivity and work potentialities of the recipients (see Becker, 1964; Walsh, 1935). That is, schools are expected to inculcate in individuals certain behaviors which should increase their economic productivity and thus elevate their earnings. The characteristics that schools are expected to develop in students are often categorized as *cognitive* and *noncognitive*. Cognitive behaviors include knowledge and skills internalized intellectually (see Bloom, 1956), while noncognitive behaviors refer to assorted social skills and personality characteristics developed as a consequence of schooling (see Inkeles, 1956). Reading is an example of a cognitive skill; motivation, punctuality, and ability to work with others are examples of noncognitive behaviors.

If the market for labor were perfect, one would expect to find that both cognitive and noncognitive behaviors have positive effects on work performance and thus on individual earnings. That is, if demand for workers is similiar in all geographic regions and based only on productivity characteristics developed through schooling, there should be a direct relation between educational attainment and individual earnings. However, a number of factors render this relationship more complex. First, only a portion of the behaviors which determine an individual's productivity are developed in school. Second, there are market imperfections (i.e., failures of the market system to operate as market theory dictates) and discriminations in the demand for labor that often lead to differences in earnings among individuals with identical capacities. And finally, to the degree that differences in individuals' productivity are reflected in nonmonetary returns, or so-called "psychic" income (e.g., some jobs are more pleasurable than others), monetary earnings will not state true returns.

When an individual supplies labor services, he supplies abilities that are derived from a variety of background influences. Inherited characteristics, parents, peers, community, and communications media all represent factors that affect an individual's skills and personality. The quality and quantity of an individual's formal schooling are also generally related to the abilities which an individual brings to the marketplace. Thus, education per se represents only one input into the quality of labor supplied and accounts for only a portion of the productivity and earnings of an individual. Any analysis of the effect of schooling alone on earnings must attempt to separate the distinct effects of schooling from those of other influences.

The quality of his labor is not the only determinant of an individual's earnings; *demand* for his labor is also a major determinant. To the degree that the demand structure differs among varying labor markets (rural vs. urban, North vs. South, etc.), correspondence between educational attainment and earnings will also differ. Moreover, to the degree that discrimination exists against particular individuals or groups, there will be lower economic returns to education among such persons and groups. Since it seems reasonable to assume that prejudicial employment practices will decrease in the future, existing evidence may understate seriously the potential relationship between educational attainment and earnings for nonwhites and other groups who presently suffer the greatest economic consequences of discrimination in the labor market.

Despite the existence of employment inequities, it is important to recognize that raising individual proficiencies through improved and prolonged schooling does raise the quality of labor service supplied. It is true that imperfections in market demand act to limit the earning opportunities of particular groups in society. The point we wish to emphasize here, however, is that equalizing the labor market opportunities available to members of racial minorities will require improvements in the productive qualifications of these groups as well as changes in employment demand. In addition to improvements in schooling, greater social investment in nonschooling inputs such as health services and housing may be required before the productive services of nonwhites are equal to those of whites.

Obviously we cannot expect differences in education alone to explain all of the differences in earning opportunities. Yet, the evidence derived from economic research in "earning functions" suggests that schooling does explain a significant share of the variation in individual income and that the equalization of levels of schooling among whites and nonwhites in combination with the elimination of employment discrimination would come close to equalizing earnings between the two groups (see Michelson, 1968). The evidence is also unequivocal in demonstrating that students who receive a higher quality and quantity of schooling show higher earnings—on the average—than do those who experience poorer quality and fewer years of schooling, even after adjustments are made for other factors that affect earning (Becker, 1964; Denison, 1962).

Research Findings on Education and Earnings

The observation that persons with more schooling receive higher earnings over their lifetimes has long been obvious to even the most casual viewer (Glick & Miller, 1956; Miller, 1960; Houthakker, 1959). In Table 1, 1960 census data are used to illustrate this simple relationship. (These dollar figures would be higher for more recent data.) In 1959, the average Michigan high-school graduate, for example, received almost $1,300 more annual income than the average male who terminated his education in elementary school. College graduates received $2,100 more than male high-school graduates who did not enter college and $3,500 more than males who did not go to high school.

This evidence is dramatic, but it does not demonstrate what portion of an individual's earnings is uniquely attributable to education. For evidence of this type, we turned first to the works of Becker (1964) and Denison (1962). Both of these researchers made downward adjustments in the returns to schooling to compensate for earning differentials due to differences in ability, motivation, social class, etc. Denison estimated that only 60% of the difference among individuals' earnings that corresponds to difference in schooling is attributable to schooling itself and that 40% is due to other superior earnings attributes of persons with higher levels of schooling. Becker reviewed a number of earnings studies that adjusted for "ability" and concluded that such adjustments did not reduce markedly the high rates of return in earnings that are associated with more education (Becker, 1964). More recent studies (Bowman & Anderson, 1969) suggest that Denison understated the significance of schooling. In fact, two statis

Table 1   Annual Median Incomes in 1959 for Michigan Males 25 Years Old and Over, by Years of Schooling

Schooling	Median income
All males	$5,269
No schooling	1,735
Elementary	
1–4 years	2,479
5–7 years	3,910
8 years	4,591
High School	
1–3 years	5,358
4 years	5,881
College	
1–3 years	6,486
4 years or more	8,091

Note.—Data found in 1960 Census of Population.

tical studies that examined the effects on income of both educational attainment and IQ reported that the introduction of the IQ measure into the analysis did not reduce the discernible impact of schooling (Griliches, 1968; Conlisk, 1968). Griliches also suggested that the impact of individual variations in ability on income is evident only at higher educational levels.

Assuming that higher earnings are partly attributable to educational attainment, it is interesting to explore how much of this differential is attributable to increased learning and how much is attributable to other noncognitive effects of schools. Since it appears that good schools can improve students' achievement (i.e., cognitive development) as measured by standardized tests as well as prepare them for and motivate them to obtain more years of schooling, it is logical to examine separately the earnings effects of achievement test scores and additional years of schooling. We assume that each additional year of schooling reinforces the noncognitive development which the schools encourage. One caution from the onset, however: to the degree that additional schooling increases achievement, the effects of the two may be confounded.

Hanson, Weisbrod, and Scanlon (1968) reported that, for a sample of males who obtained very low scores on the Armed Forces Qualification Test, the relationship between test scores and earnings was much stronger than the relationship between earnings and years of schooling. They concluded "that what one learns influences earnings more than does the mere fact of spending time in school [p. 225]." However, subsequent study of a more representative sample of males suggested that the number of years an individual spends in school does have a significant and strong association with earnings which is *in addition* to the apparent effect measured by achievement tests (Hanson & Weisbrod). Gintis (1969) drew together information from a variety of sources which supports the view that the noncognitive effects may be even more important than the cognitive in explaining occupational and economic success. The logic here is that a main objective of the schools is the preparation of students for particular behavioral roles (cooperating with fellow workers, for example) and that maximizing the cognitive goals of the school may sometimes conflict with these noncognitive objectives.

Perhaps the most ambitious analysis to date of the relation between education and earnings was done by Hanoch (1965). He used the "one in one thousand sample" from the 1960 census to estimate the income returns to schooling for American males by age, race, and region while holding constant other influential variables. Even when he employed the most stringent of statistical controls on the socioeconomic background available in the census to separate other-than-school influences, Hanoch found a strong correspondence between schooling and earnings. For example, among white males in the North, ages 35–44, the estimated effect on earnings of going beyond elementary school was substantial. High-school graduates were receiving almost $1,300 more annually and college graduates $3,100 more than elementary-school graduates (Hanoch, 1967). The average earnings for all northern males in this age category was $6,300 in 1959, so, as a proportion of total income, these educational differentials are significant. It is important to stress that these represent income increments that were adjusted for the effects on earnings of a large number of individual characteristics other than years of schooling, so these income differentials are those attributable to *education* differentials alone.

School Expenditures, Worker Productivity, and Earnings

At least two studies investigated whether individuals who attended schools in areas with higher school expenditures had higher individual earnings. The quantity of schooling was measured by the number of years completed; the quality was measured by total expenditures per pupil or teacher salaries. Welch (1966) found that money spent on teachers' salaries enhanced the earnings value of each year of schooling completed among agricultural workers.

Morgan and Sirageldin (1968) also reported that school expenditures appear to be an exceedingly important determinant of the earnings of individuals. Using a sample of 1,525 heads of family, they examined the effect of social and educational variables on earnings. They found that the combined effect of race, urbanization of background, age, sex, and years of schooling accounted for 35% of the variance in earnings. By employing an additional explanatory variable, per pupil expenditure of the state in which the respondents resided, they were able to account for 51% of the variance in earnings. They concluded that there is a high return on investments which are made to improve the quality of schools. They contended, moreover, that this finding would hold even if more elaborate efforts to remove "spurious correlations" were attempted.

Summary of Education and Earnings

The effect of schooling on earnings has been substantiated by numerous studies, some of which are described above. Better schools have fewer dropouts and higher student achievement. Both of these factors have been shown to be related to higher earnings or greater economic opportunity. Even when adjustments were made for individual ability and other intervening influences, the payoffs to better and more schooling persisted. Also, studies relating school expenditures to student earnings supported the view that investment in the quality of schooling is likely to improve individuals' productive capacities and earnings opportunities. While the studies differ in their findings on the relative magnitude of the schooling-earnings effect, virtually all studies on the subject show evidence of a significant effect. There are few social science hypotheses that have been tested so intensively with such consistent results.

EDUCATION AND OCCUPATIONAL CHOICE

Another dimension of opportunity which appears to be strongly related to schooling is that of an individual's occupational choice. Employers use quantity and quality of formal educational preparation as one basis for selecting employees. Those individuals with more or better schooling are likely to have a wider range of potential employers or occupations to choose from. There are two possible interpretations of this relationship. First, schooling credentials may be important simply for obtaining a particular position, even when the credentials bear only a slight relationship to the proficiencies required to handle the task (Berg, 1969). Alternatively, schooling requirements may be imposed as a standard for employee selection because of a direct linkage between the requirements and job performance. The significant point is that both interpretations support the proposition that the quality and quantity of a person's schooling will directly affect the range of occupational choices available to him.

Efforts have also been made in the study of this opportunity dimension to separate the nonschooling abilities that occur coincidentally with educational attainment from the unique effect of schooling. Bajema (1968) examined the interrelationships among IQ score, educational attainment, and occupational achievement. The sample was 437 males, age 45 who had taken the Terman Group Intelligence Test when they were in the sixth grade. Bajema concluded that "while intelligence (as measured by Intelligence tests) is associated with occupational achievement, the results of this study indicate that its effects operate wholly within the school system [p. 319]." In other words, intelligence is important, but unless that intelligence is manifested through the skills one acquires in school, it is not particularly useful in earning a living. Girod and Tofigh (1965) used a different sample, but also reported evidence that schooling has a unique effect on occupational choice and success.

The most extensive study of the effect of schooling on occupational achievement was the effort of Blau and Duncan (1967). Using a large sample of males, ages 20–64, who were surveyed by the U. S. Census Bureau in 1962, Blau and Duncan reported that educational level has a strong effect on occupational achievement.

SOCIAL AND ECONOMIC MOBILITY
ACROSS GENERATIONS

An interesting implication of our foregoing discussion is that an individual's increased educational attainment is likely to improve his children's opportunities. Because of this observed linkage, education represents perhaps the best means of increasing social and economic mobility over generations and of lifting people from poverty.

As Blau and Duncan (1967) demonstrated, the higher the occupational achievement of the father, the higher that of the son, and the more educated the parent, the more educated the child. Using data from a 1962 census survey, it was found that for every additional four years of school completed by the family head, almost one and one-half additional years were completed by the offspring, (Duncan, 1965; David, Brazer, Morgan, & Cohen, 1961). Supporting evidence for this phenomenon was reported by Masters (1969) in a study of social class determinants and educational achievement. Masters examined the simultaneous effects of several social class variables in explaining dropout rates. He found that the probability of dropping out of school by age 16 or 17 was directly related to the education level of the head of the household (parent or parent substitute). He also discovered that the lower the education level of the head of the household, the more likely it was that the child was at a grade level behind that of his age group.

Numerous studies point out that a child's academic performance is likely to be related to his parents' social class. The accepted explanation for this observance is that much of the education and educational motivation of a child takes place in the home. Children whose parents are more educated begin their school careers with higher achievement scores than do their less fortunate peers (see, e.g., Coleman et al., 1966). This phenomenon has been confirmed in many studies of educational performance, and is generally considered to be the result of the quality and quantity of interaction between parents and children (Peterson & DeBord, 1966).

Thus, upward mobility over generations seems to be directly affected by education. Higher educational attainment not only increases the opportunities of the individual receiving the schooling, but also enhances the prospects of his children.

EDUCATION AND POLITICAL PARTICIPATION

Since opportunity was defined earlier as the ability to affect one's destiny, the efficacy of an individual's participation in governmental processes is especially important. The determination of political issues and the choice of government representatives frequently directly affect an individual's welfare. Thus, individual opportunity in the political sphere requires political consciousness and political participation.

Schooling appears to be the predominant determinant of political consciousness and political participation. Almond and Verba (1963) described the overwhelming importance of education in determining political orientation. The more educated person tends to exhibit a greater awareness of government's impact on the individual than does the person with less education. Moreover, the more educated the individual is, the greater is his awareness of political issues, the greater is the range of persons with whom he discusses politics, the more likely he is to be a member of a political organization, and the more positive are his attitudes about the ability of people to govern themselves in a democratic fashion.

Empirical evidence of the schools' effects on political attitudes is found in the extensive study by Hess and Torney (1967). They examined the background and attitudes of approximately 10,000 elementary-school students in grades two through eight selected from 16 middle-class and 16 working-class schools in eight cities. On the basis of their analysis, they concluded that the school is the "central, salient, and dominant force" in the political socialization of the young child.

Given this background, it is no surprise that virtually all studies on the subject found a strong positive relationship between educational attainment and political participation. Agger and Ostrom (1956) found education even more significant than income in predicting political participation. Education appears to be particularly important in predicting who is likely to cast a ballot (see, e.g., Campbell, Converse, Miller & Stokes, 1964). Moreover, the greater the individual's educational attainment, the more likely he is to become involved psychologically in politics (Milbrath, 1965). Campbell, one of the best known authorities on the subject, concluded that "the surest single predictor of political involvement is number of years of formal education [1963, p. 21]." In short, the link between education on the one hand and political participation and potential efficacy on the other has been well documented. Persons with higher educational attainment are more able and more likely to become involved in political processes and to influence the outcomes of the issues that affect them. Persons with lower levels of education not only are less knowledgeable concerning political issues and thus not as likely to be aware of matters affecting themselves, but are also less well informed about the entire political process and thus not as capable of expressing their views even when they are aware of relevant issues. Clearly, lack of schooling (or lack of good schooling) restricts one's ability to exercise his political rights.

EDUCATION AND CRIME

The direct effect of educational attainment on occupational choice, earnings, and political participation represents only some of the more prominent ways in which education is linked to opportunity. Education also has indirect effects on opportunity. For example, persons with less schooling are more likely to engage in illegal activities, usually resulting in a restriction of their freedom. Low educational attainment leads to limited employment, occupational, and earnings alternatives. Given limited choices, the less educated person is more likely to pursue illegal means of achieving higher status and income. The result of this is that a person with lower educational attainment is more likely to be arrested, to be punished, and to carry a police record that further diminishes his chances of employment, his occupational choice, and his earnings. Failure in school is also likely to contribute to a rejection of the norms of the larger society, and normlessness appears to be related to crime (Powell, 1966).

This is not to say that all crime or even most of it is due to low educational attainment. Rather, the evidence suggests that since there is a limited range of legal alternatives for poorly educated individuals, these individuals are tempted to fulfill status aspirations and material needs through such illegal activities as gambling, prostitution, robbery, dealing in narcotics, etc.

A number of empirical studies have linked education to crime. One of the best of these studies was recently completed by the State of California Department of Corrections (1969). The researchers discovered that, for the years 1958–1967, the median years of schooling among newly imprisoned male felons in California remained constant at the eighth-grade level. This occurred despite the fact that the median level of schooling among all California adults was 12.1 years in 1960 and presumably has been rising ever since. It appears that those who commit felonies tend to possess substantially less than the average amount of schooling. This same study reported that in 1967 only 4.7% of all newly committed male felons had completed 12 or more years of schooling. Looked at another way, 95.3% of all convicted felons were below the average for all California adults. These figures are supported by data from a U. S. Department of Justice study (1967). Yet another finding in the California study revealed that crimes of violence are associated with level of education. Homicides, assaults, and other violent felonies are tied much more closely to lower levels of education than are less violent crimes. This is rather striking evidence that lack of schooling contributes to adult criminal behavior.

There is also evidence that relates education to juvenile delinquency. For example, an examination of juveniles in a large city (Spiegelman et al., 1968) found a high negative correlation between educational attainment and the probability of being arrested for committing a juvenile crime. Even when differences in the probability of being arrested due to other factors (e.g., race, family income, family size, presence of both parents in the home, IQ scores) were considered, it was found that high-school dropouts were three to five times more likely than high-school graduates to be arrested for committing a juvenile crime. Since delinquents do not seem to be significantly less intelligent than the general population, but are more likely to fail in school, the potential role of the schools in preventing delinquency is strongly implied (Prentice & Kelly, 1963).

EDUCATION AND OTHER AREAS OF OPPORTUNITY

Two of the many other areas in which education affects opportunity are further schooling options and military choices. Accreditation of high schools is assumed to be directly related to the breadth and quality of their instructional offerings. Low expenditure schools are less likely to fulfill accreditation requirements, frequently causing their students to be handicapped in obtaining college admission. Further, to the degree that poorly endowed schools which are accredited limit intellectual development, their pupils will do poorly on college entrance examinations. Taken together, these two effects of lower expenditure schools severely limit the postsecondary schooling options of their students. The sacrifice in earnings attributable to this phenomenon can be calculated from knowledge of the reduced probability of being able to enroll in institutions of higher education (Weisbrod, 1962).

Military choices, too, are directly affected by the quality and quantity of schooling received. Inductees are required to take the Armed Forces Qualification Test (AFQT), an instrument which purports to measure an individual's trainability. The examinee's performance on the AFQT depends in large measure on the level of his educational attainment and on the quality of his education which is reflected in the quality of school resources (Karpinos, 1966).

A high score on the AFQT enhances an individual's opportunities in two important ways. First, inductees who do well on the examination are offered many training options, and they tend almost invariably to choose courses of study which develop abilities having high payoffs in civilian life. Thus, the armed forces invest substantial resources in increasing the marketable skills of those persons who have received the best pre-Army education. These persons are given expensive instruction in such areas as electronics technology, diesel mechanics, aircraft maintenance, etc. The less fortunate inductee who scores poorly on the AFQT has fewer training options. That is, the armed forces invest less in him to raise his occupational status and earnings in civilian life. Thus, the lower scoring inductee tends to be assigned the more menial tasks or thrown into front-line combat.

Also, the more educated males avoid induction by enrolling in college and by seeking employment in critical occupations such as teaching and engineering. The less educated are drafted so that by virtue of their lower school attainments they are, at best, likely to be serving at a rate of meager pay while their better-educated countrymen are building careers and families. At worst, they are the ones most likely to become casualties or mortalities.

Finally, it is important to note that both mental health and geographic mobility tend to be educationally selective. For example, studies of social class and severe mental disorders evidenced a higher incidence of such disorders among the lower social strata, where educational attainment is lowest (see Hollingshead & Redlick, 1954). Census data suggest that geographic mobility, and thus an enlarged potential job market, is strongly related to education. The more highly educated individual has better knowledge of job alternatives and more self-reliance in seeking employment in new geographic areas. Moreover, if educational attainment is linked strongly to income, the better-educated individual is more likely to have the dollar resources necessary to move.

SUMMARY

Educational attainment and opportunity are linked in many ways. Abundant evidence supports the view that education affects income, occupational choice, social and economic mobility, political participation, social deviance, etc. Indeed, educational attainment is related to opportunity in so many ways that the two terms seem inextricably intertwined in the mind of the layman and in the findings of the social scientist.

This paper has reviewed only the individual benefits of education. It is important, however, to also note that there are enormous social benefits. As a social investment, dollars spent on education yield a higher economic return than do dollars spent on buildings and physical equipment (Becker, 1964). In addition, educational expenditures improve the functioning of a democratic society by increasing literacy, by raising the level of public understanding of complex social issues, and by increasing total political participation. The evidence is overwhelming in support of the proposition that the post-school opportunity and performance of a pupil are related directly to his educational attainment.

REFERENCES

Agger, R. and V. Ostrom. Political participation in a small community. In Heinz Eulau et al. (Eds.), *Political behavior*. Glencoe, Ill.: The Free Press, 1956.

Almond, G. and S. Verba. *The civic culture*. Princeton, N.J.: Princeton University Press, 1963.

Becker, G. S. *Human capital*. New York: Columbia University Press, 1964.

Bajema, C. J. A note on the interrelations among intellectual ability, educational attainment, and occupational achievement: A follow-up study of a male Kalamazoo public school population. *Sociology of Education,* 1968, **41,** 317–319.

Berg, I. Rich man's qualifications for poor man's jobs. *Trans-action,* 1969, **6,** 45–50.

Blau, P. M. and O. D. Duncan. *The American occupational structure.* New York: John Wiley, 1967.

Bloom, B. S. (Ed.) *Taxonomy of educational objectives, Handbook I: The cognitive domain.* New York: McKay, 1956.

Bowman, M. J. and C. Anderson. Relationships among schooling, ability, and income in industrialized societies. In K. Hüfner and J. Naumann (Eds.), *Economics of education in transition.* Berlin: Max Planck Institut, 1969.

Campbell, A. The passive citizen. *Acta Sociologica,* 1963, **9,** 9–21.

Campbell, A., P. L. Converse, W. E. Miller, and D. E. Stokes. *The American voter.* New York: John Wiley, 1964.

Coleman, J. et al. *Equality of educational opportunity.* Washington, D.C.: U.S. Government Printing Office, 1966.

Conlisk, J. A bit of evidence on the income-ability-education interrelation. University of California at San Diego, Economics Department, 1968. (mimeo)

David, M., H. Brazer, J. Morgan, and W. Cohen. *Educational achievement— Its causes and effect.* Ann Arbor: University of Michigan, 1961.

Denison, E. *The sources of economic growth in the United States and the alternatives before us.* New York: Committee for Economic Development, 1962.

Duncan, B. *Family factors and school dropouts: 1920–1960.* Cooperative Research Project No. 2258, U. S. Office of Education. Ann Arbor: University of Michigan, 1965.

Gintis, H. Production functions in the economics of education and the characteristics of worker productivity. Unpublished doctoral dissertation, Harvard University, 1969.

Girod, R. and F. Tofigh. Family background and income, school career and social mobility of young males of working class origin: A Geneva survey. *Acta Sociologica,* 1965, **11,** 94–109.

Glick, P. C. and H. P. Miller. Educational level and potential income. *American Sociological Review,* 1956, **21,** 307–312.

Griliches, Z. Notes on the role of education in production functions and growth accounting. In W. Lee Hanson (Ed.), *Education, income, and human capital.* New York: National Bureau of Economic Research, 1970.

Guthrie, J. W. Survey of school effectiveness studies. In A. Mood (Ed.), *Do teachers make a difference?* Washington, D.C.: U.S. Government Printing Office, 1970.

Guthrie, J. W., G. B. Kleindorfer, H. M. Levin, and R. T. Stout. *Schools and inequality.* Cambridge, Mass.: M.I.T. Press, 1971, in press.

Hanoch, G. Personal earnings and investment in schooling. *The Journal of Human Resources,* 1967, **II,** 310–329.

Hanson, L. W., B. Weisbrod, and W. J. Scanlon. Determinants of earnings: Does schooling really count? University of Wisconsin, Economics Department, April 1968. (mimeo)

Hanson, L. W. and B. Weisbrod. Work in progress at University of Wisconsin.

Hess, R. and J. Torney. *The development of political attitudes in children.* Chicago: Aldine, 1967.

Hollingshead, A. B. and F. C. Redlick. Social stratification and schizophrenia. *American Sociological Review*, 1954, **19**, 302–306.

Houthakker, H. S. Education and income. *Review of Economics and Statistics*, 1959, **41**, 24–28.

Inkeles, A. Social structure and the socialization of competence. *Harvard Educational Review*, 1956, **36**, 265–283.

Karpinos, P. The mental qualifications of American youths for military service and its relationship to educational attainment. *Proceedings of the Social Statistics Section of the American Statistical Association*, 1966.

Mann, A. A historical overview: The lumpenproletariat, education, and compensatory action. In Charles V. Daley (Ed.), *The quality of inequality: Urban and suburban public schools.* Chicago: University of Chicago Press, 1968.

Masters, S. H. The effect of family income on children's education: Some findings on inequality of opportunity. *The Journal of Human Resources*, 1969, **IV**, 158–175.

Michelson, S. Incomes of racial minorities. Brookings Institution, Washington, D.C., 1968. (mimeo)

Milbrath, L. W. *Political participation.* Chicago: Rand McNally, 1965.

Miller, H. P. Annual and lifetime income relation to education. *American Economic Review*, 1960, **50**, 962–986.

Morgan, J. and I. Sirageldin. A note on the quality dimension in education. *The Journal of Political Economy*, 1968, **76**, 1069–1077.

Peterson, R. A. and L. DeBord. Educational supportiveness of the home and the academic performance of disadvantaged boys. *IMRID Behavioral Science Monograph*, 1966, No. 3.

Powell, E. H. Crime as a function of anomie. *The Journal of Criminal Law, Criminology, and Police Science*, 1966, **57**, 161–171.

Prentice, N. M. and F. J. Kelly. Intelligence and delinquency: A reconsideration. *The Journal of Social Psychology*, 1963, **60**, 327–337.

Spiegelman, R. et al. *A benefit/cost model to evaluate educational programs.* Menlo Park, Calif.: Stanford Research Institute, 1968.

State of California Department of Corrections. *California prisons 1967: Summary statistics of felon prisoners and parolees.* Sacramento: State Department of Correction, 1969.

U. S. Department of Justice. *Blue print for change, annual report of the Federal Bureau of Prisons.* Washington, D.C.: U.S. Government Printing Office, 1967.

Walsh, J. R. Capital concept applied to man. *Quarterly Journal of Economics*, 1935, **49**, 255–285.

Weisbrod, B. A. Education and investment in human capital. *Journal of Political Economy, Supplement*, 1962, **70**, 106–123.

Welch, F. Measurement of the quality of schooling. *American Economic Review*, 1966, **LVI**, 379–392.

PUBLIC LEARNS WHAT FOUR AGES KNOW IN WRITING AND CITIZENSHIP*

Eighty-eight percent of the nation's nine-year-olds can write a thank-you note that Grandmother would be proud of, but only 31 percent can write a message telling their older sister when and where she is supposed to meet which of her friends. At least this is one way of looking at some of the data released in San Diego in November, when National Assessment announced national results for writing and citizenship at its second reporting session.

The results for these subject areas were made public before an audience composed of subject matter specialists, representatives of the press, and members of the Education Commission of the States, NAEP's governing organization, whose Steering Committee was meeting in San Diego. The first reporting session, at which national science and partial national citizenship results were made public, was during the July meeting of the Steering Committee.

Following are samples of the kinds of information NAEP reported in San Diego about the knowledge, skills, and attitudes of four age groups across the nation.

GROWTH BETWEEN 9 AND 13, 13 AND 17

Many of the citizenship and writing exercises were given at more than one age level. Because the tasks required in these exercises were identical, or essentially the same except for minor wording changes, the percentages of acceptable responses can be compared across ages. The results of the great majority of overlapping exercises in both subject areas show a not unexpected increase in success as age increases—at least for the three in-school ages.

---

* Reprinted from January–February 1971 *NAEP Newsletter*, Barbara Goodwin, Ed., with the permission of the National Assessment of Educational Progress, a Project of the Education Commission of the States.

For example, when 9s, 13s, and 17s were asked why it might be good to have the newspapers in a city written and printed by more than one company, the percentages of acceptable responses, by increasing age, were 37, 64, and 88. Asked why we have a government, the respective percentages of 9s, 13s, and 17s who could state at least one acceptable reason were 48, 81, and 90. When asked to listen to a recorded telephone conversation and write a note relaying the message given in that conversation, the percentages of responses providing all the necessary information were, by increasing age, 31, 67, and 79. (Responses were judged acceptable or unacceptable on the basis of predetermined categories. Examples of responses are included in the actual report for each subject area.)

The pattern that emerges from these results, and from those for many other overlapping exercises, could be taken as evidence that education is playing an important role in increasing knowledge. But one of the subject matter specialists who reviewed exercises in San Diego suggested that the increasing success shown by the results might be due simply to young people's growing older. . . .

SOME DECLINE BETWEEN 17s AND ADULTS

In general, exercises that overlapped the three younger ages showed the greatest amount of growth to occur at the youngest end of the scale— between ages 9 and 13, as the preceding results indicate. At the other end of the age range, a number of exercises that overlapped adults and at least one other age group showed an opposite trend—often the adult responses demonstrated a decrease in success.

This declining success was especially evident in the overlapping writing exercises. For example, in one identical overlapping exercise, 13s, 17s, and adults were asked to fill out an application blank. The precentages of acceptable responses increased between ages 13 and 17 (from 26 to 61), but only 50 percent of the adults completed this exercise successfully. In another exercise that asked 13s, 17s, and adults to write a letter ordering a product, acceptable responses were given by 46 percent of the 13s and 55 percent of the 17s; the rate of success then declined to 49 percent of the adults who wrote letters that included all the necessary information. When 17s and adults were asked to write directions for making or doing something, only 57 percent of the adult responses were acceptable, compared to 75 percent of the 17s.

In citizenship, some of the results also indicate a decline for adults, although this does not occur consistently enough to indicate a definite pattern. While there are many exercises in which adults did more poorly than 17s, there are also exercises in which they excelled.

The instances of lower success for adults might be explained by any

of several factors—loss of skill from lack of practice, less cooperative behavior, or improvements in school programs since the adults received their
formal education. A further reason may be that the adults were less attuned
to a "testing" atmosphere than were the in-school participants, and that
this kind of unfamiliar situation affected their responses. . . .

COMEDIANS, SONGWRITERS, POETS, PLAYWRIGHTS . . .

A number of inferences about specific objectives within subject areas
can also be made on the basis of the released data. One such observation is
that people at each of National Assessment's four age levels do some kind
of writing on their own, that is neither assigned in school nor required by
their occupation.

Nines, for example, were given a list of several kinds of writing and
asked to mark those types they did just for fun. At least one item was
marked by 93 percent of the 9s. (Jokes were the most popular among a
list that also included poems, reports, and stories.) Of 9s, 13s, and adults
who had taken a trip during the last year, 78, 88, and 71 percent, respectively, indicated having done some kind of writing, ranging from
sending a post card to keeping a diary about the trip's events. Asked
whether they had written a letter to order something through the mail
during the last year, 54 percent of the 17s said they had done so and 55
percent of the adults.

These exercises were designed to assess appreciation of writing,
with the underlying assumption that people who do unassigned writing
have appreciation for the value of writing. A built-in risk of such "self-
report" kinds of exercises, of course, is that what respondents say may
not reflect what they in fact do.

SPECIFICS A PROBLEM FOR 9s, 13s

The results for 9s and 13s indicated a high degree of success with general writing skills—88 percent of the 9s could write an acceptable thank-
you note, and 91 percent of the 13s could write an acceptable letter
inviting a friend to visit. But as the amount of specific information
required to complete the task increased, the percentages of acceptable
responses often decreased.

For example, when 13s were asked to complete an application blank
with a number of bits of information, only 26 percent filled in all the
required information successfully. Success for 9s was only about half that
for 13s—only 12 and 16 percent of the 9s' responses to this exercise were
acceptable. (Nines were given two slightly different versions of the
exercise, one asking for the first name first, the other for the last name
first.)

It must be mentioned, though, that the percentages for 9s on this exercise might not be valid indicators of how well this age group could do. To maintain National Assessment's policy of respondent anonymity, the 9s and 13s were asked to use the name Adam (or Alice) Baker Carson instead of their own on the application blank. For 13s, this seemed to cause little difficulty—56 percent of these young people used the correct name. But for 9s the percentages were much lower—only 19 and 28 used the assigned name. These percentages were in marked contrast with 9s' success in supplying other bits of information required by the blank. If any name written in the correct order—either the student's or some other— had been scored acceptable, the 9s' overall success with the application blank would have been higher.

ADULTS KNOW MORE ABOUT LOCAL AFFAIRS, CURRENT EVENTS

In general, the results for citizenship exercises dealing with state and local affairs indicated somewhat greater success among adults than among 17s and younger age groups. Asked about the political structure of their local community, 87 percent of the adults knew whether their community had a town council, compared to 69 percent of the 17s; 86 percent knew whether their town had a mayor (for the 17s, 82 percent); and 63 percent knew if their city had a town manager (42 percent for the 17s).

Adults also showed greater success in an exercise asking for the identity of persons currently holding a list of offices. The percentages of adults giving the correct names for various offices were: President, 98; vice-president, 87; secretary of state, 16; secretary of defense, 24; speaker of the house, 32; senate majority leader, 23; one senator from own state, 58; both state senators, 31; and congressman from own district, 39. This exercise was also given to 17s and 13s, and the acceptable response percentages for adults were consistently greater, for all items, than those of the two younger groups.

FEW ADULTS TAKE ACTIVE CIVIC ROLE

Adults and 17s generally demonstrated high awareness of ways in which citizens can influence the decisions of government. One or more means, ranging from writing letters to newspaper editors to signing petitions or offering opinions at public meetings, were given by 86 percent of the adults and 77 percent of the 17s. But when the two groups were asked if they thought *they* could influence governmental decisions, the rate of acceptable responses declined: 61 percent of the adults answered yes and 54 percent of the 17s.

Exercises designed to determine actual efforts made by respondents to influence government yielded even lower success rates. Adults were asked if they had written to or spoken with a government official about at least one civic issue in the past five years; only 26 percent indicated they had done so. And only 12 percent of the adults and 7 percent of the 17s indicated they had ever written a letter to a newspaper editor.

EXERCISES' ROLE NOT EXHAUSTED

The announcement of results in San Diego is not the only usefulness to be served by the citizenship and writing exercises. First, National Assessment anticipates that the results for these exercises will encourage people interested in education to examine the findings and their possible implications for areas in which education might need to improve. Second, NAEP is now in the process of further analyzing the exercise results to obtain information about educational attainments on the basis of certain group breakdowns. These include geographic region, size and type of community, sex, color, and educational levels of the parents of respondents. It is expected that such information, to be released in the near future, will be of additional use to those interested in what young people know and can do. And finally, NAEP will reuse the exercises that were not released in San Diego for future assessments. In this way National Assessment will attempt to find out how well young people are doing in citizenship and writing several years from now compared to how they did in 1969–70.

QUESTIONS AND ANSWERS ABOUT THE WRITING AND CITIZENSHIP ASSESSMENT

1. How many people took part in the assessment, and when was it conducted? Responses were collected from about 88,000 people—24,000 9-year-olds, 28,000 13s, 28,000 17s, and 8,600 young adults between 26 and 35. One person would not have had time to answer all the exercises, but for each exercise administered to 9s, 13s, and 17s, about 2,000 responses were collected; responses for adults averaged about 850 per exercise. The assessment was conducted between Spring, 1969, and Winter, 1970.
2. How were the participants selected? Field personnel traveled nation-wide to more than 2,500 schools that had been drawn through a random sample. Within each of these schools, children at the right age levels were selected, also through random sampling procedures, to complete exercises. Young adults and out-of-school 17s were selected to participate through a nation-wide random sample of households.
3. What objectives were assessed, and who decided they were important? Four main objectives were assessed by the writing exercises:
   a. Write to communicate adequately in a social situation.
   b. Write to communicate adequately in a business or vocational situation.

c. Write to communicate adequately in a scholastic situation.

d. Appreciate the value of writing.

The citizenship goals were:

a. Show concern for the well-being of others.

b. Support rights and freedoms of all individuals.

c. Recognize the value of just law.

d. Know the main structure and functions of our governments.

e. Participate in effective civic action.

f. Understand problems of international relations.

g. Approach civic decisions rationally.

h. Take responsibility for own development.

i. Help and respect their own families.

All the objectives for both subject areas were reviewed by three groups of people—lay citizens, subject matter experts, and educators. After these groups approved the objectives as important and worthwhile goals for education, exercises were written to assess how well they were being met.

4. What kinds of exercises were given? For writing, there were basically three types: (1) short answer or short essay, where the responses were scored according to whether certain pieces of information had been included; (2) multiple-choice-type questions; and (3) essays requiring writing on a given topic. The essay results were scored for general writing ability, including such things as grammar, word choice, originality, and depth of thought. In citizenship, no exercises called for lengthy written replies because the quality of responses might then have depended too much on writing ability. Thus there were a number of multiple-choice citizenship exercises. There were other types, too, a number of which asked respondents to report their behavior in various situations. Finally, there were exercises designed to find out how well individuals work with others. These were given in special group situations where the assessment administrator observed the interactions of the respondents.

5. What organizations were involved in the citizenship and writing assessment? These subject areas were assessed during National Assessment's first year of field operations, so it should be said that all the organizations and individuals involved in the project's planning stages played a part. But the organizations most directly involved, and the ways in which they contributed, are:

American Institutes for Research, Palo Alto, California—development of citizenship objectives and exercises.

Educational Testing Service, Princeton, New Jersey—development of writing objectives and exercises.

Research Triangle Institute, Raleigh, North Carolina—sample design and selection and field operations.

Measurement Research Center, Iowa City, Iowa—scoring and data processing and, under subcontract to the Research Triangle Institute, field operations in the Central and Western regions of the U.S.

6. How will National Assessment determine educational progress in citizenship and writing over time? Only some of the citizenship and writing

exercises and results were released in San Diego. For both areas, approximately half of the exercises were made public, and these were chosen to be representative of the content and levels of success shown in the withheld exercises. The unreleased exercises will be readministered during the next assessments of citizenship and writing (in 1974–75 and 1973–74, respectively). Then the results will be compared to identify the educational progress made in these two subject areas during the interim.

7. What other subject areas are within the scope of National Assessment? NAEP's current plan calls for assessment of 10 subject areas: science, writing, citizenship, reading, literature, music, social studies, math, art, and career and occupational development. Science was assessed along with citizenship and writing during the first year of field operations. This year, NAEP field staff are administering reading and literature exercises throughout the country. And by August, 1975, all 10 subject areas will have been assessed at least once.

8. Where can the results be obtained? The complete national results for citizenship and writing will appear in two separate National Assessment reports in the near future. Although costs have not yet been set, the reports will be available through the Superintendent of Documents, U.S. Government Printing Office, Washington, D.C. 20402. National results for science, which were released during NAEP's first reporting session, are now available through this address at the following prices: Science Report, $1.75; Summary of Science Report, $0.35; Commentary on Science Report (by science experts), $0.50.

HIGH SCHOOLS THAT WORK*

CHARLES E. SILBERMAN

There is clear evidence that elementary schools can be humane and free without in any way sacrificing intellectual development, and this is where the greatest change is occurring. But change is just as much needed in the

---

* Reprinted from *The Atlantic Monthly* (August 1970), pp. 85–87. Copyright © 1970, by Charles E. Silberman. Reprinted by permission of Random House, publisher of *Crisis in the Classroom*, which also contains this selection.

high schools. Because adolescents are harder to "control" than younger children, secondary schools tend to be even more authoritarian and repressive than elementary schools; the values they transmit are the values of docility, passivity, conformity, and lack of trust. These unpleasant attributes might be tolerable if one could view them, so to speak, as the price to be paid for "a good education"—good, that is to say, in academic terms. Such is not the case; mindlessness affects the high school curriculum every bit as much as the elementary curriculum. And the junior high school, by almost unanimous agreement, is the wasteland—one is tempted to say cesspool—of American education.

Reform has been slower in the secondary than in the primary schools in part, at least, because the problems are more complex and the solutions a good deal less obvious. Teen-agers arrive in school with their interests, their likes and dislikes, and their values much more clearly formed. They are far less susceptible than young children are to the teacher's influence; one of the characteristics of growth, as Jerome Bruner of Harvard emphasizes, is the "increasing independence of response from the immediate nature of the stimulus." Moreover, teen-agers are subject to a far wider range of influences outside the classroom—influences from their own peer culture, as well as from the adult culture as transmitted by parents and the mass media.

The problem is complicated still further by the fact that adolescents learn in different and more complex ways than young children. The latter can deal easily with the immediate and the concrete—with what is before them, or what they have already experienced. They find it more difficult to handle the abstract, for they do not yet have command over the mental operations that would enable them easily to go beyond the information they already have, to conjure up alternative possibilities that could occur.

During adolescence, however, roughly between the ages of twelve and fifteen, young people gradually gain command over the final stage of cognitive development. Adolescents learn how to think about their own thoughts, to think systematically about the future, to deal with concepts, propositions, and hypotheses as well as with objects, and to understand and handle metaphors.

The growth that occurs during adolescence makes possible substantial changes in both what is learned and how it is learned. Since their growing command over language, abstraction, and metaphor enables high school students to transcend their own experience and environment, high school is the place where they can come into possession of the culture, which is to say, the world created by the perceptions, discoveries, creations, imaginations, and thoughts of men. In a way and with a subtlety and sophistication that the elementary school cannot attempt, the high school can concern itself with the transmission of culture, which Matthew

Arnold defined as "the best that has been thought and known in the world current everywhere."

The "best that has been thought and known" is embodied in large measure in the scholarly disciplines. What is crucial about the disciplines, however, is that they are not mere bodies of knowledge or collections of information; they are conceptual models, or paradigms, which men have constructed to give meaning to experience. A major emphasis must be to give students an understanding of the fundamental structure of the disciplines they study.

As Alfred North Whitehead insisted, "There is no royal road to learning through an airy path of brilliant generalizations." On the contrary, education involves "a patient mastery of details." But mastery of details is the means, not the end. Emphasizing structure means emphasizing the concepts that give meaning to the details, that enable students to distinguish relevant from irrelevant details, and to apply the discipline to new situations and problems. Respect for competence is one of the distinguishing characteristics of adolescence—hence the intense interest in sports and in driving a car, activities in which standards of competence are clearly defined. Adolescents should not be denied the satisfaction that comes from competence in intellecutal and aesthetic activities as well.

If students are not to regard knowledge as dogma, they must also understand something of its ephemeral character and, even more, the degree to which the "truth" of a discipline is a function of its structure and its method of inquiry. They need to understand the different kinds of evidence and proof that different disciplines use, and they need to understand the ways in which conceptual structures produce new knowledge but themselves change in response to the knowledge they produce. In short, students need to study the grammar or syntax of the disciplines, as well as their structure and content.

But *which* disciplines? In what sequence? With what content? Taught in what way?

There is not, and cannot be, one curriculum suitable for all time, or for all students at a given time. To insist that there is, is to confuse the means of education with the end. But this is in no way to suggest that any one piece of learning is as good as any other. Knowing one thing is *not* the same as knowing another, and some things are more worth knowing than others. Surely a man cannot be considered educated unless he has at least some understanding of science. Nor can a man be considered educated unless he has at least some knowledge of the past, some understanding of the human condition, some knowledge of the nature and dynamics of human society, and some knowledge of language and the arts.

Certain skills or abilities are also essential to the educated man: the ability to learn for himself, to take hold of a subject and "work it up" for himself, so that he is not dependent upon his teacher's direction; the ability to think for himself, "to ask the right critical questions and to apply rigorous tests" to his hunches, so that he is not dependent upon the ideas and opinions of others; the ability to respond to beauty, the beauty of nature as well as the art made by his fellowman; and the ability to communicate his ideas and feelings to others. The fact that there is no one curriculum to be specified for everyone does not mean, therefore, that there should be no curriculum at all—that high school students should study only what happens to interest them.

The most frightening manifestation of the generation gap, as Paul Goodman has demonstrated in several brilliant articles, is the new generation's rejection—at times, its inability even to understand—the authority of culture and the responsibilities that follow from it. "Their lack of a sense of history is bewildering," Goodman says of the students he knows. "They do not really understand that technology, civil law, and the university are *human* institutions, for which they too are responsible"; they do not understand "that these institutions, works of spirit in history, arc how Man has made himself and is." But "if they treat them as mere things, rather than being vigilant for them," Goodman worries, "they themselves become nothing. And nothing comes from nothing."

It is absolutely crucial, therefore, to bring the young into contact with, and possession of, their culture. To do this, high schools must offer more than just a potpourri of courses. This is not to say that they should provide a single curriculum or sequence that every student must follow, come what may. Given the mood of the present generation, nothing would be more self-defeating, more likely to turn students away from the culture. Since the time of Socrates, at the very least, it has been a truism that a teacher must start with where his students are if he is to take them somewhere else. For this generation of students, it means starting with much more freedom than previous generations enjoyed.

Then to take them somewhere else, the teacher must have some convictions about where they should go, convictions about what is worth learning. The real conflict, therefore, is not between "freedom" and "restraint"; it is between rival judgments about what is most worth knowing. The conflict need not be resolved: it is not essential that teachers and students share the same educational goals, only that they *have* educational goals—goals that can be articulated into some coherent structure. For education, as Daniel Bell argues, "is a confrontation with a discipline, a confrontation with a teacher."

Education is also a confrontation with oneself. "In fact, there is only one process," the philosopher Marjorie Greene writes, "that is ourselves trying to make sense of things, trying to find significance in what would else be chaos. . . . Learning is a transformation of the whole person." For this to happen, adolescents need a good deal of freedom for personal exploration and growth.

The kind of education we have been talking about is a necessary part of this process of growth and exploration, for the adolescent passion for self-definition is a product of cognitive, not just sexual and physiological, maturation. The mental structures that emerge during adolescence, which a well-conceived curriculum is designed to enhance, make self-definition possible, for they enable young people to think abstractly—to reflect on the meaning of their own thoughts, experiences, and feelings, and to conjure up the full range of alternatives for the future.

In short, the proper kind of education gives meaning and direction to the search for identity, preventing it from being a mere exercise in narcissism. Indeed, the school has a special obligation in this regard: more than any other institution, it has the capacity, and therefore the obligation, as Edgar Friedenberg puts it, "to clarify for its students the meaning of their experience of life in their society." It does this by helping students develop the knowledge and skills they need to make sense out of their experience—their experience with themselves, with others, with the world—not just during adolescence, but for the rest of their lives.

Students at present are hardly permitted, let alone encouraged, to confront either their teachers or themselves. They are given little opportunity, and no reason, to develop resolute ideas of their own about what they learn, and in most schools they are actively discouraged from trying to test their ideas against their teachers' ideas. By and large they are expected to learn what the faculty wants them to learn in the way the faculty wants them to learn it, and no nonsense, please. Freedom to explore, to test one's ideas as a means of finding out who one is and what one believes—these are luxuries a well-run school cannot afford. As one student summed it up, "It's all a question of what they want to produce, not what we want to become." The result, at best, is to persuade students that knowledge has no relation to them, no relevance for the kinds of lives they will lead; at worst, it produces the kind of alienation, the rejection of authority, the rejection of the whole notion of culture, of disciplines, and of learning, with which we are now contending.

Fortunately, there are signs of change, in part as a response to student dissent, in part as a result of the growing distaste a number of teachers and administrators feel for the way schools are run, and their conviction that schools can be more humane, that students can handle and benefit from greater freedom and responsibility. Whatever the reasons, there would appear to be a growing ferment in high schools around the country.

HUMANENESS IN EDUCATION*

One might ask at this point, What does a school dedicated to humane ends promote? The temptation is to not define such a school because there is a great deal to be said for the process by which an individual or a faculty can arrive at its own definitions. Nevertheless, some summing up of what has been said and what will follow this section may be in order— if only to provide a point of departure. *A school that draws its energy from humanistic values is one that celebrates personal differences and, also, emphasizes human commonalities; helps the student to understand his antecedents, to grow from them, and finally, to not be restricted by them; encourages superior scholarship which allows the inquirer to contribute to his society and to strengthen his own personality; provides the resources for the individual to examine his own life so that he can enlarge his maturity and help to cause growth in others.*

BARRIERS TO A HUMANE SCHOOL

This is a new agenda for American education, one based on a new concept of education's purposes and procedures. We have termed those purposes and procedures "humanizing education"—and because a relatively new and evolving concept can often be best grasped by examining its opposite, this book is organized around the problems of education that prevent the schools from being humane institutions. Each discussion of a problem is followed by a description of various attempted solutions— options for action which, judging from the experience of the 1960's, seem worth trying.

Education in every age has had problems—large or small monkey wrenches in the machinery that prevent schools from functioning as efficiently as they might. However, some people now feel these go beyond

---

* Reprinted by permission from *Schools for the 70's and Beyond: A Call to Action.* A Staff Report (Washington, D.C.: National Education Association, 1971), pp. 20–22.

the normal category of "problems." There are those who claim that the school is genuinely sick and suggest that there is a brace of symptoms to support such an indictment. Probably, it is more correct to say that the school is rapidly becoming a social institution which is inappropriate for too many youngsters in this age. Those who are contending that major surgery and therapy are the answers are implying that the school can and should be restored to its old healthy self. That is not the path to educational excellence. The schools must be reconstructed to work *differently*— using different assumptions and different techniques for different purposes.

Here are the components which have contributed to that educational inappropriateness. The problems necessarily overlap. One cannot talk about students' attitudes toward the school without considering the educational program and the teachers on which those attitudes are based. Though the following categories do not represent the neatest classification of school problems that might be devised, they do at least offer a method of attack:

The System: Local control of education, with appropriate supervision by the states, is a hallowed American tenet. Yet the increasing urbanization of the nation, the increasing size of urban school systems, and the centralization of educational decision making in single school boards and administrations have conspired to make local control largely a fiction. The dissatisfaction of inner-city parents with school performance and the more frequent failures of school bond issues point to the necessity of loosening up an obsolescent, rigid system of educational governance.

The Instructional Program: Curriculum—the answer to the ancient question, What is to be taught? Also, *how* is it to be taught? How are schools to be organized? How is student performance to be measured, and for what purposes?

The Teachers: Teachers during the 1960's abandoned their former docility and seemed at times to compete with students in their militance. Bread-and-butter issues such as salary received most public attention during strikes and work stoppages, but most teachers' demands went beyond money to include the teaching environment itself—to bring about reform of the school as an institution. It seems self-evident that teachers cannot develop the humaneness of students unless they are permitted to function as humane individuals themselves.

The Students: Who shall be educated? For how long? In what setting? The decade's various confrontations with segregation, unemployment, adult illiteracy, and disparities in educational readiness among first-graders from varied socioeconomic backgrounds force new attention to early childhood education, desegregation, adult and continuing education —as well as to the valuable perceptions and disappointing excesses of a new generation.

School Finance: The 1960's was a period of dramatically increased expenditures for education—yet educators kept insisting that more was needed, while taxpayers began demonstrating a reluctance to provide it. More money obviously is needed for humanizing the schools. One-third of the total funds must be federal.

These barriers to a humane school were not selected quixotically for inclusion in this report. Nor were they chosen either because they are fashionable or, at the other end of the scale, because they reflect the thinking of a handful of educational theorists. They appear here because of their immediacy, their potential for solution by the organized profession, the economic feasibility of their solution—and because they forcefully prevent a concept of educational humanism from coming to fruition in the tens of thousands of schools in this country. Further, they appear to be problem areas which, if attacked systematically and energetically, will cause the dialogue necessary in coming to grips with other important issues both related to and separate from the ones discussed here.

Perhaps the greatest barrier to educational improvement is the tendency of educational reformers to say, "That's wrong; do it this way." Any method of educating, even the much-maligned self-contained classroom, is right as long as some teacher and some group of students can make it work. Rather than prescribing a single solution for every educational malady, a wise teacher considers every option available to him— what John Goodlad once referred to as "the entire pharmacy of educational alternatives." In this spirit, the Center for the Study of Instruction chooses not to dictate solutions but to present alternatives—all of which are designed to bring about the dramatic changes necessary in education's goal—to create competent, self-directed individuals who can then work to help cure the ills of society as a whole. The challenge to all of us— teacher, student, parent, and administrator—is to discuss the issues, try out solutions, and finally come up with the answers.

Chapter 2

THE TRADITIONAL HIGH
SCHOOL CURRICULUM

Review of the history of the high school curriculum, from the time of the Committee of Ten's prescription for a more uniform program of studies in 1893 to Conant's recommendations for the comprehensive high school program in 1959, indicates little change in its fundamental orientation around a program of studies that concentrates almost exclusively on the academic disciplines: English, foreign languages, mathematics, science, and social sciences. Emphasis has turned from the dominance of the classical subjects to more modern ones, especially in foreign languages. Other changes have been in regard to requirements and enrollments in different subjects, along with the addition of many electives, and, most recently, in the content of the subjects themselves. Although activity programs, counseling services, community studies, and other additions to the high school program have attracted much interest and provided valuable supplements to the program of studies, these have been essentially additions, and not substitutions, in the somewhat standard curriculum. Current movements toward different orientations of the curriculum are considered in Parts III and IV of this book.

The status of the high school program of studies in terms of subject offerings and enrollments has been surveyed periodically by the United

States Office of Education. The selection by Grace S. Wright reviews
the last two such surveys—1948–1949 and 1960–1961—and presents her
conclusions as to the trends revealed by these data. She saw the increased
enrollments in mathematics, science, and foreign languages in 1960–1961
as a result of the national quest following the launching of the first
Russian sputnik, for greater emphasis on these subjects to generate
more mathematicians and scientists and also more Americans with
foreign language skills. Undoubtedly the National Defense Education
Act of 1958 with its appropriations to aid these subjects and other
federal aid helped to bring about this swing of the curriculum pendulum.

The USOE data also show that the subject fields suffering in
percentage of enrollment included those of most recent origin, during the
decades in which the high school was seeking to become comprehensive—
health, safety, and physical education, business education, and vocational
trade and industrial education. The two vocational fields given initial
stimulus by the Smith Hughes Act of 1917—agriculture and home
economics—held their own during the 1949–1961 period.

Unfortunately there is no comparable survey for 1970–1971 to
answer Wright's provocative questions concluding this selection. The
present writer's judgment as to changes from 1961 to 1971 in the program
of studies are included in a brief statement from the 1971 book in
which he collaborated, *The High School: Today and Tomorrow*. This
comparison indicates our judgment that the social studies requirements
have been broadened, that the content and sequence in mathematics
and science have been affected by curriculum development in these
fields, that foreign languages and typing have continued to become
more popular, and that health and physical education have continued to
decline. The changing situation in vocational education (see Chapter 6)
makes judgments here very difficult, although in the early 1970s this
field is undoubtedly receiving new stimuli that may make for increased
enrollment. This summary does not reflect the various movements
continuing from the 1960s that do tend to answer affirmatively Wright's
question as to whether a functional emphasis may be reactivated "to
provide greater educational opportunity for pupils of lower ability levels,
the economically deprived, and the culturally disadvantaged?" This
emphasis, greatly stimulated by the Elementary–Secondary Education

Act of 1965 through its Title I funding for the disadvantaged, is a major characteristic of recent curriculum development and is reflected in many selections in this anthology.

The continuing dominance of the traditionally college preparatory subjects for those planning to go to college is clearly revealed in the data reported in the selection from the Educational Testing Service. The great majority of the students taking College Board examinations in the Spring of 1966 had taken English each year, and mathematics, science, one or more foreign languages, and social studies for at least three of the four high school years, and many each year. The particular focus of this survey was to determine to what extent the "new" programs in academic subjects had been adopted by the high schools? The indications were that the curriculum reform programs had definitely been adopted in mathematics and foreign languages and were affecting sizeable numbers of high schools in science and English. Whether the "new" programs are in fact becoming the "regular" or traditional curriculum is a matter of speculation in our later chapter (5) on these academic subjects.

Perhaps the most distinctive characteristic of today's high school in the United States is its continuing effort to be comprehensive. Comprehensiveness is not characteristic of all high schools, and indeed some citizens have preferred a separation of students into academic and vocational and other schools as in other national systems of secondary education and in some American cities. The post-sputnik debates in the United States as to the purposes, programs, and outcomes of high school education included the proposals of Admiral Hyman G. Rickover and others as to the establishment of more specialized high schools here. Then just returning from his stint as Ambassador to West Germany, former Harvard President James Bryant Conant undertook for the Carnegie Corporation of New York a study of the American high school focusing on the issue of comprehensiveness. In introducing the Conant report (*The American High School Today*, McGraw-Hill, 1959), John W. Gardner, then President of the Corporation, gave this excellent definition of the comprehensive high school (pp. ix–x):

> The focus of Mr. Conant's study is the "comprehensive" high school—a peculiarly American phenomenon. It is called comprehensive because it offers, under one administration and under one

roof (or series of roofs), secondary education for almost all the high school age children of one town or neighborhood. It is responsible for educating the boy who will be an atomic scientist and the girl who will marry at eighteen; the prospective captain of a ship and the future captain of industry. It is responsible for educating the bright and the not so bright children with different vocational and professional ambitions and with various motivations. It is responsible, in sum, for providing good and appropriate education, both academic and vocational, for all young people within a democratic environment which the American people believe serves the principles they cherish.

The Conant report gave hearty and influential support to the continuation and expansion of the comprehensive high school. Undoubtedly this report is a major reason for the continued dominance of this institution which in the most favorable use of the term we can now regard as the "traditional" American high school. The Conant report made many specific recommendations toward making the high school more comprehensive, and some of these with their very specific quantitative standards have also been blamed for fastening on the high school practices which are considered by some as making the high school less rather than more adaptable for the human differences the comprehensive school should serve.

Almost 10 years after his first survey, Dr. Conant, as chairman of a committee of the National Association of Secondary School Principals, made a follow-up study, this time by questionnaire alone, to determine changes being made in the high schools on items included in the first survey. This survey, also fully reported in book form (*The Comprehensive High School*, McGraw-Hill, 1967), was commented upon by Dr. Conant in an address at a National Association of Secondary School Principals annual conference which is included as the final selection in this chapter. He noted as items he considered as progress in improvement of the comprehensive high school: the reduction of the number of students per English teacher, the increased use of ability grouping, the increased inclusion of a course in Problems of American Democracy (heterogeneously grouped), the increased enrollment in five "academic solids" plus art or music and physical education, the increased use of work-study programs in vocational education, improved programs in mathematics, science, and foreign languages, and the increased percentage of academically talented students electing 18 or more academic courses, especially the increase in modern foreign languages.

Many educators question some of the Conant standards for comprehensive high schools, and some of the emphases on academic subjects and standards and ability grouping, for example, are targets for attacks in later selections criticizing the high school for its irrelevance and lack of concern for individual differences. Nevertheless his studies do reveal the characteristics of the high school curriculum as it existed very recently and as is still dominant despite the movement of the 1970s toward more relevant curriculums, alternative schools, and other developments described in subsequent chapters.

OFFERINGS AND ENROLLMENTS IN SUBJECT FIELDS*

GRACE S. WRIGHT

ALL SUBJECT FIELDS

The large increase in total pupil enrollment since 1949 was, of course, reflected in the increased pupil registrations in the several subject fields. Total registrations in all subject fields rose from nearly 42 million in 1949 to over 75 million in 1961. There was little difference in the average number of courses taken by students in the 2 years: 6.2 in 1949 and 6.4 in 1961.

Some differences in percentages of pupils enrolled in each of the subject fields occurred (Table 1), indicating certain shifts in emphasis. Seven of the 13 subject fields reported upon in 1949 increased their percentages of the total pupil enrollment, grades 7 through 12. Three subject fields— social studies, home economics, and agriculture—held their own. Three subject fields—health, safety, and physical education; business education; and vocational trade and industrial education—experienced decreases in percentage of pupils served. Mathematics had the greatest percentage increase, followed by English, science and music, in that order. . . .

SHIFT IN EDUCATIONAL GOALS AND CURRICULUM EMPHASES

The forces affecting secondary education in the late 1950s caused it to move generally from a primary concern with the whole child within a wide range of abilities, which was still the emphasis in the first half of the period 1949–1961, to a concentration on the intellectual development of that child, or from the child-centered to the subject-centered curriculum

---

* Reprinted from *Subject Offerings and Enrollments in Public Secondary Schools,* OE-24015-16 (Washington, D.C.: Government Printing Office, 1965) pp. 5, 20–21.

Table 1   Number of Pupils[a] Enrolled in Subject Fields, and Percent These Enrollments are of Total Enrollment of Grades 7 to 12 of Public Secondary Day Schools: 1960–1961 and 1948–1949[b]

Subject field	1960–1961		1948–1949	
	Number	Percent	Number	Percent
English	12,972,236	110.6	7,098,770	102.8
Health and physical education	12,081,639	103.0	7,794,671	112.8
Social studies	11,802,499	100.1	6,981,980	101.1
Mathematics	8,596,393	73.3	4,457,987	64.5
Science	7,739,877	66.0	4,031,044	58.4
Music	4,954,347	42.2	2,484,201	36.0
Business education	4,667,570	39.8	3,186,207	46.1
Home economics	3,361,699	28.7	1,762,242	25.5
Industrial arts	2,915,997	24.9	1,693,825	24.5
Art	2,576,354	22.0	1,234,544	17.9
Foreign language	2,383,703	20.3	1,219,693	17.7
Agriculture	507,992	4.3	373,395	5.4
Vocational trade and industrial education	344,704	2.9	369,794	5.4
Other instruction or courses	106,467	.9	111,053	1.6
Distributive education	38,363	.3	([c])	—

[a] Total pupil population: 1960–1961, 11,732,742; 1948–1949, 6,907,833.
[b] Alaska and Hawaii not included in 1948–1949 figures.
[c] Not reported separately.

emphasis. Concern with education for responsible citizenship and the optimum development of the individual for effective life in the community, State, and Nation gave way to a renewed emphasis on the "academics."

A major development sparking the return to the academics was the demand for increasing numbers of scientists and mathematicians resulting from the coldwar and the accelerated pace at which new knowledge was being discovered in the fields of mathematics and science, a demand given further impetus by the launching of the first Russian sputnik in 1958. A corollary to this was the need for an understanding of the advances in the field of science and technology by the average citizen who would not become a mathematician or scientist. State departments of education reacted by increasing their graduation requirements in these fields, thus affecting enrollments. Also during this period the National Science Foundation was established. Academic scholars, placed in a position of leadership, began to develop curriculums for science and mathematics from kindergarten to grade 12. At the same time a new law, the National Defense Education Act, provided funds for the improvement of instruction in mathematics, science, and foreign languages.

From the position of significance in the high school curriculum which they held between 1900 and World War I, foreign languages showed decreasing strength in each of the Office of Education's enrollment surveys since World War I. By 1949, they had reached lows of 18 percent in grades 7 to 12 and 21.8 percent in grades 9 to 12. Not until the fifties did the tide begin to turn, although following the close of World War II the country began to realize the importance of developing greater international understanding and of having a corps of people with a working knowledge of the language spoken to represent us abroad. The fifties witnessed a revision of objectives and methods for achieving them. Encompassed were the development of skills of understanding and speaking the modern languages and improving the skills of reading and writing all languages. To accomplish these objectives a longer sequence of study was advocated.

In the schools, the number of course titles in mathematics, science, and foreign language was extended and enrollments were increased. The percentages of pupils in grades 7 to 12 enrolled in subjects in these three fields, as reported in the surveys of 1934, 1949, and 1961, are as follows:

	1934	1949	1961
Mathematics	62	65	73
Science	50	58	66
Foreign language	30	18	22

At work also, and influencing the shift, was the concern of the public for a higher standard of quality in education. That high school graduates did not read and write as well as earlier graduates was a common accusation (understandable, since the high school population was indeed different in its inclusion of the lower ability levels which a generation or two earlier would have been dropouts). James B. Conant in *The American High School Today*,[1] a book highly influential in education cricles, included as one of his 21 recommendations that English composition occupy about half the total time devoted to the study of English in the last four high school years. Other recommendations were related to quality education for the intellectually gifted, including the one that such pupils take an academic program in keeping with their abilities.

---

[1] James B. Conant, *The American High School Today* (New York: McGraw-Hill, Inc., 1959).

One effect of this concern for improved quality as revealed by the current survey was an increase in enrollments in writing courses in the field of English—creative writing, journalism, and composition. The increase, 68 percent over 1949, exceeded the increase in pupil population of that period.

Another and more pervasive effect was the extension downward of the college program. In the senior year, intellectually able students were permitted, and encouraged, to take college-level, honor, and advanced placement courses. Illustrative are college and advanced placement English; advanced placement courses in social studies; advanced standing courses in mathematics, such as analytical geometry and calculus, matrix algebra, and number theory; and in science, college chemistry and physics, biophysics, bacteriology, microbiology, and research seminar.

As college courses came into the high school, the grade level at which many high school courses were offered was lowered. Elementary algebra in many schools was offered to capable eighth-graders. Biology, long a tenth-grade subject, was often moved to the ninth grade. Serious study of foreign languages was introduced in grades below the ninth.

SIGNIFICANCE OF CULTURAL CHANGES FOR THE CURRICULUM, 1949 TO 1961

During the period of this survey, education reacted quickly to changes in the culture brought about by the cold war, the defense program, and new social developments. It moved from a trend to extend upward the child development concept of the elementary school, which had existed for some 20 years, to what was, in effect, an extension downward of the college program and preparation for that program. From offerings aimed at meeting the needs of individual boys and girls, the secondary school began to emphasize a program oriented to the academic subjects.

In the child-development era, the grass roots was spoken of as the starting place for curriculum change. Local people knew the community and its needs, and thus were in the best position to determine how and to what extent those needs could be met by the school. Professional educators charted the course. Now, in the late 1950s, curriculum change began to come in response to national needs. The explosion of knowledge and the great advances in technology brought the university scholars to the fore and into the field of curriculum planning and improvement. The new partnership of professional educators and university scholars has given rise to a shift in influence from local to national needs and interests. As a result, it raises questions of Federal, State, and local roles. Will the State and particularly the local community be given freedom to design their own programs to meet those needs which are peculiar to them? Or will direction come from national planning? Or can both local and national interests be served in nationwide planning through Federal-State cooperation?

Bringing these questions to bear directly on curriculum offerings and enrollments: Will the scholars' emphasis on academic learning be expanded to include all students? Or will it be necessary to reactivate the functional emphasis to provide greater educational opportunity for pupils of lower ability levels, the economically deprived, and the culturally disadvantaged? Or can a curriculum be designed which will achieve both these emphases?

Answers to these questions will be sought by high school people throughout the Nation in their attempt to provide the best possible secondary school program for every youth.

TYPICAL PROGRAMS, 1961 AND 1971*

The 1961 USOE survey described the program of a typical twelfth-year pupil as having included in the four years of high school the following:

4 years of English
1 year of American history
1 or ½ year of a twelfth-grade social studies course, usually advanced civics
1 year of world history
2 years of science, usually biology and ninth grade general science
1–3 years of mathematics (1, general math or algebra, and if the latter 1, plane geometry and 1, advanced algebra)
4 years of physical education or health and physical education

Although enrollment data are lacking to substantiate a "typical" (that is, most frequent) program in 1971, observation of the changing

---

* From *The High School: Today and Tomorrow* by W. M. Alexander, J. G. Saylor, and E. L. Williams. Copyright © 1971 by Holt, Rinehart and Winston, Inc. Reprinted by permission of Holt, Rinehart and Winston, Inc.

high school curriculum during the 1960s indicates that the 1971 graduate's program might have differed as follows from the above:

The year of world history would have been world geography or a combination of world history and geography.

The 2 years of science would have been earth science and biology, with chances good of a third year in the physical science field.

The 1–3 years, probably at least 2, of mathematics would be less discretely divided into the subjects listed above.

A half year or year of typing would have been included.

2 or more years of a foreign language were more likely to have been included than in 1961.

2 or 3 years of health and physical education would be more likely than 4.

SURVEY OF COLLEGE BOARD CANDIDATES
REVEALS CURRICULUM TRENDS*

To what extent have high schools adopted the new programs in academic subjects? One way to find out is to ask students what and how they were taught in a field in which they have just taken a College Board examination. The courses they took, the textbooks they studied, the topics and terms they remember, the experiments they performed, the devices they used, and what they did in class and as homework will give a realistic picture of what is going on.

About 38,000 students from 7,555 high schools in 50 states were asked questions like these in the spring of 1966. The sample was random except that quotas for the tests taken by the fewest candidates were filled first. The number of usable returns ranged from 2,275 in biology to 3,769 in mathematics: a total of 26,628 cases (70%) in ten subject fields. Their average SAT scores stood at the 75th percentile of CEEB candidates who enter college. A few highlights of the findings are reported below.

---

* Reprinted from ETS Developments (January 1970), pp. 1, 3–4, by permission.

THE FIVE MAJOR FIELDS

An overview of the survey, prepared by Elizabeth W. Haven, the project director, indicates that these students took heavy but not unusual programs. English was studied every year. Almost all took mathematics, science, and one or more foreign languages in grades 9-10-11. In grade 12, 84% of the boys and 56% of the girls took mathematics; 82% of the boys and 60% of the girls took science; 53% of the boys and 68% of the girls took a foreign language. Over 80% took history or social studies in grades 9-11-12 but only 60% in grade 10.

MATHEMATICS

High school mathematics programs now include most of the curriculum reforms advocated in the fifties. For example, 75% or more of the sample had studied sets, the structure and properties of the number system, proof in algebra using axioms, and the graphical representation of algebraic inequalities and their solution. By the end of the first semester of the senior year, more than half had studied elementary analysis including elementary functions for at least two months. But only a fifth had studied topics involved in probability and statistics, and most of these had gone no farther than measures of central tendency and dispersion.

PHYSICS

Pssc *Physics*, the text produced by the Physical Science Study Committee in 1960, had been used by 37% of the juniors and 28% of the seniors; *Modern Physics*, a more traditional text, by 30% and 42%; no other primary text by more than 3%. More than twice as many pssc students as non-pssc students had studied the wave and particle models of light and the stroboscope. More of the non-pssc students had studied the "machines" used in building the pyramids.

CHEMISTRY

Modern Chemistry was the most widely used text; *Chemistry: An Experimental Science*, the text of the Chemical Education Materials Study (chems) was second; *Chemical Systems*, developed by the Chemical Bond Approach (cba) Project was third. Many schools offered a second course in chemistry of either high school or college level. Of the 2,395 students sampled, 319 had taken the college level course, 198 the second high school course—but half of these had taken the second course without the first.

BIOLOGY

The three texts developed by bscs, the Biological Sciences Curriculum Study, did not become available until 1963. They were used in that year by an eighth of the seniors sampled and in the following year by a fourth of the juniors. About half of both groups had used *Modern Biology*. The content students remembered covering showed an increased emphasis on molecular and cellular topics. Nearly 40% of the seniors were taking a second course in biology; 75% had taken or were taking a course in chemistry and 40% a course in physics.

ENGLISH

The only new development in the study of English that had attracted attention at the time of the survey was then called "structural linguistics." When this term was defined and students were asked whether they had studied it as part of their work in English, more than a third answered yes. Of 37 linguistic terms, 18 were checked as familiar by half or more. There were no surprises in their reports of what is done about writing, but in literature a fifth said they had studied no play by Shakespeare; two-fifths said only one. Of the 16 authors that more than two-thirds of the students remembered studying, only three were English, with Dickens at the top. Next in order were Frost, Twain, and Poe; also included were Sandburg, Hemingway, and Steinbeck.

MODERN LANGUAGES

The audio-lingual language laboratory was used one or two periods a week by more than half of the students of each language (French, Spanish, and German) in grades 10 and 11, by fewer in grades 9 and 12, and by some in grades 7 and 8. In their first year of study, most students said they practiced listening and speaking for as much as three months before turning to reading and writing. About half said they learned rules of grammar and then applied them; a third induced rules from their experience with the language; the rest studied no grammar in the first year. These students had greatest confidence in their reading ability, next in understanding the spoken language, least in writing and speaking.

LATIN

Although two-fifths of the students who chose the modern language tests had taken Latin in grades 9-10, not more than 35% of those who chose Latin had taken another language in any grade. Since Latin is not a spoken language, the audio-lingual approach was almost never used, and writing Latin sentences was used mainly to teach grammar. There were no surprises in the reports of classroom practices. The grammar-translation method prevails.

HISTORY AND SOCIAL STUDIES

Of the students tested, 85% had taken courses in this field in grades 9-11-12, 60% in grade 10. The courses most frequently reported were Civics in grade 9, World History in grade 10, American History in grade 11, and Problems of Democracy or Government, Economics, and other social sciences in grade 12. In American History the periods from 1787 to 1920 were emphasized. World History gave most attention to Western Europe. Elsewhere most attention was given to Russia and Asia, least to Africa south of the Sahara, and very little to Latin America. Only half the seniors had taken courses called Problems of Democracy or Social Problems; others reported courses in particular social sciences, and some were taking a second course in American History. The grade placement of courses, content covered, and texts used in this field were more varied than in the natural sciences.

THE COMPREHENSIVE HIGH SCHOOL:
A FURTHER LOOK*

JAMES B. CONANT

As chairman of your committee on the Study of the American Secondary School, I reported briefly at the last annual convention. Since then, all members have received a preliminary report based on a questionnaire sent to some 18,000 public high schools—essentially all the public high schools in the nation with a twelfth grade.

In that report I stated that your committee proposed to make a

* Reprinted from the *Bulletin of the National Association of Secondary School Principals* (May 1967), 51:22–34, by permission.

study of one group of schools by means of a second and far more detailed questionnaire. This we have done and, thanks to the prompt cooperation of the principals of just over 2,000 schools, we have obtained some exceedingly interesting information.

As I indicated at the last meeting, our interest focused on widely comprehensive high schools of medium size. The second detailed questionnaire was sent to the principals of public high schools with an enrollment of 750 to 2,000 from which not more than 75 percent and not less than 25 percent of the graduates went on with further education.

The limitations we placed on our study mean, of course, that many in this audience did not have an opportunity of participating in this study. Those principals of schools smaller than our minumum figure (750) or larger than our maximum (2,000) and those from whose schools a smaller or larger percent proceeded to a college did not receive our second questionnaire. To be specific, this means our report provides no information about (1) the over 9,000 small high schools in the country, (2) the large schools, usually located in the big cities, or (3) the schools, usually suburban, from which more than 75 percent of the graduates enter a post-high school institution.

I start off by pointing out the self-imposed limitations of your committee's study, to prevent any misunderstanding. The reasons for the limitations are set forth in the report. They are the same as those which were basic to my first study of the American high school. In a word, we focused on the comprehensive high school. It is an American invention and continues to be typical of American public secondary education. Because of its importance to the future of our society, I for one hope and believe it should continue to flourish.

SUPPLEMENTARY COMMENTS

Since the report in book form is now available and was reviewed in yesterday's papers, I do not propose to present a summary. Rather, I intend to comment on certain of our findings in the light of my experience in visiting a dozen or so schools in some 10 states in the last two years. It is not necessary to tell this audience of practitioners that there are many aspects of a high school which cannot be revealed by a questionnaire but which can be discovered by a visit. Yet, as you know from my brief report at the last annual meeting, your committee decided it had no choice but to proceed in its study by means of a questionnaire.

What I am about to say, therefore, is in the nature of a supplement to the little book which McGraw-Hill published yesterday. It will be a personal supplement, so to speak. In my visits to high schools, I was especially interested in comparing the present situation with what I encountered in 1957 and 1958. In some cases, I revisited the same school and could thus refer to my notes of nearly 10 years ago.

CHANGE IN PRINCIPAL'S ROLE

One change which I discovered may be of special interest to this audience. In more than one community, the single high school I had known had been found inadequate from the point of view of space. The increase in population of the school district has required the building of a second high school. As a consequence, in several cases, many of the decisions previously made by the high school principal were being made in the superintendent's office. One or more coordinators were concerned with the instruction in both of the two high schools. The leadership, it seemed to me, had passed from the principal to the superintendent or to one or more persons on the superintendent's staff. I have in mind not only decisions about curricula but recruitment to the staff.

As an outsider, it seemed to me that it was a pity that the role of the principal had changed. In my earlier study, I had been impressed by the importance of a school board's finding not only a first-rate superintendent, but also an excellent high school principal; and I had come to relate the degree of success of the school to the qualities of the principal. I do not doubt that under the new circumstances I have just described, good principals are still important. But their authority and responsibility is certainly diminished.

Realizing that as a layman I am inquiring into delicate matters far beyond my competence even as an investigator or reporter, I venture to raise the following question: If there are two or more high schools in a district, is it necessary to have policy made in the superintendent's office to any greater degree than if there was only *one* high school? I should think there ought to be ways of building up the importance of the position of the high school principal even in a multi-high school district. At all events, I venture to raise the issue because I have seen so many flourishing schools whose welfare clearly reflected the drive and imagination of the principal who had been given a free hand by the superintendent.

To turn now to some of the findings in the report. You will discover that many of the questions we asked were tied in with the recommendations in my study of nine years ago. At least one critical question, however, was entirely new. We asked the principal to give us the ratio of total professional staff to students. Since I made my past study, I have come to believe that this one figure tells more about a medium-sized high school than any other single criterion.

My attention was first drawn to the significance of staff-student ratios in the course of preparation of the essay on "Quality in Public Education" written by the Educational Policies Commission of the NEA and AASA in 1959. I was at that time a member of the Commission and remember very well the discussion which led to the incorporation in the report of the following sentences: "If fewer than 50 professionals are available per thousand pupils, some of the elements of a program of high quality are likely to be slighted. It should be emphasized that this ratio is a minimum." (Expressed in terms of the number of students per individual staff member, the minimum was obviously 20.)

The ratios reported from the 2,000 schools we questioned varied from 11.3 to 37.3. Since this ratio reflects quite accurately the per-pupil cost of the instruction, it is clear that the support of the schools in question varied by at least threefold. As is repeatedly pointed out in our report, our much vaunted ideal of equality of opportunity is far from being realized the nation over or even within certain states.

As is implied by the sentence in the Educational Policies Commission essay I have just read, a cross-correlation study showed that the chances of finding that a given high school offers calculus is three times as great in a school from which 40 to 59 percent go on to college if the staff-student ratio is 17.4 or less as compared with the same type of school when the ratio is 23.5 or larger. (You will find this particular comparison in Table VIII of the appendix.) Similarly, taking all the 2,000 schools together, the chances of a school providing an adequate number of English teachers is nearly six times as great if the staff-student ratio is 17.4 or less as compared with a ratio of 20.5 or more.

PUPIL LOAD FOR ENGLISH TEACHERS

What constitutes an adequate number of English teachers? As a consequence of my first study, I suggested that no English teacher in a senior high school be responsible for more than 100 students. The returns showed that very few schools have as yet met this standard. Nearly 26 percent, however, reported a "teaching load" for the English teachers of 120 or less. As compared to a figure of 150 or more which was common in the schools I visited in 1957–58, a ratio of one teacher to 120 students represents real progress. But I have not retreated from my ideal of 100, let me make clear!

There is no need to tell you ladies and gentlemen why the reduction in the number of students in English taught by a single teacher looms so large in the minds of some of us. What is really at issue is instruction in English composition. My premise was that adequate consideration of the themes could not be given by a teacher who had to handle anything like 150 themes.

On this point, I had an interesting conversation with a high school teacher of English in one school. She was fortunate enough to be teaching in a school which was sufficiently well supported to enable her to be responsible for only 110 students and, at times, only 100. She had taught, however, in a school in which the number was not 110, but 140. What she could accomplish under the two different circumstances was as different as day from night. She told me that whereas now the themes she corrected and discussed with the students (on an individual basis) averaged 500 to 1,000 words a week, previously individual conferences were rare and the themes per week had to be short (something like a quarter as long as is now the case).

I admit that the testimony of this particular teacher was reassuring; it indicated that the standard I had set for the teaching level of an English teacher had real significance. This testimony was not unusual. In general, I found a similar viewpoint in the schools I visited in the last two years.

RATIO OF COUNSELORS TO STUDENTS

Another figure which varied greatly from school to school was the ratio of counselors to students. In this case my recommendation in *The American High School Today* was far from the actuality in most of the 2,000 schools from which we obtained returns. I have had to lower my sights (but only temporarily) to a ratio of 1 to 349 or less and, even so, only 3.5 percent of the schools met this standard. But this matter is discussed at some length in the report and I have nothing to add as a result of my visitations, except to say my belief in the importance of good guidance officers remains unshaken and that I realize excellent counselors are in short supply.

ABILITY GROUPING

Both from my visits and from noting the returns from the questionnaires, I conclude that a remarkable change in attitude seems to have taken place as regards to ability grouping. A very large percentage of the schools returning the questionnaire—namely, 96.5 percent—reported that they were using ability grouping in one or more subjects. As I visited in the schools, I found the old-fashioned objection to ability grouping seemed to have largely disappeared. Now it is widely accepted that, for the good of the students and the school, there should be separate classes, depending on the rate of learning of the student in the subject.

Just how many levels there should be in the required courses, I am not prepared to say. I am prepared to emphasize once again, however, that I am opposed to a "track system" and that I would favor individualized programs according to which a boy or girl might be in the top group in

English, we will say, but in the second or third group in social studies, or vice versa, and might be in either the top or bottom group, we will say, in eleventh-grade mathematics. I must admit that if this is done, it may result in some schools in an imbalance racially as between the different classes. This is because, unfortunately, in some cities those who have recently arrived from other parts of the country have come with a totally unsatisfactory elementary preparation. Therefore, these handicapped students are not able to keep pace with those who have grown up in an adequate system.

But if there be worry among parents about homogeneous grouping being undemocratic, the attitude of the administration can be made clear if it adopts my recommendation about the twelfth-grade course in American Democracy. I believe strongly that the classes in such a course should be heterogeneously arranged so that all the youths will have an opportunity of discussing problems with those who have varying scholastic records and family backgrounds.

If a comprehensive high school is to fulfill its social political functions, there must be one course required of all in which the assignment to a class is not in terms of ability or promise, but is on a random basis. The existence of such a course stands out as evidence of the school's commitment to equality. I am glad to report that in 62.5 percent of the schools, those in charge agreed with my point of view; though, I may add, I am well aware some social studies teachers and professors of history do not.

STUDY OF FIVE ACADEMIC SOLIDS YEARLY

One of the questions we asked was designed to bring out whether or not it was possible for an ambitious student to take five academic solids in one year and, at the same time, art or music as well as physical education. The response was amazing to me—74 percent of the schools answered in the affirmative. There may have been some misunderstanding of the question and, perhaps, this figure is a little high. But on the whole, as I traveled around I got the impression that, far more than 10 years ago, people were aware of the importance of a bright student's studying both mathematics and a modern foreign language.

I have recapitulated in my report my old arguments of why, for those who have the requisite ability, it is advisable to study mathematics through grade 12 and a modern foreign language to a point where something approaching mastery is attained before graduation. If this is not done, many doors to future careers are closed. For example, without adequate mathematical preparation, engineering and science cannot be studied. Let me call my point of view the "open door policy." Let me defend it here once again.

As I travel around, I am more and more impressed by the differences between the communities served by a medium-sized comprehensive high school. I know there are communities in which no one seems to care whether the able student studies four years of mathematics or masters a foreign language or not. There are others in which pressures from parents tend to force a student who has not the ability to enroll in mathematics through the eleventh and twelfth grades. Protective devices must be installed in such a school. I found this to be the case in more than one instance. It is covered in recommendation 13 in *The American High School Today*, which reads as follows:

> Standards in advanced courses should be such that those who enroll in each successive course of a sequence have demonstrated the ability to handle that course. To this end, admission to eleventh-grade mathematics should depend upon the student's receiving at least a "C" in tenth-grade mathematics, and for admission to twelfth-grade mathematics at least a "C" should be required in the eleventh-grade course.

Similar standards should be applied to other elective academic courses. Such a regulation is important as a protection for student and teacher against undue parental pressure. Unfortunately, in one state I discovered that the chief state school officer did not believe in such a policy. He maintained that in every course a person should be entitled to the next course in the sequence unless he actually failed the preceding course. A ruling of this sort is based on a misunderstanding, I believe, of the nature of a sequential course of study and the proper role of grading in assisting the guidance officers.

ROLE OF VOCATIONAL COURSES

I should like to record another observation based on my visits as well as on the returns from our questionnaire, namely the changing role of the vocational courses. It is quite clear to me that, as compared to nearly 10 years ago, the new federal legislation has brought an improvement. The strict limits of the old Smith-Hughes Act seem to have been removed to good advantage.

I found in one school that I visited that vocational shop work had been put almost entirely on a cooperative study basis. This meant that even in such fields as tool and die work, auto mechanics, and building trades, it was possible for the boy concerned to spend the two or three or four hours of the day in the twelfth grade in a shop run by industry itself and yet receive academic credit for this work.

This is a pattern which I met in my first study only in connection with "distributive education." It seems to have spread in some cities to a wide range of nonacademic work. From what I saw, it seemed to me this was an excellent development, though it has within it dangers which were pointed out. In the first place, the arrangement depends on the employment situation and the attitude of the employers; secondly, there must be good supervision from the school or else what happens is that the employer simply exploits the cheap labor of the student.

I had an interesting experience which illustrates how impossible it is to generalize about vocational education. I visited two schools of the type I am considering in adjacent states in the Middle West on successive days. Both provided good vocational studies, which were well attended. But in one school, the training of future tool and die workers had been given up. "There are no longer any openings for graduates who are trained in our machine shop," I was told. In the other school not 200 miles away, I found a considerable number of boys in the machine shop, and was told the demand for graduates trained under what used to be called the tool and die program was never greater! Incidentally, I found that neither the teachers nor the administrators in either of the two schools had ever heard of the other school. Yet, I am sure one could have learned from the other, for the characteristics of the schools were very similar and their problems were almost identical.

VOCATIONAL STUDY WHERE?

The question of area vocational schools, I know, is agitating many portions of the country. I venture to question the wisdom of sending those who desire vocational education to a vocational school for the entire day. Such a development endangers the whole concept of a comprehensive high school. On the other hand, I recognize that in a school district which cannot afford to provide good shops and does not have cooperative facilities, it may be necessary to bus the students who are concerned with certain kinds of vocational instruction to a central spot for the use of shops. But, under such arrangements, I would hope the boy or girl would remain a member of a comprehensive high school in which he or she would do the academic work.

I should like to use this occasion to explain an attitude I developed as a consequence of my first study and which my recent visits emphasize still further. The importance of good instruction in such fields as business education, home economics, drafting, auto mechanics, tool and die work, and building trades is not to be measured by the marketable skills thus developed. As many people have said, the same skills could be developed more effectively if the vocational courses were postponed to a junior college. But if this were done a highly important motivating force would vanish from the high school.

I am of the opinion that, under proper conditions, the vocational courses I have named (and others) interest a certain type of youth who is apathetic at best about English and social studies and finds mathematics, foreign languages, and physics at the eleventh- and twelfth-grade levels too difficult. A few of the schools I have visited were not widely comprehensive according to the criteria I have used. (There were no shops, for example, except for the industrial arts.) In talking with the counselors and teachers, I got the sharp impression that in such a school a certain type of boy was far more inclined to be either a dropout or a listless student than in a widely comprehensive high school. If I am right about this, the point is not without its significance.

MATH, SCIENCE, LANGUAGES

I hardly need call to your attention the considerable change that has taken place in the instruction offered in mathematics, science, and foreign languages. The changes spelled out in some detail in the report are highly encouraging. Yet, on the other hand, their impact is uneven. I am glad that 40 percent of the schools reporting (remember their type) offer calculus. Yet, clearly, those who attend the other 60 percent of the same kind of school do not have an equal opportunity to do advanced work in mathematics.

Similarly, as regards instruction in a foreign language, there has been a vast improvement in the last ten years. Yet, in 35 percent of the schools reporting, it is impossible for a youth to study a modern foreign language for four years, according to our returns. In fact, I think the situation is somewhat worse than this figure indicates, since I have visited schools which offer a fourth year of French and Spanish but, to save money, require the few in the fourth-year class to sit with the third-year class. Adequate instruction under such conditions is impossible.

On the other hand, in a certain school from which less than half the graduates go on with further education, a third of the students are enrolled in a modern foreign language class and over 20 percent of the twelfth grade are completing the fourth year of either German, French, or Spanish. Constrast this situation with that in schools which only offer a fourth year on the compressed basis of combining the third- and fourth-year classes! Here is a striking example of the different traditions in different schools which, in turn, reflect different attitudes of the community. But I cannot help asking: Cannot the school authorities change the negative attitude of a community by offering challenges in instruction?

WHY STUDY A MODERN FOREIGN LANGUAGE?

Let me emphasize once again the significance of the study of a modern foreign language. Granted that not all students can benefit by such instruction, yet it seems quite clear to me that almost all those whom we call academically talented can. Indeed, it may well be that a good many others might study a modern foreign language to good advantage. In some of the schools which I visited, it would appear that quite a number of students elected a modern foreign language and carried it through for four years because they liked it. They had done well, although they did not have the kind of ability that would enable them to take mathematics much beyond the tenth grade. For such students, I believe, one should emphasize that studying a modern language is an essential element in the development of a knowledge and understanding of the humanities.

To my mind, those who have talked so much about the neglect of the humanities in our schools and colleges have failed to realize that the essence of the humanities is language. There is no use talking vaguely about the culture of another country. What is needed first of all is knowledge of the language. Unless one has had the experience of speaking and reading and writing the language of at least one other culture, one has not made a start in understanding comparative literature. To my mind, we went off the track some years ago when, discarding Latin and Greek, we failed to realize the cultural importance of a knowledge—and I emphasize the word knowledge—of a modern foreign language.

The inability or the unwillingness of many high school students to tackle the hard work of studying a foreign language is equivalent to students of science refusing to study mathematics; this, we now know, makes no sense. I submit that the unwillingness of those who talk the most about the humanities to prescribe the study of a modern foreign language in high school can only be bewailed by those who wish the humanities well in the days ahead.

Those of you who recall the recommendations in *The American High School Today* will remember my urging each principal to prepare an academic inventory of each graduating class. Such an inventory shows what percentage of the academically talented youth (roughly 15 percent in a school with the normal range of intellectual ability) have elected academic subjects. Some principals have used the idea and found it helpful. For obvious reasons, we could not ask 2,000 schools to prepare such inventories. Therefore, we had to be content with reporting only what were the course offerings. We had no information as to what fraction of the student body elected advanced mathematics or a foreign language, for example. Therefore, comparisons between the present and the past are expressed in general terms.

RESULTS OF ACADEMIC INVENTORY

It so happens, however, that I can provide a personal supplement to the volume. In 1965, I started but never completed a restudy of the 22 high schools on which I reported in some detail in 1959. I sent out questionnaires, and on the basis of the returns, I have been able to construct partial academic inventories of 19 of these schools and compare them with what I obtained in 1959. The changes are striking, particularly as regards the study of foreign languages. In all 19 schools with one exception, the percentage of academically talented boys electing three or more years of *one* foreign language (including Latin) increased markedly. In many cases, the change was manyfold. In several instances, it was from 0 to 40 percent or over. The results are only a little less striking with the girls.

The great shift for both boys and girls was in the percentage electing 18 or more academic subjects. Parallel to the change in the election of a foreign language (and, indeed, responsive to the change) in all but one or two schools, the increase was spectacular. Obviously, increases in the study of language had not generally been at the expense of other academic subjects. Rather, the total number of academic subjects has been increased. There can be little doubt that as far as the 19 widely comprehensive high schools we studied in some detail in 1959 and for which we have 1965 data, the change from 1959 to 1965 was most encouraging.

The other items in which we compared 1959 with 1965 were the following: four years of mathematics, three years or more of science, seven years or more of mathematics together with science. In mathematics, the changes are also in the direction of a larger percentage of able boys and girls electing four years or more. In one school, for example, the increase was from 15 to 90 percent for boys and 29 to 95 for girls; in still another, the shift was from 55 to 80 for boys and 20 to 40 for girls. Of the 19 schools, eight showed a marked increase in the able boys electing four years of mathematics, only two a decrease; the remainder were essentially constant. In the case of girls, only one school had a decrease and many of the increases were larger than in the case of the boys.

The returns in the case of science and mathematics and science combined followed much the same pattern as those I have just reported. As might be expected, the percentage of academically talented girls electing three years or more of science was found to have increased significantly in half the schools and only in three was it somewhat less.

In a word, our academic inventory has yielded specific information in full accord with the picture of the change in offerings set forth in the new book *The Comprehensive High School—A Second Report to Interested Citizens*.

Chapter 3

THE HIGH SCHOOL STUDENT

The advent of the 1970s found many American adolescents, youth, and adults facing serious problems and conflicts. The problems and conflicts of high school students are highlighted in this chapter rather than their developmental characteristics and learning processes; these should also be known to prospective and inservice high school teachers, but are probably acquired from their studies of psychology and human growth and development. The first selection, however, reports a study of the Educational Testing Service on the interests of high school juniors in 12 high school subjects; this is included to suggest as one possible source of student dissatisfaction with their high school curriculum the apparent discrepancies between their interests and the required subjects, or at least those most usually taken, as indicated by data in the preceding chapter. For example, the universally required subject, English, was ranked 11th among the 12 subjects by boys and 5th by girls. And certainly the first ranked subject—Industrial Arts for boys, Home Economics for girls—was not the most widely taken subject in either case. Granted that the ETS data represented the entire population of high school juniors, whereas some of the data in Chapter 2 referred to college-bound students, comparison of the ETS data with Wright's report of total 1961 enrollments by subjects and our estimate of the 1971 model program of studies certainly raises many questions about the gap between adolescent curriculum interests and their actual programs. Does the fact that a subject is required or strongly recommended within itself restrict interests, or at least cause many disinterested students to become more so? Do the differences between boys and girls as to these interests suggest a need for more differentiation and flexibility in requirements and recommendations? What significance do you see in these data? How do you interpret the statement: "Although the results are helpful in discussing educational and vocational plans beyond high school, they are even more helpful in assessing the effects of school programs in these fields on student interests."?

Some of the problems, concerns, and conflicts among adolescents and youth are indicated in such surveys of their beliefs and attitudes as those summarized in the short report included from *Education U.S.A.* Revealed here is the concern over the Vietnam War, the incidence of use of drugs, the interest in governmental change, and a desire for more discipline of most children in high school. Also revealed in one survey was a very small percentage of ratings of a teacher as the person most admired, but still the top rating of teaching as a chosen career. How do you reconcile these ratings? Was teaching the best job prospect in 1970?

The ghetto and its schools are focal in current social and educational discussions; the article "Like It Is—Pressures in a GHETTO SCHOOL" is based upon a taped interview with a principal and school counselor who worked with ghetto youth in an inner-city high school of a major city. They said that the very real pressures on ghetto youth— illegitimacy, black power, police injustice, sexual promiscuity, hunger, "white hats," welfare, unrealistic courses, "Uncle Toms," middle-class norms—were not perceived as such by the ghetto youth, but merely as life "like it is." For these youth, the problem is "nobody cares—people talk a lot, but they're just feeding you a line." As to the curriculum, the principal and counselor thought it not "realistic"; they felt that the work-study program for special education students was a much better model: "The special education kids are in much better shape than 75 per cent of the students who leave school with a diploma—they get a break—they get a job, they get good work habits, they make fine substantial citizens." Furthermore, they stated that the present school program relies too much on middle-class norms and standards; its improvement demands not "equal" appropriations but appropriations according to what is needed. "This 'equal business' puts the child at a disadvantage in comparing him. He is not to be compared because he is unequal to begin with—you can't equalize something that is unequal at the beginning." The article is exceedingly revealing of the problems of ghetto youth and of the school that serves them. What do you infer as to the implications for curriculum development and teacher education? Do ghetto youth require different programs from others? More costly ones?

During the late 1960s some high school students joined in the student protest movement begun in the universities, and this movement, with its varied manifestations, is still continuing in the early 1970s. Two articles in this chapter are devoted to the high school movement. The first, Diane Divoky's "Revolt in the High Schools: The Way It's Going To Be," deals primarily with the high school underground press, from which she has also edited an anthology, *How Old Will You Be in 1984?* (Discus edition, Avon Books, 1969). She relates the development of a network of nearly 500 underground papers, seen at first as "an escape from the carefully delineated boundaries of school activity and opinion" but later, especially if there was attempted suppression, as operating "confidently on the understanding that change in the schools was their first order of business, and that national issues—the cry for law and order, teacher militancy—did affect their lives as students." Divoky's citation of many papers and the situations surrounding them provides considerable insight into the problems of students, school personnel, and communities. She sees the school administrator as the man in the middle, caught between community traditions and expectations and the realities of student demands. But her sympathy is greatest for the students, and one of her closing questions is worthy of extended discussion: "If the school is to educate, can it afford not to capitalize on the increasing awareness and concern of the students?" How can student power be used to improve the high school curriculum?

Student unrest led to student disruption of the high schools in many communities, enough that in the spring of 1970 the Policy Institute of the Syracuse University Research Corporation was asked to investigate the causes of unrest and disruption and to identify strategies for dealing with them. This request, according to the preface of the report (*Disruption in Urban Public Secondary Schools*, National Association of Secondary School Principals, 1971) from which the final selection of this chapter is drawn, "stemmed from an accumulation of evidence in the hands of the U.S. Commissioner of Education to the effect that recent deportment in an increasing number of urban high schools had deteriorated to a point where the educative capacity of the high schools was seriously, if not mortally, threatened." The study involved, in addition to a search of the literature and a questionnaire study of 683 high schools, intensive research in 27 high schools located in 19 cities. The report, written by Stephen K. Bailey, includes data from previous surveys of student unrest and disruption and also its own tabulation of reported disruption in the schools included in the questionnaire study; the data are not wholly comparable but in the aggregate attest to the prevalence of many types of disruption, defined in the Syracuse study as "any event which significantly interrupts the education of students" and therefore includes boycotts, walkouts, or strikes by teachers as well as students (the types are separately tabulated in the report). The causes of disruption were identified as societal and in-school, and our selection is the discussion of in-school causes. In reading it, one should note that it was preceded by the description of these societal causes: violence in America, the success of civil rights protests in the 1960s, visibility and apparent success of college protests, the expression of ethnic-racial pride, participatory democracy, slum life styles, black revenge, racism, the television generation, and situation ethics and the new permissiveness. As noted in the beginning of the selection, "In-School Causes" discrete categorization is impossible because of the inextricable relation of school and society. Nevertheless Bailey's analysis of the in-school causes should be required reading for all high school personnel. The findings certainly confirmed some of the statements in earlier selections as to the interest of students in becoming more involved in decisions affecting them. Bailey points out that there will be increasing demands for representation of students on high school curriculum planning groups. He also emphasizes the hazards of automatic tracking and counseling systems, supporting in this instance Conant's insistence that high school students not be tracked.

Especially interesting is Bailey's development of the "politicalization" of schools and of students. One can conjecture as to whether the 18-

year-old vote will make high school students more active politically. Will Bailey's comment that "it is commonplace to note that adolescents have very little leverage on the wider society's politics, so they strike where they are and where they do have leverage" hold true? Will high school students tend to turn attention to the wider political scene? Will the newly enfranchised voter and recent graduate from the high school use his vote to effect educational reform?

STUDY SHOWS INTERESTS IN TWELVE SCHOOL SUBJECTS*

Rank Order of Interests in School Subjects Revealed by AIM, 1970

Boys' Interests			Girls' Interests		
Rank	Field	Mean	Rank	Field	Mean
1	Industrial Arts	22.55	1	Home Economics	25.35
2	Physical Sciences	20.01	2	Secretarial	22.39
3	Business	18.22	3	Foreign Languages	20.79
4	Biology	17.39	4	Art	19.76
5	Social Studies	17.34	5	English	18.75
6	Mathematics	17.09	6	Business	18.71
7	Secretarial	16.02	7	Social Studies	17.03
8	Foreign Languages	14.99	8	Music	16.57
9	Art	14.83	9	Biology	15.68
10	English	13.51	10	Mathematics	12.86
11	Music	13.45	11	Physical Sciences	11.70
12	Home Economics	12.61	12	Industrial Arts	10.96

A study of the measurement of academic interests, begun in 1966, has just been completed. It involved 15,450 juniors in a nationally representative sample of 187 high schools. When these schools were compared with the total number of U.S. high schools on various bases, some differences were found, and norms were weighted to adjust for these differences. But it turned out that there were no significant differences between the weighted and unweighted norms; hence the data now released on interests in 12 school subjects may be regarded as the present academic interests of all U.S. eleventh-graders.

True, the data on interests were secured in October 1966; the other years of the study were needed to study the stability of these scores and

---

* Reprinted from *ETS Developments* (October 1970), pp. 1–2, by permission.

their predictive value. But it is unlikely that any marked shift in interests has come about. Even for individuals, the interest expressed in these 12 fields was quite stable. Test-retest correlation averaged .86 after three weeks, .71 after one year, and .62 after two years. This amount of change shows that it is still possible to do something about interests above age 15; hence the instrument may be used to study the effect on interests of various programs. But while some students gain interest in a field, others lose it, and the relative amount of interest of all eleventh-graders in these fields is probably the same now as it was in 1966.

The instrument used to measure interests is called Academic Interest Measures (AIM). It is basically the Interest Index of the Eight Year Study, developed in 1938 but revised and updated by John French in 1964. It is a list of 192 activities (16 in each field) like the following:

Talk about books in class.
Compare accounts of the same event in different newspapers.
Collect and classify plants.
Typewrite business letters.

The principal source of these activities was observation of what was going on in these fields in many schools. About 300 activities were tried out both in the Eight Year Study and later by John French. Those selected had highest biserials with scores in their fields, lowest with other fields, and spread students out most widely.

The directions amount to marking each activity 2 if you like it or think you would like it; 1 if you don't know or don't care one way or the other; or 0 if you dislike it or think you would dislike it. The score for each field is the sum of these numbers; the highest possible score is 32, and 16 represents the level of indifference. Median standard deviations are between 8 and 9 for both sexes.

RANKING BY BOYS AND GIRLS

The [table at the bottom of page 67] shows that boys and girls differed widely in interests: e.g., Industrial Arts was highest for boys, lowest for girls. The rank-difference correlation between these two columns is—.70. Boys placed Physical Sciences, Biology, and Mathematics near the top, girls near the bottom. Girls liked Foreign Languages, Art, and English far better than boys. Both sexes preferred Foreign Languages to English by two ranks and Art to Music by two and four ranks respectively. Both gave high rank to subjects with vocational possibilities: Industrial Arts and Business for boys; Home Economics and Secretarial for girls.

USES OF AIM

AIM can be taken either in school or at home in about 30 minutes as part of a schoolwide testing program in grade 11. In that setting there is no reason to fake an interest in any subject. If desired, it can be scored and interpreted by students in about 10 minutes. Although the results are helpful in discussing educational and vocational plans beyond high school, they are even more helpful in assessing the effects of school programs in these fields on student interests.

This study, supported by the College Board, was begun by Gerald Halpern and completed by Martin Katz, both in collaboration with Lila Norris. A report on the predictive value of these scores is in preparation.

OPINION SURVEYS PINPOINT STUDENT VIEWS*

A spate of surveys has brought into focus the views and attitudes on major issues of today's students—a group that has perplexed adults more than any other younger generation in memory. Taking the opinion pulse of high school and college students has become a major activity of the nation's pollsters, and the results are giving educators one of the clearest views they have ever had of the opinions of the young people with whom they work. The results show, for example, that youth rate the Vietnam War the top issue facing the country. Integration is considered essential, but the use of busing to achieve it is unpopular. The Democratic party has gained a wide lead over the Republican party in teen-age favor.

Several surveys tackled the drug issue. A national poll conducted for the White House Conference on Children and Youth by Gilbert Youth Research found that 54% of youth, aged 14–25, would not report

* Reprinted from *Education U.S.A.*, December 14, 1970, p. 85. Reproduced by special permission from *Education U.S.A.* Copyright, 1970, National School Public Relations Association.

a known drug pusher. This figure jumped to 66% when limited to high school students. The lowest percentage of drug use was found among youth in the South (22%) and the highest, youth in the Northeast (34%). The survey also disclosed that 12% are using drugs regularly; that 26% had tried marijuana or other drugs at least once; that 60% believed at least half of their age group had tried drugs, indicating that most youths think more drug use is going on than is disclosed by several surveys, including Gilbert's. In Ohio, a survey of 10th, 11th, and 12th graders showed that only 13% had tried marijuana. Another survey, conducted in the Milwaukee area for the *Milwaukee Journal*, found that fewer than 20% of the 16–21 age group had tried marijuana. A national poll by the Merit Publishing Co. found that 10% of 22,000 student leaders had tried marijuana.

Other highlights from the surveys: only 3% of 500 ten- to 12-year-olds questioned in New England, the Midwest, and the "marginal" South by Gilbert rated a teacher as the person, among their own acquaintances, whom they "most admire." Friends in their peer group rated highest with 33%, and parents were next "most admired" with 12%. When asked to name their main achievement goal, 47% of the youth answered: "to make money." Gilbert also found that fewer than 1% of college girls selected homemaker as their main career choice; that the career most often chosen by men (13%) and women (21%) was teaching; that 42% believed our form of government needs considerable change; that 7% believed war would not be justified even if the continental United States were invaded; that 37% would not have volunteered for service in World War II; and that 23% believed violence was sometimes justified.

The Ohio survey found that 90% of the students interviewed want to be involved in decisions affecting them—curricular planning, dress codes, and rules of conduct. Conducted by R. H. Goettler and Associates, the study said students believe their major difficulty is caused by poor communication between themselves and school administrators and teachers. A national poll by the Purdue U. Opinion Panel found that 87% of students in grades 10, 11, and 12 think most children and high school students need more discipline. It also found only 19% of the students believed "the American way of life is superior to that of any other country," but 91% indicated they would be willing to work a year to help the nation solve its problems.

LIKE IT IS—PRESSURES IN A GHETTO SCHOOL*

Illegitimacy, black power, police injustice, store front church religion, sexual promiscuity, hunger, "white hats," welfare, unrealistic courses, "Uncle Toms," middle-class norms—all are discernible forces that impinge as pressures upon the ghetto child.

But the ghetto child does not perceive them this way—for him, the pressures are life "like it is."

As a principal of a high school in an inner-city setting explained, "Such things create pressures, but they aren't anything these kids are aware of. I don't think they consciously see this—because, I mean, so many people live this way. We live in a welfare state here."

Over 50 percent of the children in his school come from homes subsisting on welfare. "A lot of the kids don't have fathers, so you can look at them and say that the lack of a male image creates a kind of a pressure, for the boys especially. But, I don't think they consciously see this. Not having a father is a part of a way of life—you can't very well call anyone a 'bastard' around here.

"We are still a neighborhood school. Board policies have not changed, there has been no redistricting, no one's being bussed anywhere.

"While we are making attempts to get them out, for the most part, our kids don't see themselves in relationship to the larger society.

"For them, it's 'nobody cares.' 'People talk a lot, but they're just feeding you a line.' It's a world of 'little hope'—the kids have no idea where they're going, they're confused."

* Reprinted from *Theory Into Practice* (February 1968), 7:17–22, by permission. The following editor's note appeared in the original publication: "This article is based upon a taped interview with a principal and a school counselor who work with ghetto youth in an inner-city high school of a major city. Although the tape has been edited and rewritten by Associate Editor Grace Van Atta, the thoughts, suggestions, and pleas of the principal and counselor are, as nearly as possible, in their own words, presented as they intended them. It is because of the potentially explosive social and political atmosphere in which this principal and counselor work that they are not identified."

BLACK POWER HAS SHOOK UP THE KIDS

"This black power business has really shook up our kids. Many of them have been sucked in by this whole thing, and the anti-white feelings have regenerated.

"Although this school was not caught in the real wave of destruction during the summer riots in our city, we were caught in a few dramatic incidents when Stokely Carmichael was in town one weekend. We had a boy who got some gasoline and put a wick in it and went out to burn down a building.

"He threw it against a concrete wall. The windows were about six feet above the ground, and they not only had bars but were covered by hardware mesh. The building even had a sign on it that it was protected from fire and vandalism.

"Why did the kid do it? 'We had to do something. Carmichael was in town. We had to do something.' So he did.

"Except for isolated incidents like this one, there is no tendency for black power to formalize in the area."

SCHOOL'S THE NICEST PLACE THEY HAVE

"When we had some racial disturbances in other high schools in the area recently, a group of seniors were organized and, as some of these outside characters came into the building, the kids just bodily picked them up and brought them here to the office.

"Throughout all of the riots, we had only two windows broken in this building—this school is the educational center for the community. It's a beautiful building to the kids and their parents. They take good care of it. About all that you'll see are grease marks on the walls. For most of the kids, it's about the nicest place they have to come to."

KIDS LIE TO STAY IN SCHOOL

Some of the students in the school whose parents have prospered get a chance to move out of the area. "But, then," the principal pointed out, "they face even stronger middle-class pressures because they don't belong. Their security is here—they don't want to go.

"To stay in the school, the kids lie about their address. They behave, and their attendance record is almost perfect because they know that the only way the school can find out where they live is if they miss.

"One of the ways we discovered this was during a bus strike, when for the first time attendance referrals were made, and it was discovered some of these kids were not living where they said.

"Some of the kids walked as many as five miles to get here—this must have been a tremendous pressure. But, now we have the authority to make the decision for the child to stay in our school if he's making a good adjustment and his parents want him to.

"These kids feel uncomfortable living outside in new relationships. Here we do have a fairly stable staff. Some of our teachers have been here for years. During the most recent race crisis, when the administration started talking about in-service education—we have had a program from the very beginning of this school that was started before I came as principal. Every new teacher that comes in, we work with—we talk about where the Negro stands and the Negro image in the school—feelings and attitudes these kids have."

IT'S MAKING A FAST BUCK

"Whether it's athletics, or the yearbook, or the honor society, one thing you can't do is have this kind of activity after school, because the first thing after school, it's making a fast buck. Hustling a buck, for boys and girls alike.

"It's very difficult to get kids in right after school—it's a choice the kids have to make, and I don't think they have too much difficulty making it because wherever that dollar bill is hanging, they're going to go for that no matter what.

"But the kids will come in after 6 o'clock. They check their wraps— this is partly for security. You know what a symbol the hat is for the Negro. You check that hat and he's not going to do a thing to cause a disturbance because he has to check out that hat. All outer garments are checked and, also, this way you get at the bottles."

THEY ARE NEGATIVE TOWARD POLICE

"They have a tremendous feeling about police, tremendous. We occasionally have a problem of some kind, and the police assume that it's a Negro that does it. The way they talk to them—the way they twist and push.

"The kids have a negative attitude toward police. Whenever you say this, you have to ask if they have a right to this. And, too often, I'm afraid they have had. They see how the police treat other people, and they don't treat the Negro this way.

"The Negro gets a lot of displacement of the hostility and aggression that police feel because of the nature of their job. The middle-class white kid never experiences this kind of thing."

SOME CONFLICTS STEM FROM RELIGION

"Some of their problems stem from religious conflicts. I have two girls who are seniors who are at the point that they think they are crazy because they have had no sexual relations. One has considered suicide because she is torn by a religious belief. She has so many pressures from her church, along with academic pressures, and the pressures of experiencing her own femininity that she wishes she weren't a woman. And she is an attractive girl with a lot of personality.

"There are a lot of neurotic kids in communities like this because of religious conflict. We have these store front churches, and they have revival meetings where they don't quit until everybody is saved. Sometimes this doesn't happen before 9 a.m., and some of our kids can't make it to school because they have been up all night.

"Some kids are so religious they can't take gym."

THEY HAVE SO MANY DIFFERENT PROBLEMS

"If you're going to work with these kids, you must have the personnel to do it with. You can't lump them together—we don't have many molds here, they're really individualized because of so many different problems.

"You might have in school one hungry child. We have many. I remember a girl a couple of years ago that we had on a free lunch program in the school—we were giving 35¢. She was walking blocks and buying something with the 35¢ to share with her mother and father. The way I found out was that she was never in classes in the afternoon because she couldn't get back.

"The way they are forced to live is one of the basic reasons these children are behind academically and socially."

THESE KIDS ARE STREET WISE

"These kids have a lot of wisdom that some of us don't have in our lifetime because it's forced on them. They can spot a phony around the corner, you don't fool them, they're street wise.

"The ghetto child knows what things come first—being fed, being clothed comes first—everything else comes after that.

"He can't study if he's cold or if he's hungry—if he hasn't got a place. You can't give him a book and say, 'Your homework for tonight are the problems on page 80.' Maybe he hasn't got a place to study.

"In our failure to understand, we put the lower-class child into a situation that he can't possibly handle unless we change all the lower-class values.

"Take tardiness and attendance. It isn't important to the lower-class Negro or Appalachian white students in our school to get somewhere on time—a date—it doesn't mean a thing. This is just not in their culture, it isn't important."

HOW YOU LOOK IS A VALUE

"You'll find some of the best dressed students in our schools—because this is a value, how you look. The feeling is, I'm not really it, but I can look it.

"Nobody around this neighborhood has anything under an Oldsmobile. That they don't have anywhere to park the thing is not important. I know people who sleep in them—they don't pay their room rent but they pay their car note.

"In grocery stores in the area you'll never find the sales items prominently displayed or the cheaper merchandise. One of the reasons is that people won't buy them because they aren't brand names, and they feel they're inferior. Their point of view is that, 'if I have to work hard, and not have anything, I can eat as well as anyone.'

"These people won't go to Legal Aid Society—they pay out for legal advice and then go and plead guilty."

THEY CLIMB OUT ON WHAT THEY CAN

A lot of persons working in education—teachers, principals, administrators, boards—don't understand, the counselor said, and they are very quick to say the Negro's attitude is wrong.

"They don't have the understanding behind it, and I don't think you teach anybody's child unless you do.

"The point is that Negroes are being hemmed in by so many things that they can't climb out on, so they climb out on what they can. It's a law of nature that they're going to compensate."

THE "WHITE HAT" GETS RUN OUT

As the school counselor talked about the problems and pressures, she was critical of the way teachers' colleges prepare persons to teach in schools of predominately lower-class students.

"Teachers' colleges aren't preparing persons who have the needed understanding. The worst we get is the person who feels he's doing a big deal to want to come to this area to give us his all. So, he feels that being nice is the answer.

"These teachers get run out—they're too much with the white hat.

It's all right for awhile, but the kids don't take it for long because they really don't want it.

"The boys and girls want to know what is expected of them. It's the unknowns—when a child doesn't know what reaction should be expected—when he has not been properly informed, then he becomes uncooperative.

"They have suspicions because they don't understand, and they've had so little of the making of authority they have fallen victim to. If they are thoroughly informed and knowledgeable, they will rise above all expectations.

"They resented the fact very much when it was felt that there was a need for a security policeman in our school to keep order—they have a pride of school and loyalty that's phenomenal.

"In our school, if you want rules and regulations kept, you let the students make them. The rule is no better than the person who is going to keep it, and the teachers who use this kind of philosophy and give the children some of the responsibility for making the plans and following through with class activities don't have too many problems.

"It's the only way to operate, or you can't stay."

NEGRO TEACHERS ARE "UNCLE TOMS"

The principal said that Negro teachers in this kind of school have difficulty with their attitudes about Negro students.

"What black power says about our Negro teachers, I firmly believe—they have disassociated themselves from the race and become 'Uncle Toms.'

"While at one time the Negro teacher was quite passive, they have become kind of militant with Negro kids now. Now, it's a rejection of the kid who wears the Rap Brown haircut, and the kids feel this rejection.

"When we started the school year following the summer riots, the white teachers were physically afraid, and they were terribly threatened. Some of them went to the Negro teachers for help, but the Negro teachers were having more problems with the Negro problem than the white teachers.

"But, we work on these problems. Our teachers are in early, and many stay late at night when they have a problem and we talk about it. Sometimes we talk about it in groups, and I think this is partly what has kept our staff together over the years—sharing with and learning from the group. And, part of it's a kind of therapy, I suppose."

SCHOOL HAS CREATED A LOSS

"There are so many things that people just don't realize—many persons who are making decisions are so far from the situation that I don't see how they know what's happening—they're pie in the sky. They don't realize the way things are—what it is that we need in schools like this.

"The kids are sorely disadvantaged in terms of being up to their grade level, and as long as school systems persist in a lock-step system, they can't do anything but get farther behind.

"All you have to do is look at their records and you see this—they start out even as far as school testing and records, but as they move through the grades, they drop back at achievement level.

"School has created a loss—they haven't been anywhere but school.

"When they are starting to school, there's not much difference between the ghetto child and the affluent child. But as they grow older, this makes a big difference, and, as they go up in grades, it becomes more important to teach students of different backgrounds in ways they can learn even though they're having the outside pressures."

WE DON'T HAVE A REALISTIC CURRICULUM

Both the principal and the school counselor feel that most schools like theirs do not have a realistic curriculum. "If we could develop a more practical course that would be job-oriented—the kind of program they really need—these kids wouldn't have to go to high school four years.

"Or, perhaps a program could be developed along the same lines that we have for the mentally retarded and the child in special education. The students in special education still go four years, and they receive a certificate for the completion of twelve years of school.

"The special education pupils come to school a half day and work a half day. They're earning money, and the jobs they have while they're in the program they keep when they leave school.

"The courses they take are related to their work. These students have their own counselor who arranges their program, and he's somebody they can come to if they have a grievance.

"The special education kids are in much better shape than 75 percent of the students who leave school with a diploma—they get a break— they get a job, they get good work habits, they make fine substantial citizens.

"But the other kids, the kids we call basic, they aren't getting a thing here, or anywhere else—just a few vocational courses that are slap happy, workshop and this kind of thing."

WE RELY ON NORMS TOO MUCH

"We should take kids where they are and develop programs there— we rely on norms too much.

"When I look at my kids here—when they were sophomores, at the end of the first semester, about two-thirds were failing one or more subjects, one-third were failing two, and one-half were failing three. We took 110 of them and started them over at the beginning of the next semester, just three subjects for double periods. Their improvement was phenomenal with just this individualized attention.

"Another problem in schools like this is the drain on the very highly academic student—he goes to another school for the gifted. If he doesn't adjust there, he'll be bouncing back.

"We had a very gifted girl who became pregnant and came back to us this year. She could go back to that school, but she can't. She feels she can't face her friends there because she's had a baby.

"But, we can't satisfy her curriculum-wise because she's so advanced. For instance, she took German there, we have no German here. We're trying to offer her some enrichment, but our teachers are not that flexible.

"Also our kids going to college go through a lot of frustration in the testing procedures when they don't measure up.

"The primary problem is that there is very little in the way of creativity in programs because you are required to give them a certain number of credits."

SCHOOL IS GEARED TO THE MIDDLE CLASS

"There is a great gap between what a kid is going to face out there and what we're giving him to face it with. We aren't giving him very much.

"We've got the big American dream of middle-class society and the public school is geared that way," the school counselor said.

"The child from a wealthy upper-class family would have the same difficulty in the public school as the ghetto child. That's why he isn't in it. His family knows this—he'd be a total flop, so he goes to private school. There he can produce in a manner in which he is accustomed and expected.

"Middle class is saying point for point, time for time, issue for issue. But this is foreign, to the kids in my school. Their attitude is a sort of rule of nature—nature takes its course. 'If you go, okay.' And, 'if it's for you, you'll get it'—elusive results.

"The white student in this kind of school is likely to drop out because his parents pressure him. They don't have the feeling of the worth of education that the Negro parents do who are using the present civil rights upheaval to press for change.

"The Negro parents want their children to have more than they did and one of the quickest avenues to get this is the school—the school can give it to them.

"Our kids feel that a big job has been accomplished by just being in school. If they get an 'F' they give you an argument. They wonder why. They did the work, they say—they passed in every paper the teacher asked for. The question is, of course, what was on the paper?

"They think they have accomplished the mission by being here, by not being in trouble, and that they should be rewarded with an education that's going to come by osmosis—that sort of drifts through the skin. They don't have perseverance, their attention span is short—it's simply that many of these children have not been taught to compete because they have been felt sorry for."

TOO MUCH SYMPATHY, NOT ENOUGH EMPATHY

"Our kids have never had a chance to develop their own potential. There have been too many persons with missionary zeal, who say, 'Poor little dears. They don't have what I have and let's help them get it and make it as comfortable and as nice for them as we can and keep them happy.'

"This is like putting clothes on a native.

"Having sympathy for and empathy for are two different things and too many teachers have more sympathy than empathy. They don't have the understanding, but you can't hold this against them because no one's doing anything to tell them anything.

"Many teachers have never experienced failure, so how will they know how to deal with kids that are failing all the time. We have teachers who have never had a problem that wasn't solved or didn't have the potential for being solved—how can they handle people that have problems than can't be solved?

"You've got to know what these kids are up against."

PROVIDING "EQUAL" IS NOT THE POINT

"As long as boards of education keep talking about equal between schools and students and don't understand that there are certain areas that have to have more, three times more, four times more, in order of need, we aren't going to get anywhere.

"This 'equal business' puts the child at a disadvantage in comparing him. He is not to be compared because he is unequal to begin with—you can't equalize something that is unequal at the beginning.

"As long as boards of education sit around saying, 'You've got the same books they have—' Who says we need the same books they have? And they say, 'You've got as many teachers as they've got over at—' Maybe we need three times more in this and one less in that and somebody we don't need at all, maybe.

"But you know, we've got to be equal, and this means giving every child the same. Getting as much as other kids isn't the point. They don't understand this at the top level. I don't think there's much hope sometimes. If they did, they wouldn't make such asinine statements because it doesn't work. It doesn't work.

"You can't start in the middle."

REVOLT IN THE HIGH SCHOOLS: THE WAY IT'S GOING TO BE*

DIANE DIVOKY

The words of the school board were unimpeachable: "It is the aim of our high school to encourage students to freely express themselves, in writing or otherwise, as part of their educational program."

What they meant, in fact, was that the school board in suburban Long Beach, New York, would not allow students to distribute on school premises their fledgling independent newspaper, *Frox*. The thirteen staff members, supported by their parents, had made a formal written request to the school's principal. Their concessions were clear: "no obscenity," a promise "to publish views in opposition to our own," and a willingness "to accept a faculty adviser who is not a censor."

Backed by a new school board resolution that managed to come out squarely for both freedom of expression and full school control, the principal responded rapidly: "I feel compelled to refuse you the right to distribute *Frox* as you request and must advise you that any violation will lead to disciplinary procedures."

Bewildered by their inability to help the teen-agers come to a "reasonable, democratic compromise" with the traditionally liberal school administration, the parents have turned to lawyers. At the same time, the

* Reprinted from *Saturday Review*, February 15, 1969, pp. 83–84, 89, 101–102, by permission. Copyright 1969 Saturday Review, Inc.

students find themselves in a drastically changed role. Youngsters who get good grades and lead school activities, they are suddenly rebels confronting the adults who control their education. They have become members of a growing minority of high school students who are coming into focus as "the new problem" in the nation's schoolhouse.

Yet the mood that is nurturing a network of nearly 500 "underground" high school papers, a national student-run press service to feed them, and the proliferation of independent high school unions and chapters of Students for a Democratic Society is being set by a kind of student the school finds difficult to label. This "new problem student" is most often not a classroom failure; frequently, he is black and from a poor family but not "disadvantaged." Sometimes, when his behavior approaches its most disruptive, he resembles a juvenile delinquent, and sometimes, too, he is simply a follower, pressured by the values and styles of the dominant peer group into acting without thinking.

These students, six-year-olds when John F. Kennedy became President, were the youngest witnesses to the high hopes for a more open society that came in the early Sixties—with its battles for civil rights and against poverty. In their short span of history, they have seen on television the assassinations and funerals of three national leaders who embodied these hopes. The war in Vietnam, beginning for them as nothing much more than another TV shoot-'em-up, has become a frightening reality as they approach draft age. Still vitally young themselves, they have watched the nation's shift from a youthful sense of unlimited expectations to the middle-aged habit of assessing and conserving old strengths and former gains.

Fed by the mass media, urged by parents and teachers to inquire, the students are sensitive to the larger world—and their limited role in it—as no generation before. For them, the student council that fulfills itself by planning dances, academic work that leads only to high College Board scores, and school newspapers that highlight class elections and football games are not only artificial, but inappropriate.

The underground press is, at first, an escape from the carefully delineated boundaries of school activity and opinion. Not surprisingly, therefore, the newest papers tend to be the most ambitious in scope, boldly taking on the great issues in the national arena. The first mimeographed issue of *Alternative* in Eugene, Oregon, was almost completely devoted to opposition to the Vietnam war. The *Strobe*, an amateurish sheet published in "Baltimore's liberated zone," attacks war, poverty, George Wallace, and the "pigs of Chicago." The Appleton (Wisconsin) *Post-Mortem*, edited by Fox Valley High School students "to challenge the myths and realities of their town and society," gets a bit closer to home by focusing on local police tactics.

In their open horror and bewilderment over the happenings in the society, the articles in these papers tend to emotional or moralistic generalizations, very serious but simple truths. They convey the teen-agers' sense of the outrages happening out there in the world, but also their inability—and lack of equipment—to come to grips with problems that are so vast, so complex, so distant from their own lives.

Society seems unable to let the young stay naïve. The underground newspaper, dismissed as a potential educational tool by school administrators in spite of the student initiative and social concern it displays, teaches in another way. As they seek to express their opinions, the students discover that unlike their parents, their college counterparts, the man on the radio or the street corner, they have no right to express an opinion at all.

Last year, John Freeburg, a senior at rural South Kitsap High School outside of Seattle, Washington, began to edit and publish a mimeographed newspaper for students that reflected his own opposition to the Vietnam war, as well as to the adult Establishment's reaction to long hair. John himself was clean-cut in every sense of the word. The son of a commercial airlines pilot, a boy who spent summers working with diabetic children, he was a principal's dream: a consistent high honor student, one of three chosen by the faculty as "outstanding students," a student council representative, and ironically, regional winner of the Veterans' of Foreign Wars "What Democracy Means to Me" contest. Even in getting out his paper, he operated true to form, submitting articles to the school administration for approval before each issue.

In spite of this, three months before graduation John was suspended, and his parents' efforts to have him reinstated by the school board proved fruitless. The state Civil Liberties Union stepped in and obtained a court order for his reinstatement. An ACLU suit on his behalf for damages brought against the school district is still pending in the U. S. District Court. It claims that John's civil rights were violated; the district's counterclaim uses the traditionally unassailable argument that his activities were disruptive to school operation.

But even if his case should succeed—setting a precedent for the rights of high school students—John Freeburg has gone from idealism to skepticism about the "system" that found his exercise of freedom of the press an embarrassment to be eliminated in the face of pressures from right wing groups in the small community. His school said he was old enough to praise democracy publicly, but not to speak about its seamier aspects. Rather than practicing the ideals of freedom and tolerance it preached, the school used its power to suppress ideas. Something was terribly wrong, John decided, not just across the world in Vietnam, but in the institution that was supposed to educate him.

The staff of *Frox* is undergoing the same experience. Their crudely printed paper has worked almost painfully to link the relevant national issues to their own suburban community, to bring the big labels—"racism, imperialism, poverty"—home to Long Beach. Then they found their careful arrangements for distribution were canceled out by the refusal of the principal and the ambiguous educational rhetoric of the school board. Their own school has shown that, as Ira Glasser, associate director of the New York Civil Liberties Union, has stated: "In the classroom we teach freedom, but the organization is totalitarian. The kids learn that when the values of freedom and order conflict, freedom recedes." With what they're learning, the Long Beach students won't have to rely on clichés about freedom and repression. They now have their own gut-level issue, with all its complexities and subtleties. Unwittingly, the school system has given injustice the relevance the students themselves could not.

Once students begin to see the school as a bankrupt, manipulative bureaucracy—and themselves as its most vulnerable victims—the stage is set for the real student movement. The underground paper takes on a double role: to contradict the system that says students have no uncensored voice, and to talk with the authority of the insider about the follies of the institution and the ways it might be undermined or openly confronted. In the second issue of Ann Arbor (Michigan) High School's *Us*, the students explained what they learned from the furor produced by their first issue:

> The suppression we encountered was frightening. The savage in Huxley's *Brave New World* comments on our situation, saying to the Controller, "You got rid of them. Yes, that's just like you. Getting rid of everything unpleasant instead of learning to put up with it. Whether 'tis better in the mind to suffer the slings and arrows of outrageous fortune, or to take arms against a sea of troubles and by opposing end them. . . . But you don't do either. Neither suffer nor oppose. You just abolish the slings and arrows. It's too easy." We fear the brave new world, we fear . . . "lobotomized" education, especially in this tremendous school. The issue which was created with this publication was not one of censorship of the *Optimist*. The school paper is possibly the best in the nation. Outside of administrative demands on space and content, we do not question its excellence. The existence of anti-distribution laws for student literature is the major objection. This is a violation of our constitutional rights. If this journalistic endeavor is a failure, it can easily be forgotten. But, if you or they force us to stop, we are all failures. Then, this school, city, and country, and the principles they supposedly represent are lies.

The more seasoned underground papers operate confidently on the understanding that change in the schools is their first order of business, and that national issues—the cry for law and order, teacher militancy— do affect their lives as students. At first glance, these papers are fun. They call themselves *The Pearl before the swine, The Finger, Napalm, The*

*Roach, The South Dakota Seditionist Monthly, Big Momma, The Phil-
istine, The Bleeding Rose, Dormat Dwellers,* even *The New York Herald
Tribune.* They are fresh, crazy, biased, irreverent in their view of the world,
and often unexpectedly inventive in the way they present it. Albert Shanker,
United Federation of Teachers president, becomes a great vulture, perched
over the bodies of children. Samson Jones gets kicked out of Gaza Central
High School for his long hair—and in a rage pulls the school down.

The more stylish ones are almost a new pop art form. Print runs
around, over, and under stark drawings, viciously pointed cartoons, poignant
photographs. Sometimes the word itself becomes the design. Dreamy
poems are transposed on psychedelic drawings. Surrealistic obscene headlines fly out from the page. And often a picture stands by itself, telling
the story rather than illustrating it. This is the work of McLuhan's generation.

The national focus for the underground is HIPS, the High School
Independent Press Service (160 Claremont Avenue, New York, N.Y.
10027), which offers a weekly packet of news and illustrations of high
school uprisings, busts, dress codes, discipline, and politics. Some sixty
papers and 400 fans subscribe, at an often uncollected fee of $4 a month.
"HIPS is very much in the revolutionary bag," a staffer admits. "I suppose we're just as bad as the *Times* in being biased. But underground
papers are more interesting to read than the *Times.* They don't start with
the usual 'who, where, when, what, why.' HIPS gets people to think. Gets
them radicalized before they get into college. If that happens, chances are
a fourth of them will never get to college."

One of the slickest papers HIPS services is the *New York High School
Free Press,* which publishes 10,000 copies every three weeks (5 cents for
students, 15 cents for teachers). It introduced itself last fall with a full-
cover photo of a naked Negro baby girl holding the black flag of anarchy:
"Ursula, seven months and already foxy as hell," the editors explained.
A coupon form invites the reader to subscribe or, if he prefers, to curse
and threaten the "hippie-commie-yippie-queer-pinkos" who print it. Another reader service is a directory of pertinent phone numbers: for prayers,
demonstrations, birth control and abortion information, draft counseling,
the FBI, and "nighttime companions"—the Girl Scouts.

Yet silliness serves more serious purposes. The *Free Press,* with first-
hand reports on national and school crises and interviews with prominent
figures, is a sober attempt to reach radical and politically oriented students
throughout the city. Its mix of serious radicalism and youthful gags reflects its staff, a closely knit group of intense, quick-witted students, most
of whom attend New York's highly selective Bronx High School of
Science. In the living room of one of their homes, the students—a
balance of whites and blacks—can go with breathtaking speed from
typical teen-age roughhousing to political debate.

Reggie Lucas, the paper's fifteen-year-old music critic, talks about "breaking down the traditional teacher-student relationship" in the schools, so that by "interchanging roles, the teacher, as well as the student, could learn." Everything the adult Establishment does, he explains politely, "is not just undesirable, but repugnant to us. The real hero today is the person who can mess up the society and pervert the youth."

Leader of the group is Howie Swerdloff, at seventeen a good-natured veteran of the underground press and radical student movement, who wrote last fall:

> The main thing that's taught us in school is how to be good niggers, obey the rules, dress in our uniforms, play the game, and NO DON'T BE UPPITY! Oh, we're trained for participating in the "democratic process"—we have our student governments—they can legislate about basketball games and other such meaningful topics. Don't mention the curriculum—THEY'LL tell us what to learn. Oh, we can express our complaints in the school newspaper—but the principal says what gets printed and don't embarrass the school's reputation.

Howie's immediate fight is with the school establishment; his long-range goal is to destroy the government he finds hopelessly oppressive through a worldwide people's revolution. His mother views his position with pride tempered by concern. When he was only fifteen, she recalls, she was first called into school about his activities. Finding Howie distributing antiwar leaflets across the street from the school, she began to apologize to the irate principal. Howie stopped her: "My lawyer said it's OK, Mother."

The Swerdloffs, liberals of another generation, are hopeful about the contributions their son and his friends will make to change the society, yet are appalled by the often violent reaction of the society to the youthful protests. "You wonder," Mrs. Swerdloff said, recalling the violence in Chicago during the Democratic convention. "You teach them such good values, and then when they go ahead and act on them, all this happens."

The underground high school press represents attitudes that have generated a variety of organizations bent on changing the school and the society. Their tactics range from polite dialogue to picketing to direct confrontation with the authorities. It is, nonetheless, difficult to categorize these groups, since their degree of militancy and their deviance from accepted student behavior depend a great deal on the response of school and community officials, the particular issues involved, and on the students themselves.

There is no one approach among the black separatist groups. New York City's High School Coalition, affiliated with the Black Panther party, spews vitriolic rhetoric in its newsletter and operates on a single dogma: the necessity of black liberation by any means possible. In contrast, the Modern Strivers, a group of young Negroes at Eastern High School in Washington, D.C., talks black power, but in the traditional American terms of self-help, hard work, and foundation funding.

The degree of flexibility within a community helps to determine the degree to which a group is regarded as a problem. In Berkeley, California, the liberal, interracial Youth Council, which has a poster of Black Panther leader Eldridge Cleaver in its office in city hall, received the support of city fathers even after its president was arrested for selling drugs. In Milwaukee, however, the beginnings of a student alliance, a rather apolitical group hoping for school reform, brought shocked cries from administrators, city officials, and the state's principals' association, who were ready to accuse "subversive" outside influences of stirring up the unrest.

The students are conscious of the variety within their ranks. The New York High School Student Union, an integrated, citywide group with semiautonomous locals in 108 public and private schools, operates so flexibly that members at one school can be requesting more school dances while those at another can be out protesting the war. Its leaders tend to be disdainful of the doctrinaire approach of Students for a Democratic Society, and prefer to let their members "do their own thing."

Many groups, however, influenced by nearby college activity, have become SDS affiliates. Last year, eleven high schools in Seattle formed SDS chapters. In St. Louis, the citywide SDS group became large enough to be broken up into individual high school chapters. The Akron-based Ohio Union of High School Students, though not affiliated with SDS, has an adviser from the organization. National SDS headquarters has been overwhelmed by the flood of requests for literature from high school groups, and estimates an increase of about 800 per cent over last year. To meet the demand, the SDS national council decided in October to hire a full-time secondary school coordinator.

The schoolmen, caught offguard by the new attitude, are now rushing to diagnose the problem and find solutions. The National Association of Secondary School Principals reports the findings of a national survey of student unrest in large and small school systems at its annual convention this month. A new NASSP handbook suggests ways to make the student council more meaningful. The organization's September 1968 bulletin was devoted to student unrest and included articles about its link with college militancy, possible reasons and solutions for the "coming revolt," and even one on what to do either before—or when—the legal showdown comes. ("The handwriting is on the wall; public school students will be protected in their constitutional rights," it said.)

Reaction to the new activism by schoolmen has been as varied as the kinds of students involved, their forms of dissent, and the responses of communities. A few school administrators regard the militancy as a potentially beneficial force, an often responsible if sometimes shrill demand for a more active role in school affairs. Just as the mass media and current events have taught the students something, so too they may have learned, really learned, what the schools' rhetoric says they should—to inquire critically.

Dr. Eugene Smoley, a high school principal in Montgomery County, Maryland, puts it this way: "The activists represent a real challenge educationally by questioning the foundations of the society. They're looking for ways to be helpful, pushing for a way for their actions to have some influence, pressing for more meaningful lives. The movement is a very positive thing, because it can only be compared with the apathy of an earlier time."

Many other schoolmen, however, dismiss the activism as a fad, claim that the high school students are only imitating their older brothers and sisters in college, or maintain that because students have always complained, all grievances are on the order of gripes about the cafeteria food.

The school administrator is, indeed, the man in the middle, caught between the community he serves and a whole new set of realities. Traditionally, the community—and the society—expect him to run a well ordered, efficient institution founded on a number of assumptions: Students are children, in both the legal and educational sense. They are pretty much alike—naïve and awkward as they grow. When they learn, they learn in school. The principal is legally responsible for the well-being of school children, and educationally responsible for what goes into their heads.

Although the legal fiction that students are children to be protected remains, much else has changed. Norman Solomon, honors senior and reporter for the county newspaper, who addresses the Montgomery County school board on the system's inputs and outputs and the "serious gap that presently exists between rhetoric and reality," cannot be dismissed as a charming child. The two Berkeley high school seniors who sit as full voting members on city committees know more about the operation of bureaucracy than any textbook could teach them. After his week in Chicago during the 1968 Democratic National Convention, Howie Swerdloff can tell his teachers a good deal about violence and police brutality in this nation.

To what extent can sophisticated adolescents be considered adults when they are still legally children? If the school is to educate, can it afford not to capitalize on the increasing awareness and concern of the students? Can the school be a public forum while maintaining its tight authoritarian patterns? If the school grants more freedom to students, is it opening itself up to irresponsible—as well as responsible—adolescent judgments? Can it find a place for its dissatisfied minority without threatening its more accepting, complacent majority?

The revolt itself testifies that students have been learning more than the schools have taught: from parents who are as well or better educated than teachers; from the mass media with which the school finds itself in competition; from actual participation in the politics and culture of the society. To accept this knowledge and experience means facing up to a set of complicated problems. To deny it is to deny the students themselves.

DISRUPTION IN URBAN PUBLIC SECONDARY SCHOOLS: IN-SCHOOL CAUSES*

Stephen K. Bailey

As we have suggested earlier, the causes of high school disruption run on a circular continuum from the wider society, on through the schools, and back to the wider society. There is no sensible way to differentiate clearly among these causes. Like the strands in a marble cake, they run so closely together and take such unexpected turns and twists, that discrete categorization is impossible. For a simple example, a running quarrel between two youth gangs from different housing projects may produce a serious fight at the school which they both attend. In no real sense is this the school's "fault" even though it is the location of the fracas and indeed may get publicity that it is a "trouble" school where severe fighting often takes place.

Nevertheless there *are* some in-school causes of disruption, in the sense that certain school practices can foment dissatisfaction and trigger serious interruption of the educational process. Even more important, these in-school problems are inevitably mixed with the wider societal causes and are interpreted and perceived by students as part of that

* Reprinted from *Disruption in Urban Public Secondary Schools*, Syracuse University Research Corporation report (Washington, D.C.: National Association of Secondary School Principals, August 1970), pp. 26–33. Reproduced by permission of the publisher and author.

wider mix. It is this chemistry that makes these difficulties so pungent. In short, in the words of one rather myopic schoolman, "If we could just run *our own school*, it would be peaceful." Said whimsically, it is a pleasant remark. Said seriously, it is foolish and dangerous.

STUDENT INVOLVEMENT IN POLICY

There is healthy debate in every school we visited as to the relative weight to give student views in matters of school practices and policies. We met no administrators who felt that students should not be involved. Naturally, there is considerable and honest difference of opinion concerning both the extent of involvement and the types of practices where students should have more influence than in others. Two areas of concern popped up frequently, and a third is beginning to loom on the horizon. First, social codes, including dress and grooming regulations, and policies governing extracurricular activities are of great concern to students. When students feel that prescriptions on these matters are made by adults only, they show considerable unrest. Second, limits and restrictions governing who can and who cannot participate in athletics and cheerleading are important. Students we talked to are generally opposed to grade requirements, attendance and tardiness limits, or other ways to circumscribe such participation. (Sometimes an apparently small matter can cause serious irritation. Some high schools still require a student to pay his $1 or $2 dues to the student government as a condition of voting for representation on that government.) Serious unrest has occurred in integrated schools when restrictions cause the student government, football team, or cheerleader squad to be essentially white and clearly disproportionate to the racial makeup of the student body.

We believe that the motives of schoolmen in imposing grades and similar restrictions related to extracurricular activities, at least in the North, are purely educational. Such restrictions are an old and accepted practice, even in colleges and universities. But they are now frequently interpreted as racist practices by non-white students and are probably no longer worth the effort.

Curriculum planning is rapidly becoming a third major issue. It is undoubtedly a much more complicated problem. We found much ambiguity in the prescriptions issued by students, parents, staff, and teachers. On the one hand students seem to demand representation on curriculum bodies so as to secure a "current curriculum" which will convey high school graduates to a good paying job the day after commencement exercises. On the other hand, there is a somewhat more ambiguous demand for preparation "which keeps the options open after graduation"—for college, for specific technical careers, *or* for a good-paying job the day after commencement. High school curriculum bodies, of course, wrestle with these difficulties constantly. Whether such bodies should include voting students, the most transient constituency of a school, raises complicated and complicating issues. What we do know is that over the next few years, there will be increasing demands for such representation. If ignored, such demands can lead to further unrest.

FACILITIES

For persons not accustomed to visiting large urban public high schools, the experience can be a bit startling. Bells ringing, buzzers sounding, public address systems making all those announcements, thousands of noisy, energetic adolescents pushing and shoving their way through crowded halls and stairways, locker doors banging, books or other things being dropped, and so on—all these and many more give an impression of unmanageable social interaction in which education is effectively precluded. At the same time, after visiting enough institutions around the country one can feel a clear difference between a school which is essentially a happy one and a school which is not. The differences show up in the *tone* of the noise, not necessarily its level, and especially in the kinds of brief human contacts among adult staff, hall guards or whatever, and students moving hurriedly to their next assignment. The smiling level is important. The kinds of jocular interplay are probably more important. In the most interesting schools we visited, there was a subtle mixture of obvious respect and obvious friendliness which seemed ever present and, significantly, which ran both ways.

Some of these schools were clearly overcrowded physically. It is just plain tiring to go to classes which are clearly too large, assemblies which are merely bubbly mass meetings, bathrooms where the lines are obviously too long, and to fumble around in front of a locker shared by one or two others on the main floor of a building which was clearly not designed to accommodate such furniture. We were often told that urban people are wholly accustomed to this kind of melee. Whether they are or are not, many of them will tell you that they do not like such a mess. Whether school officials by themselves can do anything about this is doubtful. New physical facilities, clearly needed, are very expensive and attract the immediate attention of taxpayers. We merely note that overcrowding together with its attendant noise and fatigue provide a ripe climate for disruption.

RESTRICTIONS ON BEHAVIOR

We have referred earlier to efforts by schools to limit "deviant" clothing and hair styles. This remains a constant bone of contention between students and staff, and when it takes on racial or ethnic features, the contention becomes far more serious. We suspect that everyone would agree that nakedness at school is prohibited because, by itself, it disrupts education. On the other hand, restrictions against bell-bottom pants, long hair, "Afro's," and beads are probably useless and offensive.

But other restrictions can become even more sticky. One principal told us that a black group in his school wished to have exclusive use of a particular sector of the cafeteria, remove the American flag from that area, and substitute the Black Liberation flag. It is difficult to see how permission for this behavior could be given, but it was. The results were wholly predictable. Parent groups, many teachers, and school-system officials soon were outraged. The compromise was both flags at equal height in an unofficially designated, but black area of the cafeteria.

Restrictions on smoking continue to annoy students who smoke. Hall passes irritate students. Rules such as automatic expulsion from a class after a maximum number of absences have produced serious quarrels. Censorship of student newspapers, whether subtle or very direct, has produced a proliferation of underground newspapers now common to the American public high school.

Honest people of good will can argue the relative merits of restrictions on behavior and differ widely. Here again, we merely point out that these limits on adolescent life leave a running level of dispute among the many publics of a school.

CROSSCULTURAL CLASHES

One cannot visit urban high schools and not be directly aware of the clashes produced by mixing large numbers of young people and adults who come from very different neighborhoods, very different racial and ethnic strands, and very different age brackets. For example, we were impressed with the serious lack of communication often occurring when older teachers stay on in a school that has become very different in its ethnic and income characteristics. Such teachers are often called "racists" or "moralists" or worse. The basic problem, however, may simply be the very difficult adjustments such teachers and staff have to make to a rapidly changing social mix in their schools and classrooms. Many of these teachers are clearly "old pro's" in their own right, but they no longer "belong," that is, they are simply inappropriate for the kinds of demanding tasks that new constituencies and new expectations have produced.

Of course, age is not the only problem. Well-meaning schoolmen will frequently celebrate the birthday of a famous Spanish conquistador, but when a small militant group of Chicanos would also like to honor

Zapata there is only silence from the front office. Or (no analogy intended) when special ceremonies are held to honor a Booker T. Washington or a Martin Luther King, disruptions can occur not because black students dishonor these men, but because their request similarly to honor Malcolm X was ignored.

It is our considered judgment that disruptions caused by these kinds of issues will occur most frequently in moderate-income, middle-class schools into which are bussed significant numbers of low-income students, and not in either the predominantly- or all-white or all-black school settings. By way of illustration, in the southern schools visited there was little evidence of serious disruption based on racial conflict. We believe this will change as southern schools become more and more integrated. Dissatisfactions already manifest in northern integrated schools will arise in the South and will provide ready ingredients for disturbance. There is already evidence of this in recent newspaper accounts of testimony before Senator Walter Mondale's committee by black students in newly integrated southern schools.

CLASSIFICATION OF STUDENTS AND CAREER COUNSELING

One of the most difficult things that educators do is to engage in the career-sorting process. The way the process is carried out and the well-known limits on educational knowledge about the process create considerable unrest in the big city high school. Here, too, there is much ambiguity in the minds and feelings of staff, students, parents, and community organizations. Many students and parents feel that almost irrevocable and obviously crucial decisions are made as early as the ninth grade. This is the level at which curricular tracks and programs are frequently established. Counselors are clearly aware of the national controversy swirling around the whole question of tests and their meaning for central city students. Counselors are also aware of the logistic needs of the school—filling up its program quotas and class levels, for example.

In any case, with hundreds of students to consult, those responsible for the tracking and career counseling system seem impersonal, mechanical, and once more "not caring" or worse—that is, influenced by racial and class prejudice. The style of career counseling is an increasingly serious in-school cause of deep frustration and unrest.

INCREASING POLITICALIZATION OF SCHOOLS

It would come as no surprise to any big city principal to be told that a huge backlog of emotional freight produced by some very rough social conflicts in our time is being dumped on his school. Black students coming to school with the heady message of black power or white students coming to school with a "NEVER" button would only be two symbols of the inexorable process by which the public schools are being sucked into the important social quarrels of the day. The intergenerational gap, referred to earlier, adds fuel to this fire as well. The impatience level among adolescents runs high. As is the case in many universities, students want the school to be a stronger social force for goals they consider correct and necessary. Students, naturally, are politicized by the media, by local community leadership, and indeed by the more political teachers at the school.

If politicized students are deeply dissatisfied and urging action, they will probably create some kind of scene right at the school for the very simple reason that that is where they are. It is commonplace to note that adolescents have very little leverage on the wider society's politics, so they strike where they are and where they do have leverage. The management of these very important social conflicts within a school is probably the toughest problem administrators have.

Simplistic notions that trouble is caused by "outside agitators" will simply not produce constructive solutions. Among Webster's definition of "agitate" are the following phrases, "to give motion to," "to discuss excitedly and earnestly," and "to attempt to arouse public feeling." In these senses, some of the best high school students in America are agitators, and a healthy secondary school is proud of them. The best teachers and staff people we observed deftly wove these deeply felt problems into academic courses where appropriate, thus channeling emotions into behavioral insights and analyses. The worst staffs would either ignore or gloss over these matters, much to the peril of the school, and certainly to the detriment of the education of its students. To do the former is admittedly not easy; to do the latter in our time is foolish.

Chapter 4

DEMANDS FOR CHANGING
THE HIGH SCHOOL CURRICULUM

Some selections in earlier chapters have already cited various forces and problems that indicate need for further change in the high school curriculum: especially, the gap between educational objectives and attained outcomes, the neglect of some important goals, the inadequate provisions for needs of many students, and students' own dissatisfactions with their schools. Chapter 4 presents some more direct statements regarding these and other demands for curriculum improvement.

The first selection comes from a collection of articles from the underground high school newspapers edited by a high school graduate of 1969 and published in 1970 under the title, *Our Time Is NOW: Notes from the High School Underground* (John Birmingham, editor, Praeger Publishers). It is a high school student's stirring appeal for high schools to help the student "to become a better person in all facets of his future life." This plea is the familiar one of such critics of schooling as John Holt, from whose sometimes acid but popular pen a selection follows. This excerpt first appeared in an essay entitled "The Fourth R—The Rat Race" and is included in Holt's *The Underachieving School* (Pitman Publishing Corporation, 1969). In the foreword of this book, Holt, who has had extensive teaching experience, cites his credo of schooling in reproducing his answer to the *Education News* editors' question, "if America's schools were to take one giant step forward this year toward a better tomorrow, what should it be? (p. IX):

> It would be to let every child be the planner, director, and assessor of his own education, to allow and encourage him, with the inspiration and guidance of more experienced and expert people, and as much help as he is asked for, to decide what he is to learn, when he is to learn it, how he is to learn it, and how well he is learning it. It would be to make our schools, instead of what they are, which is jails for children, into a resource for free and independent learning, which everyone in the community, of whatever age, could use as much or as little as he wanted.

This point of view is illustrated by the selection here. Holt indicts the school for requiring "the adolescent to direct his attention, not to who he is and ought to be or wants to be, but who we think he is and want him to be." The pressures placed on young people, he says, make them feel "that life is a rat race." Both the high school student speaking out in our first selection, and John Holt speaking for students in the second, are demanding that the high school give adolescents more opportunity and help in discovering their own routes to the good life.

An especially urgent demand for reform in high school education relates to the totality of problems of America's large cities. The research of Robert J. Havighurst, Frank L. Smith, and David E. Wilder reported by the National Association of Secondary School Principals in *A Profile of the Large-City High School* (January 1971), is summarized in part with some statements as to its implications in the selection, "Big-City Schools, Present and Future." This selection, from its challenging opening ("The big cities of the country—those over 300,000 in population —are in deep trouble educationally") to its closing commentary on the curriculum (the probable "move away from the *instrumental* and toward the *expressive* forms of education"), is a provocative and significant report deserving serious consideration by all concerned with high school education. Because of the continuing "flight to the suburbs" and other population movements, Havighurst's observation that "it seems likely that there is more and deeper segregation and separation of high school students of different socioeconomic and ethnic groups today than there was 10 to 20 years ago" is not surprising, but frightening.

Do you agree with his final predictable goal of "greater social integration of all kinds of students"? How can it be achieved, and how can the high school curriculum help achieve it?

Other findings of this study relative to overcrowding of the large city high schools and to student conflict and activism in them, underline the necessity for change in these schools. Also seeming to demand change is the evidence of uniformity in curriculum among the schools of a city, despite the uniqueness of population configurations within particular schools. Havighurst noted that there was special support, including reduced student-teacher ratio, for some schools with high proportions of disadvantaged students, but suggested the need for more cooperative planning to provide for freer movement of students and faculty among the schools of the large city. His final observations about the curriculum—the need for greater emphasis on expressive education, learning for its own sake—seem applicable to the high school curriculum in general and in keeping with demands from others already presented. However, the data on large city high schools certainly underline the need for adolescents who attend them to have more opportunity to *enjoy* schooling.

Economic and employment problems of the early 1970s stimulated some reexamination of the college preparatory function of the high school, and indeed of the total notion of college attendance for most Americans. The problems of the "go-to-college lockstep" are reviewed in the selection by Edmund K. Faltermayer. He sees many unfavorable results of the "pernicious conformism" of the go-to-college movement, among them: "turned-off students"; prolonged dependency and the delay of "purposeful contact with the real world" after physical adulthood has been attained; the high costs of college; the "high-schoolization" of college, especially in the first two years; and the imbalance between job requirements and college training. The remedy he proposes is a greater variety of alternatives available to high school graduates coupled with a plan whereby the student who chooses college pays for his own college education out of later earnings. The alternatives to college are not fully identified in the article although there is one interesting suggestion that industry might "lower the B.A. barrier and offer interesting jobs to promising high-school graduates, along with some sort of commitment to save their jobs for them if they later decide to go to college." The

chief implication of Faltermayer's article for the high school has to
do with its goals; the "go-to-college lockstep" has undoubtedly been
aided and abetted by the prestigious college-preparatory track, whether or
not labeled, in the high school program of studies. The reform needed,
as the writer sees it, is to abolish this track and institute more programs
of studies and experiences in high school that provide the relevance
high school students and other critics demand, plus a very heavy
emphasis on learning as a way of life rather than a way of going to college.

Such an emphasis is also called for in the last selection of this
chapter, Fred Wilhelms' "Cost-Effectiveness and the Curriculum." In
a period when many forces (see Chapter 1) are calling for accountability
in education, Wilhelms' argument is a very fine antidote to treatments
of the subject that would base the evaluation of educational effectiveness
on assessment of subject matter achievement alone. Wilhelms calls for
investing our educational expenditures in teaching students to learn
and to function as persons. We ought to invest boldly, he writes, "in
teaching students to be able to learn better" and "in helping each
youngster become a *more effective person*." And he is persuasive in
his belief that schools can do these things if we can use "the common
sense to drop investments we know don't pay, and the nerve to try some
more hopeful ones."

Could it be that Faltermayer, Wilhelms, Havighurst, Holt, and the
others, including the present author, are talking to the same point,
namely demanding that the high school curriculum become much less
an arena for learning those facts, concepts, structures, which have
become ritual for the college-going, upward-bound, middle-class student,
and much more a cooperative society for students to develop their
aspirations, talents, learning skills, and human relations so as to be able
to make wise decisions upon graduation about their own destinies?
It is with this point of view that we turn now to consideration of the
specific changes currently being made in the high school curriculum, and
the ones further needed.

ATTENTION ALL TEACHERS!*

J. S. CATALINA

We recommend that all biology teachers read the last chapter in the BSCS biology text. It explains that in one year, you (the students) will have forgotten about 85 percent of the facts you learned in biology and that the purpose of the course was not to have you memorize facts, but to put you in a frame of thinking, in this case scientific.

The authors assume that if you don't go into science, you won't have much use for all the details, but that becoming a person more aware of yourself and environment will make you more easily adaptable to and comfortable in your surroundings. We wish that the course was taught on this assumption, as we wish all required courses were.

It is evident that a forced feeding of facts leads only to the forgetting of them, not to the making of a better student, or a better community, or a better world. In this age of specialization, though electives should be taught for job training, with whatever means necessary, required courses, after providing the basics necessary to life, should be a broadening influence, allowing the student to develop his own patterns of thought. School, therefore, should be a place where in addition to being trained for performing the techniques necessary for earning money, a student is allowed to become a better person in all facets of his future life. Making a living is not restricted to the accumulating of monetary wealth, but includes searching for and achieving wisdom—understanding self and environment, i.e., others—and happiness.

It is then necessary to condemn the school in which the student is removed from the accumulating of wisdom and is not allowed to discover how to achieve happiness. Such a school is only a temple to pre-twentieth century rigamarole.

* Reprinted by permission, from *Our Time Is NOW: Notes from the High School Underground* (John Birmingham, ed. New York: Praeger Publishers, 1970), pp. 205–206.

THE FOURTH R—THE RAT RACE*

JOHN HOLT

A person's identity is made up of those things—qualities, tastes, beliefs—that are uniquely his, that he found and chose and took for himself, that cannot be lost or taken from him, that do not depend on his position or his success or other people's opinion of him. More specifically, it is the people he admires; the books, the music, the games, the interests that he chooses for himself and likes, whether or not anyone else likes them, or whether or not they are supposed to be "good" or "worthwhile"; the experiences that he seeks out for himself and that add to his life.

An adolescent needs time to do this kind of seeking, tasting, selecting and rejecting. He needs time to talk and think about who he is and how he got to be that way and what he would like to be and how he can get there. He needs time to taste experience and to digest it. We don't give him enough.

In addition, by putting him in a position where he is always being judged and where his whole future may depend on those judgments, we require the adolescent to direct his attention, not to who he is or ought to be or wants to be, but who we think he is and want him to be. He has to keep thinking about the impression he is making on us—his elders, the world. Thus we help to exaggerate what is already, in most young people, a serious and crippling fault—an excessive concern with what others think of them.

Since our judgments are more often than not critical, unfavorable, even harsh, we exaggerate another fault, equally serious and crippling—a tendency to imagine that other people think less well of them than in fact they do, or what is worse, that they do not deserve to be well thought of. Youth ought to be a time when people acquire a sense not just of their

---

* From John Holt, *The Underachieving School* (New York: Pitman Publishing Corporation, 1969), pp. 39–41. Previously published in *New York Times Magazine*, May 1, 1966; © 1966 by the New York Times Company. Reprinted by permission.

99

own identity but also of their own worth. We make it almost certain to be the very opposite.

In this competition into which we have driven children, almost everyone loses. It is not enough any more for most parents or most schools that a child should go to college and do well there. It is not even enough for most children themselves. More and more, the only acceptable goal is to get into a prestige college; to do anything else is to fail. Thus I hear boys and girls say, "I wanted to go to so-and-so, but I'm not good enough." It is outrageous that they should think this way, that they should judge themselves stupid and worthless because of the opinion of some remote college admissions officer.

The pressures we put on our young people also tend to destroy their sense of power and purpose. A friend of mine, who recently graduated with honors from a prestige college, said that he and other students there were given so much to read that, even if you were an exceptionally good reader and spent all your time studying, you could not do as much as half of it.

Looking at work that can never be done, young people tend to feel, like many a tired businessman, that life is a rat race. They do not feel in control of their own lives. Outside forces hurry them along with no pause for breath or thought, for purposes not their own, to an unknown end. Society does not seem to them a community that they are preparing to join and shape like the city of an ancient Greek; it is more like a remote and impersonal machine that will one day bend them to its will.

BIG-CITY SCHOOLS, PRESENT AND FUTURE*

ROBERT J. HAVIGHURST

The big cities of the country—those over 300,000 in population—are in deep trouble educationally. Recognized until just a few years ago as the

* Reprinted by permission, from A *Profile of the Large-City High School* (by Robert J. Havighurst, Frank L. Smith, and David E. Wilder), Chapter X in the *Bulletin of the National Association of Secondary School Principals* (January 1971), 55:94–104.

home of the very best schools, they now have few of the most successful schools and many of the most problem-ridden.

These cities have two contrasting problems with their high schools. On the one hand, they have the problem of maintaining a kind of secondary education that will compete with suburban schools and thus hold middle-income families in the cities and, conceivably, even encourage them to come back to the central city from the suburbs. But, at the same time, they have to cope with a group of young people who do poorly in school, and who do not get jobs or make satisfactory adult adjustments when they drop out of school. In the central cities of the larger metropolitan areas, this marginal group may reach 25 or 30 percent of all 16- and 17-year-olds. Since this condition is further exacerbated by social considerations, the educational problem it creates is a grave one indeed.

Obviously, the solutions to such problems are not simple. Thus, for example, the *comprehensive* high school, defined and favored by James B. Conant in his two studies of secondary education, has only limited applicability in the big cities, according to Mr. Conant himself. Its values can probably be secured in certain big-city high schools, but not in most of them. The big cities may need to create models all their own.

The NASSP study of large-city high schools, which has been reported in the preceding pages, shows that there are approximately 700 public high schools in the 45 largest cities, with approximately 1.6 million students in grades 9–12 or 10–12. These schools fall into four categories, based on the socioeconomic background of the student. Student enrollments in each of these categories in 1970 are shown in Table 1.

The healthiest schools are the comprehensive type, which contain a cross-section of youth according to socioeconomic level and have a self-contained, varied, and comprehensive curriculum. These schools do a fairly satisfactory job, but many of them are threatened with "neighborhood change," which means being overtaken by the spread of inner city slums and of racial and economic segregation. Many schools which were in the comprehensive category 10 years ago have moved into the inner-city category.

The upper-middle-class schools, though dwindling in number, still maintain themselves as the high-status schools in the big cities, and middle-class parents look for them, moving their residence if necessary to keep their children in such schools. In terms of academic achievement levels and curriculum innovations, these are the "best" schools. But they lack a major ingredient of a democratic school structure, for they lack students from low-income and minority group families. Thus, they prosper to a limited degree while the rest of the city suffers.

The two lower socioeconomic status categories are growing in size as the big cities lose middle-class residents to the suburbs. Schools in such areas suffer from a variety of difficulties that we cannot do much about so

Table 1   Data on Large-City High Schools, 1970*

	No. of Schools	Enrollment
Upper-Middle Class Schools		
(over 70% middle class)		
Public	150	375,000
Private Independent	100	75,000
Comprehensive Schools		
(cross section of population in socioeconomic status)		
Public	200	500,000
Private, mainly church-operated	250	250,000
Lower Middle/Working Class Schools		
Public	200	400,000
Working Class Schools		
(over 75% working class)		
Public	150	300,000
Totals		
Public	700	1,575,000
Private	350	325,000
		1,900,000

* These data on schools in cities with populations over 300,000 are based on estimates developed by Robert Havighurst.

long as they are schools which serve an almost exclusively low economic and racially segregated student body. In this situation the student body holds relatively low expectations of educational achievement and low educational aspirations for its members. Students lack the advantage of competition with those who have greater academic motivation. These schools lack the means for encouraging common social living and common social goals for young people with a wide variety of economic and racial backgrounds. And they lack teachers of experience, because teachers with seniority almost without exception choose, when they have the option, to work in upper class and comprehensive schools.

SOCIOECONOMIC SEGREGATION AND HIGH SCHOOLS

The 1970 census reports that most of the big cities lost population between 1960 and 1970. Specifically, seven of the top 10 in 1960 lost population in the subsequent decade. These losses are accounted for mainly by middle-income young adults leaving the central city for the suburbs and by the death of people who were not replaced. At the same time, low-income people moved into the central cities, many coming from Puerto

Rico, from the Appalachians and the Ozarks, from the rural Southwest, and many from the rural South.

This process has been going on rapidly since about 1950, when the postwar economic boom began to draw industrial workers into the large cities. The result was that the proportion of youth from low-income and minority group families increased, and many high schools which had formerly contained an approximate cross section of young people (in socio-economic terms) acquired a student body that is concentrated within a narrow band of the socioeconomic spectrum.

During the years from 1950 to 1970, the migration of Southern black families to the big cities, both north and south, was a major population movement, as was the migration of Puerto Ricans to New York, Phila-delphia, and Chicago and of Mexican Americans to the cities of the Southwest and the Western states. These groups tended to find homes in low-income areas, and were subject to varying degrees of discrimination that limited their access to residential areas all over the city.

The combination of these various population movements has resulted in a remarkably high degree of ethnic segregation in the high schools, a fact which has been documented in some detail in earlier chapters of this report.

SOCIOETHNIC TYPES OF HIGH SCHOOLS

The largest ethnic group of schools in our big cities consists of 278 (42 percent) of the schools, which are 80 percent or more "non-ethnic white." This is a loose way of saying that the students—in most cases, close to 100 percent of them—are from white families whose parents were born in this country and are not Spanish-speaking. These schools are divided again along socioeconomic lines, with 110 or 16 percent being upper middle class, and 116 or 17 percent middle class comprehensive. This leaves only 52, or 8 percent, in the two lower socioeconomic categories.[1]

Quite the reverse picture is seen when one looks at the "over 80 percent black" schools; 129 or almost one in every five of all large-city high schools are in this group. The largest socioeconomic subgroup is the lowest one, which contains 10 percent of all schools, and the lower-middle/work-ing class category accounts for another 7 percent of the schools. Only 2 percent of these 80 percent-plus black schools are middle class, and these are in the "60 percent or more black" category. In other words, *there are almost no high status all-black schools, while there are 110 high status all-white schools.*

---

[1] Table 2 is reproduced here for ease of reference.

Table 2 A Typology of Schools Based on Ethnic and Socioeconomic Factors with the Number and Percent of Large-City High Schools in Each Cell

	Ethnic Characteristics of Students					
Socioeconomic Characteristics of Students	Over 80% White	61–80% White	21–60% White and Black	61–80% Black	Over 80% Black	Other Ethnic Mixtures
Upper-Middle Class SE Scale: 3–4	1 n: 110 %: 16.4	4 n: 15 %: 2.2	7	10		14
Middle Class SE Scale: 5–6	2 n: 116 %: 17.3	5 n: 39 %: 5.8	n: 18 %: 2.7	n: 16 %: 2.4		n: 7 %: 1.0
Lower-Middle/ Working Class SE Scale: 7–9	3 n: 52 %: 7.8	6 n: 43 %: 6.4	8 n: 17 %: 2.5	11 n: 19 %: 2.8	12 n: 49 %: 7.3	15 n: 20 %: 3.0
Working Class SE Scale: 10–12			9 n: 16 %: 2.4		13 n: 67 %: 10	16 n: 29 %: 4.3

"Oriental" schools (not in typology)   n: 6   %: 1.0

Other schools not used because of some missing details   n: 31   %: 4.6

All schools   n: 670   %: 100

When one searches for integrated schools with a balance of white and black, one finds 51 (8 percent) of the schools with both white and black enrollments in the 21–60 percent range. These are rather evenly spread over the socioeconomic range. Thus, there were 18 essentially middle-class racially balanced schools in the cities in 1968–69. It would be interesting to find out whether this number is changing, and whether these schools are stable, or are simply on the way toward segregation.

The other principal ethnic category of schools consists mainly of Spanish-surname students, which are located in categories 14, 15, and 16 of the typology, a total of 38 (6 percent) of the schools. These are evenly divided between schools in the Southwest with a substantial "Chicano" enrollment and schools in New York City with a strong Puerto Rican enrollment. Almost all of these schools are in the lower two socioeconomic categories.

The other discernible ethnic group of schools are those with a preponderance of Orientals—five of these in Honolulu. The West Coast cities have one or more schools with a substantial minority. Over a third of the students in one San Francisco school, which serves the whole city and admits only superior students, are Japanese- or Chinese-Americans.

CHANGE IN SOCIOECONOMIC AND ETHNIC PATTERNS SINCE 1960

School principals were asked to supply information for this study on the ethnic composition of their schools for the year 1960. A number of them did not have this information, but the majority were able to supply approximately accurate data. As would be expected, the ethnic schools have all grown at the expense of the non-ethnic white schools. For instance, the number of "81+" and "61–80 percent black" schools has increased by about 30 percent between 1960 and 1968, while the number of Puerto Rican and Spanish-American schools (21+ percent from these ethnic groups) doubled during this period.

Overcrowding. Since there has been a great increase in high school enrollment between 1960 and 1970, it is not surprising to find a considerable amount of overcrowding. Eighteen percent of the large-city high schools reported an excess of 500 or more students above their stated capacity, while 26 percent reported that enrollment was less than the stated capacity. Sixty-one percent reported that they could accommodate less than 60 percent of their students in the auditorium. Overcrowding was least common in the Southwest where 44 percent of the respondents said their schools had enrollments of less than the stated capacity, while the greatest overcrowding occurred in the Northeast where 36 percent of the respondents reported excesses of 500 or more students.

DIFFERENTIALS IN FAVOR OF LOW SES SCHOOLS

One change which is favorable to the low-economic-status schools is a result of the use of federal funds in the War on Poverty through the Elementary and Secondary Education Act and the Office of Economic Opportunity. The student-teacher ratio is now substantially lower in low-status schools than in high-status schools: the percentage of high-status schools with student-teacher ratios of 25:1 or less is about 42, compared with 70 percent of working-class schools. Also, the lower status schools are generally employing more paraprofessionals than the higher status schools: approximately 50 percent of the working-class schools employed 11 or more adult paraprofessionals, against 33 percent of the middle-class schools.

STUDENT CONFLICT AND ACTIVISM

The most striking aspect of the large-city high school is conflict among students and between students and faculty. This was reported for 53 percent of the schools during the two-year period from 1967–1969. The conflict took various forms: 29 percent of the schools were disrupted for a half-day or more; there were student strikes in 31 percent of the schools; and picketing or protest marches took place in 27 percent. At least moderate damage was done to the school building or its contents in 30 percent of the schools. Students were supported by adults other than parents in 40 percent of the cases.

The issues or concerns expressed by students as "primary" were: national policy on such matters as the war in Viet Nam or poverty (16 percent);[2] special non-academic provisions for ethnic or minority groups, such as "soul food," a separate lounge for black students, a memorial service for Malcolm X (20 percent); student relationships, such as ethnic cheer-leaders or segregated social events (10 percent); the instructional program and process, such as ability grouping, "racist" teachers (18 percent); dress-appearance codes, such as hair length and style, and mini-skirts (43 percent); and speech and press controls on such things as arm-band and button wearing, underground publications (18 percent).

There was considerable regional difference in the extent of conflict, with the highest prevalence in the Northeast, North Central, and Prairie/Western regions, and the least incidence in the Southeast.

As was pointed out in a previous chapter, the greatest incidence of conflict was in the mixed-black-and-white schools, of which 77 percent said they had experienced it. When subgroups in the typology are looked

---

[2] The base for the percentages given in this paragraph are the 355 schools that reported student conflict in 1967–1969.

at, it is seen that this phenomenon occurred most often among high-status-mixed schools (89 percent) and predominantly-black-high-status schools (81 percent). Clearly, the incidence of student conflict and activism depended mainly on the presence of black students.

The predominant issue in 10 of the 16 types of schools was student dress. The issue second in perceived importance was that of the curriculum, with demands for courses such as black studies, Swahili, and sex education. This latter issue topped the list in importance among schools with large black enrollments.

Confrontation between students and some member of the school staff—often the principal—occurred in 45 percent of the schools experiencing some form of conflict. The highest incidence of student/staff conflict was in the mixed-black-and-white schools of below middle-class status. Above-average incidence was also noted in the predominantly-black categories.

ARE THE LARGE-CITY SCHOOLS TRUE SYSTEMS?

In each city with more than 300,000 population, the number of schools ranges from 5 to 22, with a median of 11. It has been noted that the schools show a high degree of concentration of students of one race or one social class in a given school, and consequently the schools of a large city are rather different from each other. In this situation, it might be expected that some degree of specialization to meet conditions surrounding particular schools would develop, with different schools performing different functions. In fact, there is some of this. For example, a number of black schools have introduced Swahili as a foreign language, and a large number of lower-status schools offer courses of interest to students without regard to their having met certain prerequisites.

On the whole, though, the various schools of a city are remarkably similar to each other in terms of the curriculum, except where the school is a vocational school. However, when the various kinds of problems facing the schools of a city are studied, it is clear that there is a wide variation among the schools of a given city as regards the problems they must cope with. Thus, while it appears that the aim is to make the schools of a city as much alike in curriculum as possible, each principal finds himself and his staff facing a set of problems peculiar to that specific school and its situation. He and his staff are obligated to devise ways of accommodating themselves to these somewhat incompatible drives.

It might seem reasonable to expect that school systems would truly become systems in the sense that each school would perform functions that were planned or selected for it from the totality of the functions to be performed by the schools of the city. But this is hardly the case, for there appears to be very little planning that purposefully fits a given school into a broad diversified plan. It is true, though, that various schools or types of schools are treated differently by the central administration in most cities, in such matters as the numbers of teachers and other personnel provided, the student-teacher ratio, and support of certain special programs.

A LOOK TO THE FUTURE

If the high schools of a large city were to operate more as an interacting, cooperating system, some or all of the following procedures might be developed.

1. A single experimental high school might be established at a central location to serve students from all over the city who want an unconventional secondary education. This is already being done at the Parkway School in Philadelphia, the downtown Loop High School in Chicago, the new John Dewey High School in Brooklyn, and the John Adams High School in Portland. Possibly the 30 brilliant students who dropped out of Milwaukee high schools to form their own school might be attracted by such a new venture.
2. Faculty members could be shifted for a semester or a year at a time from one type of school to another, thus providing more racial integration and a more equitable distribution of people of maturity and experience among the various types of schools.
3. Students could divide their attendance among two or more schools. This might be done in terms of special interest or competence. Thus, a student with special talent in art or music might go for one day a week to a school with an especially strong program in that area; a student with a special interest in science might attend a school with a strong program in science for one or two days a week. Also, students studying special vocational subjects such as auto mechanics, electronics, business machines, or practical nursing might go for a half day to a vocational school and the other half day to a general academic school.
4. An open attendance rule could be administered with the aid of a special counselling office so as to encourage some students of the inner-city area to enroll in comprehensive or middle-class schools where they might find more academic stimulation.
5. Where enrollment is growing and financing is critical, one or more large high schools might be constructed on a kind of educational park to draw students from a wide range of socioeconomic and ethnic status.

The major source of doubt about the feasibility of this kind of system-wide program is the question of whether students would take advantage of this flexibility and enrichment to seek out better educational opportunities for themselves. Or would they choose to stay close to their homes and attend the nearest school, with those of less academic motivation dropping out of school yearly?

The evidence from other modern countries is that adolescent students move easily over rather long distances to secondary schools of their own choice in the big cities. The "neighborhood high school" hardly exists elsewhere than in the United States.

CONTEMPORARY VALUE CHANGES AND BIG-CITY HIGH SCHOOLS

It seems likely that large-city high schools will be especially sensitive to basic value changes which seem to be coming as we move from the industrial society of yesterday to the post-industrial society of tomorrow.

American society is now in the process of changing its major goal from that of productive work to that of using time in ways that maximize human satisfaction and self-realization. Having achieved the distinction of producing the greatest quantity of material goods per worker in the world, we now turn to the more complex task of consuming these goods wisely and balancing work with leisure.

Every American, if he wants it, has more leisure time (time free from work) than his grandfather had. Nobody is forced by iron necessity to work as many hours a week as his grandfather did at the beginning of this century.

This change will probably be reflected in a move away from the *instrumental* and toward the *expressive* forms of education. Instrumental education means education for a goal which lies outside and beyond the act of education. For example, the learner studies arithmetic so as to be able to exchange money and to buy and sell things and to become a competent scientist or teacher. Or the learner as a young adult studies in his vocational field so as to get a promotion, or she studies cooking so as to become a better housewife. Instrumental education is thus a kind of investment of time and energy in the expectation of future gain.

Expressive education means education for a goal which lies within the act of learning or is so closely related to it that the act of learning appears to be the goal. For example, the learner studies arithmetic for the pleasure of learning about numbers and quantities. The learning of arithmetic is its own reward. Or the learner as a young adult studies the latest dances so as to enjoy the dances he and his friends go to. He learns to dance "for fun" and not to become a teacher of dancing, or even to make new friends. Expressive education is a kind of consumption of time and energy for present gain.

We may expect a drastic shift in high school curricula which will tend to place the arts and humanities in balance with the sciences and mathematics. Just as the decade of the sixties will go down in educational history as the decade when the *instrumental aspects* of the high school curriculum were reformed and strengthened, this decade will come to stand for the strengthening of the *expressive aspects* of the high school curriculum.

As the curriculum develops, we will come to recognize a new type of successful student—the student with a high *expressive* element. This person will be somewhat different from the highly *instrumental* student who is the model of the successful student today.

Some evidence of increasing emphasis on the humanistic subjects can be seen in the information gathered in our research. For instance, in responding to questions about their school goals, principals of high-status-white schools ranked the goal of *cultural appreciation* (e.g., music, drama, and architecture) seventh, and principals of lower-status-white schools ranked it tenth. But principals of lower-status-black schools ranked this goal fifth. It is likely that lower-status schools in inner cities and upper-middle-class schools differ less in the artistic and musical abilities and interests. It is well-known, of course, that inner-city schools are not at a competitive disadvantage in athletics, which is an expressive activity.

As societal value-changes continue, principals and teachers may find it easier to bridge the gulf that exists between youth of different social classes and ethnic groups.

A FINAL OBSERVATION

It seems likely that there is more and deeper segregation and separation of high school students of different socioeconomic and ethnic groups today than there was 10 to 20 years ago. This process could conceivably continue on to the point of separating various groups into different schools or sections within schools. But that hardly seems likely in view of the conscious aims of the nation's social and political leaders to restore the central city and to bring the suburbs into closer interaction with it. The predictable goal for our large-city schools is the greater social integration of all kinds of students, with the development of the high schools of our cities into true *systems of schools* being a means to pursue this goal more effectively.

LET'S BREAK THE GO-TO-COLLEGE LOCKSTEP*

Edmund K. Faltermayer

By any quantitative measure, the expansion of higher education in the U.S. has been a magnificent achievement. An estimated 8,200,000 students enrolled at college and universities at the beginning of this year's fall semester, nearly three times as many as in 1955. Nationally, more than half of those who complete high school now enter college, and in California, with its large network of tax-supported institutions, the proportion is more than 60 percent. In just ten years the combined budgets of the country's institutions of higher education have multiplied more than threefold, to about $26 billion.

It is now appropriate to ask whether this widening of access to higher learning, hailed as one of the great accomplishments of a nation dedicated to upward mobility and the dissemination of knowledge, was soundly conceived or even desirable. Far from enlarging the choice of educational experiences available to the young or producing unprecedented numbers of joyfully enlightened citizens, the feverish expansion has reproduced, with deadly conformity from coast to coast, a system originally designed for an elite of the intellectually curious and the professionally committed— a system unchanged in basic concept since medieval times. The result is unprecedented numbers of turned-off students, far larger numbers than participate directly in campus violence. Increasingly, students see themselves as prisoners of a rigid system that virtually forces them to move in lockstep, straight from high school into college, in order to get the bachelor's degree now believed to be the minimum credential for almost any type of nonroutine work.

The restlessness on the campuses, of course, also reflects the immaturity of an ominously swollen class of young men and women subjected to sixteen years of uninterrupted formal schooling at the expense of tax-

* Reprinted from the November 1970 issue of *Fortune Magazine* by special permission; © 1970 Time Inc.

111

payers and parents. The education process extends up to ten years past the attainment of physical adulthood and is unbroken by any significant interval of purposeful contact with the real world. The cry for "relevance" in courses misses the main point. What the students really want is the sense of manhood and womanhood for which they must now wait so interminably.

The remedy is to break up the dreary pattern of lockstep education and prolonged dependency. Upon completion of secondary school, the young should have a great variety of interesting alternatives available to them, of which immediate entry into college would be only one. In large measure, students should pay for their own higher education out of later earnings, under one or another of the ingenious financing mechanisms that have been proposed in recent years. In this way, millions of students would get off the backs of parents and taxpayers by age eighteen, and would pursue their education with motivation fortified by the spending of money that must be repaid. Such a financing system would make possible a free market in higher education, a market in which student consumers, for the first time, could exert their influence to spur innovation and reduce waste.

BACHELOR'S DEGREES AT $40,000 APIECE

While precise figures are not available, it appears that annual expenditures per student have been rising three times as fast since the mid-1950s as the general cost of living. At some elite private institutions, total fees for tuition, room, and board now exceed $4,000 a year, and that still falls far short of the actual cost of educating a student. The gap must be bridged by income from endowment funds and from annual alumni giving.

And this is not the whole story. If it is assumed that a full-time student forgoes at least $5,000 of potential income during each year he spends at college, then in a sense the total cost for a four-year bachelor's degree from such an institution now comes to more than $40,000. Even in the least expensive state colleges, in which tuition is virtually free to residents of the state, forgone earnings, subsistence money from parents, and tax support from legislatures currently add up to a four-year cost of at least $25,000 for a full-time student who lives at home and commutes to and from the campus.

In return for these costs the higher educational system has traditionally been expected to perform at least three essential functions. The most basic function is to produce graduates who can go on to professional schools or who can fill jobs that require education beyond high school. But while solid information is scarce, it appears that the country may be getting a rather poor match-up between sheepskins and jobs. There are shortages in some professional fields, most notably in medicine. On the other hand, the colleges and universities are now turning out too many schoolteachers and Ph.D.'s to cite only two categories, and too few graduates with vocational certificates for technician-level jobs, particularly in the medical and clerical fields.

Another function, which many hold to be more important, is to impart knowledge—to produce a younger generation that is informed and able to think in a manner associated with a "liberal education." But it is precisely in this area that higher education has been doing an especially poor job. At many institutions, as Irving Kristol put it in FORTUNE a while back (Books & Ideas, May, 1968), "liberal education is extinct."

For many young adults the most important function of higher education has been the third one, namely talent screening. Undergraduate education is an endurance test. In the country as a whole, only about half of those who begin as freshmen eventually get a bachelor's degree, and this ratio has remained fairly constant in recent years. In prestige institutions with selective admission policies, the dropout rate is much lower because the screening is done by the admissions office rather than by a sink-or-swim educational process. Obviously there are far less costly ways to screen the nation's talent than to force millions through the undergraduate pipeline. The B.A., says Christopher Jencks of the Center for Educational Policy Research, "is a hell of an expensive aptitude test."

THE CATHEDRAL BUILDING OF OUR AGE

The growth of higher education in the U.S. has rested far more on faith than on facts. To Harvard sociologist David Riesman, the splendid edifices that have sprung up on flourishing college and university campuses in recent years represent the cathedral building of our age. If the cathedral building merely reflected the growing popularity of a consumer good bought with private funds, it would not be a matter for public debate in a nation weighing its post-Vietnam priorities. But higher education today is primarily a public enterprise. Not only do the fast-growing state colleges and universities require more and more support from government, but private institutions are beginning to appeal for government subsidies as even the richest ones begin to record red ink.

The faith has burned brightest, and taxpayer support has been most openhanded, in California. By immense efforts, the state has met the goals of its 1959 master plan, which promised higher education to all high-school graduates who want it. Under an ingenious three-track system the University of California, with over 100,000 students on nine campuses, admits as freshmen only those from the top one-eighth of their high-school classes. The state college system, with 244,000 students, draws from the top third. And the two-year community colleges (800,000 strong, counting

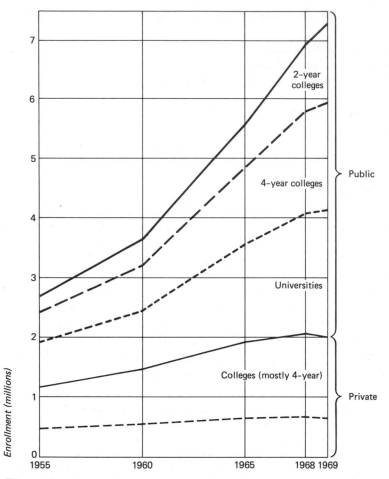

Figure 1 Higher Education—and How It Grew. As recently as 1950, enrollment in U.S. colleges and universities was evenly divided between private and public institutions. But at the start of the 1969–70 academic year, nearly three-quarters of the 7,300,000 students pursuing bachelor's degrees or higher were in state colleges, state universities, and other tax-supported institutions. As the chart also shows, colleges have grown even faster than universities. Two-year colleges, overwhelmingly public, constitute the fastest-growing segment of all. Actually, they now have an even bigger role than this chart suggests. For example, most of the students in vocational programs that do not lead to a bachelor's degree are in two-year institutions; and these students (about 600,000 in 1969) are not included in the chart, which covers those enrolled full time or part time in programs leading to a bachelor's degree or higher. Moreover, a growing number of students who go on to four-year colleges and universities start out in two-year institutions. Indeed, the two-year colleges' share of the nation's college *freshmen*, counting vocational students, now exceeds 40 percent.

a large number of part-time students) take everybody, from freshmen who hope to transfer to Berkeley or U.C.L.A. (as some do) to those who need remedial instruction.

Just when Californians are beginning to have second thoughts about the 1959 plan, New York City has embarked upon an even more ambitious act of faith. After student riots in the spring of 1969, the City University of New York agreed to begin an open-admission policy in the fall semester of 1970, five years sooner than originally planned. The undertaking is more ambitious than California's because C.U.N.Y. has only two "tracks." The better institutions in the system, such as City College and Hunter, will take any 1970 high-school graduate who had an average of 80 or higher or who was in the top half of his class, regardless of grades and regardless of the quality of the school attended. The latter proviso is a drastic concession designed to bring in more black and Puerto Rican students. The two-year community colleges will take any 1970 high-school graduate who turns up.

The students turned up in droves when C.U.N.Y. began its fall semester in September. This year's 35,400 freshmen compare with only 19,500 a year ago. An estimated one-half of the freshmen will require remedial teaching, which will raise their instruction costs about 50 percent above those for the other freshmen. With its classrooms already jammed, C.U.N.Y. is renting lofts and even bowling alleys to accommodate the influx.

Underlying C.U.N.Y.'s bold venture are the premises that a large number of disadvantaged students have the native ability to master college-level instruction, and that their initial handicaps in reading and math can be overcome in a fairly short time. The grave danger, of course, is that many of the marginal students will wash out, exiting from the system more embittered than if they had never entered it. And there is the further risk that in the meantime they will drag down the quality of instruction available to abler students. But it would be premature to predict that thousands will flunk out, or that quality will suffer severely. "We intend to run fairly competitive and tough colleges," vows Albert H. Bowker, chancellor of C.U.N.Y. And Bowker's aides emphasize that open admission at C.U.N.Y. will not be allowed to degenerate into automatic passing grades for all.

THE THREAT OF HIGH-SCHOOLIZATION

Nevertheless, it is unsettling to think what the C.U.N.Y. policy might lead to. Adopted universally, it would bring about a huge new jump in college enrollments. In most states the community colleges would take the great majority of freshmen, since this is the only way to gratify the demand for open admissions without dangerously lowering the quality of instruction in four-year institutions. In time, this development could easily lead to demands that two years of college be made mandatory for all. Such a policy, which some already regard as inevitable, would have disastrous results. If it were in effect today it would mean that colleges would some-how have to create room for about 50 percent more students. As in high schools, mandatory attendance would inevitably lead to automatic certifi-cates of some sort for all. Still more serious, the "high-schoolization" of freshman and sophomore years would further weaken whatever pressures now exist on elementary and secondary schools to turn out reasonably articulate, employable citizens in the time allotted to them. Even now, a good deal of what goes on in community colleges—and in freshman year of most four-year institutions—amounts to the reteaching of what should have been learned in the lower schools.

Even if the colleges can avoid high-schoolization, the present course of mindless, costly expansion is extremely questionable. But despite recent tightening up on the part of some state legislatures, this course still has great momentum and respected advocates behind it. In its recent reports, the Carnegie Commission on Higher Education, headed by Clark Kerr, former president of the University of California, rejected high-schooliza-tion. It would, in the commission's words, make a "captive audience" of college students. But the commission casually called for a step-up in federal, state, and local spending on higher education that would entail an added $8 billion or so by 1976, and made the proposal largely on the grounds that enrollments are expected to keep rising, and that the addi-tional students must be accommodated. Nowhere, so far, has the commis-sion dealt resolutely with the fundamental question of whether continued growth in the manner of the 1950s and 1960s is necessary or desirable, or whether the trend in enrollments could be influenced by different policies and changed patterns of education.

THE MESSAGE FROM THE JOB MARKET

The urge to go to college has been so intimately woven into the American Dream that the mere issuance of ukases limiting total admissions will not work. What might work is a series of steps to dispel the fantasies about higher education, to provide alternatives to entering college at eighteen, and to remove the subsidies that artificially stimulate going to college. Enrollments might keep climbing anyway, though they would at least reflect more serious, better-informed decision making on the part of young people than is now the case. More likely, many educators think, total enrollment would level off or even decline.

The first task of a "truth squad" on higher education would be to re-examine the validity of the bachelor's degree as a job requirement.

Superficially, the U.S. economy has been able to absorb all college graduates in recent years, and a study by the Bureau of Labor Statistics predicts that during the period from 1968 to 1980 the supply of graduates will be "roughly in balance with manpower requirements." But the B.L.S. forecast begs the question because, in its words, the projected demand reflects not only the need for professional, managerial, and other personnel who have traditionally required a B.A. or more, but also reflects "rising job entry requirements that make a college degree necessary for jobs once performed by workers with lower educational attainment." In short, some of the demand will represent not true professional need but increasing educational "credentialism"—the tendency of a growing supply of B.A.'s to create its own demand.

The B.L.S., unfortunately, has not undertaken to measure the amount of excess credentialism, but there is doubtless a lot of it. This is confirmed by Ivar Berg, a Columbia University sociologist, in a new book entitled *Education and Jobs: The Great Training Robbery*. Berg has no personal quarrel with higher education as a means of enriching people's lives, so long as it does not masquerade as a means of getting a good job. But by laboriously comparing educational requirements for the "mix" of jobs in the U.S. economy in 1957 and 1967 with the "mix" of educational attainments of the labor force, he has concluded that the U.S. is now turning out more B.A.'s than it needs. According to Berg, even the most literal interpretations of the data, taking at face value all employers' educational criteria, indicate that by around 1968 the population's educational attainments had "outdistanced job requirements." A more skeptical interpretation, he says, indicates that this point was passed "a long time ago."

Too many B.A.'s can create morale problems in some fields. Many routine jobs that formerly did not require a B.A., Berg says, are being relabeled and redefined so that they will *appear* to require one. This raises the prospect that many college graduates with high expectations of responsibility and promotion may become frustrated. Moreover, downward movement of B.A.'s into the job hierarchy is preempting positions formerly open to those without college education, and in effect walling them off from advancement. The escalation in credentials might make economic sense, Berg concedes, if it could somehow be shown that workers with B.A.'s make a greater contribution in a given job. But the skimpy evidence suggests that more highly educated workers may, in some jobs, have *lower* productivity, as well as higher rates of turnover.

Berg's study also throws a cloud over the various studies purporting to show that a college education results in higher lifetime earnings. The seeming cause-and-effect relationship, Berg says, may have little to do with what was learned in college. It may simply reflect native intelligence and the tastes of employers in hiring and promoting persons with qualities most likely to be found among college graduates—qualities these same individuals might have if they had never gone beyond high school.

What is badly needed, Berg's study indicates, is a national "truth-in-credentials" policy, so that no one would unnecessarily feel compelled to go to college in order to obtain a passport to a job. The long-term tendency of employers to keep raising educational requirements is not easy to reverse, particularly in times of slackness in the labor market, when industry can pick and choose among job applicants. But, partly as a result of Negro militance, many employers have stopped using the lack of a high-school diploma as a reason for denying access to jobs that do not really require a high-school diploma. And a few companies—far too few—have begun to take a second look at the B.A. Last year Henry Ford II, who never quite finished Yale (he left late in his senior year), called in a speech for equal promotional opportunities not only for Negroes, women, and young people, but also for those without college degrees.

By putting an end to the nonsense about credentials, the country would take a big step toward breaking up the lockstep of high-school graduates into colleges. Another essential step is to eliminate the now-or-never aspect of higher education that confronts a student of eighteen—i.e., the notion that he must go to college at once or forfeit the chance for life. The conformism about entering college immediately after high school (a conformism reinforced by college admission policies long before the draft became a factor) has a cruelty about it in that it fails to take account of different rates of maturation. Some high-school seniors are doubtless ready to attack college studies with enthusiasm, but many others need a taste of the real world. In the past, sociologist James S. Coleman has pointed out, young men and women tended to be experience-rich and information-poor. Today, twelve years of schooling and exposure to the media have created a younger generation saturated with information but deficient in some important kinds of experience. Some critics of the educational process, anthropologist Margaret Mead for one, have proposed a period of compulsory national service between high school and college. But this might result in mass, government-run make-work instead of real jobs in industry and the professions and the mandatory feature would substitute one form of lockstep for another.

BRINGING BACK THE GOLDEN AGE

A few colleges have taken a step toward flexibility by offering deferred admissions. Radcliffe College, for example, explicitly advised young women admitted to this year's freshman class that they had the option of waiting until next fall to enter; the eighteen who have chosen to wait may in the meantime do anything they wish. The draft currently rules out deferred admission for men on a large scale, but later on this and other innovations could be applied widely. Gerald Grant, a teaching fellow at Harvard, believes colleges should actively encourage a year or so of work by giving employers' recommendations equal weight, alongside high-school grades, in judging applicants. The ways in which applicants would spend the interval between high school and college, he says, might reveal more about their aptitudes than high-school grades, "which measure a very narrow slice of a kid's ability." For deferred admission to catch on in a big way, industry would have to lower the B.A. barrier and offer interesting jobs to promising high-school graduates, along with some sort of commitment to save their jobs for them if they later decided to go to college.

Delayed admission could bring a return of what old-timers on college faculties fondly recall as the "golden age" of teaching. These were the years after World War II when classes were filled with older, more mature veterans who tended to know exactly why they were in college, and who were quick to challenge facile professorial verbalizing that did not square with life. A classroom or seminar filled entirely with adolescents, confides one college president, can be "stultifying." The only feedback teachers get comes from immature, experience-poor men and women. If the instructor happens to be a young teaching assistant who has himself been continuously in the educational system since kindergarten—as is often the case in large universities these days—the adolescent hot-house atmosphere is further reinforced. Under a truly flexible system, with flexibility on the part of both colleges and employers, it would become widely accepted for people to enter or leave higher education at any time during their lives, and classes would have a sprinkling of students in their late twenties, thirties, or even forties and fifties.

LEARN NOW, PAY LATER

One way to motivate students is to make them responsible for financing their own education. Society, of course, should continue to bear the full costs of elementary and secondary education for all. But once that basic social investment is made, society's commitment to pay the costs of education should largely come to an end.

The present situation is a classic example of privilege without responsibility. An important 1967 study by a panel headed by M.I.T. physicist Jerrold R. Zacharias made the point that "most students regard higher education as something which somebody else *gives* them, rather than something they have to *get* for themselves." If students could borrow against future income to buy their education, the Zacharias report reasoned, "both real and psychological dependence on adults could be appreciably reduced." Every student, it added, "would be in much the same position

as a returning G.I. who has an 'education benefit' to spend as he chooses"
and who tends "to take college more seriously."

The G.I., of course, earns the benefit in advance by facing the hazards
of war and giving up years of his life. For everybody else, the Zacharias
panel came out in favor of an ingenious financing mechanism, which it
labeled the Educational Opportunity Bank. This proposal goes far beyond
the existing federal student-loan programs. Under the plan proposed in the
Zacharias report, the ceiling would be high enough to cover tuition, room,
and board at the most expensive institutions—$15,000 or more per student
—and repayment would stretch over thirty or forty years.

To meet the objection that students would thus be mortgaging themselves in the face of uncertainties about future earnings, repayments would
take the form of a *percentage* of future income, whatever that turned out
to be. The principle is that larger repayments from business executives,
for example, would compensate for the smaller sums collected from, say,
ministers and social workers. It has been roughly calculated that the bank
would be fully self-sustaining if it charged borrowers 1 percent of gross
income over thirty years for each $3,000 borrowed; payments could easily
be handled by the Internal Revenue Service.

The Educational Opportunity Bank concept presents some problems,
to be sure, though proponents say they could all be worked out. It assumes,
for example, that the present pattern of income distribution will continue
far into the future. Moreover, a disproportionate number of "poor risks"
might sign up—i.e., students headed for low-paying careers—and this could
bankrupt the system. Women who intend to become housewives would
present a special problem because repayment of their debt—a kind of
"negative dowry"—would become an added charge on the husbands'
income.

For these and other reasons the Nixon Administration, in drawing
up its proposals on student aid now before Congress, decided upon an
expanded program of conventional loans, involving a fixed repayment
obligation that would not vary with income. Nevertheless, the Administration bill represents a big step toward shifting more of the costs to students.
It would extend the maximum repayment period, now generally ten years,
to as much as twenty years, and permit each student to borrow up to
$2,500 a year for seven years. Some form of percentage-of-income plan
later on is a possibility, Administration officials say.

Expanded student borrowing is the best way to avert the fate that
now seems in store for most private colleges and universities—heavy government subsidies or outright take-over. Hard-pressed college presidents these
days are talking in terms of direct "institutional grants" of federal or state
money. But this kind of aid would tend to thwart the workings of the
market mechanism in higher education, since it would subsidize good and

bad institutions alike. Not only should government avoid direct subsidies to private colleges it should gradually *withdraw*, or at least stop increasing, the heavy subsidies to state and city institutions of higher learning. These subsidies have created a two-price system in higher education, which, by itself, is making it harder and harder for private colleges to survive.

Unquestionably, the public should continue to subsidize higher education to some extent. But across-the-board aid, benefiting all students, including the middle-class sons and daughters who still make up a large proportion of the students at New York's tuition-free City University, does not seem justifiable under present circumstances. If total college enrollments were dropping off or there was a danger of an "under-credentialed" work force—scarcely the problem at the moment—heavily subsidized college for all might make sense. In the meantime, subsidies should be employed in a more selective fashion.

THE HIGH PRICE OF FOLKLORE

The approximately $12 billion a year now spent on higher education by government at all levels could be reallocated to provide some fairly generous subventions to achieve important social objectives. In view of the shortage of doctors and medical paraprofessionals, there is an overwhelming case for heavy subsidization of medical-school costs, in return for a commitment by recipients to serve for a specified period in slums or rural areas. Other forms of graduate education, which tends to be more expensive than undergraduate study, might deserve varying degrees of subsidy. Students from low-income families would be able to pay college fees by borrowing, but some of them might also need grants to compensate them for forgone income—a crucial factor for eighteen-year-olds in poor families.

If the current efforts to turn marginal high-school students into college material prove successful, it would also make sense for government to compensate colleges for the cost of remedial education. Otherwise they would have to divert part of their own limited resources to dealing with problems not of their making. There is also a case for some sort of preferential treatment for students who begin college later in life, to compensate for, among other things, greater forgone income and the disruption of career and family patterns.

In assuming responsibility for most of the costs, undergraduates would in effect put pressure on colleges and universities to hold down costs. Some recent research suggests that a lot of undergraduate education may be fabulously overpriced, especially in private institutions with renowned professors, low student-faculty ratios, and magnificently accoutered libraries. The expensive colleges may offer snob appeal and a more *enjoyable* experience. But studies by Alexander W. Astin, director of reaserch for the American Council on Education (the major organization representing higher education in the U.S.), indicate that the amount of learning may be far from commensurate with the price. Astin compared students from a sample of the country's most "affluent" colleges with another group from the "least affluent." To measure the amount of learning, he compared each student's scores on college entrance examinations with his scores on the graduate record examination, given in the senior year. The results, in Astin's words, fail "to confirm the folklore concerning the presumed educational benefits of institutional quality." In effect, Astin's study says about higher education what the famous 1966 report by James S. Coleman said about elementary and secondary education: academic achievement depends far more on the intelligence, motivation, and family background of the student than on the purported quality of the school.

A HANG-UP ON SMALL CLASSES

The high-cost colleges and universities are going to have to abandon some of their costly practices, or at least prove that they are justified. One bench mark of what undergraduate education *ought* to cost, in institutions that meet or exceed the minimum standards that most American students would accept, is provided by California's huge state college system. Until the California legislature began trimming appropriations for higher education, instructional costs throughout this big, overwhelmingly undergraduate system were running close to $1,600 a year per student. For that expenditure, says Glenn S. Dumke, chancellor of the state colleges, "we think we can do a pretty good job." At Haverford College in Pennsylvania, by no means the nation's costliest, the corresponding figure is about three times as high, partly because of small classes and a student-faculty ratio of only eight to one. President John R. Coleman (not related to the author of the Coleman Report) makes no pretense of trying to prove that Haverford, with its 650 students, provides an education three times as good, though he is convinced it does a better job. And he does concede that, by increasing the size of its classes 50 percent, Haverford could cut costs without lowering quality very much. "We've got a hang-up on class size," he says.

The most important effect of long-term loans would be to bring consumerism to higher education, with students using their purchasing power to bend the system to meet their varying needs. A growing number of educators are coming around to the view that this is desirable. In a speech last spring that President Nixon passed along to his top education aides as required reading, historian Stephen J. Tonsor of the University of Michigan declared that American higher education "has become a single mechanism; its professors and students interchangeable parts." Not until the student "is forced to pay a very substantial portion of the total costs of his education," Tonsor said, will the system become "diverse and relevant to the needs of both the student and the nation."

COST-EFFECTIVENESS AND THE CURRICULUM*

FRED T. WILHELMS

If we changed our educational investments could we raise the dividends? Powerful evidence is accumulating that we could *if we invested more directly in developing the learner's ability to learn and to function as a person.*

Take intelligence: We have grown up thinking of a fixed quantity born into a baby (and surely there is some hereditary aspect). But year by year the evidence grows clearer that it is highly malleable; i.e., *teachable.* Fascinating data keep coming in from experiments on animals; whether they deal with mice or monkeys or any species between, the studies add up to this: An enriched environment will produce a better brain and increased ability to solve problems; and the effect grows more pronounced as one moves up the phylogenetic scale.

Even more fascinating is the growing evidence on young human beings. One cannot experiment on them as one does on a laboratory rat. But investigators can rig a baby's crib with stimulating things to manipulate, and watch the results; or analyze parents' teaching styles—the games they play with their children, the way they talk to them—and study the effects; or organize preschool curricula and measure the gains. All these things, and many others, are being done. The results? Well, there are many complexities, and one hesitates to oversimplify *too* much. But one generalization stands out: It *is* possible to raise the level of a child's cognitive functioning.

---

* Reprinted from *NASSP Spotlight* (May–June 1968), No. 83, pp. 1–4, by permission.

Let's throttle our inhibitions and put that boldly: It *is* possible to raise a child's IQ—substantially. Of course, the IQ is a poor steward of any adequate conception of intelligence; but, remember, it *is* a pretty good index of ability to do standard school work. So, let's convert our statement to basic school terms: It *is* possible to raise a child's ability to do school work.

How? Leave a lot of room for uncertainty and variation in this new area; but whether one looks at what good parents do naturally or at the studied efforts of preschool organizations, there seem to be a few basic ingredients:

1. *Stimulation*: rich and *varied* to reach into areas where a child might not otherwise go; *structured* to avoid confusion; *matched* with the child to yield challenge and "stretch" and yet not baffle and block him.
2. *Sensory perception sharpening*: with a kind of *forced response*, to stir up vigorous reaction; *a la Montessori*, to feel textures, to discriminate shapes, sizes and colors, to see vividly, to hear precisely.
3. *Verbalization*: a regular bombardment of it, not merely to name things but also to verbalize the abstract; emphasis on full, accurate expression that will hold an edge of precision. (This is an absolute constant.)
4. *Reasoning* and *logic* in simple form; the encouragement of *inquiry*.
5. *Warmth* and *affection* and *personal attention*, in generous dosages.

In most programs these ingredients (and others) are blended into a smooth mix of play with toys, excursions, group talk, etc. But it is *not* just the old nursery school with its emphasis on socialization. It is a *curriculum*, with every part aimed at a cumulative "cognitive push," built by analyzing the cognitive tasks children face and supplying the essential components.[1]

It works. It works so well that one wonders impatiently why we don't invest more in cultivating the *ability to learn* instead of investing only in the knowledge itself, as the standard school subjects define knowledge.

BUT WHY TELL THIS TO SECONDARY EDUCATORS?

First, even if early childhood is the *best* time for a cognitive push, it isn't the end. For example, working with older children, Suchman has been showing what can be done with inquiry training (and so have some of our high school math and science programs). Before her death, working

---

[1] If you wish to dig a little deeper, two journalistic accounts are informative and readable: Maya Pines, *Revolution in Learning* (New York: Harper & Row, 1966) and Fred Powledge, *To Change a Child* (Chicago: Quadrangle Books, Inc., 1967). Perhaps the best summary of background data is J. McVicker Hunt, *Intelligence and Experience* (New York: The Ronald Press Company, 1961). Tough going, but worth it, though a lot has happened since 1961.

through middle-grades social studies, Hilda Taba was demonstrating that even low-IQ children can be taught to use the higher processes of thought (e.g., abstracting, generalizing from data, applying inferences from one situation to predictions in another) if teachers are trained to analyze such thinking into its component skills and then build those skills systematically.[2]

Second, the basic ingredients listed above are probably just about what we need to keep the intellectual snowball snowballing. Up to now most of the organized efforts to develop cognitive effectiveness have been made with young children and with the disadvantaged. Both priorities are proper. But that is not to say that similar work with older students and the "non-disadvantaged" would not pay. In the judgment of this writer, secondary schools ought to invest boldly in *teaching students to be able to learn better.*

BUT THERE IS SOMETHING BIGGER

The news that a cognitive breakthrough is possible just has to excite any schoolman who genuinely "learns" it. Even so, it may be small potatoes compared to the breakthrough that is possible in helping each youngster become a *more effective person.* And, for this, adolescence brings special opportunity.

Words are tricky here. The layman may simply set a goal of "good personality" or "fine character." Educators may go a bit deeper with expressions like "mental health" or "self-concept." Psychologists may have still more in mind when they talk about "ego strength." Abraham Maslow raised the ante with his description of "self-actualizing people," and so did Carl Rogers with his discussions of the "fully functioning person." The difference isn't just one of words. The layman may have only a crude notion of a boy or girl who "gets along all right." By contrast, professional educators and other scholars have been poking deeper and deeper into a stirring question: Is it possible to help young people in their personal *becoming* in such a way that they can rise closer and closer to the age-old ideal of a person with all his powers free and mobilized?

The answer is "yes." And even more, investigation not only shows that potential can be released, but also that the potential itself is greater than we have thought. How bring that potential into actualization? Well,

---

[2] This is worth following up. *Teaching Strategies for the Culturally Disadvantaged* by Hilda Taba and Deborah Elkins (Chicago: Rand McNally & Company, 1966) contains a wealth of specific guides, by no means applicable only to the teaching of the disadvantaged. The Taba Curriculum Development Project in Social Studies at San Francisco State College (1600 Holloway Avenue, San Francisco, Ca 94132) developed even more explicit guides. For information on publications and prices, write to the Project.

you know better than to expect a quick, pat answer to that big question. But, just for openers, suppose every youngster in your school met these conditions:

> Saw opportunities "out there" in the world ahead of him.
> Saw himself as worthy to shoot for those that attracted him.
> Had his values and goals straight.
> Saw the relevance of his school to those goals.

Big order? Of course! But these are all things a school can do a great deal about. And adolescence opens up the chance.

For instance, the adolescent analogue of rich cognitive stimulation in early childhood may be a kind of "cultural enrichment." Young people —especially disadvantaged ones—have a meager notion of what's "out there" in the world, waiting for them. They need to see more of the opportunities, more of the resources for significance and joy, more of the choices of ways of living. They need the kind of familiarity with varied job possibilities that can get them excited about their future careers—and they need it *early*. But they also need chances to roll *life possibilities* around on their tongue and find out what tastes best. A "wake-up service" along those lines wouldn't really be so hard to mobilize.

Values are crucial—and not just in the moral sense. In a completely realistic way, a youngster's developed values form the template of the life he is going to try to lead. And adolescence is just the right time to open them up. As the years of adolescence roll on, young people become more and more idealistic not only about themselves personally but also about society, about how they can serve mankind and live lives of significance. It is the supreme time of opportunity to help them internalize goals that will literally force them to commit themselves.

Schools are full of unused opportunities to broaden horizons and raise young people's sights. Obviously guidance is central, a kind of guidance we have rarely had. Fortunately *group* guidance appears to be very effective. And something in the nature of group *therapy* may have a big pay-off. But the curriculum itself is the richest resource. Just to name any subject—whether it is "shop" or home economics or history or literature (or psychology or cultural anthropology or philosophy)—is to see a flood of opportunities to help a youngster true up his values, get a vision of what is possible, and go to work at carving out a life.

BACK TO INVESTMENTS

All the above is pretty skimpy. It neither marshals up the proofs that the breakthrough is real nor details the methods by which it can be made. But the proofs are available for anyone who cares to look, and the techniques can be learned. We never set out to detail either, in this short report. What we did set out to do was to launch a commonsense argument about educational investments and pay-offs. And, in blunt terms, here it is.

By long tradition, schools invest student time, teacher careers, and practically all their money in the business of putting across subject matter. Even when the resistance is stubborn, they fight it out on that line. If some ninth-graders read like third-graders, schools typically mount a massive remedial reading program (making some small gains, but generally winding up with low-mediocre readers after all). If students don't learn to write very well by producing "themes," English teachers press for lower student-faculty ratios so that they can have them write more of the same. Almost always, when there is trouble with subject matter, the instinct is to press harder on the subject matter.

It looks as if that's the wrong place to push. With much less cost or effort we could turn children into the kind of learners for whom reading comes easily. Even a little time spent with an adolescent in enriching his concepts of himself and the life he wants to lead may make good writing part of his personal standard of living—and ease the burden on his composition teacher's weekends. It seems such nonsense to keep pushing harder and harder against the wall of reluctance and disaffection and sheer inability to handle the subject matter when we could do so much more by making our investments in the *person*.

Having studied the evidence, I am tantalized by the certainty that we could raise both cognitive and personal effectiveness. (Hunt says we could boost the IQ average by 30 points; Taba that we could increase maturity in abstract thought by four years.) And, even though we still have a lot to learn, the technical difficulties don't look too bad. What we mostly need is the common sense to drop investments we know don't pay, and the nerve to try some more hopeful ones.

PART II

TOWARD A CHANGING CURRICULUM

The literature of high school education during the decade preceding the publication of this anthology is replete with illustrations of a "changing" curriculum. Changes were reported of so many types and in so many directions that it is difficult to establish trends. It is clear that the changes still were predominantly within the framework of a subject-centered curriculum, although several emergent areas pressed hard for a place in the curriculum limelight.

Chapter 5 presents selections reviewing and critiquing recent developments in the five academic areas that have long dominated the high school curriculum in requirements and enrollments: English, foreign languages, mathematics, science, and social studies.

Chapter 6 deals with the curriculum areas and emphases that challenge the dominance of the academic areas treated in Chapter 5. Articles are included on health and physical education, as an area sometimes required and sometimes elective but certainly not "academic" in the traditional sense, and on the usually elective areas of the arts and humanities. The chapter also highlights certain emergent curriculum emphases that were both controversial and expanding in the early 1970s: black studies, sex education, and drug education.

The final Chapter 7 in Part II is devoted to readings on the extrainstructional phases of the high school curriculum. The first article in the chapter develops and illustrates the thesis that student activities represent a major approach to "personalization" of the curriculum of large high schools; the last article reports a study showing that in practice large high schools have less participation in activities than small ones. The chapter also includes an article calling for reform of interscholastic athletics and one advocating expanded use of student assistantships. Materials in this chapter were deliberately selected to spark consideration of some of the controversial issues in a significant part of the high school curriculum that received less attention during the past decade than the program of studies.

Chapter 5

THE COMMON ACADEMIC AREAS

Stimulated by national discontent in the late 1950s with our relative position in the international competition for outer space, and the subsequent National Defense Education Act and other federal subsidies toward curriculum improvement in science, mathematics, and foreign languages, marked changes were introduced into the content and methodology of these areas first and the other standard high school offerings of English and social studies later. In the 1960s the national curriculum project became the typical mode for developing the "new" content in all of these fields: By the turn of the decade, several hundred of these projects had received various sorts of financial subsidy from the federal government, foundations, and other sources, and had produced or were still in process of producing new curriculum materials, including instructional materials for learners. The selections in this chapter have been chosen to interpret and criticize the nature of the "new" curriculum plans.

Certain emphases have been somewhat common in the various projects. First of all, there has been the common objective of updating content and, indeed, to find a means of continuously updating it. One approach to continuous updating has been the definition of a subject's structure upon which new content could be added and from which obsolescent content could be dropped. Furthermore, in all of these subject areas, there has been attention to the development and use of a broader range of instructional materials, with techniques to reach more learners more effectively. In most there has also been an increased emphasis upon the actual skills of learning, skills that would endure long after school study of the subject ends.

John J. DeBoer's treatment of "The 'New' English" is decidedly critical of some so-called "new" emphases both because they are not new and because they are not appropriate. What is really new in English, he says, is the increased support for in-service education and increased interest in the English field. He questions the utility of the teaching of linguistics for all pupils, and a general return to the teaching of the old classics in literature. He particularly doubts whether there is a universal structure of English on which its content can be hung. DeBoer proposes in lieu of such features planning for English as an "all-school function" with teachers of English bearing a very special responsibility for the improvement of students' language communication. Instead of some structure or core in the English language, he would use an "idea-centered" curriculum dealing with the personal concerns of youth and the problems of society; thus he rejects formalism in English and looks for "flexibility, irreverence, and wonder that characterized earlier periods in our educational history, and—who knows—may relax some of the tensions we are creating in so many of our high school students." Much as we recognize the cogency of DeBoer's argument for the all-school function, high school faculties have long debated the role of teachers outside the English department in teaching communication skills. How do you feel about this issue? Can, in fact, every high school teacher be a teacher of some aspects of English communication?

Walter V. Kaulfers has contributed a very comprehensive treatment of "High School Foreign Language—Developments and Prospects" to the literature on the high school curriculum. His article reviews the facts of the increased national interest and student enrollment in foreign languages, a variety of important recent developments in this field, the problems awaiting solution, and some predictions for the future. Included in his review of important developments are some conflicting findings of studies on the use and merit of the audiolingual approach popularized in the past two decades. This approach reflects the greater emphasis on use of the spoken language. Kaulfers concludes that the reevaluation of the linguistic approach "will in time lead to a better balanced, less mechanical, and more creative approach in secondary schools."

The movement toward new content in the academic subjects began in the field of mathematics and probably has had most impact there. Several major national curriculum projects have generated new sequences, materials, and methodologies widely used at all grade levels. However, as stated in the opening paragraph of the article on mathematics: "The 'new math' was clearly geared to the college bound students. It bypassed a significant group of students referred to here as the low achievers." For this reason, and in view of the wide availability of material on the new mathematics, the selection by John W. Ogle entitled "Unfinished Revolution: Mathematics for Low Achievers" was chosen for this anthology. It reviews the need for and development of "low achiever mathematics projects" and offers specific suggestions for teaching the low achievers. It also identifies relevant materials that are available for low achievers, and includes various references for students interested in pursuing this area.

The science article, "A Case Study of Curriculum Change—Science Since PSSC" by Joseph D. Novak, reviews major national curriculum projects in science beginning with the one generally regarded as a prototype of the projects in most fields, the Physical Science Study Committee (PSSC). Some elementary school projects are reviewed as well as major ones for the secondary school, and his final review is of his own work in using an Audio-Tutorial method for individualized science teaching. Novak sees the pendulum swinging from the period "when scholars in science have dominated curriculum reform and school programs have benefited" to one "where focus on students and their learning capacities will be central in science curriculum design." His article is a neatly capsuled review of the projects and also a useful treatment of curriculum design; his reference to Johnson's model may well be studied further in addition to some of the sources cited.

Developments in the social studies are summarized in the selection by Dorothy Fraser. She notes one point of agreement among all critics of past social studies instruction: *"social studies had lost touch with social reality."* Parenthetically we may note that this has been, indeed still is, a major criticism of the high school in general! But certainly among all fields, social studies would be most expected to deal with social reality. Although Fraser's article does not declare that this criticism has been wholly met, she does note the declining importance of history in comparison with the more dynamic studies of anthropology, sociology, social psychology, economics, political science, and geography. She also identifies as strong features of new social studies programs, an emphasis on nonwestern studies and world affairs and a turn from content to process goals. That the concern for improving social studies continues is attested to by a later publication of an index to 111 social studies education projects (see Bob L. Taylor and Thomas L. Groom, compilers, *Social Studies Education Projects: An ASCD Index*, Association for Supervision and Curriculum Development, 1971). The fact that this field remains in turmoil is underlined by the compilers' introductory statement that "The *Index* is not an exhaustive directory of the social studies projects, for it is virtually impossible to be current in such a rapidly changing arena" (p. xi).

THE "NEW" ENGLISH*

JOHN J. DeBOER

Few terms in the contemporary lexicon of education are so misleading as the expression, "The New English." "New" may be applied to school mathematics and to school science. The enlistment of scholars in mathematics and science for the updating of the content of elementary and high school science and mathematics is new and welcome. As for English, there is little that is new except as changes in emphasis, which have occurred for hundreds of years in American schools, may be dubbed "new." The pendulum keeps swinging, but seldom outside a fairly restricted path.

To be sure, we read about the "new linguistics," the "new rhetoric," the "new criticism." The "new criticism," a formalistic approach to literature, can hardly be called new. It is associated with well-known authors like John Crowe Ransom, Allen Tate, Robert Penn Warren, Cleanth Brooks, and others in the post-World War I period. The French school which employed *explication de texte* is even older. These writers have not had and probably could not have much influence on the way literature is taught in American secondary schools. The "new" rhetoric is really the neoclassical rhetoric, as old as Aristotle. It is not therefore wrong or untimely, but it is not *new*. Of these three, only the new linguistics has significantly affected school practices in English, thanks largely to federally supported institutes in linguistics and a growing interest in the subject on the part of teacher-education institutions. A few pioneer language textbooks are including materials from structural and transformational grammar. A few professional articles have claimed superior results for the new grammars in the improvement of student writing. But grammar (as distinguished from reading, speaking, writing, and listening) constitutes a relatively small part of the school subject called English. What is really

* Reprinted from *The Educational Forum* (May 1968) 32:393–402, by permission of Kappa Delta Pi, An Honor Society in Education, owners of the copyright.

new in English is the increased support being given to in-service education of teachers of English and the extraordinary attention that English is receiving in curriculum centers and school systems throughout the country. For this greater emphasis on research and writing on the teaching of English, we are indebted to the Modern Language Association, the College Entrance Examination Board, and most especially the National Council of Teachers of English.

Linguistics and educational scholarship relating to language is getting a better hearing today than at any time in the past. Sterling A. Leonard, Albert Marckwardt and Fred Walcott, C. C. Fries, Robert Pooley, Bergen Evans, and others vainly pleaded in the late twenties and the thirties for a more realistic and objective treatment of usage standards in the classroom. Webster's Third International Dictionary, which is based on descriptive rather than normative standards, was looked upon with suspicion by many teachers of English and denounced by sophisticated but nonlinguistic critics. Educators who summarized the negative findings of fifty years of research on the effects of formal grammar study on students' growth in language power made little impact on classroom English.

Today the linguistic scholars are being heard, but new difficulties have arisen. First the linguists have moved from a preoccupation with the practical problems of English usage to the study of syntax. Here they find themselves in disagreement on nomenclature, and indeed on the basic philosophy governing the understanding of sentence patterns. The disagreements are too technical for nearly all but professional linguists to understand. Teachers brought up on traditional concepts of sentence structure are baffled by the new science and confused as to what course they should now follow in grammar. A few have grasped some principles from one or another school of linguistics and have reported successes with them in the classroom. But most of the linguists have found it impossible to deal equally with their subject matter and the pedagogical implications of their generalizations, except in a few instances when certain of them have sought to apply linguistic principles to beginning reading.

There is at present scant evidence that the teaching of any kind of linguistics in high school will be much more effective in improving students' English expression than the Latinate grammar proved to be. If it is to be taught in high school at all, it will probably have to be an eclectic grammar, one which would not fully please any of the scholars and which would be elective for verbally minded students who have a keen interest in language. In any case, theorists engaged in planning the English curriculum will have to address themselves to the question, "Should all pupils be required to study the structure of English in order to know more about this fascinating manifestation of human behavior, or should our major effort be directed to the refinement of the skills by means of which

English-speaking people communicate?" The two objectives are by no means the same. Social pressure for the development of "language power" would predispose the curriculum-maker toward the second.

The present tendency in publications and reports on the high school English curriculum is to advocate a return to what one might call the "pre-progressive" days. This trend is not necessarily to be deplored, but it would be inaccurate to refer to it as the "new" English. It is new only because it refers to a change of emphasis from that of pre-depression days. Reading the report of the Commission on English on the College Entrance Examination Board, *Freedom and Discipline in English,*[1] one is impressed with the value of the long tradition of instruction in English, and to some extent, American literature. The names of the authors who are part of our great inheritance—Chaucer, Shakespeare, Milton, Pope, Shaw, Dickens, and so many dozens of others who are cherished in the world of the literate of the earth—abound in the report on *Freedom and Discipline.* It is not necessary for English to be the "new" English in order to be the *right* English for millions of high school students.

But those who are appealing for a return to the "old" and for deliverance from an alleged educational wasteland are often unfamiliar with the vast diversity of the American high school population. We do not know how many high school dropouts were driven to the streets by Shakespeare, Chaucer, and Milton. Many of the dropouts could possibly have been saved by teachers who did not hold them in contempt, and who knew how to discover and interpret the universal elements in the literature. The attitude of the advocates of the old English is suggested by the following passage from *Freedom and Discipline:*

> Claims are frequently advanced for the use of so-called "junior books," a "literature of adolescence," on the ground that they ease the young reader into a frame of mind in which he will be ready to tackle something stronger, harder, more adult. The Commission has serious doubts that it does anything of the sort. For classes in remedial reading a resort to such books may be necessary, but to make them a considerable part of the curriculum for most students is to subvert the purposes for which literature is included in the first place. In the high school years, the aim should be not to find the students' level so much as to raise it, and such books rarely elevate. For college bound students, particularly, no such concessions as they imply are justified. Maturity of thought, vocabulary, syntax, and construction is the criterion of excellence in literature, and that criterion must not be abandoned for apparent expediency. The

---

[1] Harold C. Martin, Chairman (New York: College Entrance Examination Board, 1965).

competent teacher can bridge the distances between good books and the immaturity of his students; that is, in fact his primary duty as a teacher of literature.[2]

Notwithstanding the brilliance and charm of this report, as it discusses the literature program for high school students who are able to find pleasure in it and to make it a part of their lives, it fails to recognize the needs of a vast number of young people to whom its recommendations do not apply. One can quarrel with the statement that the "aim should be not to find the students' level so much as to raise it, and such books [literature for adolescents] rarely elevate." The experience of many high school teachers of English contradicts the statement, which on its face is unconvincing. The only defense for it is that the authors' own experience is largely with "college-prep" students, and the report is primarily concerned with them.

A similar confusion appears in the excellent report of a survey entitled *A Study of English Programs in Selected High Schools Which Consistently Educate Outstanding Students in English,* by James R. Squire and Roger K. Applebee.[3] This report is probably the most comprehensive and detailed survey of English instruction in American high schools since the New York Regents Survey by Dora V. Smith and Robert C. Pooley's later survey of Wisconsin schools. But here again we are faced with the term "excellence," which places the study on the plane of the superior student and necessarily omits the schools which achieve superior results with students in the whole range of abilities, interests, and socioeconomic levels. Quite possibly these selected schools do well with the deprived and the retarded, but the basis for selection of the schools would not assure us of this.

A third, earlier report further describes the trend, and in my judgment demonstrates that we are dealing with the old English rather than a "new" English today. This is the report on *The Basic Issues in the Teaching of English,* produced by representatives of the American Studies Association, the College English Association, the Modern Language Association, and the National Council of Teachers of English. The report may be found in *Issues, Problems, and Approaches in the Teaching of English,* edited by George Winchester Stone, Jr.[4] Two quotations will suffice. (1) "We agree generally that English composition, language, and literature are within our province, but we are uncertain whether our boundaries should include world literature in translation, journalism, listening, remedial reading, and general academic orientation. . . ." (2) "Can agreement

---

[2] *Op. cit.,* pp. 49–58.
[3] (Urbana: University of Illinois, 1966.) (Available from the National Council of Teachers of English, Champaign, Illinois.)
[4] (New York: Holt, Rinehart and Winston, 1963.)

be reached upon a body of knowledge and set of skills as standard at certain points in the curriculum making due allowances for flexibility of planning, individual differences, and patterns of growth?" The second question is not only the basis of the old curriculum, but it is naive. How does one agree on a body of knowledge and set of skills as standard at certain points in the curriculum, and at the same time make allowance for individual differences, which may be twelve years in one high school grade?

What is lacking in many of the statements referred to is an examination of the part that literature and language plays in the life of youth. English is considered an independent discipline, the content of which has self-evident value. Thus in one report the flat statement is made that teachers of English should know the language which Chaucer used. Now, reading Chaucer in his own idiom can be a delightful experience, but reading Tolstoy in the original or in translation could be as rewarding. Why insist on Chaucer?

There is a kind of sophisticated chauvinism in the demands of college people that teachers of English should confine themselves to English literature and to a lesser extent, American. This preference for the writings of British literary men and women is quite natural, especially for two reasons: (1) Our students can understand them; and (2) English literature ranks with the best of European literature. The American writers who have been accepted generally as great artists are necessarily few in comparison. Yet is it not time for us to cultivate in our youth a feeling for the life and culture of people in other parts of the world? Graduates of our high schools who are serving in Viet Nam would perhaps be less likely to refer to the natives as "gooks."

How contemporaneous should a curriculum (high school or college) be? At the moment, many young people are concerned about sex, LSD, the revolt of youth, "Black Power," and, overwhelmingly, our invasion of Viet Nam. These concerns are likely to be with us for some time.

There are similarities and differences between the present concerns of youth and those of earlier generations. Professors in large colleges and universities have difficulty in perceiving the differences because the students are polite in their classes. Many of them are quiet and attentive and ready to absorb the knowledge and perhaps the wisdom of their academic elders. Others are smoldering but retain their self-control. (In earlier times the domination of the teacher was accepted by all, at least until the class bell rang.) The docile ones are the hopeless ones; those who are in overt or inward revolt can be either the saviors or the destroyers of our society.

But Professor Jerome Bruner tells us that every subject has a structure that must be mastered and that the procedure must be spiral from the first grade up. I will not dispute his thesis, as far as other subjects are concerned, but for school English the idea simply will not work. In the first place, English embraces many different kinds of learning. Moreover, much of the learning in English occurs when a child gradually develops language and reading skills. He does not see the outline, at any level of the spiral, of the great skeleton of language. How could he, when the linguists themselves perceive the outlines and the language behaviors differently?

Henry C. Morrison knew this back in 1926, when he categorized the language arts as something distinct from the science-type or appreciation-type subjects. To him language, in its various uses—speaking, writing, reading, and listening—was a combination of cognitive and noncognitive factors.

What kind of "structure" evolves from a reading of Frost, Wordsworth, Milton, or Norman Mailer? This is not a question of finding a "structure," but of making a response to oneself and the world. The language stimuli may gain meaning from the larger context of a person's outlook on the world of things, living beings, and the ends of human life, but individual passages or selections do not necessarily add up to a "structure."

And has anyone raised a question about the term "structure" as applied to a school subject? The word is a metaphor suggesting a building. The builders in each generation, like those who created the great cathedrals, added to their fathers' achievements until the Great Design was complete. Even a musical creation can be called a structure. Robert Browning quotes Abt Vogler saying after he extemporized on a musical instrument of his invention, "Would that the structure brave, the manifold music I build. . . ." But when is a school subject complete? Does it not constantly change and grow? A school subject is a living thing, with complex interrelations with other "subjects."

Whatever the case may be in science or mathematics, we cannot think of English as a static "structure." In the first place, the responsibility for teaching English is shared by the entire school, when English is the medium of communication. There are generalizations about language and literature which can be learned, but these do not add up to a "structure." Since language is in continuing flux, and since the language of American high school youth can be described only as a collection of geographic and class dialects, we must deal with it not as a finished product, but as a varying, ongoing behavior which can change as a result of conditioning.

If English is to be considered a separate subject, as nearly everyone believes, it must have a content of its own. It is fashionable today to assert that school English consists of three independent parts—language, composition, and literature. Many of the English language institutes are organized according to these three divisions. The influential report of the Commission on English of the College Entrance Examination Board,

Freedom and Discipline in English,[5] consists of four chapters, one on English in general, and the other three on language, literature, and composition, respectively. Certainly all three belong to English. But composition is not unique to the subject of English, and it is an art or skill rather than content. Literature belongs pre-eminently to English, but does not the content of literature embrace all aspects of human experience and deal with the content of many other school subjects? And what about speech, dramatics, journalism, the mass media of communication, remedial reading, and listening? All of these have been questioned by those who deplore the diversity of activities characteristic of modern high school English. Even foreign literature in translation and letter writing, an art which should need no defense, have been considered of dubious value for the high school student.[6]

For many years we have tried to develop strategies for reducing the extreme fragmentation of the high school curriculum. We have tried to emphasize, through various modifications in curriculum organization, the interrelations between literature and history, mathematics and science, music and art, the practical and fine arts. At the higher levels of scholarship, we are witnessing the growing trend toward interdisciplinary studies, and the development of courses in biophysics, biochemistry, physical chemistry, radiochemistry, geolinguistics, astrophysics, bioclimatology, historical geography, and psycholinguistics—and one could go on. Now the currently popular conception of English as an independent field, and the triad, or tripod, theory of English as a group of separate disciplines, would encourage a return to an even greater degree of specialization at the high school level than we have known before, just when the scholars are emphasizing the need for greater integration.

From a practical point of view, the triad theory has only limited applicability. The study of language, it is true, is fairly self-contained, although it is encountered constantly in composition and literature, and it could be included incidentally in fields other than English, if teachers have some familiarity with the subject. But composition? When we write, we need a content, which we must borrow from every subject in the curriculum. Literature? It is art, language, history, economics, psychology, ethics, religion—the whole spectrum of human concerns. Thus while language, composition, and literature are obviously central to the English program, the tripartite design is not especially helpful to the curriculum planner.

Still the search for a "core," a central organizing principle, continues.

---

[5] *Op. cit.*
[6] From *The Basic Issues in the Teaching of English.* Reprinted in *Issues, Problems and Approaches in the Teaching of English,* p. 7. Edited by George Sylvester Stone, Jr. (New York: Holt, Rinehart and Winston, 1961).

In one promising curriculum project, language has been made the center, with composition and literature revolving around it. The plan is logical and will no doubt arouse the enthusiasm of creative teachers.

Many of the efforts to find an essential "structure" for English reflect the current preoccupation with form and genre, in the spirit of Marshall McLuhan's "The Medium is the Massage," instead of significant content. Thus we are often more concerned with syntactic structures than with what a sentence says; with the organization of a paragraph or questions of mechanics than with the indignation or enthusiasm or insight which the student writer reveals; with close analysis of literary passages, often outside of social or verbal context, than with the total meaning or impact of a book.

I propose in this article that teachers of English proceed on the following three principles: (1) That English shares in the task of the high school as a whole; (2) that a certain amount of integration of English, within its own field and with other subject fields, is necessary; and (3) that English encompasses many activities which are not necessarily connected with a central organizing theme.

The first of these principles implies that we are teachers first and teachers of English second. It means that nothing human in our students is alien to us. We are "concerned," in the Quaker sense, about students' problems, attitudes, and outlook upon the world of men and events. We desire, along with our colleagues in all other departments, that students make good school citizens, consider carefully their occupational goals or their plans for college, find constructive uses for their leisure time, seek to improve the present society rather than drop out of it.

We may despair of enlisting teachers of mathematics, social studies, or science in the task of accurate communication in language, but until we secure their help in the improvement of verbal communication we will operate under a great handicap. Thus, unless English instruction becomes an all-school function, utilizing all the specialized knowledge in a high school faculty, we teachers of English fight a losing battle, and will feel isolated except in the faculty lounge and near the coffee urn.

The fact that we are teachers of English second in no way suggests that we regard English as a task of secondary importance. We bear a very special responsibility for the improvement of students' language communication. But it is a shared responsibility, one which necessarily involves in some degree all teachers who recognize communication in English as central to their teaching success.

The second principle sets forth the necessity of supplying in the English curriculum a cohesive factor which enables the students to see details in relation to a larger pattern. The question in dispute among English education professionals is what the unifying principle ought to be.

For some the "core" should be language. This viewpoint has the unquestionable advantage of providing the teacher with a reliable base from which to operate, but it deprives English of the flesh and blood which the reader finds in the assassination of Julius Caesar, the spiritual struggle of Hester Prynne, the long journey of Clyde Griffith to the electric chair, or the hegira of the Joads of California. It provides a unity, but the unity is in the package, not in the contents.

To me, a more satisfactory organizing principle is the body of human anxieties and aspirations. The issues about which students in English classes should communicate are psychological, social, political, ethical, moral, aesthetic, international. These are issues with which young people are struggling, often at the cost of derision by their middle-class parents.

Such an "idea-centered" curriculum as has been described deals with both the personal concerns of youth and the broader problems of society. It may consider love, sex, romance, and marriage; adventure, exploration, sports, humor, problems of relations with the older generation, problems of growing up, problems of personal decisions, problems of values. It should also deal with the values of nations and social classes. It should study the dilemma of moral man in an immoral society. It should honestly face the hypocrisies which repel the youth, and at the same time sternly challenge the youth to produce their own brand of honesty and rationality. Inserting blossoms into the rifle barrels of military police may be a dramatic act of faith, but a more constructive *credo* is needed. And it should not be too humiliating to consult the thousands of intellectuals, including the Nobel laureates of many countries, to discover what mature thought has to say about the means of survival.

The illustrations thus far given may seem like admonitions for social studies teachers. On the contrary, they are intended for teachers, period. If teachers of English may without feelings of guilt teach the chronicle plays of Shakespeare, Southey's "Battle of Blenheim," Hugo's *Les Misérables*, Milton's sonnet on the massacre in the Piedmont, and Whittier's denunciation of the Southern pro-slavery ministers ("Clerical Oppressors"), we can confidently refute those who say that only those issues which are dead today are fit for the English class. The *Grapes of Wrath* is recent, but it is literature, and belongs to all teachers.

Who will deny the parallel between Aristophanes' *Lysistrata* and today's Women Strike for Peace? Is the Negro marcher who is at the wrong end of a southern sheriff's electric cattle prod different from Spartacus? The eloquence and the art which ancient struggles evoked from the singers and dramatists of a Golden Age long gone can come again, probably after the obscenities of politicians have been filed in their proper places in the metropolitan newspapers' morgues.

The sharp distinction between English and the social studies cannot possibly be defended. And if the subject fields are no longer realms unto themselves, they cannot be divided into such separate subjects as language, composition, and literature. The effort made no sense in the beginning.

The question whether English should constitute a structure or a group of three substructures is less appropriate than a similar question applied to such subjects as mathematics or science. To be sure, English should have a central organizing strategy which binds its parts together, even if loosely. But this subject is unique in that it inevitably invites extemporaneous and impromptu activities of communication—reading, writing, speaking, and listening.

Two developments in the field of English teaching offer great hope. One is the Dartmouth Seminar of 1966, attended by teachers of English from the United States, England, and Canada. The proceedings of this remarkable series of meetings are reported in two volumes, one for the profession and one for the general reader.[7]

The second is the International Conference on English Education held at Vancouver, British Columbia, in August, 1967, where hundreds of teachers of English from several English-speaking countries conferred on their common problems. At this meeting Dr. James Squire, Executive Secretary of the (American) National Council of Teachers of English, told of his visits to schools in the United Kingdom. The story he tells illustrates the value of such conferences as this one, in that it corrects what must be a widespread misunderstanding of what is occurring in education in other countries. The following is a brief excerpt from his report:

> Those individuals who have a mental stereotype of British schools derived from the reading of *David Copperfield* and *Nicholas Nickelby* are in for a shock as they meet the British schoolmaster of today. Sweeping forces of reform, initiated during World War II, but reaching a crescendo during the expansion of educational opportunity of the past decade, have transformed many infant and primary schools and are now working their magic at the secondary level as well. Concern with authoritarianism, with selectivity and education of the elite, with the great literary tradition, with 'the Queen's language' that so many Americans regard as characteristic of British education, seem very difficult to discover. Rather one is struck—perhaps too struck—with the freedom, the informality, the emotional, unstructured approaches to instruction, approaches which to disciplined Americans seem determined to turn each classroom event into a spontaneous 'happening.' When the 'happening' act-

---

[7] John Dixon, *Growth Through English*, 1967. Herbert J. Muller, *The Uses of English*, 1967. Both available from the National Council of Teachers of English, 508 South Sixth Street, Champaign, Illinois 61820. Muller's is for the general reader, Dixon's for the profession.

ually happens, it is wonderfully exciting to see. But when it doesn't—! But then should any program in education be judged by its conspicuous failures?

Through such developments as the Dartmouth Conference and the visits to British schools, we may hope to find a corrective to the current trend toward formalism in American high school classes in English. They may not bring us a "new" English, but they can restore some of the flexibility, irreverence, and wonder that characterized earlier periods in our educational history, and—who knows—may relax some of the tensions we are creating in so many of our high school students.

HIGH SCHOOL FOREIGN LANGUAGES— DEVELOPMENTS AND PROSPECTS*

WALTER V. KAULFERS

INCREASED NATIONAL INTEREST IN FOREIGN LANGUAGES

The higher percentage of the secondary school population enrolled in foreign languages today as compared with the percentage enrolled in 1950 bears witness to a greater national interest in their study than prevailed at mid-century. The reasons most frequently advanced for this trend can be summarized as follows:

Increase in foreign travel. In recent years close to two million Americans have been traveling overseas annually, and some 700,000 foreigners have applied for visas to visit the United States. These figures do not include visitors to Mexico nor to the French speaking areas of Canada.

Increase in opportunities to make use of foreign languages at home. Many United States corporations have established subsidiaries abroad,

* Reprinted from *The Educational Forum* (March 1970), 34:383–393, by permission of Kappa Delta Pi, An Honor Society in Education, owners of the copyright.

thus increasing the demand for personnel with a command of a second language.

Increase in the number of Americans residing or working abroad. Since World War II some 1,400,000 Americans have been living outside the United States for extended periods. This total does not include members of the Peace Corps, nor crew members of United States merchant vessels operating abroad. However, it does include the 185,000 children of United States citizens living abroad who have been attending classes in seventeen different languages.

Increased opportunities for study abroad. Since 1960 about 80,000 Americans have been participating annually in foreign study programs ranging from summer study abroad and shipboard classes on European, Latin American, Asian, and round-the-world tours, to resident study in foreign schools for a year or more. With the recent establishment of the Foreign Language League Schools[1] in several foreign countries the opportunity to learn languages through guided travel and residential study abroad is now available to high school students on a larger scale than has been possible heretofore through student exchange programs alone.[2]

Increased need for foreign languages in the armed forces, Peace Corps, and diplomatic service. This need has led to the teaching of some 90 languages in our colleges and universities seldom included in their curricula before World War II. As a result some of the larger urban high schools have added instruction in the less commonly taught languages to their curricula.

Increased support of foreign language study by private foundations and the federal government. Examples are the grants totalling $235,000 by the Rockefeller Foundation (1952–1957) to the Modern Language Association of America, and the grants in support of foreign language teaching under the National Defense Education Act of 1958. The latter provided substantial stipends for elementary and secondary school teachers of science, mathematics, and foreign languages to attend institutes for the improvements of their professional competence, loans to qualified college students to work for degrees in the fields mentioned, and half the cost of providing equipment for the upgrading and modernization of instruction. In addition it subsidized research studies ranging from surveys of foreign language teaching to experiments in methodology.

Increased participation of Americans in international conventions conducted in two or more official languages. A survey of 1,206 societies

---

[1] For information write to Foreign Language League Schools, Inc., P.O. Box 1920, Salt Lake City, Utah 84110.

[2] See also: Work or Study Abroad Schools, Ltd., Marine Plaza, Milwaukee, Wis. 53202.

published in 1960 revealed that 346 use two official languages, 348 use three, 147 have four, 58 use five, 15 recognize six, and 11 have seven or more.[3]

INCREASE IN STUDENTS ENROLLED IN FOREIGN LANGUAGES

One of the most distinctive trends in American secondary schools since 1955 has been the marked increase in the percentage of the total high school population enrolled in foreign languages. Between 1958 and 1963 total enrollments in foreign languages (including Latin) rose by 80.9 percent, while the total high school population increased only by 36.1 percent.[4] Whereas less than a fourth of all high school students were in foreign language classes in 1959, by the fall of 1963 the number had reached close to one-third. In the modern foreign languages the gain has been marked. In 1959 only one high school student in six enrolled in French, German, or Spanish while by 1963 the ratio rose to one out of four. Since 1960 only three languages (Italian, Latin, and Russian) have experienced decreases in the percentage of secondary school students enrolled—decreases more than offset by the growth of enrollments in Spanish, French, and German.

Since the earliest days of our history, the foreign languages have occupied a more important place in independent or private schools than in public institutions. In 1963 the percentage of private secondary school students enrolled in foreign languages was close to three times as great as that for students in public high schools.

The ranking of the 50 states and District of Columbia in terms of the percentage of their total high school population (grades 7–12) enrolled in *modern* foreign languages was published by the Modern Language Association of America in 1965. The state with the highest percentage of enrollment in modern foreign languages (49.4) was Connecticut; the state with the lowest (7.7) was Arkansas. In 1965 Alaska, Nevada, and Washington most closely approximated the national average of 27.4 percent of the public secondary school population enrolled in foreign languages.[5]

---

[3] Survey of the Directorate of Information, Council of Europe, Strasbourg, 1960, reported in *Forward in Europe* (December 6, 1963).

[4] James Eshelman and James Dersham, *Survey of Foreign Language Offerings and Enrollments* (MLA Materials Center, 4 Washington Place, New York, N.Y. 10003), 45 pp. See also *PEALS*, 7, 1:3 (November 1966).

[5] Glen Willbern, "Foreign Language Enrollments in Public Secondary Schools, 1965," *Foreign Language Annals*, 1, 3:239–253 (March 1968).

REVIVAL OF INTEREST IN JUNIOR HIGH SCHOOL FOREIGN LANGUAGE

In 1965 William T. Gruhn and Harl R. Douglass received replies from 419 junior high schools in representative communities of the United States on a comprehensive questionnaire relating to curriculum practices. Their findings with respect to the foreign languages can be summarized as follows from an advance report supplied by the investigators: .

> A majority of the junior high schools offer foreign languages primarily as electives in grades seven, eight, and nine—the most commonly taught languages, in decreasing order of frequency, being Spanish, French, German, and Latin, occasionally supplemented by offerings in Russian, and Italian.
>
> In a majority of schools the introduction of foreign languages in grades seven and eight dates from the early 1960s.
>
> In a majority of schools the audio-lingual method using tape recorders and (in approximately a fourth of the schools) language laboratories is the most widely used approach.
>
> "General language" as an exploratory tryout course in two or more foreign tongues (often supplemented by a study of the history of language or of the cultures which the languages represent) are available in about a fourth of the junior high schools replying to the questionnaire.
>
> Class time for the study of foreign languages in grades seven and eight has most commonly been made available by reducing the time allotments for study periods and, occasionally, by shortening the time previously allotted to English, music, art, home economics, or physical education.

SOME IMPORTANT RECENT DEVELOPMENTS

A serious weakness in the foreign language curriculum has traditionally been the high percentage of students dropping the courses at the end of a year or two. That some improvement has been achieved is evident from the fact that only 25.7 percent of the modern foreign language students continued into the third year in 1958, whereas by 1963 the corresponding figure had risen to 39.1. As the data show, however, abundant room for improvement still exists.

Today over 79 percent of the nation's high schools offer instruction in at least one foreign language. This represents a gain of close to 19 percent since 1958. Some of the larger secondary schools have expanded their offerings to include instruction in one or more of the uncommonly taught languages, such as Chinese, Russian, or Arabic. For example, the

New Trier Township High School in Winnetka, Illinois, has been offering instruction in as many as eight languages: French, German, Greek, Italian, Latin, Russian, Spanish, and Chinese.[6]

Although the percentage of high school students enrolled in Latin has shown a decline since 1900 from 50.6 percent to less than eight percent,[7] the language is still a significant factor in American secondary schools. In recent years some 1,167,000 boys and girls in grades 7–12 of our public and private secondary schools have been studying it. Each year about 1,000 college students choose it as their major for the bachelor's degree.

In nonpublic secondary schools Latin is still the most widely studied foreign language as can be judged from the percentages of high school students enrolled in recent years: Latin 29.5; French 25.9; Spanish 14.4 and German 3.3.

At least 38 states provide coordinators to articulate the work of foreign language teachers in elementary schools, junior high schools, senior high schools, and junior colleges, and to serve as consultants and resource personnel on a statewide basis. In addition, many communities have local coordinators. These are commonly assisted by citywide curriculum committees composed of representatives from all levels at which a foreign language is taught. Leadership on a nationwide basis has been provided through guideline reports, resource materials, and bibliographies issued by the Modern Language Association of America in collaboration with the United States Office of Education. Intervisitation between high school and college teachers of foreign languages has also proved successful where tried.[8]

The use of audio-visual aids in foreign language teaching dates almost as far back as the invention of engraving and the phonograph. As early as 1904, a conversational course in French was produced on an Edison cylinder in England. Soon thereafter, recordings were being tried out at Yale University and other institutions.[9] It is only since World War II, however, that audio-visual recording and reproducing machines have become sufficiently practical and economical for widespread school use. Thanks in large part to funds available under the National Defense Educa-

---

[6] *Hispania*, 45, 2:319 (May 1962).

[7] William R. Parker, "The Case for Latin," *PMLA*, 79, Part 2, 4:3–10 (September 1964). In public secondary schools this figure is only about five percent.

[8] Joseph M. Vocolo and Douglas C. Sheppard, "High School-College Visitation: Report of an Experiment and Recommendation for Similar Projects," *The Modern Language Journal*, 50, 7:474–478 (November 1966).

[9] William R. Parker, *The National Interest and Foreign Languages*, 3rd Ed. (Washington, D.C.: Department of State Publication 7324, 1962), p. 67.

tion Act of 1958, over 5,000 of the nation's secondary schools had some kind of foreign language laboratory by 1963.[10]

Since tape recorders and projectors for showing slides, filmstrips, transparencies, or sound films are currently available to teachers in most schools, textbooks are now commonly accompanied by recordings of basic materials. In fact, audio-visual courses, in which almost every lesson makes integral use of visual aids in the form of color slides, filmstrips, or films synchronized with sound, are now available in several languages. To date, however, televised foreign language lessons have not enjoyed the same popularity in secondary schools as in the elementary grades.

Because the necessity for scheduling, the use of language laboratories frequently involves inconvenience to teachers and often results in a loss of time in moving from the regular classroom into the laboratory, the desire for self-contained "electronic classrooms" has increased in recent years. The demand has been met by two new types of classroom laboratory, both still in the experimental stage.[11]

The first, known as the Wireless Language Laboratory "consists of a transiphone passive headset, with mike, which receives the program from a lesson source, tape recorder, phonograph or teacher, via an antenna resembling a piece of masking tape that can be used to encircle the classroom." The first such "wireless" laboratory was installed in the Westwood Junior High School of Woodstock, Illinois.

The second type of installation, called the Perimeter Laboratory, is designed "for schools with problems of space, scheduling, or finance. This laboratory has a somewhat reduced capacity and modified function, but it is unnecessary for students to have control over program selection and no more than three lesson sources are ever needed. Installed around the perimeter of the classroom, it still has the same function as the traditional lab, but . . . it has the advantage that the teacher may use it when it fits into the lesson and not when it fits into the schedule."

For communities unable to provide laboratory facilities to every school, "laboratories-on-wheels," movable from school to school according to a pre-arranged schedule, have been recommended. The practicability of providing such mobile laboratories, named Rolloramas by the manufacturer, was demonstrated in 1961. The specially constructed trailer-van houses electronic language laboratory equipment, including a teaching console and student booths.

Mobile language laboratories are not unknown abroad. "Boys and girls in the rural areas around the university city of Cambridge, England,

---

[10] J. Wesley Childers, *Foreign Language Teaching* (New York: Center for Applied Research in Education, Inc., 1964), p. 78.

[11] "Notes and News," *The Modern Language Journal*, 48, 7:453 (November 1964).

are now being taught the French language by a mobile educational laboratory—a converted double-decker bus. . . . The laboratory is on the upper deck. There are separate bays for ten pupils with earphones, microphone, and a tape recorder in each. Pupils watch a film on screen, listen to a recorded commentary and then record their own attempts at the language on the tape recorder, to be played back later. . . . On the lower deck there is a classroom with two long tables, a tape recorder, and a film projector."[12]

First applied in the Army's language schools during World War II, the theories of linguistic scientists have pervaded the textbooks and most of the resource materials now used in foreign language classes. Instruction in keeping with these theories—often called teaching in the "New Key"— is characterized, according to Valdman, by five basic practices:[13]

1. Emphasis on audiolingual skills, *i.e.*, comprehension and speaking ability;
2. The assimilation of conversational style language texts through memory and memorization;
3. The presentation of authentic target language samples by the use of live native speakers in class or recordings in the language laboratory;
4. The learning of pronunciation and grammar through pattern drills; and
5. A claimed application of structural (or scientific) linguistics to language teaching problems.

Although designed primarily for instruction in modern spoken languages, the linguistic approach has been used successfully in first-year Latin by Waldo Sweet of the University of Michigan. The November, 1968, issue of the *Modern Language Journal* describes in his own words his recent experiments using programmed materials in Latin.

While most studies using achievement tests support most of the claims made for the audiolingual approach, the evidence is by no means unilateral. George Scherer of the University of Colorado, for example, found that students trained in this way did not compare favorably with students taught by conventional methods until the end of the first year, and did not begin to surpass the latter until the third or fourth semesters.[14]

Similar results were reported by Raymond F. Keating in his study of 5,000 students of French in 21 school districts of New York. In listening comprehension, reading comprehension, and speech production the students who did *not* use language laboratories scored higher on tests than those who had been trained with the aid of these facilities. In speech production the language laboratory seemed to give students an advantage

---

[12] "Foreign Language Program Notes," *PMLA*, 79, 5:A14 (December 1964).
[13] Albert Valdman *et al.*, *Trends in Language Teaching* (New York: McGraw-Hill Book Co., 1966), p. xv.
[14] Childers, *op. cit.*, p. 59.

only after a full year's work.[15] On the other hand, two experimental studies conducted at the University of Akron and at Indiana University showed that while completely self-instructional foreign language programs without teachers are unfeasible, a highly self-instructional course utilizing a language laboratory can be more effective than a course taught under traditional classroom conditions.

In a closely reasoned, thoroughly documented study of the linguistic (or audiolingual) approach to foreign languages, based upon her doctoral dissertation completed at the University of Illinois, Wilga M. Rivers has questioned many of its underlying assumptions and favorite practices.[16] Without denying the many merits of the approach, teachers in recent years have increasingly called attention to the method's shortcomings at the high school level. Among the more important complaints are the following:

1. The excessive reliance which many audiolingual textbooks place on oral pattern drills as the means for giving practice in the language, thus forcing teachers to supplement the drills with other types of exercises to prevent learning fatigue or outright boredom.
2. The excessive reliance placed on the ability of students to discover for themselves the principles of language underlying the patterns, thus making it necessary for teachers to give supplementary instruction in grammar to assure that the learner will be able to do more than parrot set phrases.
3. The sterility of many of the basic textbooks with respect to readings dealing with the people and culture of the foreign country, thus making the integral, relevant use of visual aids and other cultural resources difficult in the first two years.

On the basis of special college entrance examination board tests, 888 colleges and universities in 1964 granted college credit toward the bachelor's degree for work done in high school. In that year some 29,000 students from more than 2,000 high schools took advance placement examinations. Many of these were students of foreign languages.[17] As early as 1960, for example, the examinees in French alone numbered 780 students from 170 schools. High schools not participating in advance placement programs frequently afford students with a gift for languages the opportunity to win promotion to more advanced classes through guided independent study

---

[15] *Ibid.*, p. 60. See also: "Research Clues," *NEA Journal*, 57, 3:62–63 (March 1968). These and other limitations of the audio-lingual laboratory method were reconfirmed in 1969 by the Pennsylvania Study. For a discussion of the merits and limitations of this highly controversial research report, see Philip D. Smith and Emma M. Birkmaier, "Static in the Language Lab," *Today's Education*, 58, 7:49–51 (October 1969).

[16] Wilga M. Rivers, *The Psychologist and the Foreign Language Teacher* (Chicago: University of Chicago Press, 1964), vii + 212 pp.

[17] *PEALS*, 5, 1:1–2 (October 1964).

utilizing self-instructional programmed materials. To facilitate acceleration and advance placement, the use of specially designed teaching machines or "mechanical tutors" has been viewed with favor. Such machines, it is claimed, can provide highly individualized instruction to enable students of varying interests and abilities to progress at their own speed without holding back or being held back by others. The advantages of teaching machines using self-instructional programmed foreign language lessons (which proceed by easy stages—"step-increments"—from the simple to the complex and from the concrete to the abstract) have been described as follows:[18]

> There is strictly individual instruction, the student progresses always at his own pace; he is challenged only by his own capabilities; he is permitted to make relatively few mistakes (and knows what they are a moment after making them); he is 'reinforced' (rewarded, encouraged immediately for right answers; he cannot skip; and he is absolutely guaranteed final success (i.e., the same achievement level as that of any classmate) if he but finishes the process. . . . It is this monotonous unnatural 'inhuman' drill which the 'machine' can do tirelessly—hence more efficiently—than the 'live teacher.' Moreover, the machine's accent is always impeccable. When it has done its work, and its products come into the classroom, the language teacher will then be able to *communicate* (something different from imitation), and he will have plenty left to teach— about literature, about human values about other cultures, yes, and about the subtleties and finer uses of the language itself.

The fact that half the articles in the November, 1968, issue of the *Modern Language Journal*, (Vol. LII, No. 7) were devoted to programmed offerings and to the use of teaching machines ("computer-based teaching") shows the extent to which the profession is currently concerned with the application of self-instructional technological aids to the learning of modern languages and Latin.

Although the aims of foreign language instruction are much the same today as in previous years, the decades following World War II have witnessed a marked change in emphasis. In contrast with *reading* as the predominant (but not necessarily exclusive) linguistic skill to be developed in foreign language courses, the stress today is primarily (but not exclusively) on ability to use the spoken language, especially at the elementary and intermediate levels.

The objectives and values of foreign language study as conceived by the steering committee for the foreign language program of the Modern Language Association of America have been stated as follows:[19]

---

[18] Parker, *op. cit.*, pp. 69–70.
[19] "FL Program Policy," *The Modern Language Journal*, 50, 6:381–385 (October 1966).

The study of a foreign language, like that of most other basic disciplines, is both a progressive experience and a progressive acquisition of a *skill*. At no point can the experience be considered complete, or the skill perfect. Many pupils study a foreign language only two years; longer time is of course needed to approach mastery. At *any* point, however, the progress made in a language, when properly taught, will have positive value and lay a foundation upon which further progress can be built. It is evident therefore that the expectancy of values to be derived from language study must be relative to the amount of time and effort devoted to it.

The study of a foreign language, skillfully taught under proper conditions, provides a *new experience*, progressively enlarging the pupil's horizon through the introduction to a new medium of communication and a new culture pattern, and progressively adding to his sense of pleasurable achievement. This experience involves:

1. The acquisition of a set of *skills*, which can become real mastery for professional use when practiced long enough. The international contacts and responsibilities of the United States make the possession of these skills by more and more Americans a matter of national urgency. These skills include:
   a. The increasing ability to *understand* a foreign language when spoken, making possible greater profit and enjoyment in such steadily expanding activities as foreign travel, business abroad, foreign language movies and broadcasts.
   b. The increasing ability to *speak* a foreign language in direct communication with people of another culture, either for business or for pleasure.
   c. The ability to *read* the foreign language with progressively greater ease and enjoyment, making possible the broadening effects of direct acquaintance, with the recorded thoughts of another people, or making possible study for vocational or professional (*e.g.*, scientific or journalistic) purposes.
2. A new understanding of *language*, progressively revealing to the pupil the *structure* of language and giving him a new perspective on English, as well as an increased vocabulary and greater effectiveness in expression.
3. A gradually expanding and deepening knowledge of a foreign country—its geography, history, social organization, literature and culture—and, as a consequence, a better perspective on American culture and a more enlightened Americanism through adjustment to the concept of differences between cultures.

Progress in any one of these experiences is relative to the emphasis given it in the instructional program and to the interests and aptitude of the learner. Language *skills*, like all practical skills, may never be perfected, and may be later forgotten, yet the enlarging and enriching results of the *cultural experience* endure throughout life.

PROBLEMS AWAITING SOLUTION

In the light of articles appearing in recent issues of the *Modern Language Journal, French Review, Hispania, German Quarterly, Classical Journal,* and of periodic reports of the Modern Language Association of America, the problems still awaiting solution are of long standing. Four deserve special mention:

The need for more and better teacher preparation. As Parker[20] has pointed out:

> . . . in many states high school teachers of a foreign language are required to have a minimum of 225 'contact hours' of language instruction—as compared with the 612 or more hours in the war-time 'Intensive Language Program.' A consequence of this policy is that *the language teacher in a second-year high school class has often reached the practical limit of what he himself has been taught,* his only advantage over the class being the number of times he has taught it.

Because the modern audiolingual approach makes greater demands on teachers than the "reading method" of the prewar years, the foreign language program of the Modern Language Association has placed great stress on the formulation of standards for teacher preparation and on the means for their attainment and measurement. A comprehensive summary of the MLA's reports is contained in the Golden Anniversary issue of the *Modern Language Journal.*[21]

The need to consolidate small schools to provide high schools large enough to offer a satisfactory minimum foreign language program. To cite an example: although Illinois ranks above average in the percentage of the high school population enrolled in foreign languages, as late as 1964 only 12 percent of all downstate Illinois secondary schools had a minimum program of at least three years in one foreign language.[22] This situation exists in varying degrees in many other states.

The need for better ways of accommodating transfers from elemen-

---

[20] Parker, *op. cit.,* p. 58.

[21] "Guidelines for Teacher Education Programs in Modern Foreign Languages—An Exposition," *The Modern Language Journal,* 50, 6:323–421 (October 1966).

[22] Report of a survey by Harold C. Hand, reviewed in the *Champaign-Urbana Courier* for March 5, 1964, p. 6.

tary school foreign language classes. Because FLES programs do not always begin at the same grade level nor involve the same number of contact hours per week—even, at times, within the schools of the same district— the problem of accommodating transfers satisfactorily still remains to be solved. In general, pupils who take four years of a foreign language in elementary school, in classes meeting for an average of 20–25 minutes daily, can usually compete successfully, after a period of adjustment, with second-year students in the senior high school. However, because of the variations in pupil achievement the use of placement tests as a means for allocating pupils to classes best suited to their abilities has proved necessary in many secondary schools. Large high schools have, at times, found it practical to provide separate continuation classes for pupils who have successfully completed two or more years of a second language in the elementary grades. Needless to say, the problem cannot be solved to the satisfaction of all without close cooperation among administrators and elementary and secondary school teachers.

The need to encourage able students to continue in high school the language which they began in the lower grades, and to take as many years of the language as the secondary school has to offer. One of the chief reasons for introducing FLES and for extending the high school program to include at least three (and preferably four) years of instruction in a second language was the desirability of providing students the opportunity to acquire useful proficiency over a period of six to eight years. In reality, many transfers from FLES programs change to a different language in high school. This defeats one of the major purposes envisioned in the provision of six- to eight-year offerings in foreign languages. More effective guidance and counseling of students, involving the cooperation of parents as often as possible, is obviously needed where such situations exist.

PREDICTIONS FOR THE FUTURE

In the conclusion to the third edition of *The National Interest and Foreign Languages,* Parker[23] lists his predictions regarding the future of foreign language teaching in American education which will be realized "if enough Americans will it." His forecasts include the following:

> The certification of foreign language teachers on the basis of their proficiency in speaking, reading, writing, etc.
> The acceptance of knowledge of the nature of language as one of the highest liberal arts objectives.
> The granting of credit in high schools for study abroad.

---

[23] Parker, *op. cit.,* pp. 152–154.

The widespread provision of eight- and ten-year sequences in foreign languages in American public schools.

Experimentation with the preschool and the subconscious learning of foreign languages.

The establishment of a National Language Foundation financed by Congress.

A strong comeback of Latin and German in the curriculum and the growth of Portuguese to a position rivaling that of Spanish.

Ever-increasing capitalization of travel, television, the press, libraries, and informal education in foreign language learning.

Adoption of the audiolingual approach as the predominant approach in foreign language teaching.

It will be noted that Parker's predictions are predicated on the condition that "enough Americans will it." More recently, in a less optimistic vein, Parker warned that, "The present prosperity of language teachers, to which I made some contributions from 1952 to 1959, is, believe me, basically elusive; it can disappear as dramatically and unexpectedly as it appeared. . . ."[24]

Since the needs which have stimulated national interest in foreign language teaching during the past decade are likely to increase rather than to decrease in the years ahead, the writer is persuaded that many of Parker's predictions will eventually be realized. To the extent to which the gains made since 1960 have been achieved with massive outside financial aid, however, a plateau period of consolidation—even of temporary retrenchment—may be ahead if a serious curtailment of federal appropriations for schools occurs. Moreover, the growing demand for the elimination of a reading knowledge of two foreign languages as a blanket, across-the-board requirement for all aspirants to the degree of Doctor of Philosophy (as at the University of Illinois where this prerequisite is now optional with the candidate's major department) may in time affect enrollments not only in strictly college preparatory high school foreign language offerings, but also in college language classes proper. A similar demand for the elimination of the foreign language entrance requirement, as a blanket prerequisite to college admission (*e.g.*, Stanford University), may have an even greater impact on high school foreign language enrollment. Unfortunately the majority of secondary school foreign language courses have tended to neglect the terminal noncollege preparatory student.

In any case, the reevaluation of the linguistic approach, already underway, will in time lead to a better balanced, less mechanical, and more creative approach in secondary schools. The conviction is strong that the future of foreign languages in American education will ultimately

---

[24] *The Modern Language Journal*, 50:324 (October 1966).

depend upon the success with which teachers and administrators in elementary schools, secondary schools, and colleges are able to solve the problems discussed in preceding paragraphs.[25]

---

[25] For an overview of current efforts in this direction see Emma M. Birkmaier (ed.) *The Britannica Review of Foreign Language Education*. Vol. I (Chicago: Encyclopaedia Britannica, Inc., 1969).

UNFINISHED REVOLUTION: MATHEMATICS FOR LOW ACHIEVERS*

JOHN W. OGLE

Only within the last few years have many formal efforts been initiated to describe and develop a specific program in mathematics for a significant group of students, the low achievers. With the orbiting of Sputnik by the Soviet Union in 1957 we began a nationwide effort to develop an updated program in school mathematics. This effort, often referred to as the revolution in school mathematics, has produced modern mathematics in its various interpretations. But like all revolutions, the new mathematics program has not brought increased benefits to all, nor does it offer the promise of a more successful mathematics experience for all. The "new math" was clearly geared to the college-bound students. It bypassed a significant group of students referred to here as the low achievers.

Who are these students? What are their characteristics? What are some of the efforts made to develop a mathematics program for them? What elements should be included in a program for these students? What content and sequence should be considered? What materials and other specific assistance are available? We will look for answers to these questions in a review of recent efforts to improve instruction for low achievers in mathematics.

The term "low achievers" is used here to refer to that group of stu-

---

* Reprinted from *The High School Journal* (February 1970), 53:299–309, by permission of The University of North Carolina Press.

dents functioning below grade level but not low enough to need special education. They have been referred to as below-average achievers, underachievers, culturally deprived, educationally deprived, culturally disadvantaged, reluctant learners, slow learners, rejected learners, underprivileged, lower ability students, students of limited interest or ability, mathematically underdeveloped children, and the forgotten people of education. What they are called is not so important as the acknowledgement of their existences.

IN THE BEGINNING . . .

While program developers had virtually neglected low achievers prior to the early 1960s, teachers have been vividly, if not painfully, aware of their presence. Since the new mathematics was apparently out of step with the cadence of these students, it became apparent to many teachers that a different drummer, or at least a different rhythm, would have to be found for them. There have undoubtedly been numerous undocumented efforts made by individual teachers to provide more appropriate materials in a less frustrating setting for these students. The harvest from collecting the best ideas and techniques of these teachers would be bountiful indeed! But an effective communication system which would permit this information to be collected is almost impossible to establish. This is due, in part, to the myriad of pressures and responsibilities confronting these teachers.

Concern over the absence of a mathematics program for low achievers gradually increased with the result that group efforts began to emerge in the early 1960s. This interest was crystalized in the spring of 1964 when two conferences were held to discuss these students and their dilemma.

A conference on "The Low Achiever in Mathematics" was held in Washington, D.C. in March, sponsored jointly by the U.S. Office of Education and the National Council of Teachers of Mathematics. Reference is made to the final report of this conference in the bibliography following this article.(1) Attending this three-day meeting were 56 persons with a diversity of backgrounds including high school teachers, supervisors, college professors and U.S. Office of Education personnel.

A second "Conference on Mathematics Education for Below Average Achievers" was held in Chicago, Illinois, in April, 1964. This conference called by the School Mathematics Study Group, SMSG, was attended by 67 participants representing a wide geographic base as well as diverse backgrounds including school people and research oriented individuals from education and industry. In his statement of the purpose of the conference, the director of SMSG, E. G. Begle, acknowledged that their efforts of the previous decade had been appropriate for only a part of the school population. It was time to give attention to those students who were not doing well in mathematics. The conference program included the presentation of seven papers followed by reactions to the papers and discussions by the participants. These discussions emphasized the need for two types of programs: "Action programs based upon our knowledge and hunches as to what and how to teach, and research programs on motivation, helping youngsters to change goals and attitudes, how children learn, strategies for teaching, and what mathematics should be taught." The conference report summarizes these comments and contains the recommendations made by participants.(2)

With the impetus stemming from these two conferences and the availability of Federal money through the Elementary and Secondary Education Act of 1965, low achiever mathematics projects began to appear. Their purposes were to learn more about the low achiever and with this knowledge develop a mathematics program for him. The opportunity had at last arrived for teachers to share their ideas. They were encouraged to develop materials for those students who in the past had been condemned to boredom and frustration, if not failure.

Projects were begun to study various aspects of the problem of low achievement. Some were funded by such additional sources as private foundations and state and local education budgets. An annotated listing of many of these projects is available from the Mathematics Division of the North Carolina Department of Public Instruction.(3)

WHAT DOES RESEARCH SAY?

Recent educational research is readily available through The Educational Research Information Center, ERIC, developed in 1966 by the U.S. Office of Education. A search through ERIC reveals several reports on low achievers but in almost all cases these are merely descriptive. Much of this descriptive research is of the "advice from the firing line" variety. It consists of people sharing with others techniques which have successfully worked with their students. Other articles have been written to inspire teachers to motivate their students to learn. Because of missing data and a lack of controls, any conclusions drawn from these efforts would be somewhat dubious.(4)

Few articles approach the area of curriculum for the slow learner in a very sophisticated and direct fashion. With the efforts in the last five years to create a curriculum specifically for those who cannot produce at "grade level," some information has begun to emerge in the form of action or classroom research. This is an essential beginning before much pure educational research can be undertaken. Classroom teachers are often faced with problems which virtually do not exist in the short-term laboratory-type experiments. These low achievers, with years of limited success in school, are often required to take mathematics through the ninth or tenth grades. With its many diverse problems this group is not attractive to researchers.

Perhaps it is in the area of the affective domain that a concentrated effort should be made. What is the nature of the complex relationship between progress in mathematics and such affective factors as anxiety, motivation, and attitude? A survey of relevant research on this topic is to be found in *Elementary School Mathematics: A Guide to Current Research* and *Research in Mathematics Education.*(5), (6)

To rely on the frequency and kinds of errors made by low achievers in their computations, or to expand the diagnostic process to consider the student's growth in understanding concepts, in problem solving ability or in making quantitative decisions is inadequate. Some programs are combining the more mechanical techniques with clinical procedures. These procedures involve careful observation of the student at work, analysis of his oral and written work, and interviews. Through this type of probing it is hoped that the complex disability of low achievement might be more effectively understood and treated. Characteristics such as the short attention span and poor motivation might be attributed to emotional problems. If this is so, a team approach involving the student, his teachers, a psychologist, a social worker and, perhaps, a psychiatrist might with its collective expertise provide far more insight than is possible with objective test data. Such a team approach is presently being experimented with at a residential school, The Learning Academy, in Huntersville, N.C. The teachers on such a team are equipped to work with a student's cognitive problems. However, when a student's difficulties take them into the affective domain, the other team members bring their professional trainings to bear upon these problems.

HOW TO TEACH THE LOW ACHIEVER

The writers and teachers of the many low achiever mathematics programs have taken a careful look at their students and produced similar descriptions of the characteristics of these students. Several of these characteristics are listed below with techniques for countering them. The main objection to this approach is that it often results in treatment of the symptom without detecting the ailment which has produced it. This suggests that the student, if placed back into a regular classroom setting, might revert to his former behavior and learning patterns. As a beginning, though, here are several low achiever characteristics and the corresponding classroom strategies found to be effective by teachers in several of these programs.

History of Failure: has not functioned up to the level someone had expected him to reach; would probably like to succeed but lacks the desire.

Plan material to permit each student to experience small successes daily. Boost morale occasionally by giving a quiz of which everyone will do well. In checking papers mark only that part of a problem which is incorrect. Give credit if the student corrects his own errors.

Poor Self-Image

Never embarrass or castigate one of these students in front of the class. Regular successes for his efforts will improve his opinion of himself and increase his motivation. Course prestige can be developed by including some new and different content such as the slide rule and flow charting. Teacher should quickly learn the names of these students and be friendly with them. Since they are often overage they will appreciate being treated more like adults than children. They must be accepted and liked by others in order to like themselves.

Poor Reading Ability

Keep instructions and directions simple, specific and clear. Oral instructions will reduce the reading handicap. Practice working out word problems with the class or small groups. If the words get in the way of the mathematics, there is little hope of successful work by the student.

Little Interest in Math: has poor attitude toward the subject.

Attitude and motivation are nebulous areas. Nevertheless some ingredients to consider in developing a setting in which the students will develop positive attitudes and become motivated include fun, praise, encouragement and good grades in return for honest achievement. The teacher, if enthusiastic about teaching these students and the content of this course, will generate enthusiasm among the students. Genuine enthusiasm is like the common cold—quite contagious with some staying power!

High Rate of Absenteeism: which reflects both his feelings toward school and the randomness of his existence. He tends to live from class period to class period, or from day to day.

This haphazard attendance dictates the need for self-contained lessons which are completed daily. Evaluation of the work in class is desirable for immediate reassurance. A spiral development of the material with frequent review is necessary.

Poor Memory

Profits from drill when he knows what he is doing. Frequent review is necessary. The drill can be presented in entertaining ways involving patterns, puzzles, games and other teaching aids.

Short Attention Span: probably due to unsuccessful experiences, general disorganization and little interest in the subject.

A general plan of varying the activities two to three times each class period is strongly recommended. Capture his involvement at the beginning of the period and through successful experiences keep it. Activities might include several of the following: pleasant drill or review activity, math lab experience or group oriented work, a short worksheet assignment completed and corrected in class, followed perhaps by some game, puzzle, recreational activity, or supervised study.

Emotional and Social Immaturity: the low achieving student may be antagonistic and he is more likely to be a discipline problem if he is conventionally treated.

By working with individual students you can get to know and better understand them. This requires smaller classes. Private counseling often produces improved results. In desperation, either exchange a difficult student with another teacher, or assign materials to everyone else so that you can give sufficient attention to the disruptive individual.

Difficulty with Abstractions: often results in quick guesses without adequate consideration of the facts.

Learning new abstract concepts is difficult for most people—particularly so for low achievers. Excursions into the abstract should be infrequent, and when attempted, must be closely linked with some previous concrete relationship. Symbolism, considered by many to be the strength of mathematics, is for low achievers one of its weaknesses. These students don't jump to correct mathematical conclusions, they often can't respond well even when given a little push. They can be helped to see easier ways of doing things and to see that mathematics is a part of those easier ways.

Fails To See the Practical Use of Mathematics as It Applies to Him: To study math for math's sake is an argument he won't buy. "What's in it for me?" is his typical response.

Perhaps the best way to have mathematics become relevant to these students is to have it emerge naturally from their involvement in some activity. The most successful way to accomplish this is through a mathematics lab.

What is a mathematics laboratory? The Central Iowa Low Achiever Motivational Project offers a good answer.

"Primarily, a mathematics laboratory is a state of mind. It is characterized by a questioning atmosphere and a continuous involvement with problem solving situations. Emphasis is placed upon discovery resulting from student experimentation. The teacher acts as a catalyst in the activity between students and knowledge.

"Secondarily, a mathematics laboratory is a physical plant equipped with such material objects as calculators, overhead and opaque projectors, film strips, movies, tape-recorders, measuring devices, geoboards, solids, graph boards, tachistoscopes, construction devices, etc. Since a student learns by doing, the lab is designed to give him the objects with which he can do and learn.

"The primary goal of the lab approach is to change the student's attitude towards mathematics. Most students have become so embittered by habitual failure that they hate mathematics and everything connected with it. There is little possibility of this student learning mathematics until an attitude change has been effected. It is because of this goal that our approach is different. Some would label our approach as 'fun and games,' but I am sure that close examination will bring realization that everything in the program is oriented towards the twin goals of attitude change and mathematical improvement. Learning can be enjoyable and in fact, should be so. Once the student sees that he can enjoy mathematics, he will want to learn about it. Then, and only then, is learning possible.

"Obviously, part of our goal is to equip the student with the mathematical skills he will need to function as a useful member of society. We desire to enable the student to cope with and not fear the use of mathematics in everyday life. This entails the ability to recognize the problem, select the best solution, and compute the answer accurately. The laboratory approach facilitates the problem solving technique and motivates the students to engage in it."(7)

PROGRAMMING FOR THE LOW ACHIEVER

What constitutes an effective program for the low achiever? Here are several principles considered in the development of such programs.(8)

1. The *sine qua non* in a course for the low achiever is the skilled teacher who is well qualified in mathematics and interested in working with the low achiever.
2. Some specific objectives in terms of student behavior should be stated. To be effective these instructional goals need to be appropriate, realistic and attainable by the students if they make a consistent effort to reach them.

3. Students must be appropriately selected for the course. Flexibility in transferring students in or out of the course needs to exist. If it becomes a dumping ground or an easy credit, then the original objectives will have been lost.
4. Emphasis should be on student participation through a variety of learning activities including work in a mathematics laboratory, group discussion, discovery activities, games, puzzles, palatable practice, and numerous instructional devices. This requires relatively small classes, 20–25 students, and suitable classroom space.
5. Evaluation should consider the student's ability and effort as well as the purpose of the course. It is desirable to record the progress made by each student, levels attained, and some mention of his attitudes and habits.
6. Content should include interesting review of old topics, new material, and engaging drill. A survey of new materials now available reveals that these criteria have been consistently met.

CONTENT AND SEQUENCE

The content of these new materials is often oriented to practical, real-life situations, e.g., the adding of decimal numbers is not so much an end in itself as it is a means of keeping accurate records of money. In this utilitarian context the review of the basic operations involving the various forms of rational numbers can take on new meaning. A genuine effort is made to present many of the fundamentals of mathematics in fresh, new settings.

The following is a listing of some topics which might be included in a ninth-grade "general mathematics" class.(9)

Measurement	Equations and Formulas
Construction of Models	Mathematics and Science Experiments
Calculating Devices	Flow Charts in Problem Solving
Intuitive Probability	Mathematical Recreations
Number Patterns	Operations on Rational Numbers
Informal Geometry	Elementary Graphs and Statistics

The list is not as definite for other grade levels. One suggested four-year high school sequence included the following recommendation.(10)

Grade	Content
9	General math with emphasis on applications
10	General math with emphasis on structure
11	Simple algebra—few, if any, formal proofs
12	Consumer mathematics—emphasis on application to everyday situations

MATERIALS

What materials can the teacher use with these students? Virtually every major publishing company has now entered this field. Some of the new materials have been developed by special low achiever mathematics projects, while others have resulted from the efforts of the National Council of Teachers of Mathematics or state departments of education. Here is a sampling of these materials.

ELEMENTARY

Edwina Deans, *et al.*, *Mathematics in Action*, grades 1 through 8, American Book Co., New York, N.Y., 1969.
Glennon and Riedesel, *Essential Modern Mathematics*, intermediate grades, Ginn, Boston, Mass., 1969.

SECONDARY

Braunfeld, *et al.*, *Stretchers and Shrinkers*, Books 1–4, UICSM material developed for seventh grade underachieving students, Harper & Row, New York, 1969.
Phillips and Zwoyer, *Motion Geometry*, Books 1–4, UICSM materials developed for eighth grade underachieving students, Harper & Row, New York, 1969.
Harold Smith, *Pathways in Mathematics, Level I and II*, grades 7 & 8, Pawnee Publishing Co., One Pondfield Road, Bronxville, N.Y., 1969.
Denholm and Blank, *Mathematics Structure and Skills*, First and Second Books, grades 7 & 8, Science Research Associates, 259 East Erie Street, Chicago, Ill., 1968.
Dilley and Rucker, *Mathematics: Modern Concepts and Skills*, Books 1, 2 and 3, grades 7 through 9, D. C. Heath, Division of Raytheon Education Co., Lexington, Mass., 1968–69.
Jack Foley, *et al.*, *Individualizing Mathematics: Skills and Patterns*, series of booklets for grades 7 through 9, Addison–Wesley, Reading, Mass., 1970.
The National Council of Teachers of Mathematics, *Experiences in Mathematical Discovery*, series of booklets for discovery learning in grades 9 & 10, 1201 Sixteenth Street, N.W., Washington, D.C., 1966.
Edmonds, *et al.*, *Patterns in Mathematics*, grade 9, Houghton Mifflin, Boston, Mass., 1967.
Bezuska, *et al.*, *Contemporary Motivated Mathematics, Book 1*, a collection of clever drill-oriented techniques applicable to grades 7 through 9, Boston College Press, Chestnut Hill, Mass., 1969.
Zimmerman, *et al.*, *E.S.P., GIMMICKS*, and other materials suitable for use with students in grades 7 through 10, request bibliography of these materials from Central Iowa Low-Achiever Motivational Project (CIL-AMP), 1164 26th Street, Des Moines, Iowa 50311.

Arthur J. Wiebe, *Foundations of Mathematics*, grade 9, Holt, Rinehart and Winston, New York, 1968.
Wiebe and Goodfellow, *Explorations of Mathematics*, grade 10, Holt, Rinehart and Winston, New York, 1970.
Herrick, *et al.*, *Modern Mathematics for Achievement*, First and Second Course, series of booklets for grades 9 & 10, Houghton Mifflin, Boston, Mass., 1966–67.
Thomas Rowan, *et al.*, *Handbook for General Mathematics*, collection of ideas to aid the teacher of non-college bound pupils, grade 9, Supervisor of Mathematics, Maryland State Department of Education, Baltimore, Md., 1966.
Russell F. Jacobs, *Introductory Algebra*, Books 1 and 2, intuitively developed Algebra I course spread over two years, grades 9 & 10, Harcourt, New York, 1968–69.
Cleo Meek, Editor, *Consumer Mathematics Teaching Units*, suggestions for developing ten consumer oriented units with frequent opportunities for problem analysis, grades 11 and 12, Mathematics Division, North Carolina State Department of Public Instruction, Raleigh, N.C., 1969.

PROFESSIONAL BOOKS

Johnson and Rising, *Guidelines for Teaching Mathematics*, Wadsworth, Belmont, Calif., 1967.
Max A. Sobel, *Teaching General Mathematics*, Prentice-Hall, Inc., Englewood Cliffs, N.J., 1967.

The National Council of Teachers of Mathematics is presently preparing a yearbook on the low achiever in mathematics. At most NCTM meetings there is a swap session for people interested in these students to share information about their efforts and experiences with them. Issues of "The Arithmetic Teacher," "The Mathematics Teacher" and other journals often contain articles on this subject.

Workshops for teachers of low achievers have been held at several universities. The scope of these two- or three-week workshops usually includes experimenting in a mathematics laboratory and actually discovering, recording and analyzing data; learning new ways to present basic mathematical ideas; and practice with various calculating devices which can be used for review, drill and reinforcement. In some instances materials and equipment are prepared by the participants to take back to their classrooms. Recently produced materials are reviewed and adapted for use by these teachers with their own students. Additional information on these workshops may be obtained from references following this article.(11), (12), (13)

SUMMARY

While there is no single accepted program for low achievers, many techniques and materials are now available for use with these students. Some of the projects funded to study and find solutions to this problem have received as many as several hundred inquiries about their work. This would seem to reflect a very broad interest in the low achiever today.

No one really knows how best to cope with what has become a very significant problem in some schools. Today it may be some frustrated students confronting their frustrated teacher. Tomorrow it is likely to be these same frustrated students confronting an even more frustrated society. It is very unlikely that these students really hate mathematics. But they do hate getting the lowest grades, and are frustrated at not being able to do something others can do. They have lacked involvement. Furthermore, being unable to see how mathematics would be helpful to them other than to enroll in the next class, they have obviously failed to see its relevancy to their lives. In a society which becomes more complex each day, it is time that the revolution in mathematics include this significant segment of students. Only through a mathematics program developed specifically for low achievers will they be likely to acquire the necessary skills for holding jobs in tomorrow's labor market. Fortunately, help appears to be on the way.

REFERENCES

1. Lauren Woodby, *The Low Achiever in Mathematics*, U.S. Department of Health, Education and Welfare, Office of Education, OE 29061, Bulletin 1965, No. 31, Superintendent of Documents, U.S. Government Printing Office, Washington, D.C., Price $.35.
2. F. G. Begle, *et al.*, *Conference on Mathematics Education for Below Average Achievers*, School Mathematics Study Group, Leland Stanford Junior University, 1964, p. 117.
3. "Projects Involving the Slow Learner in Mathematics," Annotated bibliography compiled by W. C. Lowry and J. Ogle, available upon request from Mathematics Division, State Department of Public Instruction, Raleigh, N.C. Also available is a bibliography of articles on low achievers in mathematics.
4. Sarah T. Herriot, "SMSG Report No. 5, The Slow Learner Project: The Secondary School 'Slow Learner' in Mathematics," Educational Resources Information Center (ERIC) Report Number ED 021755, 1967, pp. 2 & 7.
5. Glennon and Callahan, *Elementary School Mathematics: A Guide to Current Research*, Association for Supervision and Curriculum Development, NEA, 1201 Sixteenth Street, N.W., Washington, D.C., 1968.

6. Joseph M. Scandura, editor, *Research in Mathematics Education*, The National Council of Teachers of Mathematics, 1201 Sixteenth Street, N.W., Washington, D.C., 1967, pp. 112–113.
7. Joseph T. Zimmerman, *LAMP* Booklet, Mathematics Department, Des Moines Public Schools, 1800 Grand, Des Moines, Iowa, 1968, p. 3.
8. Johnson and Rising, *Guidelines for Teaching Mathematics*, Wadsworth Publishing Company, Belmont, Calif., 1967. (See pp. 191–193 of Chapter 14, "A Program for the Low Achiever.")
9. Sol Weiss, "What Mathematics Shall We Teach the Low Achiever?" *The Mathematics Teacher*, November 1969, p. 572.
10. Sarah Greenholz, "Successful Practices in Teaching Mathematics to Low Achievers in Senior High School," *The Mathematics Teacher*, April 1967, p. 330.
11. Milton Beckman, "Teaching the Low Achiever in Mathematics," describes a three-week workshop held at the University of Nebraska in the summer of 1968, pp. 443–446, *The Mathematics Teacher*, October 1969.
12. Ruth Irene Hoffman, "The Slow Learner—Changing His View of Mathematics," describes the two-week University of Denver Workshop held during June of 1967, pp. 86–97, NASSP bulletin, April 1968.
13. Annual three-week workshop at Pacific College for classroom teachers, supervisory personnel and curriculum directors. Experimental and development work is discussed and participants engage in developing materials. For more information contact Dr. Arthur Wiebe, President, Pacific College, 1717 South Chesnut Avenue, Fresno, Calif. 93702.

A CASE STUDY OF CURRICULUM CHANGE— SCIENCE SINCE PSSC*

JOSEPH D. NOVAK

Curriculum development has a genesis extending back to the early history of man. When Childe (1951), Mead (1928), and others describe primitive civilizations, they outline the experiences required when chil-

* Paper presented at the conference on "Curriculum Development in a Changing World," Syracuse University, July 10–11, 1968. Reprinted by permission of the Editor, *School Science and Mathematics* from the May 1969 issue. Pp. 374–384.

dren transcend to adulthood. These experiences constituted for those early societies a kind of "curriculum." The history of curriculum change has been marked by contributions from many great writers during the past two millennia. This may lead one to wonder how any new contribution can emerge in curriculum design. The thesis of this paper is that we are entering a period of school curriculum design that will constitute a unique venture in planning for children's experience: newer learning theory and curriculum theory will be used conjointly with analysis of societal needs to plan curriculum. The teaching of science can be used to illustrate and develop this thesis.

To begin, I should like to refer to a model for curriculum design proposed by Johnson (1967). Figure 1 shows the culture of man as the "starting point" in curriculum design. The end-point is the set of learning outcomes desired in pupils. Learning outcomes might be described "behaviorally" as Mager (1962) would suggest, or more broadly as Atkin (1968) or Bloom (1968) would prefer. The intervening steps in Johnson's model involve application of selection criteria to abstract from the total available culture that which is appropriate, for example, for school learning; application of structuring criteria for decisions relative to which elements in the selected content should be presented first and which elements are to follow; next, specifications for design of specific school curricula are established, e.g., science for normal students in public elementary schools; an instructional system is prescribed which comprises the set of operations performed by students and teachers and defines the learning outcomes for the pupils. Evaluation is a part of this model, and decisions regarding curriculum are affected at several points on the basis of evaluative results. In this model, curriculum revision would be affected primarily by (1) changes in the teachable culture (e.g., as in that resulting from the much discussed "knowledge explosion"), (2) changes in desired pupil behaviors (e.g., resultant changes as we move from an agrarian to an urban people), and (3) changes in the instructional system (e.g., the prospective increased use of technological devices in in-

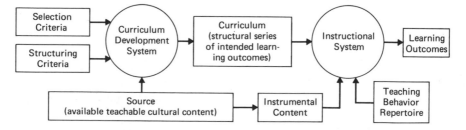

Fig. 1. A model showing curriculum as an output of one system and an input of another.

struction). Other elements would vary also, but largely in response to the latter factors noted.

Johnson's model can be illustrated by developments in science education in the past dozen years and suggestions for the future direction of change appear to emerge.

By the early 1950's there was a growing discontent among university scientists with the "antiquated" content of high school and elementary college courses. Some of this discontent was focused on college general education courses; despite repeated and occasionally successful efforts, some of which were described in two volumes entitled Science in General Education (1948, 1960), most courses for students not majoring in science failed to present important recent concepts in science and lacked completely in their presentation of the "spirit of science." They were largely what Schwab (1966) called a *"rhetoric of conclusions* in which current and temporary constructions of scientific knowledge are conveyed as empirical, literal, and irrevocable truths." By 1955, the ground-swell of opinion from the scholars was saying loud and clear that the science curriculum was not incorporating important dimensions of the "available teachable culture" and the prescribed pupil behaviors were not those that could lead to an understanding of the contemporary scientific enterprise. We were in a decade described by Hurd (1961) as a period of "crisis in science education."

Though numerous conferences were held and reports issued in the early 1950's to examine what might be done to improve science teaching, the first major step came in 1956 when the Physical Science Study Committee received financial support from the National Science Foundation. Plans were made to design a new course in high school physics. Proceeding through a series of trial editions and field tests, PSSC Physics appeared as a commercially available textbook in 1960. This was the first textbook to be made available commercially, with subsequent books resulting from national curriculum projects appearing in chemistry, biology, earth sciences, and elementary science. The elementary science curriculum programs are still in progress, and not all of these will produce pupil "textbooks," but rather, they provide instructional protocols for teaching the new materials. We therefore see the decade of the sixties as the period of national curriculum project publication in the sciences.

As noted, the Physical Science Study Committee was only the beginning of a new movement in science curriculum reform. With the establishment of the Course Content Improvement Programs within the division of Special Projects in Science Education section of the National Science Foundation, a pattern was established that rapidly spread to other areas of the science curriculum. A key figure in this expansion was the late Richard Paulson who probably commanded more knowledge about national and international science curriculum innovation than any other person. The National Science Foundation held to the precedent established with support to PSSC that curriculum projects in science must be under the leadership of outstanding scientists. So stringently was this criterion applied that almost no NSF financial support went to projects where major leadership did not reside with scientists. Richard Paulson, who had many close friends among education people, was so enamored by outstanding scientists, he tended to look very critically at any project that had majority or substantial leadership in what he regarded as the education *establishment*. With his encyclopedic knowledge of curriculum projects, Paulson was in a position to command respect on NSF advisory panels, and it is this writer's opinion that he, more than any other person, charted the course of curriculum work in science for over a decade.

Table 1 illustrates the scope of science curriculum projects supported by NSF. The seventeen projects listed do not include all programs which have received support, but these are the major projects. In 1966, these programs were receiving some $16 million annually in NSF support. The first project to receive support was PSSC and the most recent was Harvard Project Physics, the latter also receiving substantial support from the U.S. Office of Education and Carnegie Corporation, beginning in 1963. During the eight year span from 1956 to 1964, a noticeable shift in leadership and emphasis had occurred in science curriculum projects and this trend continues today.

The Physical Science Study Committee sparkled with leadership from the community of physicists. There was a tolerant posture toward Jerome Bruner of Harvard, a psychologist interested in cognitive learning, and from selected teachers at private academies. But more than any other science curriculum project the ·scientists called the shots and with the heavy emphasis focused on the first section of Johnson's model, i.e., selection of the content of physics to be included in high schools. To be sure, many excellent films were developed as well as new laboratory experiments and necessary equipment; but the focus was on transmitting a carefully defined body of knowledge. The importance of physics to technological development was played down almost to the point of exclusion, albeit, special supplementary reading materials were sponsored in the Science Study Series which included a wide range of subjects such as the "Physics of Television."

Unlike some of the curriculum groups which followed PSSC, no concise set of objectives or "themes" were defined for over-all curriculum planning. The assumption was that good physicists would automatically provide logical, if not psychological, continuity in the various aspects of the program and no further specification of goals was needed. Well-endowed financially and intellectually, the PSSC succeeded admirably, at

SUBJECT	GRADES												
	K	1	2	3	4	5	6	7	8	9	10	11	12
MATH. & SCIENCE	MATH ←(c-A)→ ←(b-A)→ ←(d-A)→ SCIENCE ←(c-A)→ ←(b-A)→ Minn. Math. and Science Teaching Project (U. Minn.)												
PHYSICS	Physical Science Study Committee (ESI) — (d-A); Harvard Project Physics (Harvard) — (b-A); Engineering Concepts Curriculum Project (CEE) — (b-A)												
CHEMISTRY	Chemical Education Materials Study (U. Calif.) — (d-A); Chemical Bond Approach Project (Earlham) — (d-A)												
BIOLOGY	Biological Sciences Curriculum Study (U. Colo.) — (d-A, c-A) (d-A)												
SCIENCE	Secondary School Science Project (Princeton) (c-A); Earth Science Curriculum Project (AGI) (c-A); Introductory Physical Science Project (ESI) (c-A); ←(c-E)→ Elementary School Science Project (U. of Illinois); ←(b-A)→ ←(c-A)→ Science Curriculum Improvement Study (U. Calif.); ←(b, c-E)→ Elementary School Science Project (U. Calif.); ←(b, c-E)→ Elementary Science Study (ESI); ←(c-A)→ Commission on Science Education (AAAS); ←(b-E)→ School Science Curriculum Project (U. Illinois)												

KEY TO SYMBOLS:

CEE Commission on Engineering Education
ESI Educational Services Incorporated
AGI American Geological Institute
AAAS American Association for the Advancement of Science

a. Planned or projected
b. Preliminary version
c. Extended trial version
d. Released for general use
A. Text and Supplementary Materials
B. Teacher Training Films and Course Materials
C. Guidelines for Curriculum & Course Development
D. Research in Learning
E. Unsequenced Units and Source Materials

*From the BSCS Newsletter, No. 28, April, 1966.

Table 1. National Science Foundation.

least in that the kinds of students and teachers who can use the program developed indicate their pleasure with it.

In the area of Chemistry, two curriculum projects began work with the recognition of the need to update the content of high school courses, as did PSSC, but these projects gave somewhat more attention to pedagogical problems. The Chemical Bond Approach (CBA) group was led by a professor in a small liberal arts college whose principal activity was teaching, not research. While the Chemical Education Materials Study (CHEMS) group was under the chairmanship of Nobel prize winning Glenn Seaborg, much of the day-to-day leadership came from college professors engaged primarily in teaching. Also, high school chemistry teachers represented a larger proportion of writing participants in CBA and CHEMS than in PSSC programs. The combined effect was that these programs, especially CHEMS, have addressed themselves to problems of teaching high school students more than did the PSSC programs. Good enrollment figures are not available, but unpublished figures from the U.S. Office of Education (Welch, 1968) indicate that many more high school students are taking CBA or CHEMS programs than the PSSC program. In fact, scientists and science educators are expressing concern that the *number* of students enrolled in high school physics now appears to be declining as well as the *percent of graduates* with physics, which has been declining for many years.

Programs in chemistry and physics did more than produce new textbooks. New kinds of laboratory activities which placed greater emphasis on the process of scientific inquiry, rather than confirmation of results reported in books, characterize these programs. Where possible, 8mm loop films have been developed to show selected phenomena where motion and/or animation has value. Obviously, then, these projects did give some attention to the "instructional program" specified in Johnson's model for achieving certain desired pupil behaviors. Though much of the new material developed was based on an intuitive rather than a theoretical approach to instructional design, the caliber of persons working on these materials necessarily guaranteed a high percentage of pedagogically successful material. In this respect, Paulson and others were vindicated in their insistence on the involvement of good scientists in curriculum programs. This result may have been at least partly fortuitous, however.

The Biological Sciences Curriculum Study (BSCS) was organized in 1959 to study the need for improvement of high school biology programs. Elementary and college biology programs were later funded under different organizations. Perhaps no area of science has experienced such an explosive advance as the biological sciences. The consequence was that high school courses were badly incongruent with the "available culture" in this area, but also, most college programs were equally obsolete. Indeed, there was some polarization among biologists as to relevance of recent discoveries at the cellular and molecular levels in contrast to the more traditional and continuing research findings in natural history and structural biology. The result was that three, not one, types of high school biology resulted under the labels of Blue, Green, and Yellow Versions, so designated by the color of the paper covers of trial editions. All versions presumably embodied the same nine *themes* comprising a kind of intellectual framework for the BSCS programs, but there is considerable debate as to the adequacy with which these themes were utilized to provide psychological structure to the programs (cf. Novak, 1966).

The BSCS programs also introduced the innovation of Laboratory Blocks. These are units of work designed to replace four to six weeks of a Blue, Green or Yellow Version program and to provide students with an in-depth study of some area, e.g., plant structure and function. The Laboratory Blocks have not been widely used in high school biology, although those teachers employing them report favorable results, and this serves to illustrate the slow rate at which instructional innovation has taken place. Moreover, the BSCS programs were designed to be largely oriented around laboratory work, not didactic teaching, but Brandwein found in his study of 1000 schools (1968) that this is seldom evident and not characteristic of BSCS classes. Small pamphlets written by experts and presenting some dynamic area of biology have been so little used as to be negligible in the over-all BSCS program. Selected 8mm loop films prepared by BSCS have had a slightly better reception.

In addition to some polarization that occurred between "traditional" and "molecular" biologists there was a degree of polarization between biology education individuals who had association with BSCS during program development. There was the strong feeling among some biology education leaders that whatever the content of BSCS programs, the primary consideration lies in the design of laboratory work and emphasis on scientific *inquiry*. Thus Schwab (1963) devoted a major section to the process of inquiry in the handbook for BSCS teachers prepared under his leadership. At a somewhat different pole (and the losers in this dichotomy) was a smaller group of biology education people who placed emphasis on structure of a discipline and the necessity for ordering student experiences so that pupil cognitive growth would be facilitated with each successive lesson or laboratory exercise. Ausubel (1966) later formalized some of the concerns of the latter group in a critical paper, but the BSCS programs were now published reality. It may be interesting to speculate how the BSCS programs may have differed if the primary source of funds was not NSF, with the polarities extant at the time.

All of the new secondary school programs placed substantial emphasis on laboratory work. The central role of laboratory work was dictated by the philosophy that opportunity for inquiry was a central objective in science teaching. Memorization of scientific nomenclature and definitions was eschewed not only for lack of relevance of much of this type of work to contemporary science but also because preoccupation with learning this kind of information was crowding out opportunity for laboratory study. Moreover, such laboratory study that did exist was seldom more than exercises to confirm textbook statements of facts or principles. All of the new secondary school science programs placed emphasis on laboratory work which was designed to show students the imperfect and tentative nature of scientific conclusions, thus characterizing science as an endless search for explanation of natural phenomena. To this end, the work of secondary school programs reflected well the reality scientists associated with the projects knew first-hand, and it was in the laboratory programs that the best efforts of the curriculum projects were evidenced.

As progress in secondary school curriculum work moved forward, programs to improve science instruction in the elementary schools began to emerge. In Massachusetts, the Elementary Science Study (ESS) was established under the same leadership that brought forth PSSC physics. In Illinois, an astronomy program for upper elementary grades (now being published for "intermediate grades") was launched. The ESS program placed primary emphasis on children's direct experience with science materials and cautioned against structured sequences of science instruction characteristic of published elementary science books. An elementary science program funded by NSF under the auspices of the American Association for the Advancement of Science (AAAS) placed major emphasis on sequential development of *process* or *inquiry* skills. Again we see the influence of NSF granting policy and scientists' preoccupation with "inquiry" emerging in curriculum design with the intentional minimization of the importance of content ordering, as Johnson's curriculum model would suggest. The AAAS program ostensibly benefited from the guidance of psychologist Robert Gagne; the hierarchical ordering of "process" skills is consistent with Gagne's theoretical views, but Gagne (1965) himself indicates that learning of an organized body of knowledge is essential:

> Obviously, strategies are important for problem solving, regardless of the content of the problem. The suggestions from some writings is that they are of over-riding importance as a goal of education. After all, should not formal instruction in the school have the aim of teaching the student "how to think"? If strategies were deliberately taught, would not this produce people who could then bring to bear superior problem-solving capabilities to any new situation? Although no one would disagree with the aims expressed, *it is exceedingly doubtful that they can be brought about by teaching students*

"strategies" or *"styles"* of thinking. Even if these could be taught (and it is possible that they could), they would not provide the individual with the basic firmament of thought, which is subject-matter knowledge. Knowing a set of strategies is not all that is required for thinking; it is not even a substantial part of what is needed. To be an effective problem solver, the *individual must somehow have acquired masses of structurally organized knowledge.* Such knowledge is made up of content principles, not heuristic ones. (Italics mine)

Unlike the ESS or AAAS elementary science programs, a program conducted at Berkeley, California under the leadership of Robert Karplus addresses itself to careful consideration of the science content presented as well as the operations or "processes" in which children are involved. Karplus combines the rare talents of physicist and educational innovator in a way that has led to some highly teachable elementary science lessons (cf., Karplus and Their, 1967). All of the new curriculum programs have found it necessary to design new apparatus and "laboratory" work, and in this respect, the program headed by Karplus has benefited not only from insights of scientists but also from thoughtful consideration of work in developmental psychology, particularly the work of Jean Piaget. Again, the NSF dictum of support only to projects led by good scientists has shown significant payoff.

As indicated earlier, the most recent of the secondary school science curriculum projects has been Harvard Project Physics (cf. Holton, 1967). Headed by three co-directors, one a physicist and two science educators, HPP based its case for financial support on the declining enrollments in high school physics, indicating that an alternative to PSSC was needed which might attract a larger proportion of the high school population. Harvard Project Physics has included in its curriculum some materials from astronomy, considerable historical development of certain concepts in physics, and a significant amount of modern technology derived from physics. Though the major emphasis in HPP is physics, as it should be, the leaders of the project sought to provide a variety of "handles" by which students could catch hold of basic physical concepts.

Another characteristic of Harvard Project Physics which distinguishes it from PSSC is the extensive evaluation program carried out during the try-out of early versions. The evaluation program has gone far beyond testing students to determine achievement levels and has included basic research questions dealing with factors related to cognitive and affective growth of students, teacher characteristics and pupil achievement, and effectiveness of certain instructional tools used in the HPP multi-media approach. Perhaps more than any other high school curriculum program in science, HPP has sought to monitor the effectiveness of alternative approaches in instructional planning and selection of curriculum substructures. In this respect, HPP has significantly involved project staff in all phases of the curriculum model suggested by Johnson and collected data on the resultant student behavioral outcomes.

At the junior high school level, the Intermediate Science Curriculum Study (ISCS) based at Florida State University is analogous to the HPP program in that considerable attention to evaluation has been directed to questions other than pupil achievement. A unique aspect of this program is that computer assisted instruction has been used to teach some portions of the program and substantial quantities of data have been generated bearing on specific aspects of pupil achievement under the CAI regime. At this time, much of the data remain to be analyzed, but we can anticipate the ISCS program will extend the focus on basic learning reasearch questions.

Most of the leadership of the ISCS program has come from individuals who are former teachers and now work primarily in Education. Most of the financial support for the project has come from the U.S. Office of Education. We see, then, in this large curriculum program a new direction of development that I believe will be more characteristic of future curriculum innovation in science, at least in terms of leadership and financial support policy.

My final illustration of the shifting directions in science curriculum design is one with which I am most familiar. Beginning in 1960, Professor Postlethwait initiated a new program for teaching introductory botany. The approach involves utilization of audio-tape for programming instruction with a full range of printed, visual and actual botanical materials for *individualized* study of botany. The "learning center" developed by Postlethwait has as an important component staff members who can serve as tutors, since much routine teaching is done by A-V devices and printed materials. The instructional approach has become known as Audio-Tutorial Instruction, or simply as A-T teaching (cf., Postlethwait et al., 1964). Some 250 colleges and universities have now adopted A-T methods for one or more of their courses.

Audio-Tutorial methods can be applied in any form of education. The use of audio-tape in language and in elementary school teaching has been with us for a decade or more, but the mix of instructional media and curriculum planning essential in A-T programming is relatively new. Based on my experience in botany at Purdue University, I initiated elementary science audio-tutorial instruction while on sabbatical leave at Harvard in 1965. While some aspects of the elementary science program we are developing resemble work done at Oakleaf School by Lipson (1966) and others, our logistic arrangements and operational procedures more closely resemble those used by Postlethwait. However, much of the work we have done up to this point has focused on the application of David Ausubel's (cf., Ausubel, 1968) theory of learning to elementary science curriculum design. We are basing our program development on Ausubel's thesis that a primary determinant of success in new learning is the adequacy of the learner's *relevant* concepts and therefore our instructional planning focuses on cognitive development. We are collecting data bearing on issues that deal with various instructional regimes and their effect on concept acquisition and relative learning efficiencies. Our assumption is that individualized science teaching with audio-tutorial methods can result in significant cognitive growth and concept differentiation in all normal elementary school students. The results from field testing to date in some twenty different schools suggest that our basic assumption is correct and that Ausubel's general theoretical constructs appear tenable. For example, data from two classes engaged in "discovery" activity as well as A-T programmed instruction showed about the same performance, with the evaluation techniques used, as did students provided only with A-T instruction. The power of carefully sequenced experience for concept learning, as suggested by Ausubel, has been borne out by our findings to date.

The Oakleaf program and our elementary science program have been supported largely by the U.S. Office of Education. Both of the projects have as central objectives the study of learning questions as well as science curriculum development objectives. Both programs make use of extensive technological learning facilities and emphasize individual rather than whole-class instruction.

In education the pendulum that marks periods of change has swung from side to side; we have been through a decade when scholars in science have dominated curriculum reform and school programs have benefited. Now the pendulum may be in transit to a pole where focus on students and their learning capacities will be central in science curriculum design. There is an acute need for training new curriculum workers who have sufficient competence in science to maintain the gains achieved through the contributions of scientists and who can add a new dimension of instruction technology and learning theory to improved curriculum designs. Those of us who have cast our lot to the field of science education must accept this as the major challenge in the improvement of school science teaching.

REFERENCES

Atkin, J. Myron. Behavioral Objectives in Curriculum Design: A Cautionary Note. *The Science Teacher* 35(5): 27–30. May 1968.

Ausubel, David P. "Evaluation of the BSCS Approach to High School Biology." *American Biology Teacher*, 28: 176–186, March 1966.

Ausubel, David P. *Educational Psychology: A Cognitive View*. New York: Holt, Rinehart and Winston, 1968.

Bloom, Benjamin S. Learning for Mastery. *UCLA Evaluation Comment*, 1(2): p. 1. May 1968.

Brandwein, Paul F. Personal Communication, 1968.

Childe, V. Gordon. *Man Makes Himself*. New York: The New American Library, 1951.

Gagne, Robert M. *The Conditions of Learning*. New York: Holt, Rinehart and Winston, Inc., 1965, p. 170.

Hahn, Robert Ray. *Science in General Education*. Dubuque, Iowa: William C. Brown, 1960.

Holton, Gerald, *et al*. Harvard Project Physics. *The Physics Teacher*, 5(5): 198–231. May 1967.

Hurd, Paul DeHart. *Biological Education in American Schools: 1890–1960*. Baltimore, Maryland: Waverly Press, 1961.

Johnson, Mauritz, Jr. Definitions and Models in Curriculum Theory. *Educational Theory*, 17(2): 127–140. April 1967.

Karplus, Robert and Herbert D. Their. *A New Look at Elementary School Science*. Chicago: Rand McNally & Co., 1967.

Lipon, Joseph I. An Individualized Science Laboratory. *Science and Children* 4(4): 8–12. December 1966.

Mager, Robert F. *Preparing Objectives for Programmed Instruction*. San Francisco: Fearon Publishers, 1962.

McGrath, Earl J. *Science in General Education*. Dubuque, Iowa: William C. Brown, 1948.

Mead, Margaret. *Coming of Age in Samoa*. New York: W. Morrow & Co., 1928.

Novak, Joseph D. The Role of Concepts in Science Teaching. In *Analyses of Concept Learning*. New York: Academic Press, 1966.

Postlethwait, S. N., J. Novak and H. Murray. *An Integrated Experience Approach to Learning*. Minneapolis, Minnesota: Burgess, 1964.

Schwab, Joseph. *Biology Teacher's Handbook*. New York: John Wiley and Sons, 1963.

Schwab, Joseph J. and Paul F. Brandwein. *The Teaching of Science*. Cambridge, Mass.: Harvard University Press, 1966.

Welch, Wayne W. "The Impact of National Curriculum Projects: The Need for Accurate Assessment." School Science and Mathematics 68(3): 225–234. March 1968.

SOCIAL SCIENCES*

DOROTHY FRASER

A PAINFUL SEARCH FOR NEW RELEVANCY

1. Importance of history declines
2. Economic emphases accelerate
3. U.S. gives way to a world view
4. Instructional materials turn multimedia
5. Process approach gains momentum

Increasing numbers of students are pursuing social studies programs which offer striking contrasts to typical programs of the 50s and early 60s.

Since the end of World War II, weaknesses of conventional social studies programs have been discussed by social studies specialists but it was not until "Sputnik fever" resulted in widespread public concern about the effectiveness of public education that demands for basic revisions in the social studies curriculum gained momentum.

While the critics often disagreed about what was wrong with social studies and what should be done, one fundamental criticism was widely accepted: *social studies had lost touch with social reality.* U.S. society had been transformed while social studies programs, especially at the secondary level, were dealing with a world of the past.

Of additional concern to critics were various surveys of student reaction to social studies which indicated that it is one of the least-liked areas of the school program.

Reform Projects of the 1960s

During the 1930s, 40s, and 50s, there were many efforts to up-date social studies curriculums.

New topics were introduced into existing courses in an effort to get some study of such significant areas as world affairs, nonwestern cultures, and economic systems.

---

* Reprinted with permission from *Nation's Schools,* July 1969. Copyright 1969, McGraw-Hill, Inc., Chicago. All rights reserved.

In the 60s more than 40 major social studies curriculum projects and many smaller ones have been financed by grants from the federal government, private foundations, institutions of higher learning, or a combination of these sources. These projects were nationally oriented—designed to produce models and materials from which local school systems could choose those most suitable to adopt or adapt for use in the particular situation.

Some have developed comprehensive K-12 programs with an interdisciplinary or multidisciplinary base. Some have planned sequences for the secondary school years. Others are concerned with specific units or courses that draw on multiple disciplines and are intended for various parts of the K-12 program. Still others work from a multidisciplinary base to deal with broad themes or problem areas, such as Asian studies, Latin American studies, or intergroup relations.

While the nationally oriented projects were developing, a number of state education departments and large school systems undertook comprehensive curriculum studies in social studies. Examples are the California Framework and Wisconsin's "Conceptual Framework for the Social Studies in Wisconsin Schools," both of which have been studied by teachers and curriculum committees in many parts of the country.

More recently, ESEA Title III programs have stimulated local school systems to undertake experimentation and innovation in their social studies programs. A review of the 66 funded shows that many emphasize the use of multimedia materials and activity-oriented instructional procedures to replace assign-recite-test routines based on a single textbook.

Tapping the Disciplines

If the flood of materials that is beginning to come from the special projects of the 60s has the anticipated impact, one result will be the end of the traditional dominance of chronological history in the social studies curriculum.

Materials from *anthropology, sociology* and *social psychology* are woven into many of the new programs for both elementary and secondary levels. Comparative studies of family and community are frequently recommended for the elementary grades as a means of introducting younger children to such ideas as cultural change, variations in ways of meeting basic needs from one culture to another, how culture affects the individual personality, and the concept of role, role expectations, and conflicts among roles.

Several of the courses prepared for the early secondary school years include study of social institutions and of the individual's relation to them. Anthropological approaches are employed in area studies for both junior and senior high school. Model courses in sociology and anthropology are under preparation. Already there seems to be an increase in the number of senior high school courses in sociology and a few in anthropology are appearing.

Even before the wave of special social studies projects began, attention to *economics* in both elementary and secondary social studies had been increasing largely due to the work of the Joint Council for Economic Education. The emphasis on economics has accelerated rapidly during the 60s. The materials from many of the special projects that are not devoted exclusively to economics treat economic concepts and topics in both elementary and secondary school years. Model courses in economics have been issued for both junior and senior high school.

Political science content has been expanded and revamped in many of the experimental programs. Concepts such as authority, conflict resolution, and justice under law are treated informally in materials for the elementary years and are dealt with systematically in units or courses for older students. Comparative study of governments, emphasizing political processes and behaviors rather than descriptions of governmental structure, is recommended in a number of the projects.

New emphases in *geographic* studies are appearing, also. Many of the experimental materials for the elementary school introduce geographic concepts and skills in the kindergarten and early primary grades. Place geography and the outmoded concept of environmental determinism are replaced by stress on man's interaction with his cultural and physical environment. New programs for the secondary school, where geography was long ignored, introduce a considerable geographic content in area study courses.

The trend toward drawing substantially on the entire range of social science disciplines will have increasing impact on new social studies programs.

A World View

Another feature of new social studies programs is a strong emphasis on nonwestern studies and world affairs. Traditional social studies programs were oriented almost exclusively to the study of the United States and western Europe. During the 1940s and 50s this situation began to change slowly. The experimental projects of the 60s have accelerated the movement by producing units, courses and materials for both elementary and secondary levels that stress world cultures and international affairs.

Other trends, such as comparative study of families, communities and regions in the elementary years, make it possible to include examples from Asia, Africa and Latin America. The increasingly popular secondary school courses in culture area studies, comparative economic systems, and comparative governments treat nonwestern as well as western peoples and nations.

Process as Content

In many of the innovative projects, teaching about the tools and methods of the various social sciences is recommended. Opportunities for learners to utilize some of these modes of inquiry, at a level appropriate to the students' maturity, are also built into the curriculum materials. Aspects of historical method, the geographer's use of maps to correlate data, sampling technics, and survey procedures are presented at points where such information is pertinent to the topic being studied. Suggestions are included for related studies that pupils may make, utilizing the tools with which they have become familiar.

The role of *content* is transformed in this approach to establishing scope and sequence. Content becomes a vehicle for developing process goals, such as the learners' ability to engage in rational decision-making. That it is a vehicle rather than an end in itself does not suggest that it makes no difference what topics or subjects are selected for study. In a program that uses a conceptual approach in establishing scope and sequence, the main criteria for choice of content will be: Will study of this topic or subject help the student increase his command of the basic concepts, generalizations or processes that have been chosen for emphasis at this grade level? In some ways, the emphasis on process as content may be the most significant aspect of the search for relevancy in selecting content for the social studies program.

Instruction Strategies and Materials

Two major emphases in teaching strategies and materials run through most of the innovative programs: (1) a stress on inquiry and discovery, and (2) the use of multimedia materials.

Inquiry and discovery—In an effort to break the stranglehold of assign-recite-test routines in social studies classrooms, many of the special projects have experimented with teaching strategies intended to encourage the learner to "find out for himself." Inductive approaches, inquiry and discovery are widely recommended. Even in the early school years, pupils are called on to collect information from a range of sources, organize it, and develop their own conclusions and generalizations. Learners are asked to formulate and check hypotheses against their data.

Multimedia learning materials—Recognizing the inadequacies of the conventional textbook, especially when used as the single source for students to consult, social studies project staffs have identified or developed a wide range of learning resources to implement their new programs.

Reading materials continue to constitute the major share of the new resources, but they take many forms. Pamphlet series and paperbacks are recommended as unit texts or for independent reading. Expository accounts are minimized or even eliminated in favor of case studies, selected documents, reading focused on a major concept or issue, and open-ended descriptions of problem situations. Some programed materials are being developed. In the realm of the audiovisual resources, many of the projects emphasize transparencies for overhead projectors, films, filmstrips, slides, tapes, kits of models and artifacts, single concept loops, sets of pictures and special-purpose maps and charts, and other graphics. Equipment for simulation games has been prepared by several projects.

Already, *commercial publishers* are beginning to respond to the emphasis on multimedia materials to some extent.

Chapter 6

ELECTIVE AND EMERGENT CURRICULUM AREAS

The traditional hold of the academic subjects on the high school curriculum was somewhat challenged during the twentieth century as high school education became almost universal, but the data presented in Chapter 3 showed their continuing entrenchment. Fresh assaults upon their favored position in enrollments and general priority were being made in the early 1970s, as proponents of vocational education, the arts and humanities, health and physical education, and various contemporary problems—race, sex, drugs, and environment, especially—pressed for curriculum status.

In 1971 the new Commissioner of Education, Sidney Marland, called for increased attention to vocational education to move it from what he called its "second-level" position. In a speech to the National Association of Secondary School Principals reproduced here as released, he called for "career education" as the function of the high school. This education was to be so provided that each graduate would be prepared "either to become properly, usefully employed immediately upon graduation from high school or to go on to further formal education." He urged the abolition of general education because it was "neither fish nor fowl, neither truly vocational nor truly academic."

For high school education to become career education, Marland further argued for eliminating "the false dichotomy between things academic and things vocational"; he said "we must purge ourselves of academic snobbery." As you read his speech, what would you expect to be the reaction of high school principals and others whose schools have long maintained academic subjects in first place? And, if you agree that each high school graduate should be ready for employment or further study, what changes must be made in the program and counseling of high school students? Marland describes some of the changes in process needed in federal and state programs of vocational education but leaves unanswered many questions as to specific changes to be made in individual high schools. How can high school faculties and their communities meet the need for "realistic exposure to the world of work, as well as to the option of general post-secondary schooling" of students "presently drifting in the general education wasteland"?

Perhaps some answers to the questions Marland leaves in the reader's mind are given in the selection on "Vocational Curriculum Development," which reports a sampling of new developments in vocational education. The programs described indicate the movement toward preparation in newer fields such as airport and airlines operation, nautical occupations, health occupations, and motel-hotel management. This survey also indicates the use of innovative techniques of individualized instruction, learning incentives, and new-type instructional materials. Certainly any marked increase in enrollments in vocational-type courses in high school will have to depart from the traditional agriculture, homemaking, secretarial, and trades and industries programs both to interest a wider range of students and to conform to occupational opportunities.

Health and physical education has had its ups and downs in interest and enrollment since first development as a credit subject in this century. Since the beginning of World War II, there has been great pressure to increase facilities, trained personnel, and course requirements in this field; however, the renewed emphasis on certain academic subjects in the late 1950s and thereafter frequently took its toll on physical education. At the same time there continues strong support for physical fitness and health education, and much concern about the nature of a good program to serve these objectives. One provocative series of proposals for physical education throughout the total period of schooling below college is presented in Ann E. Jewett's " 'Would You Believe' Public Schools 1975." Planning for her hypothetical high school program aimed for: (1) understanding and appreciation of human movement; (2) physical fitness; and (3) lifetime sports competence. The final section of the article describes the three corresponding elements of the program. Among the interesting proposals inviting reactions are those for individual programming of all students, 80 percent participation in either intramural or scholastic sports or both, and the various options for students.

The arts, too, have frequently lost ground to the academic subjects, although counterreaction to the forces of science and technology in the 1960s saw heightened interest in these fields. The author of the selection describing the changing emphases and practices in the arts, Barbara Leondar, prefaces her treatment of "The Arts in Alternative Schools: Some Observations" with the acid comment that, "The state of the arts in the public schools is even more deplorable than the state of everything else." Actually the practices she describes are believed by the present writer to be operating in some public high schools and to be of potential use in others. Leondar is somewhat disillusioned as to the provisions of the aternative schools for the arts: "For the most part the arts are withering in alternative schools, decisively in secondary though less irrevocably in elementary schools." And so she really describes "alternative programs in the arts" that might be found either in or out of schools, traditional or alternative. The four approaches to which most of her article is devoted are the open studio, the artist as schoolteacher, the student as apprentice, and the student as teacher.

For a decade or more interdisciplinary humanities courses have been offered in many high schools as an approach to more emphasis on the humanities. Charles R. Keller, author of the selection presented on these courses, subtitled the article "a needed challenge to the present separate-subject dominated high school curriculum." His article calls for substantial reorganization of the high school to make it a "liberal arts" school that would be "comprehensive—all subjects for all kinds of students" and would emphasize "release, inquiry, and discovery instead of restraint, rote memory, and regurgitation." Something more of Keller's point of view came in his March 1971 letter of permission to use his article, where he stated: "I have moved in my thinking from humanistic courses and programs to humanized education." The article indicates that he really did not have very far to go; note his argument for change in the high school, a change that would be "more in spirit than in organization": "Just when they (adolescents) yearn to be treated as individuals, they are herded together as never before. Just when they need small, flexible, intellectual communities, they too frequently end up doing the lockstep."

During the late 1960s an upsurge of concern about minority races and pressures from minority student groups, especially blacks, created black studies programs in many high schools as well as colleges and universities. Two selections from *The Journal of Negro Education* include an editorial commentary and a survey of the movement by the NAACP. These selections document some of the confusion in this movement, and also emphasize the need for clarity of purposes and research on the relative effectiveness of various programs.

A survey by *Education U.S.A.* provides the data for the article, "What's Happening Now in Sex Education." This also highly controversial curriculum area has been periodically debated and attempted for many years, but the waves of sexual permissiveness, venereal disease, premarital pregnancies, earlier marriages, divorce, and related problems stimulated many new approaches and programs in family life and sex education in the late 1960s. Various activities and programs in states, cities, and counties are briefly described in this article. Note that many of these begin in the elementary school years; some have a sequence from elementary through the senior high school. The many recent books and articles in both popular and professional journals on sex education provide an interesting body of source material for interested students.

Another old problem that became very acute was drug abuse in high schools, colleges, universities, as well as American society as a whole, which seemed almost commonplace by the end of the 1960s. As Robert Elliott points out in the selection on drug problems and education, "narcotics education is not a new responsibility which has suddenly been thrust upon us"; at least 43 states require instruction in narcotics, alcohol, and tobacco. What was new for the high schools was the greatly increased number of drug experimenters and addicts among their students, and the inclusion among the users of youth from a much wider social spectrum along with the concomitant greatly increased pressure on schools to educate against this vicious development. Elliott, viewing the problem as a school administrator in a suburban school district, offers his analysis of "Why drugs?" and proposes the essentials of an educational program. He stresses the importance of a total program of health education that should attack not only drug use, but other problems such as venereal disease, mental illness, air and water pollution, population increase, human survival, and moral and ethical values.

CAREER EDUCATION NOW*

Sidney P. Marland, Jr.

Since I intend to devote a major part of my remarks today to the subject of career education, it seems appropriate to begin by mentioning that I am finding my new job to be a richly rewarding learning experience.

Take the matter of the Commissioner's place in the Washington pecking order. I have always held the commissionership to be one of the great and auspicious positions in the Federal Government. So naturally, when I learned that a prominent Federal official is issued a brand new $30,000 bulletproof limousine each year, I immediately inquired into the nature of the transportation furnished to the Commissioner of Education.

It turned out to be rather basic—a small, misshapen, used Rebel. When I asked for an improvement, I was sent a slightly newer, small, misshapen, used Rambler.

I am not discouraged. I am merely chastened. It's really a very nice car. And, besides, I have been assured that the Commissioner hardly ever gets shot at.

Career education is an absorbing topic at the Office of Education lately. In essence we are attempting to answer a very large question: what is right and what is wrong with vocational education in America today and what can be done to build on our strengths and eliminate our weaknesses?

I will indicate to you in a few moments the major points of our reply, the steps we believe should be taken by the Federal Government and particularly by the Office of Education to strengthen your hand in refashioning the vocational or career curriculum. For we are in whole-hearted agreement that it is in serious need of reform and it is my firm intention that vocational education will be one of a very few major em-

---

* An address at the 1971 Convention of the National Association of Secondary School Principals, Houston, Tex., January 23, 1971; copy supplied by the Commissioner's Office for inclusion in this anthology.

phases of the U.S. Office, priority areas in which we intend to place the maximum weight of our concentrated resources to effect a thorough and permanent improvement.

But let me broaden the discussion a bit at this point to talk about career education not simply from the Federal point of view but from the point of view of you and me and of everyone who has committed his life's work to the proposition that education's prime task is to seek and to free the individual's precious potential. My concern with this vital area of education was with me long before I came into possession of my bent Rambler. It is the result of more than 30 years in school life, ample time to observe the vocational education problem in such diverse settings as New York City, Pittsburgh, and Winnetka, Illinois. For even in Winnetka, archetypal suburb, blessed in material things far above most communities in this country, there are many people who are worried about the logic and relevance of what is being taught their youngsters, particularly when considered in the light of the amazingly sophisticated, complex, and rapidly changing career situations they will face upon graduation from high school or from college.

Winnetkans, like most Americans, ask: what are we educating our children for?

Educators, it seems to me, have too often answered: we simply are not sure.

Uncertainty is the hallmark of our era. And because many educators have been unsure as to how they could best discharge their dual responsibility to meet the student's needs on the one hand, and to satisfy the country's infinite social and economic appetites on the other, they have often succumbed to the temptation to point a God-like finger at vocational educators and damn them for their failure to meet the Nation's manpower requirements and doubly damn them for their failure to meet the youngster's career requirements, not to mention his personal fulfillment as a human being.

Most of you are secondary school administrators. You, like me, have been preoccupied most of the time with college entrance expectations. Vocational-technical education has been a second-level concern. The vocational education teachers and administrators have been either scorned or condemned and we have been silent.

There is illogic here as well as a massive injustice. How can we blame vocational educators for the hundreds of thousands of pitifully incapable boys and girls who leave our high schools each year when the truth is that the vast majority of these youngsters have never seen the inside of a vocational classroom? They are the unfortunate inmates, in most instances, of a curriculum that is neither fish nor fowl, neither truly vocational nor truly academic. We call it general education. I suggest we get rid of it.

Whatever interest we represent, Federal, State, or local, whether we teach or administer, we must perforce deny ourselves the sweet solace of knowing the other fellow is in the wrong. We share the guilt for the generalized failure of our public system of education to equip our people to get and hold decent jobs. And the remedy likewise depends upon all of us. As Dr. Grant Venn said in his book, *Man, Education, and Manpower*: "If we want an educational system designed to serve each individual and to develop his creative potential in a self-directing way, then we have work to do and attitudes to change."

The first attitude that we should change, I suggest, is our own. We must purge ourselves of academic snobbery. For education's most serious failing is its self-induced, voluntary fragmentation, the strong tendency of education's several parts to separate from one another, to divide the entire enterprise against itself. The most grievous example of these intramural class distinctions is, of course, the false dichotomy between things academic and things vocational. As a first step, I suggest we dispose of the term vocational education, and adopt the term career education. Every young person in school belongs in that category at some point, whether engaged in preparing to be a surgeon, a brick layer, a mother, or a secretary.

How absurd to suggest that general knowledge for its own sake is somehow superior to *useful* knowledge. "Pedants sneer at an education that is useful," Alfred North Whitehead observed. "But if education is not useful," he went on to ask, "What is it?" The answer, of course, is that it is nothing. All education is career education, or should be. And all our efforts as educators must be bent on preparing students either to become properly, usefully employed immediately upon graduation from high school or to go on to further formal education. Anything else is dangerous nonsense. I propose that a universal goal of American education, starting now, be this: that every young person completing our school program at grade 12 be ready to enter higher education or to enter useful and rewarding employment.

Contrary to all logic and all expediency, we continue to treat vocational training as education's poor cousin. We are thereby prepetuating the social quarantine it has been in since the days of the ancient Greeks, and, for all I know, before then. Since the original vocational fields were defined shortly before World War I as agriculture, industry, and homemaking, we have too often taught those skills grudgingly—dull courses in dull buildings for the benefit of what we all knew were young people somehow pre-judged not fit for college as though college were something better for everyone. What a pity and how foolish, particularly for a country as dependent upon her machines and her technology as America. The ancient Greeks could afford such snobbery at a time when a very short course would suffice to instruct a man how to imitate a beast of burden. We Americans might even have been able to afford it a half-century ago when a boy might observe the full range of his occupational expectations by walking beside his father at the time of plowing, by watching the farmers, blacksmiths, and tradesmen who did business in his home town.

But how different things are today and how grave our need to reshape our system of education to meet the career demands of the astonishingly complex technological society we live in. When we talk of today's career development, we are not talking about blacksmithing. We are talking about the capacity of our people to sustain and accelerate the pace of progress in this country in every respect during a lifetime of learning. And nothing less.

The question seems to be fairly simple, if we have the courage and creativity to face it: Shall we persevere in the traditional practices that are obviously *not* properly equipping fully half or more of our young people, or shall we immediately undertake the reformation of our entire secondary education in order to position it properly for maximum contribution to our individual and national life?

I think our choice is apparent. Certainly continued indecision and preservation of the status quo can only result in additional millions of young men and women leaving our high schools, with or without benefit of diploma, unfitted for employment, unable or unwilling to go on to college, and carrying away little more than an enduring distaste for education in any form, unskilled and unschooled. Indeed, if we are to ponder thoughtfully the growing charge of "irrelevance" in our schools and colleges, let us look sharply at the abomination known as general education.

Of those students currently in high school, only three out of 10 will go on to academic college-level work. One-third of those will drop out before getting a baccalaureate degree. That means that eight out of 10 present high school students should be getting occupational training of some sort. But only about two of those eight students are, in fact, getting such training. Consequently, half our high school students, a total of approximately 1,500,000 a year, are being offered what amounts to irrelevant, general educational pap!

In pained puzzlement they toil at watered-down general algebra, they struggle to recollect the difference between adjectives and adverbs, and they juggle in their minds the atomic weight of potassium in non-college science. The liberal arts and sciences of our traditional college-preparatory curriculum are indeed desirable for those who want them and can use them. But there must be desire and receptivity, and for millions of our children, we must concede, such knowledge is neither useful nor joyful. They do not love it for its own sake and they cannot sell it in the career marketplace. Small wonder so many drop out, not because they have failed, but because we have failed them. Who would not at the earliest convenient and legal moment leave an environment that is neither satisfying, entertaining, or productive? We properly deplore the large numbers of young men and women who leave high school before graduation. But, in simple truth, for most of them dropping out is the most sensible elective they can choose. At least they can substitute the excitement of the street corner for the more obscure charms of general mathematics.

I want to state my clear conviction that a properly effective career education requires a new educational unity. It requires a breaking down of the barriers that divide our educational system into parochial enclaves. Our answer is that we must blend our curricula and our students into a single, strong secondary system. Let the academic preparation be balanced with the vocational or career program. Let one student take strength from another. And, for the future hope of education, let us end the divisive, snobbish, destructive distinctions in learning that do no service to the cause of knowledge, and do no honor to the name of American enterprise.

It is terribly important to teach a youngster the skills he needs to live, whether we call them academic or vocational, whether he intends to make his living with a wrench, or a slide rule, or folio editions of Shakespeare. But it is critically important to equip that youngster to live his life as a fulfilled human being. As Secretary Richardson said, "I remind you that this department of government more than anything else is concerned with humaneness."

Ted Bell, now Deputy Commissioner for School Systems in OE, made the point particularly well in a recent speech to a student government group. He was speculating on the steps a young person needs to take not just to get a diploma or a degree today, but to make reasonably sure he will continue to learn in the years ahead, to be an educated man or woman in terms of the future, a personal future.

Dr. Bell said:

> Here the lesson is for each person to develop a personal plan for lifelong learning: learning about the world we live in, the people that inhabit it, the environment—physical and social—that we find around us; learning about the sciences, the arts, the literature we have inherited and are creating; but most of all, learning the way the world's peoples are interacting with one another. If one educates himself in these things, he will have a pretty good chance of survival and of a good life.

In other words, life and how to live it is the primary vocation of all of us. And the ultimate test of our educational process, on any level, is how close it comes to preparing our people to be alive and active with their hearts, and their minds, and, for many, their hands as well.

True and complete reform of the high school, viewed as a major element of overall preparation for life, cannot be achieved until general education is completely done away with in favor of contemporary career development in a comprehensive secondary education environment. This is our ultimate goal and we realize that so sweeping a change cannot be accomplished overnight, involving as it does approximately 30 million students and billions of dollars in public funds. Until we can recommend a totally new system we believe an interim strategy can be developed entailing four major actions:

First we are planning major improvements in the vocational education program of the Office of Education. This program, as you know, involves the expenditure of nearly $500,000,000 annually and our intention is to make the administrative and programmatic changes that will enable the States to use this money to make their vocational education efforts more relevant to the needs of the young people who will spend their lives in careers in business and industry. We intend to give the States new leadership and technical support to enable them to move present programs away from disproportionate enrollments in low-demand occupations to those where national shortages exist and where future national needs will be high.

Right now State training programs fill only half the jobs available each year. The other half are filled by job seekers with no occupational job training of any kind. We do better in some fields than others, of course, particularly production agriculture where we are able to come closer to meeting the total need because it is a relatively static job market with little growth projected. About 70 percent of the demand in farm jobs will be met with trained help this year compared with only about 38 percent in the health occupations and 35 percent in various technical fields. This is nice if you happen to own a farm, not so nice if you run a hospital or laboratory.

We obviously require greater emphasis on such new vocational fields as computer programmers and technicians, laser technicians, and jet mechanics. We particularly need qualified people in health occupations such as certified laboratory technologists, dental assistants, occupational therapists, and the like. And, of course, we badly need men and women to capably service the rapidly growing environmental industries. Though when we speak of new occupations it is always useful to remind ourselves that even some of the newest, such as computer programming, for example, will very likely be obsolete in 20 years or so, affirming once again the need for a sound educational base underlying *all* specific skill training.

Second—here I speak of all cooperating agencies of education and government—we must provide far more flexible options for high school graduates to continue on to higher education or to enter the world of work rather than forever sustain the anachronism that a youngster must make his career choice at age 14. This demands that we broaden today's relatively narrow vocational program into something approaching the true career education we would eventually hope to realize. Vocational students need much more than limited specific skills training if they are to go on to post-secondary education, whether at the community college or four-year level. And young people presently drifting in the general education wasteland need realistic exposure to the world of work, as well as to the option of general post-secondary schooling.

Third, we can effect substantial improvement in vocational education within current levels of expenditures by bringing people from business, industry, and organized labor, who know where the career opportunities are going to be and what the real world of work is like, into far closer collaboration with the schools. Eventually, further subsidies or other encouragement to industry to increase cooperative education and work-study could greatly enhance these programs. Efforts should be made by people in educational institutions offering occupational courses to get nearby employers to help in the training. This will not only aid the students but employers as well by providing these cooperating firms a ready supply of skilled workers well prepared for the specific demands of their particular fields. I would add only this caveat: that these work experience arrangements be accepted and operated as genuine educational opportunities, of a laboratory nature, not simply as a source of cheap help for the business and pocket money for the student. Youngsters should be given the opportunity to explore eight, ten, a dozen occupations before choosing the one pursued in depth, consistent with the individual's ambitions, skills, and interests.

Fourth, we must build at all levels—federal, state, and local—a new leadership and a new commitment to the concept of a career education system. For we require leaders willing to move our schools into more direct and closer relationships with society's problems, opportunities, and its ever-changing needs. I believe these leaders will come primarily from the ranks of organizations such as yours. Not only will the present vocational-technical education leaders be partners in change, but general educators, long dedicated to the old ways, must become new champions of the career program.

In closing, a word about two very promising OE efforts to help strengthen vocational-technical education in its most crucial aspect, personnel.

The teacher is by far the most important factor in the school environment. We all know this. And we also know that voc-ed teachers are in seriously short supply.

We are also keenly aware that vocational-technical education is starved for other critical personnel, especially those qualified to develop and administer productive programs.

The first effort, called Leadership Development Awards, is a doctoral-fellowship program under the Education Professions Development Act. It seeks to identify and train a cadre of leaders for the vocational-technical career education field. As an initial move we have made the first group of awards to 160 experienced vocational educators to enable them to undertake full-time study at the doctoral level.

These men and women are attending 11 universities which share an emphasis on career education. These institutions pay special attention to the needs of the disadvantaged and handicapped; they cooperate closely with industry, the States, and the local districts; and they have established close working relationships with the surrounding communities.

Training lasts from two to three years. It is not tied to the campus but is essentially an intensive internship program with opportunities for research and exploration into the complexities of our constantly changing occupational structure.

We believe these doctoral candidates will make a very constructive imprint on the world of career education. But they will not be cast adrift upon graduation to search out their own niche in that world. Their home States will develop plans for the most strategic use of their skills—in colleges and universities which prepare career educators, in State departments of vocational education, in community colleges, and at the local level for development of the entirely new approach school systems must take to career education.

Our second effort is a program, already producing impressive results, to help the States attract and train teachers and administrators in vocational-technical education. The Leadership Development Awards I have described will produce the shapers and developers of the new career education; this second effort will produce the teachers to carry out the realistic and contemporary plans and programs they develop.

We are funding a variety of State plans. The money is helping to train personnel to work with the disadvantaged and the handicapped, to develop innovative and effective methods of exchange between teachers and businessmen, and to design and carry out more effective vocational guidance, a particularly crucial area. The funds are also being used to increase the number of trades and industry teachers in the emerging occupations that I spoke of a few moments ago.

The overriding purpose of this program is to encourage the States to develop their own capacities and their own resources to produce vocational-technical teachers in the numbers we need and of a quality we need. This new blood will energize career education, particularly in our city schools, whose revitalization is certainly education's first order of business.

President Nixon put the matter well when he said, "When educators, school boards, and government officials alike admit that they have a great deal to learn about the way we teach, we will begin to climb the up staircase toward genuine reform."

We have, I believe, begun to climb that staircase. We have begun, at least in part, the difficult, continuing work of reform. These recent tumultuous years of challenge and strife and all-encompassing change have given us lessons to learn, especially lessons in humility. But they have also taught us to hope and to act. The actions in vocational education and teacher education that I have outlined to you today are but the first in a series of reforms which I intend to initiate and carry out within the U.S. Office of Education. I solicit your reactions to what I have said for I particularly want to bridge the gulf between the Federal Government and the education leaders in the States, in the communities, indeed, in all the classrooms of America.

With a guarantee of your tolerance and support I will return to Washington and my new duties confident that the absolute need to develop a strong new program of career education is well understood by you who must understand it, that you and I agree on the kind of action that must be taken and the urgency of taking it. I respect and salute your capacity to reform the secondary schools of the land. In sum, the schools are engaged in swift change because you the educators have chosen to change them. The schools, I conclude, are in good hands.

VOCATIONAL CURRICULUM DEVELOPMENT*

Although a discouraging number of American schools still have industrial arts classes hammering out copper ashtrays or building a set of bookshelves, exciting things are beginning to happen in Voc Ed curriculums. Here is a random sampling of the new developments in vocational curriculums:

Postsecondary curriculum guides in 19 vocational areas are under

* Reprinted by special permission, from *Vocational Education,* an *Education U.S.A.* special report. Washington, D.C.: National School Public Relations Association, 1971, pp. 36–41.

development by 18 educational agencies in 14 states under 1970–1971 grants for curriculum development. When completed, the guides will be in the public domain for any public or private school to use in developing new postsecondary programs or updating existing ones. Some of the subjects being covered and the institutions undertaking the project include:

A Curriculum Guide in Air Traffic Control and Advisory Technology (Miami-Dade Junior College, Miami, Fla.)

Two-Year Post-High School Curriculum for Teacher Aides (New York University, New York, N.Y.)

Pediatric Assistant Program Development Guide (University of Iowa, Iowa City)

A Curriculum Guide in Air Pollution Technology (Santa Fe Junior College, Gainesville, Fla.)

A Curriculum Guide in Law Enforcement (University Research Corporation, Washington, D.C.)

Radiologic Technology—A Two-Year Post-High School Curriculum (St. Louis Junior College District, Clayton, Mo.)

Curriculum Guide for Urban Development Assistants (Essex Community College, Baltimore, Md.)

Cooperative Occupational Education Programs for Small Schools (University of Nebraska, Lincoln)

Aeronautical science course for high schools has been developed by California educators, and the 285-page illustrated course outline covers 11 units teachers can use to establish aviation and space programs in science classes. The outline is available for $2.25 from the Superintendent of Documents, Government Printing Office, Washington, D.C. 20402 (Order #TD 4.8:Ae8).

Airport and airline operations curriculum is being developed in connection with a unique new high school scheduled to open in New York in the fall of 1971. An existing high school near John F. Kennedy International Airport is being modernized for reopening as a comprehensive high school stressing airline occupations (pre-pilot training, pre-stewardess training, air traffic control, meteorology, purchasing, ticket sales, executive management). New York City's schools already include Aviation High School, which prepares students for aircraft maintenance jobs.

Nautical occupations are covered in several innovative Voc Ed programs in locations where such occupations are an important part of the economy.

The Gateway Borough School District, Ketchikan, Alaska, has a Sea Education program for grades 10–12, which was established with Elementary and Secondary Education Act Title III funds. Sea Ed (which won one of the 1970 National School Boards Awards sponsored by the Association of Classroom Teachers and Thom McAn Shoe Co.) features field experience trips in a 50-foot former Coast Guard boat owned by the district and in a leased fishing vessel. Tenth-graders take marine biology and a maritime-related English course; eleventh-graders cover piloting, electronic navigation devices, fish harvesting, engine trouble shooting, hydraulics, refrigeration, small business management, and navigation-related math; twelfth-graders select from specialized options which include seamanship, marine electronics, and power mechanics. Sea Ed began in 1967; the 1970 graduates all had jobs waiting for them.

Sea Resources Inc., a nonprofit corporation formed by citizens concerned about declining commercial fishing at Ilwaco, Wash., was instrumental in organizing a program which involves two local school districts— Ocean Beach and Naselle-Grays River—and Washington State's Coordinating Council for Occupational Education. Sea Resources has its own fish hatchery and a fishing boat. Eleventh- and twelfth-graders receive training in commercial and sport fishing, fish culture, seamanship, navigation, marine hull design, and engine repair and maintenance. The student-operated hatchery has already released 50,000 baby chum salmon (which will return to the Ilwaco area in two to three years) and is holding another 330,000 for additional release.

For further information, contact the Washington State Coordinating Council for Occupational Education, P.O. Box 248, Olympia, Wash. 98501.

Industrial Arts Curriculum Project, supported by USOE funds and headquartered at Ohio State University, is converting junior high industrial arts shops into laboratories for today's world of work. A two-year curriculum has been developed. The first part, "The World of Construction," was field tested in a handful of schools in 1967 and is now used by more than 300 schools; the second part, "The World of Manufacturing," is being readied for introduction into schools in 1971.

In "The World of Construction," junior high students actually tackle a "home building" project and take it through planning, technology, and management phases. They learn about purchasing land, surveying, clearing, and grading it. In five-member work groups, they construct an actual 4' x 4' building corner, including cement footings, wood framing, flooring, plumbing, insulation, siding, heating and cooling ducts, and roofing. When the project is done, the house is "sold" so that students learn about deeds and property title transfers. Each student's final project is to design his "dream house."

In "The World of Manufacturing," students devise production and assembly lines to construct such items as a small wooden rocket, a wooden land assault vehicle powered by a carbon dioxide cartridge, a buzzer burglar alarm, and a screwdriver with a plastic handle. The final project, combining all of the skills they have learned, involves production of high-intensity desk lamps. Experience thus far indicates cost of installing the Industrial Arts Project is about $40 per pupil the first year, $10 per student in subsequent years.

For further information, contact the Director, Industrial Arts Curriculum Project, Ohio State University, 1712 Neil Ave., Columbus, Ohio 43210.

Hughson (Calif.) Union High School is operating a curriculum designed for total integration of vocational and academic education, using several "learning management systems." In an individually prescribed instruction approach, each student spends 20% of his school time in large group instruction, 40% in small group instruction, and 40% in independent study. A nongraded approach is used, and students proceed at their own rate. There are no failures (a student simply recycles through a unit if he needs additional work). Results, according to "A Policy and System of California Vocational Education," have been spectacular: "The dropout rate has been reduced from 30% to two dropouts in two years; 13 previous dropouts have returned to school. . . . The continuation school, for those who had gotten out of step in the regular school program, has been closed. Hughson is now taking dropouts from Turlock and Modesto. The percentage of the student body pursuing post-high school education has increased from about half to about 70%. . . . Approximately one-third of the terminal high school graduates are presently employed in jobs directly related to their major emphasis in school."

Quincy (Mass.) Vocational-Technical School features an experimental, student-controlled curriculum providing individualized instruction that allows the student to move up a skill ladder in his chosen career field at his own pace. The instructional program is the result of a 1965 grant awarded to the Quincy Public Schools and American Institutes of Research by USOE's National Center for Educational Research and Development (NCERD). The development—know as Project ABLE—began with a study of the Quincy employment market, then built the more than 250 occupations identified into curriculum clusters. Eleven programs were constructed: business education, computer data processing, electro-electronics, foods preparation, general piping, general woodworking, graphic and commercial arts, health occupations, home economics, metals and machines, and power mechanics. All include career guidance elements. The entering student's first week is devoted to an intensive orientation session with the teacher. The many study units available are explained, and the student then chooses which units he wants to take. As he completes a unit, he is checked individually by the teacher. If he passes, he posts his success by hanging a chip beside his name on a bulletin board. At whatever point he leaves the program, he has some marketable skills, but the student understands that the higher he moves on the career ladder, the better will be his employment opportunities.

An interesting aspect of Project ABLE is that the physical facilities were being designed and erected at the same time the curriculum development was taking place. Built to meet a critical need for more high school space, the Vocational-Technical School was constructed as an extension of Qunicy High School. The result is a flexible four-story instructional space, with 43,500 square feet of unobstructed area per floor (all interior walls are demountable). The technical school contains a modern library shared with students from Quincy High; and the two physical plants are interconnected by a bridge. Also shared are auditorium and gym facilities. One recent traffic count on the bridge registered 3600 crossings in one day, indicating a genuine linkage between the academic and Voc Ed programs.

For further information, contact the Quincy Public Schools, 70 Coddington St., Quincy, Mass. 02169.

The Work Opportunity Center (WOC) of the Minneapolis (Minn.) Public Schools goes a step further, being a school that takes pains not to look or operate like one. Recognized in 1970 as one of a handful of outstanding exemplary projects by USOE and the President's National Advisory Council on Supplementary Centers, WOC was begun in 1966 with an educational research grant from NCERD. It has also been supported with funds from the Vocational Education Act, Title III of the Elementary and Secondary Education Act, and Minnesota State Department of Education. Housed in a downtown building which was once a Masonic hall, WOC is one of a growing number of experimental institutions designed to "turn on" 16- to 21-year-old school dropouts and potential dropouts and provide them with marketable skills. It appears to be working at WOC, where 3300 young people have been graduated since 1966 and where, in the words of a counselor, many students say that "WOC is where school started to make sense." Students' programs are highly individualized, and there is a built-in reward system. The student can enter at any time, attend as many hours per day as his time and inclinations dictate, and move through the vocational education programs at his own pace. Grading is on a "pass-fail" basis, but nobody fails—some just take longer to complete programs than others. High school credit is given for successful completion.

Students get redeemable 10¢ coupons for attending class and completing assignments, and the coupons are good at WOC's cafeteria, dry cleaning establishment, and service station. Student achievements are posted on bulletin boards throughout the center. Instruction is provided in electronics and electricity, small engine repair, machine work, office skills, home economics, health care, marketing and merchandising, food service, and auto mechanics and service station occupations (in an operating station leased by WOC and operated at a profit). There's a free lending library stacked with magazines and paperbacks, and students can keep the books if they want them (most read and return them). In one of the newer components, WOC is now providing part-time instruction for junior high-level students identified for help under Milwaukee's dropout prevention program.

For further information, contact the Work Opportunity Center, Minneapolis Public Schools, 807 N.E. Broadway, Minneapolis, Minn. 55413.

Department of Defense Instructional Materials are being made accessible to teachers by a Northwestern Regional Educational Laboratory (NWREL) project. Noting that military services have training programs for which many materials have been developed, NWREL investigated their usefulness for schools. An examination of 42,000 transparencies and 500 films used in Navy training revealed 12,000 suitable items. NWREL is now developing index-catalogues in seven vocational areas—auto mechanics, welding, machinist trades, basic electricity, basic electronics, first aid, and marine navigation—for distribution to teachers in NWREL's five-state region. Final phase, with cooperation of the state departments in Alaska, Idaho, Montana, Oregon, and Washington, is to establish clearinghouses for the catalogued materials.

For further information, contact the Project Coordinator, Dept. of Defense Instructional Materials, NWREL, 400 Lindsay Building, Portland, Oreg. 97204.

Taking an even more comprehensive look at military approaches to instruction was a project undertaken through a grant from USOE's National Center for Educational Research and Development (NCERD) by the Aerospace Education Foundation. Using Utah as a laboratory, the project tested whether complete Air Force instructional programs are usable in schools to teach occupational subjects. The Utah project began in 1967, using three Air Force courses from areas identified as high demand occupations in Utah. A 90-hour segment from the Standardized Electronics Principles Course was tested at Weber State College (Ogden), Dixie College (St. George), Utah Technical College (Provo and Salt Lake City), and Jordan High School (Salt Lake City). A 60-hour unit of the Aircraft Pneudraulic Course was used at Utah State University (Logan), and a 20-hour segment from the Medical Service Specialist Course was tried at Utah Technical College in a nurse's aide program.

In each, some students were given the military courses exactly as they are presented to Air Force personnel, while others were given the programs modified somewhat with conventional school instructional approaches. Teachers found they had to make some radical changes in instructional techniques to adapt to the Air Force approach, which makes extensive use of audiovisual and programmed materials and which is tightly structured to produce specific job skills. Conclusions from the project are that the Air Force materials can be adapted with good educational results by civilian schools, that their acceptance by students improves if they are modified from the strict job-orientation approach, and that use of Air Force techniques can shorten the required length of programs. For further information, contact the Aerospace Education Foundation, 1717 Pennsylvania Ave., N.W., Washington, D.C. 20015.

Emerging occupations are being met in new postsecondary programs all over the country by both technical-vocational schools and community or junior colleges. Just two of the 1970 issues of the monthly *Occupational Education Bulletin*, published by the American Association of Junior Colleges (1 Dupont Circle, N.W., Washington, D.C. 20036), included listings of these new programs:

Natural Resources Conservation (Dutchess Community College, Poughkeepsie, N.Y. 12601)
Human Services (Monroe Community College, Rochester, N.Y. 14623)
Fire Science Technology (Ohio Mechanics Institute Evening College, Cincinnati, Ohio 45210)
Organization and Administration of the Small Business (Meramec Community College, St. Louis, Mo. 63122)
Conservation and Outdoor Recreation (Wabash Valley College, Mt. Carmel, Ill. 62863)
Environmental Control Technology, Waste Water and Water Treatment (Waubonsee Community College, Sugar Grove, Ill. 60554)
Rehabilitative Medicine Assistants (North Shore Community College, Beverly, Mass. 01915)
Nuclear Medicine (Hillsborough Junior College, Tampa, Fla. 33622)
Computer Troubleshooters (Broward Junior College, Fort Lauderdale, Fla. 33314)
Radiology Training (Mesa College, San Diego, Calif. 92111)
Chemical (alcoholism and drug) Dependency Counselors (Metropolitan State Junior College, Minneapolis, Minn. 55403)
Respiratory Therapy (Weber State College, Ogden, Utah 34403).

Health occupations are included among 10 experimental projects funded for a total of more than $5 million by USOE's National Center for Educational Research and Development. One, a massive four-year, $2 million project headed by Melvin L. Barlow of the University of California-Los Angeles, is designing new courses and techniques for about 40 medical and dental jobs. One experiment involves development of a completely new occupation—ward manager, a person to relieve nurses of administrative and housekeeping tasks. Another is developing common core courses for several health programs, including dental assistant, hygienist, and lab technician. The Technical Education Research Center (Cambridge, Mass.) is devising curriculums in nuclear-medical, biomedical, and electro-optical technologies.

Hospitality occupations will get realistic treatment in the Tri-County Joint Vocational District in southern Ohio, which is constructing its own hotel-motel at Nelsonville as a vocational training facility. Funds for the $1.3 million project are coming from the Vocational Education Act, Appalachian Regional Commission, and revenue bonds. When it opens in the fall of 1971, the hotel-motel will serve as a training site for 400 student employees, including both adults (who will get classroom work at the hotel) and high school students who will take their schools' academic subjects half days and train at the hotel the other half.

"WOULD YOU BELIEVE" PUBLIC SCHOOLS 1975*

Ann E. Jewett

At the outset, it is important to recognize that we are not a wealthy school district, but a rapidly growing one in which a recently established industrial plant with substantial federal contracts has changed the nature of our population and our local economy. I have been employed in Would-You-Believe since June 1969. In the past six years we have built four new schools, two elementary schools, a middle school replacing grades 6 through 9 in our earlier organizational pattern, and a three-year high school, opened less than two years ago. Next year we will have two new physical education positions at the elementary level, one in the new Martin Luther King Elementary School and one in the Eisenhower School which was opened in 1970. We will also need an additional physical educator in one of the middle schools and are replacing one teacher in the high school.

In constructing our newer schools, we have given major emphasis to planning facilitative learning environments. Each of our elementary schools has two indoor areas suitable for group movement activities. One area (circular in the newer buildings) is equipped with a variety of hang-

* Reprinted from *Journal of Health, Physical Education, and Recreation* (March 1971), 42:41–44, by permission.

ing and climbing equipment. We have the usual stall bars, ladders, ropes, stegels, and wall peg boards, but we have also designed many pieces which can be quickly assembled from various combinations of benches, ladders, and balance or hanging bars.

The larger of the two physical education areas is rectangular or square in shape, outfitted with plastic partitioning walls which can be rolled up from the floor to form intersecting solid panels. These transparent panels divide the area into four smaller spaces. The partitions provide firm rebounding surfaces which can be converted from transparent walls into mirrors. The TV monitors, videotape recorders, and sound projection equipment are located in cabinets in the four outside walls where they offer no safety hazard and are protected from damage when not in use.

In planning outdoor areas, we have taken advantage of the different natural settings. We have left trees where this could be done. We have tried to provide each school with a grassy area of uneven terrain as well as a flat all-weather surfaced area. Municipal storehouses and local businessmen have contributed large pieces of equipment for installation on our playgrounds to supplement standard commercial climbing and hanging apparatus. The children have enjoyed participating in contests to decorate the equipment and landscape the areas. Such portable equipment as balls, ropes, bean bags, hoops, canes, tires, nets, and the like are available for both indoor and outdoor use.

We try to provide educational leadership appropriate to 1975. We believe that education at all levels should be value-oriented to increase the pupil's sensitivity and his receptivity to needed social programs, to improve his skills in group relations, and to enhance his creative use of leisure. Our goal remains individualization of instruction, and we rely upon rather sophisticated technological equipment to assist us in accomplishing this objective. Computers compile diagnostic appraisals of the relevant backgrounds, abilities, interests, and learning styles of each child, making it possible for the teacher to propose tentative goals for each student and a program of learning experiences designed to achieve them.

The activity content of our elementary physical education curriculum includes learning modules or short units of progressively greater difficulty in basic movement (locomotor and nonlocomotor) and general body awareness; elements of rhythm, response to rhythmic stimuli, and skills related to creative and folk dance; body management skills of dodging and guarding stationary and moving objects, chasing, tagging, stunts, tumbling, and apparatus; and ball and object handling activities involving striking, throwing, and catching. A wide variety of applications of these specific skills is utilized in the learning situations designed by each teacher.

The elementary schools now view communication as a legitimate core around which to plan the curriculum, so that the various areas of study may contribute to the child's ability to cope with his world on his own terms. Movement experiences in schools have come into their own in the last decade as educators have recognized the crucial role played by movement in self-expression and communication.

The roles of the physical educator in elementary education have shifted. Today's teacher works with groups of children to focus on problems, stimulate movement learning activities, and help establish criteria for solutions to problems. As a member of the teaching team, he may be contributing some television teaching, developing learning programs or videotapes, or writing scripts for learning aids.

A second major role of the teacher is that of tutor-challenger, working with individual children to help them discover their interests, their strengths, and their weaknesses. We rely heavily on self-testing in our elementary school physical education programs. Children do not receive grades but are encouraged to utilize an extensive range of self-evaluative games and devices to assess their own levels of skill achievement, fitness, creativity, and communications effectiveness.

The third role to which we urge all our teachers to give priority is that of learner. In this role the teacher is a learner about learning as he tries to make increasingly successful decisions about how to present material to children or how to encourage children to seek new personalized movement answers. Like his pupils, he struggles to know what he does not know.

The middle school offers a unique challenge to the physical educator. The typical age-range of students is from 11 to 15. Essentially the school is ungraded. For physical education learning, children are grouped according to skill achievement levels in the various areas, but we make more use of groupings which are limited to one sex than we do in either elementary or high school. Our middle school enrollment is not a great deal larger than last year, but we are employing an additional woman in one school and another man in the other school in order to facilitate team teaching, increase individualization of instruction, and provide for much expanded intramural programs and interschool opportunities for the girls. Facilities in our two middle schools are not particularly innovative, except that each has a pool designed especially for flexible instructional use and an indoor track and field area which can be converted to an ice rink.

Middle school physical education has two major elements. We focus (1) on expanding understanding of movement and refining personal skills and (2) on greater depth of social understanding through experiences in movement activities of the student's own and other cultures. We work toward a growing understanding of movement principles through situations emphasizing modifications of environmental media. Aquatic experiences comprise from 20 to 35% of individual programs. Tumbling, gymnastics, trampolining, and diving units are emphasized. Track and field activities are stressed and extended to include outdoor challenges in locomotion, balance, and skillful performance on land surfaces modified by sand, snow, or ice. All students are introduced to ice skating and skiing.

We believe that the middle school organization offers unparalleled opportunities for socialization through the development of team sport and social dance skills. We stress skill development and team strategy in the familiar team games which are popular in the community. We try to ensure that every student also participates in group games which reflect the recreational interests of young people in other societies. Social dance offerings include traditional dances, American square dance, folk dances of many lands, and current popular dance forms. Opportunities for healthful competitive sport and for corecreational social dance are varied and extensive in middle school extraclass programs.

Physical educators for the middle school need to have a commitment to the unique demands of children of this age group and enjoy working with young people who are children one moment and consider themselves adult the next, whose individual needs are as varied as their shapes and sizes. They need to be enthusiastic about guiding children in after-school programs; to feel challenged by participation in team teaching; to be well-skilled in several specialized areas; and to be competent in planning instructional materials utilizing modern technology to facilitate movement concept learning.

Would-You-Believe High School is an exciting place to work. Our facilities are unusually flexible. The emphasis is on the "pod"—or module construction—with simple basic units easily convertible to teaching stations of varying shapes and sizes. We can use a series of small activity areas for as many as 24 individual practice areas or combine two or more such areas to accommodate groups of two to six students. Our students have frequent access to the instructional materials center, which is equipped with facilities for viewing films and videotapes, carrels for independent study assisted by teaching machines, and a growing collection of books, charts, slides, films, recordings, videotapes, and learning programs, selected or developed by members of the physical education staff.

We have a few special purpose areas such as the handball courts, wrestling room, golf cages, and an adapted physical education area. We also make occasional use of a classroom in the vicinity of the physical education areas, but, for the most part, large group instruction is scheduled in the four gymnasiums lined with standard court markings and equipped with movable dividing doors. Our outdoor areas are modest in size and utilize all-weather surfacing or synthetic turfs. We make extensive use of public and private recreational facilities outside the school and limited use of the middle school swimming pools for competitive teams, aquatics clubs, special events, and remedial instruction.

Would-You-Believe High School established modular scheduling several years ago. Current schedules are built on a 20-minute module. Physical education is using two, three, and four-module blocks most frequently. We make limited use of single modules for learning activities which do not require change of attire or for particular purposes which can be accommodated by intra-departmental scheduling. Occasionally we schedule longer time blocks for elective physical education to facilitate such learning opportunities as golfing at the Real World Country Club or skiing at Snowflake Valley.

Five years ago, we survived a series of student protests. It was difficult to identify the real issues among the competing demands for black coaches, interscholastic competition for girls, varsity teams in lacrosse and volleyball, more sports opportunities for under-130-pound boys, free bowling, more basketballs for check-out for recreational use, discontinuance of regulation uniforms, and soft drink and candy machines in the locker rooms. But when the furor subsided, it turned out that what our students were really seeking was a physical education relevant to their needs in a world significantly different from that in which their teachers attended high school.

Fortunately, it was mid-May when our student demonstrations reached their peak. School was closed early and we were able to study our problems in student-faculty-parent groups during the summer. We recognized that some major changes were needed and decided to remodel our entire curriculum on the basis of thoughtful restatements of educational objectives. We employed three consultants to work with small committees in developing objectives for our total program and for the individual curricular areas. Each committee included students and parents as well as faculty members. Administrators and consultants assisted the different committees as requested.

Back in 1970, each area committee was charged with the responsibility of stating objectives which would describe the desired outcomes for each student at graduation and facilitate continuing student evaluation and guidance. The physical education committee recommended three major goals for the graduate of Would-You-Believe High School: (1) understanding and appreciation of human movement, (2) physical fitness, and (3) lifetime sports competence. As in other curricular areas, we tried to give each of our goals sufficient emphasis in a systems approach to individualizing instruction, initiated in September 1970. We have experimented with many variations in curricular patterns and a wide diversity of instructional techniques since then. The physical education curriculum in Would-You-Believe High School today, in 1975, is the result of this ongoing experimentation. We view the 1975 curriculum as subject to continuous development and change.

Our present physical education curriculum has three elements, each corresponding to one of the major goals. Students are expected to demonstrate achievements in each of these areas. The first element offers varied opportunities for developing understanding and appreciation of movement. At the initial curriculum input point, the student participates in an assessment unit during which his status with regard to each area is determined. If he already meets the minimum standards with regard to posture, body mechanics, and intermediate knowledge of movement principles, he may bypass the movement fundamentals review unit or module. He may move directly to another of the program modules in this element: movement as expression and communication, selecting a submodule in choreography or the development of new games or movement forms; or into the movement in society module, selecting a submodule in guiding movement activities of children, leading neighborhood activity programs, planning family physical recreation activities, or movement activities of other societies or particular subcultures.

The second or physical fitness element consists of three modules: muscular strength, cardiorespiratory endurance, and survival aquatics. The student who demonstrates adequate strength and endurance in the assessment unit may bypass the first two modules completely. The student who needs further development of strength or endurance may select submodules in weight training, gymnastics, jogging, circuit training, or track and field. Or he may prefer to move into other sport or activity modules to increase his strength or endurance. Most students complete survival aquatics as ninth-graders, although 20 to 30% of our high school students need additional work in this area. Many can demonstrate proficiency in the entire fitness element.

In the third element, competence in at least two lifetime sports is required of all students for graduation. A short sports orientation module is scheduled for all sophomores, emphasizing the advantages of voluntary participation throughout life, suggesting procedures for planning personal activity programs, and providing information about available curricular choices and competence standards in each sport. The student is then free to select any of the many lifetime sports activities offered at beginning, intermediate, or advanced levels, depending upon his ability level.

All students are individually programed. Except for the initial assessment module, one expressive movement module, one movement in society module, and the lifetime sports orientation module, students may select any activities for which they meet the basic entry qualifications. Physical education is a required sophomore subject; juniors and seniors who have demonstrated the required competence are not required to continue in the physical education curriculum, although most students elect additional units.

All of our classes are coeducational except for a few of the team sport sections and wrestling. Of our students, 80% participate in either in-tramural or scholastic sports or both. We field interscholastic teams in twelve sports for boys and seven for girls, in addition to mixed teams in tennis, golf, badminton, and bowling.

Physical education class instruction in Would-You-Believe High School utilizes a great deal of problem-solving. We encourage students to test different techniques for performing sport skills in order to select those which they can use most effectively. We try to refine concepts of bio-mechanics and exercise physiology through experiences in applying funda-mental movement principles and elementary knowledge of human physiology to new sports activities and specific training challenges. We place a high premium on the aesthetic aspects of movement experience, on expressive applications of movement abilities, and on creative solutions to movement problems.

We have developed numerous instructional models and individual learning programs, especially for the required modules or units. We utilize the videotape recorder and many types of teaching machines for frequent individualization of instruction and self-testing. We schedule many open laboratories for free choice activities and for conducting individual proj-ects. Our staff is working on techniques for evaluating instruction through direct assessment of student responses. All evidence indicates that our 1975 physical education curriculum is far more effective than that of five years ago.

THE ARTS IN ALTERNATIVE SCHOOLS: SOME OBSERVATIONS*

BARBARA LEONDAR

The state of the arts in the public schools is even more deplorable than the state of everything else. Friends of the arts, then, have reason to wel-

* Reprinted from *Journal of Aesthetic Education* (January 1971), 5:75, 77, 81–91, by permission.

come the educational disestablishmentarianism currently astir on the North American continent. Suddenly, from Canada to Mexico, "alternative schools" are ubiquitous. Humanistic in conception, Utopian in outlook, these schools would seem to provide a natural home for the arts. That, at least, was the assumption which led me to visit dozens of such institutions, and to study the manifestos of hundreds more. What follows is an informal account of a year's observations.

"Alternative schools" has become a generic designation encompassing a broad range of experimental institutions, public, private, and denominational. Virtually every major metropolitan school system now supports at least one unconventional school; almost every state and province, even those as educationally recalcitrant as Alabama and Virginia, now claim at least one free school. Thickets of such experiments flourish on both coasts; clusters surround the great university centers of Canada and the American Midwest. But significant numbers, following the lead of earlier Utopians, have retreated from the cities to the open land, to farms, ranches, and wilderness country. Rural or urban, they include Summerhill and Leicestershire variants, community and parent cooperatives, drop-out centers and live-in communes, peripatetic academies and ecological survival institutes. Although such endeavors tend to be aggressively independent, they have nonetheless already spawned a national and several regional information exchanges, a weekly newsletter, a handful of employment centers, and a growing number of producers of avant-garde educational materials.

Because such schools often exist on a shoestring and sometimes vanish as abruptly as they materialized, it is impossible to estimate how many lives they touch—how many children, how many teachers, how many parents. In any case, their interest does not rest on numbers alone, but rather on the influence which they may exert—indeed, *intend* to exert— upon conventional patterns of schooling. Although a few are truly counter-schools, viewing themselves less as alternatives than as rebukes to existing institutions, most regard themselves as harbingers of future mass education. For this reason, although some receive visitors in such numbers as to strain their resources, they continue to entertain with the cordiality of missionaries. Characteristically, then, alternative schools are serious, self-conscious, and principled. They are prepared to resist charges of amateurism or enthusiasm with a set of rational and internally consistent premises from which their practice derives. . . .

Nonetheless, the prospect for the fine arts is not uniformly bleak. Experimental schools sometimes offer real alternatives in aesthetic learning. Although few have attempted to educate students as potential audiences, some have evolved thoughtful, even imaginative, means for encouraging and refining the practice of the arts.[1] And where schools persist in neglecting this task, after-school alternatives—compensatory education for the aesthetically deprived—are emerging. These share the characteristic goals and style of the free school. Whether in school or out, four approaches predominate.

THE OPEN STUDIO

The open studio is exactly what its name implies—a workroom equipped with the tools and materials of one or more of the arts. Som schools will station an instructor or other adult in the studio, but r st eschew supervision on the grounds that an adult presence curtails exploration and encourages dependency. If a teacher is on hand, he is likely to remain inconspicuous, intervening only if summoned or if equipment is egregiously abused. Supervised or not, the open studio remains open to all students throughout the school day and often beyond it. No registrations, authorizations, passes, signatures, or other clerical impedimenta bar the way; the student is free to attend his Muse whenever she beckons.

The open studio has flourished in progressive nursery schools for years and, under the influence of British practice, has become increasingly common in elementary education. Among secondary schools, although still a rarity, it has at least won acceptance as sound practice. And in alert suburbs the open studio has by now become a mandatory feature of new public school construction. Generally it is one element of a more comprehensive system which includes open laboratories and industrial shops; sometimes, unfortunately, it remains the poor relation in that family. Timberlane Regional High School is perhaps not untypical. Built five years ago to serve the five hundred children of four tiny rural communities, none of which had ever boasted a secondary school, Timberlane includes two spacious and well-outfitted open shops for wood and metal work, three superbly equipped open laboratories for biology, chemistry, and physics, and a single crowded art studio. The latter, though nominally open, is scheduled for classes during much of the day, so that its accessibility is substantially reduced. By contrast, the Sanborn Middle School in affluent Concord reserves the entire basement of its two-story plant for the arts. Here, in an architectural setting as elegant as any on the continent, alcoves are equipped for easel painting, for

---

[1] Implicit in this approach (and explicit, too, in the emphasis on learning by doing) is the assumption that potential audiences should be educated by doing what the artist does. Whether this practice also implies, as Dewey argued, that reader and listener are in some sense author and composer *manqué*, re-creating the work in the act of responding to it, is a question schools prefer to ignore.

wood, metal, and clay sculpture, and for pottery, leaving available for elective use a large central space with movable work tables. In a studio of these proportions, two or three classes (limited, as a rule, to ten children) can meet simultaneously without disruption of privacy and without curtailing spontaneous use of the facility by individuals.

Obviously the open studio is best suited to the visual arts. Nowhere is dance popular enough to merit its own space, while music requires rather different arrangements. Creative writing, however, remains a puzzle. Two Newton teachers claim considerable success with a modified version of the open writing lab. Although institutional rules require that students register for and attend the lab, once enrolled they are under no compulsion to write nor will they receive formal instruction in technique. On an ordinary day, perhaps a quarter of the class, gathered in corners or on the fringes of the room, will be otherwise occupied. The rest, sprawled over tables, hunched above typewriters, or strung out on window seats according to their bent, will be in the throes of composition. What they compose is under their own control, as is the amount and kind of assistance they receive. Some students will submit work in progress to a friend or teacher; some will display only finished artifacts. Some seem to want the merest nod of approbation, some a detailed critique, some the applause of the entire group. Although flexible enough to accommodate such diverse preferences, the laboratory setting nonetheless puts the writer on public view, a circumstance which would seem to multiply the psychic discomforts of composition. For the graphic artist, on the other hand, such a milieu seems nourishing. The young observer in the studio can incorporate in the most casual and offhand fashion a rich knowledge of media and technique. His fellows are, as a rule, happy to discuss or to demonstrate. If several students confront related problems, they can constitute themselves an informal class and request appropriate instruction. But perhaps most desirable of all is the opportunity afforded by the open studio to explore at leisure, to pose one's own problems, to fail, if need be, and try again or try another way, always without penalty to the ego or damage to the academic record.

THE ARTIST AS SCHOOLTEACHER

The open studio system abandons formal instruction or at least minimizes it. This, of course, is consistent with the more general goal of reducing constraints and expanding choices. But at the same time it reinforces—or in any case does not ameliorate—the aimlessness and dilettantism which may afflict the free school student. Least of all does it offer him a model on which to pattern his own behavior, or provide him with a sense of the practicing artist as an embodied human being. Adding to these considerations the further one that the practitioner is likely to prove the most ardent advocate of his calling, many schools have sought to attract working artists to their faculties. Estimating the success of such recruiting efforts is precarious, since the distinction between artists-who-teach and teachers-who-paint or act or dance is necessarily a fine one, ultimately decidable only by the practitioner himself. Still, certain patterns emerge.

The most common is one borrowed from university practice—that of the artist-in-residence. In return for work space, and perhaps board and housing, the professional makes himself available to students. He will offer tutelage if requested but, from the school's point of view, his most important function is merely to be visible and, within reason, amiable while doing his own thing. Obviously such an arrangement once again favors the visual and certain of the performing arts, since what the composer or poet does is not readily accessible to observation. Obviously, too, such activity as *is* observable will vary in quality from school to school and, within the school, from month to month, artists being men of disparate talents and uncertain inspiration. Thus, although the Sudbury Valley School numbers among a staff of twelve a musicologist, a painter, a sculptor, and a photographer, a random visit may find the art studio bare, devoid even of signs of recent occupation, while the only music emanates from the stereo set in the smoking room. Even when the artist's activity is prominent, his apparent effect on students may remain negligible. In fact, so perverse are the ways of adolescents that the continuing presence of a practicing artist—his very ordinariness in the school setting—may discourage rather than excite students' interest. Nonetheless, the salutary influence of a devoted professional upon a youthful community can scarcely be discounted. If he never answered a question nor offered an explanation (though it is hard to imagine that happening), his example as a man who takes himself and his work seriously ought to guarantee his welcome.

By contrast, the visiting artist imported into the school for a single performance appears as an exotic and can exert a lively impact. Unfortunately, the impression often conveyed by such visitors is a compound of glamour and mystification, designed to dazzle rather than enlighten. The very conditions of the visit may thrust the artist into the role of entertainer rather than of teacher. Even if he resists the temptation to preserve a professional distance between himself and his audience, his interchange with the numbers of children who will have something to say must necessarily be abbreviated and fragmentary. Still, enlightenment need not be dull, nor communication superficial, provided the artist is himself clear in his intentions. The Arena Stage of Washington represents perhaps the happiest conquest of the hazards of an isolated visit. Veterans of nightly improvisational performances for general audiences, the Arena troupe spends its days in schools and its weekends in teachers' workshops. Experience has taught the troupe to reject engagements shorter than half a day or audiences larger than two hundred. Given this number, each member of the troupe will engage a group of ten children for approximately two hours in the creation of improvised roles and situations around themes suggested by the children themselves. For a final hour the entire group will reconvene so that adults and children together can perform for their fellows. Because the Arena company sees its purpose as teaching children to make dramatic art of their own experience, its members avoid censoring the children's themes. In racially tense Washington where most teachers are white and most students black, theirs could be a disastrous course. Instead, they have learned to coax from the incipient explosion itself the conception of art as a paring and shaping of life, an imposition of coherence on chaos. That they do so without preaching, almost without language itself, is a tribute both to their skill and to their art. Unhappily, the momentary transformation wrought by Arena Stage is rarely sustained by the schools it visits. Though the company may suggest what schools can aspire to, its brief performances cannot, after all, affect children deeply and permanently.

Like Arena Stage, the Teachers and Writers Collaborative of New York sends its members into conventional public schools to offer children an unconventional experience. But unlike the theater company, the Collaborative's teacher returns to his class once a week. He thus maintains continuity while escaping the invisibility which may cloak the resident artist; his arrivals become celebrations interrupting the weekly routine. In fact, he occupies much the same position as the art or music specialist supplied by the school system, with the important difference that he is not a part of the system nor is he a certified teacher. Instead he is likely to be a young poet with a published volume or two to his credit, a growing reputation, and a serious commitment to his craft.

The Collaborative's teachers come into the classroom to help children write poetry. That they succeed, often beyond anyone's predictions, is substantiated anew by each issue of their monthly newsletter, which regularly displays samples of student work. Although suspicious of mechanically applied methods and sceptical, as poets will be, of generalizations, they have nonetheless evolved a loose technique which, in one variation or another, dominates the Collaborative's practice. Its elements will be familiar to readers of Herbert Kohl, a founder of the Collaborative, and to fans of *the New York Review* where Kenneth Koch recently described his classroom adventures:

. . . Rhyme is wonderful, but children generally aren't able to use it skillfully enough to make good poetry. It gets in their way. The effort of finding rhymes stops the free flow of their feelings and associations, and poetry gives way to sing-song. There are formal devices which are more natural to children, more inspiring, easier to use. The one I suggested most frequently was some kind of repetition: the same word or words ("I wish") or the same kind of thing (a comparison) in every line. . . .

A poetry idea should be easy to understand, it should be immediately interesting, and it should bring something new into the children's poems. This could be new subject matter, new sense awareness, new experience of language or poetic form. I looked for other techniques or themes that were, like wishes, a natural and customary part of poetry. I thought of comparisons and then of sounds, and I had the children write a poem about each. As in the Wish Poems, I suggested a repetitive form to help give their poems unity: putting a comparison or a sound in every line.

Some things about teaching children to write poetry I knew in advance, instinctively or from having taught adults, and others I found out in the classroom. Most important, I believe, is taking children seriously as poets. . . . Treating them like poets was not a case of humorous but effective diplomacy, as I had first thought; it was the right way to treat them because it corresponded to the truth. A little humor, of course, I left in. Poetry was serious, but we joked and laughed a good deal; it was serious because it was such a pleasure to write. Treating them as poets enabled me to encourage them and egg them on in a non-teacherish way—as an admirer and fellow worker rather than as a boss.[2]

One clue to the Collaborative's success, manifest in Koch's remarks, is its desanctification of poetry. Koch relieves verse-making of the burden of holiness too often imposed on it by teachers whose reading ceased with Tennyson; he returns the poem to the world of discourse and to the arena of children's immediate concerns. At the same time his attitude is thoroughly practical; he sets forth without preconceptions to find a technique that works, and he tinkers about until he has found it. How much his search is aided by professional intuitions can scarcely be guessed, though they would seem to be crucial. While that fact magnifies the value of his insights for teachers who are not poets, it also underscores an important gap in the Collaborative's procedures. Explanation has been systematically ignored; no attempt has been made to understand, in logical or psychological terms, why one approach works and another fails,

---

[2] "Wishes, Lies, and Dreams: Teaching Children To Write Poetry," *The New York Review*, Vol. 14, No. 7 (April 9, 1970), 18–22.

or even to examine what it means for a technique to "work." Doubtless it is unjust to accuse the Collaborative of slighting a task it never chose to undertake. Yet the neglect of so unique a fund of experience is surely regrettable. What that experience, diligently combed, might reveal about the sources of children's aesthetic capacities, their nature, development, and variation, needs to be known. As long as the Collaborative continues to tinker without conceptualizing, its success must remain local and isolated, unexplained and unexplainable.

THE STUDENT AS APPRENTICE

Both the open lab system and the introduction of professional artists into the classroom imply an acceptance of the school as a world unto itself. An opposing view, however, regards the school as an artificial, sometimes noxious enclave which, by isolating young people from the real business of life, unduly prolongs helplessness and dependency. Some argue further that teachers who merely teach, those whose sole occupation is schoolmastering, will never be taken seriously by adolescents since they lack the authority conferred by genuine achievement. John Holt is among those who have lately arrived at this view:

> . . . What is most truly and deeply nutty about schools and schooling is not the idea that someone decides what and how and when someone else should learn something, or even the idea that all this should be done in a building shut off from the rest of the world, but the idea that learning should or can take place in an institution *that doesn't produce anything but learning.* . . . Any game, or puzzle, or activity, that is not worth the time and attention of the adults will soon be seen by the children as not being worth their time either. No one can get children truly interested in reading, or writing, or whatever it may be, who does not himself do these things regularly, and in their presence, and not for their good and pleasure but for his own.[3]

These two beliefs, taken together, underlie the "school without walls" exemplified by Philadelphia's widely imitated Parkway Program. Parkway has no classrooms of its own. Instead, its students learn science in research labs, mathematics in engineering or insurance offices, and languages in foreign consulates. And of course they study art history in museums, music in recording studios, writing in newspaper offices and television stations. Other smaller schools sometimes apprentice individual students to local master craftsmen. Although particular arrangements vary, there exists a common underlying intention: to evict the arts from

---

[3] *New Schools Exchange Newsletter,* No. 36 (no date), p. 2.

schools, where they are alien and embarrassed, and to send children forth to encounter the artist on his own turf.

Where schools have failed to provide such opportunities, after-school alternatives are emerging. Their appearance is perhaps the newest wrinkle in aesthetic education. Saturday piano lessons are not, of course, strikingly novel; out-of-school instruction has long prevailed as the dominant pattern of training in the arts. But except for a gifted elite, those children lucky enough to discover the arts out of school generally did so under tutors whose accomplishments were pedagogical (or commercial) rather than creative. What is novel, then, is the inauguration of out-of-school centers where serious, committed artists stand ready to initiate children into their crafts. All of these, however, are still too new to permit evaluation. The Cherry Street Studio, for instance, came into existence earlier this spring and for the present remains only a building housing sixty painters, sculptors, and printmakers whose studios are always open to young people. The Voice of Children, a creative writing project, has expanded sufficiently in the last year to contemplate publication of a monthly journal. The Touch-stone Center, an even more ambitious experiment in authorship now getting under way, expects to produce a journal of international children's writing. These endeavors all emanate from New York City, but rumors suggest that their counterparts on the West Coast and elsewhere are already being planned.

Again, it is perhaps unjust to require of a new and precarious enterprise that it add to its other vexations that of systematic analysis and research. Yet fundamental questions need answering, and the day-by-day accumulation of events which might supply those answers may be difficult to recapture in later retrospective study. While the practical goals of these experiments merit applause, they need not preclude, as they now do, the equally worthy purposes of research and evaluation.

THE STUDENT AS TEACHER

Big kids have probably always taught little ones. In primitive societies they may be the primary tutors; in our own popular folklore the role of big brother, though invested with lofty condescension, will also require as its price some tutelary responsibility. Lately a convergence of events has sparked a new interest in the effectiveness of juvenile teachers. Among those events was Dolores Durkin's study of children who learned to read before entering school, a study which found the preschoolers had been instructed by siblings as often as by parents.[4] This discovery had already shaped the practice of some British infant schools where instruction in

---

[4] Dolores Durkin, *Children Who Read Early* (New York: Teachers College Press, 1966).

reading—and in almost everything else—proceeded very informally, relying less on teachers than on the willingness of peers to share their skills.
Again, Ivan Illich has recounted the success of Spanish-speaking Harlem
teenagers in teaching their native language quickly and efficiently to adult
volunteers.[5] And experiments in cross-age tutoring in American public
schools have suggested that tutors learn at least as much as their pupils
from such an experience.

Much of this needs to be said only in order to be dismissed. Peer
teaching in alternative schools—and there is much of it—proceeds from
entirely different motives. It is the product not of a concern with the
efficacy of teaching and learning, but rather the expression of allegiance to
a cause. In fact, its symbolic importance may outweigh its practical effects,
for the student-as-teacher embodies an egalitarian principle high in the
scale of free school values. "All may learn and all may teach," proclaims
one school's brochure, announcing its elimination of distinctions based on
academic rank or achievement. Clearly, unless students are empowered to
teach—and moreover, to teach their teachers—that proclamation will be
hollow.

Proclaiming away all such distinctions, however, does not erase them.
Perhaps it is a tribute to innate human modesty that the student who
chooses to teach is, as a rule, one who has already achieved substantial
competence. Since, in academic subjects, such expertise will be rare, the
young instructor is likely to be teaching a performance skill—typing,
dressmaking, sports, auto repair, or one or another of the arts or crafts.
At the Palfrey Street School in Watertown, an eighteen-year-old painter
of great promise teaches a beginners' class of fellow-students. In an experimental school in Los Angeles, a sixteen-year-old guitarist joins with
a literature teacher to offer a course in poetry and song. At the Murray
Road School in Newton a high school filmmaker receives academic
credit for teaching animation techniques at a nearby junior high. In
many schools, individual tutoring or casual instruction in an open lab has
grown so routine as to attract little notice.

But if in alternative schools and in conventional ones the rationale
for peer teaching differs, its practical effects do not. The most predictable
of these is wretched teaching—wretched, that is, if teaching is valued
for its clarity, logic, and coherence. The young teacher does not begin
at the beginning, does not proceed in sequence, does not define his terms
or explain his assumptions or offer reasons for his judgments. He does
not, in short, lay bare the workings of a mature intellect; patently, he
cannot. Countervailing strengths, however, may offset these shortcomings.

---

[5] Ivan Illich, "Why We Must Abolish Schooling," *The New York Review*, Vol. 15,
No. 1 (July 2, 1970), 12–13.

Not the least of his assets is enthusiasm. Scarcely a substitute for coherence when the instructor is an adult, enthusiasm may nonetheless count importantly in the young teacher. His obvious pleasure in his activity, his eagerness to pursue it despite recurrent and inevitable frustration, his patience and shrewdness, intensity and persistence, all provide that model of discipline and purpose so rare in free schools. Moreover, the young teacher's bumbling may lend his example extra weight: he is not so far ahead of his students that the gap appears forbidding. They rightly see him as one of themselves, distinguished from them by will and perseverance. Some surely must recognize, at least subliminally, the latent presence of those qualities in themselves, and the consequent possibility of a corresponding achievement.

The greater benefits, however, may accrue to the tutor. The worn observation that one learns his subject best by teaching it still nurtures a kernel of truth. Under the questioning of students, the teaching artist must seek words to describe habits, assumptions, and intuitions which lie on the fringes of awareness. He must, however incoherently at first, explain and justify what he is about. In the process of finding language for this peripheral knowledge, he brings it into conscious focus, gains insight into his own procedures, and can alter or refine them voluntarily. He must also begin to formulate his own aesthetic, to demonstrate why *this* is better than *that*, and to support his judgment with reasons sufficient to withstand his pupils' challenges. Assuming that critical self-consciousness is to be desired in the artist, this early training would seem invaluable.

Peer-teaching in the arts is an innovation of a different order from those described above. Less amenable to planning and more dependent on a spontaneous confluence of circumstances, it cannot be programmed into a curriculum. It need not, however, exclude other modes of instruction; in fact, it probably serves best as a supplement to a more nourishing diet. How rich a supplement it is remains to be discovered. Once again, its consequences need to be better understood, if only because it is a style likely to prevail for some time.

A final distinction—between alternative schools on the one hand and, on the other, out-of-school alternative arts programs—perhaps needs to be emphasized. For the most part the arts are withering in alternative schools, decisively in secondary though less irrevocably in elementary schools. Many alternative schools have traded the formalism of conventional institutions for an equally forlorn disorder. Theirs is an extreme response to desperate circumstances. But pessimism would be premature. Lively minds populate both camps; where they have attained influence, reform follows—in the public schools, reform inspired by the experimenters, and in alternative schools, reform stimulated by students' incapacity to bear the burdens of self-determination. But reform is slow, and if despair is unjustified, impatience is not.

Alternative programs in the arts, however, are another matter. Whether operating, like the Teachers and Writers Collaborative, within schools ossified by habit and custom, or like the Cherry Street Studios, entirely outside the system, these approaches bring a new and welcome vitality to the teaching of the arts. Especially heartening is the readiness of practicing artists to bare their mysteries to children. If such programs flourish and multiply, they may yet undo the mischief of generations of schoolmasters.

INTERDISCIPLINARY HUMANITIES COURSES— A NEEDED CHALLENGE TO THE PRESENT SEPARATE-SUBJECT-DOMINATED CURRICULUM*

CHARLES R. KELLER

If young people are to have a lover's query with the world, to paraphrase a line from Robert Frost's poem, "The Lesson for Today," they need to be in liberal arts secondary schools. They need the humanities.

What do I mean by the humanities? The humanities have to do with making man more human. Indeed, one writer has defined the humanities as "those activities that label us as human."

The humanities embrace literature, languages, music, art, philosophy, and history. They acquaint us with the thoughts, creations, and actions of our predecessors and of our contemporaries. They impel us to raise basic questions and to search for answers to them. The study of man's relationship to his natural environment, including himself, brings the social sciences and science into the area of the humanities.

Involvement in the humanities enables us not only to meet the unexpected and unusual in life but also to do something even more difficult —to live day by day with the expected and usual.

The humanistic approach puts man at the center of things, provides him with needed strength outside himself, and gives him confidence that

---

* Reprinted from *Today's Education* (January 1968), 56:19–20, by permission.

men make history. Ralph Waldo Emerson revealed the essence of the humanities when he wrote, "Every revolution was first a thought in one man's mind . . . every reform was once a private opinion."

The appearance of interdisciplinary humanities courses here and there throughout the country is, I believe, one of the most interesting and significant developments in American education. These courses are a needed challenge to the present domination of the curriculum by separate subjects.

We need creators. We also need creative readers, listeners, and seers to respond to things that other people have created.

Humanities courses give students chances to wonder, to do creative work, to find new interests. So much good reading, looking, and listening can be part of these courses. And art and music get a deserved new position in the curriculum. Education can be deep involvement rather than superficial exposure. Education can become the kind that William James liked, "knowledge by acquaintance," rather than the kind he disliked, "knowledge by description."

The interdisciplinary humanities courses devised for both going-to-college and not-going-to-college students have no set pattern of content or organization. Most are for high school seniors, but some appear in the early years of high school and, occasionally, even in elementary schools. In fact, humanities courses are so numerous now that they may be called "the wave of the present."

I know of a low-achieving seventh grade class in which a music teacher and a social studies teacher worked together whenever they could. In a unit on the American West, they used art, music, and poetry—Grant Wood's "American Gothic," a section of Ferde Grofé's "Grand Canyon Suite," and a portion of Carl Sandburg's "Chicago." The result? A low-ability group learned something about the characteristics of an area—a bit of geography—and they *felt* art, music, and poetry.

And then there was a twelfth grade humanities class of able students who were discussing how Lord Jim in Conrad's book of the same name ignores his responsibilities as ship's mate and jumps overboard when he thinks his ship is sinking. Even though the vessel does not sink, ever afterward he has to live with his decision to abandon passengers committed to his charge.

Previously the students had read *Paradise Lost*. Suddenly inspired, one boy said, "I wonder whether there isn't a great similarity between Lord Jim's jump and Adam's fall." An animated discussion arose, and soon the students began to talk about the problems *they* were facing and would face, the decisions *they* were making and would make, and the factors affecting their decisions.

In interdisciplinary humanities courses, education can be discovery, and among the things young people discover are themselves. One of the chief aims of education should be a constant questing for the answer to that basic but elusive question, "Who am I?"

The fact-by-fact approach to education does little to aid in the quest. Students need ideas; they need "knowledge by acquaintance." Bring Socrates into high school and let the young—of all abilities—become acquainted with him. Then get them to think about Socrates in relation to Lord Jim and to Sir Thomas More in the magnificent play and movie, *A Man for All Seasons*. Do this, and a philosophy of life may begin to emerge.

A small high school with a senior class of 72 students gave a humanities course for the second time last year. A counselor there wrote:

> All our seniors are embarked on the most stimulating, enriching experience of their school years. Their involvement with ideas, their growing awareness, and their sometimes painful discomfort (caused by the abandonment of traditional classroom procedure, which called for little "stretching" of the mind) is an exciting and humbling sight. . . . Each student is pursuing in depth some phase of the course—music, art, philosophy, literature—and the projects for the first quarter dispelled any doubt I may have had about provision for differing abilities.

In one humanities course, attention centers on two buildings and their times: Chartres Cathedral in France and the rebuilt Coventry Cathedral in England. In another, students are considering change in twentieth-century America as seen in Thornton Wilder's *Our Town* and Leonard Bernstein's *West Side Story*.

Almost without exception students call their humanities course their most worthwhile high school experience. One spoke for many when she wrote from college, "The course really hasn't ended. The questions raised, the things learned, are still with me as I go about my work in college."

In my desire for an *inner* space program to match our outer space program, I have been hoping that the experiences with interdisciplinary humanities courses might bring a real change in secondary education and might lead to liberal arts secondary schools. We have long had liberal arts colleges, and, in many ways, elementary schools are liberal arts educational institutions.

With seventh grade, however, the bells, the subjects, the fears of not getting into college take over. Just when young people should be learning how to use freedom, they have less of it. Just when they need more unity, they get more diversity. Just when they need to develop internal controls, external pressures increase. Just when they yearn to be treated as individuals, they are herded together as never before. Just when they need small, flexible, intellectual communities, they too frequently end up doing the lockstep.

The change will be more in spirit than in organization, but liberal arts secondary schools, as I envision them, will be different. They will be comprehensive—all subjects for all kinds of students. Students will see relationships as they learn, will be involved in what they study rather than exposed to it. We must break the present monotony of five classes a day, five days a week, 36 weeks a year—with the same teacher at the same hour daily.

Let's give four groups of students to four teachers of different subjects for four blocks of time each day. Allow the teachers, and perhaps the students, to decide how to use the time. Bells can be ignored; lockstepping can be lessened; small intellectual communities can be created.

Let's have at least one art teacher and one music teacher with a maximum of two definite class assignments each during the day. The rest of the time they will be available to work with other teachers in these small intellectual communities.

With such flexibility, schools will emphasize release, inquiry, and discovery instead of restraint, rote memory, and regurgitation. Dealing with a few things in depth will begin, and the cover-everything practice will end. Much independent work will be featured; individual creativity will be fostered. Large, well-equipped libraries are a must; and art rooms, shops, and space that men can use and direct rather than space so divided that it dictates what men can do.

Teachers and students will become associates-in-learning. Emphasis will be on dialogues in the classroom rather than on the traditional question-and-answer technique. Life should be a series of dialogues. Students should be having dialogues with one another and with plays, poems, paintings, buildings, musical compositions, TV programs, news items, newspaper editorials—in *and* out of the classroom. Place students in the midst of ideas and they will learn; place them in the midst of facts and they will memorize.

During a fine four-week summer program in the humanities participated in by 65 high school students from 11 schools, I asked one of them how she liked the program. She smiled as she replied, "It's wonderful. I thought it was going to be like school but it *isn't*." I found myself thinking that if we develop the humanities in our schools, if we establish liberal arts secondary schools, a day will come when a student in such a summer program will say, "I hoped it would be like school, and it *is!*"

EDITORIAL COMMENT: BLACK STUDIES IN AMERICAN EDUCATION*

Walter G. Daniel

One of the most sweeping changes characterizing American education today is the establishment of black studies programs in elementary, secondary and higher educational institutions. As is true of most movements, this emphasis upon knowledge about and appreciation of Afro-Americans is not new, for many Negro writers and educators have promulgated such ideas for many years. The responses in the early years were feeble; only in the recent period has there been widespread interest. As the demand for black studies has gained momentum, it has become increasingly evident that many advocates and their supporters have little knowledge of the large number of scholars, black and white, who have long been concerned with the history of the Negro in American society and who have endeavored to secure for Afro-American history and literature a respected place in American education. Now that there is a new attack the black experience provides a context broader than the study of history and literature. Schools take into account the total background of learners and the ethnic group. Emphasis goes beyond knowledge to action.

It has been said that the current demand for black studies is a manifestation of discontent with the present system in its entirety and that it is really much more a symbol of discontent with the total society. Indeed, it does seem that this movement has achieved its current priority as an outgrowth of protests originally aimed at obviously discriminatory practices in such areas as public accommodation and voting. For some, however, separation as a social objective has replaced the demand for integration and an immediate end to segregation and discrimination. Many, particularly students, have become immersed in the revolutionary spirit which pervades the international scene and sharing in the rising expectations of

* Reprinted from *The Journal of Negro Education* (Summer 1970), 39:189–191, by permission.

227

disadvantaged people throughout the world. Some see black studies as based primarily on an ideology of revolutionary nationalism with liberation and self-determination for black people as the ultimate goal. In fact, the concept of black power exerted considerable influence on the black studies movement. While many people—Negroes and whites—rejected this extreme view, those who embraced the black power thesis saw black studies as the training ground for the leaders of the black revolution. Recognizing the need for the analysis of social, political and economic conditions affecting black people, they gave highest priority to the action aspect of the black studies program—action which would lead to black separation by revolutionary means. At the other extreme were those who saw the introduction of black studies as a means of peaceful change and reconciliation. Between these positions other views of more moderation and balance developed. The result has been the vastly individual black studies programs, with each institution determining the unique form and substance of its own efforts in this field.

The rapidly escalating demands for black studies programs have been called an intellectual crisis. Programs have often been instituted in great haste, frequently without focus, without clearly defined objectives, and without administrative and financial provisions required for effectiveness. There is little agreement on the specifics of such programs but such general terms as "need" and "relevance" recur in justifications. The great variety in the actual structure, offerings, administration, and admissions policies in higher institutions and the differences in curriculum and community involvement in elementary and secondary schools provide testimony to the vastly different viewpoints from which persons responsible for programs see their task. That these programs are necessary on all levels of education if the black person is to develop cannot be disputed. It is also true that other Americans should learn about and appreciate the Afro-American's contribution to the life of our country. In responding to these needs, however, educators must provide purposeful and well organized programs.

On the elementary and secondary level, educators must concern themselves with innovations which are required if the program of black studies is to be effective. Curricular changes take into account the black experience and aim to place the role of black people in proper perspective. The preparation of appropriate materials is given high priority. Staff development programs aimed at the education and re-education of teachers will be required if the instruction is to be balanced. Textbooks, books for leisure reading and magazines containing pictures and illustrations with which black children can identify must become more generally available and be sufficient in quality and quantity to be more than tokenism.

There are equally pressing imperatives on the university level. Decisions concerning important issues should precede the actual implementation of a black studies program. Careful attention should be given to the establishment of general policies with regard to recruitment of faculty and admission of students. Many pertinent questions may be raised. Significant among them are the following: How will the competence of a prospective teacher be measured? Should the program be open to any student who desires to enter? How will programs be related to the total college or university structure? Is there any justification for an autonomous department of black studies? For what kinds of positions will the graduates be prepared? Finally, will the program stress (1) community involvement, (2) scholarship, research and historical analysis, or (3) a balance between the two?

As the offering of black studies continues and spreads in schools and colleges, some procedure for evaluating their effectiveness must be evolved. Admittedly, objective assessment of such recently established programs which spring from opposing principles and objectives will be difficult. Nevertheless, it is imperative that they be examined to ascertain the extent to which their purposes are being achieved and are educationally valid. In spite of the many variations in stated purposes and forms of black studies programs, a common aim seems to be the development of race awareness and pride on the part of Negroes. All advocates of black studies see them as an initial step in the black man's attempt to control his own institutions and life. Thus, any measure of the effectiveness of such programs must consider whether they have contributed to the improvement of the black community in terms of its own sense of identity. Another important consideration would be the effect a program would have on persons who are not black—the white majority and other minority groups. Has the larger society's understanding of the Afro-American's position in American society been increased? Have relations between the races been improved as a result of a program or has the polarization among the various elements been exacerbated?

In addition, objective research is needed to test the validity of goals, to establish criteria for judging programs, to determine relative values and to refine techniques for testing results. Such research will, hopefully, provide a sound academic and educational basis for Afro-American studies. If black studies are to survive as a separate discipline or as a combination of disciplines or allied fields, the move from subjectivity to objectivity is critical.

THE PRESENT STATE OF THE ART
IN BLACK STUDIES*

William L. Smith

In general, Black studies is seen as a new dimension of already existing disciplines. In the post-secondary school level history, psychology, anthropology and sociology tend to be the base root from which Black studies flow. It is, in fact, construed as having an inter-disciplinary foundation; not as a new discipline but rather as a procedure and theoretical basis for describing a new condition, or better yet, a new dimension to human conditions. It is viewed as the new perspective of a discipline, format, and philosophical base to describe a new phenomenon. The fact that at present there is no unilaterally accepted theoretical base at either the post-secondary or secondary level accounts for the lack of consensus on a national basis for the development and implementation of Black studies programs.

There is a profound disparity in the articulation of basic concepts from the independent writers, the universities and colleges, the junior college, State departments of education and the secondary schools. In most cases the academic constraints placed upon the hierarchical structures from the university down to the secondary school have produced greater innovation in Black studies program development in the local school districts than in either the State education agencies or junior colleges, and especially in the universities. What has resulted is a great proliferation of individual curriculum development in the local secondary school systems with no sharing or coordination of efforts with other school systems. There are volumes of materials and recommendations for implementation produced. There is some evidence that a few State departments of education have attempted to assume the leadership for the integration of Black history and culture into the regular American history curriculum in the secondary schools. Evidence, at the time of this writing, of the coordina-

---

* From "Critique of Developments at the Secondary Level," *The Journal of Negro Education* (Summer 1970), 39:240–243, by permission.

tion or sharing of these integrating activities among State departments of education does not appear to exist.

The greatest efforts to date to provide secondary school teachers with comprehensive analyses of the literature and limited research in Black history and race relations seem to have been made by the offices of the National Education Association, the American Federation of Teachers, the National Association for the Advancement of Colored People and the National Urban League but each organization seems to have done its work independently.

There does not seem to be any indication of a systematic quantitative or qualitative national or local assessment of comparative data or strategies presently developed. On the local level, one of the overriding factors that accounts for this is the lack of criteria agreed upon for determining such an assessment. There appear to be as many sets of criteria as there are school boundaries or kinds of school populations—e.g., black inner-city, white inner-city, suburban and rural. In addition, the philosophic and political intent for such a program plays a major role within a single school system with regard to what actually goes on in that school system. For example, in the large urban school system where there is an extremely high percentage of minority populations the psycho-sociological orientation receives the greatest impetus. Materials are developed to enhance the cognitive, positive self-esteem and affective responses of the student population; while in the predominantly white schools within that single school system coursework is structured primarily from history for cognitive response and tends to be left to the option of the student, as an elective, rather than as a required course.

This lack of unanimity of approach even within a single school system compounds the problem of field testing or evaluating curricula. What is of even greater complexity in the evaluative process is the fact that, in many cases, after curriculum committees have spent an inordinate amount of time and effort, with student groups and the like in the developmental process, these materials are then placed at the disposal of teachers to be used at their discretion in whatever ways they feel are satisfactory for *them* as teachers. There, obviously, are a number of instances where the materials are not used or are used in such a superficial way that the entire effort is aborted. What seems abundantly evident is the lack of a definitive training program for teachers who do use or are scheduled to use these materials. The other overriding constraint in the utilization of materials comes from the traditionally oriented subject matter specialist who views the integration or restructuring of curriculum material in American history as being in conflict with State regulations.

The National Office of the NAACP conducted a survey of some 250 school districts in the Fall of 1969, taking a cross section of urban, rural and suburban school systems with different kinds of ethnic populations.[1] The response from these 250 schools was overwhelming. The survey addressed itself to what these systems were doing with regard to Negro history. Eighty-five percent of the 250 school systems responded to the survey which asked the following general questions:

> Have social studies and history curricula been revised to include greater emphasis on the participation of Negroes in American life and history?

> Are copies of the revised curriculum guides and resource materials for social studies and American history classes available?

> Are there other courses (i.e. American literature) that have been revised along these lines?

> Are revised curricula materials now being prepared but are not yet available? Are there approximate dates when they will be available?

> Have new courses on Negro history been prepared?

> Are copies of the new curriculum guides and resource materials available?

> Please indicate if social studies or American history curricula have not been revised.

> Please indicate if new courses on Negro history have not been prepared.

> What training is being done?

A preponderance of the voluminous material sent to the NAACP had been produced from Federal monies, especially Title I and Title III, ESEA. These materials suggest that it will require a massive undertaking to qualitatively and quantitatively evaluate what has been done. There appears to be as much variance between what was produced as there were school systems responding. In almost every case, training components proved to be the missing ingredient as a strategy for implementation on either a system-wide basis or a selected school basis for most school systems. These data do indicate that for the secondary school students, especially, a multi-racial, multi-ethnic perspective for infusion into American history was preferred by secondary school personnel in urban, suburban and rural school systems. The rationale for such a point of view is supported by most of the major organizations involved in secondary school education, both within and outside the educational establishment.

---

[1] June Shagaloff, "Survey of Negro History in Selected Secondary School Systems," Unpublished Report of 212 School Systems Responses. NAACP—1790 Broadway, New York, N.Y., Fall, 1969.

Across the country, teacher and student committees are revising social studies curricula to give a more honest interpretation of the role of the Black man. With this growing awareness of the Black minority has also come an awareness of the roles played by other often overlooked minorities —the Early American, and the Spanish speaking American. Since 1964, six states—California, Connecticut, Illinois, Kentucky, New Jersey and Pennsylvania—have either passed laws or strongly recommended that the role of America's minorities be accurately depicted in the teaching of United States history. Needless to say, all States have not been willing to recognize what these minorities have contributed to this society and civilization.

A survey was made of the 50 state departments of education, the District of Columbia and some high density cities.[2] State offices were asked what steps were being taken, if any, to implement the teaching of Black history and if samples of any curricular material were available at the State level. Where curriculum materials were not available at the State level, curriculum or social studies personnel were asked to suggest cities in that State which had some type of program.

Of the 50 States and the District of Columbia, 28 had some type of material available; 19 States had no material available nor had any plans for developing any in the near future; four states were either in the process of developing material or had established what type of material would be needed.[3]

To determine if there existed regional patterns to the availability of material on Black history in the States and the District of Columbia, the States were divided according to Federal regions and analyzed. By regions the States in the Northeastern, Middle Atlantic and Great Lakes areas of the country had, statewide, more available material than any other areas. Of the 21 States noted, 16 had material available for use, two were in the process of preparing material and three had no material.

No material was available from four Southern States—Louisiana, Mississippi, Alabama and Georgia—at the State level; however, State officials indicated that some local districts did have programs in preparation. Nor was material available from five of the plain States—Montana, Wyo-

---

[2] Jewell Chambers, *The Teaching of Black History in the U.S. Public Schools*, Report of Survey for the Office of Programs for the Disadvantaged, (memo form) Fall, 1968, U.S. Office of Education.

[3] *Material Available*: California, Colorado, Connecticut, District of Columbia, Florida, Hawaii, Idaho, Illinois, Iowa, Kentucky, Maine, Michigan, Minnesota, Missouri, New Hampshire, New Jersey, New York, North Carolina, Ohio, Oklahoma, Pennsylvania, Rhode Island, South Carolina, Texas, Vermont, Virginia, Washington, West Virginia. *No material available*: Alabama, Alaska, Arkansas, Delaware, Georgia, Indiana, Louisiana, Massachusetts, Mississippi, Montana, Nebraska, Nevada, New Mexico, North Dakota, Oregon, South Dakota, Utah, Wisconsin, Wyoming. *Materials in preparation*: Arizona, Kansas, Maryland, Tennessee.

ming, the Dakotas, and Nebraska. Two State officials commented that they were aware of no need for such materials as there was not, nor had ever been, a "sizable" Black population in their respective States.

In the 28 States reported having available materials, the type of curricular aids which could be used by the public school teacher varied greatly. To help teachers of both elementary and secondary schools, more had been prepared at the local level than at the State level. The most frequently mentioned State aid was the bibliography, and the quality fluctuated. Some were well organized and included not only books, but also periodical references and audio-visual material. From the bibliography it was expected that the local school district or concerned and interested teachers would be able to alter or adopt the existing course of study to include more Black history.

In reviewing the available curricular aids in the 28 States which had materials and the 22 cities suggested by State education officials, the first consideration was whether they provided either written material to guide teachers or lists of audio-visual material for classroom use. Written material was further delineated into the categories of bibliographies, teacher resource material from which the teacher could draw up their own units and formal syllabi which provided the teacher with preconstructed units.

In evaluating the programs used in the teaching of Black History, grades K-12, it was found that the approach most frequently used was the integration of material on Black Americans directly into the regular social studies or social science curricula. At the secondary level, separate courses in Black history were sometimes offered as an elective in the 12th grade. It should be noted, however, that these courses were offered primarily to Black students attending predominantly Black schools. In two instances special Afro-American literature courses were also offered as high school electives. Again, these were available to Black students in Black schools. Frequently mentioned as the best guide for history teachers was William Loren Katz's *Teachers' Guide to American Negro History* and one state, Iowa, purchased 800 copies for the use of its teachers.

WHAT'S HAPPENING NOW IN SEX EDUCATION*

"If we feel that sex is an important aspect of life, then it is important to enable people to think clearly about it. This the public school systems can do if the parents of America will let them," says Professor Reiss.

Part of the problem, thinks Elena M. Sliepcevich, director of the School Health Education Study, Inc. (SHES), may be that changes in education come about "slowly and painfully." Some of the groups most energetically pushing sex education in the schools, she says, have very little knowledge either of how schools operate or of the pressures from other special interest groups constantly being exerted on school boards and administrators. She notes that there are some 25,000 different organizations in the health field alone, many of which would like to insert their specialty into the school curriculum.

Recognizing these pressures, the Joint Committee of the National School Boards Association and the American Association of School Administrators passed a resolution in 1967 calling for "one sound, interrelated, and sequential program in health education, including sex and family life education" which would operate from kindergarten through grade 12, and which would avoid "bandwagon approaches, crash programs, and piecemeal efforts focused on one or a few topics that happen to be enjoying popularity or extensive press coverage."

The resolution framers noted that, in the field of health education, boards and administrators are being urged more and more to provide special time in an already overloaded curriculum for as many as 30 categorical topics, including smoking, drug abuse, alcohol education, venereal disease, accident prevention, tuberculosis, cancer, and nutrition, as well as sex and family life education.

---

* Excerpts reproduced by special permission from *Sex Education in Schools*, an *Education U.S.A.* special report. Copyright 1969, National School Public Relations Association.

Literally, the resolution adds, if something new goes into the curriculum, something must come out, and it states flatly: "There is neither time nor justification for separate courses in categorical areas of health . . . which should be a unified concept."

One of the School Health Education Study's earliest steps in 1962 was to survey small, medium, and large school districts in the United States, selected by random sampling, to determine the emphasis being placed on health topics in the curriculum.

In the sex and family life field, SHES found that although medium size districts were emphasizing family life education in grades 1–6, more than half of both the large and small districts were omitting this area of learning in the elementary grades.

A majority of schools in all size districts, the study showed, were teaching about boy-girl relationships, the structure and function of the human being in the seventh grade. Instruction about marriage, parenthood, and child care was generally delayed until grades 10–12. And even at that, a majority of the big city school districts were not including units on preparation for marriage in the high schools.

A companion SHES study of 18,000 elementary and high school students, which turned up many distorted ideas and a general lack of knowledge about health, also revealed that the students lacked confidence in either their parents or the schools to help them gain more knowledge and perspective on sex questions. Three fourths of the boys and one half of the girls said they would never, or only sometimes, turn to either their parents or a school counselor for answers.

Miss Sliepcevich suggests that there has been a tendency in schools to underestimate the ability of students to deal with more advanced and complex health concerns at earlier ages. If students, throughout their school career, were given factual knowledge upon which to base their conduct, she believes the tragic "had I but known" consequences of ignorance might be lessened. Accurate knowledge dispensed early and often is desperately needed, she says, in an era when more women marry in their eighteenth year than in any other and have their first child in their nineteenth year, and when 40 percent of the unwed mothers of this country are between 15 and 19 years of age.

Deryck Calderwood of the Sex Information and Education Council of the United States criticizes some so-called "sex education" programs in the words of a student who told him: "They give as little information as possible as late as possible to as few as possible." Calderwood makes a practice, when visiting a school, of asking if it has a sex education program. Adults may say yes, but students say no. He concludes the program is often handled in such antiseptic terms students never know what they are receiving.

Things are changing, however—perhaps not as fast as some of the publicity suggests—and broader programs of the type favored by AASA, NSBA, AAHPER, and other concerned groups are being initiated.

Some have been encouraged by state legislation. Illinois enacted its sex education law in 1965, followed by Maryland and New York in 1967, Michigan and Ohio in 1968.

The editors of *Education U.S.A.* surveyed the states in September 1968 to discover whether the state board of education had adopted (a) a policy statement on sex education; and (b) guidelines to help local school districts develop programs in sex education.

Of 31 replies, 16 states—Connecticut, Delaware, Florida, Georgia, Iowa, Illinois, Maryland, Michigan, Minnesota, New Jersey, North Carolina, Ohio, Oregon, Virginia, Washington, and Wisconsin—reported that they had developed or were developing policy statements.

Six additional states reported to *Education U.S.A.* or to another survey by the State University of New York at Albany that, while they had no policy statements, there were state guidelines for local districts to follow. These were Alaska, Colorado, Indiana, New Mexico, South Carolina, and Utah.

Another four states—Mississippi, Montana, New Hampshire, and South Dakota—said they were planning workshops, providing speakers and/or materials, or otherwise getting ready to consider broadened programs of sex education and family living.

Much of this activity has been encouraged by the U.S. Office of Education. It announced in 1966 that schools, communities, and state agencies wishing to establish or improve programs in sex and family life education might be eligible for federal grants. Teacher and counselor institutes, graduate fellowships, state leadership training, adult education, library improvement, curriculum development, research, and demonstration were given as examples of projects that might qualify for federal funds under Titles I, II, III, and V of the Elementary and Secondary Education Act; Titles III, V, and XI of the National Defense Education Act; Title I of the Higher Education Act; the Cooperative Research Program; and various vocational and library services acts.

The *Virgin Islands Department of Education* is developing a cooperative program in family life and sex education for all grades. In preparation are a curriculum guide, inservice education for teachers, and a pilot program for the schools. The program has had the help of SIECUS and a grant from the Public Welfare Foundation, Inc. Community planning is developing concurrently with the school program, under the aegis of the Unitarian-Universalist Fellowship and the St. Thomas Mental Health Association. The latter has been actively sponsoring community-wide institutes to help keep the public informed and interested.

The local school districts are beginning to move, too. Two of the biggest—Chicago and New York City—have inaugurated family life and sex education programs in the last three years. San Francisco is in the tryout stage. Baltimore, Maryland, Washington, D.C., and Kansas City, Missouri, have had programs under way for some years.

Chicago, moving cautiously with a carefully chosen advisory committee of civic, medical, religious, and educational representatives and keeping the parents informed all the way, started its program in the fifth grade of one elementary school in each of the city's 27 districts. That was in 1966–1967. The following year it was extended to a total of 108 schools and was further broadened in 1968–1969. It will expand until, by 1971, the education will begin in kindergarten and continue through the twelfth grade.

As part of the preparation, and before their children started the course, Chicago parents were shown all the material to be used, including three films. They were given the option of having their children excused but, only 16 were withdrawn out of a total of 3,167 youngsters.

Teachers were prepared in a series of after-school training sessions (for which they were paid) by psychiatrists, physicians, and experienced teachers. Of 90 teachers asked to teach, only four requested to be excused.

The course itself consisted of one period per day over three weeks taught by the regular fifth-grade classroom teacher as part of the regular health education and science curriculum.

The reception so far, says the director, Barbara Hawkins, has been "fantastic." Many parents told her that sex education is *the* dinner table topic for the three weeks the course is in operation and that now they can "talk to their children again."

Asked to evaluate in writing their reactions to the course, parents made such comments as: "I know my job is to pick up where you left off, but what a wonderful start you have given me!" "The main advantage, I feel, is that my son and his friends have similar information and won't confuse each other." "I think my daughter will benefit greatly by being taught sex education as matter-of-factly as arithmetic or any other subject."

In 1967, *New York City* introduced into 166 selected schools at all grade levels its new curriculum area entitled "Family Living, Including Sex Education." In the early grades, this instruction is included in the science, health education, or social studies time allotments. Beginning in grades 5 and 6, the teaching is more direct, with teachers given flexibility in planning how best to schedule it. In junior and senior high schools, one period per week is devoted to various aspects.

For example, seventh-graders learn about endocrine glands, sex glands, hormones. Getting along with others of both sexes, what to do about crushes on older persons, puppy love, and how to behave on a date, along with discussions of "how to say 'no' " and how to "vary the tempo on a date," get emphasis in the eighth grade.

Near the end of the eighth-grade curriculum comes a subject to be introduced, says the curriculum guide, with "great sensitivity"—the subject of homosexuality.

Ninth-grade teachers have the task of dispelling "common fallacies about sex"; e.g., that sowing wild oats is a good preparation for marriage; that sexual intercourse is necessary for development, health, and happiness; that inhibition and control are harmful, and the like.

For children in some New York City neighborhoods where dropout rates are high, study of marriage and parenthood will be telescoped into the tenth grade from the eleventh- and twelfth-grade curricula. Tenth-graders also will be given intensive instruction on the reproductive system through charts, transparencies, and manikins, and will be asked to do independent research on "old wives' tales" about prenatal care.

Eleventh-graders will discuss everything from virginity and the double standard of morality for men and women to why engagements are broken and how to plan a honeymoon.

In the twelfth grade, buzz sessions on such subjects as promiscuity, prostitution, venereal disease, homosexuality, contraception, abortion, and divorce will be backed up by books and studies of the work of family planning agencies.

The *Baltimore, Maryland,* systemwide program of family life education, say spokesmen, represents the results of planning that has gone on for more than a decade. Where learnings fit into special disciplines, that is where they are taught. For example, units on population pressures occur in studies of the social sciences; education about venereal disease, in secondary school science and health classes. Baltimore uses team teaching in this field and conducts regular workshops and seminars for teachers.

Washington, D.C., schools have been teaching health and family life education from kindergarten through the twelfth grade since 1958, but teachers feel information is not enough. They believe they must go beyond the four walls of the schools and work with the parents in raising the standards of behavior for young people. In 1966 there were almost 5,000 live births to unwed mothers in the District of Columbia, almost half of them in the 15 to 19 age group. And there were more than 2,200 cases of gonorrhea in the 10 to 19 age group.

Kansas City, Missouri, has a unique and practical angle on the sex education of its seventh-graders. It teaches them by television, two sessions per week throughout the school year. Included in the TV lessons is material on emotional and social growth, understanding emotions, physiology of sex, the male/female reproduction systems, VD, understanding human sexuality, boy-girl relationships, and so on. Boys and girls are separated for the TV lessons on human growth and reproduction. Parents are informed when these are to be aired and asked to notify the school if they do not wish their youngsters to view those particular segments. Teachers follow up on the TV lessons with guides keyed to each program.

San Francisco is still in the tryout stage, having begun its planning in 1967 with an advisory committee of 30 persons representing a broad spectrum of the community. An inservice course in family life education was held in 1967, enrolling some 600 teachers and administrators, and the schools have enlisted support of the local educational TV station to develop a TV series on family life education.

The 25-year-old sex education program in *San Diego, California,* was developed from requests from parents. The local PTA routinely requests the principal to provide sixth-grade social health lessons (one hour per day for one week). Group counseling sessions and informal discussions are held once a week in the high schools. Although the program is optional, it has more than 99 percent student participation.

The 20-year-old sequential family life program in *Hayward (Calif.) Unified School District,* sparked by a student petition in 1947, is a community endeavor where, as one observer put it, if the schools cannot cope, other agencies are asked to join in—doctors, clergy, parents.

Hayward's director of secondary education, Don Oakes, says sex education teachers are advised in advance of certain pitfalls to be avoided—for one, use of questionnaires that could be misinterpreted as personal inventories on sex habits. Also avoided is any advocacy of birth control, mechanically or medically. The schools' position is that the individual must make this decision with the advice of physician or clergy. The schools discuss birth control as an international problem, a controversial issue, an item in current events.

Another item avoided is the teaching of anything approaching sex techniques. This task, says Oakes, "is better reserved for an experienced marriage counselor or qualified medical doctor."

In *Evanston, Illinois,* an extensive program in family living has operated for 16 years with particular emphasis on reproduction at fifth, seventh, and eighth grades. Also offered is a comprehensive inservice training course for teachers. Support has been good, thanks to an effective community relations program and to the fact that the courses are continuously evaluated by parents, along with the superintendent, principals, supervisors, teachers, and nurses.

Keokuk (Iowa) Senior High School has had an elective marriage and family living course for 25 years, and in all that time teacher James D. Lockett has had no opposition from parents. His superintendent, Elmer C. Gast, concurs that there has been no vocal opposition and indeed admits that "our main criticisms are coming from people who want us to do more on the elementary level."

Lockett says the basic purpose of his course, which covers premarital sexual relations, reproduction, implications of the moral code, VD, and family planning, is to "bolster the teaching of the parents who have done a good job, and to fill in the gaps for those students whose parents have done an inadequate job." When he surveys students early in the course on whether their parents have done an adequate job in teaching them about sex, 50 percent regularly answer no.

The *Anne Arundel County, Maryland,* public schools are working toward county-wide implementation of a K-12 program in family life and sex education. At the end of the year 1968 the board of education, with a group of outstanding teachers, was preparing some tentative units for selected situations at grades 5 and 6.

Flint (Mich.) Community Schools have a program of sex education extending from the fifth through the twelfth grades, conducted by a staff of special teachers who provide instruction in all elementary and secondary schools. Using a developmental and sequential philosophy, teachers emphasize sex education at the fifth-, eighth-, tenth-, and twelfth-grade levels. Only the twelfth-grade segment is elective; all other portions of the program are required, although children may be excused from sequences on human growth and development under parental request.

Moorestown Township, New Jersey, public schools are in the second year of a three-year plan to introduce a "Personal Growth Program" into the elementary schools. Correlated with all areas of the curriculum, K-6, the goal is to provide sequential learning experiences in social, physical, emotional, and intellectual growth and "to promote communication between adults and youth as students progress to junior high school."

In September 1968, the *Fayette County, Kentucky,* schools inaugurated a basic sex education program for grades 6, 8, and 10. Units are taught in special classes or seminars, and not necessarily as a specific part of any course. Teachers are prepared in a five-day workshop for which they are paid. The system will have a comprehensive sex education program extending through all grades, beginning in 1969.

A citizens task force in *Arlington County, Virginia,* strongly recommended in 1968 that the schools give increased attention to human growth and development from the "earliest ages," in order to "present each pupil with the fundamental information he needs for a well adjusted life." The task force felt that boys and girls should not be separated for such instruction and that they needed information much earlier than has been customary. For example, the facts of menstruation, said the task force, should be given at the fourth-grade level.

"Getting Ready Time: Preparation for Family Living" is one phase of the K-12 family life and sex education curriculum of *Summit County Schools, Akron, Ohio.* A 14-week course presented one hour each week to fifth- and sixth-graders, it is initiated as a health club with the idea that information learned is club business, not playground talk. Parents are honorary members of the club and students are encouraged to continue their discussions each week at home. There are no books, homework assignments, or tests. Facts are transmitted by "broadcasts" from the graduate registered public health nurses who teach the course. Games played with factual concepts and terminology questions keep interest high. Almost 50,000 youngsters have taken the course in the 18 years it has been offered.

NARCOTICS: A NEW AREA OF SECONDARY SCHOOL RESPONSIBILITY*

Robert Elliott

My talk today is undertaken with mixed emotions. I welcome the opportunity to discuss a subject which has long been of interest to me, and one which must be resolved if we are to continue to produce young people capable of assuming the awesome responsibilities that will face them. I feel some frustration, too, in acknowledging that this is a school responsibility, one more chore in a seemingly endless stream that flows from the parents to the school. I also feel some disappointment at the failure of educators, you and me, to face up to the problem before it reached the crisis level. If the schools are to be blamed for drug abuse, it is because we have brought it on ourselves. Our guilt is in omission, not in commission.

"Narcotics: A New Area of Secondary School Responsibility" is not an accurate title for this presentation. Narcotics education is not a new responsibility which has suddenly been thrust upon us; it has long been our responsibility. At least 43 states require instruction in narcotics, alcohol, and tobacco. In Illinois the school code specifies:

* Reprinted by permission from Robert Elliott, "Narcotics: A New Area of Secondary School Responsibility," *North Central Association Quarterly*, Vol. XLIV, No. 4 (Spring 1970), pp. 325–334.

> The nature of alcoholic drinks and other narcotics and their
> effects on the human system shall be taught . . . in all schools
> under state control . . . for students of high school grade (text-
> books) shall give not less than 20 pages to this subject. . . . In all
> state universities and teachers' training classes . . . adequate time
> and attention shall be given to instruction in the best method of
> teaching such subject and no teacher shall be certificated who has
> not passed a satisfactory examination in this subject. . . . Any
> school officer who neglects or fails to comply with the provision of
> this section shall pay for offense the sum of not less than $5 nor
> more than $25.[1]

Twenty years ago I was teaching a quiet unit on drugs and trying to
persuade parents and students that this was an important and worthwhile
topic for study. The problem then was heroin and was confined mostly
to the poor ghetto areas of the city where poverty and human misery
motivated an escape through hard drugs. It is ironic to recall that an
appeal to the Federal Narcotics Bureau in Chicago was answered with the
statement that narcotics was not a concern of youngsters. Certainly it was
not a problem that affected youngsters outside of the densely populated
inner city, not youngsters with good suburban homes, money, and fine
educational opportunities. Our present problem is a reversal of that condition. Most of today's users are from better than average homes, have
higher than average intelligence, and have money—none of the apparent
reasons why the epidemic of 20 years ago was rampant in the poor and
disillusioned and discouraged slum dweller.

The present drug problem is, to say the least, confusing. The
avalanche that hit us a year or more ago is still vivid in our minds and
we are still bewildered by what took place. Cliches like "generation gap"
and "lack of communication" are used to explain our plight. There is not
a *lack* of communication, there is *too much* communication. Everyone is
talking, everyone is an authority on the subject, but too few are listening.
At this point we are not even sure how many students are using drugs. A
teacher made headlines in California by stating that 60 to 70% of the
students used drugs. A girl reported:

> Last year it was beer parties, this year it's pot parties. I don't smoke
> marijuana myself, but I'd estimate 50 to 60% of the kids here have
> tried it one time or another. Not just hippy long hair types, but
> everyone, athletes, student government leaders, honor students . . .[2]

---

[1] *The School Code of Illinois*, 1967. Section 27–10, p. 261. State of Illinois, Spring-
field, Ill.

[2] Connie Myers, "How Drugs Peril Suburb Teens," Chicago *American*, February 23,
1969.

"I don't smoke marijuana myself but I know others who do." This is a familiar statement, and one that we accept as legitimate; a student said it so it must be true. We overlook the fact that students, too, can carry gossip and transmit rumors. Chicago suburban police estimate that at least 50% of the boys have tried some form of narcotics at least once.[3] The so-called liberal colleges, such as the University of California, Wisconsin, Harvard, Yale, Princeton, make the headlines because large numbers of students use drugs openly and defiantly. A survey at these schools indicate that perhaps 25% of the students have had experience with drugs. We have about six million college students, less than 5% of them attend these schools; the other 95% attend colleges where the drug problem is rare or nonexistent. When you read of 40 students arrested for drug usage in a high school of 4,000 you are reading about 1% of the student body, far less than the 35% who smoke cigarettes.

The news media do little to produce a climate of thoughtful concern. The drug story is a "hot" one, and in their haste for deadlines they concentrate on headlines. How does one counteract, for example, the influence of the *Today* show? On that show, Hugh Downs reported that he had been unable to find any real harm in marijuana. Downs commented:

> . . . Most of the evidence unfolded on my television programs appears to point to one immense danger; since young people are particularly sensitive to truth, and since for over 30 years patently exaggerated myths about marijuana have been circulated by an establishment toward which many of the young already feel rebellious, great harm has been done through destruction of credibility.[4]

Commenting on Downs's view a research physician noted: "It is almost criminal for those so far from the field of medicine or pharmacology to be so dogmatic about something they know nothing about."

Experts like Downs are too numerous, and they always seem to be heard. In a recent conference in this city a lawyer proclaimed that young people have been given the wrong idea about the dangers of marijuana and that reports on damage from LSD were premature. Our pseudo-experts emphasize, for example, that marijuana is not physically addicting; they do not emphasize that physical dependence is far less important in addiction than the psychological/emotional factors. Some outstanding personalities openly admit the use of drugs, even advocate their use, and others suggest that marijuana is harmless, perhaps even beneficial.

Whatever its size or scope we have a problem and it is clear that the

---

[3] *"Parents Guide to Marijuana,"* Western Electric, Rolling Meadows, Ill., Public Service Pamphlet, p. 4.

[4] Jess Stearn, "The Seekers," Chicago *Today*, Friday, January 12, 1969.

schools are expected to lead the way to its solution. The command has been passed from a concerned public to a worried Board of Education to a frenzied superintendent to a befuddled principal to an unprepared teacher, "do something, teach 'em about drugs." To get the public off our back we engage in some educational practices that, in retrospect, seem rather ridiculous. We were pressured into "crash" programs involving mass teaching by movie and lecture. We bring in the "junkie" to talk with our students because he is the only one who "can tell it like it is." There is little preparation for these programs, and even less follow-up. Some schools go to the point of hiring private concerns to do the job for them. Fine teachers who have identified effectively with teen-agers over a period of years are, suddenly, no longer credible; they are not addicts or users so they can not teach about drugs.

WHY DRUGS?

The most perplexing part of the problem is *why.* Why should youngsters who have so much to gain in life want to escape through drugs? The natural process of growing up must be considered an explanation. Kenneth Keniston of the Yale Medical School observes that adolescence is a "turbulent period of transition between childhood and adulthood."[5] This transition involves the accomplishment of two tasks: *rebellion* and *search.*

Rebellion is the essentially negative task of breaking the many deep bonds that link a person with childhood. This is a difficult task, and a final one, for once the bonds have been broken nothing will ever be the same again—the support, love, permissiveness, irresponsibility, and dependence of childhood will be gone. In some cases the bonds are broken only by violent and convulsive wrenching from those with whom they are most closely tied.

The search for identity, meaning, significance, relevance, and values is more positive in nature. The teen-ager seeks understanding and recognition from his peer group, and his status within that group depends to a great extent upon the very conformity he often seeks to escape. Unless he has been grounded with the right values, unless he has good judgment, and unless he understands himself and others, he may act with others in defying legal, social, and parental authority. The search often leads to experimentation with drugs, especially if this is what the group does, and if such actions are seen as a defiance of authority. The theory of rebellion and search is valid only up to a point. You and I rebelled by sneaking a

---

[5] Kenneth Keniston, "Rebellion and Search in Today's Youth," address to Headmaster's Association Meeting, February 2, 1968.

smoke in back of the barn just "for the hell of it," and I suppose we, too, searched for ourselves. But it seems to me that the rebellion and search theory falls short of the mark.

A more compelling reason, in my judgment, lies in the affluence of our society. The nature of our sufficiency is, indeed, unique to our time and place; it is based upon "material sufficiency, not . . . economic deprivation." It states that our youth have little to be concerned about except themselves. They can contemplate the weaknesses and hypocrisy of the establishment, the future of mankind, and the failure of our generation because they have little else to do. The youth of today is almost completely free from any worries about providing for himself; he is well-fed, well-clothed, well-housed, and well-educated. He is a parasite, living off the efforts of others and depending upon others for support and comfort. Our standard of living has produced a generation which has financial power; the teen-ager buys an impressive number of cars, clothing, and records. He commands the immediate attention of the press and television. We spend more time, money, and energy on him than on any other age group. As a result we have a generation which is extremely self-centered.

Unfortunately, some of our adults see them *only* as spoiled kids made soft by too much too soon: "They don't have the guts to face life like it is, they have been insulated against the outside world and when the going gets tough they fold." This explanation may suffice for some but it doesn't answer the question clearly.

Knowing material sufficiency and having time to reflect upon a system which they have had no part in building and no responsibility in maintaining some of them pronounce it "bad." They see something wrong with a system which they perceive to be designed only for high income and social status. We see our accomplishments; they see only our failures.

Perhaps we should take a look at what they see: A gain in the gross national product means little if it is not equally distributed or if all people do not have access to its rewards. We place a man on the moon but our earthly environment is dying. How explain a higher standard of living and material accomplishments to a young man who knows that it has been purchased at the price of polluted streams and lakes and air? How explain the death of Lake Erie or the eight years of life remaining for Lake Michigan? The air we breathe is foul; acquatic life is dying; man is drowning in the junk heaps of used cars and tin cans. Supplies of drinking water are sharply limited in some parts of the country.

We have taught him, and he has learned well, that our science and technology can accomplish almost any task. Then why, he asks, is our environment in peril? Is it because we do not know how to clean it up? But what has polluted air to do with using drugs? The natural rebellion of youth has found an adult weakness and with his tunnel vision and black or white reasoning, he seizes upon it as a condition he cannot accept. It doesn't meet his standards and not being able to accept it he has an excuse for enjoying the exotic pleasures now, for getting turned on now.

Another explanation lies in the fact that we seem to condone the use of drugs. We are a drugged society. We use them to go to sleep, wake up, slow down, and speed up. We use more tranquilizers than aspirin. As one sociologist noted:

> Both the actual miracle and myth of modern medicine have made the use of drugs highly legitimate, as something to be taken casually . . . our children, in being casual about drugs, far from being in revolt against an older generation, may in fact be acknowledging how influential a model that generation was.[6]

We condemn the use of some drugs and condone the use of others. Hypercritical youth, with time on his hands, wonders why we condemn the use of his drugs but not alcohol and tobacco? We have not answered the question. Certainly his drugs are bad, and we must not veer away from this fact, but ours are just as bad. A young girl asked: "I get my highs on 'Mary Jane,' you get yours through alcohol. What's the difference?" A young man commented bitterly:

> You hypocrites. How can you tell me not to try marijuana when you know damn well alcohol and nicotine are more dangerous. Nine and eleven billion dollar a year businesses say you're a man of distinction or you're masculine or sexy . . . if you smoke, or use brand X.[7]

Equating alcohol and tobacco with marijuana, heroin, and amphetamines does not in any way diminish the seriousness of the drug problem. It's not that we should emphasize their drugs less but that we should emphasize alcohol and tobacco more.

Alcohol is used by a majority of the adult population and creates more problems than all other drugs combined. We have at least six million alcoholics and probably an equal number of problem drinkers. More than one-half of the crimes are associated with alcohol; the majority of homicides are committed by persons under the influence of alcohol; and at least a third of all traffic fatalities involve a drinking driver. Alcohol is classified as an addicting drug. Eddy writes:

> Physical dependence on alcohol definitely occurs, and the abstinence syndrome resulting when the intake of alcohol is reduced below a

---

[6] *Time* Magazine, "The Junior Junkie," February 16, 1970, p. 36.

[7] George D. Demos, "Drug Abuse and the New Generation," *Phi Delta Kappan*, December 1968, p. 214.

critical level is manifested by tremors, sweating, nausea, tachycardia, rise in temperature . . . and in severe grades, convulsion, and delirium . . . characterized by confusion, disorientation, delusions, and vivid visual hallucinations.[8]

Alcohol is addicting and alcohol is consumed by a majority of adults—this is the model that youth sees. In his one-way approach he cannot perceive any great difference between his choice of drugs and ours. But *too* many of them are using our drugs. The number and frequency of high school drinking parties is a far greater problem in my judgment than the use of drugs.

The problems associated with smoking are of even greater importance. If we really want to protect youth we should concentrate on the cigarette. As soon as I suggest this many of you will "tune me out" because you smoke and your initial reaction will be that I am comparing apples and peaches. You are right, I am comparing apples and peaches but with one common element—both are deadly. So why isn't smoking a suitable topic of concern for this meeting? Perhaps it's money that gets in our way—big money, respectable money—not the dirty money of the drug trade. A few years ago we could only speculate as to the effects of tobacco but now the facts are clear. Dr. Luther Terry, former Surgeon General, commented:

The period of uncertainty is over . . . there is no longer any doubt that cigarette smoking is a direct threat to the user's health. We know for certain that lung cancer, which is climbing to almost epidemic proportions throughout the world, is directly associated with cigarette smoking. The rising number of deaths among men and women in the prime of life is related to cigarette smoking. The toll from bronchitis and emphysema can be traced to cigarette smoking.[9]

About 300,000 persons die annually because of cigarette-induced diseases such as heart disease, bronchitis, and emphysema.[10] The mortality rate from lung cancer has increased in men more than 15 times in 35 years. This is a disease which is largely preventable; it is caused by smoking.

---

[8] Nathan B. Eddy, H. Halbach, Harris Isbell, and Maurice H. Seevers, *Drug Dependence: Its Significance and Characteristics,* pamphlet, reprinted with permission of U. S. Department of Health, Education, and Welfare, Public Health Services, p. 727.

[9] Luther Terry, (Opening address at World Conference on Smoking and Health) *A Summary of the Proceedings,* September 11, 1967, p. 1.

[10] The Tuberculosis Institute of Chicago and Cook County, 1440 West Washington Blvd., Chicago, Ill.

Estimates suggest that 62,000 will die from this disease in 1970.[11] Forty percent of our adult population, 51 million people, now smoke. And why do teen-agers begin:

> . . . We do not see enough real freedom on this decision in our cigarette infiltrated world. Adult example, peer invitation, glamourous advertising make it too easy for youngsters to start cigarette smoking . . . farmers, merchandisers, manufacturers, advertising agencies, newspapers and magazines, publishers and broadcasters draw large income from cigarettes. Tax benefits are considerable to federal, state and city governments.[12]

The tax return *is* considerable. The federal government collects almost two billion from tobacco taxes, another 1.5 billion is collected by state and local governments. The combined effects of example and advertising produce 4,500 new teen-age smokers every day. Nationally about 35% of the boys and 30% of the girls smoke by graduation time, over one-third of them smoke half a pack or more per day. Parents set the example. By high school graduation 44% of the boys and 37% of the girls smoke when both parents smoke, as compared to 29% and 16% whose parents do not smoke. To gain new smokers the tobacco industry spends about 30 million annually for advertising. Surprisingly, they are assisted by the Department of Agriculture which, according to the *New York Times*, spends about 30 million a year to support the tobacco industry in various ways and another 30 million for tobacco shipments through the "Food for Peace" program.

And, it is interesting to note that *almost* no person smokes marijuana without first smoking cigarettes. If tobacco were *not* an important part of the economy, if it were *not* a big money-maker, it would have been declared illegal years ago. Cyclamates were banned overnight, without fanfare, appeal, or discussion because there was the possibility that they were cancer-inducing. Our inconsistency is best summarized by one commentator who suggested:

> Parents are educating by example and precept, the mass media are educating seven days a week . . . Since society holds conflicting and ambivalent attitudes toward drugs and since there are large discrepancies between what is said and what is done, the impact of all this education undoubtedly is to produce confusion and conflicts for the students.[13]

---

[11] American Cancer Society, *1970 Cancer Facts and Figures*, 219 East 42nd Street, New York, N.Y.

[12] "A Statement on Cigarette Smoking by the American Cancer Society," Approved by the Board of Directors, American Cancer Society, October 23, 1968.

[13] Marvin R. Levy, "What Can Schools Do? A Time for Relevance," a paper presented at the American Public Health Association Meeting, Detroit, Mich., November 12, 1968, p. 7.

AN EDUCATIONAL PROGRAM

We now face a critical problem with drugs. About ten years ago we had a sudden increase in venereal disease among teen-agers all over the country. And we went through a harried period of innovation to provide the necessary instruction. The crisis passed, and with it the instruction in venereal disease. But still another crisis threatens. The director of The National Communicable Disease Center says:

> Gonorrhea has been increasing dangerously all over the nation for the past several years and is now "out of control" in the United States. Teen-agers and young adults (24 and under) account for nearly half of the total cases reported, 23,000 out of 42,000.[14]

Unlike some kinds of drugs there is little mystery about the eventual effects of this disease: blindness, crippling, malformation of babies, damage to the reproductive system. If the present trend continues the schools will again be under pressure to alleviate this problem.

And so it goes, crisis following crisis. It is past time for us to recognize that we have a frightening responsibility to teach youngsters the facts of life *outside of our structured academic courses.* We cannot continue to wait until a problem reaches epidemic proportions before we act. Youngsters must be taught to make choices and decisions about the quality of life they will lead. Decisions must be based as much upon old-fashioned moral, ethical, and spiritual values as hard logic. The sophisticated lessons of our traditional curriculum are not valid if one can not make those personal decisions that keep him free from drugs and disease.

Knowledge in college-level physics is not as important as the knowledge that LSD doesn't reveal new insights into life; creative writing is not as important as knowing that marijuana is not a creative drug. Alcohol twists the tongue whether speaking Spanish or English. The fact that over two-thirds of our hospital beds are occupied by persons suffering from emotional disturbances should alert us to the fact that we need to do much more in teaching the person about himself.

We must begin *now* to develop effective programs that are imaginative in concept and attractive in presentation. This is necessary, not simply to obey existing laws, but because it is essential to the welfare of our students. For years we have been piously accepting health instruction as a necessary part of the curriculum, and for just as long we have been treating it as something akin to the "village idiot," always there, hovering in the background, occasionally being recognized. We *say* it is important but we have never granted it full membership in our organization. When a problem related to the subject appears we hastily improvise a solution.

---

[14] John B. Hall, "Gonorrhea on the Rise," Cook County Department of Public Health news release, December 31, 1969.

We take some time from the nearest related department, usually physical education because they are nonacademic and will not protest as much, and show a film or hear a lecture.

This is a luxury we can no longer afford. There must be a massive move toward establishing fully credited courses of study in the health-related area—whether you call it health education, social problems, human values is not important. The crisis in narcotics is only one problem; the increasing rate in venereal disease is another; and perhaps the greatest is the ever-increasing number of emotionally ill people in our society; and all projections promise an even greater rate of increase as more and more people are jammed together. Is health education not a logical place for attacking our problems of air and water pollution, population increase, human survival, and moral and ethical values?

Such a course can be as intellectually stimulating as any course in our school. It must be a combination of psychology, sociology, physiology, which stresses human values, human problems, and human solutions. Do we have room in our program for a required course of this kind? Can we afford the time and teachers? We found the resources for teaching by TV, for complicated electronic hardware, for AP courses for a few students. Since Dr. Conant's report we have intensified our offerings for the bright and college-bound students It is now time to provide a program for *all* students on how to make choices and decisions covering personal matters. Ironically in *many* cases it is the bright and gifted and college-bound who exhibit the greatest need for such a course. In our lust for academic excellence we have made our schools sterile of human values, of moral and ethical values, of the importance of recognizing the uniqueness of each student. But the first hurdle usually stops us. *Where* will it be taught and *who* will teach it? In this age of innovation, with constant emphasis upon change, isn't it possible for us to solve this problem?

In setting up a drug education program, I would insist on the following essentials:

1. Emphasize people, not drugs.
2. The course should be taught in the school by school personnel.
3. Let the students discuss the subject.
4. Provide alternatives.
5. The approach must be varied and community-wide.

1. *Emphasize people, not drugs.* A program of instruction in narcotics, alcohol, tobacco, and/or sex must be based on self-instruction. The student must learn about himself: his brain, nervous system, intelligence, emotions, and attitudes. He should know that he is primarily an emotional creature motivated by love, fear, and anger; and that it is emotion, often operating subconsciously, and not intelligence that causes most problems.

Thousands of years ago the caveman killed his enemy with a club;

we have advanced to the point where we can now kill the world by pressing a button; but the emotions involved are the same, fear and anger. We have the capacity to visit the planets, harness the ocean depths, produce abundance in food, clothing, and shelter—but our emotions get in the way of realizing utopia. The need today is not more technology but more understanding and compassion. The crying need for understanding and compassion is no less critical in teaching youngsters about themselves. Unless the student has an insight into himself, all the drug facts are of little value.

Of course we must incorporate valid facts into our discussion. The local and state laws, as well as local judicial practices, must be covered. The physiological and psychological effects of drugs must be presented accurately and objectively. Medical facts should be included. And what are the facts? I have covered some effects of alcohol and tobacco. The addicting properties of the opiates and the effects of amphetamines, tranquilizers, LSD, and barbiturates can be found in any number of publications. The big hang-up is marijuana. Here you will have to take your choice of sources: the researchers in both government and private sectors and law enforcement officers who pronounce it a dangerous drug or the pseudo-experts who with a limited knowledge of its effects play upon our incomplete knowledge in stating that it is harmless. These are the people who previously advanced a similar argument for LSD, tobacco, and thalidomide.

As I say, you will have to take your choice because the two sides seem to be polarized. Over the years I have done extensive reading on marijuana and I have yet to find a legitimate medical research report that states marijuana is a safe drug. By the same token, police officers who see the first-hand effects of marijuana have long condemned it as a highly dangerous drug.

This much is certain: marijuana is an unpredictable intoxicant, an hallucinogenic drug. It produces a psychological dependence which is far more difficult to conquer than physiological dependence. It is outlawed in most countries in the world. Only the long-lasting effects of the intoxication are in question, not the intoxication itself.

We have a small, stubborn core who persistently defend the use of marijuana. I can not understand how, or why, Hugh Downs or Mayor Lindsey of New York City, where 224 teen-age heroin deaths occurred last year, can call it harmless and censure those who get "up-tight" over its use. What is the case for marijuana, beyond the fuzzy area of individual rights?

A few years ago I taught that marijuana was dangerous because it could lead to heroin. This argument is no longer valid, according to some, because it "ain't necessarily so." Ain't it? We are now witnessing evidence of heroin addiction in teen-agers the scope of which may be unlike anything we have seen in the past. Federal officials say that heroin addiction has increased 40% from 1968 to 1969. One official calls it an epidemic. And youngsters do not begin their drug usage on heroin; all the youngsters involved have a history of drug use and all of them have, at one time, used marijuana. Perhaps marijuana doesn't always lead to heroin, but over 90% of all heroin addicts smoked marijuana before they used "H." Those who defend and rationalize the use of marijuana can not, if they are sincerely concerned with the welfare of young people, discount the relationship between their advocacy and the growing heroin problem.

We in education must take some of the blame for our drug problem, and our society bears some guilt, but the permissive sector which advocates freedom to experience all pleasures and to hell with the consequences must now face up to an increasing number of young addicts who will spend the rest of their existence more dead than alive. "There is no cure for heroin addiction," a comment from an official of Synanon, a statement echoed by virtually all those who work with drug addiction—a very unrealistic sentence for a 17 year old who has been assured that "pot" is harmless.

Another physician who specializes in drug treatment noted "if a young person smokes marijuana on more than two occasions, the chances are one in five that he will go on to more dangerous drugs."

But facts alone are not enough; it's the attitude that's important. The emphasis must be upon the person understanding his needs, motivations, and limitations. Most important, it must be emphasized that drug use is only a symptom, only the outward response to internal turmoil.

2. *The course should be taught in the school by school personnel.* This does not preclude using physicians, pharmacists, or even drug-users as resource persons, but they must be supplemental and not central to the program. The belief that only a drug addict can communicate with youngsters is simply not true. (The drug addict is no more an expert in drugs than the diabetic is an expert in diabetes.)

We should ask several questions about any outsider coming into the schools: has he had training in the physiological, psychological, and medical effects of drugs? Doctors, lawyers, police officers are not qualified simply by the nature of their positions. The most erroneous information on drugs I ever heard was delivered by a doctor. Has the speaker had a previous successful experience as a teacher? Can he teach, can he understand those youngsters to whom he is going to impart information? Does he realize how much influence he will have upon them? Who recommends the speaker? Have other schools heard him and do they recommend him? There must be a planned preparation before the speaker arrives including some factual knowledge of the subject. There should be a systematic follow-up to the talk, including an evaluation of whether or not the speaker made an accurate presentation.

Can this material be taught by a staff member? The answer is yes, it must be. It is the school's responsibility to teach and it can not be contracted like a plumbing job. The material is not so exotic and the presentation so sophisticated that it can not be handled by a good teacher with modest preparation on the subject. Give your teachers an opportunity to enroll in the many excellent courses now being offered all over the country. Give them sufficient time and incentive to study the materials and prepare their own course of study, and let them teach. Publications from the National Institute for Mental Health and from the Federal Bureau of Narcotics and Dangerous Drugs are excellent. Your State Health Department will also provide valid and effective teaching materials.

I would also recommend that the school, through its Board of Education, prepare a policy statement on drugs. A written policy is vital in informing the public of the school's stand regarding the use or possession of narcotics on school property. Robert Ackerly's *The Reasonable Exercise of Authority*, published by the *National Association of Secondary School Principals* gives some excellent information on this topic.

3. *Let the students discuss the subject.* It sounds trite to remind teachers that any subject is best covered by allowing the students the opportunity to discuss it thoroughly and completely.

We must not lose faith in the good sense of our students to arrive at an intelligent and reasonable decision when given the opportunity to thoroughly explore a subject. This *is* education, teaching youngsters to make choices and decisions. The world has changed much in the past few years; the teen-ager is a little more sophisticated, and perhaps more eager to challenge authority, but human nature has not changed, most students are capable of making sound decisions. Let them discover the facts about drugs, let them ask the questions, and let the teacher participate. Most of our young people are seeking our guidance whether they say so or not. They want direction and support in arriving at their decisions. And they want realistic controls. There is no better way of teaching than by reinforcing the consensus over such questions as: Would you want your brother or sister to use drugs? Why? Or what would you tell your son or daughter if they asked "should I smoke or drink?"

4. *Provide alternatives.* The choices and decisions about drugs and sex must be personal ones, they must be internalized. Our infallible argument is that drugs have failed to provide the better life, and students know this. The decrease in use of LSD indicates that students are aware of effects. We still need to show them, however, that the fullness and richness of life can be attained through non-chemical means and so we must present reasonable alternatives to drugs. We can show them that "cloud nine" or "turning off" or "turning on" can be achieved in other ways.

Youth are frequently bored because they have so little to do; they have little to contribute and our expectations of them are slight. They are neither children nor adults; they are expected to exist on books alone until they are out of school. Dr. Bruno Bettelheim asks "is youth obsolete?" It is not by accident that many drug abusers are deeply involved in the liberal causes of civil rights, tutoring projects in slum schools, voter registration, and collecting food and clothing for needy families. Many of them, more by instinct than intelligence, have expressed an interest in helping the less fortunate and have given much of themselves in this effort. Perhaps this is our best clue as to possible alternatives. Perhaps we can direct the attention of youth away from himself by involvement in constructive projects where they are busy doing something they want to do, something they feel is important and worthwhile. The user just might realize that helping others is a better escape than injuring himself. As one sociologist commented, "the real solution is in finding ways for young people to become active members of our civilization."[15] If the school is to be an agent for social change, perhaps it can be more effective by initiating programs in which students actively participate to help others rather than by policy-making decisions by the Board of Education.

5. *The approach must be varied and community wide.* While I have insisted that direct instruction in this area is necessary and that the final responsibility be vested in one area, the problem can not be solved by the school alone. All areas of the community must be involved. Schools can not assume the ultimate and final responsibility for solving this problem. Parents and community must realize that simply studying and discussing a problem doesn't solve it. We can do little about the problems occurring in the home or community that create a climate favorable for the first use of drugs. Parents must be aware of what is being taught and how it is taught, but they must understand that the school's jurisdiction and responsibility in narcotics are limited. The courts must cooperate in removing drug offenders from the public schools, especially pushers who in some schools openly sell their wares in corridors and escape to sell again. Churches and community agencies must be alert to provide needed services.

We must also make a concerted effort to enlist the help of all our teachers. All concerned teachers want to help students through this period. Such an approach, coming naturally from many sources in the school, and supplemented by a thoughtful program outside the school, *must* have an effect on our teen-agers. But I return to my first point; it must start somewhere; some course and some teacher must have the final responsibility for covering the essential material in depth.

We have not fulfilled our obligations to youth. We have time for all subjects necessary for college entrance but less time for subjects of more

---

[15] *Time* Magazine, "The Junior Junkie," February 16, 1970, p. 36.

importance to the personal lives of our students. We need more emphasis on alcohol and tobacco because they are a more important problem to a larger number of our youth than all other drugs. I hope there was urgency in my message, because we must prepare our students to make the final decision and to understand clearly that:

> Meaningful control rests not with the law, the Federal Bureau of Narcotics and Dangerous Drugs, the police, nor is it the ultimate responsibility of your doctor, your parents, or your teachers. The on-the-spot decision of whether or not to take drugs is clearly yours. The drugs go into you. The responsibility is yours . . . to make a rational choice, you must have respect for yourselves, your mind, your body, and your future.[16]

---

[16] David C. Lewis, "Drug Education," *The Bulletin of the National Association of Secondary School Principals*, December 1969, Number 341, p. 98.

Chapter 7

THE EXTRAINSTRUCTIONAL
PROGRAM

This writer's definition of the curriculum as the planned program of learning opportunities provided by the school includes learning opportunities that do not always involve direct instruction. The direct instructional program has been treated in Chapters 5 and 6; in Chapter 7 we turn to the extrainstructional program.

The opening article, by Robert R. Ford, principal of a large California high school, views student activities as a way of "personalizing" the high school program. At his school personalization starts with articulation activities prior to registration and with orientation ones for new students. In addition to various personalized opportunities relating to the instructional program—program selection, independent study, merit program, use of laboratories, and individualized advanced courses—various other possibilities are described.

The high school activity generally best known to the community and to students is the interscholastic athletic program. The article, "Interscholastic Athletics—Tail That Wags the Dog?" by another California high school principal, echoes a frequent criticism that seems to have been little deterrent to its proliferation and status in American high schools. James R. Solberg notes that there is "an impressive case for the discontinuance of interscholastic sports competition as it is presently constituted." He cites six reasons traditionally given for the program, and then states how the assumed advantages could be accomplished in other ways. His criticisms are bold. How do you react to them? Can the values usually attributed to athletics in fact be otherwise and better sought? Is it, as Solberg contends, "time for a reordering of educational priorities"?

Theodore W. Hipple describes and argues for a still somewhat innovative activity: "A massive involvement of students at all levels of education above fourth grade with students at all lower levels." He calls this "participatory education": he would have students earn credit toward graduation for experience in assisting teachers. He gives a number of examples of such a program and explains various ways of administering it. He also resolves some of the more difficult problems: teachers who resist such help, and the legal responsibility of the certificated teacher. But Hipple sees great value for both the participant and the teacher and students helped. Especially cogent is the point that some of the student participants will become teachers themselves after this experience, "with an awareness of what they can expect," so that their career choice is better made. Hipple's enthusiasm was confirmed by a 1971 report of a study in Montgomery County, Maryland, of the use of about 4500 high school students as student aides, indicating generally favorable reactions from both teachers and the student assistants.

The final article in this chapter deals with the problem of student participation in the activity program of large high schools. A study by the author, E. John Kleinert, had indicated decreased student involvement in activities as high schools grow larger. Many specific findings are provocative of discussion, too. For example, the proportionate number of student leaders decreased with size of the school; clubs and athletics, throughout all sizes of high schools, showed the greatest student participation of all the classifications surveyed. The entire study is quite revealing of the relatively acute problem of large city high schools. Here, where the tendency toward institutionalization is greatest, the program generally considered to offer most opportunity for developing individual interests and special roles has had proportionately the least participation. As Kleinert concluded: "The very large high school, with its institutional character and impersonal masses, is less likely than the small school to help the average individual student with problems of personal identification." Obviously more large schools need the efforts toward "personalization" described in the first article in this chapter.

To improve the situation Kleinert offers several suggestions: use of the "school-within-a-school" plan; broader involvement of faculty in the activities program; expansion of facilities for activities; increased student responsibility for the activity program; and more systematic evaluation of the program. He lists three fundamental questions for the evaluation of a program which might serve as useful bases of a curriculum class discussion of specific high school activities known to members of the class.

The articles in this chapter illustrate major themes and problems of the extrainstructional program of the high school but deal with only samples of the great variety of activities offered in American high schools. In view of the many articles and reports available in the general educational literature, students of the high school curriculum may well select specific activities for more intensive investigation. A classification that may be useful for this purpose includes the following types:

Assemblies
Athletics
Clubs (curriculum; service; social; national youth affiliates; hobbies; honor societies)
Contests, fairs, festivals, tournaments
Homeroom
Public programs
Publications
Service organizations
Social programs
Student-directed periods, days, weeks
Student government
Travel-study programs

PERSONALIZING STUDENT LIFE
AND STUDENT ACTIVITIES*

ROBERT R. FORD

Personalization of the high school program has been a long-term concern of educators as high schools have tended to increase in size. The growth in maximum enrollment has been a phenomenon wherever the availability of school sites is at a premium whether it be in the inner city or a suburban area of high real estate values.

The latter situation pertains to West High School which is one of four high schools in the Torrance Unified School District located close to the ocean in southwest Los Angeles County. This four year high school serves a middle-class suburban community. It opened in 1962 with a thousand students; present enrollment is 2,300, and it is master planned for an enrollment of 3,200.

The following article is a result of a discussion among the administrators of West High School to review present practices for personalizing student life with particular emphasis on student activities. We do not proffer a panacea for the ills of impersonality in the large school. Rather, the reader is invited to use our experiences as a springboard toward additional questing for his own school in a matter that requires concerted effort on the part of the faculty and of the student body.

When freshmen enter high school in Torrance, they come from the security of community K-8 schools. At West High School they meet freshmen from eight feeder schools and might or might not have contact with friends from their former schools. Personalizing or individualizing a student's experience so that he does not feel like a bent punch card becomes both an immediate and long-range task.

* Reprinted from the *Bulletin of the National Association of Secondary School Principals* (November 1968), 52:76–82, by permission.

ARTICULATION

Individualization of student life at West High for incoming eighth graders starts in the spring prior to registration. Principals of the eight feeder K-8 schools share at a luncheon meeting hosted by the high school opinions and ideas on changes in curriculum and registration. When the need arises, departments host their counterparts from the elementary schools to adjust scope and sequence of the curriculum. Counselors visit the feeder schools to confer with eighth grade teachers and to explain registration procedures and materials to students. Counselors are accompanied by representatives from the music and athletic departments who explain special try-out enrollment procedures. Parents are invited to the high school for an evening meeting where counselors speak to them in small groups to provide information similar to that received by their students. Providing registration information to both parents and students promotes home discussion and involves parents in the decisions of their student. Parents are taken on a tour of the school. This is followed by a reception where they have an opportunity to meet the staff and other parents.

Parents and students are invited to meet with a high school counselor during the summer months to discuss student achievement and goals, and to finalize the selection of courses for the fall semester. Students are encouraged to give direction to their high school career by developing a tentative four-year program which, of course, may be modified as interests and abilities develop.

ORIENTATION

Freshmen are invited to school the day before classes begin for an orientation program. The principal welcomes the class, and officers of the student body are introduced. In class groups, freshmen are provided with a West High School identification card, a copy of their class schedule, the student handbook, and their book locker combination. Teachers assist students who are unable to operate locker combinations. Members of the student service group, the Chieftains, help alleviate the "butterflies in the stomach" feeling by taking freshmen on a guided tour to locate their classrooms. At the conclusion of the program, cokes and cookies are provided by the student body and freshmen are encouraged to make new friends among the students of the several feeder schools.

PROGRAM SELECTION

Academically talented students are given an opportunity to become acquainted with the high school by enrolling in a limited choice of summer school subjects at the end of the seventh and eighth grades. During their eighth grade, academically talented students may study one course at the high school, choosing algebra, earth science, or a foreign language. Fifty percent of the student body elect to individualize their instructional programs by enrolling in summer school courses. A few enroll to raise a grade. Others take courses offered only in summer school or enroll for courses which they cannot fit into their schedule during the school year. A further opportunity exists for students with a C or better average to individualize their programs by enrolling for seven instead of the usual six subjects.

INDEPENDENT STUDY

Independent study is an accommodation to a student's desire to focus his interest. Students as individuals or in small groups may be released from class to develop a special report or a unit of the course in which they are particularly interested. Those who are interested in longer-term independent study may receive credit for directing their own learning from a course outline, or developing a special project under the guidance of a faculty sponsor. Special project reports are bound and added to the library collection. Students in independent study have, for example, composed music, written up research on holograms, the Mormons in San Bernardino, the nature of a sophisticated mathematics formula, and composed books of poetry and stories. Some recent independent study project titles have been: "Julius Caesar: Patriot, Statesman, or Opportunist Dictator?", "The Ruby Laser," "The Presidential Role and the Proposal and Direction of Legislation," "Nationalism and Communism in China," "Compulsory Arbitration," "India's Religion," "A Study of the English Novel Since 1900," "Observations on Eugene O'Neill," and "Was Reconstruction Radical?"

MERIT PROGRAM

A merit program augments the independent study program. Students who have demonstrated the ability to direct their activities without supervision may apply for admission to the merit program. A merit student is provided an identification card to be presented to the teacher when he would like to be excused from a class. With the approval of the teacher, the student may be excused to visit the library, a laboratory, a shop, or another class in pursuit of a special interest.

LABORATORIES

The use of laboratories suggests the accommodation of individual needs. Science and language laboratories are open before and after school, as well as during regular class periods. The shorthand laboratory enables the teacher to provide dictation simultaneously at four different speeds and allows students to receive taped dictation from business executives. Experience has indicated that this laboratory has significantly increased proficiency and reduced the shorthand drop-out rate. Students are more proficient in one year than they used to be in two.

All ninth grade students are provided a reading laboratory experience for five weeks. They receive developmental reading instruction, and problems are diagnosed for instruction as needed on an individual basis. A mathematics laboratory has been established for students who have a history of difficulty in comprehending mathematical concepts.

ADVANCED PLACEMENT OR VOCATIONAL TRAINING

Qualified seniors may choose to individualize their program by enrolling for a course at El Camino College. Students with an interest in vocational preparation may select from the courses of six shops. A maximum twenty credits are available to those who choose to earn while they learn with on-the-job training. Courses planned which will provide added individualization of student programs are nursing skills, business occupation skills, chef's training, and plastics. Students may elect to augment their program with instruction at the Southern California Regional Occupational Center. The Center is a cooperative venture of seven school districts to provide the greatest possible scope in the development of saleable, vocational skills.

ACTIVITIES ADVISER

The services of a full-time activities adviser are of increasing importance in a large high school, because he deals most directly with students in matters affecting school spirit and morale. It is through the efforts of his office that students have an opportunity to broaden their interests, deliberate on ways of accomplishing goals, and learn techniques for dealing with other people. Students presently are interested in more than athletics, assemblies, clubs, and dances. Today's students need the guidance of an effective activities adviser in their quest for individual expression, involvement with the operation of their school, and concern for the well-being of their fellowmen.

STUDENT GOVERNMENT

Individualization of student life, through the presentation of challenge and opportunity, is no more explicit than in the current atmosphere of student body elections. Students seem to be interested more in a candidate's proposals for improvement of the organization and welfare of the school, or his suggestion of worthy projects, rather than in campaign promises of more social activities for the student body. The structure of student government provides meaningful individualization. During orientation, social science classes serve as a medium for dissemination of information about campus life and after orientation as sounding boards for opinion and as represented groups in student government. Opinions expressed in social science classes and carried to the house of representatives may result in a bill acted upon by student council or a proposition of a student body election. As an example: considerable involvement preceded an election when the student body voted to lower the grade point average required to run for student office.

MEANINGFUL ACTIVITIES

Students have demonstrated their interest in school and community operation by participation in administrator-teacher day and junior citizens' day. As the titles suggest, students become involved with the operation of the several school offices; some prepare lesson plans under the direction of teachers and actually teach classes. This experience has developed an interest in a teaching career for several students. Junior citizens observe the problems confronting their adult counterparts in municipal government and attend a meeting of the city council. Establishment of a Youth Advisory Council with representation from each high school has been an outgrowth of this activity.

Student interest in their fellowmen has provided two opportunities for creative participation. A principal of a school in Nepal visited West High as a guest of the United States Government. Upon learning of the meager equipment at his school, students raised funds for the purchase of a microscope which was sent to Nepal. A framed expression of gratitude was delivered by a member of the Peace Corps, returning to California.

Last Christmas, students desired to be involved in a project of more lasting effect than, and in addition to, donation of canned food to families in need. They elected to earn money individually to contribute 500 toys to a Head Start center. A bus load of students delivered the toys to the children at the center.

SATURDAY SEMINARS

Enlarging horizons and developing self-realization were accommodated this spring at a series of Saturday morning seminars involving such programs as a trip to the computer research facility. As a result of this visit one of the students is now carrying on correspondence about computers with a member of the corporation. At another Saturday program individual interaction between pairs of black, white, and brown students led to enthusiastic participation for an hour beyond the allotted time.

STAFF-STUDENT RELATIONS

The adults of a school, through display of a warm and accepting attitude, help students regard school as a place where they belong. Creating a sense of identification is individualization in its most meaningful form. Regard for students is expressed in many forms: eye contact and a smile extended to a number of students while crossing the campus, a faculty talent show to portray the "human side" of people past thirty, and the increased understanding by teachers who participated in a sensitivity group with the school psychologist.

Personalization was the concern of many during student deliberation of dress regulations. Concurrence was reached on regulations which permit expression of personality within the framework of "good taste."

A similar opportunity was recently presented when need for an editorial policy regarding the student newspaper became evident. When students pitted their desired "freedom of the press" against their responsibility for the well-being of their school, they were not found wanting.

Individualization of student life through involvement provides opportunity for great strides toward mature concerns. Once a month before school the principal meets with students to learn of their concerns and answer questions. The year started with questions such as, "Why don't we have a senior square at our school?" and has progressed to, "What additional programs would assist the student body in developing better communication among people of different color?" The foregoing considerations have resulted in plans to extend personalization of student life and activities by:

Extending the opportunity for independent study to students of average academic ability;

Experimenting with the merit program to provide for greater student self-direction;

Involving students to a greater degree on faculty committees;

Charging Student Council and the Associated Student Body to continue and extend their school and community service;

Developing additional elective courses to meet the growing variation of student interests;

Working toward development of course outlines and materials at varying levels of complexity to make success available to all students;

Providing additional vocational information by increasing the number of speakers from business and industry who visit the campus throughout the school year to give information to interested students;

Engaging in a project to reaffirm an appreciation for our American heritage;

Extending the activities of the student exchange club to include exchange
with other parts of the United States as well as foreign countries;
Establishing a student body account toward the funding of a project in another
country.

INTERSCHOLASTIC ATHLETICS—TAIL THAT WAGS THE DOG?*

JAMES R. SOLBERG

Interscholastic athletic competition at the senior high school level has
become the tail that wags the dog. Unconscionable expenditures of the
time and energy of countless school teachers, coupled with soaring costs of
maintaining the athletic program make an impressive case for the discontinuance of interscholastic sports competition as it is presently constituted.

It has reached a point in many schools where classroom instruction
is predicated upon coaching competencies of the teacher. One principal
complained, "It's impossible for me to hire a woman teacher. I must staff
24 coaching positions each year, and as my faculty gets older and more
reluctant to undertake coaching duties, I find that normal replacements
must be found among men who can coach."

The traditional reasons for athletics in the schools fall into four
categories: (1) self-realization and development of the individual through
participation or observation; learning skills, techniques and information
necessary to enjoy sports. (2) Involvement of the athletes with others
in real experiences; attainment of positive attitudes regarding group efforts.
(3) Exposure to vocational possibilities. (4) Cultivation of respect for and
need for regulations; encouragement of a sense of civic responsibility.

Other reasons often provided include: (5) The motivating power of
athletics for students who find little success in the classroom. (6) The

---

* Reprinted from *Journal of Secondary Education* (May 1970), 44: 238–239,
by permission.

expectations of the tax paying public regarding appearances of school athletes, especially in communities with a long athletic tradition.

It is not unusual for a moderately sized high school to expend $20,000 annually on coaches' salaries. Additional costs are incurred in transporting teams to away competitions that may readily reach $4,000 each year. Beyond that are expenses for scouting, coaches' conferences, team luncheons and uniforms and equipment.

Taxpayers' public dollars alone do not support interscholastic athletics. Students are also required to make considerable cash outlays for insurance and occasional pieces of gear. This is particularly true of tackle football.

The purpose of this essay is not to launch a campaign against interscholastic athletics. There can be no doubt that sports programs, as distinguished from physical education, have played a significant part in the development of today's comprehensive high school. However, one must ask whether the traditional place held by interscholastic athletics is appropriate in the contemporary secondary educational scene.

Of the six frequent apologies for interscholastic athletic competitions, all can be accomplished other ways. A thoroughgoing intramural program would accomplish every educational objective presently sought by athletic programs. Additional advantages would be the involvement of greater numbers of students, considerable reduction in the level of financing and conservation of teachers' energy by virtue of the utilization of recreational personnel or other para-professional aides for supervision and training as needed.

It may be argued that the money presently spent by school districts in athletics could be better spent by up-grading classroom instruction. Consider what could be accomplished in a school with the $24,000 that would be otherwise spent on coaching salaries and transportation costs. Given what is known today about teaching and learning, surely we could tailor classroom instruction so that every student can succeed.

Do the schools have the responsibility to serve as a training ground for collegiate and professional athletics? If so, might not other agencies assume the role? A community recreation program could more readily provide the experience required for such training. Its broader base of fiscal and moral support would enable a community to support community athletics at a more realistic level than is possible on an interscholastic basis. Obviously, the possibility of abuse would need to be policed just as interscholastic programs are presently supervised.

Dads might be expected to be the greater deterrents in viewing athletic activity in its proper perspective. Perhaps schools are in the sports business because fathers need the vicarious satisfaction that obtains from sons' participation. If so, that is not a proper function for the schools.

In short, it would seem that interscholastic athletics, by virtue of their popularity and magnitude, have outgrown their place in the school setting. We have tended to subordinate other educational needs in deference to the sports program. It is time for a reordering of educational priorities.

PARTICIPATORY EDUCATION: STUDENTS ASSIST TEACHERS*

THEODORE W. HIPPLE

Anyone even slightly familiar with education today knows that a critical teacher shortage exists. The increase in the absolute number of teachers in recent years has been more than offset by both the greater number of students and the longer stay in school of these students. Nor does it appear likely that the larger salaries, better working conditions, and improved public images teachers may now look forward to will significantly reduce the shortage. It becomes necessary, then, to work within the framework of this given—a shortage of qualified teachers—to try to improve education. If, however, we can begin using all the vast human resources we have in our education enterprise, there is good reason for optimism.

I propose that those who administer America's education begin offering, as many already have, approved programs for school credit that will permit students to leave their own schoolrooms and go to work for part of the day in another room in their own school or in another school altogether. Why must a trained kindergarten teacher have to sift through 60 boots, 30 scarves, 30 stocking caps, and 59 mittens each wintry day when it is time for her charges to go home? Two fifth graders from the class down the hall could be released from their work to help her. Why must several reading groups in a primary grade sit idly by while their busy teacher works with just one group? Certainly a seventh or eighth grader

* Reprinted from the *Bulletin of the National Association of Secondary School Principals* (September 1969), 53:80–89, by permission.

could listen to some of the reading groups part of the time and thereby extend their reading exposure; also the teacher, freed from having to create some seatwork material, would have more time for teaching reading.

A high school math whiz could leave school one hour early one day a week (This arrangement could be built into his schedule.) and grade papers for the seventh grade math teacher or privately tutor some of his students who need special assistance. Two business students from the high school could go to an elementary school and help teachers there complete attendance records or balance milk money accounts. Several members of the high school future teachers club could be released to a grade school to offer their services in whatever capacity the schools can use them.

On the college level, where most students have transportation and reasonably flexible schedules, the opportunities are limited only by the extent of the imagination employed in the program. I suggest that college students be allowed to enroll each term, for credit toward graduation, in a program that places them in local schools for at least two hours each week, there to use their talents in helping the teachers and students alike. The college senior majoring in French could provide content help for the high school French teacher whose professional training included only a minor in French, completed 20 years ago. The college theatre major could help the overworked English teacher direct the school play. The library science student could work in a school library, the future chemists as special assistants in a high school chemistry lab, the prospective engineers in a shop program, and on and on. These college students of whom I write are not prospective teachers; future teachers, with their special talents and commitments, could be utilized even more, and possibly be allowed to earn credit for four or six hours a week.

In short, what I am proposing is a massive involvement of students at all levels of education above fourth grade with students at all lower levels. This proposal, for what I call "participatory education," can, I believe, be the means of effecting significant educational and social improvements. I am not proposing a volunteer system at all, in which the only rewards are personal satisfaction, but rather an elective system which offers, in addition to that personal satisfaction, some substantial coin of the educational realm: credit toward promotion or graduation. It seems sensible to me that our schools, which now teach virtually everything, also should present students with opportunities for helping fellow students and for doing so for credit. If the development of good driving habits is an appropriate function of the schools, and I believe it is, then surely the development of good living habits, including those of helping other people, is equally legitimate. The ideal, I suspect, is somewhat tarnished by my system of offering credit for this help; to do less, however, is to continue to rely on a voluntaristic behavior that most students, regardless of their altruistic inclinations or lack of them, do not have time for. When the students can earn credit for helping students at lower levels in the schools, I think they will jump at the chance to participate.

PROGRAMS IN OPERATION

What I am suggesting is already in successful operation in some schools. For example, in Lexington (Mass.) High School a "Student-Helping-Student" program provides tutoring on an individual or small group basis. At the same school, a student organized program provides assistance to local elementary schools in the form of tutoring, supervision, and service as teachers' aides. El Camino High School in Sacramento, California, involves over 200 of its students in a program called "Inside Work Experience" that includes many of the kinds of activities I have mentioned above. At Bethesda-Chevy Chase (Maryland) High School, National Honor Society students even leave the state to tutor other students; they go to a junior high in Washington, D.C. At Denby High in Detroit the sociology classes have "adopted" one of the inner-city elementary schools; the sociology students plan and teach not only the traditional subjects but also such extras as guitar, tap dancing, cheerleading, and pop art. At the University of Florida, four of the five education courses, excluding student teaching, required for secondary certification involve participation in local schools.

Schools, then, are using participatory education and are reporting satisfaction with the programs they have established. I don't know of any school which is thinking of dropping such a program; indeed, many have plans for expansion to include more schools, more students, more projects. The idea of participatory education does work at the level of practice.

But one could still ask, why *education?* Why not some other institution of society, like the church? Or why any organized institution at all? Why not urge students who want to, to go to slum areas on Saturday to paint and refurbish tenement apartments or tutor children? Such church-sponsored or volunteer programs can be good ones, but they are often complicated to arrange; they involve only a few students for irregular, short periods of time; and they have an aura (though usually not an intentional one) of condescension and self-righteousness about them.

A national participatory education program does not have these weaknesses. Thousands, indeed millions, of students can be involved, students in fifth grade or eighth grade or in high school, college, or graduate school. Such a program can become as common in the schools as physical education or Friday night dances. Everyone—the bright and the dull, the rich and the poor, the white and the black—can work together to improve the American school system they are still a part of. Education is America's biggest endeavor in the numbers of people involved, one much deserving an effort toward its improvement commensurate with its size and importance. Such improvement is indeed possible if the human elements in education are put to use in ways far more imaginative than in the present scheme of things.

ADMINISTERING THE PROGRAM

Participatory education has one advantage not available to most other programs: Schools are usually in close proximity to other schools, often within walking distance. Thus, students can leave one to travel to another. Even if distance *does* present problems, they ought not to be insurmountable. After all, schools regularly transport pupils across town or country for sports activities and music events. Why not, then, for a program like this one which would benefit even more students in more educationally significant ways?

Nor would participatory education be a difficult program to administer. Most schools have articulation arrangements with nearby schools and meet regularly to discuss curricular offerings or to effect joint calendars. Participatory education can easily become an agenda item at such meetings and plans can be created that take into consideration local problems, such as varying school day lengths. Arrangements can be made, for example, for a high school to send out 40 students every day at 2:15 to various junior high and elementary schools. These schools will use the high school youth according to the needs of the schools and the talents of the students coming to it. The time the student helpers lose from high school will be more than compensated for by the enrichment derived from the experiences at the lower grades.

If it seems to some that I have glossed over possible administrative entanglements, it is simply because I have great faith in the capacities of school administrators to handle what are, at bottom, logistical problems. When the basketball team goes to the state tournament, its fans somehow get there, too; the transportation arrangements, not unlike massive troop movements, may be a headache for the principal, but he gets the job done. So, also, can he manage the time and transportation elements in participatory education.

POTENTIAL BARRIERS

A difficulty slightly more complex than the administrative arrangements or transportation is the reluctance of some teachers to accept any help at all from outside the walls of their rooms. A degree of masochism resides in a few teachers that causes them to delight in relating how hard they must work, how many themes they must grade, how much daily preparation they must do. Others, unfortunately, are so insecure and threatened as to be rendered almost helpless if someone else (even if it's only a student just a few years older than those they teach) comes into their rooms. The vast majority of teachers, however, will welcome help of any kind, just as those teachers already using student assistance have welcomed it. They recognize that it is more important that their students learn than that they teach; anything, or anyone, which helps them effect that learning, deserves and receives their earnest consideration. Success on the part of some teachers in utilizing student help in their teaching and supervisory tasks will result, I think, in persuading reluctant teachers to join the program; success begets success.

A more serious barrier is the legal one operative in most states which requires that certificated personnel be responsible for and in charge of students in *all* school activities. My proposal, however, in no way violates this principle, as it does not provide a teacher with the option of turning over her class to an older student and retiring to the teacher's lounge for coffee and cigarettes. The certificated teacher will still be very much in evidence and will still be responsible for what goes on in her classroom. But now she will have help, help that she can use as she thinks best. Teachers can have older students help them grade objective tests or distribute supplies or assist individual students in special projects or lead small group discussions. The list of possible activities is endless, but always the certificated teacher will be in charge, both of her students and of her student assistants.

The dimensions of the improvement possible with the implementation of participatory education are limited only by a school's effort and imagination. Assuming it subscribes to the program and commits itself to its success, a school can achieve for its students an education simply not possible under today's conditions of overworked teachers in overcrowded classrooms. Of greatest significance, of course, is the educational improvement. When teachers are not doing tasks that virtually anyone a few years older than their students can perform—e.g., attendance taking, putting on leggings, helping supervise recess activities—they can be doing other things that more properly are the responsibilities of trained teachers—e.g., preparing lessons, providing individualized instruction, examining new materials, establishing curricular priorities.

Teachers are human and their energy is limited. When that energy is spent in the necessary but easily performed routine tasks, it cannot be brought back for the really crucial concerns of teaching. An analogous example might be that of the doctor in whose office there are nurses and nurses' aides and receptionists who perform many of the important but less difficult aspects of the work. The doctor is saved for that which only he can do. So also can it be for the teacher and her team of student assistants. The teacher does the teaching, but students a few years older than those she teaches are given duties in accord with their abilities. The teacher now has more time for her central task: teaching.

MORE INDIVIDUAL ATTENTION

The students in a class where the assistants work will gain much from participatory education. They will be the beneficiaries of the efforts of an entire instructional team, one composed not only of their regular teacher, but also of older students. They will be able to secure increased individual attention from their less beleaguered teacher, will benefit from the extra time she has for preparing lessons and, possibly, most significant, will experience a sense of personal worth from knowing that their learning is considered vital by an entire team of people. It is not Mark Hopkins on one end of a log and James Garfield on the other, but it is a whole lot closer than our present education structure permits.

The subsidiary members of this team, the student assistants, will themselves benefit considerably. An old saw in education has it that one learns something best by teaching it. This has been true of Shaker Heights (Ohio) High School science students who are working in teams of five to seven students and are teaching science several days a week to elementary school students. This program, by the way, grew in five years from one team of six high school students and one elementary classroom to over 100 students and 20 classrooms. But even those who help in ways that involve little subject matter content will experience the thrill and satisfaction of helping others learn. They will know that their work has freed teachers to perform better the important duties for which they have been especially educated. Additionally, they will be getting school credit for their work, and it is at least a debatable point whether school credit could be given for a more worthwhile human endeavor.

ATTRACTING STUDENTS TO TEACHING

There is, happily, the possibility that some of these student assistants will become teachers themselves as a result of their experiences in a participatory education program. Nova High School in Fort Lauderdale, Florida, requires that its program of participatory education include considerable teaching experience, the better to attract students to teaching; happily, many high school boys are entering the program. The Green Bay (Wisconsin) High Schools even develop printed schedules of what student is *to teach* with what teacher at what schools. Gainesville (Florida) High

School has made wise use of an unfortunate split-shift situation; many high school students spend several hours a day in local elementary schools. Eisenhower High School in Decatur, Illinois, refers to its program of participatory education as "exploratory teaching." Similarly, Tenafly (New Jersey) High School labels its participants "Cadet Teachers." Mt. Lebanon High School in Pittsburgh even secures written evaluations of the teaching performance of its student participants. Students in these and other programs who have seen both the problems and the promises of teaching from the teacher's side of the desk before they have completed their career plans may choose education with a zeal and commitment not always found among those who become teachers because they think they will "like it." These student assistants who become teachers will do so with an awareness of what they can expect, of likely achievements and probable failures. They will become, I submit, good teachers. Moreover, they will be interested in maintaining the program of participatory education.

To the degree that people who would not have chosen careers in education without participatory education will become teachers with it, it will have eased the teacher shortage and its attendant problems. But even if few of these people ever again enter classrooms after their own schooling has been completed, education and society will be the better for their having been student assistants. Lawyers, butchers, owners of cleaning establishments, engineers, salesmen, housewives, adults in all walks of life who, as students, experienced the role of a student assistant will view education with a more nearly complete perspective. It is a legitimate expectation that they will support education.

Wilbur J. Cohen, Secretary of Health, Education, and Welfare in the latter months of the Johnson administration, repeatedly urged Americans to put their priorities in order and place education spending at least on a par with that for tobacco or liquor. A new generation, having been involved in participatory education, may not reach Cohen's goal, but they will be more aware of, and possibly more sympathetic to, the financial burdens most schools face.

A VARIETY OF BENEFITS

And there can be some immediate benefits. High school students who report to their parents about their experiences in elementary school where they helped overworked, ill-equipped teachers in overcrowded classrooms may be far more persuasive than any referendum-motivated school board press release. With participatory education, a student's knowledge of schools and their problems, and hence, his parents' knowledge, goes well beyond an awareness of the situation in the single school building he attends. It is feasible that with massive participatory education can come massive public support of education, a support brought about by a concerned parentage whose children are no longer only students but also student helpers in the schools in need of financial assistance.

The immediate benefits for society from participatory education also include some significant improvements in human understanding. When students of varying backgrounds help other students, their joint efforts, their interaction, may better the relationships among the groups they represent. Newton High School in Newtonville, Massachusetts, reports favorable relationships growing out of its participatory education program, which cut across class and race boundaries; so also does the Denby High staff of the program mentioned above. This bringing together of many disparate groups can be participatory education's most worthwhile aspect.

Then there are the benefits to the individual as he comes to understand and to accept himself more fully. It may even be that high school students of low ability who would be potential dropouts can receive enough positive experiences from their work in a grade school that their self images will be improved sufficiently and they will stay in school. The Whittier School in Oak Park, Illinois, for example, intentionally chooses junior high students of low ability to help younger students; the preliminary reports indicate that the tutors' self-images have become more positive as an important side benefit in the program. Some of the apathetic high school boys sent from John Marshall High School in Cleveland to teach science in elementary classrooms have now become enthusiastic about their own schooling. Through the assistance these students have given others has come their own improvement. Helping others is a part of the American tradition, though one that some recent thinkers have almost given up on. Participatory education is rooted in this tradition.

It takes little to implement this proposal. Few innovations in education which involve as many students as participatory education can be put into practice with so little administrative effort and expense. There will be some scheduling problems, some transportation difficulties that might necessitate a school's buying a station wagon or two, some psychological unwillingness on the part of both teachers and student assistants that will have to be overcome, but, on balance, the goals that can be achieved far outweigh these minor concerns.

And outweigh them they must. Participatory education has so much to offer America's schools and to America itself that its immediate implementation ought to be considered in every school district. It will not solve overnight all of the shortcomings of American education, but it will ease many of the problems and, over the long haul, may entirely remove some of them. Of more importance, it will involve millions of Americans in the human task of helping millions of Americans. And that, after all, is what America is all about.

EFFECTS OF HIGH SCHOOL SIZE ON STUDENT ACTIVITY PARTICIPATION*

E. John Kleinert

One aspect of the booming school enrollments of the post-war years has been the increase in the proportion of large high schools in the United States.

The reasons for the emergence of the large high school are as familiar as the reasons for the increased enrollments themselves. Most common among factors contributing to this growth is the lag that inevitably occurs between the need for a new high school building within a district and the acquisition of funds for its construction. In spite of advance planning, a community often waits until a high school becomes overcrowded before it votes affirmatively on a bond issue to build another one.

A second reason for the existence of more large high schools relates to the uncertainty of most school administrators concerning maximum desirable enrollment for a high school. This uncertainty frequently manifests itself in a compromise solution: structural additions are made to existing high school buildings. This may occur several times until the school site becomes overburdened by congestion within and without the buildings. Congestion is not the only result of rapid growth; other problems arise. One such complication is administrative understaffing. The situation demands that new rooms be added and additional teachers be employed, but the high school administrative staff often remains largely the same in number.

Because of the obvious physical problems which arise when a high school becomes large, and because so many more high schools are large today, there is need now for greater research effort to be expended towards determining what effects these schools have upon students. After determining their effects, it will be possible to estimate the maximum size a high school can be if it is to have the best influence on students.

---

* Reprinted from the *Bulletin of the National Association of Secondary School Principals* (March 1969), 53:34–46, by permission.

In years past a great deal of research was directed at the small high school in an effort to understand its strengths and weaknesses. That research produced criteria upon which minimum high school size could be established by districts. Now similar benchmarks are needed to tell us when a high school is too big.

A SINGLE INDICATOR

This article is the result of studying one aspect of the large public high school: student participation in extracurricular activities. It must be said that student participation in a school's activity program is but a single indicator of the effectiveness of a high school—and it is not even that unless the premise is granted that extracurricular activities are, in fact, valuable components of a high school education. Therefore, the results of this study of one particular effect of a high school's size on the experiences of its students would of course have to be joined with studies of other effects before the determination of maximum high school size could be attempted. The investigation which produced this paper may be significant as an initial attempt to evaluate what the large high school can or cannot do for its students.

My findings indicate decreased student involvement in activities as high schools grow larger. This is usually viewed as undesirable by students, parents, teachers, and administrators who believe that participation in student activities is basic to learning cooperation and leadership, as well as to having a rich and enjoyable high school experience.

In order to make my study, I selected by random sample 63 high schools, with enrollments in the upper three grades from 87 to 3,063, from all southern Michigan high schools. This was done in such a way as to assure equal representation of "small" (0–599 students), "medium" (600–1,499 students), and "large" schools (1,500 students or more). Through this procedure I established three sub-groups of the total sample.

I then selected seven classifications of student activities: music, athletics, student government, dramatics and oratory, publications, clubs, and service committees. These included almost all of the activities traditionally considered extracurricular. Names and numbers of students who participated in each component of each school's activity program were the basis for the analysis of student involvement in the 63 schools.

The findings, based upon correlation coefficients computed at the University of Michigan Computing Center, revealed a striking decrease in student involvement in the activity programs of larger high schools as compared with those of smaller schools. These findings are summarized below.

Total Participation

The extent of total student participation bore a strong negative correlation to school size. The fall-off in this overall participation, however, was seen to be considerably greater when small schools (less than 600 students) grew larger than when the large schools (600 or more students) grew still larger. This was indicated because of the overwhelming advantage noted for the small schools in terms of student activities. A continued, but less obvious, trend of reduced participation in the middle group of schools was seen as they became larger. However, only a slight drop in the magnitude of student involvement was distinguishable in schools as they pass the 1,500-student level.

The scattergram for this relationship is shown in Figure 1. Note that the relationship with the size groups varies, the strongest existing in the smaller schools. The graph in Figure 2 shows the differences in actual participation between the three size groups.

Proportion of Students Participating

The relationship between the proportion of individual students who participate in school activities and the size of the high school was found to be high and inverse for schools with enrollments of less than 600, and moderate and inverse for schools with enrollments of more than 600.

As the small school approaches medium size the study revealed a sharp drop in the proportion of high school students engaged in at least one activity; as the medium-size school grows larger individual student participation was shown to follow a less significant trend.

In the larger schools studied, an average of only 32 students per hundred participated in one or more activity; whereas 76 per hundred did in the small schools and 49 per hundred did in the medium-sized schools.

Extensive Participation

When considering various specific aspects of the activity program, the results were similar to those reported above. Smaller schools, for instance, had more students participating in several activities (2, 3, 4 or 5) in a given year than did larger ones.

Interestingly, no relationship with size existed for student participation in 6 or more activities. This finding leads to speculation about an unexpected strength of the activity program in the small high school; the danger of overinvolvement in student activities appears to be no greater in the small school, where total participation is high, than in the large high school, where total participation is lower.

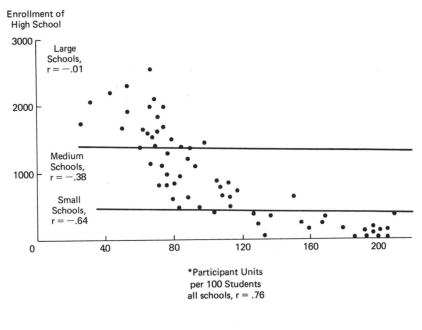

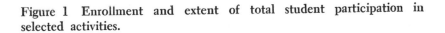

A "participant unit" is one student
participating in one activity.

Figure 1 Enrollment and extent of total student participation in selected activities.

Student Leadership

The findings also supported a strong inverse relationship between school size and the total number of leadership roles available to students. A high and significant negative correlation was found for these factors when the total range of school sizes was used, as well as when only the medium-sized and large schools were considered. Further, the means for the three groups show the average number of leaders in activities per 100 students as 25.4, 10.0 and 7.1 for small-, medium-, and large-sized schools. The fact that the average middle-sized school in the sample had 10 student leaders per 100 students, whereas the average large school had but 7.1, indicates a 40 percent gain for the medium-enrollment school. Contrasted with the 25.4 student leaders per 100 students for the small schools, the difference in the various sized schools' influence on leadership potential is noteworthy.

The consistently significant correlation figures for leadership and size factors give support to one of the most conclusive findings of the study: the proportionate number of student leaders decreased as schools of

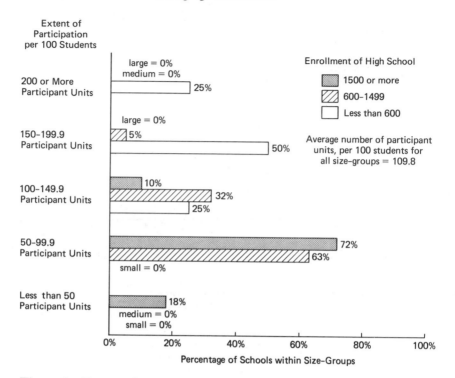

Figure 2   **Extent of total student participation in selected activities for three size-groups of high schools.**

the sample grew larger. The strength of this relationship is illustrated by the graph in Figure 3.

External Participation

A statistically significant inverse relationship was observed for the entire range of schools in the sample when external participation (performance before the general public) was related to high school size. This factor included all activities that are normally performed before audiences which include people from outside the school.

Kinds of Activities

Pertaining to activity classifications, the larger the high school gets the fewer, proportionately, students are found participating in clubs, athletics, and school publications. The size of the high school, however, appears to have little influence on the students' participation in service committees and student government functions.

Clubs and athletics, throughout all sizes of high schools, showed the greatest student participation of all the classifications surveyed, and these two groups of activities also yielded the highest negative correlations for extent of participation and size of the high school.

It is interesting to note that the small schools in the sample averaged 55 and 50 participant units per 100 students in clubs and athletics, respectively, while the larger schools averaged 18 and 13 for the same activity classifications.

The correlations computed for extent of student participation in the five previously mentioned activity classifications and size of the high school were almost as significant for the schools surveyed with 600 or more students as for the total sample.

When school clubs in the sampled schools were divided into three basic types, those devoted to recreation-performance and future-occupation purposes carried a marked negative correlation with high school size, while those clubs of an academic nature were found not to relate as significantly to size.

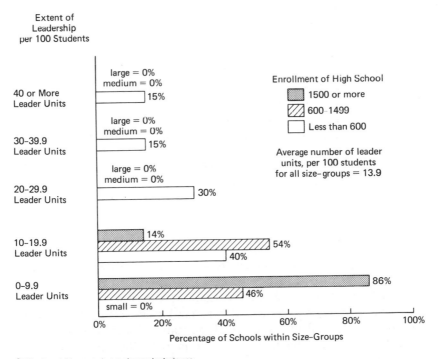

*A "leader unit" is one student serving as a leader in one activity. A student thereby may be counted more than once.

Figure 3 Extent of student leadership in selected activities for three size-groups of high schools.

Number of Activities Offered by School

A distinct difference in the total number of different kinds of activities per 100 students was observed between the small- and medium-sized schools, and between the medium- and large-sized schools. The strength of the inverse relationship for the size of school and the proportionate number of activity offerings is indicated by a −.73 correlation coefficient computed for it from figures obtained from the sampled schools. A −.25 figure would have been statistically significant at the 5 percent level of significance.

CONCLUSIONS

From these findings, I conclude that the student's opportunity to participate in a number of activities becomes less as the high school grows larger. The very large high school, with its institutional character and impersonal masses, is less likely than the small school to help the average individual student with problems of personal identification. That is, it fails to provide him with opportunities to take initiative, to enjoy recognition, to exercise leadership—in short, to gain honor and glory. The eagerness of a student to participate in those school activities which are essentially voluntary in nature is understandably affected by his being one of 2,500 persons, recognizing only a few faces outside his classes. Also, his sense of identification with a school enrolling thousands is undoubtedly weaker than it might be where he is counted as a larger fraction of the whole.

If the student's extracurricular activities are considered one of the important features (supplementary to course offerings) in the total effect of the high school on the growth and development of the child, and if the results of this study are taken as valid, then educators should feel concern in the face of ever-increasing numbers of high schools with enrollments of over 1,500 students

TWO ASSUMPTIONS

Before making some proposals for dealing with the problematic situation of lessened participation in student activities in a large high school, I want to clarify my assumptions regarding the situation.

My first assumption is that organized student activities in the high school program enhance the overall educational experiences of the individual student because they provide him with the opportunity to work cooperatively and informally within student groups. This opportunity would be denied him where the program is restricted to the formal classroom experiences of the curriculum. I would assume that the goodness of these activities is the result of their enabling students to obtain certain learning experiences that are closely related to the academic functions of the school and their providing opportunities for the individual student to identify with a social group in a more mature and independent way than his classroom experiences would allow. Ameliorating the increasing problem of the high school student's anonymity in urban America can occur only if the leaders of our schools recognize the extracurricular program as a vital part of the whole educating process.

My second assumption is that high schools cannot be made small again. The school districts in this country that are able to afford regular construction of new high school facilities to keep pace with booming enrollments are almost without exception able to do this only by constructing large plants that will centralize the modern services of a secondary school. Leaders of most contemporary institutions sense the nostalgic desire of many for a retreat to an earlier, less complex America where the standards of the past could be applied to our institutions, where each staff member would know the names of all of the people with whom he worked, and where the leader would be able to identify most of the human personalities and characteristics of his organization—an unrealizable desire, unfortunately.

PROPOSALS

On the basis of these premises, I now make suggestions which are compatible with the direction of the American high school in the 1960's. They are consistent with most of the innovations which have characterized the New Look of the modern secondary school.

The first proposal has to do with the growing trend to divide high schools into several sub-schools. This is frequently called "schools-within-a-school" or the "house plan." Among its most widely known examples are the Newton (Massachusetts) and the Evanston (Illinois) high schools. One of the primary intentions of those who have been instrumental in developing house plans for their high schools has been to bring about the individual student's closer identification with his school. The intention has been to create a warmer, more intimate atmosphere among the student body. The underlying theory is that students benefit more from their high school education when they are in more regular contact with a smaller group of teachers and students than is customarily the case in the very large school.

Usually this change in high school organization brings about an increase in student participation in extracurricular activities. However, the evidence indicates that this increase is not particularly significant. The most common practice in schools with the house plan is to keep the activity program about the way it was, with the difference that student government and intramural athletic units are established within each house. Opportunities are not increased for youngsters to participate to a greater extent in the varsity athletic program, the music organizations, the social and academic clubs, and the service organizations of the school. By and large, these activities retain their single school unity, and it remains just as difficult as ever for the student to participate.

Therefore, I propose here that high schools in the process of considering house plans resolve to divide their activity programs much in the way they divide their academic departments and curricular offerings to suit the location and solidarity of each house. This means, in many cases, the creation of four high school bands and four varsity football teams. This can be accomplished by reducing the school community's aspirations for developing state and regional award-winning, recognition-gaining student organizations. This reduction in aspiration would certainly be commensurate with a major reduction in the cost of each organization, even though the overall school budget would certainly have to be increased somewhat to accommodate the multiple organizations. Also, the loss of state and regional awards would be compensated for by a major increase in student participation.

A second suggestion for improvement applies to schools not anticipating a change in structural organization. These schools should consider putting a special kind of emphasis on their student activity programs by involving their faculties to a greater extent in extracurricular activities. It would seem desirable, in terms of the basic educational objectives of a high school, that fewer specialists and more regular teachers be used. This broader base of faculty involvement in the extracurricular program presupposes that schools would consider activity sponsorship a regular part of the teaching assignment. In many schools this is already common practice, but too seldom is this portion of the assignment stressed by the leadership of the school and articulated as a basic part of the total education program. It is suggested here that this kind of assignment represent at least 10 percent of a faculty member's load; that he be given complete choice of which, if any, portion of the activity program he wishes to involve himself in; and, most importantly, that these assignments not be spare time, extra pay tasks.

Schools placing greater emphasis on their activity programs as their student bodies increase must devote more attention not only to staffing for these activities but also to expanding their recreational facilities. These facilities should include not only gymnasiums but meeting rooms and social areas as well. This expansion of facilities is entirely consistent with the wide-spread tendency to develop flexible scheduling and independent study programs in schools across the country. Wherever these organizational changes in curriculum occur, there is need for all-purpose areas and spaces for students to function in unsupervised circumstances. It is specifically these spaces that would be most important for the operation of such activities as additional student government bodies, clubs, and discussion groups.

NEW RESPONSIBILITY FOR STUDENTS

This current tendency of secondary schools to develop new programs requiring building additions with specialized facilities is also compatible with the third solution offered here. When schools are anticipating neither house plans as organizational changes nor staffing an expanded activity program, serious consideration should be given to assigning to students themselves new kinds of responsibilities for organization and leadership. The attempts of high schools in recent years to provide students with unsupervised time whereby they may study or relax between classes is leading toward greater realization of the potential of young people to operate independently within the framework of the high school. In regard to the student activity program, this tendency would suggest that schools may tap more and more of their student leadership potential for sponsorship and leadership functions within the extracurricular program. It is entirely conceivable, for example, that the Honor Society, the French club, the ski club, and the intramural basketball league could function beyond the gaze of the usual sponsor. It is interesting to speculate what the benefits of such wholly student-run organizations might be for those who are members of them. For some of the activities, the use of students in real leadership roles (rather than in the pseudo ones they often hold in name only while the sponsors, remembering their classroom functions, actually do the leading) would represent a bold effort on the part of the school administration to recognize and tap in an unusual way the rich potential of youth. For many, the opportunity to attempt expanded student leadership opportunities in order to create a broadened activity program in the large high school would be an exciting venture.

Finally, any attempt to provide the student in the large high school greater opportunities for participation in the life of that school would almost surely require a concerted effort to evaluate the established activity program of that school. This evaluation would result in a sharper focus on those activities which should be stressed or broadened, and the elimination of those activities less beneficial in terms of the overall objectives of the high school. One important outcome of this evaluation would be the emphasis of those activities which are most significant for the greatest number of students. In effect, there would be an effort to consolidate the energies of the school staff and the facilities of its buildings so that the greatest usefulness could be gained from the activity program.

It should be noted that this kind of activity program evaluation should be carried out regularly by every school, whether or not it is intending to put more or less stress on extracurricular activities. This evaluation should be based on the same criteria used to evaluate the school's entire educational program. Basic to this evaluation would be the following questions:

a. Which aspects of the activity program are consistent with the aims of the school and its curriculum?
b. How does each activity relate to specific contemporary demands of American society?
c. How does each activity relate to specific contemporary needs of young Americans?

Each of these basic questions should be answered to the satisfaction of a school committee composed of members who are sensitive to the reasons for formal schooling in late twentieth century America and who are aware of the need for new efforts to prepare youth for the uncertain age that lies ahead.

In conclusion, it must be recognized that many American high schools in recent years have relegated their activity programs to the status of a forgotten step-child. The defense made for this neglect usually is based on the severe challenges made on schools during the 1960's: challenges to improve academic programs so that high school graduates will have a better chance of success in college. What is too often overlooked by those who make this defense is that the active participants in our American democracy who over the years have had the most to offer society are people who have had the opportunity to be active participants all their lives. When we confine the education of our young to formal academic experiences only, we deny them the opportunity to participate in meaningful social activities related to the school community which help them develop into contributing, mature citizens.

PART III

TRENDS AND ISSUES
IN CURRICULUM
IMPROVEMENT

The avalanche of criticisms from within and without the high school has generated a host of innovations in the curriculum and especially in its facilities and organizational setting. The chapters in Part II reviewed current changes in the curriculum itself; in Part III we turn to the issues that are being debated as further change is demanded by many, and also to the trends toward change in the facilities and organizational setting.

Chapter 8 reflects the popular demand at the advent of the 70s for more "relevance" in the curriculum. Included are selections that explain the need for greater relevance to youths' problems today and tomorrow, and also several descriptions of changes needed, proposed, or in process.

"Individualization" is also the keynote of much curriculum change in the early 70s and the predictable future. Chapter 9 presents analyses and descriptions of several approaches toward the "individual self-fulfillment" goal its first selection sets for the high school. Independent study, learning activities packages, and modular scheduling, respectively, are considered in articles that describe each approach and look toward further improvement of its use.

Chapter 10 deals with the continuing, at times controversial, development of roles in curriculum improvement. The selections included pertain to the roles of national curriculum projects and their involvement of academic specialists, of the learning industry, of industry-education partnerships, of the parties involved in performance contracts, and of students.

Chapter 11 turns to today's trend toward establishment of schools and educational programs outside the regular high school system. Represented in the articles are: a "humane" campus laboratory school; an urban "school without walls"; the nonpublic school; the so-called "alternative" schools beginning to emerge in the late 1960s; the street

288

academy of New York City, as one variety of the latter; and the education voucher plan for providing parental choices of schools for their children.

The final chapter, 12, is devoted to several readings that relate to the role of teachers and technology in curriculum change. The several selections point to or attempt new role definitions for teachers as curriculum and instructional developments continue to involve increasing use of technology.

Chapter 8

MAKING THE CURRICULUM
RELEVANT

"Relevance" had become the most popular criterion of curriculum
evaluation by 1970. The high school curriculum was assailed by students,
laymen, and educators because of its lack of relevance to such overlapping
but at times conflicting concerns as the major contemporary problems of
the nation, the ambitions, interests, and problems of adolescents,
and the immediate and acute racial, economic, employment, and other
problems of particular communities, especially urban ones. The selections
in Chapter 8 state some of these criticisms and concerns and also
describe some approaches to making the curriculum more relevant.

In his chapter for The Brookings Institution report, *Agenda for
the Nation*, Ralph W. Tyler based his proposals for improving the high
schools on the charge that "the high school at present is failing to serve
effectively more than half the youth who are of high school age."
He derived this figure from the number of dropouts plus the one-third
of the graduates who "do not develop the skills and attitudes required for
higher level employment and for civic leadership." Among various
factors preventing the success of past efforts in providing "a meaningful
and relevant program" has been "the tradition that the high school should
be an adolescent island outside the major currents of adult life." To
correct the situation he proposes "a major effort to furnish high school

students with significant adult activities" in community and work experience programs. The article includes consideration of specific changes needed in the high school and in school-community relationships to implement such a program.

Two selections are focused on programs for students about to drop out, or forced out, of high school. "They Don't Have To Drop Out" by W. Stanley Kruger describes some of the projects supported by Title VIII of the Elementary and Secondary Education Act Amendments. The article indicates some of the major problems dealt with in these dropout prevention programs and some of the major approaches used. The reprint from the *Dade County Teacher* of the description of Dade County's Douglas MacArthur School (Miami, Florida) extolls this school as one "where the 100 percent would-be dropout stays—and succeeds." The article describes the school's objectives, program, and instruction; although fully as laudatory as would be expected in such a local source, the article actually reflects observations known by the present writer to be common among those who have visited the school. Readers may note from these two articles the concern in all these programs for an improved and different relationship between the potential dropout and his teachers, for departures from stereotypes of the school structure itself as well as the curriculum and instruction, and for work experience opportunities. Do you see differences, too, between these programs? What problems may be incurred in relation to one of Kruger's principles: "Each of these demonstration projects must influence, continuously and increasingly, its entire school system"?

The usual method of high school curriculum change—the addition of elective courses—is utilized in the proposal by James L. Fenner on "Reconnection for Relevance: A Proposed New High School Curriculum" which is excerpted here. But Fenner's proposed new courses are different: they would be open for everybody rather than according to some curriculum track, and they are also "intended to cut across interdisciplinary boundaries, to bridge some of the gaps between subject and subject or between school and the 'real' world, to combine and recombine the world, the media, the person, and the school in new and significant configurations." His descriptions of the first 13 of the 40 such courses he proposes are included in the selection. Among the most interesting of the other titles are: "Do-It-Yourself Household Repairs and

Improvements"; "Getting Your Money's Worth"; "How To Get a Job and Get Ahead"; "Everyday Law"; "Nutrition, Diet, and Partymaking"; "The Stock Market"; "Protest Literature"; "Rock and Folk Survey"; "Variety in American Society"; and "Emceeing, Newscasting, and Discjockeying." In concluding his presentation of the 40 courses, Fenner notes that he has dealt primarily with their content but that "much must be done to make the manner as strongly integrative as the matter." He also comments that the new electives would not be a complete solution to the problems of the high school curriculum. Discussion of his proposals will undoubtedly raise questions about the staffing of the courses: Who is to teach them? What qualifications are required? How could teachers prepare themselves to teach such courses? What help could be given through team teaching arrangements and the use of community resource persons?

"Education for relevance," as developed in the articles in this chapter is no one program and not even very new. What is new is probably the concentrated attention to the notion of relevance, undoubtedly strongly stimulated by student dissatisfaction with the high school curriculum. The proposals herein assume the continuation of some traditional curriculum elements hopefully changing as described in our Part II selections, and the addition or partial substitution of new curriculum elements, largely functional or experiential in nature. Is such a mix of the old and new inevitable?

Should increasing relevance be sought through more programs that serve already dissatisfied youth, as those described in the articles on the Title VIII dropout prevention projects and the Douglas MacArthur School, or by organization of new and intriguing courses such as suggested by Fenner, or by broad expansion of the school program into community work and service experiences as proposed by Tyler, or by some combination or other approach? As the new programs are developed, what should happen to the old? Will a more relevant work experience make the traditional, required course in English, for example, more or less tolerable? Is it possible that the competition of Tyler's community service corps or Fenner's electives would force change on the rest of the curriculum? What do you propose?

IMPROVING THE HIGH SCHOOLS*

Ralph W. Tyler

The second problem is education at the high school level. Society needs a much higher percentage of its youth educated beyond the elementary school. As the demand for unskilled and semiskilled labor has sharply diminished, there are increasing employment opportunities that require at least a high school education—health services, education, recreation, social services, science, engineering, administration, accounting. Such an education also contributes to constructive citizenship and to competence in other areas of living.

In spite of the need, the high school at present is failing to serve effectively more than half the youth who are of high school age. Over a million of them drop out each year before completing high school, and an equal number of those who remain make no measurable progress on standard tests in high school subjects. The dropouts include 60,000 unwed mothers and 80,000 already identified as delinquent. The largest part of the nation's expenditures for welfare and unemployment go to persons who dropped out before completing high school, and a considerable part of the cost of crime is associated with them.

Of those who remain in the high school to graduate, one-third do not develop the skills and attitudes required for higher level employment and for civic leadership. Many of them are from minority groups, but the largest fraction includes young people from white middle-class and working-class families of city, country, and suburbs. During the depression years the number of students who were learning little in high school was attributed to limited employment opportunities. With the present demand for people with training and education, it is clear that this is not the case.

* Reprinted by permission, from "Investing in Better Schools," in *Agenda for the Nation* (Kermit Gordon, ed.); © 1968 by The Brookings Institution, Washington, D.C., pp. 213–219.

294

Our current failure to educate approximately one-third of the youth enrolled in high school is not due primarily to the inadequacies of the students but to the inappropriateness of the program to supply them with the kind of learning required. They are concerned with becoming independent adults, getting jobs, marrying, gaining status with their peers, and helping to solve the ills of the world. They perceive little or no connection between the educational content of the school and their own concerns. "What has algebra to do with me?" they ask. "Why should I try to remember the chief battles of the Revolutionary War?" Even the high school science laboratory appears to be a place for following the directions of the laboratory manual to see if they can obtain the results reported in the textbook.

Because they do not see the relevance of the high school to their present and future lives, they do not become actively involved in the learning tasks assigned. They turn their attention to other things such as athletics, social activities, artificial stimulants, or they may become quiescent, enduring the school routine until they can drop out.

This problem has been recognized by many secondary schools over the years, but the steps taken have not been adequate to solve it. For fifty years the Smith-Hughes legislation has provided federal aid for vocational education in the high school, but even after significant revisions in 1963 only 10 percent of high school age students profit from vocational technical offerings.

Some schools have tried to provide a meaningful and relevant program for the student by broadening the offerings of the high school but without transforming the curriculum as a whole. Courses have been added, but within the same framework, so that the new courses were also outside the real concerns of the student. The history of Africa can be as lifeless as the history of Colonial America if both are seen as little more than events to memorize. Spanish can seem as irrelevant as Latin if both are treated as routines for acquiring vocabulary and remembering grammatical rules.

Another effort to attack the problem has been based on the assumption that the root of the difficulty was in the boy or girl, not in the school and its program. Hence, the focus of effort has been on counseling and other treatments administered to the student without making any basic shift in school attitudes and practices. Some students by dint of teacher and counselor efforts have been able genuinely to perceive the school tasks as being vital to them; but most of them, under stimulation, put forth more effort yet still viewed the school work as having no connection with life outside of school.

One factor standing in the way is the tradition that the high school should be an adolescent island outside the major currents of adult life. Modern society has increasingly isolated adolescents from the adult world. Yet this is the time of life in which young people are looking forward to being independent adults; they need opportunities to work with adults, to learn adult skills and practices, and to feel that they are becoming mature and independent. Hence, the restrictions on youth employment, the limited opportunities to learn occupational skills at home, the segregation of civic and social activities by age groupings, all add to the difficulty of the adolescent and increase his anxiety about attaining adult status and competence. The secondary school should help to bridge this gap.

Experimentation and research suggest practices that seem likely to increase the effectiveness of the high school in giving a functional education to more young people. Primarily these practices involve developing a close active relation, not simply a formal one, between the school and the responsible adult community, so that the student will find questions and problems outside the school that can be attacked by what he learns in school. The emphasis is upon learning that is relevant to his life, not upon grades, credits, and other artificial symbols.

What is required is a major effort to furnish high school students with significant adult activities—job programs, community service corps experience, work in health centers, apprentice experience in research and development, and in staff studies conducted by public agencies. It will be necessary to redesign the high school in order to open it to the community and to utilize many kinds of persons in education. The school will need to serve a wider range of ages and allow students to vary the amount of time devoted to studies. To supply a substitute for grades and credits as qualification for employment opportunities, a certification system will need to be developed to validate the student's competence in various major areas. This will also tend to reduce the emphasis upon purely formal requirements such as class attendance and the completion of prescribed courses.

This proposal is not simple and it may be misunderstood. It proposes to use work and other areas of life as a laboratory in which youths find real problems and difficulties that require learning and in which they can use and sharpen what they are learning. It does not propose to substitute learning on the job for the deeper insights and the knowledge and skills that scholars have developed. The teacher, the books, other materials of the school, and the intellectual resources of the community are to be employed by the student as he works on the problems of his job and carries through projects on which he is engaged. When he is actually doing work that he finds significant, he can see for himself with the aid of those who know the field that many kinds of learning are helpful and even necessary. Coordinators are needed to connect education with the world of work, and teachers need to learn to select the content of school subjects and assist students to use it in connection with the activities in which they are engaged.

The student is concerned with civic and social service activities as well as with gainful employment. In these areas he will meet problems that involve values, ethics, aesthetics, public policy, in fact, the many facets of real life. The opportunity is thus provided for the student to comprehend the perennial areas of educational concern—social-civic understanding and commitment, health, personal integrity, and the arts, as well as the skills of occupational competence.

To provide for the varied interests, abilities, and career plans of students, corresponding variations can be made in the selection of school assignments related to the job, and in the division of the student's time. For example, John Brown, a well-read student, who has been very successful in most of his previous school work and plans to enter a university, might work twenty hours a week for one year in an industrial laboratory and another year in a community service corps providing supplementary educational services to the children of an inner city area. He might be taking advanced high school courses, or he might be doing independent study in one or two fields. On the other hand, Tom Smith, a student who is skeptical of book learning and the relevance of schooling to his life, might work twenty hours a week in a data processing center for one year and another year in a community health center. His school studies should furnish a basis for finding other interests to be pursued in more intensive study, perhaps helping him to select a technical institute for further occupational preparation.

The proposal assumes an extension of the hours per day and weeks per year devoted to high school education. The present five- or six-hour day, even in concentrated vocational laboratories, is little enough to satisfy the level of skill now required for job entry. With the proposed variety of activities in and out of school, the student should be able to work eleven months per year without undue weariness. Since he would receive pay appropriate to the service rendered, summer vacation jobs would not be important.

Some of the major features of this proposal are currently used in imaginative programs of vocational-technical education in some high schools. Unfortunately, even in these cases the benefits are limited to the few students enrolled in these programs. But they demonstrate the feasibility of work programs, wider adult involvement in the education of youth, and closer relation between learning in school and activities outside. They also demonstrate ways in which federal funds may be used to furnish added support for constructive educational improvements.

It should be stressed that the proposal does not imply a sharp separation in educational goals and methods between elementary and secondary schools. Beginning at the fifth or sixth grade, opportunities should be provided all students to explore content and activities related to vocational-technical offerings, increasing in depth through grades eight and nine toward major field specialization at grades eleven and twelve.

Parts of the program have been employed in various places and subjected to impartial evaluation. The kind of education described here has been shown to arouse greater interest and effort in many students than classroom study alone, to increase student understanding of the subjects studied, and to develop maturity of responsibility and judgment. Community service corps experience such as that developed by the Friends Service Committee has been found to arouse in many students greater motivation to learn and to develop social skills, social responsibility, and maturity of judgment. Communities have constructed the Neighborhood Youth Corps program to serve a similar purpose with young people from backgrounds of poverty and limited opportunity. The involvement of a broad range of people in the educational activities of youth has proved helpful, as has the provision of a variety of patterns to include, in addition to full-time enrollment, part-time school attendance while holding full-time or part-time jobs, and enrollment in high school, full time or part time, after a period of work, military service, or other activity. This varied pattern of experience and competence can be utilized constructively in an institution open to the community, whereas it is likely to be a handicap to a school operating in isolation, with study confined to textbooks and related materials.

However desirable this program may be, national efforts may be required to eliminate or reduce the obstacles.

One major impediment involves making new institutional arrangements and training the personnel. For the development of cooperative work-study education, surveys of job opportunities in each community are necessary. Coordinators need to be trained to work out with employers the outline of job experiences and their relation to the educational resources of the school. Their primary concern is the utilization of job experience to enhance the student's development. The high school curriculum itself will need rebuilding to make it relevant to the problems encountered by students in their work, not only in business and industry, but also in public agencies and nonprofit institutions. In many cases, a community service corps will need to be established to provide young people with opportunities for social service. It will take three to five years to open the school to the community and to train coordinators who will serve as middlemen between the school and the comunity.

A second impediment is the fear by both school people and parents that a new and unorthodox educational program will not be recognized by colleges or employers. The criteria for college admission have broadened greatly from those of the early 1930s, which commonly prescribed the courses to be taken and required an examination based on specified textbooks, to the present policies that prescribe broad fields of study and examine a candidate's verbal facility and ability to handle quantitative relations. Furthermore, employers rarely look for particular courses or kinds of high school programs in considering job applicants. Nevertheless, the program recommended here would be more easily adopted and developed if there were an acceptable means for certifying the educational achievement of the students. Tests and other devices are now available to measure educational accomplishments in terms of most of the knowledge and skills that contribute to success in college or competence in handling a job. Federal government support of the development and standardization of the tests of competence in various major areas would help in gaining approval of the necessary changes in the school and also provide a means to institute the certification system.

A third obstacle is the lack of curriculum content and instructional materials for teachers to use in a program departing so markedly from the traditional high school courses. This is discussed at length in the next section. In addition, states will need resources to aid local high schools to obtain the materials and continue their development. The national interest in this aspect of secondary education might take the form of federal grants to state departments of education to support a high school curriculum resource center in each state.

A fourth impediment is offered by child labor laws, which in many cases will need to be modified to permit a student to do work related to his schooling. Similarly, practices and attitudes among employers and labor organizations will need to be changed, but earlier work-study programs and some of those developed for disadvantaged youth demonstrate ways in which they can be effected without too much burden to employers and other employees.

The provision of funds to get started, the development of appropriate measures of the student's educational achievement in the new program, and the establishment of curriculum service centers should furnish significant incentives to the hundreds of high schools concerned with providing a functional education for young people not now getting much from school. Their experience can be expected to influence another group of high schools to undertake the transformation. Within ten years practices and doctrines for these programs will be established, even though the number of schools involved to that time will likely be less than half the total in the country. When this situation is reached, a review of progress can be made to plan the next stage in still wider adoption of this kind of program. The problem is a national one, but the actual implementation is so dependent upon the initiative and resources of the local schools that the attack must depend upon the voluntary efforts of the local groups.

THEY DON'T HAVE TO DROP OUT*

W. Stanley Kruger

Problems concerning high school dropouts, like the somewhat related problems of the poor, seem to have been with us always. In both cases the needs are longstanding, wide-spread, and persistent, and these factors tend to make solutions even more difficult.

In education, however, some progress has been made toward alleviating the dropout problem. The high school graduating class of 1969 had a dropout rate of 22 percent, compared with a rate of 38 percent for the class of 1959. Yet much remains to be done. That our educational system loses approximately one of every five potential high school graduates is a tremendous waste. It's even more grievous in view of the penalties assessed against those who are unskilled and uninformed by our increasingly complex way of life.

As the dropout rate decreases, the educational task actually becomes more difficult because the salvage effort converges upon those who make up the very "hard core" of the problem. Some contend that in every social action arena, whether education, employment, health, housing, or law enforcement, there is a hard core consisting of the alienated and the unable that cannot be dissolved by any means. As educators and citizens we must decide whether we will view these problems as beyond solution or as the prime challenges to our educational system today.

Amendments to the Elementary and Secondary Education Act, approved in January 1968 as title VIII, authorized Federal money for "demonstration projects involving the use of innovative methods, systems, materials, or programs which show promise of reducing the number of . . . children who do not complete their education in elementary and secondary schools." Congress appropriated $5 million for dropout prevention programs to begin in fiscal year 1969, and so far, 10 school systems have been awarded funds for model projects.

---

* Reprinted from *American Education* (October 1969), 5:6–8.

The new projects are located in Baltimore, Md.; Batesland, S.D.; Dayton, Ohio; Fall River, Mass.; Fredonia, N.Y.; Miami, Fla.; Paducah, Ky.; St. Louis, Mo.; Seattle, Wash.; and Texarkana, Ark.

No single model was developed in the Office of Education for these title VIII dropout prevention programs. Numerous studies and experimental programs have made it clear that no simple cause-and-effect relationship explains why some students leave school. No socioeconomic level, intelligence strata, physical classification, or ethnic group is immune from the problem. No panaceas have been discovered, and few situations are responsive to short-term or inexpensive remedies.

An analysis of the problem does, however, lead to the conclusion that most students leave school for two basic reasons: alienation and disability. They may be alienated or disinterested because they do not care for the physical environment, the organizational goals, the activities, or the personal relationships they perceive at school. Or they may be unable to succeed academically because of poor mental or physical health (including pregnancy), low scholastic aptitude, pressing financial or social circumstances (including marriage), or disturbing family situations. Some of the most serious disabling factors begin affecting a chuld during his earliest school years, and if treatment is to be preventive, it too must begin early.

The conditions that contribute to the alienation-disability syndrome are many, and they are interwoven in complex fashion. From the early stages of program planning, it was apparent that if title VIII projects were to be effective, they would have to establish a comprehensive range of program goals, utilize unusual teaching and learning approaches, and apply a diversity of ameliorative actions. Although these programs vary from location to location, each attacks the basic conditions that seem to contribute most to the student's decision to drop out. These conditions, along with some of the remedial approaches, are described below.

TEACHER-LEARNER INTERACTION

Many students leave school in reaction to the behavior of adults encountered there. In some cases the difficulty seems to center around teachers, counselors, and administrators who cannot easily accept normal student-age behaviors. In other instances the trouble appears to lie in traditional instruction procedures, which are generally directed toward forcing a student to conform to the school's pattern rather than letting him develop his own potential.

Several of the title VIII projects are working to improve the crucial relationship between students and teachers. Through sensitivity training, for example, teachers in the Paducah project, which now also operates in

Louisville, learn to be more appreciative of their students' special needs and to look at things from the dropouts' perspective.

In Baltimore, teachers receive sensitivity training and also are being prepared to use contingency-management techniques. In this process, the teacher makes a "contract" that allows a student to do something he wants to do in exchange for performing skill-building tasks. The objective is to establish cooperative planning relationships between students and teachers in which students take part in scheduling their own work. Baltimore is also installing special resource centers where students who need something different from the regular classroom environment can be assigned. There, teams of experts in remedial instruction, guidance, and social work, join with personnel from the community to help the student resolve his emotional plight through a low-key approach to instruction. In Fall River and Dayton, dropout-prone senior high school students are staffing tutorial and recreational programs in an effort to build "cross-age" bonds of support with younger children.

INSTRUCTIONAL ENVIRONMENT

Educators are aware that many young people, by the time they reach junior and senior high school, have developed an intense dislike for the school as a physical institution. It is a place where they have had far more frustrating experiences than successful ones. In many of the title VIII projects, the school is conceived of as a place that offers instruction custom-tailored for each student. It may or may not be located at a physical site that would be readily recognized as a school building.

For some of the dropouts in Seattle, the change involves shaping new patterns of organization within the traditional classroom setting: Students are split into small groups; then each group elects representatives who work with teachers in designing instructional programs. In Miami the dropout prevention program is conducted within the regular school building but uses special resources classrooms. In Texarkana, students in the special program go to intensive training centers in a separate building of the school campus.

In some of the projects, educators are utilizing a variety of places where learning can occur. For youths whose estrangement from school is well advanced, Seattle is making use of storefront, or satellite, classrooms. In Fall River, a recreational park is being used year round where students study plants, animals, physical education, and conservation. Home instruction and counseling for the sick, retarded, or pregnant are being provided in Baltimore. Some of the title VIII projects are arranging student exchanges that will give dropout-prone youths an opportunity to start in a new school, free of the obstacles that previously hindered them.

CURRICULUM CONTENT

The key word in revising a curriculum to prevent students from dropping out is relevance. Oftentimes a student's interest in schoolwork fades because he can't see what value his studies have for him. The usual curriculum of today's schools is simply too futuristic to attract or provide motivation for potential dropouts. Title VIII projects use different provisions to bring a "here and now" perspective to the curriculum. To help the schools do this, student-advisory councils have been established for all the projects and involve not only potential dropouts but other students, high school graduates, and youths who have already dropped out of school.

In some of the projects, educators are restructuring curriculum materials to deal with topics that are pertinent to the students' everyday lives. Skills and knowledge usually found in the compartments of mathematics, science, social studies, and language arts are, instead, organized around things that interest the students. For example, in Dayton, inner-city youngsters learn academic skills by analyzing welfare problems. In Fredonia, these skills are taught in a rural life context.

Increased attention is also being given to curriculum areas that have been nonexistent or weak with respect to the immediate needs of the potential dropout. Thus, the relationship of the Lakota Indian heritage to the general culture is the focus of concern in the Batesland project, and vocational education receives a high priority in St. Louis. A new curriculum in health education, including sex education and family living, is being developed in Dayton. Remedial instruction in mathematics and language arts is an integral component of all the dropout prevention activities, so that students may experience success with the basic academic tools.

INSTRUCTIONAL METHODOLOGY

If the dropout problem is to be solved, some means must be found for overcoming a student's sense of defeat and failure in schoolwork. Schools must find a system that motivates students by rewarding them for success instead of penalizing them for failure—but, at the same time, does not neglect their educational requirements. Baltimore, for example, is coupling contingency-management techniques with a reward system called "Earn and Learn." High school youths receive extra income for doing schoolwork and even in elementary school, youngsters who do their lessons accrue points which may be exchanged for school supplies.

Materials used in such instructional systems must have high interest for the student and must be pitched to an ability level at which he can begin to succeed immediately. This calls for individualized materials sequentially ordered so that each student can proceed along his own path of achievement. The Texarkana project will depend heavily on educational technology, using teaching machines, programed instruction, and other "non-teacher" devices. In Miami, an automated system is being designed for the constant collection and analysis of data about each student's performance, thus helping teachers prescribe learning experience suited to individual abilities.

At the secondary school level, title VIII projects are emphasizing work-study programs as a means of dropout prevention. Work stations that have real learning potential are being sought throughout the communities involved; arrangements are being made so that students can advance through a variety of career-ladder experiences in organizations or clusters of organizations. Often, regular content instruction takes place at the job site, conducted by qualified staff from the employing organization. These work-study programs also help potential dropouts meet their financial needs.

PUPIL PERSONNEL AND OTHER ADDITIONAL SERVICES

All students need a variety of services beyond those which the instructors of a school staff are able to provide. The more alienated or disabled the student, the more he needs special services in guidance and counseling, school psychology, social work, and health and therapy. Attempts to increase pupil personnel services and to individualize their application are evident in all the title VIII projects.

Schools are using other approaches to counter personal problems that may contribute to a student's decision to drop out. For example, some of the projects are trying to minimize the adverse influence that dropout-prone students are likely to have on one another. One of the most promising attempts is in the Paducah-Louisville project where "Self-Enhancing Education" techniques are being used to help potential dropouts learn to work together and, in the process, build bonds of mutual confidence, trust, and responsibility. St. Louis project planners are trying to change the attitudes of youths who are prone to leaving school by involving them in high-interest extra-curricular activities. In Dayton, college students from inner-city backgrounds have been hired to encourage younger students to stay in school.

SCHOOL-HOME-COMMUNITY LIAISON

The lack of parental and community support for continued school attendance is another facet of the dropout problem that title VIII programs are trying to counter. Additional social workers and community liaison personnel are being assigned to target schools, and teachers are given release time for home visitations. Parents and community leaders are being employed in the schools as aides and community liaison personnel, providing badly needed adult models with whom students can usually relate better than they do with school professionals. Parent and community advisory councils are used in overall planning and implementation of the projects, and some council members participate in instructional teams with professionals and students to determine curriculums.

These, then, are the primary problems the dropout prevention programs will be dealing with, and some of the major approaches that will be used. In administration of these projects, careful attention will be given to maintenance of resource inventories, continuing evaluation, periodic educational audits, and considerations of economic feasibility. Through various quality control devices, it is hoped that cost-effectiveness analyses will indicate those program components that offer the greatest potential for adoption elsewhere.

Even the best-laid plans, however, are of little avail unless the school systems involved are committed to basic system change. The title VIII project schools have made such a commitment, indicating a willingness to abandon unproductive instructional procedures, outmoded curriculums, and even the physical plant of the school as the primary site of instruction. Each of these demonstration projects must influence, continuously and increasingly, its entire school system. This cannot be done if the project is viewed as a foreign operation, staffed by strangers, operating under artificial conditions, concerned with tangential issues, and surviving only by the availability of unusual amounts of money.

In one sense, a certain amount of isolation is necessary when dealing with dropout-prone students and their special needs. However, extreme care must be taken so that separation for valid pedagogical reasons does not result in de facto segregation of educational groups, fragmentation of the educational environment, or abdication of educational responsibility for the special programs. The dropout prevention programs must provide for continuous interchange of ideas with other students and staff within the school system. Otherwise, the new ideas that are generated will never be incorporated into the rest of the system.

It has been suggested that we do the dropout a great disservice in failing to recognize his display of courage in disassociating himself from a situation which seems intolerable to him. Perhaps the greater concern should be reserved for those equally alienated students who passively "sit in" the confines of a system that has ceased any functioning in their behalf. It may be that our only sure approach to educational improvement is to consider *every* student a potential dropout. Certainly every student could benefit from the changes in our schools suggested in the dropout prevention programs.

If these projects can stimulate corrective change within all school systems, then perhaps their greatest value will be realized. If this were to happen, it would not be the first time in our history that concern for a minority group resulted ultimately in betterment for us all.

NAME OF THE GAME IS "MAKING IT"*

GEORGIA COOPER

Douglas MacArthur Junior-Senior High School.

It's a school where the 100 per cent would-be dropout stays—and succeeds.

It's a school that picks up the county's potential failure and through insight into his needs along with a pat on the back transforms his record of high absenteeism and apathy into one of good attendance and involvement.

It's his last opportunity to make it—and that's the name of the game—making it.

Douglas MacArthur Junior-Senior High School exists as an opportunity school. "A spirit of freedom permeates the curriculum—freedom to create, explore, experiment, to consider one's self in relation to others; freedom from a lockstep, regimented atmosphere."

The opportunity school opened its doors January 7, 1965 to 135 students. They came from every part of Dade County—all boys—grades 7-10, who were getting nowhere in their classes.

Today, a good five years later, the opportunity school has an enrollment of 350 students—grades 7-12—who now have a chance to go somewhere and be something.

* Written by Georgia Cooper, published in *Dade County Teacher*, Volume XXII, No. 9, January 1970, official publication of the Dade County Classroom Teachers' Association, Inc. Reprinted with permission.

The slow learner is in the spotlight at the school. The "failure" is getting the opportunity to reverse his field, and the potential dropout is "in."

Edward N. Blews, principal from the day the school opened its doors, says:

"MacArthur is a special adjustment school. It's a school unlike any other in Dade County. It teaches the academic subjects needed for graduation, but it places much more emphasis than other schools do on employable trades and skills. But that's not the whole of it—that alone doesn't explain the school's success."

A pervasive spirit of enthusiasm, apparent to even the most casual observer, can be seen in the way MacArthur students enjoy what they're doing and take pride in doing it well.

One of the school's original objectives was to provide the opportunity for boys to find success in themselves as well as to succeed in a particular endeavor by making progress within the range of their abilities. Set requirements for admission stressed that boys of all intelligence levels would be acceptable only after careful screening; and provided that all regular school resources for helping them adjust had been exhausted. The school planners' chief intent was to help boys experience success in some aspect of the instructional programs, centered around industrial arts, agriculture, music, art, physical education and academics.

It was hoped this would change the boys' attitudes toward school— that is, these attitudes would become more positive.

Four basic objectives for Douglas MacArthur were established by the early planners of the school. These remain unchanged. They are:

1. To provide a worthwhile curriculum for deserving and earnest boys who have not been able to succeed in the regular school program.
2. To overcome disabilities—emotional, physical, psychological, sociological or environmental—in certain boys so that they can return to their regular schools and find success there.
3. To provide a worthwhile junior and senior high school curriculum for boys who may not necessarily be of the clinical or special education type, yet who need a special curriculum that will include basic saleable skills for future livelihood.
4. To provide a school, obviously experimental, which would demonstrate the at that time unproven theory that through vocational rehabilitation, the boys would be able to plan a future.

Now, five years later no one dares debate the wisdom of these early objectives.

The barometer of the school's success rests on the willingness of the students to attend school.

The teachers at Douglas MacArthur have a creative approach toward curriculum. Experience has shown that the traditional approach just doesn't work with these students. Proof is the fact that they have already rejected the traditional school.

At MacArthur the basic academics presented are those required by state regulations so a student can earn a standard high school diploma. English and history are combined in a basic course called Communications. In this course, instructors use non-graded materials for the typical failure-ridden student, whose reading ability ranges from non-reader to tenth grade level. The team of academic teachers operates within a framework of language arts, social studies or science.

Each week a theme is selected and presented via a film, film strip, a school produced tape or a team lecture. Taped theme materials are often stenciled and each student receives a working copy. Recent themes include: Conservation in Florida, the F.B.I. and Law Enforcement, The Working Man in the Large City, Communism and the War in Viet Nam and Jobs and Job Careers in Dade County. The emphasis is placed on the present rather than the past, but frequently the boys' own questions lead to their searching into the past for a better understanding of the present and future. All four basic communicating skills—listening, speaking, reading and writing—are employed in this most important part of the MacArthur program.

The mathematical program is also based on a flexible plan of ability grouping. A large portion of the math program is geared to a shop-related basis. Measuring, estimating, learning to use micrometers, scales, depth gauges, and other tools are motivational experiences in these classes.

There are formalized blocks of time for teaching mathematical skills as well as periodic visits to the shops by the mathematics teachers to see the boys at work and to become more familiar with the shop programs. In this way, the mathematics teachers are able to determine shop-related mathematics skills which the students will need.

In other words, they teach the mechanics rather than the theory of math. The students learn how to figure area and volume and circumferences of circles. They learn to work with measurements and fractions in the shops.

Science is presented as an "Earth Science" in the agricultural classes. The agricultural program deals with farm machinery, farm supplies, nurseries, landscape gardening, and the production of crops and livestock. It also includes those industries and businesses involved in marketing, processing, and distributing agricultural products. All students in the eighth grade are involved in the countywide E.T.V. science offerings and all tenth graders participate in a basic course in biology in order to meet the state requirements for graduation. Animal husbandry and the study of poultry are also included in the program.

Shop electives constitute a popular aspect of the programming at MacArthur. Among the shop electives offered are courses in motors, metals, woods and small motors. In all these areas, the teachers strive to teach the boys skills that will be saleable.

Boys are not taught to do by hand jobs that are done by mechanized equipment in industry. Although MacArthur has been able to secure some of the needed machines and equipment for teaching the boys how to operate then safely and efficiently, more are desperately needed.

The metal classes stress the following objectives:

1. To teach students about the metal working industry—how metal products are designed and produced and how people earn a living in metal working.
2. To teach students how to design, plan and carry through a project.
3. To teach basic hand and machine skills and to encourage students to develop their own talents and interests as they relate to metals both vocationally and avocationally.

The metal shop includes sheet metal instruction, electric, acetylene and arc welding and lathe operation.

Beginners, after the initial orientation period, are given a series of small inexpensive jobs that include riveting, sheet metal forming, light acetylene welding and, of course, close tolerance measurements. Most often a small barbecue grill is the beginning task.

After the first semester in the metal shop, the boys are usually assigned to individualized projects which can either be original or selected from shop magazines.

Older students, advanced in this area, often launch into such projects as making beach or swamp buggies, metal outdoor or patio furniture, or one of a myriad of turret lathe projects.

The main objective of the wood working laboratory is to place the student in a situation where he can become acquainted with the tools and processes of industry and related trades. While products are made and constructed by the students, these products become secondary and a means to an end. The main function of the lab experience is for the student to learn to work for himself, to make decisions and—most important—to get along and work with others.

In the wood shop, the instructor tries to involve his advanced classes in such projects as furniture repair and re-finishing, manufacturing of "put it together yourself" kits for a number of furniture companies, various jigs for local wood shops, construction of self-inspired unique furniture maker's benches, etc. It is important to mention that the individual projects selected by the boys are independently and formally planned, including detailed dimensions and evaluations to be considered, perhaps criticized, and finally approved by the instructor.

The junior or beginning classes stress safety and efficient shop procedure especially where small inexpensive items that include assorted joints and wood welding operations are called for. MacArthur's shop instructors stress the importance of safety above all, and are proud of their five-year record of no serious accidents in their workshops.

The automotive and basic power mechanics programs, by far the most popular, have a continual waiting list of applicants.

Small motors is a suggested preparatory course for those desiring to take automotive mechanics. In these classes, basic mechanical procedure is stressed. Acquaintance with the many types and uses of tools, safety procedures, and a thorough knowledge of the principles of two- and four-cycle gasoline engine operation are mastered. Lawn motor repair and small outboard motor overhaul are also a part of this course.

The automotive program has been continually expanding since its inception. The usual automotive programs offered elsewhere require courses of theory before actual shop experience is undertaken. The neophyte mechanics at MacArthur, however, learn theory interspersed with actual shop experience.

Beginners in the automotive courses progress through a program designed to prepare them to be topnotch service station mechanics. Boys showing sufficient aptitude and interest are permitted to enroll in the more advanced phase of mechanics which involves complete engine, transmission and rear-end overhaul.

In the past, advanced students have participated in a six-week training course offered by the Outboard Motor Corporation. This training is normally offered only to regular working mechanics as a refresher course.

Cooking is another popular offering on the MacArthur curriculum. Boys accepted for the unusual training are closely screened and are required to have health permits as they engage in preparation of food for the school itself. There are approximately 30 students in the five cooking classes. They are rotated so that all may engage in preparation of food, serving and clean-up duties. Short order cooking is also included.

The kitchen is equipped with a large grill which allows the boys to gain the necessary experience to get employment eventually in the many restaurants in this vacation area.

The boys are also taught baking. Cooking instructors of MacArthur are constantly receiving fine progress reports from former students now working as full-time bakers.

The Douglas MacArthur Music Department is unique. Where other study programs may fail, for whatever reason, to bring students out of their "shells," the music program always seems to work.

The department offers instruction in band instruments, as well as guitar, bass guitar and drums, the latter being an innovation in Junior-Senior High School music programs.

The classes are especially popular among the students. Three levels—beginner, intermediate and advanced—are offered. These classes foster development of worthwhile character traits by a carefully planned, interesting, easy group method of teaching these instruments.

Classes are conducted in a workshop format. Students study and work together in the spirit of close, friendly cooperation, a strong tie (and motivation) being the power of music itself.

The basic textbook is a workbook written especially for the class by MacArthur music teacher Charles Kinzel. The workbook introduces chords first, with single string melodies coming later. Simple American folk songs are taught starting with the first lesson period. As the students learn, they eventually progress through all different phases of musical form from early folk songs up to modern rock.

At the advance level, the classes are organized into small performing groups. Here vocal participation is encouraged and developed. As performing groups emerge, neighborhood programs and concerts are arranged. The bands play for teen dances in junior and senior high schools throughout Dade County, and in this way are able to supplement their income.

By way of example, the Douglas MacArthur String Band this past year (1969) presented a series of 25 concerts in local junior and senior high schools.

Each such musical program obviously requires extensive preparation, order, timing, and above all talent.

Many leading educators, as well as State Vocational Rehabilitation Department officials recognize and support the view that MacArthur's program of music therapy is an ideal vehicle for vocational rehabilitation, improved self-image, cultural enrichment and, in general, wholesome character development.

The art classes at Douglas MacArthur are taught in a relaxed studio atmosphere. Activities for beginning students are designed to promote the greatest amount of individual success possible for each boy.

After the boys have gained confidence, they work in all of the major areas (ceramics, sculpture, painting, etc.).

When they have completed the basic course requirements, they may then work in any media they choose. Boys who show potential in the art program are placed in related jobs through the cooperation of Vocational Rehabilitation. Several of the school's former art students have taken advanced work at the Miami-Dade Junior College; and two students have found jobs in the Educational Television System.

Douglas MacArthur is not a new school with carpeting and all air-conditioned buildings. On the contrary, it's a makeshift structure held together more by a sense of purpose, dedication and concern than anything else.

Anne Montanari, guidance counselor and communications instructor says, "The school is attempting to help each boy find the individual within himself. And the boys are saying, in different ways, that that is what's happening."

One cannot rely on mere photos or word descriptions to learn what Douglas MacArthur is all about. One must talk to the students themselves.

Joe, who has been at Douglas MacArthur only a short time, previously attended North Miami Senior High. "I didn't like the module system. My grades were low," he says. "I like it here. It's really great. Here you're called by your name—not by number. They care about the individual. If you need extra help, they'll come around and give it to you."

Joe says he "definitely would have dropped out of school" had he not transferred to MacArthur.

The bonds which hold MacArthur together are fourfold—teacher, counselor, student and principal. And it's reflected in the way the students greet the adults. They are at ease, they're involved, they're interested.

And in one way or another, they all say, "MacArthur is one of the best things that's happened to me."

Despite the feeling of closeness, the almost warm family relationship which prevails, the main objective of the school is never forgotten. The first and ultimate objective of the school, as Principal Blews sees it, is "to get as many boys as possible out of MacArthur and back into regular schools. Some boys attending MacArthur are able to return to their former schools after only a few weeks because the individualized attention MacArthur furnishes enables them to gain the necessary confidence to attack problems which once overwhelmed them at their regular schools."

"There are several reasons why Douglas MacArthur is succeeding where other schools have failed. Both teachers and students realize that the school might well be the students' last chance to receive an education. This creates extra effort in every direction on the part of both groups. A low student-teacher ratio allows for more individual instruction while lending itself to a closer relationship between faculty and student body. Flexibility of curriculum permits the school to adapt to the students' needs more readily than in a regular school. The staff is guidance-minded and is sincerely interested in the welfare and future of each student. The philosophy of the school is one of accepting the student as he is and assisting him up the educational ladder as far as possible."

While these same successes may be approached in other high schools in Dade County, they are far more difficult to attain there. Most of the boys arrive at Douglas MacArthur displaying a defeated attitude, the result of many years of loss of confidence in themselves and loss of status in their schools. Literally, they come with chins dragging. Without question, Douglas MacArthur provides the individual attention so desperately needed by these boys. Here they are noticed and their personalities are enticed out of hiding.

Perhaps the whole crux of the story is just this—it is necessary to build realistic worthwhile dreams for those who may want them. Without question, Dade County needs not only continued support and funds to maintain Douglas MacArthur—it needs many more schools like it.

RECONNECTION FOR RELEVANCE: A PROPOSED NEW HIGH SCHOOL CURRICULUM*

JAMES L. FENNER

The following proposed elective courses for high school are intended . . . as electives because I believe students—at least *some* students—would find them—at least *some* of them—intrinsically interesting enough to make them want to take them. This alone would relate them, as far as the nature of their appeal went, to out-of-school interests. They are intended as courses for everybody; and that means a heterogeneous student body. This too would relate them, if only superficially on an organizational basis, to life outside the school. And, most important, they are intended to cut across interdisciplinary boundaries, to bridge some of the gaps between subject and subject or between school and the "real" world, to combine and recombine the world, the media, the person, and the school in new and significant configurations, so that adolescence need not be the nightmare that Jules Henry,[1] John Holt, Paul Goodman, and Edgar Z. Frie-

---

* Excerpt reprinted from *The Teachers College Record* (February 1970), 71:428–432, by permission.
[1] Jules Henry. *Culture Against Man.* New York: Vintage Books, 1963.

denberg assert it to be. It is this feature of the proposals that, I hope, would make these courses valuable for the society (because its youngsters would be able to experience some sense of synthesis), for the school (because students might not feel so hostile to an institution that is giving them an education with a little life in it), and for the young people themselves (because they would be able to see some purpose, some pattern of interrelationships, some relevance to reality, in what the school is offering them). Here are the proposed electives, with brief descriptions of each:

1. ENTERTAINMENT

This course would deal with current films, with TV, with radio (very much a source of adolescent entertainment today: "We're portable!" as the "good guys" put it), records, with the theater, and with the entertainment aspects of the mass-circulation magazines. Sebastian De Grazia[2] underlines the hollowness of our leisure. A course like this one wouldn't cure the malaise he describes, but it might be a start, and it would surely be popular. Its purpose would not be primarily to entertain the students; it would be aimed at helping them to understand and assess and respond knowingly to what the entertainment media offer. Materials would be plentiful; they constitute a major part of the out-of-school life of youngsters already, and in class they could be analyzed as to their methods, their craftmanship, their social implications, their psychological impact, and their visual, verbal, rhetorical, sensory, and kinesthetic structures.

2. PERSONAL RELATIONSHIPS

This subject would explore the many levels and values in personal relationships. Carl Rogers[3] insists upon the essential importance of self-discovery. "Psychology" would have been the traditional name for a course like this, and there would still be that aspect to it, but in addition it would deal with the style and content of relationships within the family and the peer-group, and with personal concerns such as love, sex, friendship, ambition, the draft, and perhaps it would touch upon the philosophical as well as the psychological aspects of such matters. Here too, the content of the course would be life as students actually and personally live it outside of school. Although it would deal with these situations in general and in principle instead of attempting to guide pupils in their personal lives directly, it most certainly would bear a direct and magnetic relationship to the reality with which they are in daily contact.

---

[2] Sebastian De Grazia. *Of Time, Work, and Leisure*. Twentieth Century Fund, 1962.
[3] Carl Rogers. *On Becoming a Person*. Boston: Houghton Mifflin, Inc., 1961.

3. MORAL ISSUES

This would be a study of ethics as exemplified by the personal re-lationships of the previous course, or by political questions, or by school or business problems. The course would aim to present issues and analyze them with penetration and clarity rather than to present solutions. Any kind of written or other material could provide the basis for a sequence of discussions: magazine articles, news items, TV, radio, or film shows, excerpts from philosopical writings, the Bible—whatever. These would be grouped into "topics" representing different *kinds* of ethical issues, and presented in discussion as they relate to adolescent concerns both im-mediate and future. Here the ethics of business, politics, international affairs, child-rearing, sex, and school could be subjected to the kind of analysis that might make even school look relevant.

4. WASHINGTON POLITICS TODAY

This would combine the current events that the media inundate us with, the national aspects of what used to be called "Civics," political theory, debates on national programs and/or bills before Congress, bio-graphical and/or political studies of national figures, a little history as the need for it arose in discussion of the day's issues, and perhaps some class predictions of future political developments. The text for the course would be the daily paper, the newsweeklies, the radio, TV, and perhaps some traditional textbook material on the structure of the Federal govern-ment.

5. LOCAL POLITICS TODAY

The emphasis here would be on state and municipal politics, in-cluding education, the police, welfare, the courts, and the tax structure. City and neighborhood newspapers would provide the texts. TV and radio coverage of local events would be monitored daily. Local politicians might be asked to address the students. Jury duty would be discussed, possibly in connection with the film *Twelve Angry Men*. Magazine articles on such topics as corruption in politics would certainly be of value and interest. An aspect of such a course that would capture the interest of young peo-ple and seem relevant to their real concerns and out-of-school experience is the discovery and discussion of ways of "fighting city hall" effectively: how to mount an effective campaign, when to write letters, when to ob-struct, when to visit whom—how, in other words, to make one's weight felt as a citizen.

6. INTERNATIONAL AFFAIRS TODAY

All the media would provide material for this course. Propaganda analysis would form a considerable part of the subject-matter, as would the metaphors of international discourse. The foreign press could be studied for alternative points of view. WNYC has an interesting suppertime "Foreign Press Review" several times a week. The course would not try merely to acquaint students with international events; it would seek to help them understand the rivalries, pressures, aspirations, and other motivations that they reflect. And it would undertake some evaluation of the thoroughness, effectiveness, objectivity, and reliability of the media's presentations of international news.

7. HOW TO THINK STRAIGHT

The traditional name for this course is "Logic," but here a common-sense rather than a technical approach would be stressed. Books like Stuart Chase's *Guides to Straight Thinking*[4] or Robert Thouless' *How to Think Straight*[5] could be used as texts, and issues and examples for analysis could be found in every news presentation or public document, whether political, social, religious, or whatever, published in America. The popularizers of Korzybski[6] have provided interesting case studies in straight and crooked thinking. In this kind of course, the "purely" intellectual enterprise of thinking accurately could be given a contemporary applicability to social and personal issues that vitally concern young people, thus serving to help integrate in-school and out-of-school learning and experience.

8. THE FUTURE

Nothing concerns teenagers more than the future; probably not even the present. This course, cutting across many subject-matter boundaries, would explore and speculate about the future of technology, or politics,

---

[4] Stuart Chase. *Guides to Straight Thinking*. New York: Harper & Row, 1956.

[5] Robert H. Thouless. *How to Think Straight*. New York: Hart Publishing Company, 1939.

[6] See Alfred Korzybski. *Science and Sanity*. Lakeville, Conn.: Institute of General Semantics, 1958; and the following: Wendell Johnson. *People in Quandaries*. New York: Harper & Row, 1946; Stuart Chase. *The Power of Words*. New York: Harcourt, 1954; Hugh R. Walpole. *Semantics*. New York: Norton, 1942; S. I. Hayakawa. *Language in Thought and Action*. New York: Harcourt, 1964.

or school, of personal relationships, of sports, of communications, of America, of the Negro, of practically everything. It would draw upon the present as depicted in the media, upon the past as researched out of books for this or that investigation, upon logic, experience, and intention. It might help pupils to feel that they have some realistic possibility of contributing to the shaping of their own futures if they understood more fully the processes and probabilities in accordance with which the future tends to unfold.

9. OUTER AND INNER SPACE: A SCIENCE SURVEY

In descriptive rather than technical terms, the principles, discoveries, and chief theories of the social and natural sciences would be presented and discussed here. The course, while relying to a degree on historical material about previous discoveries and innovations in the sciences, would be kept rigorously up-to-the-minute via regular scrutiny of current material presented in the media. Thus, new advances in the technology of space exploration, communications, computerization, automation, or even recent re-evaluations of theoretical systems could be made a part of the course. Biology, psychology, sociology, and anthropology might justify the "inner" part of the title; mechanics, chemistry, sub-atomic physics, and astronomy would be the "outer" space. The point of the course would be not to introduce the technical aspects of the sciences, but to give some pupils some familiarity with underlying concepts of scientific understanding, such as the "reflective thinking" of Dewey[7], so that they will be better able to follow and comprehend the technological society in which they live.

10. HOW TO USE FIGURES

The computational problems of everyday existence stump many pupils because they have learned in school to fear and hate quantitative subject-matter. But computational math and useful arithmetic, if presented afresh in the guise of "tricks" or "speed math" or "mental arithmetic" or "short cuts to accuracy," might grab youngsters and sustain their interest. The Trachtenberg System and other computational devices could be made the basis of a truly useful arithmetic course that would be of value to academic, commercial, vocational, and "general" students. For some, its value would be vocational; for others, academic; for still others, perhaps just recreational or curiosity-satisfying. Certainly it would help relate school to actual student needs.

---

[7] John Dewey. *How We Think*. Boston: Heath, 1933.

11. LOCAL RESOURCES: INFORMATION, RECREATION, SERVICE

The aim here would be to engage directly in the task of acquainting students with what is real in their surroundings. Particularly among the poor, many students have had limited experiences outside their immediate neighborhoods. In this class, they would have a chance to take the trips their elementary-school teachers never took them on: walking tours through their city's neighborhoods, to the underground cinema, night court, domestic court, the Chinese New Year celebration (if there are such), and scores of others. It would acquaint them with where and what the tourist attractions are; it would take them to the airport; it would show them how to file for services when they need them; it would give them a sense of their city. Here they would find out how to call an ambulance, how to get psychiatric emergency service, how to apply for these or those benefits, whom to complain to about this or that: the Better Business Bureau, the Rent Control Office, the District Attorney's office, and so on. It would acquaint them with the services offered by the Housing Authority, the Board of Health, adult education programs, the Legal Aid Society, private and public family service organizations, the Department of Hospitals, the Civil Liberties Union, out-patient clinics, the Visiting Nurses' Association.

12. ADVERTISING AND PROPAGANDA

Here students would practice analyzing and interpreting the political and economic persuasions that flow around them incessantly. They would deal with local and international propaganda pitches, with the relationship, as Ellul[8] describes it, between technological progress and propaganda, with advertising's protean forms: radio and TV commercials, printed ads, direct mail, billboards, packaging and point-of-scale promotions. They would practice reading between the lines, understanding what is *not* said, understanding the *purposes* of the message-originator, understanding the weaknesses of the receiver. Students would consider the interrelationships inherent in the multiple appeals of advertising: visual, verbal, auditory, etc. A course like this is bound to have practical value and intense interest for adolescents. Chase's *The Power of Words* and Hayakawa's *Language in Thought and Action* might be used as texts with average classes. Even as demanding a work as Ellul's *Propaganda* might be used with superior groups.

---

[8] Jacques Ellul. *The Technological Society*. New York: Knopf, 1964.

13. CHILD DEVELOPMENT AND FAMILY PSYCHOLOGY

Here girls would study family resources, sources of outside help on personal and family problems (medical and psychiatric clinics, marriage counseling, etc.), principles of child development, cause of family friction, etc. As texts, the class could use not only popular books like Spock's *Baby and Child Care*[9] and Gesell and Ilg's *Child Development*,[10] and the U.S. Government pamphlets, but they could also study popular presentations in the magazines, papers, and on TV to evaluate their worth and seriousness.

---

[9] Benjamin Spock. *Baby and Child Care*. New York: Pocket Books, 1946.

[10] Arnold Gesell and Frances L. Ilg. *Child Development*. New York: Harper & Row, 1949.

Chapter 9

FOCUS ON THE INDIVIDUAL
STUDENT

Vying with "relevance" as the central aim of curriculum planning and the priority criterion for evaluation of curriculum and instruction is the notion of "individualization." In fact the causes and antecedents of these emphases are inextricably related. The increasing size of the high school, as well as that of the population in general, and the school's institutionalization threaten the identity of the individual student. He wants, and his parents and teachers want for him, individual attention and learning experiences relevant to his concerns and problems.

High schools have long sought, of course, to serve the individual student, which can be witnessed by the steady addition of elective courses, activities, counseling and other services, and a plethora of plans for individualizing instruction. But these have not been enough for the "individual self-fulfillment" goal of the high school, especially in the large high school. This is the subject of the first selection, "Individual Self-Fulfillment in the Large High School" by Allan A. Glatthorn, who argues, with convincing clarity and supporting suggestions, that "the large high school through its multiplicity of resources can be the optimum environment for maximum self-fulfillment." He develops two principles as basic to this goal: multiplicity of alternatives and freedom of choice.

Glatthorn sees as most important in the use of these principles, the development of a climate for self-fulfillment "which encourages each individual to become his own true self." For this climate, the open school is needed: "Open to visitors, open to criticism, open to change, and open to new ideas." In such a climate teachers see students as individuals rather than as members of groups, and Glatthorn suggests specific means of developing this teacher perception of distinct personalities. He questions grouping practices because of their threat to individualization, and holds that students need opportunity to be associated with many groups and to move among them.

Among the means suggested and described by Glatthorn for contributing to individual self-fulfillment are: wide electives; diversity of content in the curriculum fields and a corresponding diversity of media and materials; use of self-instructional materials; independent study plans; small group activities. Several of these means are dealt with in more detail in other articles in this chapter. Glatthorn closes with 10 steps for immediate action by the principal of any high school.

Independent study is considered by the present writer as an especially significant approach to individualization. In the publication *Independent Study in Secondary Schools* by Alexander, Hines, and Associates (Holt, Rinehart and Winston, Inc., 1967) we suggested five patterns as follows:

1. Independent study privileges or option
2. Individually programmed independent study
3. Job-oriented independent study
4. Seminars based on independent study
5. "Quest-type" program for development of special aptitudes

In the several years since completion of the Cooperative Research project in which this classification emerged from our survey of practices, the independent study idea has spread markedly. However, the greatest spread has probably been in connection with flexible scheduling practices which assign independent study time (type 1 above) to students but do not necessarily assure that independent study really occurs.

The plan of independent study in English by David W. Berg in his "Independent Study: Transfusion for Anemic English Programs" could use all but the first of the foregoing types. He would set up the English class on an independent study basis, differentiating the types of independent work according to the needs of the students. Diagnostic and practice materials might be used as in programmed independent study, for those who need it; many students might be working on projects that could be reported on in seminar fashion; others might be following interests relating to jobs or to Quest-type intellectual interests. Major requirements for a good independent study program, one infers from Berg's article, are respect for students' individualities and interests, the teacher's serving as "a source to whom the students can turn when the need arises," and a wealth of materials. These requirements square well with the concept of independent study presented in the publication cited:

> *Independent study* is considered by us to be learning activity largely motivated by the learner's own aims to learn and largely rewarded in terms of its own intrinsic values. Such activity as carried on under the auspices of secondary schools is somewhat independent of the class or other group organization dominant in past and present secondary school instructional practices, and it utilizes the services of teachers and other professional personnel primarily as resources for the learner. (Alexander, Hines, and Associates, p. 12.)

Berg's article also presents the rationale of his proposal for the program of independent study in English for virtually all high school students. He would start "by throwing out the curriculum guide and burning the course of study," which he believes is usually "outdated and irrelevant anyway."

Glatthorn's article described the trend toward development of materials for pupil self-instruction as one of the means of moving toward individual self-fulfillment. This newer and growing practice is specifically illustrated in the article by Richard V. Jones, Jr., on "Learning Activity Packages: An Approach to Individualized Instruction." He relates several types of materials to the objective of continuous progress: the teaching-learning units (TLUs) of the Westinghouse-supported PLAN project of the American Institute of Research; the "UNIPACs" of the IDEA Project, Kettering Foundation; and the Learning Activity Packages (LAPs) of the Nova High School, Fort Lauderdale, Florida, and their adaptation in the Hughson, California, High School LAPs. The article gives a detailed description of the writing of these Learning Activity Packages, and thus explains their nature and use in high school curriculum and instruction. Although Jones considers the writing of

LAPs "difficult, tedious and time-consuming work," as indeed it is, he believes that the result is "a system which at once individualizes instruction for the students, and structures the curriculum so that the teacher is free to be a guide to the learners rather than a controller of groups." His article, coupled with some LAPs available from sources he mentions, should be a valuable resource for teachers interested in exploring the possibilities of this approach or actually engaging in the writing of LAPs. Do you see this as a desirable approach to individualizing instruction? Have you written or could you write a LAP? How would it affect instructional procedure? In what subject fields could LAPs be used most effectively?

The inflexible uniform period high school day so widely decried as a barrier to flexibility of curriculum and instruction, is giving way to modular scheduling, which still uses periods of uniform length, the shorter modules, but assigns them for quite different instructional purposes and arrangements than the standard daily class period of the traditional high school. Scott D. Thomson's article, "Beyond Modular Scheduling" notes that "computer-generated modular scheduling" was initiated in five institutions in 1963 and has subsequently "moved forward the quest for a flexible, individualized structure for students." He reports the reactions of students to the new scheduling, and various other favorable results. His concern, however, and he documents it, is with the problems of individualization that have not been solved by new scheduling arrangements; the benefits of individualization, he observes, "do not automatically arise from free time." And so he proposes the development of a "client-centered school" which would have as a central component a diagnostic center and process that would give direction to each individual's program. The presentation of his model is provocative and should lead curriculum discussants to search for the alternative arrangements to the present modular scheduling plans Thomson feels essential.

INDIVIDUAL SELF-FULFILLMENT IN THE LARGE HIGH SCHOOL*

Allan A. Glatthorn

The educational cliché which seems to have the widest currency these days is "Individualized Instruction." Several major research centers and curriculum projects are developing materials and methods to achieve this goal, and the most prestigiously innovative schools are at least doing a lot of talking about it.

I would acknowledge at this stage a growing sense of uneasiness about individualized instruction as I have read about it and as I have seen it operate in some schools. Although the theoreticians are quick to disavow the forms it takes in these schools, it most frequently seems to manifest itself in this form: a learning laboratory replete with media gadgetry, with 25 youngsters sitting at individual carrels, each working at his own pace through a linear series of learning packages. I would reject this as a description of an ideal learning situation. I see it as too mechanistic, with too much stress given to pacing as a factor in individualization, with too little socialization in the learning process, and with too narrow a view of the nature of growth and learning.

I would suggest instead that the schools should dedicate themselves to a different kind of goal which I would phrase thusly: *maximum self-fulfillment for each individual learner.* Such a goal suggests that each learner is unique; that each youngster has some undeveloped potential, some special self which only he can become; and that the job of the school is to deploy all its resources—curriculum, staff, materials, schedules —to facilitate this self-fulfillment. And while arguments about big schools versus small schools are not quite as interesting as those about old mistresses versus young mistresses, I would argue that the large high school through its multiplicity of resources can be the optimum environment for maximum self-fulfillment.

---

* Reprinted from the *Bulletin of the National Association of Secondary School Principals* (March 1969), 53:47–56, by permission.

PRINCIPLES OF SELF-FULFILLMENT

Before discussing these resources and how they might best be deployed in the large high school, I would like to comment briefly about the basic principles of self-fulfillment and then try to describe the optimum climate for such self-fulfillment of the individual.

It seems to me that there are two fundamental principles basic to all aspects of individual fulfillment. The first is the principle of multiplicity of alternatives. This principle suggests that man has the greatest chance to develop his unique potential when he has the greatest number of options from among which to choose. And the principle embraces options of all sorts: books to read, models to imitate, careers to begin, philosophies to adopt, groups to join, subjects to study, clothes to wear, art to enjoy, paths to follow. The antithesis of such diversity in uniformity—and uniformity is the death-knell of individuality. Such a principle helps us realize that the teacher who shows a group of 30 students how to discover their own interpretations of a poem is doing a better job of "individualizing" than the teacher who has written a self-instructional program which leads the student to "discover"—at his own pace—some single predetermined "truth" about the poem.

The second principle of self-fulfillment is freedom of choice. This principle suggests that the individual will achieve true self-fulfillment only as he controls his own destiny by making his own choices. It is absurd to develop a mulitplicity of alternatives if we then paternalistically deny the individual the right of self-determination. Others who decide for us—whether they be administrators, government officials, parents, or friends—limit our freedom and diminish our chances to grow.

All schools regardless of size can, of course, grant the student freedom of choice, but the very size of the large high school makes it more likely to offer a multiplicity of options. And together these two principles—multiplicity of options and freedom of choice—give us in the large high school a sense of direction in developing a climate for individuality.

CLIMATE FOR SELF-FULFILLMENT

This ambience for creative self-fulfillment which encourages each individual to become his own true self is far more important than any gimmicks for self-instruction or gadgets for self-pacing. Such a climate enhances growth by saying in effect, "Each of you is different, and we will allow you all enough growing room to become yourself, for this school is big enough to tolerate a great deal of idiosyncrasy."

How is such a climate developed? Probably it is most simply the projection of a principal and his faculty who believe in the sacred right of each person to be himself—and who are quite willing to grant that right even to the immature. What are the characteristics of such a climate? There are probably a minimum number of rules and policies, for rules by their nature ignore individual differences, and policies become a substitute for individual decision making. There is no dress code, for such codes attempt to standardize dress and hair style, the most prized aspects of the teenager's individuality. There is an intellectual freedom which manifests itself in an uncensored student newspaper, a forum for outside speakers representing all points of view, and the open discussion of controversial issues in the classroom.

The climate for individuality is best found in the open school—open to visitors, open to criticism, open to change, and open to new ideas—and is probably best produced by the principal who is willing to defend the open school against the narrow-minded of all persuasions who really believe only in the freedom to express their particular brand of the truth. Such a climate, of course, can be found both in the small and the large high school, but I would argue that it is more likely to be found in the larger school where the diversity produced by sheer numbers is often the most effective counteragent to uniformity.

In such an open climate for individuality we are most likely to find teachers who see students as individuals, not as members of a group. A few teachers are totally blind to individual differences. Their faculty lounge griping is replete with phrases like, "they're all the same," "the trouble with kids these days," "this younger generation." More typically we find teachers who perceive students as members of a group; they are quick to label, and the label blinds them to individual differences. Such a teacher admits that differences do exist, but he maintains that they exist between groups, not between individuals. His professional talk resounds with such phrases as "my low ability class," "all our Negro students," and "the trouble-makers in our school." These attitudes, obviously, render ineffectual any tinkering with "individualized curriculum" or "individualized instruction," for real individualization can come about only when the teacher sees students not as members of groups but as unique personalities.

RECOGNIZING INDIVIDUALITY

There are some ways that all schools can foster teacher perception of distinct personalities. Faculty meetings can be set aside to discuss the manifold ways in which learners do differ: one technique in such a meeting is to ask a cooperative teacher to select one of her "average" classes and to try to characterize it for the faculty, following her description with a detailed report on each member of that class which would illuminate dramatically the fact of individual differences. Another tested technique is the case conference, which draws together all staff members who have contact with a student for mutually profitable sharing. Occasionally such a conference should be presented before the faculty.

I also think that administrators should give serious consideration to providing sensitivity training for their faculties. While there is some disagreement about the extent to which such training can effect permanent change in attitude, there is little doubt that T-groups led by an effective trainer can help members become more open to themselves, to colleagues, and to students. Another technique which has worked in some schools is to select five or six members of a readily identifiable group (Negroes, gifted students, chronic discipline cases) and have them appear on a panel in a faculty meeting to discuss frankly their attitudes and opinions. Such a discussion will likely reveal sharp differences within the group.

GROUPING POSES THREAT

As implied above, grouping practices in a school typically militate against individualization. Most large high schools have fortunately departed from "tracking" or "curriculum groups" procedures which channel students into totally separate streams called "nonacademic" or "gifted" or "business education." However, most of us do cling to rigid ability grouping despite two significant and substantial pieces of research: the Coleman report which indicated that the prime factor in a student's learning is the composition of the group, and the Rosenthal study which demonstrated that the label placed upon a group directly affects teacher expectations and grades awarded. And I don't believe the pernicious effects of ability grouping are mitigated by assigning new labels like "Quest Phase" or "Basic Learnings Phase."

I am not arguing here for an end to all ability grouping; it may have to endure simply as a pedagogical compromise, but I do think we need to be aware of the threat it poses to true individualization. In fact, perhaps we can find in the large high school some solutions which retain the efficiency of grouping while avoiding the dehumanization of ability grouping. Some schools—graded and nongraded—find that students can reliably select their own learning group. Others might wish to follow the suggestion of Herbert Thelen and explore the possibilities of "teachability grouping," by which we try to match teachers and learners who can best work together. (Herbert A. Thelen. *Classroom Grouping for Teachability*. New York: John Wiley and Sons, 1967.)

In summary, the thesis here is that the more groups there are for a student to be a part of and the more the student has freedom of choice about membership in such groups, the greater are his chances for maximum self-fulfillment. Here again, it seems obvious that bigness is an advantage—the larger the school, the greater the number of groups to choose from.

Perhaps at this juncture a summary is in order. The real goal of all schools, and one most readily achieved in the large school, is maximum self-fulfillment for the individual, a self-fulfillment optimally achieved when there are a multiplicity of options and a freedom of choice. And more important than instructional gimmicks or curricular tinkering are an open climate fostered by a committed principal and the teachers' ability to see learners as individuals—a perception often perniciously influenced by inflexible grouping procedures. All this is not to suggest that curricular and instructional matters are of no consequence, for kept in perspective they can make a significant contribution. It is to these matters that we now turn.

CURRICULAR DIVERSITY

There are two important ways in which the curriculum can contribute to maximum self-fulfillment. The first is through a diversity of subject offerings brought about by an extensive program of electives. While the required academic majors are essential in producing the necessary intellectual competencies, the program rich with elective subjects of all sorts offers more opportunities for the cultivation of idiosyncrasy. So the student to develop most fully needs a wide array of electives from which to choose—and he needs the time in the school schedule to study those subjects of his own choice.

The second way in which the curriculum can contribute to maximum self-fulfillment is through diversity of content. If all students must study the same mathematics, follow the same bscs biology program, read the same literary classics, then we have severely limited the opportunities for individual self-fulfillment, no matter how clever we are in finding ways to individualize the pace of learning. We come more and more to see, in fact, that there is little content that is absolutely essential for all learners— as long as they can learn the critical cognitive processes.

Consequently, we can individualize content as much as we choose, without undue concern about the student's missing something essential. The black student can read black novels, as long as he is learning how to read novels—and he can study black history, as long as he is developing an understanding of historical processes. Here again, it seems clear, the larger high school can offer more electives and more content options than the more limited smaller institution.

Concomitant with curricular diversity is the need for a diversity of media and materials. The astute teacher determines the learning objectives—and then provides for the learners a wide variety of media and materials options, for he knows that learners differ markedly in their preferences for, and their ability to learn from, the various kinds of learning resources. Here, I think, the principal again must provide leadership for his faculty by helping them develop sophistication in the use of media and multiple resources. One way is to begin by a simple examination of present practice: ask a reading consultant to determine the reading level of one of the basic texts—and then present to the faculty the reading scores of the members of the class who have to read it. A more positive approach is through a continuing program for faculty inservice which shows the faculty how to provide the multiplicity of learning options requisite for optimum learning.

SELF-INSTRUCTIONAL MATERIALS

Perhaps a word needs to be added here about self-instructional materials. Many schools are finding that much of the cognitive content of a given unit of learning can be put into self-instructional form, thus giving the teacher more time for those aspects of learning where his presence is essential—and giving the student the opportunity both to learn at his own best pace and to develop the skills needed for self-directed learning. Such self-instructional materials are becoming increasingly available from major publishers, ranging from simple programed textbooks to elaborate multimedia packages and kits.

Teachers are finding, however, that they can develop their own self-materials for pupil self-instruction. These take many different shapes. Nova schools develop Learning Activity Packages, each of which encompasses about a two-week unit of study; the Materials Dissemination Center of I/D/E/A is helping teachers write and share what it calls UNIPACS, about the same length as the Nova packages. Some elementary and secondary schools in Duluth, Minnesota, are using shorter, single-objective materials. And in a few schools, teachers have worked out entire curricula in self-instructional form. While there is much variety in length and complexity, all successful self-instructional materials have the same basic ingredients:

> clearly stated learning objectives
> pre-test to determine readiness and level of present achievement
> content to be mastered
> means for frequent feedback to the learner about his progress
> post-test to measure final achievement.

From all the evidence I can see, it is the large high school again which is able to offer an array of media and materials resources—and whose teachers are taking the leadership in developing self-instructional materials.

So curricular and media diversity is important in the school committed to individual self-fulfillment. However, even more essential are two aspects of the instructional program—independent study for all students and small group learning in all disciplines. Let us conclude our discussion of ways to bring about maximum self-fulfillment by examining these two critical avenues for maximizing growth.

GROWTH TOWARDS AUTONOMY

My commitment to independent study for all students stems from my belief that the student can best fulfill his potential as he becomes more and more self-directed in his learning—as he makes more and more decisions for himself about when to study, what to study, where to study, and how to study. All students need this growth towards autonomy, and it is achieved not by reading about it or listening to sermons about it— but by experiencing it under the direction of an instructional staff which knows when and how to keep hands off.

School administrators interested in developing independent study programs have a wide choice from which to make a selection: William M. Alexander has identified five patterns, and his associate James D. Wells has set up 10 categories, based on their relationship to regular class work. (William M. Alexander, Vynce A. Hines, and Associates. *Independent Study in Secondary Schools.* New York: Holt, Rinehart, and Winston, 1967.)

In view of the importance I attach to independent study and as a consequence of my belief in self-fulfillment for all learners, I would advocate a comprehensive independent study program including all students, involving all the disciplines, and affecting all areas of the school's program. While our school's independent study program still needs much improvement, I think it has a richness and diversity produced by the multiple resources that a large and able faculty can bring to such a program. Last year during any given week all the students in our school had the chance to select from a long list of activities such as the following:

1. Read in library
2. View single concept film in English center
3. Listen to audio tape in social studies center
4. Play game of On-Sets in mathematics center
5. Meet with small group of students for student-led discussion in humanities center
6. Work with own teacher in remedial session
7. Listen (in student lounge) to faculty member discuss contemporary rock poetry
8. Enroll in short-term, no credit, no-grade independent study course
9. Work on long-range project in science laboratory
10. Paint in art room

11. Listen to speaker from community discuss medicine as a career
12. Meet with guidance counselor and small group of students to discuss a common problem
13. See a student production of a play.

At the risk of being tedious, I would again argue the virtues of bigness: a strong independent study program requires the multiple resources that the large high school can best mobilize.

LEARNING IN SMALL GROUPS

Finally, I think the large high school can most effectively mitigate the undesirable effects of bigness by extensive use of the small learning group. In fact, it is difficult to exaggerate the importance of the small group in promoting maximum self-fulfillment. As Jerome Bruner pointed out in "Culture, Politics, and Pedagogy" in the May 18, 1968, issue of the *Saturday Review*, the "unpredictable" dialog between teacher and student is probably the single most important function of the human teacher. And this dialog can take place most effectively and most excitingly in the small group, as all students have maximum opportunity for meaningful involvement.

So important is the small group that I think it should be used in all subjects, and as I have indicated elsewhere (*Learning in the Small Group*, Dayton, Ohio, Institute for Development of Educational Activities, 1967), it can provide the ideal setting for practically all kinds of learning activities —not simply discussion. When headmasters of small independent schools boast of "small" classes of sixteen, I counter with the retort that English students in our North Campus school meet four times a week in seminars of 12 students. Some small schools can have small classes; large schools, with wise deployment of staff, can have small seminars.

But there has been perhaps too much discussion of a theoretical and an abstract nature. At the risk of seeming simplistic, I would like to conclude by extracting from the theoretical discussion 10 steps for immediate action that any principal can take, regardless of the size of the school:

1. Eliminate the dress code and weed out unnecessary rules.
2. Organize a "Forum for Controversy."
3. Organize a faculty inservice course on "Individual Differences."
4. Let students select their own learning group.
5. Add elective courses.
6. Help teachers provide diversity of media and materials.
7. Work with teachers in developing content options.
8. Show teachers how to develop self-instructional materials.

9. Provide independent study time for all students.
10. Schedule small groups for every discipline.

There is one final suggestion: work for your own self-fulfillment—but that's another story, for another time.

INDEPENDENT STUDY: TRANSFUSION FOR ANEMIC ENGLISH PROGRAMS*

David W. Berg

> I've got too many kids in my classes Jane just sits there all day and does
> nothing Billy's too smart for the rest of the class Sally isn't too bright
> but she sure is a good worker Sandy is very bright but she sure isn't
> a very good worker Sammy could care less about anything but cars if
> that kid smarts off one more time either he goes or I go half my
> class didn't even bother to bring their books. . . .

So goes a typical English teacher's conversation in the lounge or at the lunch table or to his spouse at dinner. And under the typical English curriculum these complaints are only too valid. The sad but unavoidable fact of pedagogical life that causes most of our problems is the much abused concept of individual differences, and the even sadder fact is that we are not even coming close to providing for these differences. At best, we make a feeble attempt at coping with the situation by so-called ability grouping for our English students. What we are actually accomplishing, if this is our approach, is simply eliminating gross disparities among the students in a particular track, usually on the basis of IQ. This by no means confronts the reality of individual differences in the classroom.

* Reprinted from *English Journal* (February 1970), 59:254–258. Copyright © 1970 by the National Council of Teachers of English. Reprinted by permission of the publisher and David W. Berg.

For example, consider one of your own English classes for a moment. Look at Jim, sitting in the corner because he's a troublemaker. Half his school career has been spent in corners or in hallways. Have we compensated for his individual difference? Next compare Suzy, with her love of poetry and romance, with Bill, the captain of the football team. They both have similar IQ's; they both have similar scores on English achievement tests; they both qualify for the "regular" track in our system of ability grouping: therefore they both shall read and study *Great Expectations* for four weeks this year. Are we providing for their individual differences? Are we providing for the difference between Julio, an extremely bright boy who fled from Cuba without a knowledge of English, and Mike, a boy with an IQ of eighty and a court record, when we put them both in our "basic" track and give them both the same book? In your "honors" track you have above-average plodders who make it on the basis of hard work and good study habits; you also have brilliant students who gain nothing from a comparative study of Cyrano and Romeo. These are only a few of the real, nitty-gritty individual differences that we in the profession are not providing for. These are differences not in IQ or reading ability or English skills alone, but in personality, interests, and learning styles.

"But I have thirty-five students in my classes. The best I can do is teach for the middle of whatever range I have." So goes the pitiful cry of the English teacher. And I sympathize. I agree that you have too many students. But I maintain that it's a pathetic excuse, one that can no longer be accepted. English teachers have too long used this as a crutch and, having justified themselves to the world and cleared their consciences, wait for the never-never land when school boards will suddenly listen to the NCTE and give them four classes of twenty-five students each. So what do we do in the meantime? We have two rather obvious choices: we can sit back on our dangling modifiers and continue to bemoan our unlucky fate, *or* we can use a little imagination, free ourselves of our individual and professional anachronisms, and do something with what we've got.

Specifically, I would propose launching a program of Independent Study in English for virtually every student in Grades 7 through 12, and I would start by throwing out the curriculum guide and burning the course of study. Unless yours is an exceptional school system, these are outdated and irrelevant anyway.

Why on earth should every tenth-grader—or every tenth-grader within a given "ability" range—be forced to study *Silas Marner*, for instance? Because it's good literature? Perhaps it is, but so are many other novels that are infinitely more relevant to today's youth. Even more significant, a novel that is relevant to one individual may well be meaningless for the student sitting next to him. Are there any inherent values in *Silas* that cannot be found in other books? I doubt it. Our professional judgment of what is or is not "good literature" fades to insignificance if it results in a distaste for this good literature, as it often does. Our omnipotence in decreeing what is good for all simply does not face up to the realities of modern society. Similarly, it is no more justifiable to prescribe *Hot Rod* for an entire low-ability class than it is to prescribe *Great Expectations* for an entire "regular" class.

Another lame rationalization that we offer to defend our literature offerings is that unless the students are exposed to ——— (Dickens, Shakespeare, Twain, Eliot, Faulkner, or whoever) in school, they will never get this exposure. I think the realistic approach here is to admit first that for some students it will never matter one iota if they don't get exposed to this type of literature. I also believe that the students who will benefit from this type of exposure will arrange to fulfill this need at the appropriate time. Our mission as teachers would better be to encourage and make available this exposure—to offer it rather than force it.

The second stumbling block in the English curriculum is grammar. My personal prejudice on this topic is that grammar should not be taught on the secondary level at all, except to those students who might benefit from a humanities approach to the English language. I find the study of our language fascinating and rewarding; this is one reason why I am an English teacher. I do not expect all my students to feel this way, however. I also cannot believe that intensive study of grammar year after year will help a student write better. There is no other subject that a student encounters for as many school hours with as meager results as grammar. If you feel that you must teach grammar, go ahead. But do one of two things: either teach it for the same values that we teach art or music—as a humanities course and not as a shop course—or individualize your approach so each student is studying the specific aspects of grammar in which he is deficient. Don't force half your students to sit through material they already have mastered for the benefit of the other half who probably won't learn it again this year. An individualized approach fits in well with an Independent Study program, since it will involve diagnosis and prescription for each individual student. You will have students who will do no work whatsoever on grammar this year, because they will demonstrate that they have already mastered that material. You will have other students who will be doing considerable work on grammar, starting with the basic rudiments. If you do feel that grammar must be a part of your class, this is the only realistic approach.

Think for a moment about how your English classes went today. How much involvement was there? Was the day exciting or enjoyable or meaningful for your students? Did you have a good time and end the day satisfied with what went on? Now consider this: What would happen if tomorrow you came into class and said, "Beginning next week you may elect to work in any area that interests you. Since this is an English class, the only requirements are that whatever you work on should include some reading and writing." What would happen? You would at first be greeted with stunned disbelief. Never in their entire school career of seven or nine or twelve years have they been offered this kind of choice, and chances are they will never have the opportunity again. It will no doubt take some of them quite awhile to realize that you really mean it and to realize the full implications of such a "non-assignment."

What will they do with this golden opportunity? Some will start by doing nothing. So be it. These are the do-nothings anyway. One advantage to this approach is that they are electing this option of their own volition. A major learning experience for them will be that, come grade time, you can say to them, "You elected to fail." For once in their life you have stripped them of the excuses "The-teacher-doesn't-like-me" or "I-just-don't-understand-this-junk." You are also removing the rebellion motive from this type of student. You must accept their daily option of not doing anything as a legitimate choice, as long as they don't interfere with the rest of the class. Your responsibility to them is to encourage them to take a more desirable option, by suggesting more attractive alternatives. A second advantage of this approach with this type of student is that you are not asking any student to do the impossible. It is literally impossible to threaten, cajole, or in any way convince certain students that it is to their advantage to do some of the things that are required in the traditional English class. And I'm not sure that they aren't justified in rejecting things like how to write a friendly letter, or what is a participle, or what are the conflicts in *Great Expectations*. Why *should* they bother with these?

On the other hand, I doubt very much that you will find a single student who has no interests at all. They may not be what we would consider teaching in English class, but they are interests that are real and vital to that individual; therefore, they are important. If you have a student who is interested in cars or dogs or snowmobiles or airplanes or whatever, why can't you use that interest to accomplish whatever it is an English teacher is supposed to accomplish? Do you want them to read? Then let them read a car manual or a book on maternity care if this is what they feel a need for. Do you want them to write? Then let Suzy write a poem and let Joe write an essay on deer hunting. The day may come when Joe too will write a poem, and you may certainly encourage and suggest it, but don't sit him down on a Friday afternoon and tell him he has to write one.

If you do elect to try Independent Study, you are not abdicating your rights and responsibilities as an English teacher. You are in fact taking on more responsibilities and work than in a traditional classroom.

You are basically readjusting your philosophy to serve more realistically the needs of your students. You are for one thing a source to whom the students can turn when the need arises. Does Ken want to learn about the 1970 car styles? Then you might suggest that he write a letter to General Motors requesting some pictures and brochures, and you would show him where to find out how to write a business letter. Is Sally enthusiastic about what she found out about her topic? Then give her the opportunity to tell the class or part of the class about it. Has Harry found a book on animals that is too hard for him? Encourage him to improve his vocabulary and his reading comprehension, and show him how to do it. He will respond, because he knows he needs it. He will learn because the motivation comes from himself, not from a teacher who says, "You need help in reading. Report to the remedial reading teacher for nine weeks."

If you do accept the rationale behind an Independent Study program for your classes, there are several approaches you might adopt. After explaining what Independent Study is and the responsibilities it involves, you might begin by allowing those who have met certain criteria to proceed. You should, if you follow this procedure, encourage every student to become involved eventually in the program as soon as each one meets your standards of behavior. You should also be very specific about delineating the path to follow to qualify for the Independent Study program, and make it very clear that it will not be restricted to the smarter students.

A second approach would be to assume that all your students are capable of pursuing Independent Study and allowing all to begin simultaneously. Although you would realize that your assumption is very probably false, this approach has the psychological advantage of not isolating those about whom you may have reservations—the less mature student or the discipline problem. Your expressed expectation that they all will succeed is a much more positive approach than beginning by implying that they could not succeed at this either. It would however entail your keeping a close eye on those students and revoking their Independent Study privileges if the occasion should arise. After a suitable waiting period you should by all means give them a second and a third chance if necessary. A primary objective of this type of program is to develop the ability to work and learn independently, and as with any other skill it will take more effort to develop it with certain individuals than with others.

As the year progresses, you will be able to encourage and develop greater sophistication in the students who are involved in the program. If a student's written work indicates a need for work on sentence structure or spelling, for example, you can both point out the need and its importance and encourage him to undertake independently a course of action that will remedy the problem. If he does elect this course of action, you will of course need to have resources available and you will have to show him how to find the information he needs. You might also have one of your students who is skilled in this area tutor him by mutual agreement only in that specific skill area. This could very well serve as an Independent Study project for both students. You could further expand this idea by asking different students to become "experts" or resource persons for various skill areas, if they so desire.

Perhaps the most fascinating aspects of an Independent Study program in English are the limitless ramifications and possibilities it offers both the teacher and the students. Intensive reading in one area or by one author may lead one student to other areas. Reading short stories may lead another student to investigate how to go about writing one himself. Having the opportunity to read about hot rods (and pass English at the same time) may bring a potential dropout to the realization that school does not have to be a threat, that there is something here of interest and value to him after all. The sense of accomplishment of a slow student at achieving his own set of objectives may encourage him to try harder at whatever his next project might be.

What are the logistics of implementing an Independent Study program in your classroom? The major requirement is a wealth of materials conveniently located in the classroom. To accomplish this does not necessarily involve the expenditure of a large sum of money. A "wealth of materials" should include as wide a selection of paperbacks as you can accumulate (ask the students for donations; ask the PTA for a paperback drive; put an ad in the local paper—you'll get hundreds); it should include a variety of textbooks from all subject areas (check the textbook storeroom; ask your fellow teachers; send for sample copies); it should include a variety of practice materials (make some yourself; take apart sample workbooks and staple the lessons in manila folders; ask other teachers to run off a few extra copies of a lesson each time they make one; use magazine articles for reading comprehension exercises, stapling them in folders and writing a few questions for each; have your students help in any way they can).

If you are including skill materials as options for Independent Study, and you should, diagnosis is the order of the day. Again, use sample materials such as tests, or make your own diagnostic tests. They don't have to be of professional caliber; they should be designed to indicate to the student areas that he might need work on. Your practice materials should then be keyed to the diagnostic test, so the student can see that if he does poorly on section one of the test he can find help in a specific place. Used in this way, your classroom becomes more an English laboratory than an English classroom.

Individual conferences are a necessity to operate successfully a program such as this one. These can be held during class time for some, before or after school for others, and during homerooms or study halls for the rest. If you object to seeing students before school or during your planning period or even once in awhile during your lunch period, you probably aren't the kind of teacher who would be willing to try a program like this anyway. You might be pleasantly surprised though at what might happen if you asked one or two of your students to bring their lunches to your room and talk over their projects with you.

What are the possible outcomes of such a program? These might be a few: more fun for you as a teacher, excitement and enjoyment for your students, skill development for those who need it, enthusiasm, interest, and a much-needed revitalization for your English curriculum.

LEARNING ACTIVITY PACKAGES: AN APPROACH TO INDIVIDUALIZED INSTRUCTION*

RICHARD V. JONES, JR.

Recent writers in the field of education have emphasized the need for more individualized approaches to the instruction in our public schools. These writers assail as inhibitors to learning the traditional lock-step procedures which are typical of both elementary and secondary schools across the nation. Rather than providing for the learning needs of each student, the segmented and rigidly enforced age-grade kind of school organization tends to inhibit the learning of both the more advanced and/or interested students, and for the low ability or uninterested students. Research in the behavioral sciences is re-emphasizing the uniqueness of the person and the general lack of our present instruments in education to define even a majority of these unique characteristics of people.

* Reprinted from the *Journal of Secondary Education* (April 1968), 43:178–183, by permission.

The philosophy of the non-graded or continuous progress program is based upon at least four assumptions:

1. Schools as organizations in society are held responsible for the maximum development of each individual.
2. Each individual learns at a rate and in a manner that is characteristic of that individual.
3. Each learner utilizes a unique set of experiences in the learning process.
4. Effective learning occurs only when the learner participates actively in the learning processes.

While most practicing school administrators and teachers would agree with the ideals presented above, there is in our schools an increasingly large number of students with increasingly wide variations in backgrounds, experiences, interests, and abilities. If school personnel accept the philosophy of non-gradedness, an immediate question arises: *How is the teacher to survive in a classroom full of students, each progressing at different rates within individualized programs?*

The education profession must accept the responsibility for suggesting answers to this question. If we concede to the need for more individualized programs, we must also develop strategies to implement these programs with present facilities, present organizational structures, and present funding. We must look to possible alternatives to the apparently overwhelming needs facing the educational organization, and take first steps.

Embryonic programs have been developed and are evolving in the educational community to provide for both the needed instructional strategies and for the necessary management of student groups. One example of that approach is being studied by the American Institute of Research in Palo Alto, California.[1] This group, through funds provided by the Westinghouse Corporation, is developing and testing "teaching-learning units" (TLUs) in selected schools in California and Pennsylvania. Teaching-learning units can be generally described as individualized, two-week units designed to guide the learner toward the achievement of specified behavioral objectives. The AIR anticipates producing thousands of TLUs so that teachers and students may choose from a variety of units depending upon the individual needs and capabilities of the student who will use the material. A computer is used to supply detailed information on the progress of each student involved compared to his capabilities.

---

[1] John C. Flanagan. "Functional Education for the Seventies." *Phi Delta Kappan.* XLIX (September, 1967), 27–31.

Another approach is being encouraged by the Kettering Foundation through Project /I/D/E/A.[2] Here, the development of self-guiding units called "UNIPACS" has been initiated. UNIPACS are sets of self-instructing materials written by teachers which are sent through a quality-control system within the /I/D/E/A project and then made available to all participating teachers. These curricular materials include sequenced and self-directed programmed activities also designed to guide the learner as an individual toward specific behavioral objectives.

A third approach to an individualized instructional program revolves around the concept of "Learning Activity Packages." Developed initially at the Nova Schools in Ft. Lauderdale, Florida under the direction of Dr. James Smith, and most recently incorporated into the Continuous Progress Program at Hughson High School, Hughson, California, Learning Activity Packages, called "LAPs," are sets of alternative activities for students. Individualization is provided by allowing the student optional learning modes, and by utilizing a variety of instructional media, subject content, and activities from which he may choose. Each LAP is designed to bring the learner toward the understanding of a single major concept. The remainder of this paper will discuss the writing of LAPs as a device to individualize instruction.

One of the first requirements in writing Learning Activity Packages is to explicate a scope of major concepts or "learnable ideas" to be understood by the learner, and then to sequence these concepts. Typically, ideas are included which will generate about one month's effort for the "average" student moving at an "average rate." The complete set of concepts constitute a "structure," (to use Bruner's term),[3] to which the data and facts of the subject may be interrelated by the learner. This is the basic idea of conceptualized learning.

When this has been accomplished for each subject area and for all levels of instruction, the result can be a scope and sequence of primary ideas moving from pre-school education into college programs. Each primary idea that has been identified becomes the topic of a Learning Activity Package, and is subsequently sub-divided into a set of secondary ideas.

Included as secondary ideas are those supporting ideas which are appropriate for the consideration of any primary idea. For example, at the ninth-year level, if the concept "Living things interact with their environment" were identified as a primary idea, then some appropriate *secondary*

---

[2] The Institute for Development of Educational Activities. A Charles F. Kettering Foundation project. Materials Dissemination Center, 27965 Cabot Road, South Laguna, Calif. 92677.

[3] See Jerome S. Bruner. *The Process of Education.* New York: Vintage Books, 1960.

ideas might be: (1) living things adapt to their environment; (2) living things are changed by their environment, and; (3) different environments support characteristic living things. These secondary ideas become the sections of a Learning Activity Package called "LAP segments." The composition of these segments will be clarified below.

Following the identification of the secondary ideas, the teacher-writer outlines in performance terms the kind of behavior the learner will demonstrate once he knows the "secondary idea." Robert Mager has written a most informative book[4] which describes in an interesting way the characteristics and writing of such objectives. Simply stated, these objectives, called "Instructional Objectives" in the LAPs, include (1) the kind of behavior which will be demonstrated by the learner when he has "learned," (2) the acceptable level of performance which will be demonstrated by the learner, and (3) the sets of circumstances which will be in operation when the performance is demonstrated. This latter segment delimits the performance to certain times or places, to certain kinds of equipment, or with certain necessary materials.

In LAPs, a set of instructional objectives is typically written for each segment. These objectives, if properly developed, can suggest the kinds of activities which might be included. They will certainly outline that behavior which is to be tested.

After the instructional objectives are listed, the writer prepares the evaluation instruments. The evaluation program in LAPs consists of three major procedures: exemption, student self-assessment, and teacher tests.

First is the *exemption*. Any student who after reading the concepts under discussion in the Learning Activity Package, and reading the kind of behavior he is expected to demonstrate, may decide that he already understands the knowledge involved and is able to demonstrate the kind of behavior required. These students would be encouraged to exempt the LAP by passing selected skill and knowledge tests. If the LAP is successfully exempted the student would move on to the next LAP and receive credit for having finished the one for which he has just demonstrated his competence.

A second kind of evaluation in a Learning Activity Package is the *student self-assessment test*. This instrument commonly includes a set of questions with the answers readily available, which can be used by the student to examine his own level of achievement. Self-assessment tests may be included for the entire LAP or may be included within each LAP segment. Obviously, students attempting exemption of a LAP would use this instrument before presenting himself to the instructor to bypass the LAP.

---

[4] Robert Mager. *Preparing Instructional Objectives*. Palo Alto, Calif.; Fearon Press, 1964.

The third major phase of the evaluation program is the *teacher test*, given either at the end of each LAP segment but certainly at the end of the entire Package. These tests determine the degree of achievement attained by each student completing the LAP. The teacher test is parallel in content, form, and type of question to the student self-assessment test. Commonly, teachers write one examination and then merely use alternate items for the student assessment and the teacher test.

Once the critical but preliminary steps of defining the primary ideas, secondary ideas, instructional objectives, and evaluational procedures are completed, the writer of a Learning Activity Package must turn his attention to the development of a variety of activities from which a student may choose to learn the content, skills or material involved. The activities included in this section of a package are of two general types: (1) the *core activities*, (2) the *depth opportunities*.

Core activities include those instructional methods and materials through which the student may conceptualize the secondary ideas by a confrontation of stimulating and valid content within the conceptual area. It is imperative that the learning activities outlined in the package provide the student with the opportunity for decision making. This element is critical; for if the student is not provided with alternative routes to the attainment of the learnable idea, then little has been gained beyond the traditional lock-step approach to curriculum development. Not only must alternative modes of learning be included, but also must a variety of materials and specific content fields be provided for the student.

For example, if a student is to work with a set of ideas outlined in a specific book in order to gain some needed experiential background, then the LAP writer must provide for students who find reading difficult by allowing the student the option of (a) having the book read to him, or (b) listening to an audio tape or recording of the book, or (c) seeing a film about the book (if one is available), or (d) reading a less difficult book or a book within his reading level which discusses similar ideas. A major problem for writers is encountered at this point. Many teachers traditionally trained and oriented tend to define single kinds of activities as the most appropriate for learning and hesitate to allow other routes for students; some teachers are unaware of alternative approaches to major ideas; and many just do not have a variety of instructional materials at their disposal.

Included within this set of activities must be the option for students to participate in group-learning of a wide variety, type, and purpose. Of significance here is the use of "ad hoc" small groups. By allowing groups of students to self-organize as they arrive at a particular point in their learning, the teacher is able to cause the kind of learner interaction that is necessary to attitudinal change. Kimball Wiles suggests that the use of small groups is one of the more effective ways to change peoples' attitudes.[5] Therefore, it seems imperative in this individualized type of learning that the student be provided the opportunities to interact with his peers and with his instructor. Without this opportunity, a Learning Activity Package becomes little more than a set of programmed activities, and the student soon finds himself uninvolved and in need of testing notions, concepts, and attitudes which have been internally defined.

Another critical aspect of the core activities involves the inclusion of teacher-student contact points. At several significant and predetermined crossroads in the course of learning the student must be brought into contact on a one-to-one basis with the instructor. The necessity for this particular procedure is dictated by the diagnostic responsibilities of the teacher's role. It is at these crucial times that the teacher must professionally assess the progress of the student's efforts and suggest other activities to lift him from plateaus of learning or help him over barriers to his progress. In addition, teacher-student contact points assist in the developmental stages of the self-reliant behavior that is crucial to individualized instruction, by providing limits or boundaries to independent action.

Each set of core experiences utilizes several choices of specific content for the student to study. Students might be allowed to investigate, for example, cultural aspects of American Indians, African natives, or Eskimos, in order to arrive at some concept of social structure in primitive societies. Indeed, the significance of studying birds, bees, or bison when investigating the concept of the inter-relationship of living things to their environment seems less than critical. As students are given this freedom to choose specific content, the conceptual framework is emphasized rather than the examples of data which support and clarify the concept.

Typically, when the student completes a set of core experience activities required of him within the LAP segment, he is directed to one of two points. If the secondary idea is so significant that the teacher decides some assessment of progress is necessary, he may be directed to a teacher test. This evaluation may be an oral, written or practical test and typically covers only that part of the Package completed (a "LAP segment teacher test"). If the secondary activity is not deemed critical or the completion and understanding can be assessed later, the learner is directed to the next LAP segment. Included either throughout the Learning Activity Package or localized on a few pages in the package are the second set of activities, the *depth opportunities.*

Depth opportunities allow the student to (1) apply knowledge gained and skills developed in some kind of activity which he finds particularly interesting, or (2) develop further theoretical competencies in some

---

[5] Kimball Wiles, unreported lecture at Ceres, Calif., September 3, 1967.

area of interest, or (3) organize some type of quest activity which he designs himself. These activities are typically wide-ranging and diversified. Most certainly they should not include "more of the same." That is, depth opportunities should allow the student to develop a skit around an idea, or paint a picture to express an idea, or produce a play, or participate in a play, or become involved in some student-oriented project which will further clarify the concept under consideration, and will bring him to a fuller and more complete understanding of the primary idea of the LAP. Many times students will proceed with depth opportunities as they proceed through the core experiences, so that they find themselves spending more time, putting forth greater effort, and experiencing an increased joy in learning a particular subject than has been previously all too typical in our schools.

Finally, the student arrives at the point where he decides that he has mastered, to the degree indicated in the instructional objectives, the primary idea and secondary ideas of the LAP. He is then directed to a conference with the teacher, and to the final LAP teacher test. Upon successful completion of this examination, he proceeds to the next Learning Activity Package. If at any time, but more particularly at the end of the LAP, he does not demonstrate a level of competency that the teacher has defined as the level of acceptance, he is recycled into those kinds of optional activities he has not chosen but which he and the teacher together feel can provide the level of achievement desired. If after recycling the student still does not achieve the required degree of competency, he may be cycled into remedial work, given individualized optional activities to complete, or in some instances, directed to other LAPs or other subjects. In any event, the student must participate in this decision, and the teacher must have clearly in mind the particular learning needs of the student and communicate to the student that "failure" has not occurred.

Student grades are a combination of at least three factors: (1) his score on the teacher's test; (2) the amount of time it took to make his way through the Learning Activity Package as compared to the mean completion time in the class, and (3) the quality of work completed within the Package. In addition, any depth study work would be an additional factor toward the grade received. The specific determinants which make up these three factors will vary from subject to subject. In this manner, laboratory study, shop work, etc., can all become logical parts of the final grade. If a student's total of all three of these elements of the grade is still below passing level it should indicate to the teacher that he was working in a LAP beyond his present capabilities. He has not failed, the teacher has. Therefore, he is recycled "back," or "over" to material more appropriate to his present capabilities.

A Learning Activity Package is designed for student use. Students will have them, write on them, keep them, or throw them away. Therefore, each LAP must have directions for the students to read and follow. Typically, these directions include grading procedures, how to submit assignments, a description of the entire LAP, and any specific directions needed for more effective and efficient use of the LAP by the student.

Before the directions are outlined for the student, the LAP must be "presented" to the student. This presentation is called the "Rationale," and recalls for the student where he has been in the subject area, where this LAP will take him, and why he should occupy his time with the idea to be studied. It is vital that this material be written in the learner's terms. Brevity and relevance are the guidelines to the over-ambitious writer-teacher.

Many other elements may be included within the covers of a LAP: visual aids; a bibliography of all applicable and available resources; work sheets; an achievement record; and a large dose of motivational drawings, anecdotes, and cartoons. The insertion of these items is limited only by the imagination of the writer and the availability of time to think them up and write them down.

As we proceed from grouping systems which limit intellectual growth of all students to the boundaries of a group lesson to more individualized instructional procedures, we will need a new structure within which to operate. The Learning Activity Package can be one of these new operational patterns. These materials are being used now at the Nova Schools in Florida and Hughson High School in California. Writing this material is difficult, tedious and time-consuming work. The resultant, however, is a system which at once individualizes instruction for the students, and structures the curriculum so that the teacher is free to be a guide to the learners rather than a controller of groups.

Readers who are interested in further information about the project using Learning Activity Packages at Hughson High School should contact:

Mr. Jerry Carpenter, Curriculum Director
Hughson High School
Hughson, California 95236

BEYOND MODULAR SCHEDULING*

SCOTT D. THOMSON

September, 1971, will mark the eighth year of computer-generated modular scheduling in American secondary schools. Initiated by five pioneering institutions in 1963,[1] the modular approach has moved forward the quest for a flexible, individualized structure for students. It has opened the traditional lockstep schedule to allow for independent study and for significant alternatives in class size and in length of class period. And it has provided teachers with new perspectives about instruction as well as new opportunities to employ resources.

Student attitude and achievement under modular scheduling tend to be positive, although longitudinal studies are in short supply. Students like modular scheduling, as do most teachers. Students under the system make wide use of libraries and other special facilities, and they tend to score significantly higher than do students in traditional classes on tests of critical thinking. There appears to be no systematic difference in mean achievement scores between students in flexible modular schools and those in traditional schools, although students in the modular schools generally make a greater percentage of both high grades and low grades than do students in traditional schools where the "average" grade is dominant.

The most visible change occurring in a school with modular scheduling comes from placing students in independent study for approximately one-third of the school week. Visible change extends also to the 80-minute or longer laboratory periods, to seminar classes of 15 students, to open laboratories and mediated self-taught units, to the personally initiated projects of many students both at school and in the community, and to the continual ebb and flow of students from area to area throughout the day.

---

* Reprinted from *Phi Delta Kappan* (April 1971), 52:484–487, by permission.
[1] Overfelt High School, East San Jose, California; Homestead High School, Cupertino, California; Lincoln High School, Stockton, California; Marshall High School, Portland, Oregon; and Virgin Valley High School, Virgin Valley, Nevada.

Beyond these obvious encounters with change can be found the more subtle and important aspects of modular scheduling: the student who suddenly recognizes that learning is more than sitting in a classroom, or the student who pursues for the first time a problem to the limit of interest and capability; the teacher who exchanges the security of the carefully manicured daily lesson for experimentation with new course structures, or the teacher who recognizes anew the importance of discussing class objectives with students; the department that moves decisively into developing a variety of media for content delivery or that creates new minicourses; and the faculty who, as a group, recast their techniques to take advantage of new opportunities for tutoring and for interaction with small groups.

Hard on the heels of these heady strides toward better instruction, however, rise some dust clouds of concern. Each year the high hopes of students and teachers wrestle with contradictions in human behavior—the desire for freedom and an aversion to obligation, the hope for motivation and the reality of insidious lethargy, the radiance of a new idea and the necessity for dogged pursuit. Would the attractive images of theory wash out with experience? Would it be possible to shuck the shell of tradition and to push forward anew? Could schools learn the practical gains as time passed and define the major impediments which remain?

PLANNING THE NEXT STEP

With modular scheduling it was hoped that students would respond to unscheduled time by using it to direct advantage, depending upon individual needs. It was thought that some students would concentrate on special interests, others might explore broadly, others would review and tie down uncertainties, and still others could secure special help to strengthen basic skills. Not only would students be free to use this time to personal advantage, but teachers, also, would be unburdened from the monotony of continuously scheduled class time. Teachers could provide personal help to students as well as lead them to the multitude of resources found in school libraries and laboratories and in the community at large.

Many students responded well to this concept. For instance, by all ordinary criteria, scholarship at Evanston Township High School, now in its fourth year of modular scheduling, continues at a high level. The graduating classes of 1969 and 1970 qualified more National Merit semifinalists, 62, than were qualified by any previous two classes. The class of 1970 outpaced its predecessors in Illinois state scholarships. College admissions continue to rise. Recent achievement scores remain up.

A more careful analysis, however, dampens the optimism. It appears that some students do not fare so well. Those who achieved poorly under a traditional class schedule tend to achieve even more poorly today under the modular schedule, according to a careful investigation at ETHS by Ronald Walden. When given free selection time, this group of students invariably choose activities of a purely social or antisocial nature. They tend to waste time. Opportunities for independent study are ignored even when the student enjoys the freedom of selecting the area of exploration. According to Walden, these "retrogressed students" are an identifiable group, tending to score poorly on achievement tests and on the responsibility and social maturity scales of the California Psychological Inventory.

Under modular scheduling it was anticipated that the availability of free time, together with abundant resources and the direct encouragement of a teacher, would stimulate all students. Everyone, it was assumed, would desire to explore his particular interest or to improve himself along some lines. Every student, hopefully, would respond to responsibility.

Now it becomes apparent that independent study is not synonymous with individualization of instruction. The benefits of individualization do not automatically arise from free time. Rather, these benefits come from a more thoughtful design of instructional strategies. The need for considerable structure in some instances and modest structure in others, depending upon the nature of the student, must be a part of the scheduling picture to achieve true individualization.

Schools moving into modular scheduling ordinarily replaced a highly structured, traditional schedule for everyone with an open, modular schedule for everyone. In actuality, one monolith had been traded for another. In each instance all students were forced into a single mold. While it could be argued that a majority of students benefited from the open schedule, it must be accepted that perhaps 20% of the student body had actually fared better under the traditional system. Many of these are students with the most pressing need for assistance as they enter high school, if their prior records are to be believed.

Understanding this, modular schools began to crack the monolith. One common step was to expand the number of reading classes and to schedule students with weak reading skills into these classes for part of their "free time." Often, immature students were assigned to tutoring centers or to study halls during unscheduled time. The results, however, were not spectacular. Students often resented what they considered to be new intrusions upon their personal freedom. Concerning student attitudes, it should be understood that modular scheduling is popular with the unsuccessful as well as the successful student. According to a poll taken at ETHS, 93% of the students prefer modular to traditional scheduling. In the same poll, however, these students suggest that freshmen be scheduled in class 75% of the time, as compared to about 50% for seniors. These attitudes correspond to the opinions of the faculty, who feel that immature and low-achieving students use unscheduled time unprofitably.

Acting more boldly, some districts (Hopkins, Minnesota, for one) have developed special schools to assist the low-achieving student. Designed especially for uncommitted learners of all abilities, these schools recombine the elements of freedom and structure. Because the best individual program for uncommitted students includes considerable structure, independent time is minimal. Students' accountability to the teacher is increased. Within this external framework, however, broad student initiative is encouraged. A project approach based upon student interests ordinarily is used, with the separate subject areas serving as resources to investigate the problem. Community resources are tapped, but always under the direction of a learning contract. Group counseling and close teacher contact with the home buttress the effort.

These approaches, together with the modifications in class structure, especially those to provide additional scheduled time at the freshman level, are seen as significant steps toward a program of instruction tailored to the nature of individual students. The search for adequate pliability must continue until a series of instructional strategies exists which will accommodate the particular needs of various unique groups of students. An institution stressing individuality will provide several distinct modes of instruction, because each mode would be optimal for some student. Breaking forward into a new realm of several concurrent and discrete programs should allow a fuller utilization of the potential of computer scheduling as well.

THE CLIENT-CENTERED SCHOOL

Many schools currently possess the resources to design and implement a continuum of instructional modes including dimensions other than the teacher-directed/student-initiated axis. The appeal of such a system, however, is tempered by the limits of our current knowledge about students. Before students are slotted into one of a highly sophisticated series of alternatives, the school must be professionally confident that the student is aimed correctly. Were we in possession of comprehensive student data and a competent diagnostic system, we could become more aware of the components of various student typologies. We would then be more confident about designing a series of legitimate instructional modes for the students in these various groups.

Central to illuminating these matters would be the formulation of diagnostic teams and the establishment of a diagnostic center. The diagnostic team, a group of professionals who know the student well, would act in a manner comparable to an admissions committee at a private university. Gathering facts about a student's objectives, skills, maturity, interests, work habits, attitudes, psychological needs, and family expectations, the diagnostic team would begin to form an image of their client. Additional data would be sought until the image achieved focus. The approach would be comprehensive and would include both objective and subjective diagnoses. There would be no single person sitting down to advise whether or not a student should take Speech I or Typing. Rather, a larger group would be looking in careful detail at a broader picture. Important dimensions would be added to the scene. Sound judgments could be made upon perceptions of greater depth and accuracy than those we presently possess.

Once the nature of the client was ascertained and once the desired behavioral goals were established in conference with parent and student, the information could be held in a data bank. After a number of students were similarly profiled, central tendencies would emerge in these profiles, allowing a manageable collection of student typologies. For these typologies, then, a continuum of finely honed instructional modes could be designed to provide a generous degree of individualization within the total school program.

The beginnings of such a diagnostic system would be modest and would focus initially upon the cognitive dimensions of a student's profile. The diagnostic capability should eventually reach beyond these limits, however, toward the affective, psychomotor, and maturational aspects of student personality. In like manner, the instructional modes would focus first upon the cognitive dimension of student differences. Even then the mix of content, methodology, technology, and structure considered appropriate for enhancing the academic growth of separate and identifiable groups of students would vary because the student typologies would vary. Initially the choice offered might be between highly structured English III and non-structured English III at two levels of difficulty. In an experimental school, however, the choices could be much broader, including instructional modes focusing upon social problems.

The term "client" in this approach is used as traditionally defined by the professions. A client is a person who solicits assistance from a knowledgeable source. An ill patient seeks help from his physician. A man with income-tax problems seek the advice of an accountant. Two persons forming a partnership seek an attorney. A student desiring beneficial learning experiences seeks a teacher.

A client-centered school is directive. It provides specific programs for students based upon the nature of that student as professionally diagnosed, and based upon a program professionally designed to guide the student toward objectives defined jointly by his family and by society. Many important dimensions of personality are included in designing an appropriate instructional mode, not student interests alone. The focus is upon achieving desired student behaviors once they are identified by a comprehensive diagnostic input.

The total instructional system of a client-centered school, operating

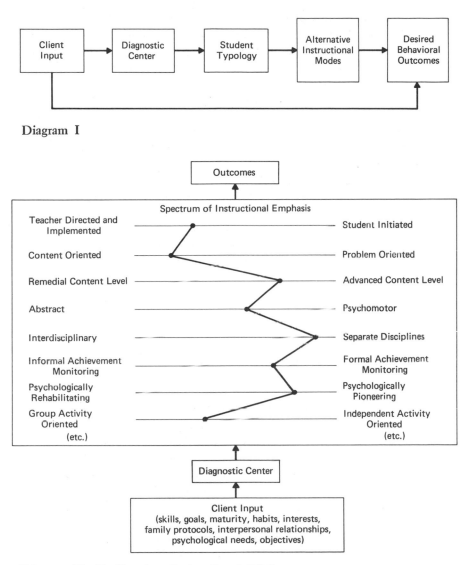

Diagram I

Diagram II   Profile of an Instructional Mode

upon information supplied by a diagnostic center, is illustrated in Diagram I.

The accurate definition of various student typologies and the development of alternative instructional modes to service these typologies is central to the concept of this system. The nature of individual students can be determined by achievement, attitude, interest, and maturity measures; by personal interview; by anecdotal records; through the insight of teachers;

and in conference with parents to gain a picture of family protocols and objectives. These elements of the student's total personality can be identified and scaled on a comprehensive form. After a group of students are profiled, central tendencies will emerge, upon which the school may design the series of alternative instructional modes.

The instructional modes must be highly adaptive. They must provide the framework most conducive to the success of each individual student. They must provide not only for the intellectually "bright and dull" but for a variety of attitudes, values, psychological patterns, and life styles. A hypothetical instructional mode, placed upon the spectra of eight important elements, is shown in Diagram II.

As a practical matter to functioning schools, the variety of distinct instructional modes would necessarily be limited to a manageable number. A restricted scale of elements could keep options from ballooning. Certainly more alternatives could be offered than at present, however, in any genuine attempt to provide professional direction to the goal of individualization.

It should be emphasized that a client-centered approach extends to aspects of student life beyond the usual limits of "individually prescribed instruction," where the focus tends to be on mastery of subject content by individual effort. Some student profiles in a client-centered school might call for very little independent course work, yet the client's program would be highly individualized and most appropriate to his needs. Other student profiles, based upon the desire of some families for a minimum of structure, may require only occasional student attendance in a formal classroom.

A considerable degree of student and parent commitment should arise from the client approach, particularly today when educational goals vary significantly from family to family. The parent needs to be involved with input and the definition of desired behavioral outcomes. With these pinned down, the school can better understand and meet individual parental expectations. The student also should provide input. He will discuss thoroughly the diagnostic outcomes prior to his assignment to an instructional mode. Thus fully apprised, he can see the value of, and gain a commitment to, the particular instructional mode prescribed for him to achieve his objectives. He may also gain valuable personal insights by the process of diagnosis and discussion.

Wise schools build upon careful planning. The practicality of a diagnostic center and a client approach to individualization will have to be weighed as our collective experience grows. What does appear to be true from the present vantage point, however, is that unscheduled time and independent study at present do not benefit a significant number of students. Alternative arrangements must be found. The search will continue for new approaches. The client-centered school seems to be a promising direction to pursue.

Chapter 10

NEW ROLES IN CURRICULUM DEVELOPMENT

The greatly increased interest in curriculum improvement of the past decade has brought new partners into its processes as well as greatly expanded efforts by some old partners, the scholars, and the students. Today business and industry are the new and very aggressive partners in curriculum improvement, while students are the old but equally, if differently, aggressive ones.

Beginning in the late 1950s, with the post-Sputnik stimulus of federal funds and national defense movements, the national curriculum project became a major approach to curriculum improvement in the standard high school disciplines. We reviewed its popularity and impact on the subject fields in Chapter 5, and turn here to a review and prospectus of its role in continuing curriculum development. Arthur R. King, Jr., who has been director of one of the major centers for curriculum development, the Hawaii Curriculum Center, provides the article, "Curriculum Projects: A Perspective." He explains the rationale of the projects and gives a helpful identification of their characteristics. Note herein the influence of the academic specialists: "Whether the effort is mounted by a professional society of academic scholars, a regional laboratory, a consortium of school districts, a joint university-state agency, or a publishing firm, it is members of the academic disciplines who set the approach and put the stamp of authenticity on the materials

package." King also regards as characteristic a relatively common process of development of the curriculum area and of approaches to curriculum design. He draws various implications for roles of teachers, supervisors, and teacher educators, including possible "interchangeability of roles."
He sees the continuance of the national curriculum project as "an exciting new day" for the education profession, and urges educators to take full advantage of this "potent new technique of the large-scale curriculum project to enliven our entire educational enterprise."

During the 1960s the need for new instructional materials and equipment to implement the new curriculum programs plus the increased funding of education attracted new industries and new combinations of publishers and hardware manufacturers to form new learning industries. These new industries and combinations had uneven success, and by the end of the decade many had withdrawn from the field. The article by Gabriel D. Ofiesh on "The New Education and the Learning Industry" reviews these developments and presents the thesis that cooperative effort by the learning and education industries is sorely needed. New models must emerge, he feels, rather than "the same old pedagogy packaged in new cartons." If education and industry can cooperate and have government subsidy, he writes, "the necessary revolution in American schools will almost inevitably occur."

Cooperation for somewhat different purposes is described in the report on " 'Partnership' High Schools: The Search for New Ways To Cooperate" excerpted here. This publication from the Institute for Educational Development, reported more than 30 partnership projects in 23 cities and 19 states. Although the report seems to beg the question of the purposes of these partnerships, perhaps because of their diversity, it does make reference to the desire of industries to help their cities and their high schools, to help students prepare for employment, and to find more effective ways of participating in education other than their traditional "largesse." Common points of resemblance in the projects are listed in the introductory section of the excerpt; the key notion of cooperation is the distinctive and promising idea. Other articles in this anthology offer abundant evidence that urban high schools need much help in meeting the needs of their students; certainly industry can help greatly in funds, personnel, and opportunities, and in cooperative planning and evaluation of specific projects.

In the early 1970s "accountability" had become a widely-used and debated force in education. The schools had long been legally accountable for their students and technically accountable for the handling of funds and records, but they had neither been expected to account specifically for results nor accustomed to doing so. Rising taxes and taxpayers' resistance combined with national problems that caused a questioning of most social institutions and systems, brought mounting scrutiny of the schools and school budgets. Leon Lessinger, author of the selection "Engineering Accountability for Results in Public Education," says "how to engineer accountability for results in public education is the central problem for the education profession." One aspect of the matter is performance contracting, which he sees as "*one* process for which accountability is the product." The article describes and illustrates this process in some detail; note its utilization of private enterprise (although, as he states, the contract can be with teachers, universities, and nonprofit organizations) in meeting specific educational goals. He cites six advantages of the use of performance contracts, apparently leaving the reader to cite any disadvantages. Do you see any?

Lessinger is positive that the use of performance contracting will increase, and thus far his predictions seem justified by reports of contracts executed and in process. Therefore he develops other new roles, possibly for industries or combinations of industrialists and educators. He sees the necessity for management support groups (MSGs) to give assistance to program planning and development, project management, and communications between the contracting-parties. Accountability through the performance contract should also entail an independent education accomplishment audit (IEAA) that would also involve some group independent of the contracting parties. This whole notion of performance contracting itself is relatively new in education and decidedly controversial, and its further development through funding and engineering operations recommended by Lessinger seems highly problematic. What does the reader perceive as possible uses of this approach to improving the high school curriculum?

The role of high school students in the improvement of their curriculum may seem a far cry from that of the professionals and industrialists we have been considering, but it is a role, too, that came into greatly increased prominence as high school students began open protests against their schools in the late 1960s. "Why," many educators asked, "haven't we been consulting students all along?" Others could point to efforts here and there to use student representatives on planning committees, to turn some questions (frequently fairly routine ones) over to the student council, and perhaps to have really effective involvement of students.

Hopefully, once instituted and for whatever reason, student involvement in curriculum development will be a lasting, constructive one rather than a short-term defensive measure to be terminated when the unrest ends. The high school curriculum should have no more active participant in its development than the students whose own needs, interests, and aspirations are being served. Certainly the influence of adults representing a wider spectrum of concerns and having the view of many students and their needs is not to be forsaken or minimized, but a steadily improving high school curriculum requires continuous cooperation of the students, educators, and community.

CURRICULUM PROJECTS: A PERSPECTIVE*

Arthur R. King, Jr.[1]

The large-scale curriculum project is a dominant fact of contemporary schooling. Projects abound in mathematics and the sciences; social studies, English, and vocational studies are increasingly being served; fewer projects are undertaken in art, music, and health.

These major projects have, over the past dozen years, put into the hands of teachers and supervisors a wide array of packages of materials from which selections may be made, have spawned an entirely new professional specialty, and have aroused a host of reactions. These reactions run the gamut from cries of outrage, to well-conceived challenges, to full acceptance and delight.

The range of emotions expressed is paralleled by the range of interpretations of the phenomenon itself. Much of the dissonance springs from the "new" label, as in "new math," for example. Actually, the two essential elements in schooling have gone unchanged for decades, perhaps centuries. These are a teacher and a methods/media/materials set.

The teacher remains the master of the instructional situation, despite such innovations as team teaching, instructional television, computer scheduling, paraprofessional assistance, programmed materials, and now the products of large curriculum ventures. The sum of the teacher's professional knowledge, skill, commitment, insight, experience, values, attitudes, fears, aspirations, and other deeply personal characteristics makes up a *gestalt* which structures and permeates the instructional event.

The other element is the methods/media/materials set assembled by the teacher for classroom purposes. The individual's skill in manipulating

* Reprinted from *Educational Leadership* (February 1969), 26:493–499. Reprinted with permission of the Association for Supervision and Curriculum Development and Arthur R. King, Jr. Copyright © 1969 by the Association for Supervision and Curriculum Development.

[1] Acknowledgment: The author is indebted to Edith Kleinjans for valuable editorial assistance.

357

and personalizing this set of techniques and devices to achieve objectives fuses the two essential elements into a single context in which children learn.

This brings us to the key consideration: the source of the methods/media/materials sets or packages. Both traditional theory and conventional beliefs of school men hold that the individual teacher, or the group of colleagues in a single school, determines educational purposes, plans courses and sequences of courses, designs and tests materials, selects media, evaluates instruction, and controls the entire cycle. In reality, however, methods/media/materials sets have been assembled largely from the shelves of educational suppliers, including textbook publishers, equipment firms, testing agencies, and the like. Rarely in my experience have I encountered teachers who produced substantial amounts of original materials or who had any means of effectively disseminating their ideas or products to the profession at large.

If this picture is accurate, then the potential impact on large curriculum development projects can be simplified. The input of materials and media from national sources is not new; rather, we have control over the design and construction of teaching materials in the hands of disciplinary scholars and educational professionals and only distribution in commercial hands.

I emphasize the teacher's traditional role of augmenting and personalizing the use of instructional materials sets in producing the learning situation. Schooling still proceeds essentially by the interaction of persons, and in fact the teacher's role as exemplar or model in the field of study enhances his or her importance in teaching the "new curricula."

THE LARGE-SCALE CURRICULUM PROJECT

Large-scale curriculum enterprises have certain distinguishing marks. A first mark of the project is the use of some variant of the systems approach, which attempts to account for the full set of parts in relation to an organic whole. The project usually maps out and follows the full sequence of (a) the definition of subject matter and inquiry skill by scholars, (b) the design of the course(s), (c) the selection of teaching strategies, (d) the selection of media, (e) the design of evaluation strategies and materials, and finally (f) the preparation of plans and materials for retraining teachers who will use the sets or packages.

Second, in their general approach to the curriculum problem, the projects reflect the dominant role played by specialists in disciplinary fields. Whether the effort is mounted by a professional society of academic scholars, a regional laboratory, a consortium of school districts, a joint university-state agency, or a publishing firm, it is members of the academic disciplines who set the approach and put the stamp of authenticity on the materials package. In contrast to commercial publishing ventures, which usually expend relatively little on design and development but much on promotion and sales, the major curriculum projects put millions of dollars into theory, design, development, and testing before they release materials for dissemination.

Thanks to large grants from government and foundations, they have had "risk capital" to use in conceiving new strategies for solving perennial problems. Project teams are practicalists. Hence they focus on such "useful" matters as the essential concepts and characteristic methods of their field of inquiry and how to make these comprehensible to students. They are not too interested in such traditional concerns of educators as an overarching, total design to the curriculum, children's needs, societal concerns, or vocational requirements.

A third characteristic is an apparent consensus about approaches to curriculum design. Most developers have taken some variation of the Brunerian stance, affirming the disciplines of knowledge as the functional divisions of intellectual activity today. Most projects have been in single disciplines (PSSC, CHEM Study, SMSG, and BSCS are examples). Some more recent projects are trying general approaches to families of disciplines (AAAS, SCIS, and COPES in elementary school science, for example). A new project at the Hawaii Curriculum Center takes "a pluralistic view of sciences."

The scope of the projects varies. Some develop single units for incorporation into existing programs. Others aim at a one-year course. Still others provide a sequence for two or three years of schooling or even the whole span from kindergarten through grade 12.

The intended audience typically consists of students of average to superior ability. A few programs are pegged specifically to college aspirants, a growing number to slower or less able students. There is some interest in preparing "culturally relevant" materials for minority or "disadvantaged" groups, but with little solid accomplishment thus far.

The lack of a total framework into which these instructional "components" are to fit is lamented by some writers. Of this I have more to say later.

A fourth characteristic of major projects is a more or less definable range of approaches to instruction. Project staffs typically stress "inquiry" or "discovery," "heuristics of learning," "concepts orientation," "inductive approaches," "critical analysis," and "authentic laboratory approaches." Although these notions are far from new, either in the educational literature or in the practice of teachers, it is only recently that such approaches are being incorporated into the actual design and production of the materials package.

The fantastic rate at which knowledge is piling up has prompted curriculum makers to shift instructional strategies. Hence new project materials have emphasized (a) depth of experience in a few topics ("post-holing"), in contrast to broad coverage, (b) concepts and generalizations rather than memory, and (c) inquiry and analysis rather than the accumulation of the "rhetoric of conclusions."

Few projects to date have exploited the use of "big media" such as instructional television, computer-assisted instruction, or whole filmed courses. Science packages usually include laboratory equipment; some attempt "academic games." Programmed learning materials are rarely used.

All courses assume a better-than-average to excellent teacher to make effective use of the materials which, one designer says, go only ten percent of the way toward "true inquiry" orientation.

On the other hand, observers report that only a small proportion of teachers using the materials exploit their full potential; most use them rather as a better textbook in the traditional way.

IMPLICATIONS OF THE MOVEMENT[2]

The curriculum project movement has a number of implications for teachers. Teacher roles are becoming more precisely defined, requiring, for example, a "physics teacher with background in PSSC" rather than a "science teacher who can do physics."

Consequently teacher education, both preservice and in-service, becomes more specific and demanding. Depth of knowledge of one's discipline, including both conceptual and methodological structures, is called for. Language teachers without oral/aural command are unemployable. In some areas near-native speaking competence plus experience in the language culture is required. These demands are especially acute for the teacher in the self-contained classroom or the jack-of-all-trades in the small departmentalized school.

Many teachers find the professional and intellectual challenge stimulating; others are fearful and resistant.

The curriculum supervisor also finds the large-scale curriculum movement a force for change in role. The professionalism of the new materials makes it impossible for the "curriculum generalist" to pose as an expert

---

[2] This change of roles is discussed at greater length in: Arthur R. King, Jr., and John A. Brownell. *The Curriculum and the Disciplines of Knowledge: A Theory of Curriculum Practice.* New York: John Wiley & Sons, Inc., 1966.

in the curriculum of any disciplined field. He has his choice of two ways to go: he can identify with curriculum administration, oiling the machinery for the selection and installation of curricula; or he can become a curriculum philosopher, attempting to build theoretic structures of what the whole curriculum might be like, or what approaches to the curriculum problem are adequate. The curriculum subject specialist must achieve a scholar's grasp of an academic field which will equip him to "translate" that field into instructional strategies and courses.

Teacher educators' roles are undergoing change. Methods and materials courses are increasingly relating the more specific demands created by the project curricula. The teacher of teachers finds it necessary to hustle to keep abreast of happenings in the school.

Ironically, while much of the impact of the recent developments in curricula has been to pomote depth of specialization for all concerned, interchangeability of roles is also increasingly possible. The insights and skills required of leadership teachers, curriculum supervisors, teacher educators, and educational materials designers and evaluators are overlapping to the extent that a total professional career may well include playing all of these other roles.

Several noted critics have deplored the lack of an overall curriculum pattern into which new components might fit. The situation, they say, is chaotic, unstructured, unbalanced, and unpredictable. But I venture a contrary view. I see the large number of curriculum development centers as a force for creativity.

What could be more sterile than to have some supergroup impose by fiat a scheme into which subsequent efforts must fit in order to secure funding and access to the schools? I can imagine a very healthy "open set" concept of the "whole" curriculum, with opportunity always open for the newer way, the more credible approach, and the fresher idea to break into the standard pattern. If I must choose, I prefer chaos with creativity over order with ossification.

In the organization with which I am now identified, two classroom teachers and one curriculum specialist, not too many years away from the classroom, are in operational control of four projects commanding five million dollars over a period of five years. The opportunity for individuals to create for their fellow professionals is enhanced beyond the wildest dreams of teachers and curriculum specialists of just a few years ago.

Clearly, an exciting new day is here for the education profession. We can seize the opportunity boldly, ready ourselves for our task, and make use of the potent new technique of the large-scale curriculum project to enliven our entire educational enterprise. If we are not ready, the educational industries are.

THE NEW EDUCATION AND THE LEARNING INDUSTRY*

GABRIEL D. OFIESH

A recent article in *Barron's* (November 18, 1968) by Ralph Kaplan related to the new learning industries. Its headline was, "Learning the Hard Way: In the Knowledge Industry, Most Corporate Freshmen Have Flunked." Not only is education in a crisis; the new knowledge industry (which I prefer to call the new learning industry) is also in a similar state of ferment. Only a few years ago, many looked with hope to the profit motive and aura of accountability which permeated industry for help in overhauling an archaic educational establishment.

There is an acute awareness that the crowded classrooms, the split shifts, and all the other undesirable yet expedient measures which were forced upon schools to meet today's needs will be *totally* unacceptable tomorrow. To continue the traditional system, in which individualized attention has become a rarity, could ultimately force us to limit educational opportunity to a "choice" segment of the population.

This prospect of deviation from a philosophy of free education for all the people is definitely untenable. Yet, we must continue to try to reach satisfactory solutions to the critical problems which prevent our achieving this goal.

The rapid accumulation of information in almost every discipline and endeavor has forced the field of education to search for new methods of acquiring, assembling, analyzing, and disseminating information. Such methods in our technological age must include audiovisual means in order to have any persuasive impact. Techniques and devices, such as educational television, teaching machines, audiovisual communication, and

* Reprinted from *Educational Leadership* (May 1969), 26:760–763. Reprinted with permission of the Association for Supervision and Curriculum Development and Gabriel D. Ofiesh. Copyright © 1969 by the Association for Supervision and Curriculum Development.

above all, the programmed instruction process, have been hailed as revolutionary and capable of solving problems associated with the knowledge explosion. Some educators have considered these devices and aids not to be revolutionary in themselves but in relation to the needs of education. This potential was unfortunately not as quickly realized as many persons had thought it would be.

However, in spite of the failures of the rather fragmented efforts by the new learning industry, and the inability to arrive at a rapprochement with education, the demand for dramatic change in approach is mounting. Recognition of the need for a marriage not only between technology and education, but between educational technology and industry, has become more acute rather than less so.

Many of the industrial giants who sought to take part in the emerging learning industry are withdrawing from the fray at a most inopportune time. Rather than critically analyzing the reasons for the failure of their efforts of the past few years, they are giving up without a struggle when a little more effort, properly directed, well might bring success. One of the mistakes such industries have made was the naive supposition that simply uniting the conventionally oriented publishers of the past with electronically oriented firms of today would somehow bring the systems approach into education. This of course was not a viable probe.

Conventionally minded publishers of print media did not understand the implications of the new technology and the need for materials that would be adaptive to individualized learning. Electronic firms, steeped in the systems approach which was borrowed from the weapons acquisition process, were unable to make the transfer to the problems posed by the demands for the new education. Consequently, little more than lip service was given to the development of individually adaptive learning systems. Yet, at a time when the demand for change is gaining momentum, there is no question that a new learning industry will survive, and that it will meet the needs that are being identified on a national scale.

The U.S. Office of Education recently established a national commission on instructional technology to look into the problem. Senator Ralph Yarborough has proposed a bill for $475 million to establish an Office of Educational Technology. Further, there is a growing movement to individualize instruction through independent learning programs. Of 746 superintendents who responded to a recent survey, top choice was given to individualized instruction as the most promising development among 15 innovations.

What is needed now is a recognition, on the part of corporate heads of the new learning industry and on the part of educators, that the learning industry, in order to survive and make a significant contribution to the challenges of American education, must be based upon the best of educational engineering, which itself is based upon the best of educational technology. Yet there first must be an understanding of what educational technology is all about.

The word technology is a derivative of "techne," meaning "art" or "craft," and the word "logos," indicating "a study of." Therefore, technology literally means "a study of art." To all appearances, it seems a harmless word. Yet, technology is a dangerous word; it gives the impression of being scientific while it is not. Technology is the systematic application of scientific knowledge to the solution of practical problems. Educational technology is therefore the application of scientific knowledge toward the solution of problems in education.

An immediate objective of education must be to communicate knowledge more efficiently and more effectively in order to increase learning. The traditional art of education is insufficient to create this result. Methods must be designed which will optimize approaches to developing and understanding the behavior of all the minds we are committed to educate. To accomplish this task, we must develop a science and technology of education. The validity of education as a science is still being probed, and a technology of education is emerging therefrom—one which allows education to become an applied science of learning.

Both the learning industry and educators must maintain the distinction between technical specialists and genuine technologists. The latter are specialists in the entire body of technological knowledge, and are responsible for the continued in-depth study of growing relationships between the "techne" and the contemporary problems surrounding themselves. Included in the rubric of educational technology are presently known technologies (and those *as yet* unfeasible), and their application to educational problems.

The overwhelming nature of developments in instrumentation may cause "hardware" concerns to dominate our thinking, in preference to the "software" concerns which should have primary interest at this stage in the development of educational systems. Two other technologies—biochemical and information—are at this time only tangential in their impact. The more we learn about mapping the human brain, about the structure and function of the central nervous system, the impact of drugs, and the heuristic and synergistic nature of the elements of information theory, the greater impact we can expect these elements to have on the rubric of educational technology itself.

Considering such future developments, educational technology should be "process," rather than "machine" or "hardware," oriented. Failing to recognize this principle, the learning industry expected exaggerated profits almost instantly, on the order and scale of print media. Another obstacle was the reluctance of educators and veteran publishers to constitute interdisciplinary teams.

TO SHARE IDENTITY

Just as a single person must experience independence before he will voluntarily give up some of his freedom for the benefits derived from interdependence, so a professional group must feel secure before it is willing to share some of its identity. The medical world is managing to do this: most doctors now concede that a hospital can be run just as well by an administrator trained for management rather than for medicine; and on research projects, doctors work with psychologists, biologists, and physiologists.

Yet educators seem to cling to each other. Is there a public elementary or secondary school in the United States which has hired a business administrator to run its school? Or a psychiatrist to head its guidance-counseling staff? Or an educational technologist to direct its learning program?

When such questions are asked, the reply comes back: "Education isn't a business, or a therapy center, or a science. Education is an art." The problem of unwillingness to communicate with scientific disciplines is one of long standing. Travers reports an early example of this attitude:

> Joseph Mayer Rice was the first to discover that the results of research do not bring about educational change, however persuasive the results may be. The educational subculture is basically resistant to the efforts of an agent such as a research worker to produce change. . . . Rice was a physician by profession but he became interested in problems of education and made a two-year visit to Europe in the 1890's, where he studied pedagogy and psychology. His book which followed, *The Public School System of the United States* (1893) . . . summarized the observations he had made on 1200 teachers located in various schools from Boston to Philadelphia in the East to St. Louis and Minneapolis in the Middle West. Educators paid no attention to the opinions of a layman; legend relates that he was met with jeers when he attempted to present his findings to a meeting of the National Education Association . . . Rice's effort to produce educational reform had absolutely no effect on his contemporaries.[1]

Finally, a realistic understanding is required of what the systems approach to education fully entails. Engineers, or quasi-educational engineers, simply drawing flow charts, do not provide us either with an educational system or a learning system—and gathering a variety of media and tacking them together does not provide us with a multi-media learning system.

The "systems approach to education," in brief, involves the specifi-

---

[1] Robert Travers. In: *Training Research and Education*. Robert Glaser, editor. New York: John Wiley & Sons, Inc., 1962.

cation of behavioral objectives, the assessment of student repertoires, the development of instructional strategies, testing and revision of the instructional units (validation), and finally packaging and *administering a validated learning system.* This approach results in the development of learning experiences for students, which are adjusted to students' needs and learning modes. The learning experiences, however, are designed to produce the behaviors specified; in other words, the specified behavioral objectives are the constant in the system.

The task is a formidable one and we have yet to find a single industry that is tackling this task in a forceful manner. Until these models emerge, educators are going to ask the learning industry what is new about the product—or do they have to continue to accept the same old pedagogy packaged in new cartons?

It is strikingly clear, then, that if both industry and education recognize the nature of their convergence, and if the government commits itself to endow this marriage between educational technology and industry, the necessary revolution in American schools will almost inevitably occur.

"PARTNERSHIP" HIGH SCHOOLS: THE SEARCH FOR NEW WAYS TO COOPERATE*

DONALD E. BARNES

INTRODUCTION

In a little more than 18 months, something new has appeared in American education generally known, at least for the time being, as "high school partnerships." Other names and sometimes no names have been attached to the phenomenon, which now consist of more than 30 ventures with a common origin and similar attributes in over 20 cities and 19 states. More, perhaps many more of them, may be expected.

---

* Reprinted with permission, from Institute for Educational Development, Industry and Education Study No. 2, 1969 (New York: The Institute for Educational Development), pp. 1–3.

Despite their family likeness partnerships come in many varieties. They can be recognized by main points of resemblance which include: (1) an understanding or exchange of commitments, (2) between representatives of a corporation and an urban school, usually a high school, (3) to the effect that they will try to cooperate over a period of years, (4) in an organized group of projects intended to improve education in the school, (5) for the benefit of the students.

THE DETROIT STORY

Before the smoke had cleared from the skies of Detroit following the summer riots of 1967, Edward N. Hodges III, general employment supervisor for Michigan Bell Telephone Company, began an outline of possible projects for building a new Detroit. His suggestions had been sought by William M. Day, board chairman of Michigan Bell.

High on Hodges' list was the "need to reach juveniles and young adults . . . cut off from the mainstream of life with no hope, no future and, in many instances, no feeling of social conscience." Among the possible measures which he outlined was the "adoption" (quotation marks his) of an entire school by a single company. At that time he did not elaborate on the suggestion.

A period of soul-searching and intensive study on the part of Detroit's civic leaders produced several large action-programs in that autumn and winter. The best known and most widely imitated idea to emerge from the effort was Ed Hodges' suggestion of a new kind of relationship between a corporation and an inner city high school.

When the proposal reached Dr. Norman Drachler superintendent of schools, a quick and favorable response was forthcoming. On October 24, 1967, an agreement between Detroit's public schools and Michigan Bell was announced. Northern High School, on Woodward Avenue in the heart of the Northside ghetto, had been "adopted."

Little more than a month later Chrysler Corporation announced completion of negotiations with the Detroit Board of Education for a "partnership" arrangement with Northwestern High School to "help students to perceive the relationship between what happens in school and what awaits them in our complex technological society." The understanding with the Board of Education went on to say, "There is every reason to anticipate that this joint effort will result in higher aspirations and achievement among Northwestern students."

And within a few weeks Illinois Bell announced that its BEACON program would include similar arrangements with two high schools and an elementary school, all within impacted poverty areas of Chicago.

GOING NATIONWIDE

Nearly every month thereafter has brought news of one or several new partnerships. Newark, New Orleans, Pittsburgh, Hartford, Minneapolis, Milwaukee, Atlanta, Albany, Miami, St. Louis, Cincinnati, San Jose, Indianapolis, Charlotte, Oakland, Jacksonville, Charleston, Wilmington, Philadelphia and most recently New York City and Los Angeles—all are numbered among the cities in which partnerships of one kind or another have been organized in the meantime. Some of them have been operating quietly and without publicity. Some of them came into being gradually, via informal, on-the-scene understandings.

It is especially interesting that many of these ventures, at least 19 of them at this writing, have been initiated by affiliates of American Telephone & Telegraph Company apparently as a result of similar estimates of local needs and opportunities by related companies in cities widely separated by geography, history, and economic characteristics. Other companies and combines which have made commitments to a partnership include Chrysler Corporation and Boron Oil Company, Aetna Life and Casualty, Kaiser Industries, Procter & Gamble (with General Electric, Avco, Ford and others), Quaker Oats Company, Minneapolis Honeywell, Inc., General Mills, Inc., Boeing-Vertol Division, E. I. du Pont de Nemours & Company and the Economic Development Council of New York City, an agency representing more than 80 member corporations.

The phenomenon, then, amounts to a wave of informal experiments, conducted nationwide yet locally inspired and controlled, searching for and testing new and improved relationships between industry and public education in American cities.

ENGINEERING ACCOUNTABILITY FOR RESULTS IN PUBLIC EDUCATION*

Leon Lessinger

An important change has taken place in what Americans expect of their public schools. The optimism about the value of education is still there and continues to be strong, but serious doubts have arisen about the public school system's ability to actually deliver on its promises.

The shift in attitude becomes apparent through analysis of the questions being asked at hearings by elected officials of both parties at every level of government, from Congress to state legislatures and local city councils. The same line of questioning can be heard among businessmen, at school board conventions, at various citizen group meetings, and in the highest circles of the executive branches of government. Seekers of educational funds have always talked in terms of books, staff, materials, equipment, and space to be acquired or used, together with students to be served and programs to be offered. Questioners in the past were content to listen to accounts of resources allocated. This has changed. Today the questions focus on results obtained for resources used. The questions are pointed, insistent, and abrasive. The public school system is being held accountable for results. Accountability is the coming sine qua non for education in the 1970s. How to engineer accountability for results in public education is the central problem for the education profession.

It would be interesting to speculate about the reasons for the growing demand to link dollars spent for education to results achieved from students. Increased and accelerating costs, poor academic performance of minority children, and inconclusive results of federal compensatory education projects (totaling, since 1965, in the billions of dollars) are probably important causal factors.

Accountability is the product of a process. At its most basic level, it

---

* Reprinted from *Phi Delta Kappan* (December 1970), 52:217–225, by permission.

means that an agent, public or private, entering into a contractual agreement to perform a service will be held answerable for performing according to agreed-upon terms, within an established time period, and with a stipulated use of resources and performance standards. This definition of accountability requires that the parties to the contract keep clear and compete records and that this information be available for outside review. It also suggests penalties and rewards; accountability without redress or incentive is mere rhetoric.

Performance contracting is *one* process for which accountability is the product. The idea of contracting is older than free enterprise. Its appeal to both liberals and conservatives revolves around its attention to two things that leaders agree are desperately needed in education—quality assurance and knowledge of results.

At its most primitive level the process works like this: A public authority grants money to a local education agency to contract with private enterprise[1] to achieve specific goals within specific periods for specific costs. The money is targeted at pressing needs which are not being adequately met, such as dropout prevention among disadvantaged groups or bringing the underprivileged and undereducated up to competitive educational levels.

Seen from this vantage point, accountability appears to be merely the utilization by education of private enterprise for getting things done. Of course, such utilization is not per se a new development. For example, any superintendent of schools can show that performance contracts have long been used in school operation and maintenance. The use of performance contracts to achieve accountability is, therefore, not new to education. It is the extension of this idea into the realm of learning through a particular process, called in this paper educational engineering, which represents what some are calling the "coming revolution in American education."

EDUCATIONAL ENGINEERING

Since World War II several fields have been developed to enable managers of very complex enterprises to operate efficiently and effectively. These emerging fields of knowledge and practice are commonly known as systems analysis, management by objectives, contract engineering (including bids, warranties, penalties, and incentives), logistics, quality assurance, value engineering, and human factors engineering, to name a few of the more important. If to these are added instructional technology and modern educational management theory, a new and valuable interdis-

---

[1] Performance contracting need not be limited to private enterprise. The principles are applicable for arrangements with teachers, universities, and nonprofit organizations.

ciplinary field emerges. This body of knowledge, skill, and procedure can be called educational engineering. It is the insights from educational engineering that makes it possible for performance contracting to achieve accountability for results in education.

Why couple the term "engineering" with education? Why more apparent dehumanization? It is not appropriate here to treat this question at great length. But I note that engineering has traditionally been a problem-solving activity and a profession dedicated to the application of technology to the resolution of real world difficulties and opportunities. While the teaching-learning environment differs from the world of business and industry, some rationalization of the two subcultures may be beneficial. A major objective of educational engineering may very well be to arm educational practitioners with both the technological competence of essential engineering generalizations, strategies, and tools and the professional practice of a successful instructor or educational manager. From this point of view, educational engineering can be a symbiotic art—a marriage of humanism and technology. It is this possible symbiosis that makes performance contracting for learning accomplishment feasible.

ACCOUNTABILITY IN OPERATION

The application of one educational engineering process to achieve results in the basic academic skills can be used to illustrate the concept of accountability in operation. This accountability process can be engineered as follows:

1. The local education agency (LEA) employs a management support group (MSG), whose members have competency to assist them in political, social, economic, managerial, and educational matters. The relationship between the management support group and the local school leadership group resembles that of long-term consultants on a retainer account.
2. The MSG works with staff and community (or other groups as required by a particular local situation) to produce a request for proposal (RFP), which is a set of specifications indicating as clearly as possible the service to be performed, the approximate amount of money to be invested, the constraints to be observed, the standards acceptable, and related matters. The RFP is the local education agency's blueprint for action to meet pressing priorities.
3. The next stage of the educational engineering process occurs when the RFP is set out to bid. The pre-bidding conference becomes the forum for educational exchange. Here a rich and varied communication through competition occurs between elements of the private and public sector. The bidding process is flexible to the extent that allowance is made by LEA officials for new insights and better elements to be incorporated into a revised RFP.

4. Following the bidding conference, a revised RFP is issued and actual bids are entertained. The MSG assists the LEA in operating the conference and reviewing the bids. The local board "hears" the top bids in a manner similar to the process used in the employment of an architect.
5. The local school board selects what it considers to be the best bid and enters into negotiation for a performance contract with the successful bidder. The MSG assists at this stage.
6. Concurrently with the signing of the performance contract, an independent educational accomplishment audit team is employed by the LEA both to monitor execution of the performance contract and to provide feedback to the LEA to certify results for purposes of payment.

It may now be helpful to analyze the structural elements of this process in more detail.

The *performance contract* is the managerial tool to assure the achievement of results, while encouraging responsible innovation. The approach is simple in concept although complex in actualization. With technical assistance, the learning problem is analyzed, and a delineation of achievement outcomes to be expected is specified. An RFP is developed and sent by the LEA to potential contractors who have demonstrated competent and creative activity in the specific and related fields. The RFP does not prescribe how the job must be done but does establish the performance, financial, administrative, and legal parameters of the operation. The RFP requires that the bidder guarantee specific results for specific costs. The confidence that the bidder has in his approach is reflected in the level of the guarantee, the social practicability, the time, and the costs indicated in the bid he presents.

The program to be bid, including the specified number of students, is described in the contract. Incentives are provided for the contractor to bring each child up to specified levels of performance, at the lowest cost. Provision is made in the performance contract to develop a program for which the contractor will guarantee results.

After the demonstration period is completed and all relevant costs, procedures, achievements, and performance data have been validated, the contract requires that the contractor guarantee an effective, fiscally responsible program. Then, on a "turnkey" basis, the LEA incorporates the instructional program into the school. Thus performance contracting is a capability-creating resource for public education.

The *management support group* is the catalytic and buffer agency which provides not only technical assistance to the district, but a communication link between those who determine priorities, such as a federal agency, and the school system that is developing program proposals. The group has access to new developments in the field, especially in industrial and governmental sectors, and assists the LEA in developing the RFP to assure that conditions and constraints in the RFP do not preclude but actually encourage the opportunity for these new developments to be demonstrated. The MSG also plays the role of a buffer between the LEA and community groups, as well as between the LEA and potential bidders. It provides assistance to the LEA during the proposal evaluation and operational stages on an "as needed" basis.

As operational results during the initial stages are determined, the group provides program planning assistance to the LEA so that the instructional programs are effectively and efficiently "turnkeyed" into the school. In this way, the school can achieve the potential benefits which have been demonstrated. Too often school systems either adopt programs not proven or acquire techniques proven in pilot programs only. Later they sometimes discover that the results erode over time. The MSG can provide critical technical assistance to the school officials during the adoption or turnkey process, ranging from projecting administrative costs required within the system to the implementation of performance budgeting techniques that will insure continuing quality assurance.

The *independent education accomplishment audit* (IEAA) is a managerial tool to assist quality control of the program. By reporting on results, this procedure encourages responsibility, creating a need for clearly stated performance objectives and an accounting for the costs incurred in achieving results. Just as the performance contract allows the school to monitor the contractor, the IEAA is designed to assure the lay board and the community it represents that the school leaders and the contractors are doing their work. The independent accomplishment audit, first introduced through ESEA Title VIII by the U.S. Office of Education, is a practical recognition that education is an important investment in human capital. Just as fiscal audits certify that public school resources and expenditures are (or are not) in balance, the IEAA certifies that investments in human beings are (or are not) successful according to stated goals and demonstrated accomplishment.

Patterns of funding the educational engineering process are critical. The flow of federal, state, and local funds must encourage the creation and responsible control of process components. Budgeting must be based on clearly defined criteria for "go" or "no go" decisions to be made at the end of each discrete stage. Three-stage funding as a facilitating device consists of resources and the timely freeing of previously earmarked funds for other new starts or operational programs.

THE TEXARKANA MODEL

The Texarkana Dropout Prevention Program, under ESEA Title VIII, was the first to use performance contracting with private enterprise in instruction. A number of new ventures have since been started, including those in Dallas, Texas, and Gary, Indiana, as well as the 18 centers funded by the Office of Economic Opportunity. These "second generation" approaches make use of performance contracts that are independently audited. They are built on the Texarkana approach and have employed techniques and strategies to overcome difficulties exposed during the first year of operation of the Texarkana experiment.

The assumption behind the Texarkana program and those of the second generation is that a private contractor will have greater freedom to innovate and thus be more successful in motivating students than the regular school system has been. A direct instructional service and a self-renewal function are the dual objectives of the projects.

Let me turn next to some of the wider implications of engineering accountability into public education.

ADVANTAGES OF PERFORMANCE CONTRACTS

The advantages of performance contracts are inherent in the nature of the serious problems that confront education today.

First, contracting facilitates the targeting and evaluation of educational programs. Many good instructional programs have not been given the opportunity to demonstrate their potential due to the lack of an effective delivery system at the school level. Recent critical evaluations of Title I of ESEA note this operational inadequacy. The performance contract approach, which utilizes a separately managed and operated center with separate accounting procedures, fosters the objective evaluation of educational results and also the managerial processes by which these results were achieved.

Second, performance contracting for instructional services could introduce more resources and greater variability into the public school sector. Now, new programs are being offered to the public outside the school system; the process of fragmentation and competition has begun. Several large corporations are establishing franchised learning centers across the country. One company, for example, has at least 40 centers operating in the major cities of this country; 10 others are establishing centers in other cities. Performance-type contracts to improve student achievement in compensatory education are usually enacted between the parents and the franchisee. As a result, the parents pay for the schools' operations. As these franchised centers expand, parents may refuse to pay property taxes by defeating tax and bond issues. On the other hand, the performance contract approach would allow the school system to utilize the services and products of a particular firm or firms so that the public schools could be renewed through a turnkey process. Performance contracting can be looked upon as a means to foster and catalyze institutional reform within a school system, allowing systems to continue operations and to become competitive with private schools and franchised learning centers.

Third, the performance contract approach allows a school system to experiment in a responsible manner with low costs and low political and social risks. Both school officials and critics have expressed the need to determine the relative cost effectiveness of various instructional methods in contractor-operated centers, as well as upon incorporation into the particular schools. The performance contract approach not only allows for determination of these costs and benefits but also provides the bases for projecting initial adoption as well as operating costs when the system is introduced into the schools. In this way, the approach allows policy makers to make rational choices when choosing new techniques for extension into standard classroom practice.

Fourth, the new "bill of rights in education," proclaiming the right of every child to read at his grade level, will undoubtedly generate great pressures upon school resources. If our schools are to make this right a reality, they might want to consider using performance contracting for the development and validation of new reading programs. Upon successful demonstration, districts can then adopt the program or portions thereof. The success of these programs will in large measure depend upon the ability of the school to skillfully design and execute performance contracts and then effectively incorporate the projects into its normal operation.

Fifth, performance contracting can play a significant role in school desegregation. One of the major fears of the white community (rightly or wrongly) is that black children, upon integration, will hold back the progress of white children. Through the performance contract approach, many of the previously segregated black children will have their academic deficiencies, if any, removed on a guaranteed achievement basis while they are attending the newly integrated schools. From this point of view, performance contracting would allow communities to desegregate in a non-disruptive, educationally effective, and politically palatable manner.

Finally, the approach creates dynamic tension and responsible institutional change within the public school system through competition. Leaders will now have alternatives to the traditional instructional methods when negotiating salary increases; performance contracting and its variant, performance budgeting, permit the authorities to couple part of a salary increase to increase in effectiveness.

PROBABLE TRENDS

Whatever may be the merits of performance contracting, dramatic increases in its use are virtually certain in the immediate future.

Proper guidance, in the form of descriptive material as well as guidelines for implementing performance contracting and/or performance budgeting, is essential to avoid a potential backfire. For example, certain firms which develop tests and sell curricula might bid on performance contracts; other firms might develop specific reading and math curricula around specific tests. Franchised learning centers are bidding on performance contracts with schools in order to force state agencies to accredit their programs. Certain schools facing desegregation problems are considering very seriously the establishment of performance contract projects without a capability or an in-depth knowledge of the concept.

Two actions on the part of public policy officials would be helpful. First, additional operational proposals and planning grants should be funded, not only to legitimize the concept of performance contracting in education, but also to develop a "learning curve" on the "do's and don'ts" of developing RFP's for large urban schools. Because of the Texarkana project, those associated with its development have amassed a stockpile of knowledge; yet the applicability to diverse urban school systems is limited. Second, concurrently with the development of additional planning exercises and based on the experience of Texarkana, a booklet describing performance contracting and a procedures manual that could be made available to schools across the country should be written. The demand for such documents will increase dramatically over the next few months.

THE MANAGEMENT SUPPORT GROUP

The concept of the management support group is new to education. Its precedent was established in the defence-aerospace area when, in the mid-Fifties, the Aerospace Corporation was created to act as a buffer and technical assistance team between the Air Force and weapons systems suppliers for the Air Force. The Aerospace Corporation's major functions were to develop programs, design requests for proposals based on performance specifications, assist in evaluating proposals, and provide management services to contractors. The major functions of the MSG in education under the concept of educational engineering would be in the following areas:

1. *Program planning and development assistance.* School systems generally lack such a management capability, or, if such is available, "day to day" operations prevent effective utilization of that resource. Moreover, an outside group provides new insights and a different perspective in analyzing educational and other problems and in developing alternative solutions. For these and other reasons, it is advantageous for the school to have an MSG develop the RFP. The MSG could assist in the following

ways during the program development and planning:

a. analyze and determine the community's educational needs and the desired levels of student performance;

b. conduct program definition phase studies and determine sources of funding;

c. develop the RFP and experimental design to be used for turnkey purposes as well as national dissemination;

d. develop and recommend "program change proposals" on a continuing basis during the initial stages;

e. develop means for gathering and maintaining political and community support for the program during all phases;

f. contact potential bidders in the education industry and R & D laboratories to insure that the latest innovative techniques are considered and are encouraged for application by the direction and flexibility allowed in the RFP;

g. determine the qualified bidders and send them the RFP.

2. *Project management assistance.* Too often, proposals are developed by outside groups who curtail relationships with the school once the contract has been awarded. The management support group has to provide extended and sustained services in the areas ranging from establishing the project management office to developing evaluation techniques. The project management services would be in the following areas:

a. develop a multi-year management plan for the conduct of the demonstration and turnkey effort, including an administrative system for the LEA's project management office;

b. conduct, when appropriate, preproposal development and bidders' conferences with all interested parties;

c. establish a proposal evaluation procedure and assist in the evaluation by presenting strengths and weaknesses to the LEA;

d. continually evaluate the contractor's progress and assist in contract renegotiations as required;

e. manage pilot programs when specifically requested to do so by the LEA;

f. analyze the administrative and managerial changes required when the techniques proven in pilot programs are integrated into the school systems. This turnkey phase is critical to overall success and requires careful analysis and program planning and budgeting.

3. *Communications link.* Because many firms of unknown or questionable reliability will be entering this newly created multibillion-dollar market, the MSG is a necessary mediator and "honest broker" between the firms and the school systems. At the community level, the vested interests of powerful groups and important decision makers must be determined. Here, the MSG, acting as a buffer between the LEA and these interest groups, both inside and outside the school system, can obtain such information in an effective and politically advantageous manner. (For example, the superintendent could point to the MSG as a scapegoat if specific ideas or recommendations are not accepted by the board.) The MSG can

provide an on-call, as-needed manpower pool during planning and implementation. It can hire potential school employees in order to allow officials to see them in action. Moreover, the MSG has access to consultants around the country; on short notice it can provide their services while bypassing cumbersome district procedures.

In short, the politics of experimentation where private industry, local schools, and the federal government are all involved creates the need for unofficial advocates and buffer mechanisms to protect politically all parties concerned, while insuring that the project does in fact become a reality.

PROBABLE TRENDS

The concept of the management support group was made legitimate by the Title VII and Title VIII ESEA grant guidelines. Only a few firms have the capability to perform this function on their own, although many individuals do have this capability and could form a fertile cadre to advise and train others. The concept of catalytic buffers was included in the enabling legislation for ESEA Title III, presented to Congress in 1965–66; however, it was deleted in final legislation. Many people attribute the failures of Title III projects to the lack of a mechanism that would have provided the necessary political and technical skills to insure effective planning implementation and eventual adoption by LEA's of successful projects. A strategy for developing this capability within school systems across the country would reap enormous cost savings, reduce time wastage, and effect early adoption of new programs.

INDEPENDENT ACCOMPLISHMENT AUDIT

Similar to the earlier demand for fiscal audits is the public's present demand for an accounting of student accomplishment. Just as the independent fiscal audit of schools has eliminated most fiscal illegality and has forced fiscal management changes, the IEAA group can also be used to create a demand for necessary instructional reforms. The concern for results in education among the electorate is a recent development, but it is gaining momentum. "Equal opportunity" in education no longer mollifies the majority: some "equity of results" is demanded. This is especially true of the educational benefits conventionally called the "basic skills." Even though Title I language reflects a traditional concern over inputs such as equipment, teachers, space, and books, the subsequent questions raised by Congress have moved beyond how the money was spent to whether the students have learned, have secured jobs, or are falling behind. This is the political soil from which the independent accomplishment audit has grown.

The independent education accomplishment audit is a process similar to that used in a fiscal audit. The emphasis, however, is on student performance as a result of financial outlays. The IEAA relys upon outside independent judgment and has six essential parts: the pre-audit, the translation of local goals into demonstrable data, the adoption or creation of instrumentation and methodology, the establishment of a review calendar, the assessment process, and the public report.

1. *The pre-audit:* The auditor selected by the school system starts the IEAA process by discussing with the staff, students, and community the objectives and plans of the particular program to be reviewed. This phase produces a list of local objectives and a clear description of the programs in some order of priority. In performance contracts, he reviews the project's "procedures" manual.
2. *The translation:* In concert with local people, the auditor determines what evidence will be used to indicate whether the objectives have been met and decides what methods will be used to gather the evidence. This phase produces a set of specifications indicating what the student will be able to do as a result of the educational experience, the manner in which the evidence will be secured, and the standards which will be applied in evaluating the success of the program in helping students to achieve the objectives.
3. *Instrumentation:* Along with the translation, the auditor, working with the LEA, determines the audit instruments, such as tests, questionnaires, interview protocols, and unobtrusive measures, which will be used to gather the evidence. The product of this activity is a set of defined techniques and procedures for data gathering.
4. *Review calendar:* An agreement is secured in writing which indicates the nature of the reviews, where they will be held, how long they will take, when they will occur, who is responsible for arrangements, the nature of the arrangements, and other logistical considerations. It is essential that the calendar be determined in advance and that all concerned be party to, and have the authority to honor, the agreement.
5. *The audit process:* This is a responsibility of the auditor. In this phase, the auditor carries out the procedures agreed upon in the preaudit, translation, and instrumentation phases as codified in the review calendar.
6. *The public report:* The auditor files a report at a public meeting giving commendations and recommendations as they relate to the local objectives. The report is designed to indicate in specific terms both accomplishments and ways in which the program may be made more effective.

ADVANTAGES OF THE IEAA

The IEAA is a new technique designed to put local school personnel and the clients they serve in a problem-solving mode of thinking. It is built around a financial core, since money is a common denominator for the heterogeneous elements of input, but its focus is upon student attitudes, skills, and knowledge. From the IEAA, a whole range of useful by-products is anticipated. First, it may lead to a knowledge of optimum relationships between outputs and inputs—for example, the "critical mass" in funding different types of compensatory programs. Second, it can form a basis for the discovery and improvement of good practice in education. Third, the IEAA creates the need for performance-type contracting and/or budgeting in the basic academic and vocational skill areas. Finally, it can renew credibility in the educational process by effecting more responsiveness to the needs of children and supplying the understanding necessary to produce change. The power of the electorate over public education must be politically, not administratively, derived: If techniques can be developed to convince the community of the benefits of responsible leadership through accountability for results, those interested in furthering education can better support the educational enterprise.

PROBABLE TRENDS

The IEAA concept is now a reality. Over 20 groups or individual auditors across the country are receiving special training and guidance at USOE-sponsored audit institutes. Most of these groups will serve as auditors in Title VII and VIII of ESEA. However, if Title I and Title III funds were made available in a way that would allow LEA's to use performance contracting, and a large number (say 500) decided to do so, the existing resources for training and conducting professional educational audits would probably be inadequate. A superficial survey of existing USOE resources (Title III service centers, the regional laboratories, and resources of private firms) indicates that the auditing capability is limited. A full-scale inquiry should be undertaken. At the same time, university-based graduate studies on educational engineering with heavy emphasis on educational audits should be instituted in a select number of qualified universities. Such curricula must be developed in light of the political and social milieu in which the audit must take place and must be conducted by qualified individuals who understand the concept from a theoretical as well as operational point of view.

DEVELOPMENTAL CAPITAL

For too long a period of time, the public schools have been funded and operated in such a manner that educators and administrators have been discouraged from providing efficient and effective instructional services. Federal funding—despite a plethora of regulations and guidelines, proposals and reports—actually supports and, in some cases, encourages inefficiencies and inequities in public schools. At all levels of financial support, money has been directed toward specific problems as they emerge, rather than being systematically used to reform the institution. Hence, taxpayers and legislators find themselves in the tragic position of throwing "good money after bad"; while school costs have never been greater, the problems emerging from public education have never been more numerous.

The hard lesson to be learned from the past five years of major federal funding of educational programs is that the way in which the money is delivered is as important as the amount. If the cycle of more money and ever greater problems is to be broken, political authorities should realize that discretionary money must be used not only for successful programs, but also for system renewal. Writing in the Fall, 1969, issue of *The Public Interest*, Daniel Moynihan admonished: "The federal government must develop and put into practice far more effective incentive systems than now exist whereby state and local governments, and private interests, too, can be led to achieve the goals of federal programs." Properly conceptualized, therefore, federal aid to education should be viewed as capital, which, when made available in a predictable and systematic manner, will provide the energy for educational engineering. The basic purpose of developmental capital is to provide a financial resource to stimulate and sustain reexamination and modernization of the educational system. The investment of "risk" capital can generate new educational traditions by applying the developmental aspects of business success to the public sector.

Effecting necessary change requires discretionary funds which are not now available to local school leaders. In the absence of an infusion of new monies for development, dissemination, and installation of new products and practices, the gap between the demand for higher quality education and performance is likely to widen even further.

With developmental capital set-asides, renewal can be directed through federal, state, and local channels, and activity can be aimed at improving management leadership capabilities. All three sectors of government can work in conjunction with each other to attract the best minds and resources to the renewal of the system. Funds at the federal level can be applied to "high risk" investments, for this is the only governmental level that can commit the necessary amount of money and manpower to accomplish research and development.

USING DEVELOPMENTAL CAPITAL

Developmental capital, available in a three-stage process, is the means of responsibly fostering change and renewal. If educational engineering is ultimately to have any impact, it must receive its "energy" from a pattern of funding.

Three-stage funding of projects is one way to maximize the effectiveness of this developmental capital. In this process, the first step is to provide small amounts of money to the agency so that a management support group or technical assistance can be used in the planning process. These planning grants accomplish two purposes: First, schools can afford to attract the resources necessary for good planning. Second, they equalize opportunities among schools that are competing for project approval. No longer will wealthy schools have an unfair advantage over poor schools in the competition for developmental dollars, as happened in the Title III and Title I ESEA application process.

Program operation and management funds are then made available to schools that have demonstrated the best use of the planning grants. There are two major criteria for awarding this money: First, the schools should demonstrate skill in the assessment of system needs and imagination in relating expected program outcomes to the identified needs. Second, the request for proposal should be a clear and comprehensive document. The heart of the RFP is in the clear statement of outcomes, not only for the program but also for the renewal of the school system. The art is in setting parameters in such a way that the bidder is able to make his best response to this statement of need. The third stage of the funding would automatically follow the money for program operation and would be for the independent educational audit. There must be no chance for the auditor to be involved in either program planning or operation; rather, the accomplishment audit group must be independent.

Grants management, funded by a risk capital account at the local level, must also follow this three-phase process if sustained innovation is to be accomplished. Risk capital can be used by an administrator to build an inhouse innovative capability or at least to utilize that which exists on the outside under contract as a management support function. If the administrator could make this risk capital available in three stages, talented and ambitious teachers would be encouraged and would have the resources to bid on requests for proposals. This process could take on a myriad of forms.

PROBABLE TRENDS

The need for new patterns of funding in education is receiving widespread attention. Congress has already taken limited action by requiring planning grants and educational accomplishment audits in the provisions of ESEA Title VII and Title VIII. The expansion of this new pattern of funding to ESEA Titles I and III should be given high priority if these programs are to achieve their original objectives.

While these new directions at the federal level support the concept of educational engineering for accountability, action is also required, and is already occurring in some instances, at the state and local levels along the lines previously mentioned. The trend for states to assume an increasingly greater role in educational financing will provide an opportunity for a more cohesive and systematic approach to school funding. Even with total state responsibility for financing education, this three-stage funding process would prove to be just as important as the proposed equitable redistribution of education resources.

At the local level, a developmental capital approach to grants management would foster a responsible strategy of educational innovation. LEA's are caught in a fiscal crunch; since most school budgets can be altered only slightly, any sudden increase in discretionary money would probably have an insignificant impact upon the system, because the money would be treated as an "add-on" under the current lump-sum dispersal of program money. If promising innovations are to have a marked impact, money must be programmed so that innovations are comprehensively planned and implemented, objectively evaluated, and then effectively turnkeyed back to the schools when appropriate.

This sort of approach will lead ultimately to modernizing reforms, such as program budgeting and performance evaluations. School decision makers have not enjoyed the freedom of choosing among alternatives. If a developmental capital approach to program funding were adopted, responsible innovation could begin to produce relatively unambiguous results. As alternatives are generated through developmental capital and performance contracting, the way will have been prepared for the installation of PPBS and other necessary reforms.

SUMMARY

The educational engineering process described above is consciously directed toward increasing the capability of the schools. Thus it is that a turnkey arrangement is called for in every RFP and is incorporated into every performance contract. With costs underwritten by the local education agency, provision for adaption, adoption, and installation of a successfully completed performance contract is assisted by using school personnel as consultants and as trainees in the process successfully bid by the contractor. The turnkey, or turnaround, feature is potentially a bodkin's point to pierce the armor of resistance to change and innovation that is so permanent a feature of school life. The objective of the standard turnkey feature of all performance contracts with private enterprise is simple and clear: to arm the school with the know-how of better instructional practice and to see that validated practice is adopted.

In general, educational organizations are influenced by three basic factors: the cultural or belief system, which sets policy in the form of goals and creates the mind-set by which activities are accepted; the technology, which determines the means available for reaching these goals; and the social structure of the organization in which the technology is embedded. An educational engineering process to produce accountability for results in the public schools attends constructively to these three basic factors.

Chapter 11

ALTERNATIVE SCHOOLS
AND PROGRAMS

Dissatisfaction with the established public high school is producing many alternative approaches to high school education, including several described in the selections of this chapter. Some alternatives, of course, have long been available in the form of nonpublic schools and one selection presents the contributions of these schools. However, some alternatives are found within the public school system. The first article describes the innovative program of a state university campus laboratory school, tax-supported, although independent of a school district, and the second one is illustrative of the school-without-walls plan in several urban school districts. Another article presents various types of summer programs, some sponsored by or conducted in public high schools. The last three selections deal directly with the movement from public schools to newer alternative schools.

Don E. Glines' article, "Implementing a Humane School" describes the somewhat revolutionary program of the Wilson Campus School at Mankato State College, Minnesota. Citing the public school system as "the worst example of a monopolistic police state in America," Glines holds that "what is needed in every community in America today is a philosophy of alternative educational programs" so as to have "a wild upside-down school, a semi-innovative school, and a structured school available to all students, parents, and teachers on an optional basis." Some 63 changes in the Wilson School have moved it toward the "wild upside-down" model. Among the more innovative changes are: students' "window-shopping" in the selection of study areas; courses that can be "mini or maxi"; student selection of his teachers; optional attendance; daily "smorgasbord scheduling" in which "the student determines the amount of each course he desires to study in a given day." One of the most lasting impressions of the present writer's visit to the school was the mixture of ages seen in many classrooms, with high school students frequently participating with young children in some activities. Glines intersperses many criticisms of conventional school practice, and also various policy suggestions that readers may find controversial and worthy of extended discussion. For example, do you agree that to implement such a program, teachers "must be allowed to come and go and have optional attendance, freedom, responsibility, and a great deal of individualization and self-selection, the same that we preach for students"?

A new concept of "a school without walls" was implemented in the Philadelphia Parkway School in 1969. At Parkway, which has been described in several publications, there is no conventional arrangement of classrooms, but students had tutorials for basic skills and were guided for most of their learning experience to various resources (libraries, museums, hospitals, newspapers, businesses and industries, and others) strung along a two-mile stretch of the Benjamin Franklin Parkway in the heart of the city. Several other cities, including Chicago, made plans to establish similar schools; included here is a preliminary description of the Chicago Public High School for Metropolitan Studies (Metro). It, too, has no conventional school building, and its students by individual placement participate in learning experiences throughout the city. Each student participates in various learning units or courses, and is also a member of a counseling group, meeting three hours per week. A sampling of the courses during 1970–1971 included "Game Theater," "People of the U.S.," "Black America," "Stock Market and Economy," "Let the Buyer Beware," "Penal Justice," "Math Applications in Business," and "Marine Biology." Other significant departures in the Metro program are identified in the selection; almost unique is the evaluation plan.

C. Albert Koob, then executive secretary (later president) of the National Catholic Educational Association, offers an interesting brief history of nonpublic schools in the United States, and then discusses their relationships with public schools and their unique contributions. He feels that competition between public and nonpublic schools could be wholesome, but that it really has not existed outside of sports and in a few competitive cultural events. He suggests four purposes that the nonpublic schools can serve for the improvement of all education: (1) cooperative planning for sharing talent; (2) opening private doors to the inner city; (3) sponsoring joint training programs; and (4) orienting education toward values. Koob closes with a strong argument for cooperation in strengthening all schools.

The article by Donald W. Robinson entitled "Alternative Schools: Challenge to Traditional Education" is a benchmark of the movement toward these schools which had taken on considerable momentum by 1970. His first paragraph, which cites the establishment of over 700 independent schools in the past three years, documents the movement, as do other facts. Included is an estimate that approximately 80 percent of the schools are for children from preschool through high school. More detail as to one type of alternative school is given in Jonathan Black's article, "Street Academies: One Step Off the Sidewalk." He identifies the street academies as "storefront schools . . . for high school dropouts." His article deals with these academies in New York City, 14 of them operating at the time, 8 in Harlem and the others elsewhere in Manhattan and Brooklyn. He relates the seven-year history of the academy program and the expansion plans under way. Although cooperation with and contributions to the public school program are mentioned, its image is "as an *alternative* to public education." In fact he sees as the danger of "the academy's doubling back into the school system" a loss of its "uniqueness and intense personal involvement." Black's concluding comment that the questions about the academies "must be faced with a courage and a confidence in the concept of storefront schools, because the educational system needs the academy desperately" seems to sum up well his very favorable view of the street academy.

A new development in the movement toward educational alternatives is the *education voucher plan* proposed by several persons named in the selection by Robert Havighurst. In general, this plan provides that the state would give parents an education voucher, which they could use for payment of their child's school costs at any school of their choice, within whatever limitations the state plan sets. Thus the plan tends to make all schools competitive and to an extent, publicly supported, and it provides alternative choices for parents and their children. Havighurst's article appeared as one of three in *Phi Delta Kappan* for September 1970, and is selected here for his brief critique of the various proposals of voucher plans and also to spark the reader's more detailed investigation of these various plans. Havighurst's espousal of a plan that would force mixing along racial and socioeconomic lines may also stimulate discussion.

These various selections regarding alternatives in education clearly indicate the mood of dissatisfaction with conventional public schools that was affecting educational choices and decisions in many communities in the early 1970s. What is the situation in your own community? What choices of high schools and programs within high schools are available? Are the alternatives adequate? If not, what other alternatives should be available, and how would you have them get started?

IMPLEMENTING A HUMANE SCHOOL*

Don E. Glines

The Wilson Campus School at Mankato State College, Minnesota, is not the best school in the nation. We have all the obstacles facing education today, just as the American society in general has problems with pollution, conservation, drugs, budgets, cities, and minorities. We lack quality, we are not a model; but Wilson is an example of education's need for the ability to make rapid, massive, dramatic change. It represents a serious attempt to apply the concept of *humaneness*[1] in the day by day operation of a real school. If the principles given in the ASCD 1970 Yearbook are "right," then a great majority of the present schools are "wrong."

Wilson is challenging many education practices today. Monopolies are not always the big industries in America, nor are the only police states found among some foreign powers. Unfortunately, the worst example of a monopolistic police state in America is the public school system. We require students to attend school, require certain courses, require certain books, put "minus 10 wrong" on the paper, and give the child an "F"; we no not allow selection of teachers or rooms or materials. We have tests on Friday and dress codes every day. We still even paddle and expel students in some schools.

What is needed in every community in America today is a philosophy of alternative educational programs. In 1970, we really do not know what is best. Therefore, there should be a wild upside-down school, a semi-

---

* Reprinted from *Educational Leadership* (November 1970), 28:185–190. Reprinted with permission of the Association for Supervision and Curriculum Development. Copyright © 1970 by the Association for Supervision and Curriculum Development. See also Don E. Glines, *Creating Humane Schools* (Campus Publishers, Box 1005, Mankato, Minn.) for fuller development of the ideas in this article.

[1] Mary-Margaret Scobey and Grace Graham, editors. *To Nurture Humaneness.* 1970 Yearbook. Washington, D.C.: Association for Supervision and Curriculum Development, 1970.

innovative school, and a structured school available to all students, parents, and teachers on an optional basis.

The current Wilson effort grew out of a previous conservative mold. Wilson, until 1968, had national exams and percentage comparisons. Our pupils went to college; the parents were satisfied; we had the usual share of strong and weak teachers. We had self-contained classrooms, "A" through "F" report cards, textbooks, required seventh-grade courses, period 1-2-3 schedules, dress codes, bells, and other examples of ritual and ceremony which still exist in most schools.

Wilson is engaged in about 63 changes. A few of them involve personalized programming, matching students and teachers, student development of curricula, optional attendance, smorgasbord scheduling, individualized learning, 12-month school year, student freedom, individual progress reports, all-day kindergarten, emphasis on the affective domain, five-phase instruction, and a nongraded K-12 country school environment.

THE PROPER MATCH

Of these, the most important is *the match between the teacher and the student*. Learning occurs if there is a good relationship. Personality, perception, interest, sex, age, and skill are the factors to match. If the student relates to the teacher, the battle is on the way to being won. If there is an improper match, positive learning does not occur. At Wilson, each student selects all his own teachers and his advisor. No teachers are "assigned."

With the proper match, the *affective* domain then becomes the focus. Self-image, attitude toward life, being "turned on," good peer relationships, positive motivation, and perception of others are crucial. Wilson programs concern themselves first with this aspect.

The *psychomotor* domain closely follows the affective domain in importance. Gross motor, fine motor, visual motor, auditory discrimination, and others are keys in learning. Therefore physical education, industrial arts, home economics, art, and music are important courses at Wilson, especially in the primary years. Many even learn to type during this period.

Then comes the *cognitive*. Learning is easy in this area, limited only by the individual's potential, assuming that the match and the affective and the psychomotor areas are taken care of, and assuming the school has a continuous progress program and that the home environment allows the school to function with the individual.

Creativity is another concern here at Wilson. Why is it that in the conventional schools more dropouts occur among those classified as creative? Who said that math and social studies are more important than drama, speech, music, art, chorus, and other fine arts areas? At Wilson, courses growing out of the Creative Studies Team have great importance. We truly believe in a balanced curriculum; English, social studies, and math are not kingpins, but are only equally important.

Further, we are concerned about individual learning styles, especially as these relate to progress in a self-paced program. Very few schools have paid attention to *learning styles*, but it is becoming more evident every month that this is an important factor in learning. Even simple illustrations, such as the fact that some students need quiet concentration and some prefer to study to the tune of noisy records, show the complexities, without even discussing the impact of listening, discussion, reading, writing, and seeing methods as these affect various individuals.

Being concerned with the affective, psychomotor, creativity, and learning style factors, as well as the cognitive, has probably done more to enhance *motivation* than any other single issue, with the exceptions of allowing students to choose their own teachers and develop their own courses of study.

Relevancy is another key at Wilson—the belief that the student best learns that which is meaningful to him at this moment in time. We are concerned about interest and frames of reference; we believe that curricular development should not be dictated by publishers, supervisors, legislators, parents, school board policies, and experts, but rather heavily engaged in by students. After all, whose education is it?

Wilson is concerned about the problems of students in urban, suburban, exurban, and rural settings. But as an example of the need for involvement in change and humaneness, look at Indian education, which a U.S. Senate subcommittee report stated "could hardly be worse" and labeled "a national tragedy—a national challenge." Indian education has been called "sterile, impersonal, and rigid" and seems to be part of the cause of some Indian problems. What have we done as a total national concern to enhance the Indian culture, art, costumes, customs, history, dances, legends, weapons, and beauty and to bring about a better understanding of the Indian in America? If the analysis in a recent book, *Our Brother's Keeper—The Indian in White America*,[2] is valid, the answer can only be summarized as pitifully little.

A JOINT PROJECT

Staff interest in helping in this area led to the selection of Wilson as one of six schools nationally to participate in a project on innovation

---

[2] Edgar S. Cahn, editor. *Our Brother's Keeper—The Indian in White America*. Cleveland, Ohio: The World Publishing Company, 1969.

in education, sponsored jointly by the National Association of Secondary School Principals and the Bureau of Indian Affairs (BIA). Wilson, along with two other schools, is to contribute innovative educational ideas to three BIA schools; the Indian schools are to help the public schools develop new curricula and further understanding as related to the Indians in America.

To implement some of the programs and philosophies, Wilson follows a system of window-shopping regarding the selection of study areas. Students window-shop as any adult might do in looking for the right set of clothes. There is a shopper's guide available to help him select, such as the ads one might find in the supermarket. If the student cannot find what he wants, he asks the management to help him order a special program.

Tied in with all of the efforts is the development of the early childhood years. Wilson has limited programs for three- and four-year-olds. But the five-year-olds are in school all day. We do not have a "mother hen" (six of the ten teachers are male) with them constantly; they wander throughout the building. We are interested in freedom, responsibility, and self-selection for these youngsters, but with some structure based on diagnosis, prescription, and guidance.

Further, part of the Wilson program calls for options. Courses can be mini or maxi. Pupils can go duck hunting whenever they want during the duck season, take vacations anytime during the year, work, sleep, stay at home, and generally "do their thing" as long as it does not hurt others. The opportunity for options is available to students K-12. We believe that humaneness involves choice of teachers, choice of courses, daily schedules, optional attendance, freedom of dress, and individualized evaluation (no report cards), as examples of some of the changes toward a humane school.

In this program, the year-round school concept is quite important. Students operate on a continuous progress, self-paced learning cycle; they may plug in, plug out, slow up, speed up, drop in, drop out, cycle in, cycle out whenever they desire. They may spend 3, 13, 33, 103 weeks pursuing an area. Wilson is open 12 months a year, closed only for two weeks during the winter, one week in the spring, and two weeks in the late summer.

Requirements at Wilson are quite fluid. We do not agree with the state department requirements and, therefore, do not specifically follow them. We argue against college entrance required courses and disagree with the present legislative requirements. We do not believe that all ninth graders in Minnesota need English, social studies, math, science, physical education, and one elective; nor do we believe that all second graders need an extra big chunk of language arts, a big chunk of math, some social studies, minimum "book" science, and a little physical education, music, and art built around lunch and recess. What about home economics, industrial arts, foreign language, typing, environmental studies, and drama for elementary students? Wilson includes these and the instruction is on a 1–1 basis as much as possible. Groups are arranged when needed. The 1–1 and group arrangements are complemented by open lab and independent study opportunities.

The schedule is a daily smorgasbord menu. The student selects as much as is needed or desirable, when it is needed, for as long as it is needed. Students select the amount of soup, salad, hamburger, cottage cheese, milk, cookies, steak, peas, eggs, backed potatoes, jello, etc., that seems desirable for that day. Putting it in educational terms the student determines the amount of each course he desires to study in a given day. For example, he may spend all day in the art center. Each day a new schedule is developed for students to select the opportunities which they desire to pursue. They may go home for part of the day, if that best suits their needs.

THE LIGHTED SCHOOL

We are concerned about community involvement and the lighted school. We have Parent, Student, and Faculty Councils operating now, and we coordinate these through a Joint Council. They are not as effective as we would like, but we are working to improve communication. We still have not done a good job tying the non-parent taxpayers, the legislature, the state department, and the school boards into the school. Some parents are still not convinced. Usually in the second year of an innovative program, there is a "revolt" from the minority who are against change. Wilson recently had such a reaction, and again this proved to be true of a small but very vocal percentage. Schools interested in change must be willing to face such unpleasantness.

Wilson believes strongly in evaluation. There is more research to support a Wilson type program than the conventional kind, but there is not enough of either. We cannot prove that Wilson's is the right program; yet neither is there proof that it is wrong. Conventional schools cannot prove they are right, but Wilson cannot prove they are as bad as we think they are. Wilson's evaluation is based on 1–1 relationships, diagnosis, prescription, affective domain, and student evaluations of teachers, plus outside evaluation by the Office of Institutional Research. Conventional schools have group comparisons, Iowa tests, "A" through "F" report cards, and emphasis on the cognitive, conformity, and authority. There is a great deal of research still needed in education.

To help a student through this type of program, each student selects a teacher who serves as his advisor, counselor, and consultant. Each teacher has 5 to 15 counselees; the teacher is involved in this selection process in that he or she agrees to work with the individuals who have made the requests. At Wilson, most students have a great deal of 1–1 contact, whereas in a conventional school, where there may be one counselor for 300 students, there is very little 1–1 contact for most students. If it were attempted, there would be a long line outside the door each day.

Do schools really need to make such a dramatic change as that which has occurred at Wilson this past year? In the 1970's, communication systems will be available by which, through home TV and push-button phones, we will receive instant answers from a regional retrieval information center. We will have an attachment to the TV sets to plug in home video cassettes so we can watch the Late, Late Show early, or any other favorite program or lesson we want to store on a cassette. The 1980's will find signed checks and credit cards on their way out. Electronic money is not far off. Should schools keep pace with the changes in their surroundings? We at Wilson believe we should. Not everyone agrees, but remember, Socrates was forced to commit suicide by drinking hemlock after he was accused of impiety and *innovation.*

To implement such a program, teachers must be treated as professionals; they must be allowed to come and go and have optional attendance, freedom, responsibility, and a great degree of individualization and self-selection, the same that we preach for students. Teachers are human, too. This changes the whole authority structure—all present administrative designs must be revised.

Though each faculty member has gone through much frustration in the past year and a half, there have also been glimpses of the pot of gold at the end of the rainbow. Wilson teachers are convinced that there is somewhere, somehow, a better way to educate boys and girls; for this ray of hope they continue to strive. The efforts at implementing a humane school can probably best be summarized by a note received from one of the staff members during this past year. It read, "Don, I am staying home tomorrow. This day has been hell!"

CHICAGO PUBLIC HIGH SCHOOL
FOR METROPOLITAN STUDIES*

The Metro High School is an experimental four-year "high school without walls." The school has no conventional school building; it does have a headquarters in a downtown office building that serves as office space for staff, a student-staff work area, and a student-staff lounge. Metro students participate in learning experiences throughout the city—with businesses, cultural organizations, and community groups.

Metro is a Chicago Public High School with full-time responsibility for 350 students. Students who graduate from Metro fulfill all Chicago Board of Education requirements for a high school degree. The students come from every neighborhood in the city. They closely reflect the diversity of Chicago's school population in terms of ethnic background, interests, and previous school achievement. Students who are now attending Metro were chosen *randomly* from approximately 3,000 applicants.

The nature of Metro's educational program reflects a number of ideas about learning that the students and staff of Metro are testing and developing:

1. The possibilities for meaningful education are enhanced when such education occurs in real-life situations, including the businesses, cultural institutions, and neighborhoods of a city.
2. Students can learn from people with varied skills and interests—lawyers, electricians, artists, newspaper reporters. A skilled teacher can help a student use the talents of these people to gain a rich and individualized education.
3. An urban school must be developed with student involvement in decision-making. Students become more independent and motivated learners by helping make decisions about how their school will be structured and how their own education will proceed.

---

* Mimeographed statement sub-titled "A Brief Description, February 1, 1971," provided this writer upon his request to James F. Redmond, General Superintendent, Chicago Schools.

4. A fairly small learning community of teachers and students must be the basic unit to which the student relates. This community of learners must provide both constant support and constant evaluative feedback to the student regarding his directions for learning.
5. The diverse backgrounds of students provide a resource for education that should become an integral part of a school program.

To implement these innovations, Metro has developed a three-part program consisting of learning units, individual placements, and counseling groups.

The *learning units* are the basic learning experiences in the program. They are taught both by the school's full-time staff and by staff members of participating organizations. Some units deal with traditional subject areas, such as geometry and chemistry. Some units deal with basic skills such as reading. Well over half of them deal with topics that are not usually covered in a high school curriculum: Studying the current show at the Museum of Contemporary Art, studying probability with a group of insurance actuaries, learning filmmaking techniques from television film producers, and learning about a community's problems from a neighborhood organization. Except for a few distributional requirements, a student is free to choose whatever he wants from the Metro catalogue, which currently includes about 100 courses.

Individual placements are a recent development at Metro. They provide an opportunity for a student to find out about a place in the city in which he is interested, perhaps an occupation in which he thinks he might want to work. Individual placements have been made in secretarial pools, animal hospitals, zoos, preschools, industrial laboratories, community organizations, political campaigns, lawyers' offices, etc. Ideally, the student is given some real responsibility in the organization and an opportunity to understand how it functions overall.

Counseling group is, in one sense, the core of the program. This group consists of 15 to 20 students who meet for three hours each week. This time is devoted to group discussions and other group activities, individual counseling, and planning of the student's program. The counseling group allows students from diverse backgrounds to become well acquainted by sharing past experiences and discussing present problems and future plans. It is the fundamental forum where students make themselves heard on decisions pertinent to the school's organization and curriculum.

These varied activities constitute a student's program; they may send him from one end of the city to another during a typical day. A typical student could begin his day interviewing inmates at a state prison as part of a course in "Penal Justice." He then heads for the Loop, where his counseling group meets in a conference room provided by Montgomery

Ward. He ends the day photographing buildings as part of a class in city planning. His next day could consist of a math lab experience at Metro headquarters, a class in electronics at the telephone company, and a free period spent at the library or just relaxing at Metro headquarters.

A second student could have a completely different set of experiences chosen to suit his interests and abilities. His program might consist of a journalism course taught in part by practicing reporters, a physics course using lab facilities at the University of Illinois, a placement in a quality control laboratory in a chemical company, and a course in improvisational theater at Second City.

The Metro calendar is divided into four ten-week learning cycles. At the end of each cycle, the student sits down with each of his teachers, and they fill out a detailed evaluation of his work. The teacher, after consulting the student, gives him either CREDIT or NO CREDIT for that ten-week learning cycle. Each learning unit fulfills requirements for graduation in a major subject matter area, like English. Thus, a student's year of English credit may (for example) come from work in filmmaking, creative writing, and American literature.

One interesting aspect of the Metro school is an attempt to evaluate the program's development carefully. This evaluation has two parts: (1) a long-term comparison of Metro students with a control group of students who applied to Metro but weren't admitted in the random drawing and (2) a short-term "formative" evaluation that attempts to provide information bearing on decisions that must be made about the school's development. The formative evaluation seeks to answer questions like the following: What do students think about counseling group? What are the characteristics of classes which students like? What are the most successful alternatives for getting information to students? How much interracial contact is there at the headquarters compared to six months ago?

Another interesting aspect of the school is the involvement, from the initial stages of planning, of outside consultants. Consultants from Urban Research Corporation of Chicago have worked on planning and carrying out all phases of the Metro program, including contacts with participating organizations, curriculum planning, staff development, teaching classes, student counseling, development of administrative procedures, and evaluation.

It is much too early to make any definite judgment on the success of the Metro program. Students and staff constantly confront difficult problems making the transition from traditional patterns of education. For example, some students have particular difficulty in taking the responsibility that comes with Metro's freedom. Teachers find it difficult to assume the multiple demands of their role: teaching, counseling, curriculum development, and making outside contacts. Crucial decisions confront the school concerning how to expand in size while maintaining a sense of community and a flexible program.

It will require several years of bold experimentation before the nature of the Metro experiment can be clearly evaluated.

THE CONTRIBUTION OF NON-PUBLIC SCHOOLS*

C. Albert Koob

In confronting the massive problems facing education today there is need to gather together all forces which can be of service to the nation. In recent years many possibilities for cooperation between the private sector and the public sector of education have come to the attention of the American people. This, of course, has been largely the result of federal legislation, particularly ESEA, the Elementary and Secondary Education Act. Whatever the reason, it augurs good for the nation that educators are beginning to think in terms of cooperative endeavor and better use of talent, rather than in terms of the "we-and-they" separation between public and private education.

The non-public schools today are facing a crisis the like of which they have never faced before. It is not only a crisis of financial limitation but also a crisis which involves the very reason for the existence of private schools. It is of little consolation to the average private school administrator to know from the history of American education that the first schools in America were indeed private schools. It is of little consolation for such administrators to know that there will always be some people who prefer to send their children to a non-public school for good and valid reasons. What is very much the concern of the private school educator is the justification for his entire system, and the contribution that his system makes to society at large. While he may be personally convinced of both the justification and the contribution, the truth of the matter is that both

* Reprinted from the *Bulletin of the National Association of Secondary School Principals* (December 1968), 52:74–82, by permission.

educators and non-educators have begun to take a much more critical look at private schools than ever before. The pros and cons of the existence of private education are quite frequently matters for debate today, where once a peaceful, perhaps complacent, sort of existence was the lot of private school educators.

POSSIBILITY OF CHAOS

It is not my intention here to discuss the agonizing controversies, political and otherwise, of recent years nor to attempt to justify private education. It might be noted, however, that one basis for private education does lie in the concept put forth by William W. Brickman, head of the School of Education at the University of Pennsylvania and editor of *School and Society*. He points out that America very much needs the possibility of choice in education. The dualism in education which America has experienced in the past two hundred years is, then, not just something to be tolerated, much less to be explained away as a historical anachronism. It is, rather, a vital part of American life.

Yet non-public schools have not fully sold themselves to the American public in many instances. This has been especially true in recent years when all educational programs have been subject to public scrutiny. All too frequently they have appeared to be expressions of a "ghetto" mentality. They have appeared to be divisive in so far as they catered in some cases to particular ethnic and religious groups or to an exclusively upper middle class clientele. The charge has been made that such schools exist only for the elite. While there is undoubtedly some justification for these remarks, especially if one considers the academically talented as elite, there is a deep regret on the part of private educators that such conditions have existed.

The history of education in America provides a helpful background for answering the question of how the non-public schools came to be what they are today. Following an era of exclusively church-related education, the common school appeared on the scene in the early nineteenth century and came into prominence about 1840. From that time on, the common school, or (as we know it today) the public school, developed rapidly. Yet despite the tremendous and largely successful efforts of Horace Mann, one of America's truly great educators, the common school did not achieve an educational program divorced from religious indoctrination. The local educational leaders of that day tended to be men of strong religious convictions and quite often ministers of various denominations. It is not surprising, then, that while the common school became "non-denominational," it remained strongly oriented to Bible reading, chapel service, and ethical precept, all of a distinctly Protestant cast.

REACTION TO PUBLIC SCHOOLS

Reaction to this movement was inevitable on the part of those not sharing Protestant beliefs and even on the part of those Protestants who had very strong convictions about their own sectarian teachings. It is interesting to note that a Catholic bishop, John Hughes of New York, was the instigator of legislation which ultimately led to the abolishment of state aid to sectarian education. In 1842, following a prolonged conflict within the State of New York over the support of schools that were teaching Protestant beliefs, the New York State legislature finally passed a law prohibiting the use of state funds for sectarian education.

Immigration patterns helped to strengthen the conviction that ethnic groups and religious groups could best protect their rich heritage by setting up their own schools. As wave after wave of Europeans reached the shores of America, the private schools shouldered a great deal of the responsibility in assisting the foreigners, usually poor and uneducated, and enabled them to adjust to the new culture in which they had to live. Far from being divisive, as ethnic schools of today are sometimes considered, these schools were in many cases the greatest exponents of what we have all come to know as the American way of life by simultaneously cushioning against cultural shock and fostering Americanization.

A SECOND SCHOOL SYSTEM

It was in 1852 that the largest movement toward private schools, as a kind of second school system, really took form. Because of the controversy over whose brand of religion should be taught in the common schools and because of the large number of Catholic immigrants, the Catholic bishops of the United States decided that every parish should have it own elementary school. Orthodox Jews and many Protestants who feared that too little religion was being taught in the public schools likewise elected to follow the pattern of an entirely separate school for their children rather than be content with a few hours a week for religious instruction.

When the emphasis toward secondary education for all students became nationwide, the various states established compulsory education laws, which usually required a child to remain in school until he was sixteen years old. This meant that the teenager would now have to be cared for by the private schools, also, if they were to be consistent with the public schools. In the 1920's, then, the nation saw the beginning of a huge movement toward non-public high schools. Today there are approximately four thousand of these non-public secondary schools educating just a little less than two million American youths. These figures would take into account all non-public schools, whether religiously oriented or non-denominational, that follow a state approved secondary school curriculum.

Today within private education, many are asking what the private schools can and should contribute to the educational system of our country. This questioning reflects the changes within our society. Some years ago, Robert M. Hutchins, in addressing a group of Catholic parochial school educators, pointed out that the failure of private education to experiment and try new forms of educational technique was probably its greatest shortcoming. In this regard the nation's schools were the real losers. In a similar vein, Myron Lieberman has observed that the private sector of education has failed to be the spark that would challenge public education to do a better job.

PRIVATE EDUCATION'S SELF-VIEW

Private education never really saw itself either as competing with public education or as sparking it toward better quality. Rather, it saw its purpose as serving a particular segment of society by giving adequate and perhaps excellent scholastic training to those it enrolled. Many of the fine programs that now exist in private schools across the nation did indeed have their beginnings in the public schools (although in not a few cases the private schools themselves did some pioneering in better educational programs). Professional training for administrators, the movement toward better counseling programs, advanced placement, team teaching, and modular scheduling are the direct result of the leadership of public school educators. Most of the private schools have moved to incorporate these changes for improvement of educational outcomes. The non-public schools have followed these trends not only to conform to an emerging pattern but also to take advantage of such programs as their desirability became increasingly obvious.

What about the "competition" that one hears of between public and non-public schools? Is it good or bad? Is it desirable or not? Can it be a healthy means toward improved education? Unfortunately, if we are to be perfectly honest, we have to admit that the only real competition that one finds to document an answer to these questions is that described on the sports page of the local newspapers. Competitive sports, and in a few cases competitive cultural events, represent about the only sort of recorded, measured competition. Academic and scholastic competition, where it has existed at all, has been very much hushed up. The number of finalists in the National Merit Scholarship Program, in spite of all professional recommendations to the contrary, did for a time provide some rather unhealthy applications of the competitive spirit, even though criteria for competition were totally misused and the resulting comparisons grossly inaccurate.

ADVANTAGES OF COMPETITION

But competition *can* produce a better product. At least Madison Avenue has convinced us of this bit of elementary economic wisdom. Why shouldn't it be possible to challenge our nation's schools toward improvement by exploiting the advantages of a competitive system? This is exactly what a task force of the Chamber of Commerce urged in its 1966 report. Recent developments in secondary education have indeed illustrated the attraction that well advertised programs of innovation can have for all educators who are trying to find new and better ways to organize their schools. Teachers and administrators have traveled for miles to look at new programs. It seems to have made little difference whether the school was public or non-public when an exceptional idea was given due publicity. Perhaps this phenomenon simply indicates that modern educators like to travel, or perhaps it is the result of an "over-sell." But whatever the reason, the basic concept looks good: build a better program and the principal down the street is going to have to do something about his own school's weaknesses.

As we look ahead to the changing society in which our educators must live for the next decade, there appear many hopeful signs that the non-public sector of education will serve in a notable way the purposes which they are best able to serve for the improvement of all education. Four of these purposes are outlined below.

1. COOPERATIVE PLANNING: SHARING TALENT

The private sector of education will supplement the efforts made by public schools by joint planning for team projects. Better programs will be mounted in each of the disciplines covered by modern secondary education. When campus schools and "super schools" become a reality, the private school will undoubtedly maintain its normal role of independence but it will also engage in cooperative endeavor with the public school. Such planning makes sense in an era where every amount of talent available must be used to the fullest extent. Such educational operations could guarantee the widest possible use of all the experience and skill at the disposal of education. Excellent teachers are rare and should be shared.

2. OPENING PRIVATE DOORS TO THE INNER CITY

Social action programs will make use of the private educational facilities to a much greater degree. America is confronted with the enormous problem of what to do for education in the inner city. Large metropolitan public school systems will profit from the use of facilities and personnel which until now have maintained a segregated kind of existence catering only to the few. The use of specialists, highly trained and tremendously dedicated people, will be on a much wider basis than just the individual school. The religiously oriented school will open its doors widely to anyone of any race, color, or creed. Such schools will put at the disposal of the public their gymnasium and playground facilities, their specialized services, and their dedicated teachers. Some of this will be done during the regular school day, but more of it will be done in evening programs, Saturday programs, and summer specialized programs.

To be more specific on this point, Commissionr Harold Howe has publicly stated many times that he firmly believes that the U.S. Office of Education should serve all of education and not just the public schools. In addressing the assembled delegates at the National Catholic Educational Association Convention in San Francisco in April 1968, Howe stressed the urgency of keeping alive the private schools as a source of help in the inner city. He emphasized that these schools enjoy some unique advantages over the local public schools in today's inner-city crisis by way of mobility of personnel, lack of red tape in meeting problems, meaningful contact with ethnic groups, and an innate dedication which was responsible for their existence in the first place. In the opinion of Commissioner Howe, the educational problems of our metropolitan areas will be more readily solved when all forces that can help to effect an improvement are brought into a working relationship.

Sociologists like Christopher Jencks and David Riesman have likewise argued along the same lines, maintaining that the massive problems of the public schools in huge metropolitan areas are so complex and so deeply rooted in socioeconomic, racial, and religious backgrounds that only a new effort, involving the private sector of society, will suffice to alleviate the conditions.

3. SPONSORING JOINT TRAINING PROGRAMS

In-service training programs for better administrators and for specialists of every kind will be carried out under the joint sponsorship of both private and public schools. Private enterprise may well be added as still a third partner in getting better programs set up for in-service training. Educational television, computer assisted instruction, and similar ventures in the field of telecommunications require expensive equipment and highly qualified personnel. Cooperative efforts are not only desirable but will be necessary. Specialists who have been trained for private schools will work with and for public education. The development of joint institutes and workshops for improvement of administrators is already underway. The National Association of Secondary School Principals was one of the first groups in education to recognize the advantages of joint sponsorship of this kind of in-service training. As educational planning becomes truly comprehensive, elements of the business world, private education, and indeed the average citizen will all be combined to effect a better educational system for our nation.

4. ORIENTING EDUCATION TOWARD VALUES

All educators today are concerned with learning how an individual communicates a set of desirable values to those under his care and teaching. But the non-public schools rest their case for existence on the premise that they are able to identify and communicate specific values. With the aid of a large and significant research effort, the private sector of education must find and disseminate more complete information on this process. Hopefully it will come up with some meaningful answers. The whole nation must be concerned with the way youth appraises past values and formulates new ones. We must learn more about how a teacher assists young people to select the proper values.

RESPONSIBILITY FOR MEANING

Student revolts, lack of respect for authority, and scant regard for heroes of the past are all symptoms of a generation that is groping for meaning to life in an automated society. The private sector of education treasures as part of its philosophy the responsibility for giving a meaning to life. And as the private sector combines forces with the public schools, we will see more joint ventures to examine such very delicate problems as the meaning of life and which values are worth cultivating.

Within the field of non-public education there is already a marked degree of cooperation. The federal legislation which has emphasized the child benefit theory greatly encourages those in the non-public schools. If aid and assistance can be given from public funds to help children develop into better citizens physically, intellectually, and academically, then the case for non-public education is greatly enhanced. The child-benefit theory has a great deal to say for all children of this nation. What is involved in aid to non-public schools is far greater than merely financial aid for textbooks, guidance services, and things of that nature. It is not a question of catering to minority groups. Rather, the issue truly concerns better education for all of society.

The child-benefit theory has significant implications for the private school educator concerning what his school is, what it should be, and how it serves. Every course that is given by the non-public school ought somehow to contribute to the making of a better America. The excellent teacher on the staff of a private school must find the way to use his talent for the benefit of all children. Every exceptional program under the auspices of a private school ought to add to the common store of good education.

STRENGTHENING ALL SCHOOLS

We Americans, who treasure the free enterprise system, like to say that competition makes for a better product. We treasure freedom of choice which allows us to select one product over another. The average citizen truly desires good education for youth. He may not know how to articulate his own thoughts on the matter, but the average American would probably welcome cooperation to achieve good education, once he understands that cooperation will strengthen all schools, and not weaken public education.

As public school administrators become aware of the potential of the private schools in their area, and as private schools begin to know something about the problems of the school district in which they operate, there will emerge a much better spirit of cooperation and a oneness of purpose. This will make good civic planning far more possible. Shared facilities and shared time programs, which are now just on the cutting edge of new educational ventures, will undoubtedly become quite common. There is every reason to believe that the nation will see the wisdom of avoiding unnecessary duplication while it still cherishes the element of competition. The non-public school has something to contribute. It has now begun to see its way toward making that contribution.

"ALTERNATIVE SCHOOLS": CHALLENGE TO TRADITIONAL EDUCATION?*

Donald W. Robinson

Over 700 independent schools have been founded during the past three years, as teachers, parents, and students seek alternatives to the stultifying

---

* Reprinted from *Phi Delta Kappan* (March 1970), 51:374–375, by permission.

climate of so many public schools. Two or three new "alternative" schools are born every day, and every day one dies or gives up its freedom, claims Harvey Haber, founder of the New Schools Exchange.

In existence less than a year, the New Schools Exchange (2840 Hidden Valley Lane, Santa Barbara, Calif. 93103) describes itself as the only central resource and clearinghouse for all people involved in "alternatives in education." The exchange publishes a directory of experimental schools, acts as a placement bureau for teachers, and publishes a newsletter (29 issues to date, 2,000 subscribers, $10 per year).

The exchange provides a sense of community among radical educators. As one visitor recently expressed it, "The information that is moving through things like the *New Schools Exchange Newsletter* is primarily a feeling, and only incidentally a body of data. It's that Woodstock complex, a ritual magic to ward off the stunning desolation that sweeps across the land sometimes like a cold wind. But then feelings are very powerful. They can swell and topple empires."

These feelings constitute the fuel that is firing the revolution that manifests itself not alone in the New Schools movement, but equally in the student revolts and in the writings of such authors as Leonard, Kohl, Kozol, Holt, Herndon, and Glasser.

The feelings are of frustration and resentment because schools are so regimented, administration so unsympathetic, teachers so hamstrung, and learning climate so sterile.

The directory issued by the New Schools Exchange lists several hundred innovative schools and educational reform groups in 28 states, the District of Columbia, and Canada. The largest number, over 100, are in California. There is also a considerable concentration in New England. (The private schools springing up in the South are not experimental in the same sense!)

A similar directory is available (for $10) from the Teacher Drop-Out Center (University of Massachusetts, Amherst, Mass. 01002). This center is operated by two graduate students, Leonard Solo and Stan Barondes, who queried 400 reputedly innovative schools and published statements from 60 replies.

These replies reflect the spirit of the schools:

"We believe in the right of every individual to be free to experience the world around him in his own way."

"We encourage kids to live their own lives. Classes are not compulsory; self-government runs the school."

"We believe that in a loving, accepting environment in which emotional needs are met, children will feel free to grow; and that feeling free, they *will* grow, *will* follow their natural curiosity, *will* do whatever they find necessary to meet their needs."

More extreme is this statement from an Oregon school:

"Philosophy: A cross of Skinner and Neill and Leary and IWWW. The school is an integral part of a farm commune research organization crazy house. Prospectus and appropriate political material available."

Of course not all of the reform movement lies outside of the public schools, and several city systems are listed in the Drop-Out Center's directory of innovative situations. The statement submitted by John Bremer, director of Philadelphia's much-publicized Parkway Program ("School Without Walls"), includes this unconventional bit:

"It is true that we teach some unconventional subjects, but the study groups are mostly small, under 10 students, and the old ways of classroom teaching just do not make any sense. So students and faculty are redefining what we mean by teaching and learning. Our faculty members teach, but when they do, it is not in a classroom; it is in the city, in an office building, in City Hall, in the street, depending on what they are teaching."

Such statements exemplify the sentiments of Solo and Barondes, whose goal is "to identify the schools—elementary and secondary, public and private—that want the unusual teacher, the teacher who believes in letting students grow into individual, alive, and aware humans, the teacher who breathes controversy and innovation." Their second goal is to locate these unusual teachers and to serve (without charge) as a clearinghouse to bring innovative teachers and free schools together. They find that the number of eager teacher applicants far exceeds the school openings. The center receives eight to 10 letters a day from teachers wanting to move to a freer school.

Still another manifestation of the freedom movement is *The Teacher Paper*, a quarterly publication produced by high school English teacher Fred Staab, assisted by his wife and a volunteer staff. *The Teacher Paper*. (280 North Pacific Ave., Monmouth, Ore. 97361, $2 per year) exudes a tone of congeniality with the spirit of the new schools, though its constituency is essentially the corps of teachers who have elected to reform the public schools rather than desert them. Staab started his paper last year to provide a forum for teacher expression and to improve communication between teachers and the public. He feels that too much of the local communication about education is filtered through the administration and that even in national education journals the teacher's voice is much too muted. He claims his publication is neither anti-administration nor anti-establishment, only pro-teacher and pro-student. And indeed both the feature article in the December, 1969, issue titled "Bulletin Boards as a Guerilla[1] Tactic" and a foldout "Guerilla Manual" listing 162 disruptive tactics should provide a modern superintendent with more chuckles than scowls. Militant rhetoric has become part of the scene.

---

[1] Webster spells it "guerrilla," but "free school" people tend to apply the same standard to spelling that they apply to conduct: Do your own thing.

Staab predicts that the rapid growth of *The Teacher Paper* will continue and is seeking a part-time job so he can devote more time to making it grow. His present 1,200 subscribers in 30 states include roughly 900 teachers and 300 parents, two-thirds of them Oregonians. He is confident that circulation will expand because other journals lack style, seriousness, and bite and do not reflect teacher views.

These three voices of dissent, the New Schools Exchange, the Teacher Drop-Out Center, and *The Teacher Paper* are heralds of a protest movement that is gaining steam in its crusade to humanize education. (The founders and managers of all three are over 30.) While some educators are dedicated to extending the applications of computer assisted instruction and systems analysis, these teachers and parents are more concerned with humaneness, sensitivity, and freedom of the student to be a free, inquiring person, with human help from teachers.

The New Schools Exchange is beginning to attract attention. It has been visited by writers, foundation representatives, and government consultants, and dares to hope it may receive some grant money, while admitting that without additional support it cannot survive many more months.

Most representatives of recognized establishment groups admit that they know too little about the new schools to hazard an opinion. However, Cary Potter, director of the National Association of Independent Schools, recognizes them as one segment of the current wave of frustration with traditional education. "They represent a mixed bag," he says, "a terrific spectrum, out of which may come some useful ideas. Some of the black schools especially show something about independence which is good."

Perhaps the best opportunity to learn about the alternative schools movement is offered by the workshop conference the New Schools Exchange has planned for April 4 and 5 on a 1,200-acre ranch in Santa Barbara County, California. Director Haber invites inquiries.

Many of the conspicuous demands of the new school movement are being pushed in public schools also, but too slowly, too uncertainly to satisfy the mood of "action now." Some public schools are becoming ungraded, introducing sensitivity training, calling on parents and other adults to contribute their expertise as resource people, and even taking school completely out of the school building, as in the Philadelphia Parkway School already referred to.

One advocate of experimental schools has prepared a list of ways these "alternative schools" can relate to the public schools. The suggestions include: providing community resource specialists to supplement public school activity; giving creative parties for students from public schools; supporting radical students and teachers, if for no other reason than to let them know they are not alone, odd, insane, or whatever else the "system" might be trying to make them believe of themselves; organizing joint experimental school and public school student projects; offering student teachers practice teaching opportunities in experimental schools; and exchanging services of experimental school and public school teachers in after-hours activities.

The names of the new schools reflect the tone of the movement: Student Development Center, All Together New Free School, Alternative Foundation, School for Human Resources, Community Workshop School, Halcyon School, Involvement Education.

They represent a fairly wide spectrum of educational thought, with a heavy sprinkling of super-Summerhills. About half of them are inner-city schools. Haber estimates that approximately 80 percent are designed to accommodate students from pre-school through high school. Organization, curriculum, and financing vary widely. Some operate entirely on tuition, some rely wholly on other sources, and many combine the two.

Many of these new schools are not carefully planned; many do not survive. Haber estimates the average length of life of a new school at 18 months, after which it may die completely, merge with another school, or alter its course so severely as to cease to be a radically innovative institution.

The entire movement may prove ephemeral. But even if few alternative schools survive, the movement will have made its contribution to reform, much as third parties in our political history have forced the established parties to adopt social reforms.

STREET ACADEMIES: ONE STEP OFF THE SIDEWALK*

JONATHAN BLACK

Like so many large cities, New York is in the midst of educational ferment. The bitter teachers' strike of last year only underlined the terrible failure of formal education to reach the children of the ghetto. Those ghetto stu-

---

* Reprinted by permission from *Saturday Review* (November 15, 1969), pp. 88–89, 100–101. Copyright 1969 Saturday Review, Inc.

dents who do persist through the indignities and irrelevancies of the public school system generally end up with a fairly worthless scrap of paper—the general diploma. Those who graduate with an academic diploma may be scarred in subtler ways, with their imaginations blunted, their enthusiasm cauterized, and their hostilities toward the system aggravated beyond repair.

The imposition of decentralization from above has proved a decisive political failure in New York, and it may be some time before the experiment of community control can regain its momentum. But there is a dynamic decentralized school system sprouting from below, a string of storefront schools in three boroughs, that threatens to restructure the roots of education.

The idea of storefront schools is derived partially from economic and physical necessity, but more significantly from a belief in the critical relevance of education. Schools *should* be only a step off the sidewalk. Where the step between a community and its schools has widened into a chasm, it is crucial that that intimacy be restored. The ghetto school has only a fragile hold on its children, and if the realities of ghetto life are ignored, even that tenuous communication is lost.

Street academies are storefront schools. They are schools for high school dropouts. Each academy has from fifteen to thirty students, three teachers, and usually one street worker. The academy program envisions a three-step process: several months at a local street academy, additional time at a more formalized Academy of Transition, and finally "graduation" to either Newark or Harlem Prep (privately funded high schools, the latter a recent outgrowth of the academy system). But college education, although it may be the ultimate goal, is only one of the levels on which academy staffs operate. The genesis of the academy idea is in street work, putting together a dropout so he *wants* to get his high school diploma. The academies are built up from the kids, shaped by their needs. The street worker is not a seven-hour-a-day caseworker. He lives in the dropout's world, shares his sidewalk and his problems, and not infrequently ends up in night court with bail money. Eventually, if he is good, he may succeed in coaxing the kid to an academy where he can start picking up the pieces of his education.

There are now fourteen operating academies, eight in Harlem, the others elsewhere in Manhattan and Brooklyn. The style of one academy may differ substantially from the style of another. Sometimes this is dictated by the demands of the neighborhood, sometimes by financial expediency, and frequently by the individual preferences of the head teacher who still retains a high degree of autonomy in the academy system. At one of the Harlem storefronts, the teacher explains his line: "How do you get these kids to college? I tell 'em, dig me. You want money, you want to talk black power, you want to make it in the system? You gotta have that degree. These kids have to be hipped to a lot of stuff: the Jews, the Mafia, basketballs. Every cat bouncing a basketball around Harlem thinks he's gonna be a pro. Forget it!" Educational philosophy? "These cats are bored. Everyone's bored. You gotta excite 'em. You give them pride. You make them think black is worth something."

A typical social studies lesson in this academy was an informal rambling brew that slid over Vietnam, Biafra, the French Foreign Legion, the concept of civil war, capitalists in Texas, Indians in Mexico, drugs in Mexico, academy students in Mexico (a summer trip organized by this teacher), American imperialism, white imperialism, etc. When asked who sponsored this academy—each school is funded separately by a sponsoring corporation—the black teacher leaned over sheepishly and whispered under his mustache, "Chase Manhattan." Obviously, this teacher has a friend at Chase, but the freedom within this academy is apparently typical of a non-interference policy of all sponsoring corporations. And a little illogic is a small price to pay.

The tone of a Lower East Side academy is quite different. The school is housed temporarily in a church while its old building undergoes renovation. There is not much talk of black power, and the twenty students enrolled for the spring term are as mixed as the neighborhood. The head teacher here is white (about one-fifth of the forty-two academy teachers are white), and he puts great emphasis on revitalizing a formal curriculum. His style is more teacher than revolutionary. He believes in a deep personal involvement with his kids, but is skeptical about the practicality of the academy functioning as a full-time family surrogate. As in many individual academics, the effectiveness of this academy's program is difficult to evaluate. This is a transitional phase, and the academy as a fully funded, fully staffed unit is only beginning to gel. The entire academy program is still an experiment, still relatively small, still groping. Its potential is only beginning to be explored.

A Brooklyn academy, located in Bedford-Stuyvesant and sponsored by Union Carbide, exemplifies the program at its best. As in all the academies, the four or five rooms are a pleasant eyeful, crisply renovated by an imaginative group of young architects called Urban Deadline, sportily furnished and brightly painted—in pale lavender, sky blue, and lemon—with little resemblance to the fermented green of most school buildings. Posters clutter the walls, and partitioning creates a varied and exciting use of limited space. As in all the academies, there are people just lounging around. And there is a charge of excitement here. "It's just beautiful," says the street worker from the area. "These kids would be lost. Now they're working; they're back in school. They're worth something." Perhaps the most unlikely smile is spread all over a white face, an attorney from Union Carbide now working at the academy. Initially sent for a limited three-week training period, he now stops in at Carbide about once a week and spends most of his time teaching English at the school, taking kids to ball games, and bailing students out of jail.

Carbide has been more than cooperative. Beyond their basic contribution of $50,000, they have donated three cars, furniture, movie equipment, and an elaborate "wine and dine" affair with Carbide executives when students graduate from the academy. Carbide is considering setting up a completely black-owned factory in the area. And from Carbide's point of view, the association has been equally fruitful. They have a handy information laboratory to test out ideas and familiarize themselves with expansion into ghetto communities and a direct tap on a vast employment pool. IBM, which also sponsors a Harlem school, is as deeply involved with the operation of its academy, and other corporations, notably banks, are taking advantage of the job link for recruiting ghetto employees.

The history of the academy program has been brief, hectic, and explosive. It started seven years ago with a white street worker, Harv Oostdyk —himself a college dropout—and a suburban Christian movement called Young Life. The initial organizers simply picked up kids off the streets and organized a tutorial center for dropouts at the Church of the Master on Morningside Avenue, where the Reverend Eugene Callender was an enthusiastic sponsor. Ford Foundation money—$700,000 in grants—kept the program alive and growing. The academy was a going thing when Callender, appointed executive director of the Urban League of Greater New York in 1966, took the program under the aegis of the Urban League. Since then, the Urban Coalition has become involved, and through its contacts corporations now provide the lifeblood of funding—about $50,000 a year to operate each academy; Callender has left the Urban League; Oostdyk has left the academy; and the academy idea, boosted by the enthusiasm of New York Urban League Director Livingston Wingate, is being carried nationwide by the National Urban League.

In New York, a variety of expansion plans are under way. There is an informal goal of at least one academy in each of the city's five boroughs, and the possibility of twenty schools by the end of 1969. The role of the street worker is being explored, and an institute to train street workers may be set up soon. There is talk of either expanding Harlem Prep— seventy students graduated this year—or of developing an additional prep school fed by satellite street academies. A committee of sponsoring corporations has been formed and meets once a month to pool resources and evolve new strategies. And finally there are broad plans for meeting the continuing needs of academy students, in school and out, during studies and after graduation. "We're just beginning to look at the total needs of our kids," says Wingate. "We've guaranteed that they'll not only be picked out of the street, but sent through college."

One of the success signals of academy work has been a growing cooperation between storefront schools and the New York City Board of Education. Ordinarily, there is an informal relationship between academy staff and the high schools. Street workers may talk to students outside school, during lunch hours, in their homes, around the neighborhood. There is an obvious advantage, however, in establishing some liaison directly with the high school to facilitate contacting dropouts, present or future. A Rockefeller Foundation grant permitted the Urban League to set up a cadre of eighteen salaried street workers, assigned to be physically present in three high schools, Haaren, Brandeis, and Charles Evan Hughes. In Haaren, where the dropout rate averages 60 per cent, the principal, Bernard V. Deutchman, has been particularly pleased with the relation between his school and the McGraw-Hill Street Academy a few blocks away. Deutchman views the academy not only as a second chance for kids who are having trouble, but also as an invaluable laboratory, a training ground for "sensitizing" teachers to dropouts' problems. As the relation between Haaren and the academy develops, Deutchman envisions the academy being physically located within the school, offering credit courses, and serving as an alternative to those who for some reason or other cannot make it in the public school system.

This program touches a shared ideal among a number of disparate academy staff and consultants. The thought is that as the academy reaches its maximum utility as an educational model, and, as its methods are deemed successful, it will be incorporated into the city board of education. "You can't just tell the system what's wrong," explains Robert Rogers, acting head of the academy system. "You've got to show them."

There is no question that the academy can serve a vital role as a teacher-training ground. The first teacher to "return" to Haaren under Deutchman's program was bubbling with enthusiasm, and exchanges between the school and the academy will increase. The academy can serve as a school for both dropouts and teachers. There are problems, however. For one thing, although the teachers in the academy program are highly qualified in their work, some are not college graduates, few meet certification requirements, and probably only a handful have any interest in teaching in city schools. The methods of a number of academy staff probably would not be palatable to the board of education, and it is unlikely that the United Federation of Teachers would welcome the newcomers with much enthusiasm.

More fundamentally, however, the orientation of the academy program from its inception has been socio-psychological, demanding a twenty-four-hour-a-day commitment to its students. Much of the academy's success is undoubtedly attributable to its image as an *alternative* to public school education. It functions personally, tutorially, remedially. It has the

leisure and the dedication to explore education in the broadest of contexts—
the total life of its students. Ideally, this should be the function of a public
school education as well, but the danger of the academy's doubling back
into the school system is that this uniqueness and intense personal involvement may be lost.

A similar challenge faces the Urban League. One of the rare qualities
of the academy has been the extraordinary richness and diversity of persons
attracted to its programs, from black militants to white seminarians, from
corporate attorneys to ghetto junkies. Much of the energy and vitality
comes from this dialectic. Teachers learn and learners teach. The Urban
League provides an attractive umbrella organization to manage the academy
program and facilitate smooth and controlled expansion. But street academies have always sprung from grassroots concerns. Much of their success
is due to this "building up" process, institutions shaped by human needs,
the very opposite of a formal public school education. Academies have
remained diffuse, flexible, and relatively autonomous in operation. Con-
ceptually, the Urban League is not opposed to this orientation, but control from above threatens the decentralized richness of any such program.
The very success of the academy has undoubtedly made such an institutionalization inevitable, but established organizations, wary of a public image,
have a sluggish dynamic of their own and sometimes a gluttonous politic.
So far, frictions have been minor, but there are pitfalls to be aware of.
Similarly, the growing involvement of the sponsoring corporations must
be continually probed, lest the academies become just another item in a
corporate publicity brochure.

As the academies develop, these questions must be faced. And they
must be faced with a courage and a confidence in the concept of storefront
schools, because the educational system needs the academy desperately.

THE UNKNOWN GOOD: EDUCATION VOUCHERS*

ROBERT J. HAVIGHURST

> Now all the Athenians and the strangers sojourning there spent their time in nothing else, but either to tell or to hear some new thing.
> And Paul stood in the midst of the Areopagus and said, "Ye men of Athens, in all things I perceive ye are very religious. For as I passed along, and observed the objects of your worship, I found also an altar with this inscription: TO AN UNKNOWN GOD. What therefore ye worship in ignorance, this I set forth unto you." Acts 17:21–23.

The similarities of contemporary America and the Athens of St. Paul's day have been remarked before. One of the more engaging characteristics of both societies is their openness to new ideas. In the U. S., we like to "tell or to hear some new thing," and we also have the money to go a step further—to try out new things.

In our present state of urban malaise, we find ourselves discontented with most of our social institutions, including our schools. Some people are concerned about the poor reading and arithmetic and speaking of the children of our urban slums. Others complain about the schools in the middle-class sections of metropolitan areas, charging that the boys and girls are being regimented into a faceless conformity to materialistic values.

With the ranks of the discontented being recruited from such diverse quarters, the educational Establishment finds itself caught in the middle, pushed from different directions to make basic school reforms. Furthermore, the Establishment cannot weaken its already difficult position by saying that the public expects too much of the schools—at least half of what the child learns and more than half of his attitude toward learning come from the home. However true this may be, the educators *have to* claim that the school system is *very* important, and they *have to* claim that

---

* Reprinted from *Phi Delta Kappan* (September 1970), 52:52–53, by permission.

the schools can do *much more* than they are now doing for disadvantaged children.

While the educational Establishment slogs along, trying to do things a little better here and a little better there, the critics and the discontented demand drastic reforms. This is fertile soil for the idea of giving parents public money to find better schools for their children. Thus the current discussion of voucher schemes gets a start; it is amplified by the readiness of the American public to listen to new ideas.

Within a very short space of time, the voucher idea has proliferated into several quite different proposals for practice. Carr and Hayward[1] have described and criticized five different voucher schemes—those of Milton Friedman, Theodore Sizer and Phillip Whitten, Henry Levin, James S. Coleman, and Christopher Jencks.

The "free-market" proposal of Friedman would provide every child with a flat grant or tax credit which his family could use to pay tuition at the school of its choice. The public schools would continue to exist and would charge tuition equal to the amount of the grant. But private schools would be in a good position to compete with public schools, since they would get the same amount of public money per pupil as the public schools. Thus, it is argued by Friedman and others, the quality of education would be improved by removing it from its present status as a near-monopoly of the public schools and subjecting it to the competition of the free market.

But a critical look at this unregulated free-market proposal has led to something like the following judgment:[2]

> . . . an unregulated market would redistribute resources away from the poor and toward the rich, would increase economic segregation in the schools, and would exacerbate the problems of existing public schools without offering them any offsetting advantages. For these reasons we think it would be worse than the present system of public schools.

This quotation comes from the report of a team headed by Christopher Jencks which was supported by a grant from the U.S. Office of Economic Opportunity. This report is a model of careful and critical analysis of a variety of voucher proposals. It starts with the proposition that public money might well be used to support a *variety* of schools, but this has not been done in the United States. "As a result, we have almost

---

[1] Ray A. Carr and Gerald C. Hayward, "Education by Chit: An Examination of Voucher Proposals," *Education and Urban Society*, February, 1970, pp. 179–91.

[2] Center for the Study of Public Policy, *Financing Education by Grants to Parents. A Preliminary Report.* Cambridge, Mass.: The Center, 56 Boylston St., March, 1970.

no evidence on which to judge the merit of Adam Smith's basic principle—namely, that if all parents are given the chance, they will look after their children's interests more effectively than will the state." It concludes with a proposal for a voucher system that, they contend, "would make it possible for parents to translate their concern for their children's education into action. If they did not like the education their child was getting in one school (or if the child did not like it), he could go to another. By fostering both active parental interest and educational variety, a voucher system should improve all participating schools, both public and private."

The Jencks report proceeds with an exhaustive analysis of "seven alternative economic models," which include the five analyzed by Carr and Hayward. It comes out in favor of the "regulated compensatory model" summarized by Jencks in the *New Republic* article reprinted in this *Kappan*.

This would require a school that participates in the program to accept at least as high a proportion of black or other minority group students as had applied, and to fill at least half of its places by a lottery among applicants. It would also give a higher-value voucher to low-income children than to middle- and higher-income children.

The program would be sponsored and supervised by an Educational Voucher Agency (EVA), which would act like a school board in some respects and might conceivably be an arm of a local public school board.

Now, with this proposal before it, the Office of Economic Opportunity will presumably try to locate several communities that will set up EVAs to organize voucher plans supported by public funds for a major experiment, which should continue for a minimum of five years, and preferably for eight years.

The proposal assumes that about one-sixth of the families would choose privately controlled voucher schools under the ground rules that are proposed. This 16% compares with the estimate this writer has frequently made, that no more than 20% of American parents would bypass the nearest school in sending their children to school, given some freedom of choice. An experiment that included as many as 15% of children from a socioeconomic and racial cross-section of society would be impressive. This writer hopes it will come about.

Thus the *unknown good* about which there has been so much interesting discussion would be explored and would become known. Is there in America a modern Athens to take this challenge seriously?

Chapter 12

TEACHERS AND TECHNOLOGY
FOR THE CHANGING CURRICULUM

Each expansion of the use of technology in education has been accompanied by the quandary as to its effects on teachers' roles and even their jobs. Yet, despite radio, television, a host of audiovisuals, and today the computer, teachers continue to have significant roles and the number employed continues to increase. The persistent problem, however, is one of role definition as new curriculum and instructional developments involve an increasing sophistication in the use of technology. Chapter 12 presents several selections relevant to this problem.

One of the recently most publicized and debated developments in teaching is differentiated staffing, which classifies those involved in teaching according to their different roles. This practice is generally related to a plan of curriculum and instruction that utilizes a variety of organizational and technological facilities. The article by Fenwick English deals with various "Questions and Answers on Differentiated Staffing" and highlights the Temple City, California, plan of which English was director. In this writer's judgment, differentiated staffing is primarily justified by its provisions for separation of professional and nonprofessional tasks; on this score note Temple's argument: "The use of auxiliary personnel will relieve teachers of many of the nonprofessional tasks that now consume much of their time and energy and will permit them to concentrate on the instructional program."

Dwight W. Allen's paper for a conference on "Humanizing the Secondary School" related curriculum, instruction, and technology in a comprehensive proposal for "A Technology and Performance Curriculum." As indicated in the editor's introduction to the conference report, Allen argued strongly that educators should "seek to shape the development of technologies to anticipate educational needs" rather than refusing to accept or remain indifferent and disengaged toward technology. His discussion of specific uses of technology in scheduling, individualizing instruction, differentiating staffing, and performance criteria is provocative. Teachers who read the selection and consider the applicability of Allen's proposals may well ponder whether his model can be introduced piecemeal or whether the entire plan must be adopted at once. Obviously many schools have tried to do one without the other, and perhaps with some success. However, cases are known in which computer-made schedules have created independent study time but not individualized instruction, and in which differentiated staffs still use content rather than performance objectives, with little individualization. How can a high school move to change its entire system to such an operation as Allen proposes? Should it?

The selection from the *Survey of Computing Activities in Secondary Schools* confirms our earlier point that technology alone or any other group of organizational and facilitating changes does not within itself produce change in curriculum and instruction. For example, Darby, Korotkin, and Romashko conclude that "merely introducing computers into a school does not automatically cause innovation to take place." They also concluded that "the computer is more frequently used as a *tool* in instruction rather than as the *object* of instruction." Among the controversies they commented upon with reference to the instructional use of the computer are: the mode of use—informal or formal; whether the computer must be actually within the school; merits of small versus large computers; the type of computer language to be used; and, especially, the funding of computer use. Among interesting questions raised by this survey for possible discussion and further study is the motivational impact of the computer: Why is the computer so

effective in motivating students? For example, the authors reported that
"teachers mentioned that some students get so involved with computers
that they neglect their other courses." What is the attraction, and can
it be utilized for other purposes? Another question relates to the survey
finding of "the dominance of computer applications by the mathematics
curriculum" and the subsequent suggestion of training programs
designed to encourage computer use among teachers in other curriculum
areas: What applications would be desirable in other areas, and how
could their teachers be interested in computer training?

A very significant and innovative use of the computer in curriculum
planning developed by Robert S. Harnack and others at the State
University of New York at Buffalo is reported in the excerpt from
"Computer-Based Resource Units—An Overview" selected for inclusion
here from the complete report of a Title III, ESEA project directed by
Harnack. This project, and the innovation it involved, is based on the
marriage of a much earlier, now almost traditional practice in curriculum
planning—the resource unit—with today's dominant technological tool—
the computer. Harnack and his associates devised a plan whereby a
characteristic barrier to effective development and use of the unit approach
in teaching—its time-consuming planning—could be minimized through
use of the computer. As the report documents, the unit approach
itself has been long and widely espoused and much used—but not used
enough, since it is agreed with Harnack that there is not known any
"pertinent statement which refutes the unit approach concept, degrades
its usage, or speaks ill of its potential for efficient learning."

The technical procedures involved in computer-based resource unit
planning are fully described and the research thereon fully reported
in the complete report from which the selection is taken, and in
other articles and studies by Harnack and his associates. Enough of the
general rationale as to teacher functions and computer functions and the
objectives and design of the project are included here to help the reader
understand the general nature of the process. Note that it involved
the development, coding, and programming of specific resource units, so
that a teacher having access to the computer-stored units can by
identifying his objectives and the characteristics of his pupils receive
from the computer a content outline, suggested large group activities,
small group activities, instructional materials, measuring devices, and also,

with proper imput as to learning objectives and individual pupil characteristics, "suitable instructional material and individual activities for each student, per each objective chosen." The excerpt also includes the authors' views as to implications of their study for further utilization of computer-based curriculum planning in teaching and in research. Elsewhere in the report they suggest a national network of computers which would, they state, "probably promote more diversity in the curriculum than it will promote similarity." Indeed they state that "tomorrow's teacher will have tremendous planning help because of the recorded teaching-learning suggestions from all other teachers, to say nothing of the suggestions of instructional materials at his disposal—literally, the resources of the world." What are your reactions?

QUESTIONS AND ANSWERS ON DIFFERENTIATED STAFFING*

Fenwick English

As many pioneering school districts around the country are trying differentiated staffing, a variety of approaches to differentiation have developed. The models vary according to basic staff structure and the philosophy of the different schools and districts. My answers to the questions below are a reflection of the philosophical position of one district, the Temple City (California) Unified School District, and its teachers; they do not necessarily reflect professional consensus.

The Temple City plan, the result of an 18-month study by the staff and administration financed by the Charles F. Kettering Foundation, went into effect at two Temple City schools last year.

What does differentiated staffing mean? Is there one definition?

To differentiate a teaching staff means to separate by different roles. There is no set definition of a differentiated staff, since at this time many models, with a variety of bases, are being proposed, developed, and tried.

What is the purpose of differentiated staffing?

The basic purpose of differentiated staffing is to provide a more individualized program. Differentiated staffing makes it possible to make maximum use of teacher talent. Although all teachers are not equal, the tendency has been to pretend that they are—to say, "A teacher is a teacher." Organizationally, this has led to inefficiency in using human resources. Differentiated staffing corrects this by assigning teachers on the basis of matching their various combinations and degrees of talent to children's needs.

Differentiated staffing serves a further purpose by creating an organizational incentive system that makes teaching a career and permits teachers to advance as *teachers* rather than having to move out of teaching into administration in order to progress.

* Reprinted from *Today's Education* (March 1969) 57:53–54, by permission.

What are the essential ingredients of a plan for a differentiated staff?
These may vary for different models. The Temple City plan is based
on the following principles:

1. Differentiated staffing is a means of producing more relevant student learning.
2. Teaching must be the primary function of all teachers.
3. Teachers must become formal professional partners with administrators in the decision-making process.
4. Teachers must be relieved of many nonprofessional functions now required of them.
5. Teachers must perform the self-disciplining or regulating activities of their own profession.
6. Organizational flexibility must be created through the use of flexible scheduling.
7. New kinds of teacher in-service and preservice programs need to be developed to prepare teachers to be able to function in different roles.
8. The advanced positions in the teacher hierarchy are service rather than supervisory positions.
9. Some teachers should earn more than school administrators.

Can roles be differentiated? Vertically? Horizontally?

Teaching roles can be differentiated just as other professional roles
can be. Teachers are already familiar with a number of means of differentiation. Most of these bring about vertical differentiation, using additional responsibilities as the basis for upgrading assignments. This kind of
differentiation may be in the form of extended contractual periods or of
extra pay for such services as developing curriculums, acting as leader of
a teaching team, or performing a special function, like coaching football
or directing the band.

How will levels of competence and responsibility be determined?

The first step is to develop a set of generic models that separate
teacher roles. These models can then be tailored to the needs of individual
schools by the teachers, who are the best judges of what services are
relevant to their problems. If the advanced roles are being created in order
to help classroom teachers upgrade their teaching, the teachers should be
the ones to say what help they need.

Who will evaluate the various levels of competence?

Evaluation is a professional responsibility and should be practiced
by the professional teacher. Competence is measured in terms of the degree
to which the staff receives the services it has determined it needs.

Some will question whether good teacher relationships can prevail
when teachers evaluate each other. The Temple City plan, however,
assumes the responsibility of teachers, as competent, mature adults, to
engage in appraisal of each other.

Will differentiated staffing help teachers to do a better job?

Yes, if teachers have defined the help they need to do a better job, and if they are actually involved in the selection, evaluation, and retention of their colleagues. A differentiated staff will help create organizational self-renewal, for teachers in their new roles will feed into each school a steady stream of promising new ideas and practices to improve the quality of the instructional program. The use of auxiliary personnel will relieve teachers of many of the nonprofessional tasks that now consume much of their time and energy and will permit them to concentrate on the instructional program.

Will it merely introduce a new administrative level?

Not if teaching remains the prime function and if *all* personnel have regular teaching responsibilities. A differentiated staff in which differentiation is based on additional responsibilities cannot very well be superimposed upon the traditional school structure where teachers are with children all day long. Some type of flexible scheduling will allow all teachers to have regular teaching duties and will permit those with additional responsibilities to meet with more children than at the present time. In this way, the talents of teachers are expanded rather than reduced as they advance. Teachers are not promoted away from children.

Where is it being tried? What models exist?

Prototypes of differentiated staffing have existed for some time. Most early models have used additional duties as the method of separating teacher roles beyond the staff level. The models being developed now are more sophisticated and more formal, in that they involve a teacher hierarchy. As the profession gives more attention and thought to staff differentiation, far-reaching and perhaps more creative models will be conceptualized.

One model recently proposed by Bernard McKenna utilizes a five-level learning-task hierarchy, and identifies the teacher technologist; the liberal enlightener (analyzer of areas of knowledge considered important by the general population); the identifier of talents; the developer of talents; and the facilitator of attitude and interpersonal behavior development.

In another proposal, a daring and provocative one, James Hall conceives of a differentiated staff as an exemplar of ethnic balance and harmony for students to emulate.

Dwight W. Allen, dean of the School of Education at the University of Massachusetts, has proposed a model in which the teaching staff is divided into four levels of responsibility, as well as one in which separate schools would be organized vertically around a subject or discipline. Students would transfer from one school to another during the school day for various types of in-depth learning experiences. Teaching responsibilities would be delineated for each discipline within each school.

How can models for differentiated staffing be evaluated?

Differentiated staffing is not an end in itself but a means of improving learning, so the best way to evaluate a model is through the development of curriculums that can be measured in student outcomes. In the meanwhile, because schools cannot wait until this task is finished (if it could ever be considered finished), alternative models can be compared with each other. It can be assumed that any model that allows teacher talents and time to be used more effectively enhances learning, since the teacher is the key facilitator of the learning process.

What are the colleges doing about preparing teachers for differentiated staffing?

Few teacher preparatory institutions are graduating candidates who understand how to teach in a flexible school requiring team teaching, how to use auxiliary personnel effectively and delegate responsibilities to them, and how to engage in colleague evaluation or organizational decision making. Most colleges are still producing graduates who can function only in the traditional organizational patterns.

New training programs need to be initiated not only for teachers, but for school administrators as well. Differentiated staffing implies decentralized decision making; it removes the administrator from many unilateral decision-making situations and places him in a group-centered collegial environment. Traditional schools of administration with their accent on conventional organizational theory, which considers authority as the central criterion of controlling and motivating people, must retool with a more modern theory that is in harmony with the desire of teachers to be formally included in the decision-making process, and to be considered as mature, competent professionals.

A TECHNOLOGY AND PERFORMANCE CURRICULUM*

Dwight W. Allen

Dwight W. Allen discusses alternative strategies for educators in their attitudes toward using a wide range of technologies in education. They can:

1. Refuse to accept the technologies under a presumption that they are an unorthodox encroachment on the humaneness of American education;
2. Remain indifferent and disengaged until the technologies are perfected; or
3. Seek to shape the development of technologies to anticipate educational needs.

A strong argument is made for the latter of the three alternatives. The paper goes on to discuss specific uses of technology in:

1. Scheduling to provide teachers and students with a greater range of alternatives for educational decision making
2. Individualizing instruction by providing appropriate instructional content, opportunities for learning experiences, materials, resources laboratories, and teacher-pupil interaction
3. Rethinking and redefining the role of teachers by recognizing different levels of performance and differentiating the responsibilities of teaching
4. Establishing performance criteria as a basis for developing more

* Reprinted from *Humanizing the Secondary School*, Norman K. Hamilton and J. Galen Saylor, editors (Washington, D.C.: Association for Supervision and Curriculum Development, 1969), pp. 79–88. Reprinted with permission of the Association for Supervision and Curriculum Development and Dwight W. Allen. Copyright © 1969 by the Association for Supervision and Curriculum Development.

precisely identified measurement tools for student achievement of the broad instructional objectives of the school.

The paper is concluded with the proposition that "unless secondary schools meet the challenge posed by curricula based on performance and not just innovation, the danger is that such schools will cease to serve adequately the society whose future citizens it is their responsibility to educate."—N.K.H.

American culture is organized around active mastery rather than passive acceptance. Its peculiar genius in the external world is manipulative rather than contemplative. And although our contemporary society marvels at and prizes creativity and those who have its gift, we reserve our greatest admiration for the glories of mass production.

The resolution of this conflict between the more humane and liberalizing pursuits of man, which free him from ignorance, fear, prejudice, and pettiness, and the so-called dehumanizing aspects of automation, which impersonally organize more of his waking hours, is now education's crucial concern. Educators have to deal with both quality and increasing quantity; not merely with man's production, but with the production of men who are free to create new images of freedom. The present condition in education argues against such freedom.

Students are now bound to the arbitrary masters of time, control, and supervision. We have channeled students into archaic mazes that contract rather than expand their individual freedom and consequently their initiative and potential for creativity.

The beauty of the technologies now available in education is that they can do for educators what, because of insufficient time and money, the educators cannot do for themselves. Technologies can do for students what the students cannot do for themselves by giving them the freedom to choose and new alternatives to choose from.

Among the democratic ancients only the free men and citizens were permitted to pursue the higher arts. Now, at least theoretically, all have the choice to pursue liberal arts. Yet the paradox is that the process of education has been enslaved to the system by which it is transmitted, a structure outmoded by a least five decades.

Various technologies can free students from the arbitrariness, routineness, similarity, and monotony of unbroken hour-long instruction.

THREE STRATEGIES TOWARD USE OF TECHNOLOGIES

We can assume three strategies or attitudes toward the use of a wide range of technologies in education:

1. We can refuse to accept the technologies under the presumption that they are an unorthodox encroachment on the humaneness of American education;
2. We can remain indifferent and disengaged until the technologies are perfected; or
3. We can seek to shape the development of technology to anticipate educational needs.

Historically, a patient, conservative, and hesitant attitude toward technology has characterized educational policy.

The danger of refusing to accept technology means that we must wait until a given technology has thoroughly proven itself in every other discipline and enterprise before applying it to education. If, on the other hand, we anticipate the potential of technology in our schools, the advantages are not only earlier use but, more important, that educators have the initiative in developing the *direction* of technology. The advantage of shaping the technology, of determining the methods by which it can best be used, of deciding how it will best be used, will ensure that education will not be subject to the decisions made by others, but that it can take the initiative in shaping, not in being subject to, or shaped by technology.

To limit the uses of technology to the mechanics of education— scheduling, report cards, or personnel records—is to neglect the more imaginative development of the technology in relation to the learning process. *Educators must take the lead in developing the technology to humanize mass education.* We must find means to individualize instruction more effectively, to continually reexamine and revise the curriculum, to synthesize common and overlapping disciplines.

The computer is an example of a complex technological tool used in education. What are some of its uses? One of the most advanced applications to education is a system that develops computer generated master schedules. The Stanford School Scheduling System, developed by Robert Oakford, has been recently planned in the public domain. Educational Coordinates in Palo Alto, California, the largest user itself, scheduled more than 100 schools, double the number of schools scheduled two years previously by the Stanford group totally.

A computer-generated flexible schedule provides teachers and students with a greater range of alternatives for educational decision making. Students freed from significant portions of classroom sessions have greater opportunities to:

1. Meet in individual conferences with teachers (at Marshall High School in Portland, Oregon, a recent survey showed that each teacher spent an average of three hours and twenty-five minutes a week in student conferencing);

2. Go to a resource center to pursue a project independently or under the direction of a teacher;
3. Go to an open laboratory and remain as long as necessary to finish an experiment or reach a conclusion;
4. Confer with others in an open classroom on a joint assignment.

Teachers, structured less, can meet with individuals for longer periods to adjust to individual needs, and have more time to prepare instruction. Students, structured less into classroom patterns, can choose from among the entire school's resources, including a wider range of teachers.

INDIVIDUALIZING INSTRUCTION

The majority of secondary schools are not oriented to individualizing instruction, though all would claim to be. Students act and react collectively. The teacher may be the only real learner in the high school because he is often the only real *active agent*. Because of organizational structures, groups of students must conform to patterned procedures so that, at least ostensibly, the majority can benefit. Students, as a result, must be passive in relation to the learning activity of the teacher. Nor are materials in the school established to accommodate the individual, but to accommodate the time blocks that regulate the day's pattern, the staff, and all the students. The system is an administrative convenience.

What kind of opportunities for humane, individual experience does the school provide for a student who lacks an adequate reading background? Most commonly the school structures him into a remedial reading course which he often finds as defeating as any other course because he still must compete for grades when he really lacks the training and encouragement necessary for real advancement. The argument is not with the tremendous current efforts of teachers but with the inflexible structure of the system. A remedial reading student in his remedial reading course still carries around his reading handicap with him to all his other classes. How do we justify our actions as humane? How can we say we are freeing the student from his deficiency? The curriculum is not designed around the individual's needs. We only make the curriculum cumulative by adding on course after course to "enrich" or to compensate for gaps in the already overburdened structure.

Variation in interest and ability is related to both length of time and availability and accessibility of materials and instructional aids. If the length of time a student takes to learn a specific skill is irrelevant to learning it, neither does it make much sense that a student is unable to have access to shops or laboratories for experiment and for independent and individual study. Unless shops and laboratories are open most of the school day, students will not be able to use them to optimum advantage. Although the availability of shops and laboratories does not in itself create a course design based on performance, it is clear that student interest will be stimulated because the student can work at his own speed and during his own time. This is but one example of how organizational variables preempt performance and the individualization of instruction.

It is imperative that the structure of the school not be anti-individual. If the concept of human development is important to our thinking, if it is urgent that people not be lost in process, then each student's integrity, uniqueness, and at least partial self-determination must be recognized in the educational program. Students themselves must be responsible for certain levels of decision in their education.

One method of individualizing the instruction is to let achievement, not time spent in class, be the criterion for educational progress. If educators can recognize and provide for new levels of individualization within the school program, then students can realize the continuous development of responsibility so essential to human growth.

The concept of individual instruction does not mean necessarily that the teacher must deal with students one at a time. It does mean that presentation and choice of materials for the individual student should be appropriate for him at that time. The goal of individualization is an appropriate instructional content for each student. If a basic and common presentation is given to all students, some are immediately ready for the next presentation, some need individual and independent study, some need additional presentations, and some need discussion of the material in a group situation. The problem here is to identify which individuals are ready for which of a series of alternatives and to provide them with that appropriate series. Some might need repetition; some, elaboration; some, a presentation of the same material from a different viewpoint or perspective.

The unfortunate organizational restraints of many current administrative arrangements have prevented us from gaining any real perspective on individualized instruction. Providing more varied instructional groupings—larger and smaller classes, longer and shorter classes, meetings of varied frequency—suggests wider ranges of alternatives which will allow for individualized instruction. Individualization can be stimulated within the formal classroom or it may take place as one phase of laboratory instruction. It can be developed by efficient grouping practices for either short or long terms. Classroom facilities can be utilized on an individual basis with the requisition of unused spaces for individual and independent study or for formal or informal small groups which are also particularly adaptable to this type of instruction. Resource centers may be planned specifically for individual study in a given subject with individual carrels and technical centers for such activities as programmed learning or linguistic practice.

The emphasis on individualization of materials and independent study as a basic format of instruction assumes facilities and organizational alternatives not commonly provided at present. There is a need to develop new concepts to individualize and humanize the high school, and the progress of this development will depend largely on our ability to identify and adapt technologies.

ROLE OF THE TEACHER

Another issue at stake in humanizing the high school is rethinking and redefining the role of the teacher. The present state of the profession has not changed dramatically in the twentieth century. Since the skills which a teacher uses are largely the same for all teachers of a particular subject and for a given grade-grouping level, the job of preparing a beginning teacher has been an enormous and, considering all aspects of the job of teaching, unrealistic task for teacher education institutions.

A recent study of the present characteristics of teachers in California[1] revealed that the general dissatisfaction with professional limits and conditions is at least as important as, if not more important than, salary as a cause of teachers' moving out of the profession.

The requisite step, toward individualizing teaching and recognizing different levels of performance, is to differentiate dramatically the responsibilities of teaching. There is a wide variety of ways in which to arrange a differentiated staff. One way is now under development at Temple City in greater Los Angeles. Administrators and teachers in the Temple City School District are involved in a study to determine the specific roles of the differentiated teaching staff, the roles of administrators, the objectives and responsibilities of incumbents of each of the varying levels of responsibility. Task forces are already at work on the legal implications, communications, and finances. A salary schedule has been adopted by the board of education which provides for a maximum teacher salary higher than that of the superintendent. One school in the district has already implemented the differentiated staff plan.

The educational system must be reanalyzed to allow new alternatives of staff use—alternatives which technology can enhance; alternatives which lead to a more humane use of staff resources and their interaction with and utilization by students.

---

[1] Robert J. Addington. "Sampling Techniques for Administrative Decision Making in Education." Unpublished thesis. Los Angeles: University of Southern California, 1965.

PERFORMANCE CRITERIA

But whatever other concerns we have, our preoccupation must ultimately be with student performance. Performance is the execution of the functions required of a person, the exhibition of a skill. A criterion is the standard of judging, the measure or test of a thing's quality. Establishing performance criteria for secondary schools is not necessarily just a curriculum problem but a problem of determining objectives and of establishing human appreciations.

Present methods of evaluation leave unanswered questions about a student's learning development. How do secondary schools measure, besides the learning of the *content* of a course, a student's social development? What about his increasing ability to learn? What is the standard of value for measuring this elusive quality? How do secondary schools measure a student's ability to make decisions—one of the most important functions of a civilized man? To define his immediate and future goals? Are not all these special qualities a part of the integrated pattern of educational objectives?

It is likely that secondary schools will in the future continue to place emphasis on what the student knows in any given subject area and will test him accordingly. And tests will largely determine his placement. Hopefully, such tests will seek to gauge performance. Actually, tests now tend to be obstacles along an educational track. If too many pupils fail, we lower the barrier. It is irrelevant to ask whether a test is easy or hard if its purpose is the accomplishment of an educational objective. Yet students now speak of tests as easy or hard, which reveals to what extent our objectives perhaps follow the line of least resistance. Moreover, schools need tests which determine the limits of achievement and which set the floor, not the ceiling, of the understanding of chemistry, of English, or of government.

The irony is that even as we become more expert in the development of factual transmittal—more successful in teaching students more information which they may learn better—our need to do so, in fact, may be decreasing sharply.

One way in which technology may ultimately serve to summarize education is to make factual material so accessible, so external to human memory—through computer data banks, electronic retrieval and analytical systems—as to reduce the premium on human knowledge in all but the highest of conceptual levels, even as mechanical and electronic calculators have eliminated the intellectual premium on mental arithmetic. We must take care lest we solve well the wrong problem.

As I see it, current widely accepted educational objectives may not identify the most relevant student performance. A syllabus, a curriculum guide, a stated bit of philosophy governing, supposedly, the "game of school," are the creatures of administrators and teachers—not of students. Proceeding from premises with which students are often unfamiliar, the teacher attempts to evaluate student performance using low level factual abstractions of unspecified objectives within a course. The result is unsatisfactory from almost any point of view, though admittedly most easily measured, sorting students into piles of relative "success."

Lewis Carroll in *Alice in Wonderland* depicts a scene startlingly simple and yet profound in its simplicity. Alice, in her journeys through Wonderland, came to a fork in the road. She asked the smiling Cheshire cat, perched on a limb in a nearby tree, which way she should go. "That depends," the Cheshire cat replied, "on where you're going." Where we are going in education might not have, in actuality, any pertinence to what we are presently doing.

It is difficult to overestimate the importance of formulating clearly stated objectives. An instructional objective should specify under what conditions and to what extent performance will take place. For example, "A student will be able to write a paragraph in English with two or less syntax errors in every 300 words." We must replace something called "three years of French or German" with criteria of some measurable degree of fluency in French or German.

As performance criteria are more precisely identified, present practices of evaluation become less tenable. Transcripts which reflect standards of performance frozen in arbitrary time units are often actively misleading. Subsequent modifications in performance are certainly relevant in judging student competence. One alternative is to consider a transcript record as temporary—reflecting a current learning status—but subject to revision without prejudice. It would be interesting to compare predictions of future success based on updated transcript records as contrasted with traditional fixed records.

The barriers to performance are fractured and conditional verities. What is true for a student in history is not true for him in mathematics. But it might be next year. The truth upon which schools operate is segmented according to time and, therefore, is conditioned and determined by the very fluidity of its foundation. Something more accurate and functional is needed.

In our curriculum development, how do we "grade" a student's ability to cross-transfer his knowledge from subject to subject? Is his knowledge an embodiment that can be transferred from place to place as though it were corporeal; or is it rather like a seed that can be sprouted anew in a different climate and under different conditions?

In vocational education, performance criteria have been delineated better than in other subject areas in the high school. Each instructor attempts to differentiate within his vocational course according to the individual abilities of his students and their performances. The standard progress-chart reports of the vocational shop teachers represent a significant effort to individualize instruction according to performance, which is what future employers demand. Yet, the blocks of time in most secondary schools encourage teachers to set the tasks in a pattern of time uniformity. This allows the average student to finish the allotted task only in the time prescribed. The better student finishes in less time and the slower student perhaps never finishes.

The Center for the Study of Instruction, established by the National Education Association, in its publication, *Schools for the Sixties*, makes several relevant recommendations. One recommendation is particularly significant here:

> The vertical organization of the school should provide for the continuous, unbroken, upward progression of all learners, with due recognition of the wide variability among them in every respect of their development. The school organization should, therefore, provide for differentiated rate and mean of progression toward achievement of educational goals. Nongrading and multigrading are promising alternatives to the traditional graded school and should receive careful consideration.[2]

Performance criteria will change within a historical context. Unless secondary schools meet the challenge posed by curricula based on performance and not just innovation, the danger is that such schools will cease to serve adequately the society whose future citizens it is their responsibility to educate. Automation and the resources of technology will bring with them not so much less production as they will more leisure. As educators and free men, we will be less structured by employment and occupation. We will be able to portion out less time to business and to "busyness" and more to speculation and the patient pursuits of wisdom and their applicability in an industrialized world.

If we can direct the role of technology in education and if we can match the performance of our students with the needs of society, we can spend less time, paradoxically, on power and more on potential; less time on consumption and more on education; less on learning and more on being human.

---

[2] Project on the Instructional Program of the Public Schools. *Schools for the Sixties*. New York: McGraw-Hill Book Company, Inc., 1963. p. 78. Used by permission.

SURVEY OF COMPUTING ACTIVITIES IN SECONDARY SCHOOLS*

Charles A. Darby, Jr.
Arthur L. Korotkin
Tania Romashko

CONCLUSIONS

Extent of Administrative and Instructional Applications

From the 12,396 responses received from the 23,033 secondary schools in the continental United States, it can be concluded that more schools are not using computers than are. The ratio of nonusers to users is roughly 2 to 1. Among those schools that are using computers, administrative applications dominate. This domination of administrative over instructional use is of an approximate 2½ to 1 ratio. Although no other survey of this nature and scope has ever been performed, some previous studies provide a rough estimate of instructional use of computers in secondary schools. Comparison of the present survey with these earlier studies indicates that instructional use of computers is growing rapidly in the secondary schools in the United States. In order to chart this growth, future surveys are necessary to provide additional data points. A set of computer use indicators, similar to the economic indicators used by government, might be developed to chart computer use. Educational planners at all levels would find such information quite useful.

* This material is the Conclusions Section of the Final Report, "Survey of Computing Activities in Secondary Schools," October 1970, prepared by the American Institutes for Research under contract (Contract No. NSF-C584) for the National Science Foundation. The material reprinted here remains in the public domain.

435

Degree of Administrative and Instructional Use among Computer Users

Although the number of schools using computers is still in the minority, the degree of computer use in these schools is quite high. There is, of course, wide variation in the degree of use among these schools. However, indicants, such as number of computers used, number of applications, number of students involved, amount of computer time used, and frequency of use show a fairly high degree of computer use.

Nature and Purpose of Instructional Use

At the same time, the diversity of applications and subject areas in which computers are being used instructionally is not at the same high level on the average. Problem solving and EDP skills training applications dominate instructional use of computers in secondary schools. EDP skills training is of two types. Some EDP skills training is provided to students in preparation for entering a career in the computer field. More frequently, EDP skills training is provided to students in conjunction with the use of a computer in problem solving applications. Problem solving and EDP skills training form the core of classroom instructional uses. Occurring somewhat less frequently are CAI and gaming and simulation applications.

The other core of computer use centers on guidance and administration applications. Management of instruction applications occur less frequently in conjunction with these core applications.

The dominance of computer applications by the mathematics curriculum is even more marked than that of problem solving and EDP skills training. In most of the schools surveyed, computer applications have been well integrated into the mathematics curriculum. However, applications have very rarely spread to other subject matter areas to any extent.

Most typically, instructional use of computers starts with mathematics departments in the schools. If use does spread to other departments, it is normally through the efforts of mathematics teachers. Why computer use has not spread more rapidly is very difficult to determine. Mathematics teachers indicated that they have met with considerable resistance when attempting to encourage colleagues in other departments to develop computer applications. It is evident that the computer quite readily lends itself to use in the mathematics courses. On the other hand, applications in areas such as social studies, English, etc., are less obvious, and probably require considerable imagination and interest on the part of teachers in these subject areas.

It is known that the computer can be threatening from the standpoint that students frequently learn more about it than teachers do.

Therefore, a teacher undertaking a computer application must have sufficient confidence in himself not to be bothered by such an occurrence. Possibly, training programs designed to encourage computer use among teachers in subject areas other than mathematics, as well as among mathematics teachers might help break down some of the resistance to the spread of computer use.

At least one other factor which stands in the way of computers being used more throughout the entire curriculum is concerned with the structure and content of the curriculum. The curricula of most schools, as presently constituted, make it difficult to introduce innovations. In many schools, the schedule is already packed with traditionally required courses, particularly for college bound students. Several teachers stated the need for modular curriculum scheduling. This approach divides the school day into smaller time periods than the common 50 minute class sessions presently used in most schools. With these additional units of time, the curriculum planners have more flexibility to introduce curriculum innovations. A number of computer users have gone to modular scheduling quite successfully. Providing short so-called mini courses or introducing modular scheduling permits the inclusion of computer uses in their tight schedules. It may be concluded that merely introducing computers into a school does not automatically cause innovation to take place. Many schools, in fact, may be realizing less than full benefit from instructional computer use because of the structure of the class schedules.

It is safe to conclude that the computer is more frequently used as a *tool* in instruction rather than as the *object* of instruction. Therefore, the purposes of the computer applications tend to concern themselves with the subject matter such as mathematics, science, and economics. The computer simply aids the student in accomplishing the content goals of the subject area. Another way of describing the nature of computer applications is to describe what students actually do in these applications. Most typically, students write and run programs on computers, using it as a tool to accomplish the goals of the course they are taking.

A number of interesting controversies surround the instructional use of computers in secondary schools. One of these deals with the mode of use of the computer. At one end of the continuum is the mode in which the computer is used in the classroom on a highly formalized basis. At the other end of the continuum appears the use of the computer in a laboratory setting in a very informal way. In the former mode, the use of the computer is normally planned by teachers and scheduled for use on homework and classroom assignments. When used more informally, the computer is simply made available to students. They are instructed how to use the computer if and when they come to the laboratory to use it. In this way, students may use the computer in a variety of classes as they feel they have a need to use it. In this latter mode of operation, it is the students, rather than the teachers, who spread the use of the computer into various subject areas. Schools and individual applications may fall at various points along this continuum. Which mode of use is most effective for which educational settings and objectives is a question worthy of investigation.

Another controversy concerns the necessity of actually having a computer present in the school. Some schools actually do have a computer in the school, others use the computer through a terminal or take their computer programs to an off-site location to be run. Still other schools use both on-site and off-site computers. Some teachers feel that it is important that the computer be present in the schools so that students can actually see the computer and interact with it on a direct hands-on basis. Others feel that this is not as critical as having access to a large scale, sophisticated computer which is probably too expensive to actually have on-site in the school.

Many schools have introduced the use of a mini computer, which normally is a small scale inexpensive machine which can be used in the school. The controversy here centers around the instructional merits of the small scale computer versus the large scale computer discussed in the context of cost-effectiveness. Regarding this controversy, it was interesting to note that one can not judge the sophistication and educational significance of a school's computer use simply on the basis of the sophistication of the computer being used. A more important factor determining the quality of the instructional application is the expertise and imagination of the teachers involved in the application. This is not to say that more sophisticated computers in the hands of competent and motivated teachers will not improve the quality of instructional applications. However, good teachers can produce good instructional applications without the use of sophisticated computer equipment. Conversely, access to sophisticated computers will not result in effective instructional applications unless used by competent and motivated teachers.

One additional, particularly interesting controversy centers around the type of computer languages which students should be taught. At one end of the continuum are those who believe that students should be taught assembly language. At the other end are those who feel students should be taught compiler language. The reason set forth by most assembly language proponents suggests that students learn about the logical operation of the computer more thoroughly when using an assembly language. On the other hand, advocates of the compiler language indicate that understanding the logic of the computer is less important than understanding the logic of programming evident in compiler languages. Assembly languages are used most frequently by teachers who wish students to learn about the computer itself, i.e., EDP skills training for vocational purposes.

Compiler languages are frequently taught to students who will use programming in the solution of problems. Teachers of compiler languages can teach the essentials of such a language fairly quickly. This permits them to turn to what they consider to be the most important aspect of the computer use, that is, actually using it for the solution of problems. Each approach seems appropriate when used in the way described here.

One of the greatest benefits derived from the use of computers in instruction results from its capacity to motivate students. Why the computer is so effective in motivating students is not easy to answer. This question provides an excellent area for further research. Some have suggested that it is the hands-on experience that computers provide. Others suggested that it could be that computers make the subject relevant. This may be particularly true of mathematics. Whatever the reason, investigation into this area should prove fruitful for continuing to improve computer-based instruction, as well as instruction which is not computer-oriented.

In general, it appears that computers have not been introduced into the school curriculum after a careful and systematic evaluation of the instructional needs within schools. As indicated before, someone in the mathematics department frequently initiates the use of computers. If the use spreads, it does so in a relatively unplanned manner. Introduction and spread of computers in this fashion has resulted in a large number of worthwhile computer applications. However, there still is a need for the development of a means of systematically determining educational needs and objectives and applying computers where they can be most effective. As part of the systematic application of computers in the instructional process, there is a need for evaluating the effectiveness of computers. Based on such an evaluation, computer applications can then be revised and improved.

Level and Source of Support of Instructional Use

Information regarding the level and source of support of instructional computer applications indicates that even within the sample of schools which are using computers for instructional purposes, only a minute percentage of the educational dollar is being spent on instructional applications. The overwhelming bulk of the money being spent comes from local sources. There are also a variety of cooperative arrangements which have been developed for the sharing of computers and information about computer applications. Many schools see the need for developing these types of cooperative arrangements, although there is some difference of opinion as to whether these cooperative arrangements should involve sharing of computer facilities. There are some schools that prefer to have sole access to a computer rather than share one.

Previous Use

Possibly the most revealing finding regarding previous use of computers concerns itself with how instructional applications develop. Many have been of the opinion that instructional applications have developed as a way of getting more use out of a computer which is already being used for administrative purposes. Information from the schools surveyed indicated that this is probably not the case. Most instructional applications have developed independently of administrative applications within the schools.

Future Use

Regarding future use, schools tend to show preference for expanding present applications further rather than initiating new types of applications. In addition, they report the intention of continuing to turn to local sources for the bulk of their support in the future. To some degree, this may be due to the lack of knowledge as to where one can obtain funds for computer applications. Information regarding source of funds might prove useful. Teachers may be inclined to continue their present applications because they indicate that they are generally satisfied with the applications that they have. They do, however, point out that there are problems and that they have certain needs which should be filled to enable them to continue to expand instructional use of computers. These needs most frequently concern funding, space, and training, in addition to a need for information. Money, of course, is normally the largest problem. However, project staff were impressed by the fact that many teachers indicated that fairly minor needs stand in their way of gaining full advantage from their computer use. For instance, many are blocked by the need for an additional keypunch. This suggests that, quite possibly, a small expenditure of funds could significantly improve the computer use of a fairly large number of schools. In these instances, there is a need for funds to be made available in small amounts.

One problem which schools have with their computer applications results, in part, from solutions to these problems. Frequently teachers who receive training in the use of computers will leave the educational community to take jobs in industry where they can be rewarded more handsomely. Such an occurrence only makes the need for trained teachers more severe. Teachers must be rewarded more for developing and implementing computer use in order to keep them employed in the schools.

With the heavy emphasis on teaching programming, one specific problem takes on considerable importance. Several teachers mentioned the inadequacy of diagnostics produced by compilers and assemblers.

Present program diagnostics are geared toward the operational programmer rather than the student. There seems to be a need for program diagnostics which are more instructional in nature. Some efforts along these lines have been made, but more must be done.

Teachers mentioned that some students get so involved with computers that they neglect their other courses. This causes tensions and jealousies among departments within the schools and frequently has considerable effect on the students' overall academic performance. It must be recognized that the computer is a tool which is designed to aid instruction, not control it. At the same time, computers present a challenge to students and teachers alike. Teachers must meet the challenge to continue to guide student learning. If they fail to meet the challenge, students will learn unguided and thus possibly ineffectively.

The use of computers for instructional purposes appears to be growing rapidly. However, if it is to continue to grow and we are to continue to derive the fullest benefit from its unique capabilities, its introduction and use in the instructional process must be carefully and systematically planned. Also, much more must be done so that schools can share information about the problems and promises of computers. Finally, the effectiveness of computer applications must be evaluated to derive the fullest benefit from every educational dollar spent on them.

COMPUTER-BASED RESOURCE UNITS*

Robert S. Harnack

AN OVERVIEW

During the past decade a fascinating revolutionary movement has been evident in professional education. Changes in subject matter structure

---

* Excerpted by permission of Robert S. Harnack, Director, Center for Curriculum Planning, from *Evaluation of An Innovation in Education—Computer Based Curriculum Planning* (A Special Report of the Center, State University of New York at Buffalo; Joseph M. O'Connell, editor, February 1970), pp. 1–5, 23–26.

and organization, staff utilization and school organization, instructional materials and techniques, as well as the philosophical and actual move toward individualization of instruction, have been so alarmingly rapid that the normal evolutionary pace has been disrupted. This revolutionary change, *per se*, has caused an unusual amount of curriculum planning confusion and has complicated the decision-making which must be done by elementary and secondary school personnel.

The following pages describe a program which may help the teacher with this complicated planning task. This program employs the computer as a tool to aid the teacher in pre-planning teaching-learning situations for the total class, small groups, and individual students. Basically, the computer serves as a retrieval system designed to aid the teacher in his decision-making about classroom objectives, subject-matter content, instructional activities, materials and testing devices. The purpose of this report is to describe this project, to present reports of specific studies which indicate its potential for improved curriculum planning, and to acquaint the reader with an information feedback system devised to improve the units.

Background

In January, 1963, Cooperative Research Program, Project No. D-112, sponsored in part by the U.S. Office of Education, was begun. It was titled: *The Use of Electronic Computers to Improve Individualization of Instruction Through Unit Teaching.*[1]

This volume points out that the teacher in the elementary and secondary school today is confronted by dual expectancies. On the one hand, he is expected to organize and present subject matter with imagination and authority; on the other, he is urged to individualize instruction in such a way as to assure the best development of pupils' special talents. Too often, neither of these expectancies is achieved.

In an effort to assist the teacher in his performance of both of these roles, an original proposal was made to demonstrate the effectiveness of applying electronic processing equipment in such a way as to relate pre-planning of subject matter, materials, and means of presentation and evaluation to the needs and receptive abilities of individual pupils, small groups, and large groups within the context of the unit approach.

The Unit Approach.—The unit approach has always been highly

---

[1] Harnack, Robert S., *The Use of Electronic Computers to Improve Individualization of Instruction Through Unit Teaching.* Buffalo, N.Y.: State University of New York at Buffalo and Research Foundation of State University of New York, Cooperative Research Project No. D-112, 1965.

respected as a curricular vehicle which encouraged the professional teacher to make these pre-planning decisions about teaching-learning situations. Lack of teacher pre-planning time to make intelligent decisions has resulted in rendering this approach ineffective. Local experience has shown that data processing equipment can be employed by teachers to overcome the time-consuming disadvantages of the unit approach.

Unit teaching has been of consistent concern to teachers and students of professional education. The authors who have written about this subject since the early 1930s are many and well known. In their writing, Morrison, Wynne, Hopkins, Giles, Quillen, Miel, Krug, Gwynn, Lavone Hanna, Leonard, Alberty, Burton, Noar[2] have shown vital concern for unit teaching.

Today hundreds of experienced teachers are using nothing but the unit approach. The author knows of no pertinent statement which refutes the unit approach concept, degrades its usage, or speaks ill of its potential for efficient learning. Nevertheless, all who believe in and practice the unit approach have spent many fascinating but fruitless hours seeking answers to why this approach has not been universally adopted. The answers certainly are not simple, but one can hazard several guesses.

First.—Successful use of the unit approach is dependent upon teacher decision-making which requires high level capabilities. For example, teacher decisions have to be made in regard to the choice of subject matter for the unit and the relationship of this subject matter to (1) the major social functions, (2) the immediate needs and characteristics of the pupils in the classroom, and (3) the unit objectives (provided these

---

[2] Henry C. Morrison, *The Practice of Teaching in the Secondary School*, (Rev. Ed. Chicago: The University of Chicago Press, 1931). John P. Wynne, *The Teacher and the Curriculum*, (New York: Prentice-Hall, Inc., 1937). L. Thomas Hopkins, *Interaction, the Democratic Process*, (Boston: D. C. Heath and Co., 1941). Harry J. Giles, *et al.*, "Adventure in American Education," *Exploring the Curriculum*, (New York: Harper Bros., Inc., 1942). James I. Quillen, *Using a Resource Unit*, (Problems of American Life Series; Washington: National Association of Secondary School Principals, National Education Association, 1942). Alice Miel, *Changing the Curriculum: A Social Process*, (New York: Appleton-Century Co., 1946). Part II. Edward A. Krug, *Curriculum Planning*, (2d Ed. New York: Harper & Row, Inc., 1957). J. Minor Gwynn, *Curriculum Principles and Social Trends*, (3d Ed. New York: The Macmillan Co., 1960). Lavone A. Hanna, *et al.*, *Unit Teaching in the Elementary School*, (Rev. Ed. New York: Holt, Rinehart and Winston, Inc., 1960). J. Paul Leonard, *Developing the Secondary School Curriculum*, (Rev. Ed. New York: Holt, Rinehart and Winston, Inc., 1960). Harold A. Alberty and Elsie Alberty, *Reorganizing the High School Curriculum*, (2d Ed. New York: The Macmillan Co., 1962). William H. Burton, *Guidance of Learning Activities*, (3d Ed. New York: Appleton-Century-Crofts, 1962). Gertrude Noar, *Teaching and Learning the Democratic Way*, (Englewood Cliffs, N.J.: Prentice-Hall, Inc., 1963).

screens are used as a basis for selection in regard to the total scope and sequence of the school's offerings). Additional decisions have to be made regarding the organization of subject matter, curricular approaches, developmental activities, culminating activities, instructional materials, classroom techniques, and evaluating (measuring) devices.

Second.—A reservoir of ideas is essential to such decision-making. The lack of this reservoir prevents the adoption of the unit approach. Obviously, a specific outline of subject matter, a specific textbook, a specific classroom methodology, and specific measuring devices, remove any necessity for decision-making, and when a teacher is professional enough to know and use the screens of selection, a reservoir or a collection of objectives, activities, materials of instruction, and measuring devices focused on a series of topics must be made available for the teacher. This need, of course, led to the development of the resource unit concept in 1938 and the subsequent writings and studies on resource units by Hanna, Biddick, Quillen, Klohr, and Harnack.[3]

Third.—Although the resource unit offers in itself a vague planning guide for intelligent direction of classroom activities, teachers find it necessary to explore and canvass beforehand the narrow "live" possibilities of these instructional reserviors. When a teacher moves from a limited base for selecting, organizing, and developing learning activities for the classroom to a much broader base which permits many kinds and degrees of development, pre-planning time is realistically necessary in order for the teacher to gain some confidence and security before he steps before the pupils in the classroom.

During the years many a professional, experienced teacher, trying desperately to use unit teaching, found that he knew enough professional education to employ with some sense of precision the broader screens of selection; and he found, by working with others, that he could identify and gather some of the ideas and materials necessary for classroom teaching-learning experiences; but he could not find the professional pre-planning time to do the whole task of unit teaching intelligently.

Can something be done to overcome the time-consuming disadvantage of the unit approach?

Defining Teacher Functions and Computer Functions.—The partici-

---

[3] Lavone A. Hanna, "Source Units," *Stanford Social Education Investigation* Bulletin No. 1 (mimeographed), September 1939. Mildred Biddick, *Preparation and Use of Resource Units*, (New York: The Progressive Education Association, 1940). Quillen, op. cit. Paul R. Klohr, *The Resource Unit in Curriculum Reorganization*, (Unpublished Doctoral Dissertation; Columbus, Ohio: The Ohio State University, 1948). Robert S. Harnack, *The Role of the Resource Unit in Curriculum Planning*, (Unpublished Doctoral Dissertation: University of Wisconsin, 1951).

pants in the Cooperative Research Program felt that electronic equipment can be used to overcome the obstacles inherent in certain functions a teacher performs as he organizes a teaching-learning situation. If this is true, then one of the most difficut tasks which a teacher faces—finding the time for pre-planning the actual teaching-learning situations in the classroom—can be alleviated. In other words, the basic purpose for experimenting with electronic data processing equipment was to help teachers overcome this lack of time for pre-planning.

Prior to the development of project plans and procedures, particular attention was given to separating the pre-planning functions of the teacher from the retrieval functions of the computer.

The teacher's functions are four:

1. To identify the subject of the teaching unit and to identify the basic unifying theme which would serve as the center of interest in the classroom during a specific period of time.
2. To define the students' abilities, needs, characteristics, and interests, as these items relate to the selections to be made within the total unit.
3. To suggest possible learning outcomes in the form of behavioral skills, understandings, information, and peripheral objectives which may reasonably be expected to result from the teaching-learning situations developed throughout the unit.
4. To make, if necessary, certain professional decisions related to those tasks or areas which the teacher deems important for the objectives and the students in the classroom.

On the other hand, the electronic computer must serve the following functions:

1. To provide the teacher with a subject matter outline or problem census related to the learning outcomes identified by the teacher.
2. To suggest a significant (related to the learning outcomes and characteristics of the pupils) number of large group introductory and developmental activities.
3. To suggest a significant number of introductory and developmental small group activities.
4. To suggest a significant number of individual learning activities which might prove to be helpful.
5. To suggest suitable instructional materials, including reference materials, for individual students.
6. To suggest appropriate equipment, audio-visual materials, and the like, for large group and small group instruction.
7. To suggest suitable references and other materials for the use of the teacher.
8. To suggest how achievement of these proposed outcomes may be evaluated.
9. To suggest "leads" to other related units (continuous activities) which might grow out of the proposed unit.

Once the specific functions of teachers were separated from the functions of the electronic data processing equipment, the next step was to define and organize the data for the computer. The sets of variables requiring top consideration were obviously related to the teacher's pre-planning functions. Thus, it was clear that the equipment would have to contain a coded reservoir of items regarding learning outcomes, subject matter, instructional activities, instructional materials, measuring devices, references for the teachers, and suggestions for further units of instruction—in short, a *resource unit*.

Objectives

Basically, this program is designed to help elementary and secondary school teachers in their pre-planning of large group, small group, and individual teaching-learning situations within the context of unit teaching. To overcome the obstacles connected with the unit approach to teaching was the other obvious purpose. In order to accomplish the above, five specific objectives served as a guide for project activities. They were:

1. To gather from all sources the component parts of resource units.
2. To identify the specific variables, or categories, whereby all items in a resource unit could be coded for purposes of eventual retrieval by a data processing machine.
3. To code all items in the resource units.
4. To program the electronic data processing machinery in such a way as to relate pre-planning of subject matter, materials, means of presentation, and measuring devices to the specific objectives of a classroom teacher.
5. To program the electronic data processing machinery in such a way as to relate pre-planning of materials and means of presentation to the needs and receptive abilities of individual pupils.

Directly tied to the objectives stated above were ancillary purposes which were concomitants of this developmental program. They were: (1) to improve the selection of variables related to coding and programming, (2) to assess the coding and programming in order to make the entire process more efficient, and (3) to gain information from teachers regarding the use of this innovation.

SOME TENTATIVE IMPLICATIONS

Unit teaching, as a concept, emphasizes teacher planning and decision-making for the individualization of instruction. In the classroom, individualization of instruction requires that the teacher use the individual learning variables of his pupils as well as professional knowledge about subject matter in order to select objectives, content, classroom activities, and instructional materials which will benefit the individual pupil's depth and breadth of learning. Such decision-making by teachers requires millions of man-hours of work; and, therefore, in most instances, individualization of instruction within the concept of unit teaching becomes an ideal which is unattainable.

To make unit teaching and the individualization of instruction work in the classroom involves a two-fold problem: is there a process which will enable the teacher to pre-plan for individualization of instruction within a framework of sound education theory and practice, and does such pre-planning by the teacher result in actual improvement of student learning?

In an effort to assist the unit teacher in his pre-planning for individualization of instruction and to insure depth and breadth of the individual pupil's growth in an area, the Center staff has tried to invent a process whereby electronic processing equipment could be applied in such a way as to relate the pre-planning of a teaching-learning situation to the needs and receptive abilities of individual pupils.

In the original D-112 project, the Center for Curriculum Planning of the State University of New York at Buffalo developed, coded, and programmed six computer-based resource units and supplied over one hundred teachers with resource guides (specific printed suggestions taken from a resource unit) related to the six resource units on the 3rd grade and the 11th grade, social studies, level. (Since then, 25 more resource units have been developed and coded and many more resource guides have been generated and used in the schools. More are being developed as this is being written.) The suggestions contained in all of these resource guides are keyed to the analysis of the composition of the class members as a whole, as well as to individual learner variables, the specific instructional objectives of the unit chosen by the teacher and/or the learners, and to other decisions of a professional nature which the teacher might choose to make. The electronic computer, properly programmed, can accommodate the numerous variables involved in each classroom situation.

In sum, the electronic computer can perform the three functions in this context:

1. Responding to the learning objectives identified by the teacher and/or pupils, it can provide an appropriate content (subject matter) outline.
2. By taking into consideration the variables of learning objectives and the characteristic composition of the class, it can suggest:
    a. significant large group activities
    b. significant small group activities
    c. significant instructional materials for the total group
    d. significant measuring devices for the total group
3. By taking into consideration the variables of learning objectives and the characteristics of each learner, it can suggest suitable instructional material and individual activities for each student, per each objective chosen.

Generally, the implications of this study are fascinating because they open a clutch of curriculum studies. The limitless work to be done revolves about the use of electronic computers as a tool to foster the improvement of instruction. In like manner, this study encourages an examination of the relationship between computer-related curriculum developments and basic curriculum theory and design. Such an analysis is needed at this time because many of the present developments related to computer technology in education are peripheral in the sense that only single factors or subdivisions of these factors of a total curriculum design are being studied. One cannot minimize the use of computers to reorganize subject matter content, to experiment with linear programming for individual students, to develop multi-group scheduling, and the like. All such developments either have a useful function already or, as a result of careful study and analysis, may serve the educational community in the future. However, the lack of studies related to a total pattern tends to give the existing peripheral studies a "side show" atmosphere. Therefore, in many instances, studies related to only one factor or a subdivision of a factor in a total curriculum pattern are often given the label of "gimmickery." In other instances, as a result of this activity, such studies are seen out of context and are often lightly dismissed as insignificant because many practicing professionals do not see the relationships.

Specifically, this study has implications for the following areas in the field of curriculum planning.

Teacher Decision-Making.—Further study of this process may foster and improve teacher decision-making. Experienced, well-educated teachers have always made decisions for classroom operation. These decisions define the subject matter to be taught, the purposes to be served, the methodology to be used, the instructional materials needed for the learner and the methods of evaluation. Such decision-making is limited by many factors such as time available, physical facilities, and the prevailing philosophy of administration and supervision. However, as the profession of teaching becomes just that and as the physical facilities, materials, and educational philosophies lean toward the individualization of instruction, teacher application of the screens of selection necessary to make intelligent decisions will become exceedingly difficult, if not impossible. Computer-based resource units may provide a pre-screening process for sifting thousands of suggestions in such a way that the more useful suggestions finally provided for the teacher will enable him to practice his decision-making with more finesse. It would seem logical that further development of the retrieval processes would lead to further improvements and refinements of the decision-making process.

Individualization of Instruction.—A rapid perusal of this study indicates the hope for the development of better instructional programs for individual learners. This project has many implications for individualizing instruction. These include an increased adoption of the basic philosophy of individualization, the use by practicing teachers of the characteristics of learners, the identification of independent study activities, and the identification by students of objectives related to a unit of instruction.

Professional Teaching-Learning Situations.—The development and use of resource guides may lead to the improvement of teaching-learning situations. All staff members in professional education strive to identify more pertinent specific instructional objectives, subject matter content, classroom methodologies, instructional materials, and measuring devices. Even the very process of identifying the initial theme for a resource unit, to say nothing of the remaining tasks, causes the professional staff member to employ the factors of a curriculum design. For example, a selection of the unit topic would require the professional worker to consider the characteristics of contemporary society, the general characteristics and maturity of the learners, curricular approaches, and the like. Certainly the implications of this study are such that stronger emphasis may be placed on the development of professional teaching-learning situations as well as a more complete consideration of curriculum design and theory.

Research.—Finally, the implications for further research in the area of curriculum planning and development are so numerous that one hardly knows where to begin or end. *First,* this process may enable curriculum workers to study the individual learner's variables as these variables relate to all aspects of the teaching-learning situation already incorporated into the resource unit. The reverse of this application would enable the researcher to analyze the ingredients of a resource unit to determine the obvious gaps and lacks related both to learner's variables and the objectives of the unit. *Second,* a host of research studies are suggested by the relationship of the resource guide to teacher pre-planning. The major goal in curriculum research has always been to aid the teacher in his pre-planning. The basic questions still remain. Does such a process as herein described aid the teacher? If such a process does aid the teacher, in what areas? If it does not, how can computer technology be employed to aid the teacher? *Third,* development of this process leads to the definition of research studies related to the individualization of instruction. The most fascinating point to explore in this area is the extent to which the use of resource guides leads to the dispersion of learning away from a central theme. *Fourth,* what happens when numerous resource guides are used in a practical situation in a specific school system by many teachers over a period of one or more years?

Stated succinctly, a resource unit, as a memory bank, can be coded for an electronic computer; and specific suggestions related to various types of objectives and the individual variables about each learner can be retrieved. The challenge is to find out whether or not the application of such resource guides leads to improved learning for individuals. There are some indications that a unique method has evolved to help teachers plan teaching-learning situations for individual students, the small group, and the total classroom. There are general indications that this process has helped teachers to overcome millions of man-hours of work; and, to that end, it should be further developed.

PART IV

THE HIGH SCHOOL
CURRICULUM
OF THE FUTURE

This final part focuses on the high school of the future—its possible directions and programs, and ways and means of achieving them. Chapter 13 includes four glimpses into the future, from one that would utilize and systematize what we now have to one that would reconstruct education on a personal curriculum continuum, ultimately eliminating formal levels of education such as now exist. Each article calls for a highly individualized approach to high school education, although the formulae for individualization vary sharply.

Chapter 14 includes various reports and proposals as to the steps toward change. One project, ES'70, would utilize a systems approach in a consortium of school districts; another a community-centered program. Other articles espouse other emphases, and one article deals somewhat comprehensively and very constructively with program development in rural high schools. The anthology closes with articles that respectively advocate the roles of students, teachers, and people in general in changing the curriculum.

For the most part readings in Part IV were chosen to represent points of view and processes that exist in theory rather than practice. As in other chapters of this book, many of the ideas and suggestions are actually in opposition to the present consensus. Hopefully these readings in particular will stimulate reflection, discussion, and even action by readers who do or will work in American high schools.

Chapter 13

SOME PROPOSALS FOR THE FUTURE

Although many articles already presented in this anthology have
offered suggestions, even brief dreams, for the high school curriculum
of the future, several more comprehensive and futuristic selections have
been held for this chapter. The first selection is a partial presentation
of the Model Schools Project of the National Association of Secondary
School Principals and is taken from an article by the Director and
Associate Director of this project, respectively, J. Lloyd Trump and
William Georgiades. This project, supported partly by the Danforth
Foundation and involving 34 schools, aims to help the schools in
"Doing Better with What You Have." It is also building upon what the
NASSP already has—an accumulation of ideas, materials, and affiliations
through previous projects in staff utilization and other studies. Thus
this model is less revolutionary than some, but it also deals with the high
school broadly as compared with some proposals tending to focus on a
particular program for the future.

The outline of the model of the NASSP Model Schools Project gives
relatively little detail as to the characteristics of the curriculum sought.
Two goals are relevant, *e* and *f*, and several points indicate steps
expected to be taken toward these goals. Quite specific curriculum
planning is apparently anticipated in the project schools with much
emphasis on individualized instruction and systematic evaluation.

Galen Saylor's high school of the future is "a humane school." Unlike many writers on the high school, he calls attention to the accomplishments of American secondary education, commenting that much current writing "is highly critical, tearing the high school apart for its failures and entering strident pleas for rebuilding." Acknowledging that there may be faults, he argues that they "should not be considered apart from the real accomplishments." Saylor, too, places more individualization at the beginning of his proposals for change, and he offers a new suggestion to this end. He recommends that every high school have a "corps of top-quality staff" whom he would call "Directors of Personal Development." He lists the responsibilities of these persons, and describes the major aspects of the program for personal development: the program of common studies, extracurricular activities, community experiences, and tutorial seminar. In the latter, of which the director of personal development would be in charge for his group of about 30 students, "whatever is done must be interesting, important, and significant to the members of the group, who must work together in a complete interactive relationship." What do you think of the proposed "director of personal development"? What qualifications would be necessary for such a person?

Fred Wilhelms' paper, "Some Hunches of a Revolutionary," focuses on curriculum reform in four basic "streams": vocational education, science-mathematics, social studies, and humanities. He would have an area committee, with a majority of its faculty members from outside the field of specialization concerned, work over each stream; their first job "will be to shuck off the stereotypes that have accumulated, including the traditional sequence." Wilhelms' ideas for improving the streams are indeed revolutionary, and should provoke much discussion. Note some samples: "the community is a better shop for most purposes than anything we could have in our schools"; "our adolescents are unquestionably, in my mind, the best source of energy to mount an early childhood program that would go well beyond the model of Operation Head Start"; "the danger is not aiming too high over his (the adolescent's) head, the real danger is arrested development"; "I want to build into this six-year program a sensitivity-training program which would make the popular $500 program that industry is so eager to use for its junior grade executives look like peanuts." Which of his ideas are most challenging? Most feasible? Least?

The final article, "Curriculum Continuum: Possible Trends in the 70s" by Harold G. Shane, envisions the possible elimination of grade levels as we have known them and the substitution of "a carefully reasoned and well-designed continuum of experience for the learner." Shane distinguishes between the "personalized curriculum" he sees in the curriculum continuum and "individualized instruction," which "was intended to help a child meet group norms or standards, but at his own rate of progress." In the personalized curriculum, teachers would help the student to "create himself" without reference to norms. Shane points out some of the full implications of a curriculum continuum, such as the elimination of failure, acceleration, special education, remedial work, annual promotion, dropouts, compensatory education, and report cards and marks. He also describes the organizational changes involved, including the elimination of discrete elementary, secondary, and higher education programs.

Shane's continuum seems the logical outcome of the movement toward nongradedness and individualization that has been occurring somewhat unevenly in schools at all levels. As his comments also indicate, much of this movement has still assumed fixed norms and learning sequences. Will they, can they, disappear in the future? Can there indeed be a curriculum continuum for each learner? What guidelines would the school employ in marshalling its total resources that Shane says the adolescent would be guided in wisely exploiting? What resources?

At this point in the use of this book readers will hopefully begin to construct their own model of the high school curriculum of the future. Which if any of the ideas in this chapter would you incorporate? What goals would be set for students? What formal learning opportunities— courses, units, organized experiences of any sort—would be included? What informal, personalized ones? What would happen to classes, periods, credits, grades, and all the other paraphernalia of the traditional high school curriculum?

DOING BETTER WITH WHAT YOU HAVE
NASSP MODEL SCHOOLS PROJECT*

J. Lloyd Trump
William Georgiades

Our purpose today is to help anyone in any place to improve the quality of teaching and learning. Your school, old or new, in ghetto or suburb, poorly supported or richly endowed, can be better than it is. How to do it is our mission. The basic requirement is that you know where you are going, that your educational goals are clear.

The NASSP has developed a model to help you. We'll tell you about that model and, in the process, suggest some alternatives for you to consider in making changes *in the right direction* in your school—*doing better with what you have.*

Some persons argue that any change is better than no change at all—but that is a useless controversy. The directives from pupils and teachers are too clear these days. Schools *will* change.

The NASSP Model is being implemented in a project, supported partly by the Danforth Foundation—with 34 schools participating. How will these schools be different? What should we call them—more *humane* schools because each individual gets more attention? Some people in one of the model schools, a junior high school in southeast Washington, D.C., call it the NOW School.

Here are the words to a song they have written, under the direction of Thelma E. Robinson, music teacher:

> There's a crazy little rumor
>   And it's spreading everyday;
> That the school where I am going
>   Wants to change to a new way.

---

* Reprinted from the *Bulletin of the National Association of Secondary School Principals* (May 1970), 54:106–113, by permission.

Where they say that I can study mostly
    What I want to know—
And if that is true that school will be
    The place I want to go!

Teachers there will be a help to students
    Who will really want to study,
Yes, really study.
And it might be fun to want to know something
    That causes me to study,
Oh, really study.

And so if that crazy rumor
    Means that school will change its rules—
I will gather all my friends
    And we will fly right to the school.
We will call our school The NOW School—
    And we'll go there everyday!
And God bless the Model Project
    That has shown us our new way!

SOME OLD IDEAS

The National Association of Secondary School Principals has the Model for the NOW School. No one else has such a comprehensive program. We have been working a long time with some very old ideas. The roots of our Model are deep.

Quintilian stated the philosophy almost 1900 years ago:

> Moreover, by far the larger proportion of the learner's time ought to be devoted to private study. The teacher does not stand over him while he is writing or thinking or learning by heart. While he is so occupied, the intervention of anyone, be he who he may, is a hindrance.

The foundations also are in pronouncements of Plato, Socrates, the Humanists, in Herbart, Rousseau, Morrison, William Wirt, Carl Rogers, and thousands of others, past and present.

Our contribution in the NASSP is to put a lot of those old ideas, and some new ones, into a total commitment for a model—or system—where changes in all aspects of schools have to occur. We have been working on quite a number of school improvement projects, for a long time. A few examples are the work experience project with the NYA in the late 1930's; *Planning for American Youth* in the 1940's; the staff utilization studies in the 1950's and 1960's; and the Administrative Internship as a means for better schools, also in the 1960's.

The NASSP staff utilization studies developed several publications that attracted world-wide attention. The first, *New Horizons for Secondary School Teachers*, suggested a broad spectrum of studies while indicating some important choices that principals had to make. The second publication, *Images of the Future*, attracted even more attention. We put ideas from the staff utilization studies, supported by the Ford Foundation, into a frame of reference and described our teaching and learning system. The report at the end of the project, *Focus on Change—Guide to Better Schools*, still sells a lot of copies with translations into several foreign languages.

AND NO BELLS RING

Ten years ago, at the Portland, Oregon, NASSP Convention, we premiered a film, . . . *And No Bells Ring*. Hugh Downs, the narrator of this film, was then with Jack Parr on the Tonight Show. He went from there to the Today Show. Incidentally, at that time I had just left the University of Illinois (having been employed part-time by the NASSP) to be in Washington as a full-time NASSP employee. Ten years later the NEA film service finds that this film is still in considerable demand.

We produced a number of additional audiovisual programs with accompanying booklets to clarify further the instructional system we proposed. Starting in 1962 we had a new vehicle for working with the schools: a project also supported by the Ford Foundation, The Administrative Internship in Secondary School Improvement. We developed two film strips: *Focus on Change* and *Focus on the Individual—A Leadership Responsibility*. A 16mm sound, color film, *The Present Is Prologue*, told principals how to organize their schools differently and proposed methods for working more effectively with teachers. A recent film, *Answers and Questions*, deals with curriculum irrelevancy and other problems that pupils and teachers face and suggests some questions for further discussion.

We tell you these things that you may understand better the origin and development of our NASSP Model. A lot of so-called new ideas today need the model because a failure to change all aspects of the school program limits the possible gains of such innovations as television, programmed instruction, flexible scheduling, micro-teaching, and the use of varied learning strategies—including educational games, total environment education, various curriculum projects, the school-within-a-school, year-round school, and many more. These innovations fail in most cases to produce pupil gains and to help teachers because they try to function in self-contained classrooms, or with poor staff utilization, and with principals who sometimes have the wrong priorities.

So now we return to a more detailed explanation of the NASSP

Model, to show you how you can take steps toward it in your school and do better with what you have.

OUTLINE OF THE MODEL OF THE NASSP MODEL SCHOOLS PROJECT

1. Basic Goals

a. To provide a program with varied strategies and environments for learning through which all pupils, regardless of differences in individual talents and interests, may proceed with gains.

b. To provide conditions for teaching that recognize differences among teachers and capitalize on the special talents and interests of each person.

c. To define clearly the role of the professional teacher as separate from the roles of clerks, instruction assistants, and general aides.

d. To separate the principal's role in instructional improvement and general supervision from management tasks that can be done by other persons.

e. To emphasize in curriculum revision the distinction between those learnings that are *essential* for all pupils, and those learnings which are *specially relevant* for some of them.

f. To reduce required learnings in all subjects to provide more time for pupils to follow their own interests and talents.

g. To develop better methods and materials for evaluating changes in conditions for learning, teaching, and supervising, as well as changes in the use of the things of education; also for evaluating the effects of the program on pupils, teachers, and principals.

h. To utilize school funds, supplies and equipment, and other school facilities differently to produce better results as described under Item "f" *without* necessarily having more of the things of education.

i. To discover better ways of utilizing outside consultant help not only within a given school but also through audiovisual devices to spread the consultants' talents among other schools.

j. To analyze the process and the progress of change among schools.

2. Basic Characteristics of the Program

a. The principal spends three-fourths of his time working directly with teachers to improve instruction and learning.

    1. He organizes learning for teachers according to the same general principles that he expects teachers to follow with their pupils.

    2. He selects assistants qualified to handle the school's managerial and other tasks only indirectly related to instructional improvement.

b. Differentiated staffing and other arrangements produce changed roles for teachers.

    1. Instruction Assistants (average of 20 hours per week per teacher) oversee pupils' independent study, etc.; Clerks (average of 10 hours per week per teacher) keep records, etc.; General Aides (average

of 5 hours per week per teacher) perform tasks *not* requiring competence in subject areas or clerical skills.

2. Teachers are scheduled an average of not more than 10 hours per week with pupil groups (2 hours with large groups, 8 hours with small); the balance of 20 hours, mostly on school premises, are for keeping up-to-date, developing materials, evaluating, conferring, and supervising.

3. Most teachers serve a new role as teacher-counselor (helping about 35 pupils *individually* to plan, schedule, and change their independent study time and collecting information about each pupil's progress and difficulties).

4. Teachers work individually in offices or in groups organized by departments or on some other basis.

c. Individualized learning methods emphasize motivation, continuous progress, self-direction, individual scheduling, personalized evaluation, and attention to personal needs and interests, *while maintaining pupil accountability.*

1. Pupils are required, all the years they are in school, to attend 8 hours of motivational presentations and discussions each week in all 8 areas of human knowledge (30 minutes in a large group and 30 minutes in a small group per week in each area). These groups are scheduled by the school office.

2. Pupils have 22 hours per week for scheduling independent study in the school or community (distribution decided by pupils and their teacher-counselors, changeable by them at will with joint approval). A professional counselor or the principal resolves disagreements, if any, between a pupil and his teacher-counselor. These pupil schedules are made, changed, and recorded by teacher-counselors and their secretaries.

3. Each pupil covers required content at his own pace, using specially prepared materials. Much of this work may be done cooperatively in various-sized groups, as established by students themselves.

4. Evaluation for each pupil is in relation to his own past achievement in a variety of educational goals. Since teachers cannot evaluate every aspect of learning, priorities are established.

5. Attendance of pupils is regularly checked and the amount of each pupil's progress systematically reported by the instruction assistants who supervise independent study.

d. Curriculum revision separates basic, essential learnings from other learnings that mainly are appropriate for pupils with special talents and interests.

1. Materials are organized to provide self-direction, self-motivation, self-pacing, and self-evaluation by pupils themselves.

2. The amount of *depth* and *creative* studies in relation to *required,*

basic studies increases with the age and maturity of individual pupils.

e. Improvement of teaching and learning requires that money and facilities be utilized differently.

 1. Financial input is analyzed in terms of gains (product output) in the foregoing items "a," "b," "c," and "d" (principal's role, teaching roles, individualized learning, and curriculum revision). Improvements in those areas do not necessarily cost more.

 2. Most conventional classrooms become learning centers (both kinds: *study* and *work*) for independent study; a few rooms are divided for small-group meetings and for teacher offices and workrooms; a few spaces are needed for large-group instruction (motivational presentations).

 3. Priorities for new construction or for purchase of supplies and equipment are based on what will produce the most good for the most pupils, in terms of the goals of the teaching-learning methods in the Model.

f. Increased emphasis on evaluation is essential to provide feedback for directing further improvements, and to produce confidence in the changes.

 1. The emphasis is on behavioral changes when evaluating individual pupil progress.

 2. Analyses will reveal changes made in conditions for learning, teaching, supervision, curriculum development, and use of funds and facilities in school and community.

 3. The effects of the changes on pupils and teachers en masse, on principal and assistants, and financial efficiency will be measured.

3. Underlying Conditions

a. Only as administrators, teachers, and pupils are totally committed to all of the project's goals will there be basic comprehensive changes as envisioned in the Model.

b. Each school will provide reports evaluating the project's effects on pupils, teachers, supervisors, curriculum, facilities, and money. The goal is to produce improvements as compared with past accomplishments in each school as measured by earlier data gathered in the school and by new evaluation techniques that the project will develop.

c. In return for more comprehensive evaluation reports, the parents, community leaders, central administrators, board of education members, and other persons in the community power structure will offer constructive assistance and suggestions based on the data they receive.

d. The school will work to achieve the Model as rapidly as is reasonable in the local setting. A two-year transitional period, or less, should be adequate.

e. The schools will refrain from seeking unnecessary publicity, especially during the transitional period, but will cooperate in preparing reports for distribution by the project.

f. Two additional key words for progress are *self-study* and *professionalism*. Conversely, the following methods of stimulating change are de-emphasized: visits to other schools, use of outside consultants for motivating change, purchase of externally developed technology and materials, construction of new or additional facilities, and substantial increases in school expenditures per pupil. However, communications among the schools with similar interests and problems is encouraged to further the goals of self-study and professionalism.

THE HIGH SCHOOL OF THE FUTURE: A HUMANE SCHOOL*

GALEN SAYLOR

I define the humane high school as one that contributes as fully as it can to the maximum development of each youth and young adult within its jurisdiction, assuring him a full measure of self-actualization in terms of his unique talents, capabilities, and potentialities. Although an individual is the product of native endowment interacting with a culture in all of its manifestations—institutions, values, modes of living, political structures, legal requirements and definitions, media for communicating, and so on—society nevertheless expects the schools in the modern era to accept major responsibilities for development of the total personality. What the school does through its institutional arrangements, its social climate, its formal program of education, its administrative structures and policies, and the quality and character of its interpersonal relationships will therefore be a most significant factor in the quality and nature of human development. Society should be, and must be, greatly concerned about its schools and how well they fulfill their primary purpose.

The scope of the task the high school faces today in order to fulfill its social responsibilities may be illustrated merely by citing numbers.

---

* This article first appeared in *The Humanist* May/June 1971, and is reprinted by permission.

Currently about 15 million youth are enrolled in grades nine through 12 of our schools. This number will remain fairly constant for the remainder of the decade. Then, rather large increases will occur annually, with enrollments totaling about 22 million by the end of the century. Endeavoring to help this mass of young people analyze as fully as possible their capabilities and potentialities is, obviously, a Herculean task. But beyond that, to provide the kinds of schooling needed to develop each individual to his fullest possible measure of self-realization is a social burden of a magnitude never before faced by a nation. The Soviet Union may have as many youth to educate, but, at least at the present time, it does not attempt to provide the many possibilities for human development that we do.

Before I state some changes that I think are needed in our program of schooling, I would like to call attention to the accomplishments of American secondary education. So much of the current writing about the high school, especially writing done for the nonprofessional, is highly critical, tearing the high school apart for its failures and entering strident pleas for rebuilding it. (See, for example, Charles E. Silberman's *Crisis in the Classroom.*) This is not to say that the criticisms and attacks may not be validated by what happens in some of the more than 20,000 secondary schools throughout the country and in classrooms within individual schools. But these faults should not be considered apart from the real accomplishments of the American high school. The contributions of the high school to the development and advancement of the nation, and to the socialization of its people, have been extensively examined by scholars. (See especially, Henry Steele Commager, "A Historian Looks at the American High School" and Lawrence A. Cremin, *The Genius of American Education.*)

During their evolution through the past three centuries, the schools, particularly the secondary schools, have exemplified Frederick Jackson Turner's generalization that the people of the United States constantly readjusted their institutions through a series of recurring social evolutions in diverse geographic areas. The academies of the late 18th and 19th centuries and the high schools of the last half of the 19th and first quarter of the 20th centuries were élitist institutions, serving a very limited number of youth. The high school of today, illustrating Turner's concept of social evolution, did not emerge or establish itself as an agency to serve the educational needs of all youth until the second decade of this century.

But, in all honesty, we must recognize that even today the high school has not fully, successfully, or even adequately met these needs. It has not contributed significantly—often, it has not contributed at all—to the self-realization of many youths in a community. Particularly, but not solely, it has contributed little to those in the central city of urban areas.

Nonetheless, the high schools—their governing boards, administrators, and teachers—are already, in my opinion, developing new forms of schooling, new types of programs, and new modes of working with youths in a manner that will continue the kind of social evolution about which Turner wrote.

What, then, are some of the changes that will enable a program in secondary education to foster the maximum development of all youths within its jurisdiction?

Obviously, the program must be individualized as fully as possible. We shall continue to have a central building or complex of buildings known as a high school, and we shall continue to educate youths in large groups. How else could we provide for the complete education of 15 to 20 million people in the years ahead? Despite this, however, high schools have already developed a much greater measure of individualization than they had in the past, and many innovative high schools are already initiating some significant new programs.

In my opinion, every high school should have a corps of top-quality staff whom I would call "Directors of Personal Development." Each of these directors would be fully responsible for guiding and directing the development of a group of students—hopefully not more than 30, but, at least at the outset, considering the cost, perhaps more than that. The director would have the following responsibilities:

1. To utilize all of the expertise available among psychologists, evaluation experts, and other types of specialists in human behavior, and, in full cooperation with the family (who, hopefully, would already have been involved in similar endeavors with the elementary school), to help each student analyze, assess, diagnose, and fully understand the nature and character of his talents, potentialities, and capabilities. Such an appraisal would be a continuing process throughout the student's school career.
2. To plan with the student and his family that total educational program which best promises to contribute to his fullest possible development.
3. To supervise and direct the student's activities while he is under the jurisdiction of the school.
4. To be in charge of a tutorial seminar that would include all of his students and that would serve not only as the focal point of the entire program, but provide exciting and challenging opportunities for the students to work together on studies of many pressing problems, issues, and interests.
5. To work closely with parents, community agencies, and other staff members in planning and directing the program.

The major aspects of the program for personal development are as follows:

1. The program of common studies. This part of the program encompasses the basic school subjects. It should provide general education and specialized

programs for individual development. Its subjects may be grouped in seven broad areas: humanities, social sciences, science and mathematics, family life, physical and mental health, specialized studies, and career development. Each of these areas should offer ample opportunity for individual development, with methods of instruction emphasizing inquiry, discovery, and research; the students should be encouraged to engage in self-directed individual study, experimentation, creative activities, and so on. Each area of study would offer seminars and problem-oriented courses that provide an abundance of possibilities, particularly at the advanced levels.

An area of career development would include a skills laboratory, which would help any student achieve an adequate level of skills in reading, self-directed learning, computation, social relationships, leadership, and group participation. The principal function of this aspect of the program would be to provide appropriate opportunities for prevocational study, and, if part of the career plan, for work experience or vocational preparation.

An area of specialized studies would encompass courses in languages, advanced work in the arts (beyond a general treatment in the humanities), and additional subjects not falling within the other areas.

The principal concern in all areas is that students have those vastly enriched and extended experiences for self-directed learning that are so seriously lacking in many high schools.

2. Extracurricular activities. These programs should provide rich opportunities for pupil-directed experiences that enhance self-development.

3. Community experiences. If at all possible, every student sometime during his high school career should participate in meaningful and significant community activities. With more than 15 million students enrolled in the high schools, accomplishing this objective may be difficult, but every effort should be made to provide such opportunities. For some students this program will provide work experience in conjunction with the program of vocational education. Other students may participate in any kind of worthwhile program. They may intern in government offices, work with all sorts of community agencies that provide services to people, or simply participate in any business or professional enterprise or office that could provide desirable experience. The Director of Personal Development would be responsible for assignments, but a special community service bureau would need to be established to direct the total program.

4. Tutorial seminar. As stated previously, each Director should be in charge of a seminar for his group of students. This program should be flexible with respect to time and schedule, topics and matters to be considered, and seminar procedures. Whatever is done must be interesting, important, and significant to the members of the group, who must work together in a complete interactive relationship. This seminar would also serve as a center for discussing community experiences, matters of guidance and counseling, school problems, or other important topics of general interest.

Finally, the high school of the future must be a humane institution; it must regard each of its students as a person of dignity and inestimable worth who can, and should, attain perfectability. While it must do many other things, everything that it does should be directed toward fulfillment of this basic purpose.

THE TARGET OF THIS REVOLUTIONARY— THE CURRICULUM*

FRED T. WILHELMS

It is those resources I want to talk about now. What I am going to say is not the whole answer to the problem. I do not mean to ignore or minimize the things we have been talking about. There are many lines in which we must fight: the endless battle for more money for schools; the politics of centralization in some parts of the country and of decentralization in other parts of the country; the whole question of organization; the use of media. These and many other fronts are important. Yet, I think we often use some of these issues as an evasive gesture, to avoid the central job.

Ultimately we must concern ourselves with the curriculum, not with some courses thrown in at the edges as a kind of sop, but with the basic curriculum itself. The logic behind this is simple and common sense: that is where the school and the young people meet; if we want to help a young human being in his development, we are not going to do it somewhere else on some special day. We are only going to do it in the long, dusty process while he is in his algebra class or wherever he actually is.

For simplicity in proposing to you some basic curriculum reforms,

---

* Excerpt from "Some Hunches of a Revolutionary," in *Student Unrest: Threat or Promise?* Richard L. Hart and J. Galen Saylor, editors (Washington, D.C.: Association for Supervision and Curriculum Development, 1970), pp. 70–76. Reprinted with permission of the Association for Supervision and Curriculum Development and Fred T. Wilhelms. Copyright © 1970 by the Association for Supervision and Curriculum Development.

I should like to think of the six-year program of the junior and senior high school in terms of four basic streams: vocational education, the science-mathematics stream (recognizing some difference between the two components, yet relating them basically to the technology), the social studies stream, and the humanities stream.

Let me ask you to make a practical check: if each of those broad streams in our curriculum had been fulfilling in the past 30 years the goals and objectives that you privately think it could and should deliver, how much of a problem would student unrest still be in our schools? Then, why don't we tackle each stream and make it into what we want? We frustrate ourselves by talking about fixing the whole school all at once, or changing the whole curriculum at one time; the whole curriculum does not hang together that well.

I would like to suggest a model for working on any one of these four streams. I suggest that you form an "area committee" in your school, on, say, social studies. We shall, of course, wish to involve lay persons and students, but let us think first of the faculty. Not more than about 45 percent of that area committee should come from the field of specialization under consideration. A little more than half ought to come from faculty members in other fields. This committee will be looking at the whole sweep of the social studies program for the six years of junior and senior high school. They are not to be concerned with the course of studies for the ninth grade, but to think of the six-year program as a whole.

Their first job will be to shuck off the stereotypes that have accumulated, including the traditional sequence. It is time we realized that in most of these fields (the sole exception *may* be science-math) there is almost nothing to lose. We have a sterile social studies, a sterile vocational education, a sterile English program, all of which have been rank failures; so we have plenty of reasons to start from scratch, to start barehanded, with no prior commitments to any body of subject matter at all. I know there will be some legal requirements around the edges and college entrance requirements will have to be reckoned with, but those things will take care of themselves when we really get to them. The committee's real job is to figure out in gutsy terms a few basic purposes we want the social studies program to accomplish.

SOCIAL STUDIES

To start with, assume that we want the social studies to make people into good citizens, and then look realistically at what a good citizen is like. I think we will discover that a good citizen is not about 98 percent conformity and nice-Nellyism, but that he is often the toughest questioner and dissenter in the crowd. Whatever we found out about the traits of citizenship, we could then hammer out little by little a sense of purpose that students and teachers and the lay community would genuinely believe in, and begin to plan some kind of organization of the field and imaginatively and deliberately to gather materials—a procedure that we do not ordinarily follow in curriculum planning. We act as if we should start with *materials to teach*; what we need is *materials to teach with!* The purpose in a literature program is not to teach a body of literature; it is *to use literature to do something for human beings.*

In a six-year period of schooling teachers have a huge amount of time. Assume that you have about a quarter of the school day for six years, and that you have a set of purposes. Then you begin by saying, "What could we do during that time that would make sense in terms of what we want to do for the youngsters?"

VOCATIONAL PREPARATION

Suppose one of these area committees is concerned with the field of vocational preparation. Long ago our predecessors had the insight to realize that you could not talk vocational competency into existence; you had to have shops and laboratories. But then we got stuck with those shops and they determined what constituted vocational preparation in the schools. For years we have been teaching sets of skills which are often unrealistic and which become obsolete so fast it makes us look silly.

So we need new insights. Certainly one is that the community is a better shop for most purposes than anything we could have in our schools. Another basic premise must be that real success in a vocation is highly dependent on trained intelligence in problem solving. And that it is a matter of genuine, open, effective communication, and being able to work comfortably with other people. Success in one's vocation is also a matter of being able to swing with change very rapidly because change is going to keep on happening very rapidly. These are skimpy ideas about vocational education. But certainly we all know in our hearts that it is much more important that the elementary school and the junior high school succeed in revealing to the pupil the possibilities of the life he could lead vocationally, getting him excited about himself and getting him energized about his future, than how well we teach him to handle a lathe when he is in senior high school. We need a kind of vocational Higher Horizons program that would be exciting, using all of the imagination and confidence-building opportunities we have at our command.

SCIENCE

Let us switch to the sciences. Here again we saw long ago that there must be laboratories. You could not do the job in science by just lecture-discussion. But it was only a few years ago that we began to realize that instruction should start in the laboratory and stay in the laboratory. And precious few schools have yet accommodated themselves to that new approach to the sciences. We were accustomed to studying the chapter on life and then going into the laboratory and running through some workbook exercise to "prove" the chapter. I wonder if we got mousetrapped on another thing, too? Was it, perhaps, the schools that let the idea get abroad that science is amoral, that it has no moral responsibility in our society? Don't we need a science program which discovers life purpose as well as life processes? Isn't that just as legitimate a function of a science teacher as teaching youngsters how to bend glass without breaking it?

SOCIAL STUDIES, AGAIN

Let me go back to the social studies. Oddly enough, having long since decided that in home economics, vocational education, science, and physical education, we could not do the job by lecture-discussion but had to have a laboratory of some sort, in the social studies we have never been that discerning. If social studies mean anything they must connect with the community somehow. I don't know why we have been so slow about this. A social studies program that is worth its name must use the community laboratory. Once we make that basic decision, we will find so many things to do.

In San Francisco about 12 years ago, I was serving simultaneously on two committees. One conducted a Community Chest survey of the day care available in the community. We found that only about a third of the known demand was being met. We needed day care centers desperately. The other was a student committee of the San Francisco Youth Association which was earnestly trying to find outlets for adolescent energy. They would have been delighted to staff child care centers. We never could find enough jobs for them—not even unpaid, volunteer jobs.

Right now our adolescents are unquestionably, in my mind, the best source of energy to mount an early childhood education program that would go well beyond the model of Operation Head Start. These young people, under some supervision from a home economist, a nurse, a nutritionist, a psychologist, and other specialists, could do a far better job than has been done so far. They would be making a terrific contribution, they would be earning some money, they would be learning how to handle their own youngsters when they have them five or six years from now. We have all kinds of outlets for youth in our communities.

This is not the whole story in the social studies; I do not want to abandon the scholarly disciplines. In a recent conference, we saw a group from Southern California working on ways of teaching the Bill of Rights. They started with a short film in which the police do certain things with a dope addict and his friends; then they stopped the film every once in a while and raised questions as to what constitutes a violation of rights. Under what conditions would you let a policeman come into your house? Try sometime to think your way through to a good statement of how citizens should be protected *against* their own government and yet be protected *by* it too. This is truly a difficult thing to do. That kind of social studies material is beginning to pop up from all around. The project called "Man: A Course of Study" (Education Development Center) seems to me to be one of the most inspiring things that has ever been done. We do not have to settle for anemic, boring social studies programs.

HUMANITIES

I would like to concentrate on the field that happens to be my pet—the burgeoning, very young field of the unified humanities. Several thousand high schools around the country have developed the beginnings of such programs in the past five or six years. Generally speaking, this is only a one-year course with a pitifully small conception of a humanities program. Obviously, it ought to be a six-year program. (Really, the elementary school ought to be engaged and so should the college.)

Again, suppose you had a fourth of the school time for six years to devote to a unified humanities program, and you had a real vision of what you were trying to do. This is the part of the school day when you are going to help youngsters—not just *let* youngsters, but *help* youngsters—come to grips with their own personal values, with their own sense of the significance of life, with their own personal worries.

You are going to use whatever will help them in this search. Obviously you will use literature, the arts, music, as they fit. Just as obviously, you are going to use psychology and the other behavioral sciences. The program will require a team. I think you are going to have to have a kind of laboratory; better, it would be a suite of laboratories. Think what you could do if you had a library setting, a room or a series of rooms where books were in prominence, all kinds of them. The *New York Times Book Review* (if that was appropriate to your group) would be there and the *Saturday Review*. Reviews of the latest play on Broadway that would depict it as a happening noted with excitement. You would have the finest recordings of all kinds of music for use on the best stereo equipment. You would have, either in transparencies or in those wonderful paper prints that you can get so easily from galleries now, the best art of all time, including the modern. We brag a lot about the fact that 90 percent of all the scientists who ever lived are alive today. We do not seem to be as aware that a lot of the best poetry and the best music that have ever been composed were composed by people who are alive now.

We could have all these resources. We could have an atmosphere in that room or suite of rooms that would be as different from the typical dried-up English class as that English class is different from the physical education class out on the playground—an entirely different mode, a totally different way of life. I would like the humanities period to be a tranquil time when youngsters could read whatever interested them. We would have to put on one whale of a treasure hunt to find things that would be meaningful to students with different kinds of backgrounds and different reading abilities. We have gone way off the track in insisting that boys and girls should not read anything in school except the great things and then interpreting "great" to mean *Silas Marner*. With the cooperation of the youngsters, if we really settled down to it, we could find things. Audiences of educators, teachers especially, always seem to go into a special hush if I use the example of *Catcher in the Rye*. Each generation of youngsters seems to discover it by themselves. There is a kind of built-in validity about that book. If we don't have guts enough to use that kind of material we might as well go out of business, because we are going to have to use things much farther out than that to guide youngsters to the joy and excitement of books, music, and painting.

The question of where a boy or girl is *now* is given undue prominence. The danger is not aiming too high over his head; the real danger is arrested development. If we get him on the track, get him reading a lot, get him excited about ideas, get him looking to art as a personal resource, we do not need to worry. He will come through to a full and rich adulthood.

I would build into this humanities program a very extensive use, not only of psychology, but of other behavioral sciences such as cultural anthropology. I want these youngsters to have time and knowledge enough to sit around and talk about not only their personal values but also the values of their culture. And I don't know that there is any better way to do it than to give them fascinating glimpses of a variety of cultures, to externalize a bit, to look at the values of this group and that group, to see the differences, and by this process to be able to perceive and examine our own cultural hang-ups in a calm and civilized way. I want to get the vision of some very sophisticated psychologists into the act. I want to build into this six-year program a sensitivity-training program which would make the popular $500 program that industry is so eager to use for its junior grade executives look like peanuts. You could move into such a program slowly, very tenderly, without any prying or pushing or bruising— moving as kids get ready for it in various stages over a six-year period. You could develop in a high school graduate a sensitivity to other human beings that no generation has ever even dreamed of before our time.

And we could do the same thing with writing and speech. We now have a clumsy, sterile composition program, self-defeating, geared to a kind of sanitary correctness. I have hired many of the products (fired most of them later)—people who freeze up in front of a piece of paper, freeze up in front of a microphone, who can't think on their feet, who haven't the slightest idea, really, of communication. This is not surprising, considering that they have been taught over a twelve-year period that it doesn't matter much what you say, and that it doesn't matter at all why you felt like wanting to say it; that what matters is to put it into proper form and proper grammar. In the context of what I have been talking about, it would be easy, with much use of the arts and music and sensitivity training, to develop boys and girls who had a real flair for communicating out of the center of themselves into the center of you. A lot of young people today have this wonderful instinct, the yen of the flower children to get right from me to you without anything between us. The traditional composition program as it now stands is the worst thing that could happen to them in that respect. I guess you think I am exaggerating, but I have made about half my life's living writing and editing. I know what I'm talking about: we are killing communicators.

A CURRICULUM CONTINUUM: POSSIBLE TRENDS IN THE 70s*

HAROLD G. SHANE

For generations most education in the U.S. has been divided into arbitrary segments. It also has been given labels such as "the elementary school" and "the secondary school." A century or more ago, in view of what was then known about teaching and learning, and when the school population was expanding rapidly in urban centers, such grade-level divisions instituted for administrative purposes made a great deal of sense. However, education now has reached a level of sophistication at which serious thought

* Reprinted from *Phi Delta Kappan* (March 1970), 51:389–392, by permission.

can and should be given to the development of a carefully reasoned and well-designed continuum of experience for the learner, one which can replace the disjointed divisions of the past and the present.

Such a curriculum continuum presumably would provide an unbroken chain of ventures and adventures in meaningful learning, beginning with early childhood education. It would extend through post-secondary education and on into later-life education.

Urgent priority should be given to studying and experimenting with the development of genuine continuity in education for several reasons. First, learning itself is a continuous process. It begins no later than at birth and extends through time until one ultimately learns the meaning of death. Since the input of experience is continuous, there is no reason for sectioning the curriculum into four- or six-year time blocks and for "keeping school" on the basis of a nine- or 10-month academic year.

Second, we have been wasting our time. Despite decades of talk about "articulating" the units of public education, this objective has never been achieved because it *cannot* be achieved. We have simply squandered our time and energy on refining the errors inherent in the graded school when we should have thrown away the "graded" and "segmented" concepts years ago.

Third, if we intend seriously to improve the psychology of teaching and learning (a task which is difficult enough in itself), we need to remove the uncoordinated divisions which presently serve as barriers or hurdles to the educational progress of children and youth.

A fourth reason for giving priority to the task of bringing continuity to education is perhaps more subtle than the first three. The challenge of building a sound, well-conceived curriculum continuum is one *which can help educators to find themselves* in a confused and confusing culture. Today most educators over 30 years old are pioneers in a new, unfamiliar pedagogical world. Whether we be elementary teachers or college deans, all of us have three educational deficiencies carried over from the pre-1940 period to overcome: (1) an experientially limited, hence inaccurate, concept of the past, (2) a perception of the present diminished by our incomplete auditory and visual input related to education during the last three decades, and (3) a concept of possible educational futures which is defective because it is based on faulty, linear projections of the past into tomorrow.[1]

As we move toward better continuity, the implications for changes in contemporary, arbitrary segments of education (such as the secondary

---

[1] For example, the "over-thirties" in education are likely to think of the computer as an addition to our stockpile of resources in the education warehouse rather than as the foundation for an entirely new warehouse.

school) become tremendous. Indeed, as the curriculum continuum becomes a reality, such divisions as the elementary school and the secondary school will literally cease to exist as academic or administrative units. Since this may strike some persons in elementary and secondary education alike as a draconian type of educational reform, careful heed must be given to an explanation of the nature of the curriculum continuum concept, its psychological value, and the desirable changes toward which increased continuity can carry educational practice.

WHAT IS A CURRICULUM CONTINUUM?

As indicated above, an educational or curriculum continuum may be described as an unbroken flow of experiences planned with and for the individual learner throughout his contacts with the school. Much current thought and research suggests that the program should begin no later than in early childhood and should continue to provide educational opportunities as long as the school has anything to offer the learner. In other words, persons in their sixties or even older would be served methodically when the continuum concept is eventually extended to its upper ranges.

Continuity in learning implies that schooling shall extend throughout the year. Furthermore, it may begin officially at any time during the year that a child is deemed mature enough to be present (e.g., at age three), not at a legislated date such as "by the year in which he becomes six years of age on or before midnight on the 30th of November." Vacation periods would be scheduled at any time during the calendar year and for any length of time upon which agreement was reached. This would constitute no problem when the young learner is assigned to a team of teachers rather than to grade level or to a class. Teachers likewise could be off-duty during any interval for study, travel, rest, and so on. Deliberate "overstaffing," i.e., five teachers attached to a basic four-teacher unit or team, woud permit one to engage in non-tcaching activities in February just as readily as in July.

In a curriculum continuum, educational experiences also are personalized. The *personalized* curriculum differs from *individualized* instruction in at least one major respect. Individualized instruction, which has been attempted for many years, was intended to help a child meet group norms or standards, but at his own rate of progress.[2] The personalized curriculum continuum serves as a means of making the school's total resources available

---

[2] In the "Winnetka Plan" as begun by Carleton W. Washburne, for instance, the curriculum was basically the same for all children in a given grade, but the *rate* of progress varied. The rapid learner was kept from moving beyond the company of his age-mates by providing him with enrichment activities and similar paracurricular experiences.

to a child so that his teachers can figuratively help him to "create himself" without reference to what his "average" chronological age-mates may be accomplishing.

The meaning of a personalized continuum type of curriculum can be clarified further by means of literary allusion. The curriculum of the 1930-vintage graded school was one in which the child was forced to fit the program. That is, it was analogous to the mythological bed of Procrustes. This was an iron bedstead on which the ancient, unfriendly Greek giant bound the unwary traveler, then cut off his victim's legs or stretched them to fit.

The individualized, and sometimes nongraded, approach to instruction was a distinct improvement, since it endeavored to shorten or lengthen the Procrustean bed to fit the child. The personalized curriculum continuum, on the other hand, is one in which the child, with teacher guidance, is encouraged—indeed expected—*to build his own bed.*

SOME PSYCHOLOGICAL VALUES OF THE CONTINUUM CONCEPT

"Continuity" in education is not merely a mechanical or organizational plan for locking together or more closely articulating the present arbitrary units of education which precede and follow the secondary school years. Rather, in many ways, it is a psychological concept, a way of conceiving the learner's ongoing experiences as a smoothly flowing stream with an "educational current" that is properly paced to match the skill and speed with which he can ride its eddies and rapids.

In a school characterized by the psychologically supportive qualities of the continuum, the learner begins to find answers to three questions which during the past decade have begun to be recognized as queries of basic importance:

1. "Who am I?" (self-identity)
2. "What am I doing?" (self-orientation)
3. "Where am I going?" (self-direction)

Self-awareness and, hopefully, a wholesome self-concept are developed as answers are found to question one. Through seeking and gradually acquiring an answer to point two, the learner progressively "finds himself" in the process of searching for inner integrity. He likewise develops the skills of social interaction and the coping behaviors in which self-confidence resides. Finally, in discovering answers to question three the learner establishes a personal compass course or sets in motion an inner gyroscope which, if all goes well, leads to desirable personal-social contributions, to acceptance by others, and to consequent personal happiness.

It may be conjectured that only through a personalized curriculum continuum can we construct a humane educational milieu or matrix in which the learner can safely, and with a sense of security, *discover* the world and *create* himself. We do not know enough, we cannot clearly predict enough, of the twenty-first century world (in which the infant, child, or adolescent of the 1970's will spend the larger portion of his lifetime) to gamble on a less flexible concept of the curriculum than the one proposed here. We must eschew in the realm of content the impossible dream of *what* explicit fundamentals children and youth shall learn; we must espouse the more tangible goal of teaching them *how* to learn.

And we ourselves need to unlearn the unexamined educational *beliefs* that often guide our conduct, while striving to learn the value that resides in *believing* in what education can accomplish.

NEW DIRECTIONS TOWARD WHICH CONTINUITY IN EDUCATION CAN LEAD

In the years immediately ahead, the educational world seems likely to continue to be invigorated by continued change. Probable future developments which research and trend-projection suggest include substantial increases in whatever it is that I.Q. tests measure, in the continued spread of man's 13 major languages (especially English, Spanish, Mandarin, and Russian), and the development of a phonetic English alphabet with approximately 30 consonants and 15 vowels. The schools also seem likely to be influenced by major improvements in the status of women, by legislation requiring compulsory psychiatry, by a five- or six-hour day and an eight-month working year, and by the growing need to cope with problems stemming from overbreeding, pollution, accumulating garbage and diminishing resources, and man's ancient propensity for attempting to settle his disputes through warfare.

To the exciting and sometimes unnerving educational mix of the future, bona fide continuity in the curriculum is likely to bring further vitality. To illustrate, in schools with a curriculum continuum:

There Would Be No Failure or "Double Promotion"

One learner would merely live differently, and at a different rate, from others.

"Special Education" and "Remedial Work" Would Cease To Exist

All education of all learners would be "special," regardless of whether they were handicapped, gifted, or in the wide "normal" range between.

Annual Promotion Would Become a Thing of the Past

What we now speak of as promotion would become a *direction* rather than a yearly hurdle.

There Would Be No Dropouts

At present we have created a needless dropout problem. In a personalized program, with suitable guidance resources available, the secondary school student would not drop out to accept a position. Instead, the school, employer, student, and (when possible) his family would reach a consensus that it was desirable for him to extend the flow of his curriculum continuum outside the school to include the world of work. Weeks or months later he could, if he chose, pick up the thread of his in-school experiences. The absence of grades, formal class assignment, and so on, would encourage his return with no stigma attached.

Compensatory Education Would Terminate

There would be no need for compensating, since education in a continuum is designed to maximize talents, minimize environmental inequities, and be inherently "supportive" in the sense that it builds on and sustains the unique assets which each learner acquires because of his membership in any given U.S. subculture.

Report Cards and Marks Would Vanish

In a continuum, reporting becomes a "spot check" on where the learner appears to be rather than an invidious semestral agony foisted on individuals clumped together for purposes of comparison.

And so on. . . .

CHANGES THE CONTINUUM CONCEPT CAN BRING TO EDUCATION IN THE FUTURE

What are some of the changes that are likely to occur in today's high school as the fact of continuity in learning and in education is more widely acknowledged and as teachers and administrators frankly face the opportunities—and problems—of a transition to an uninterrupted and personalized sequence of learning for children and youth?

Organizational Changes

For one thing, as noted earlier, a discrete secondary school program would cease to exist. But so would the elementary school on one hand and college on the other. Graduation exercises would become obsolete, since one cannot graduate from a continuum.

Almost inevitably, there would be a significant downward extension of education. Ideally, the school would establish its first contacts with the child no later than at age two during a "non-school pre-school" interval. Here children would be examined for psycho-physical or environmental impediments to learning prior to beginning direct school contacts in the "minischool," at age three, for their first methodically planned sensory input.

Patently, when schooling begins for children three to four years sooner than is now generally the rule, the structures we now call elementary and secondary schools will be dealing with a psychologically different type of client with a distinctly different background. He would not have been enrolled in kindergarten, for instance. Instead, he would have spent an indeterminate "make-ready" period in a pre-primary continuum and entered the primary years anywhere between, say, five and seven or even eight years of age. By the end of the middle school era (i.e., at the close of what is now grade eight), he may have spent anywhere from seven to 12 years in elementary education following a seamless personalized program. He has worked under teacher-team guidance, and, quite conceivably, is the beneficiary of technological developments which have helped to widen and deepen his background.

The organization of the secondary school and the nature of its curriculum, as they exist in 1970, seemingly will need to go through a complete mutation as a continuum approach spreads upward. It is not too soon to begin speculating as to how the coming splice between elementary and secondary education can be made both smoothly and so as to serve the potential new product as he moves from early to later adolescence.[3]

Almost certainly, there will be major changes in the traditional high school-college relationship, too. At present, the college often expects U.S. secondary schools to provide a subject-content background so that the adolescent can achieve his "real education" during his university years, i.e., examine, expand, and apply the "beginnings of knowledge" presumably supplied by the time a diploma is conferred. As early childhood education becomes commonplace, as the personalized continuum becomes established, it may not be illogical to expect that, in effect, the secondary level of the 1980's will, with a more sophisticated clientele, be reorganized to replace

---

[3] One is led to the tentative conclusion that, as education attains the continuity it has lacked, the portion of education now thought of as "secondary" will become at least as flexible as the "elementary" portion. Thus it would be of indeterminate length, without a graded structure—in short, a part of the stream of personalized, seamless education that would lead into post-secondary programs of many kinds.

the college years of today so that the "college-bound" secondary student of a decade hence can immediately enter upon a program at the university which is of graduate school caliber.

Changing Policies and Practices

Imbedded in the concept of continuity are various changes in policy. Typical of these is a decrease in age homogeneity among children working together. In the absence of rigid allocations of subject matter (e.g., studying the Middle Ages in grade six, biology in grade 10) the continuum may well draw together in year-long or in short-lived special purpose groupings children and youth who differ in age by as much as four or even six years.

Pupil interchange from school to school, district to district, and even country to country also becomes feasible if not essential when a personalized educational continuum replaces graded and nongraded schools. Teacher exchanges at an unprecedented level are a concomitant. By the 1980's it may be little more than routine to find a mature student (who today would be in high school) doing a year's work in Scotland or Ecuador. Perhaps his textual material would be transmitted from his home campus in facsimile form at appropriate intervals.

Undoubtedly, education will draw upon various instructional systems centers associated with the schools as supportive agencies for a continuum. Perhaps by the Eighties some forms of computerized instruction and information retrieval will be in general use.

The practice of making adult education an integral part of what is now secondary and collegiate education comes to mind when one extends a lifelong educational experience-chain to the middle years (40 to 70) and to early old age (70 years plus). With increases in leisure time, with rapid change making some skills and knowledge obsolete in a few years, and with the active life-spans of many people due to extend into the 90's within a decade or two, it seems reasonable that some people may profitably enroll in a secondary school interval appropriate to their personalized curriculum. Such re-enrollments, for as long as a year or two, might occur in the forties for the person seeking new vocational avenues and in the sixties or seventies as partial retirement draws near and new interests and hobbies are in need of cultivation. Who knows? We may have *old* married housing projects opening on the 1988 campus!

New Deployment of Faculty Members

There will probably be much more vertical deployment of teachers in the continuum school as it becomes evident that learners need access to a greater variety of stimulating faculty minds. Today's second-grade teacher may find herself on a team working with a mixed cluster of 12- to 18-year-olds twice weekly in a human development-sex education project, working with senior citizens on several afternoons, and helping to supervise paraprofessionals working with three-year-olds in a minischool complex during the remainder of the week.

The effective use of paraprofessionals seems certain to be an important challenge to the school which uses differentiated staffs to achieve personalized instruction.

Perhaps the most demanding task, and certainly one of the most important as the seamless curriculum materializes, is that of redirecting teacher education—including in-service re-education. Particularly, some secondary teachers and many college teachers who have been predominantly subject-oriented may find it difficult to become skilled in the flexible, creative use of educational resources, in identifying with interdisciplinary teams, and in working with groups of students in situations in which new criteria for group membership and for assessing success are taking form.

Selecting Content for a Curriculum Continuum

For decades, research studies have suggested that, except for central tendencies created by widely used textbooks, the U.S. curriculum has been a Joseph's coat sewn of many pieces. Even now there is little agreement as to what should be taught and when. As a result, it is unlikely that conceptualizing the curriculum as a continuum can increase the general disarray. In fact, it is likely that a continuum will bring a measure of order.

One reason that much disagreement has marked curriculum development is that schools generally have grouped children chronologically, then failed to find any way of coping with problems of instruction brought about by the inevitable range in ability that ensued. The personalized curriculum reduces this problem to a minimum, since it rejects, as an undesirable goal, any idea of increasing the correlation between chronological age and uniform achievement norms.

As continuity is brought to education, the scope and sequence of the child's inner curriculum, i.e., the sum of what he has internalized from his school-sponsored experience, becomes uniquely personal. In the secondary continuum school, the individual adolescent would be guided in the wise exploitation of the school's total resources. His program would be *derived* from his status and needs, not predetermined by impersonal requirements.

Better Tomorrows through Greater Continuity

In a recent book, Peter F. Drucker referred to the present as an age of discontinuity. His purpose in writing was to ask *not* "What will tomorrow look like?" but "What do we have to tackle *today* to make tomorrow better?"

Likewise, in education we should not speculate about tomorrow until our speculations become an opiate that keeps us from improving the schools as they exist today. At the same time, decisions made today shape the future. Since this is so, it seems prudent for educators at all levels, including secondary education, to give consideration to the idea of an uninterrupted, personalized flow of educational experiences, a seamless curriculum. Decisions that create greater continuity are likely to lead to the distinctly better education that the U.S. has always relied on the schools to produce.

Chapter 14

MOVING TOWARD THE HIGH SCHOOL OF THE FUTURE

The current literature of high school education includes many proposals and reports many projects for moving the high school toward such programs as projected in the previous chapter. The last chapter of this book turns to a sampling of these proposals and projects.

ES'70, described in a paper prepared by Gabriel Reuben for this anthology, is an attempt to apply a systems approach to the redesigning of the high school program. The sixteen autonomous school districts involved in this project were selected to be representative of the geographic regions and the types of school districts of the nation. Some disappointments in federal funding restricted the full development of the original plans, but school district contributions kept the project alive. Reuben notes that "the greatest impact of ES'70 has been its catalytic effect in promoting a climate for change." The consortium or network pattern is reminiscent of earlier cooperative efforts such as the Eight-Year Study, the Horace Mann-Lincoln Institute of School Experimentation, and various other projects supported by philanthropic foundations and utilizing shared problems and problem-solving approaches. Gabriel reports that in ES'70 "all network members have benefited from the experiences of their counterparts throughout the country as evidenced by a sharing of locally developed materials, strategies, and techniques."

The systems approach of ES'70 involved "adherence to behavioral outcomes as a prerequisite to the design of a new instructional system." Each district operated training programs to help teachers learn to prepare performance-related objectives and criteria, which would lead in turn to the development of individualized learning packets. Other features of the project mentioned by Reuben include the use of emerging technological tools and the development of new management systems. Increased cooperation among school districts on a consortium basis as an approach to school improvement is the possibility developed by this article. What advantages and disadvantages do you see?

A major impetus to and support of innovations in the schools came from the federal Elementary and Secondary Education Act of 1965 and its subsequent amendments. To indicate the problems associated with this stimulus and support as well as its accomplishments and promise, a selection is presented here from an address made at a National Association of Secondary School Principals annual conference by Nolan Estes, then Associate Commissioner of Education. The first problem he cited is "far too many programs funded under the Elementary and Secondary Education Act are simply additions which tend to perpetuate more of the same." He also noted the fragmentation incident to categorical federal aid supporting quite disparate programs in the same high school through different Acts and Titles, and the related problems of "distorting priorities at the local level" and "divisiveness." Nevertheless he maintained "that the system that we have now—the system of local control, state responsibility, and federal concern—is worth saving." To make it better, Estes called for developing in every school and district "the capability for comprehensive planning—comprehensive planning for the wise use and wise expenditure of our funds." In effect he was anticipating the movement toward "accountability" (see Chapter 10), which developed soon afterwards.

Many educators and laymen believe that the fundamental effort toward improvement of the high school—the effort without which no amount of systems analysis, federal funding, or other external planning and aid would fully succeed—must be made by the local community. Representing this point of view is an article by the author of this anthology, entitled "The Community Can Save Its High Schools from Mediocrity" included in a series of articles in *The Humanist* devoted to the theme, "Can We Save the Public High School?" "Yes," we say to this question, if "more and more parents and citizens in general care about their high schools and cooperate to improve them." The article reviews past experience with the community high school, and holds that today's need is for "a *comprehensive, community-centered* high school model that is relevant to the students and community of the 1970s." Several specific cooperative actions are suggested for moving toward this model, including the creation of a community council for each high school that would interact with student and faculty representatives, fuller use of community media, student forums on community issues, student participation in community activities, community work experience, use of community resource persons and facilities, and opening the school for adult education and recreation.

This anthology, being representative of the contemporary high school literature, has included several articles emphasizing the problems of urban schools and proposals for meeting these—for it was these problems and proposals that occupied attention in the early 1970s and seemed certain to continue to do so in America's urban society. But there are also many rural high schools and it can be expected that large numbers of American adolescents will continue for the foreseeable future to have their high school curriculum in small schools in rural environments. The article by Ward Sybouts is an analysis of the problems of these schools, with many provocative suggestions for improving their programs. He notes that "a massive educational system for rural youth" will continue to be needed and that "it is incumbent upon the educational enterprise to provide quality education for all youth, *rural* as well as *urban*." He reviews past improvement projects for small schools and finds them good, but inadequately disseminated. His suggestions for future program development highlight innovations in organization and administration, the revitalization of the community school concept (is this the same concept as Alexander's?), the use of shared services, a consortium arrangement for inservice education, and evaluation programs.

The final three articles of this book emphasize the role of people, and especially students and teachers, in improving the curriculum. James E. House gives a resounding "Yes" to his title question, "Can the Student Participate in His Own Destiny?" He reviews studies of students' interest in being involved in decision-making that affects them, and identifies the ingredients for participation. Among the needed ingredients found in his research study were: an open communications link providing for a grievance procedure; student participation in setting rules and regulations; "an exciting and relevant curriculum"; and "an understanding and knowledgeable teacher." Charles H. Hill's article focuses on "Teachers as Change Agents," reviewing some research and other publications that minimized or criticized adversely the role of teachers. Hill also reports his own use of a survey instrument "to investigate the teacher's perception of himself as a change agent," which led him to conclude that the teachers surveyed "(a) want to institute changes: (b) do not wish to make changes which require additional time or effort on their part; and (c) feel thwarted by authoritarian principals and quagmire-creating bureaucracies." The remainder of the article documents the requirements and strategies for teachers who would persist as change agents, the author contending that teachers can be in fact change agents but that "mastery of one's own professional destiny is not without its price."

For the final article in this book the same selection is used as in the first edition and for the same purpose: to emphasize the role of human beings in change processes. Especially in the 1970s, with the greatly augmented technological resources, the trends toward organizational innovations, and the conflicts in society and education of competing forces, Alice Miel's "Innovation and People" is a highly useful and impressive reminder of the importance of the human element in change. Hopefully this closing article will challenge each reader to make his own role in educational change an important, constructive, and satisfying one.

ES'70*

GABRIEL H. REUBEN

ES'70 is a consortium of sixteen autonomous school districts[1] which have formed a corporation for cooperative effort toward the design of an organic curriculum.

The ES'70 Corporation logo bears the legend, "Educational System for the Seventies . . . A Cooperative Program for Educational Innovation." It is difficult to pinpoint exact dates and credit everyone involved with the conception of ES'70, as is frequently the case with good ideas and sometimes with organizations. It should be noted, however, that at an ES'70 network meeting in Willingboro, New Jersey, in June of 1970, a plaque was presented to a representative of the Ford Foundation in recognition of its thinking and assistance which served to stimulate the formation of the consortium. Major credit, though, for the early planning, the architecture of the organization, and the impetus for ES'70's prenatal development and birth, must go to David S. Bushnell and Robert M. Morgan, formerly director and deputy director, respectively, of the Division of Comprehensive and Vocational Education, Bureau of Research of the United States Office of Education. These two men, as "parents" of the concept called ES'70, viewed it as an application of the systems approach to the redesign of the total educational program of the high school. "Selected schools were to serve as a flexible staging area where

---

* Manuscript prepared especially for this anthology.
[1] ES'70 School Districts: Baltimore, Maryland; Bancroft School (Haddonfield), New Jersey; Bloomfield Hills, Michigan; Boulder Valley, Colorado; Archiocese of Chicago, Illinois; Houston Independent, Texas; Institute of American Indian Arts (Santa Fe), New Mexico; Mamaroneck, New York; Mineola, New York; Monroe, Michigan; Philadelphia, Pennsylvania; Portland, Oregon; Quincy, Massachusetts; San Mateo, California; University City, Missouri; Willingboro Township, New Jersey.

486

the interactive effects of the important components of the educational process can be tested and revised in terms of both contribution to student learning and cost benefits."[2]

The schools selected to participate were to be representative of every region in our nation and to include virtually every type of district: rural, suburban, and urban; diverse cultural mixes; and varying levels of community educational financial support, from the very poor to the very wealthy. Further, each district was to be one which had some experience with and commitment to innovation. When the first network meeting was held in May of 1967, at the Nova School in Fort Lauderdale, Florida, a design for cooperative effort with the U.S. Office of Education, universities, foundations, private nonprofit institutions, business and labor organizations, and state education departments was presented as a guarantor of success.

As the consortium has developed, the purpose of ES'70 has been broadly interpreted to include the improvement of the learning situation for all boys and girls so that each student's school experience will be effective, will be relevant to his needs and aspirations, and will make him a useful, functioning adult able to cope with, contribute to, and benefit from a fast-changing society. Further, an integral part of the program is the assistance of teachers in keeping their skills abreast with an increasingly complex educational enterprise.

To support this mammoth undertaking, a grandiose scheme was prepared, including a PERT chart identifying the major classes of activities which would be completed before the entire program could become operational. These activities fell generally into four broad classes: (a) staff development, (b) instructional management, (c) school management or environment for learning, (d) evaluation. Specific tasks structured in this plan ranged from the preparation of inservice training programs to the exploration of computer potential to instructional and school management situations.

A $30 million[3] five-year plan was proposed as the U.S. Office of Education's contribution to the support of the undertaking. Unfortunately, only a fractional percentage of the federal funding was provided. Changes in the administration of the nation, combined with what appeared to be virtual continuous reorganization of the U.S. Office, and turnover of its personnel ended USOE's commitment by early 1970. What was for the first two and a half years a marriage between the organization and the

---

[2] R. Morgan and J. Morgan, "Systems Analysis for Educational Change," *Trend*, Spring 1968, p. 28.

[3] D. Bushnell, "An Education System for the Seventies," Speech at Aerospace Education Foundation Conference, Washington, D.C., September 12, 1967.

U.S. Office of Education ended in divorce with only the barest liaison continuing through persons who have maintained interest in specific projects and through the personal relationships of individuals in the U.S. Office of Education with some of the superintendents and coordinators in ES'70.

Despite the drying up of the flow of federal funds, sixteen school districts determined that their association and cooperative endeavor in ES'70 had been fruitful enough to continue to function. In order to maintain an administrative office and a management team, each school district was assessed a sum ranging from $2500 to $6000 depending upon its total school budget for the first year of operation without federal funding for the management of the consortium. After that the assessment was reduced to a $2500 annual figure for all districts regardless of size.

Since the inception of the ES'70 program nine major network meetings have been held at a variety of sites throughout the country. Deliberations at these sessions have focused on specific educational issues, problem-solving strategies, and a review of relevant research and development projects. In addition, separate conferences have been provided; one for superintendents, six for coordinators, and two for principals. Three major curriculum training institutes were sponsored for teachers in the ES'70 schools (Duluth, San Mateo, Willingboro). A two-week workshop was convened for principals of the ES'70 high schools. Additional opportunities have been made available to representatives of ES'70 schools to attend conferences or institutes dealing with Achievement Motivation, Harvard Project Physics, computerized guidance systems, behavioral objectives in English, and arts curriculum development.

Since November, 1969, an executive office of ES'70 has existed to provide cohesion and centralization to the network. From this office have emerged materials, reports, and newsletters in an attempt to maintain a vital internal communications network. Effective that same month, the U.S. Office of Education, the National Endowment for the Arts, and the JDR 3rd Fund awarded the corporation a grant for an arts curriculum development project.

A review of school district progress reports, reinforced by on-site visitations, reveals that the greatest impact of ES'70 has been its catalytic effect in promoting a climate for change. Most coordinators report the greatest efforts at the local level are directed at staff development activities. Each district has designed a local strategy or program to involve staff members to some degree in the planning of a new instructional program. Boulder and Willingboro have developed their own self-instructional training materials. Several districts have worked cooperatively with nearby colleges and universities. Many schools have utilized commercially prepared materials for staff training (VIMCET, Deterline) and several districts have brought to their staffs "experts" from other ES'70 schools to assist in their local inservice programs. All network members have benefited from the experiences of their counterparts throughout the country as evidenced by a sharing of locally developed materials, stategies, and techniques.

A number of ES'70 districts have recorded their success at conducting interdistrict visitations with designated staff members. Visits to innovative locations have served to inspire many skeptical staff members to a more positive outlook toward the "newer methods." Distribution of *ES'70 News* and other related documents and filmstrips has assisted many coordinators in their efforts to stimulate faculty members to take a new look at their present mode of operation.

It is significant to note the wide variety of strategies employed by local change agents to foster a positive climate for change. There is no doubt, however, that the exchange and interaction among the coordinators greatly facilitated this process for many districts. In the absence of "trial runs" many school leaders would certainly have been reluctant to attempt tactics which were ultimately employed and determined to be quite successful.

There is no doubt that a major impact of ES'70 has been the effect of its adherence to behavioral outcomes as a prerequisite to the design of a new instructional system. Practically every school district has launched a training program to develop the skills in teachers to write performance objectives, prescribe performance criteria, etc. This in turn has produced a plethora of materials incorporating such objectives into various forms of "individualized" learning packets. Locally developed curriculum materials have been supplemented by access to other resources (IOX, IDEA, BOE) which augment the rather voluminous supplies already stacked on shelves.

Further progress seems to be prevalent in many ES'70 schools with regard to a wide use of emerging technological tools. Willingboro and Mineola have demonstrated their application of television as a viable instructional medium. Other ES'70 districts are exploring the potential of the computer and all are exposing themselves to an examination of a wide range of audio-visual resources. Many have commented how their identification as an ES'70 school has brought them a parade of hardware and software vendors.

Particularly noteworthy are the many comments which reflect how ES'70 involvement has triggered a special or renewed contact with State Education Departments. Many local districts have established close linkages with state and federal personnel as a result of their affiliation with ES'70. In more than a few cases this has extended to other agencies as well as including universities, private industry, and foundations. To some districts this has produced additional sources of funds and to others valuable resources and talent pools to draw upon as conditions require.

A few districts indicated a certain degree of progress in the area of school management—environments for learning. To districts such as Monroe, San Mateo, Philadelphia, and Portland, this has meant a focus on planning new buildings which would be appropriate for a learner centered program. To others it has meant the formulation of new management systems to accommodate the emerging demands of an individualized school setting. Several ES'70 schools have already benefited from Dr. Walter Foley's work at Iowa City with Houston as a site projected for implementation. San Maeto is piloting the California PPBES program and other districts have monitored its progress in this area. Other management schemes are emerging in Quincy and Portland which aim to maintain a data flow to allow for optimal diagnosis and prescription of students' activities. It is significant to note the extension of such management practices into the instructional phase where it has been so sorely lacking. Also, several districts are upgrading their business, accounting, and bookkeeping functions, but this follows a general conversion practice from industry.

In retrospect, there is no question but that ES'70 has provided an impact to its members. It is clear that climates have been created, teacher interest has been stimulated, instructional activities are being formulated, and new designs are emerging.

The superintendents of the ES'70 School District believe that ongoing association with other forward looking administrators of innovative school districts is highly stimulating and continually self-renewing. It is this, plus what might be regarded as the security of working with others who are heading in the same directions, utilizing the same vocabulary, and meeting similar problems, which bodes well for the continuation and growth of ES'70 . . . for the benefit of the professionals participating, the school district involved, and, utimately, education as a whole.

ESEA: ITS PROMISE, ACCOMPLISHMENTS, AND PROBLEMS*

Nolan Estes

PROBLEMS

Let's look quickly now at some of the problems related to federal aid to education. It is true that we have an appropriation of more than $2 billion this year for elementary and secondary education activities. It is true that this represents a 300 percent increase over the last four years, but still the $2 billion appropriation represents less than eight percent of the total expenditures for elementary and secondary education in this nation. We anticipate that some $26 billion will be spent for all elementary and secondary activities this year. The $2 billion from the federal government is only a small piece of the total pie.

Let me turn to some of the problems we encounter in administering our slice of the pie. First, far too many programs funded under the Elementary and Secondary Education Act are simply additions which tend to perpetuate more of the same. Frequently we find programs being added at the end of the day, programs or courses being taught on Saturday, courses being taught during the summer in the same old way, when it would have been more effective to make some basic changes in the instructional programs which were already in operation.

It's entirely possible for a local secondary school to have a program in Title I for the disadvantaged, and another program under Title II providing library books. It's possible, in addition, to have a demonstration program under Title III, to provide and purchase equipment under NDEA Title III, to have guidance counselors partially paid for under Title V, to provide institute programs for teachers under Title XI of NDEA, and to participate in all of the programs under the Vocational Education Act.

*Excerpt reprinted from the *Bulletin of the National Association of Secondary School Principals* (May 1968), 52:83–86, by permission.

Frequently, this results in fragmentation, a handicap that makes it difficult for us to have great impact on programs at the local level. Because of this fragmentation, federal funds can fail to meet the most pressing local needs. A guidance counselor might be hired when perhaps a school social worker is most needed. And it's possible that a librarian or an administrative assistant might be more valuable in a particular situation than some of the personnel provided under our programs.

Federal categorical aid programs can run the risk of distorting priorities at the local level. Those of you who were involved in the National Defense Education Act when it was first passed in 1958 are well aware of the problems that resulted when foreign language and science education were the emphasis of the program, which required dollar-for-dollar matching. Many of us found ourselves seeking funds from other budgets in order to qualify for these particular funds, and as a result there was a great distortion in our program and a great imbalance in our curriculum.

Another major problem with federal aid to education is the divisiveness that may result from the number of programs. Many school districts and many state departments of education have established separate staffs to administer these funds. As a result, if you want to talk about social studies or language arts in the regular program, you go to one staff member. If you want to talk about social studies or language arts for disadvantaged students, you go to another staff member. This divisiveness doesn't encourage a unified effort to improve education.

EVALUATION

As you know, there has been discontent in the Congress during the last two years about the educational world's inability to evaluate programs under the Elementary and Secondary Education Act. More and more, we are being pressed by the Congress to provide specific data on the achievement of pupils, on the change in attitudes of staff members, and on the change in characteristics of leaders, facilities, and organization. We have been hard pressed to provide the data that is necessary and desired by members of Congress and, too often, the planning and staffing for these programs have been inadequate.

Administrative overburden can result from our present method of providing federal aid to education. Three weeks ago *Nation's Schools* published a survey of 16,000 school districts throughout the country. They asked administrators what their most pressing problems were, what they worried about the most. Unfortunately, one of the top five items which most concerned administrators was the federal red tape involved in securing and developing programs under the Elementary and Secondary Education Act.

But solving these problems does not depend on eliminating categorical aid. In spite of the problems connected with it, categorical aid is still the will of Congress and it is still the most effective means of insuring that serious, nationwide needs are not neglected. Our task is to find ways to use categorical aid wisely so as to avoid the problems I have mentioned and eliminate the red tape. And we are doing just that. For one thing, we are encouraging states and local school districts to take a new look at the way their funds are now being used and to consider the advantage of careful, long-range planning on a comprehensive basis.

CHALLENGES

One of our greatest concerns related to programs under the Elementary and Secondary Education Act is the fact that, frequently, principals and teachers are bypassed in planning them. Principals and teachers may not even have an opportunity to participate in the decision-making process in relation to these programs. The most significant plans and decisions all too often are made at the superintendent's level or in the state department of education.

It seems to me, then, as we take a look at federal aid to education in the next decade there are at least two challenges that face us. The first relates to adequate planning for the wise expenditure of federal funds. The second deals with the concentration of these funds on our most critical problems.

There's no doubt that the federal government has a very important role to play in American education. Congressman Perkins said recently that, instead of $2 billion, he anticipates some $10 billion in federal aid to elementary and secondary education by 1972. He put one qualification on it, however. He said whether we can achieve this goal will be determined, to a large extent, by the way we as educators show that we can use these funds efficiently and effectively.

The President's Advisory Commission on Intergovernmental Relations in its Annual Report, submitted January 31, put it another way. This report says that the local, state, and federal system is on trial today as never before, in this century of crisis and change. It indicated that, while hopeful signs can be found, progress seems discouragingly slow in the light of the advancement that needs to be made. It concluded that "the manner of meeting these challenges will largely determine the fate of the American political system. It will determine if we can maintain a form of government marked by partnership and wholesome competition among national, state, and local levels or if, instead, in the face of threatened anarchy we must sacrifice political diversity as the price of the authoritative action required for the nation's survival."

FOR MAXIMUM EFFECT

I maintain that the system that we have now—the system of local control, state responsibility, and federal concern—is worth saving; but it will require our best efforts. These efforts include developing at the secondary school level, in each school and each school district in this country, the capability for comprehensive planning—comprehensive planning for the wise use and wise expenditure of our funds.

When we talk about comprehensive planning, we are talking about the assessment of priorities and then the development of strategies to satisfy some of the needs that have been identified. The assessment of needs, of course, has to take place within the framework of well-identified goals, beliefs, and expectations. It includes the collection of all sorts of data, including manpower requirements, economic as well as demographic data.

After needs have been assessed and priorities assigned, then we need to develop change strategies to improve our program. In many instances, significant change in our schools does not take place because insufficient attention is given to the technical factors. These include psychological strategies for change; that is, developing ways to involve teachers and principals in decision-making and to provide for adequate feedback. It is true that change does not take place in an organization until there is change in people. It is also true, however, that if you want change, you have to develop an organizational pattern that facilitates rather than blocks improvement.

The next challenge facing us involves a concentration of federal funds on our most difficult or most critical problems. Less and less flexibility is available at the local level as higher and higher percentages of funds go into salaries. We suggest that federal funds which are available to local school districts and to local secondary schools be concentrated into a discretionary account in order to make it possible for a principal to have the flexibility that's necessary for him to explore, to experiment, to try out promising approaches.

Frank Brown [moderator of the session] asked a moment ago if every local school district in this country would have, one day, an innovation account. I submit to you this morning that if properly organized, if properly coordinated and concentrated, there could be now through the use of federal funds an innovation account for every local school district and every local secondary school. School districts have an option with regard to federal funds. They can either concentrate on fewer programs and fewer individuals in the hope of effecting substantial improvements, or they can spread out these funds more thinly and reach more students.

It seems to me that the philosophy of the greatest good for the greatest number, as it becomes an attempt to reach more students with minimal results, it a poor use of federal funds. There's a critical mass of effort required to produce clear results. The use of prototype programs and models and the concentration of federal aid programs on fewer children is a much more effective way to demonstrate successful tactics. Once these successful practices have been demonstrated, they can be used in the regular ongoing program to bring about improvement systemwide.

THE COMMUNITY CAN SAVE ITS HIGH SCHOOLS FROM MEDIOCRITY*

William M. Alexander

The greatest danger most high schools face today is not extinction, but threatened, perpetuated, or deepened mediocrity. The public's yearly investment of several billion dollars in over 16,000 public high schools will not be cut off, however much disenchantment may exist. But mediocrity can become more widespread and deeper unless more and more parents and citizens in general care about their high schools and cooperate to improve them.

Earlier in this century, as high school education rapidly became almost universal, the high school was extolled as a community school, as a school the people of a community built and supported for the good of their children, the community, and the nation. It was where the youth were to learn to become good citizens, as well as to prepare for college or to take their first steps toward earning a living. The high school was the center of many community activities, frequently the showplace of the small town and suburb. People hoped it was their offspring's means to the good life. In emergency periods some high schools even became major centers for survival-oriented enterprises. Thus, in the 1930's many high schools in the South became community centers for food preservation and

---

* This article first appeared in *The Humanist*, May/June 1971 and is reprinted by permission.

other vital activities of a depressed economy. During World War II the high schools everywhere provided manpower for wartime industry, Victory Corps for varied community services, and assistance in salvage and rationing. Since World War II the high schools have more frequently been turned to for solving national rather than community problems. Indicative of this shift are the National Defense Education Act (1958) for increasing support to science, mathematics, foreign languages, and other fields deemed critical for national defense, and the recent and current federal programs to reduce poverty, racial segregation, and related social and economic problems.

Many factors other than national problems and federal funding, of course, have tended to lessen community interest and participation in the high schools. The bureaucratic control that inevitably came in states, counties, and cities with increasingly concentrated populations set up attendance areas that could not correspond to natural communities, which tended to disappear anyway in urban areas. Life, particularly in urban communities, became very complex, and fewer adults turned to their high schools for any purpose not directly related to their own children. As college attendance became more and more common, high school became less and less the focal point of many parents' dreams and concerns. The pressure to meet college requirements produced a curriculum fitted to the academic track, and the high school could less easily be bent to community needs and issues. In too many cases, it could also not fulfill the needs of youths not choosing or not needing a college preparatory program.

The high school curriculum would more likely be considered relevant today if its community focus of the 1930's and 1940's had been more fully developed and continued, and if the still popular 1918 statement of the Cardinal Principles of Secondary Education were really the basis of today's community high school program. The aims of this statement—health, command of fundamental processes, worthy home membership, vocation, civic education, valuable use of leisure, and development of ethical character—need renewed and successful formulation in a *comprehensive, community-centered* high school model that is relevant to the students and community of the 1970's. Such a school would offer a variety of learning opportunities in which each student could find a program relevant to his needs and aspirations. It would also reflect the highest aspirations and critical concerns of parents, organizations, and institutions that, even if not located within a contiguous area, constitute a type of community served by the school.

High schools have not achieved this dream, but they can move closer to it and avoid greater mediocrity provided that the people of their communities care and cooperate. Here are some possible cooperative actions that could help:

Establish a community council for each high school in a district that includes more than one school. The necessary decentralization of bureaucratic school districts is occurring too slowly to help most high schools relate more closely to the community groups they serve. An intermediate step is a community council, created by the district board of education and reporting to it. As central boards and local community councils learn to work together, the people will have more opportunity to create their own high school.

Have periodic reports made to the community council by representatives of the school's student council indicating how students believe the community can help the school. One wonders if many high school disturbances of recent years might not have been averted if there had been good channels of communication between students and community representatives. Under most present school district organizational patterns, student complaints and suggestions proceed up school channels, not to groups of parents and citizens who might better interpret these ideas and counsel the students and school leaders.

Similarly, have reports made periodically by representatives of the school faculty. Interpretation of school programs, practices, and problems by responsible faculty members can help to facilitate understanding between members of the school and the community. A report might demonstrate, for instance, how videotapes and different audiovisual aids are used in instruction. These media, and carefully written descriptions, might also be used as a means of presenting reports to other groups.

Use community media as fully and objectively as possible for reporting school programs, accomplishments, problems, and needs. Recent Gallup polls concerning public information about the schools, and interest in them, underline the need for more and better reporting. Although a friendly press appears to be the most useful medium, all available media can help. More direct communication between parent and teacher is perhaps most urgently needed, but school personnel also need to clearly explain their goals and processes of education to the public at large.

Promote and service student forums on community issues. The high school should be a major forum for debate and discussion of local, state, national, and international issues significant to the people of the community. Especially since 18-year-olds can now vote, the student need for information on current issues is critical. High school courses, especially in the social sciences, have been assailed most frequently, and described as sterile, principally because of their lack of relevance to these issues.

Provide maximum opportunities for high school students to participate in community activities. The high school should have extensive arrangements for setting up student apprenticeships and other roles in community organizations. To accomplish this, it might conduct an annual inventory of community groups to find out whether they could accommodate students as members, assistants, or apprentices. Undoubtedly only a minority of the total high school population would be involved in such activities at any one time, but successful involvement might result in more opportunities for additional students. Other students might have summer occupations as interns in various government offices. Some might have part-time employment during the school year in such offices or in social agencies.

Cooperate in providing meaningful work experience for as many high school students as possible. Granted the enormous difficulty of providing significant work experience for youth in a society lacking full employment for its adults, this does not obviate the fact that lack of work experience is a major problem for youth growing up in our culture. We can be more resourceful. For example, grave concern about environmental pollution and ugliness has already produced many youth corps, who have been cleaning up neighborhoods, beaches, and waste heaps. This kind of program might serve those students who do not have other work opportunities.

Use community resource persons to give expert service in curriculum planning and instruction. One might consult the community to obtain: advice of psychologists, psychiatrists, medical doctors, and other specialists in planning counseling services (and in actually counseling when school services are lacking); assistance of various specialists in planning programs related to recreation, home and family living, sex education, drug education, consumer education; guidance of practitioners in fields of vocational education.

Open the community to students who wish to use its facilities for independent study. Such programs as that initiated by Philadelphia's Parkway School need to be widely adopted. At Parkway, students learn not only through experiences in community agencies, business, and industry, but through academic tasks in libraries, museums, and other centers. All of the educational resources of the community ought to be available to the high school students whose teachers encourage their use of these resources on an independent study basis.

Throughout the year, open the school, after hours, for adult education and for recreation. Despite the growth of adult education programs throughout the country, many rural areas, small communities, and parts of inner cities still lack educational facilities other than their public schools. High schools closed to adults and to students after hours and during the summer are incompatible with contemporary life styles and schedules. The community's high school cannot continue to operate only six to eight hours per day, 200 days per year, when the people of the community need its facilities for continuing education and recreation.

For proposals like the above to be implemented, substantial public opinion must be aroused in support of the comprehensive community school concept. The sparks to bring this about may come from emergencies, even from student activism, but might best and most constructively come from enlightened school board members and competent school administrators. Perhaps a community's first step should be the election of school board members who will choose and support administrators able to mobilize community resources for creating or re-creating a strong high school. The combination of good board members, able school administrators, and active community representatives is almost certain to produce a high school that serves its students and community well and is served well by them.

PROGRAM DEVELOPMENT IN RURAL SCHOOLS*

WARD SYBOUTS

During our time of urban crisis we can see numerous indications that the needs of rural areas and smaller communities are being moved down the list of national priorities and concerns. The sheer magnitude of the urban problem looms so large on the national horizon that it cannot be ignored. By contrast, the dispersed nature of rural areas, which do not yield great concentrations of humanity, has tended to dilute the urgency of rural needs in education. Such a diversion of immediate concern for rural education is inherently dangerous because of the interrelatedness of our dynamic cultural structure.

Small schools will continue to exist in the coming decades. One may question the projected figures about the number of students in rural schools, but it remains apparent that a massive educational system for rural youth will be demanded. It is incumbent upon the educational enterprise to provide quality education for all youth, *rural* as well as *urban*.

* Reprinted from the *Bulletin of the National Association of Secondary School Principals* (October 1970), 54:116–130, by permission.

The fact that there is a smaller percentage of rural youth in no way removes the mandate for adequate education.

Before examining some processes of program development, however, it may be well to consider what small schools have done in the past.

School reorganization and consolidation have been carried forward to a satisfactory level in many areas. By contrast, other sections of the nation still demonstrate glaring reorganization needs. In those areas in which reorganization has not moved ahead with sufficient vigor, we can see very clearly that professional educators have not exerted leadership adequate to the task. Reorganization must be carried forward to an optimum level of completion and, once districts are reorganized, programs need to be developed that take advantage of all the opportunities a reorganized district affords.

The distinction between an "essential" as compared with a "non-essential" small school has been considered by state department personnel for years. Essential small schools can be defined as those which must be operated in order to provide education for isolated youth, while the non-essential small school is one which can be closed through consolidation or school district reorganization without placing education beyond reasonable limits when transporting youngsters. On the one hand, the distinction is crucial when considering needed state-wide programs for reorganization or curriculum improvement; on the other hand, it becomes a moot question when considered by the student who is forced to attend a "non-essential" school. The student forced to attend the "non-essential" school is just as real and has the same needs as the student enrolled in an "essential" small school. Under the guise of educational humanitarianism, boards and administrators have repeatedly claimed that the "non-essential" small school is justified. To combat the continuation of the "non-essential" high school and to enable the "essential" small school to develop a more adequate program, there should be criteria established in each state which could be used to determine which schools' continuation is justifiable and which is not. Support formulas need to be applied which will provide adequate financial assistance to "essential" small schools and discourage the continuation of the "non-essential" small school.

IMPROVEMENT PROJECTS

During the past decade there has been a number of special small school improvement projects. These projects have ranged geographically from the Catskills to the Rockies and from Texas to the Northwest. The focus of the small school projects has extended through multiple classes, small group techniques, flexible scheduling, shared services, programed instruction, correspondence courses, filmed courses, ETV, tele-lectures, amplified phone seminars, community resources, film centers, and building design, to ear phones for bus riders. Many excellent and outstanding results have been achieved in project schools as a result of these special efforts. Unfortunately, the pattern of dissemination of small school improvement techniques has been limited and spotty. The vast majority of small school administrators have not adopted project innovations. The reluctance or hesitation to make changes and improvements in small schools may stem from many causes (i.e., excessive internal orientation, excessive per-pupil costs, uninformed school patrons, and high rate of turnover in positions of leadership). Whatever the causes, the fact remains that the vast majority of the nation's rural schools have not adopted many of the techniques that have been developed in project schools.

Program development in rural schools is faced with significant cultural forces. The mobility of our population, particularly the rural-urban thrust, has serious implications for rural school curriculum. The mass media have moved the information level outside the classroom to a level which has been viewed by McLuhan,[1] as higher than in the classroom. Studies that focus on the nature of rural youth and their reactions to school reveal important similarities between urban and rural youth involved in delinquent behavior.[2] These studies also give important insights into the needs of youth that must somehow become incorporated into the curriculum of the rural school.

All too often the view is expressed that small schools become as good as large schools when they become as comprehensive as large schools. This can be a futile effort and a fatal mistake. The small school will be much more successful in program development if the curriculum is limited. For example, large schools may offer three years of French, German, Spanish, and Russian. All too often, rural schools have offered one language one year, and two different ones the next year in a frantic effort to duplicate the big school. The rural school would be much better off to offer three years of only one language, but take great care to ensure quality instruction. Rural school leaders will be wise to remember the implications of the *Eight Year Study*[3] and work toward fewer offerings while ensuring quality.

---

[1] Marshall McLuhan. *Understanding Media: The Extensions of Man.* New York: Signet Books, 1954.

[2] Paul Ford, Herbert Hite, and Norman Kock. *Remote High Schools: The Realities.* Portland, Oregon: Northwest Regional Education Laboratory, April, 1967. And *Rural Youth in America.* Eugene, Ore.: Youth Study Project, December 13, 1963.

[3] Wilford M. Aikin. *The Story of the Eight Year Study.* New York: McGraw-Hill Book Company, 1942.

RURAL SCHOOL BALANCE SHEET

Rural school proponents have devoted a considerable amount of time contrasting rural schools with urban schools and debating claimed strengths and weaknesses. There is no value in such a debate beyond the point of identifying weaknesses which can be corrected and strengths upon which one can capitalize.

Areas of disadvantage in rural education center around staffing problems, program limitations, and inadequacies of facilities, all of which have been reflected in less than complimentary results as reflected in follow-up studies of graduates from rural schools. Patrons of rural schools are often quite defensive about the quality of their graduates and refute claims that larger schools are doing a better job by pointing with pride to rural school graduates who have gone on to college and been very successful. Such claims of individual success are true, but it is also true that small school graduates, as a group, experience less success in college than do graduates from larger schools. It is incumbent upon the rural school administrator to recognize the facts in the face of emotion and develop the school program accordingly.

Potential strengths in rural schools are as readily identified as are the disadvantages. Size, flexibility potential, accessibility to interpersonal relations, the advantages of rural living, and information via modern media and transportation all give distinct advantages to rural schools. Teachers have an opportunity to become well acquainted with each student in a rural school. In like manner, the family can become a better known quantity to the rural teacher, and better understanding and accessibility can be derived. Learning can be organized with much greater access to flexibility in a small school than in a large school. Large schools find it difficult, in comparison with rural schools, to avoid institutionalizing the program and to guard against the loss of individualization. Modern media and transportation have done a great deal to remove the isolation shock of rural areas and have given small communities the opportunity of providing modernized rural living to its patrons. Education leaders in rural areas must capitalize on every potential strength as they go about the task of program development.

PROGRAM DEVELOPMENT

Program development in rural schools is based on several assumptions:

1. Rural schools will continue to exist.
2. No rural school can function adequately as a self-contained entity.
3. Leadership for rural schools must be developed on a base which provides continuity as well as a progressive posture.

4. Rural youth need and deserve an education that will enable them to develop to their full potential—which takes into account the fact they may attend a rural school and move into an urban center.
5. There is a need for improving the quality of rural education, and program improvements are within the capabilities of our education system.

There are several areas of program development which can be identified and sequenced through a school year. The following discussion will be limited to a few areas of program development which include:

1. Planning and organizing
2. The implementation of the community-school concept
3. The relationship of a rural school to a service unit
4. The establishment of an in-service consortium of schools
5. Providing guaranteed financial support to all high school graduates
6. Follow-up and evaluation of program.

PLANNING AND ORGANIZING

Planning and organizing for program improvement is certainly not new. There are numerous examples of rural schools in which careful planning has led to major program improvements. It is within the realm of planning that the rural school administrator has an opportunity to take advantage of small numbers, for the size of the rural school becomes an advantage when arranging and planning for the use of time within the master schedule.

Many rural secondary schools contain grades 7–12, which are in turn organized as six-year high schools or junior-senior high schools. Roughly defined, a six-year high school is one in which the program is continuous, grade 7–12, as one school with one staff, and there is actually no clear distinction between the junior high program and the senior high program and no separation of students. By contrast, the junior-senior high school has two distinct but related programs operated by one staff in one facility in which there is separation of junior high students from senior high students.

Six-year secondary schools which are organized as junior-senior high schools are better able to provide for the needs of young people. Age difference, which is reflected in different developmental tasks, can be more realistically considered and accommodated in the program of the junior-senior high school than in a six-year high school. Ideally, there should be a classification of buildings and facilities, as well as staff, into three categories in a junior-senior high school. Certain areas of the building and certain staff should be utilized primarily for junior high school students, while other areas of the building and staff members should be available for senior high students. Specialized areas and staff such as band, shops, art, home economics, library, office, guidance facilities, and lunch rooms should be used by junior and senior high school students. Facilities used by junior and senior high students should be scheduled, whenever possible, so that junior high students use them at one time and senior high students use them at other times. Of all facilities to be used jointly by junior and senior high students, the library is the one which does not generally afford student separation. Basically, the junior-senior high school should function with well-articulated yet separate programs operated in one building with one staff under the direction of one administration.

If there is validity in the arguments which have been used to justify the junior high school, there is validity in keeping separate programs in the junior-senior high school. The key to accomplishing separation between junior high and senior high students is found in the scheduling of time. Although most buildings have not been built as junior-senior high schools, experience has demonstrated clearly that two programs can be scheduled in one facility in a way that fosters student separation at desired and appropriate times in the schedule.

Breaking away from the traditional block schedule in which the student attends four or five classes and one or two study halls each day for five days per week is also proving to be a means of program improvement in rural schools. In this respect, smallness is proving to be a real advantage. Where urban schools require computer assistance for counting, sorting, and developing a schedule conflict matrix, and loading the schedule, it is possible to accomplish the same scheduling chores in a rural school in much less time while keeping control of all the variables. Many rural schools are finding the blocks of time in which a weekly demand schedule can be arranged by teachers to be very beneficial. The weekly, or in some instances daily, demand schedule within the block-of-time is particularly advantageous when accompanied by a carefully planned independent study program with an adequate independent learning center.

The steps employed at the Wisconsin State University at the River Falls Laboratory School illustrate one approach to developing a daily demand schedule. Inflexible demands, which resulted from utilizing part-time or shared staff, were identified and placed in the schedule as a first step, within a framework of 240 minutes total teaching time divided into 15 minute time divisions or modules. Inflexible areas included were physical education, art, music, industrial arts, and home economics. Secondly, blocks of time were deducted from the total time available and reserved for independent study time. Independent study time varied with each student from 20 percent to 33 percent, and was a reflection of his ability to utilize independent study. The third step involved the establishment of the coming day's instructional needs and time pattern by the teachers. These demands were then placed on the master schedule by a coordinator familiar with the inflexible schedule components and other restraints such as facilities and staff. The daily master schedule was placed on a color-coded bulletin board in a central location. Scheduling unusual time demands required, on occasions, that teachers negotiate their needs.[4]

As previously mentioned, flexibility in scheduling and the encouragement of independent learning require adequate instruction materials. Only a few rural schools have been fortunate enough to boast adequate resource centers for realistic independent study. Rural schools, where small numbers of students are enrolled for courses other than basic required courses, have a tremendous need for independent study facilities. Special student interests in rural schools can only be met through independent study conducted in adequately equipped laboratories.

Even the most elaborate rural school independent learning centers will require supplementary materials. All rural schools have accredited correspondence courses or filmed courses available. Such courses can do a great deal to extend and enrich the curricular offerings for the small high school. In some areas, intermediate or service units have been established that have, among the various services they provide, an instructional materials center and courier service which make available great quantities and varieties of instructional materials. What is indicated here is the fact that rural schools must draw upon resources from outside their own districts.

Extending the school year provides innumerable opportunities for program enrichment. Rural youth no longer fit the stereotyped "hard-working, pitch-fork-in-hand, sun-tanned" youth needed on the farm. Summer employment is difficult to locate in many rural areas. Within recent years, census figures have shown there is a sizable proportion of our rural youth who are classified as non-farming. These factors along with the total cultural scene clearly point to a need for extending the school year.

One approach to extending the school year which has a great deal of potential for program development is the pattern of employing part of the staff for an extended period of four to eight weeks during the summer. Staff on the extended contract are assigned two areas of responsibility— teaching and planning. Summer classes, workshops, seminars, or independent study projects can be conducted during half the day and the remainder of the day used for teams of teachers to plan curriculum and instructional materials for the coming year. During the course of the regular school year, the daily demands of teaching take so much time and energy

---

[4] James W. Stewart and Jack Shank. "Daily Demand Modular Flexible Scheduling for Small Schools." Unpublished report, River Falls: Wisconsin State University, 1970.

that teachers do not have an adequate opportunity to make major curricular improvements and revisions. Summer planning time for teachers can constitute one of the most valuable techniques for the improvement of instruction.

Summer classes give students and patrons in the community many educational opportunities which would otherwise be lost. A rural community of a few hundred or a few thousand people could very possibly have a summer program which contained a reading clinic, a remedial mathematics course, a seminar on economics and the stock market for advanced high school students and adults, a lapidary workshop with accompanying field trips, a summer theatre involving vocal and instrumental music for students and adults, and various independent study projects under the direction of summer staff. It is easy to see that summer programs extend the curriculum in terms of breadth, time, and clientele. The combination of extending the school year into instruction and program development presents one of the most productive arrangements.

COMMUNITY-SCHOOL RELATIONSHIP

The community-school concept is an important one to incorporate into the priorities for program development in rural schools. Unfortunately, school personnel and board members have all too often demonstrated behavior which has illustrated their concern over "territorial imperatives." Policies as well as rules and regulations have been set up by boards and administrators which restrict and limit the use of school facilities by the patrons in the community and reduce the two-way flow of ideas and advantages. The school and community have become separate entities in many respects. Those responsible for the education of people should recognize:

that the school cannot be isolated, and
that if education is to prepare people to live in a community, rural or urban, then the closer the education process can become involved with the community the better.

There are strong arguments to support the contention that the family is the most influential force shaping an individual. Culture, with its mass media, styles, values, and innumerable other facets, is often considered the second most influential force which shapes an individual. The peer culture may be referred to as a third most influential force in the environment of the adolescent. The school may well be the fourth most important environmental force. If, when all the evidence is exposed, we find that the home and cultural factors are the two most influential environmental forces, it then becomes incumbent upon the school to take advantage of these forces in every possible way. Logic then leads to the conclusion that the community-school concept, which incorporates home, community, and school, is one which maximizes the opportunities for program development.

> The community is a learning laboratory which we could not possibly duplicate in what we call a school plant. It includes the environment, the problems, people who live in it, values, and experiences which are all factors in the educational process.
>
> Leadership is a key ingredient to bring about the full fruition of the community-school concept. Once the direction is established, however, needs which encompass all the people in the community can be identified. Program, facilities, and personnel can be organized to meet the needs of the people in the community. Such programs will no longer be fragmented or overlapping but will be coordinated and far reaching to include all residents of the community without regard to ages 5–18 or grades kindergarten through 12. *Educational needs*, broadly conceived; *recreational needs*, for all ages; *community development projects*, which may not necessarily be educational efforts in a direct sense; and *cooperation with the various agencies which exist in the community*, i.e., churches, lodges, labor unions or farming organizations, chamber of commerce as well as many others—can all be reached through the utilization of the community-school concept with the avoidance of duplication of effort on the one hand or the omission of needed programs on the other hand.[5]

INTERMEDIATE OR SERVICE UNIT

The intermediate or service unit has an important role to play for rural school program development. It does not take very long to establish a rationale for the inclusion of a support system capable of providing services to rural schools which cannot be provided economically from the district resources. Service units, referred to by various names around the nation,[6] have provided help in many ways to rural schools. A few of the more common services have included:

1. special education
2. psychiatric services
3. family counseling
4. testing
5. subject area specialists

---

[5] Dale K. Hayes and Loren R. Bonneau. *The Nebraska Community Education Project: The Curriculum Experiment*. Lincoln: University of Nebraska, Teachers College.

[6] W. E. Inman. *Selected Characteristics of Emerging Intermediate Units of School Administration*. Department of HEW, Office of Education, Washington, D.C.: Government Printing Office, 1967.

6. cooperative purchasing
7. computer services
8. IMC (including motion picture libraries, ETV models, copying services, pro-
    duction facilities, equipment loan and service, consultation and courier
    service)

The resources required for an adequate educational program are so expensive and varied that the typical rural school can only have them available through the assistance of some cooperating agency, such as an intermediate service unit. Small districts need not worry about losing their autonomy to a service unit. The very nature of the legal provisions for establishing service units placed the emphasis on "service" to "member schools" and has recognized these services should be those "which individual school districts cannot efficiently or economically provide by themselves."[7] Administrators in rural schools need to employ the service unit to its fullest extent in developing program.

IN-SERVICE CONSORTIUM

An in-service consortium is an idea that will provide a number of schools an opportunity to bring together their resources. Staff in-service and program development are difficult to achieve in rural schools. However, if a group of schools works together, the programs can be strengthened by a cooperative interchange.

Quite simply, an in-service consortium works as follows:

1. A number of schools form a cooperative group with a willingness to share
    resources;
2. A grid is developed in which needs are shown along one axis. Resources,
    either available within the personnel and facilities of the member schools
    or which the finances of the member schools are capable of acquiring, are
    shown on the other axis;
3. From the needs-resource grid those in-service and program development
    topics with the highest priority are selected; and
4. Programs are developed, conducted, and evaluated.

In some situations it may be found that all member schools wish to participate in a given topic, while in other instances some schools may not see a need and so choose not to take part. The important thing is that each school determines its own needs. Within the in-service and program development consortium framework there is an economically feasible way for a number of rural schools to have available the resources and special personnel talents of member school districts.

---

[7] *Ibid.*

COMMUNITY SCHOLARSHIP PROGRAM

A community scholarship program is a unique and interesting way to extend the school program in a meaningful dimension. Areas which have developed community scholarship programs have found obvious benefits. Every young person needs to be assured the opportunity of continuing his education, whether it be in a trade school or four-year college. A variety of community scholarship programs is currently functioning which gives each graduating senior the assurance that he will have available the needed financial resources to further his education.

The operation of a community scholarship program need not be complex. A community group can form a non-profit corporation for the purpose of receiving and distributing scholarships. The articles of incorporation should establish the membership and organizational framework. Funds can be solicited from a variety of sources and in various ways which are most appropriate for the community. An application with the Internal Revenue Service making contributions deductible for income tax purposes is often helpful. The criteria and procedures for awarding scholarships need to be carefully developed so that the needs of students are met and the wishes of the community served.

Through such a program many groups that normally award scholarships can be brought together so that a more adequate program can be made available. Every graduate who wishes to go on to some form of education can be assured of the opportunity through the establishment of a community scholarship program.

PROGRAM EVALUATION

Evaluation of program is an area which has been greatly neglected. It may be that evaluation has not been practical because of a lack of precision in determining what is to be accomplished in program development. Most assuredly, program effectiveness will never be known unless more adequate means of evaluating are devised. It may be that through intermediate service units, along with in-service consortiums and community education efforts, better program evaluation techniques can be developed. Once these evaluation techniques are available, valuable feedback information for further program improvement will be possible. The habit of considering program development without adequate evaluation must be avoided.

The process of evaluation is complex indeed. No evaluation program should be established until it is known what is to be evaluated and under what set of circumstances. There are some generalizations about evaluation which can be outlined:

1. The principal of the rural school must have a research posture. All too often, the administrator who attends graduate school does a research paper, a field study or thesis, and gives a sigh of relief when the paper is finished and approved, with the comment that he never wants to be bothered with that sort of useless exercise again. If more administrators could see the relevance of evaluation and would apply known research techniques to their programs, there would be much better results and fewer program failures in our schools.

2. A variety of research tools and techniques is required for program evaluation. For many years it was the practice to evaluate all segments of the school program with a standardized achievement test. It is now abundantly clear that such tests, when used alone, are inadequate.

3. Evaluation is an area in which special competencies are required. Rural school administrators will do well to call upon consultants to help design evaluation systems. To avoid the bias that always surrounds any research, it is advisable to use persons other than those conducting a program to do the evaluation.

4. The design for evaluation needs to be established before a project or program is started. There are numerous reasons for collecting data before the fact as well as after. Frequently, programs are never assessed, simply because no one thought of evaluating until it was too late.

5. The evaluation of both methods and results is justified and has value. Evaluation becomes inadequate, however, when only method or procedure is assessed. Results, the end product, in terms of stated objectives, should be known. When considering the end product, evaluation of school program virtually requires a follow-up study of graduates. Some of the most important feedback can come from follow-up studies.

6. Evaluation results must be applied for future program improvements. The research posture of the school administrator is important in the analysis, interpretation, and application of evaluation findings. Valuable programs frequently have been discarded because some symptoms, or isolated variables, were not yielding satisfactory results. When the carburetor on a new car is not working properly the car is not junked—the carburetor is fixed. When program elements fail, the program should not be abandoned —the failing element should be corrected on the basis of evaluation feedback.

SUMMARY

Rural school leaders carry a heavy load and shoulder a major responsibility for program development. The accomplishment of acquiring and developing improved programs will come as rural school administrators find ways of capitalizing on inherent strengths to overcome weaknesses. The isolated rural school can no longer cope with the realities of our culture. It is possible for a small rural school, small in student enrollment and separated from other schools by many miles, to be a "good" school if its program is in the mainstream of our society, traced by a network of relationships with other small schools, with an intermediate service unit or its equivalent, with a total community-school relationship, and with evaluation for continual improvement.

Rural school leadership is the key ingredient to program development. Without adequate leadership rural school program development will never come to full fruition. Several recognized difficulties continue to contribute to the problem of leadership. Outstanding young administrators generally stay for only a few years and then move to larger districts. Salaries, living conditions, facilities, and isolation are only a few of the contributors to high turnover in administrative positions in rural areas. It is doubtful that adequate leadership for the majority of the rural schools in our nation will come under present conditions. Each necessarily existing rural school will need to receive special financial assistance through adjusted state-aid formulas. Every rural school, with adequate leadership and appropriate ties to support facilities, should become a "project school" in which program development becomes the *modus operandi* rather than the exception.

CAN THE STUDENT PARTICIPATE IN HIS OWN DESTINY?*

JAMES E. HOUSE

"I'm only a U.S. citizen enjoying my rights, until I come to school."[1]

Educators have been "foot dragging" and divided in rendering an opinion about the ability of students to participate in determining their own

---

* Reprinted from *Educational Leadership* (February 1970), 27:442–445. Reprinted with permission of the Association for Supervision and Curriculum Development and James E. House. Copyright © 1970 by the Association for Supervision and Curriculum Development.

[1] This quote, and others which appear not documented, was extracted from a doctoral dissertation prepared by the writer. These were responses by ninth- and twelfth-grade pupils to a survey about participation.

destiny. Students have sensed this dividedness and confusion, and have proceeded to seek answers to the question for themselves. Their answers have been manifested in student protest and demonstrations.

STUDENTS WANT TO PARTICIPATE

Last year, more than 2,000 high schools across the nation experienced walkouts, sit-ins, boycotts, or other means of student expression in an attempt to prove that they are important and want to participate. A careful analysis of the protest movement would indicate that many of the demands and concerns of students are indeed legitimate, and would suggest that a complete evaluation of how we do business with youngsters in school is needed. In fact, to deny a student the right to participate in his own destiny is an infringement of his constitutional rights, as described in the Fourteenth Amendment and the Bill of Rights, and reflected in a growing body of court opinions. Our judicial system has called for a halt to the flagrant abuse of student rights in school.

Clute advocates that

> Students must become partners with us in the process of their education. Partners, in that students must share in the vital decisions of school life. Particularly those that affect his privacy and his precious constitutional rights, and equally important in his participation in the decisions which affect the rights of others. Responsibility grows out of the respect for one's self and an understanding of the meaning of personal freedom. *Responsibility cannot develop prior to the granting of freedom.*[2]

"I think the students should be consulted more about the problems we are having. Just think, we might be able to come up with something."

One very simple, but fruitful, way of resolving some of the problems in the educational arena is merely to seek answers from our clients—the students. Folks in the business world spend millions of dollars annually to gather consumer opinions about their products. New directions are charted as a result of these findings. Research tells us that students want to be consulted as "consumers" of our educational "wares."

---

[2] Morrel J. Clute. "The Rights and Responsibilities of Students." An unpublished paper, Wayne State University, Detroit, 1969. (Mimeographed.)

In a recent study conducted for *Life*[3] magazine, more than half of the students polled in one hundred schools across the nation revealed that they were unhappy with their limited participation in school policy making. Moreover, more than 60 percent of the same students wanted more say about making rules under which they must live, and a greater share of involvement in making curriculum decisions. The issue of decision making is relevant for pupils, as 54 percent labeled it "very important."

This student poll compares very favorably with one conducted by the writer for a dissertation, in which more than 60 percent of the pupils revealed that in their schools, pupils really wanted to decide what happened to them. Only 30 percent of the pupils in the same survey felt that they "usually" or "always" had a chance to participate in decision making on policies and rules under which they must live.[4] The conflict between students and adults is crystallized, as described in the *Life* poll, where only 20 percent of the parents and 35 percent of the teachers felt that students should have more participation in policy making. Only a mere quarter of the adults polled placed student participation under the "very important" category as compared with 54 percent of the pupils. This accounts, in part, for the generation gap that exists, hence student unrest.

INGREDIENTS FOR PARTICIPATION

"The students themselves should organize and use their group power to attain the goals they feel are necessary, and truly run their own school and get rid of the toy government, the student council."

Some secondary schools value student participation, and every effort is made to have this participation become a significant part of the educational process. How do these schools differ from other schools? One quick observation of these forward-looking secondary schools is that you will find an open communication link to help students participate in a significant way in their school operation.

Teachers and administrators in these schools seek student opinion and use this to strengthen the fibers of togetherness. Students are trusted and encouraged to be different, because being different is one way of testing what one really believes. Decision making is seen as a cooperative venture by all who are affected by the decision. An open communication

[3] "What People Think About Their High Schools." *Life* 66 (19): 24–25; May 16, 1969.
[4] James E. House. "A Study of Innovative Youth Involvement Activities in Selected Secondary Schools in Wayne County, Michigan." Unpublished Ed.D. dissertation. Detroit: Wayne State University, 1969.

link in the secondary schools provides for a grievance procedure—a system of redress. This procedure is known by all students in school; it shows no favorites. We know that where communication is missing, it always breeds suspicion and a lack of trust.

In spite of the difficulty in establishing a workable communication link, some secondary schools have initiated student-faculty-parent advisory councils that are concerned with such problems as discipline, classroom conditions, and human relations. One superintendent in an Ohio school district invites student representatives to his office to talk and listen to one another on a regular basis. Still other schools have appointed an ombudsman, have conducted open forums, and are sharing more power with the student council. Communication is beautiful, but tough to accomplish.

"The students have great ideas about rules and regulations, they just don't have a chance to express them."

A second glance at these forward-looking schools would reveal the existence of human rules and regulations. If rules and regulations are to be more acceptable and workable, students must have a chance to help set the regulations. Rules and regulations must not be viewed as a means of keeping people in line, so that undesirables can be suspended when they do not toe the mark.

Every effort would be made to eliminate those regulations that may be classified as annoyances, such as hall passes and permission to go to the rest rooms. Self-discipline would be the goal of every student, if the professional staff would help him to achieve this goal. Students would, in fact, determine regulations such as the length of hair, wearing apparel, and beards, and would set up their own discipline procedures.

Educators are rightfully proud of the Freedom School being operated in Washington, D.C., by students. Not only do students determine the rules under which they must live, they also select teachers, develop the curriculum, and make other important decisions.

"I don't think the school faculty listens very much to our student council. I think our student council should have some say in our curriculum."

Another characteristic of forward-looking schools is an exciting and relevant curriculum. It would show evidence of being responsive to the current sociological problems on the educational scene. Students do not understand why they cannot deal with problems related to poverty, racism, black studies, sex, drugs, and the Vietnam war. Instead of placing emphasis in these areas, educators have been forced to revise the academic disciplines (science, math, foreign languages), and make them tougher. This process has placed a great deal of pressure on students to succeed. Nonclass activities, in which many children find a sense of accomplishment, would be an important part of the curricular experience. Such activities would not be viewed as something tacked on, after the fact.

In some schools, pupils are reshaping the curriculum by calling for the elimination of the track system that segregates pupils. Still others encourage pupils to teach courses without credit, to volunteer for essential community services, to attend department meetings as advisors, to suggest course content for black studies, and to share the spotlight with teachers on curriculum advisory councils.

Teachers and administrators in one Maryland school eliminated the regular schedule for a two-week period. A student-recommended curriculum was initiated which included a visit to Congress, listening to jazz music, working with deprived children, debating the war, and a broad spectrum of exciting educational experiences. The curriculum can be relevant.

"The teacher should not look to the bright kids all the time. The other kids feel hurt and not wanted."

A final ingredient that would be found in these forward-looking schools would be an understanding and knowledgeable teacher—a teacher who felt comfortable with pupils helping to run the class. Pupils do not like to sit still and listen to teachers talk all the time. When students have a voice in decision making they are more eager to raise questions, explore options, and make value judgments about issues for the love and satisfaction of it all.

If the class engages only in oral discussion and answers the questions at the end of each chapter, then something is gravely missing in the educative process. Students know what activities "turn them on"; teachers need only to ask.

In the classroom, there are factors related to grading practices, student-teacher planning, teaching methods, and the future-oriented curriculum that tend to prohibit pupil participation. A grading practice in the classroom that is used as a weapon, rather than an effort to evaluate pupils in terms of their own accomplishments, would be rejected. Pressure to participate solely for the sake of a grade has a tendency to reduce meaningful participation.

Teachers can, most of all, help pupils to participate in their own destiny by helping them to acquire a feeling of dignity and worth. No student in the classroom should feel belittled. Each pupil must have a feeling that he is the most important person in the classroom. His teacher can help him feel wanted and important, thereby giving him the skills he needs for determining his own destiny in school.

Some teachers are using students as aides, assistants, tutors, evaluators of teacher performance, and in other creative roles. Other teachers are meeting the challenge by providing experience in independent study and small group discussions.

The evidence is starting to mount that pupils can participate in their own destiny if the school environment is one of trust, which recognizes the dignity and worth of students. Student demands to participate in their own destiny provide a real chance for us to correct an injustice that has existed for too long. We should be proud that a pillar of democracy—student participation—is moving closer to reality.

If students are to participate in their own destiny in school related matters, students must choose ways and opportunities to use their talents, interests, and feelings. Here is something that you can do in your school now: See that

> *Students have a voice* in planning, deciding upon, implementing, and evaluating experiences in which they participate.
>
> *Youths* have opportunities to *work with other youths and adults* in a variety of situations, in a variety of relationships.
>
> *Leadership is shared.* Youths share with teachers and other adults the responsibility for guiding and leading activities to the reasonable maximum of their potential.
>
> *Youths* are encouraged to *originate plans and ideas* for enhancing their role and participation in school and community activities.[5]

Why not try it?

---

[5] Dolores Paskal, Leonard S. Demak, and Edwin J. McClendon. *New Roles and Relationships.* Detroit: Wayne County Intermediate School District, 1969, p. 3.

TEACHERS AS CHANGE AGENTS*

CHARLES H. HILL

An appropriate subtitle for this discourse might be: "Training for Frustration." Each year thousands of teachers attend summer school, federally financed institutes and workshops. As a result of this ritual, teachers become informed about new methods, materials, and technological advances. What happens to a teacher, filled with desire to make changes in the education of children and trained to use the desired innovations, who returns to a school district? The answer to this question requires an investigation of the historical role of teachers' involvement in the change process.

Teachers have been regarded as unimportant in the change process. Thomas Woods (1967, p. 54) stated, "The impetus for change originates from outside the educational system and within the system the pressure for change comes from the top down." Commenting on the role of teachers, Henry Brickell (1961, p. 22) observed, "New types of instructional programs are introduced by administrators. Contrary to general opinion, teachers are not change agents for instructional innovations of major scope." Nearly all literature discussing change in the public schools assumes a vertical, authoritarian organization with both the intent and the execution of change coming from the administration. Teachers are cast, not only in a passive role, but frequently in the role of active obstructionists.

Richard Carlson (1965, p. 77) reported on the unanticipated consequences of a new program for individualized instruction. Concerning the activities of the teachers involved, he stated, "Some of these practices should be classified by the cynic as sabotage." Literature is replete with pleas to teachers to change their practices, or at the minimum, not obstruct change (Battle, 1968, p. 23; Taba, 1962, p. 460; Fishburn, 1966, p. 272; Shannon, 1968, p. 177). Teachers, who are among the most highly educated individuals in any community, have gained the reputation of

* Reprinted by permission from the March 1971 issue of *The Clearing House*.

opposing change. Many writers feel that teachers have, in fact, carefully cultivated their state of relative powerlessness.

Teachers have invited suppression. Cunningham (1961, p. 127) noted that teachers have sought well-defined roles which do not leave them accountable for their actions. The administrator who is authoritarian and directive has been the most popular with teachers. "Authoritarianism in the schools," according to Lanter and Howe (1969, p. 23), "is imposed more by the teacher himself than by anything else." Teachers have dehabilitated themselves by seeking security at all cost. They have historically been mute about their needs and desires (Wirtz, 1965, p. 163). Some teachers have made an uproar about making changes, but according to Cunningham (1961, p. 120), they allow themselves to be easily suppressed. This teacher passivity has extended in other directions.

The sociologist Chilcott (1961, p. 390) described the teachers in the community as vague, formless and conforming. Teachers have sold their right to innovate for the serenity of being non-controversial. Teachers who do gain new knowledge and skills would often rather run than fight. Kastrinos (1967, p. 621) surveyed 50 participants of an NSF Institute for Biology Teachers. He found that within a year, most of the participants had moved. Some responded that they moved in frustration, unable to implement their new ideas. Others had apparently used their new training for personal advancement. When I was in my first year as an elementary principal, the superintendent gave this advice: "Don't forget, your teachers are like little children. They have to be led by the hand." It would appear that teachers have worked hard to attain their present reputation. The pendulum, however, is beginning to swing.

The 1965 *Education Index* introduced a new sub-category under "Teachers"—"Teacher-Administrator Conflict"—which may be prophetic of the emerging teacher role. To assist in clarifying the perceptions of contemporary teachers, an informal questionnaire was administered to a group of teachers enrolled in the 1970 Summer Session at Washington State University.

The informal instrument was administered to 28 teachers who met two criteria. Each teacher was experienced and committed to return to the school district in which he taught the previous year. The range of experience was 1 year to 18 years; the range of age was 23 to 54. The mean experience was 5 years and the mean age was 33. Twenty S's were female, 8 were male. The questionnaire was administered during the 5th week of a 6 week session. The S's were enrolled in one of two graduate level courses, "Innovations in Reading" and a "Demonstration Teaching" course.

The instrument was designed to investigate the teacher's perception of himself as a change agent but did not lend itself to formal statistical analysis. The press of time prevented refinement of the questions or assessment of validity or reliability. The questions were purposely very general, creating some difficulty in quantifying the responses. The results, therefore, are reported here as generalizations drawn from the most frequently appearing responses.

1. Most teachers want to make some changes in the curriculum when they return to school. The changes are equally distributed among: changes of emphasis of content, changes of teaching method, and institution of major innovative programs.
2. By almost unanimous consent, the respondents named individualized programs as a change they do not desire to make and will not attempt.
3. The most important criterion for selection or rejection of a new program was the amount of extra work required by the teacher. The effect of the change on the children and the presence of positive empirical evidence was frequently mentioned.
4. The person most frequently mentioned as either facilitating or obstructing teacher-instigated change was the principal. Principals were most often characterized as authoritarian and capricious. The teachers under 33 frequently mentioned older teachers as obstructionists. Parents and other teachers were considered to be positive influences toward change.
5. The procedure for making a change was viewed as beginning with the principal, moving through a teacher committee and then upward to the superintendent. Using such phrases as "and then wait" and ". . . around it goes," cynicism was frequently expressed by the respondents. Teachers felt that their proposals would somehow be processed out of existence without ever culminating in a definite yes or no.
6. The availability of money was perceived as being of prime importance. Most respondents felt that the money necessary to institute new programs is in existence but not available because of administrative priorities.
7. Most of the respondents felt that they have cooperated fully with past changes imposed on them by the administration. The respondents felt that they had been involved in the decision making but had not received in-service training to help them make the changes.

The basic impressions that I gained from the responses were that the S's: (a) want to institute changes, (b) do not wish to make changes which require additional time or effort on their part, and (c) feel thwarted by authoritarian principals and quagmire-creating bureaucracies. Literature suggests some definite steps which must be taken by these and other teachers who wish to become change agents.

Many authors have agreed that teachers must be willing to speak out and make their wishes clearly known (Fishburn, 1966, p. 275; Lanter & Howe, 1969, p. 23; Wirtz, 1965, p. 163; Hunt, 1970, p. 73). Recently, a more militant faction of the teaching profession has been using language to describe the desirable action of teachers such as: "confrontation" (Dodson, 1965, p. 30), "aggressiveness" (Koontz, 1968, p. 12), and "revolution"

(Lanter and Howe, 1969, p. 23). Regardless of the moderation or extremism expressed, the role of the teacher is changing toward having a more important role in decision making (Miller, 1966, p. 533). The critical feature seems to be the willingness to become more vocal and demand the attention of the administration, regardless of the consequences. Something more than an outburt of words will be needed, however, for a teacher to institute change.

If a teacher desires to make a change, he must be willing to accept the consequences of that action (Cunningham, 1961, p. 128). The sociologists Brookover and Gottlieb (1964, p. 255) noted that teachers have traditionally used their administrators as buffers against criticism. A teacher who is asking for the authority to make an important change must also be accountable for the effects of the change. It seems reasonable to assume that some teachers are not in a social-financial position to ask for the right to create change. The teacher who has property or family ties which cannot be sacrificed in the event a move becomes necessary, the teacher who is fighting for tenure, the teacher who is fighting against formal evaluation; all of these have disenfranchised themselves from the decision-making process. These teachers do not have the freedom to be held accountable for their actions. The changes proposed by teachers must also meet certain criteria.

It is easy to become enthralled with an idea through the enthusiastic orations of a professor or the glittering promises of a salesman. The teacher-instituted change most likely to be accepted by administrators is one which is well supported by empirical evidence (Cohler, 1967, p. 97). Changes which are arbitrary, capricious, or influenced by irrelevant facts will not be well received. Approaching an administrator with data from other systems using the proposed innovation is more likely to succeed than an emotional, "I think we need to do it for the benefit of the children." Fishburn (1966, p. 275) suggested that whenever possible, the innovation should first be tried by the teacher in his own classroom as evidence for the probable success of the change if it is adopted by the system. Teachers may also achieve their goals by deliberate wielding of political power.

Miller (1966, p. 533) has pointed to a source of teacher-power which was mentioned only one time in the informal survey—professional negotiation. As teacher organizations mature, concern over salary increases will be shared with teacher-instigated changes of organization, curriculum, and facilities. Brookover and Gottlieb (1964) have outlined informal power groups which are also significant in the decision-making process. These are called "cliques." Some of these cliques, most commonly based on teacher-age or recreational interests, can bypass the whole administration in order to execute changes. The teacher who desires to make a major change would do well to analyze the system power structure and attempt to influence key individuals. Guba (1967, p. 31) has outlined strategies which may be applied to influencing key individuals. These strategies are not unique. When used by politicians, they are known as propaganda. When used to hawk vacuum cleaners, they are known as sales techniques.

Assuming the principal or some other key person is the focal point of a teacher who desires change, there are essentially six strategies open to the teacher. In a simplified paraphrase of Guba's strategies, the teacher may:

1. Persuade the person that he is obligated to make the change because it is consistent with his publicly announced value system. The proposed change may be, for example, what is best for the children.
2. Present hard research data to the person who attempts to make rational decisions.
3. Carefully explain the proposed program and provide the information necessary to carry out the change. Some innovations are opposed because they are not understood.
4. Appeal to some basic need—peer acceptance, esteem, power, security, etc.
5. Point out the personal economic advantages (promotions, job opportunities) which attend the making of the desired change.
6. Allude to the influential people who are in agreement with him, or prestigious systems which have made the adoption.

These strategies may be applied to any key individual—teacher, board member, administrator, or patron. Knowledge of the target person is implied so that the appropriate strategy may be used. Teachers have historically attempted to claim a "divine right" to exercise leadership within the educational system. The right has been denied; teachers must study and apply the science of influencing people. The power to make changes will not come easily, but the teacher who desires to make a change is, to a real degree, the master of his own destiny.

Mastery of one's own professional destiny is not without its price. Willingness to do the required work, exposure to accountability for one's actions, courage to speak up, academic diligence and honesty, and premeditated application of the science of persuasion are some of the costs to the teacher who wants to be a change agent. All things do not come to he who sits and waits.

Bibliography

1. Battle, J. A. "What Is Good Teaching," *The New Idea in Education.* eds. Battle and Shannon. New York: Harper & Row, Publishers, Inc., 1968.
2. Brickell, Henry M. *Organizing New York State for Educational Change.* New York State Department of Education, 1961.

3. Brookover, Wilber B. and David Gottlieb. *A Sociology of Education,* 2d ed. New York: American Book Company, 1964.
4. Carlson, Richard O. *Adoption of Educational Innovations.* Eugene, Oregon: University of Oregon Press, 1965.
5. Chilcott, John H. "The School Teacher Stereotype: A New Look!" *The Journal of Educational Sociology,* Vol. 34, No. 9 (May 1961), 389–390.
6. Cohler, Milton J. "Administrative Review and Professional Decision Making," *Illinois Schools Journal,* Vol. 47, No. 11 (Summer 1967), 95–99.
7. Cunningham, Luvern L. "The Teacher and Change," *The Elementary School Journal,* Vol. 62 (December 1961), 119–129.
8. Dodson, Dan. "To Work Effectively as Agents of Change," *Social Action,* Vol. 31, No. 6 (February 1965), 30–31.
9. Fishburn, Clarence E. "The Classroom Teacher's Commitment to the Educational Renaissance," *Journal of Secondary Education,* Vol. 41 (October 1966), 268–276.
10. Guba, Egon C. *The Basis for Educational Improvement.* Unpublished Monograph, 1967.
11. Hunt, Douglas W. "The Premise of Change," *Criticism, Conflict and Change.* eds. Hurwitz and Maidment. New York: Dodd, Mead & Co., 1970.
12. Kastrinos, William. "Summer Institute—A Follow Up," *American Biology Teacher,* Vol. 29, No. 8 (November 1967), 621–622.
13. Koontz, Elizabeth D. "Why Teachers Are Militant," *The Education Digest,* Vol. 23, No. 5 (January 1968), 12–14.
14. Lanter, Paul and Florence Howe. "Teacher Power—An Agent of Change," *Changing Education,* Vol. 4 (Fall 1969), 20–24.
15. Miller, William C. "Curricular Implications of Negotiation," *Educational Leadership,* Vol. 23, No. 9 (April 1966), 533–536.
16. Shannon, Robert L. "Are You Doing What You Should or What You Could?" *The New Idea In Education.* eds. Battle and Shannon. New York: Harper & Row, Publishers, Inc., 1968.
17. Taba, Hilda. *Curriculum Development: Theory and Practice.* New York: Harcourt Brace Jovanovich, 1962.
18. Wirtz, Marvin A. "Something for the Special Child," *Principles and Practice of Teaching.* ed. John Ohles. New York: Random House, 1970.
19. Woods, Thomas E. *The Administration of Educational Innovation.* Eugene, Ore.: University of Oregon Press, 1967.

INNOVATION AND PEOPLE*

Alice Miel

An unusually large group had turned out for the meeting that evening. All were busy people—curriculum workers from the city and surrounding suburbs, professors of curriculum representing the many colleges and universities in the area. They had come expecting a lively discussion with a professional critic of education. They had hoped for a sophisticated probing of ideas, but instead they were treated to insults, some open, some covert.

The more the audience showed an intention to listen carefully and to find points of both agreement and disagreement, the more extravagant the speaker's attack became. According to him, teachers in the elementary school are and should remain mere baby-sitters. Since high school and college teachers do nothing but miseducate, their best contribution would be to stay out of the students' way. School administrators are hopelessly bad. The speaker left a strong impression that education is to be saved only by ignoring all persons specialized in that field.

A SOBERING REVIEW

Those who insult others while promoting an innovation often do not intend to do so. They get carried away in their zeal to sell their particular road to salvation and they forget to show respect for other people in the process.

Alienation of others may be the inevitable and unenviable lot of the innovator, inside the profession or out. Yet it is possible that awareness of assumptions and behavior that appear insulting to others may help in minimizing alienation and in facilitating the process of change.

* Reprinted from *Educational Leadership* (May 1965), 22:585–591. Reprinted with permission of the Association for Supervision and Curriculum Development and Alice Miel. Copyright © 1965 by the Association for Supervision and Curriculum Development.

The guest at the meeting was speaking in a way familiar to educators. He typified a few of the kinds of insults frequently encountered, but it is possible to compile a somewhat longer list by searching the memory for other words and deeds in other times and places.

As the list is examined, it is sobering to review one's own behavior and that of colleagues while calling to mind treatment at the hands of certain lay citizens.

These Approaches Are Injurious

1. The writing off of the educator's professional preparation and experience as of no value in bringing about change. The notion that no good ideas for innovation in education can be expected from educators themselves is insulting to an entire profession and denies the record.
2. The assumption that others can always be counted on to turn a deaf ear to proposals for change and that therefore they must be bypassed and presented with a *fait accompli*. An individual or group might be given a chance to listen before being discounted.
3. The assumption that any question asked or objection raised in relation to a proposed change can be automatically dismissed as foot-dragging. The objector is not necessarily resistant to all kinds of change and may have a much more constructive purpose than preservation of a comfortable status quo.
4. The assumption that those close to an operation have been entirely unaware of problems until such difficulties were pointed out by an onlooker.
5. The assumption that those close to the operation have no ideas of their own for solving problems seen by themselves or pointed out by others. Why not provide a hearing for everyone's views?
6. The typing of an entire group as performing at the level of the least competent among them or as performing like those encountered in one's own schooling a generation or two ago.
7. The stereotyping of individuals on the basis of age alone, as outdated and useless, or the blaming of persons for not having acted in their earlier days in the profession on the knowledge only when available. Each individual deserves to be judged for himself alone.
8. The placing of a premium on only one or a few types of competence, for example, specialization in mathematics or in research skills. All who are serving usefully in various capacities in an institution or a system have a right to assurance that their particular competence also is valued.
9. The advising of knowledgeable individuals to return to an antiquated solution, long ago discarded for good and sufficient reason.
10. Being told that some simple, mechanical solution will suffice when the problem is extremely complex and perhaps perennial. One who thinks of education as an enterprise requiring the willing cooperation of intelligent human beings rightly resents the implication that education is a machine to be repaired by some all-knowing tinkerer.

11. Being treated as a button to be pushed, as a body to be deployed, in short, as a *thing*. Only the individual with some measure of autonomy can maintain his human dignity.

THE HUMAN ELEMENT IN CHANGE

The foregoing analysis is negative and distasteful, but the external and internal climate in education just now calls for a forceful reminder. We have lost much ground gained during an earlier period when there were sincere attempts to build a profession of self-confident, thinking people. In the general haste for reform in education, people in large numbers are being distrusted and ignored. Their potential contribution is being wasted. The motive power that comes from being considered important in decision making is going untapped.

Even though shortcuts appear to be achieved through disregarding the human element in change, a high price may be paid in later resistance at the critical point of putting an innovation into effect. Few worthwhile changes can be made in education without accompanying changes in the beliefs and capabilities of a number of people. Furthermore, changes of any moment require the most careful planning and preparation.

After the innovator has done the best he can in developing a logic for his proposal, working it out in major outline, and analyzing the requirements for implementation, he will do well to submit his complete prospectus to a wide assortment of people for a preview.

If something is to be tried out with six-year-olds in mathematics, for example, the specialist in that field may save time for children, teachers, and himself by inviting the questions and cautions of those wise in the ways of young children. He also needs the help of those who will most likely think in terms of the total curriculum and schedule of the school.

If a school is to be reorganized, it will take many different persons to see all the angles, anticipate all the possible difficulties, and force the proposal maker to complete the meticulous planning warranted when such a large investment of human energy is to be demanded. Most appalling is a current argument for bringing about change by plunging teachers into a new situation to sink or swim. Equally appalling is the type of brainwashing which guarantees that teachers will profess to like any change foisted upon them.

If someone believes that a great deal of money should be invested, say to provide facilities for statewide broadcasting via closed circuit television, it is intelligent to secure the widest range of experience in evaluating the proposal in advance. Alternative ways of using such a sum, with the possible consequences of each, would be useful to consider.

Nothing appears so simple as an operation little understood. To the uninitiated or to the one somewhat removed, many things seem easily possible. It is the people on the scene of action—those who must carry out a new idea—who know certain questions to ask, who may have improvements to suggest at the planning stage, who can anticipate details to be thought through in advance, who realize some of the things it will take to do the job, who can advise on timing.

The one who is to implement a change needs a thorough understanding, a commitment to the importance and rightness of an attempted change, a view of what he himself will be doing under new circumstances, and the proper tools and training. Only the person who has an opportunity to use considerable judgment of his own in how he carries out his responsibilities—judgment as to the ways he will use time, energy and resources—can operate as the kind of professional person we need in the schools. Only such a person can, in turn, deal with each student as an individual whose dignity is to be maintained and advanced.

INDEX